HEALING OUR DIVIDED SOCIETY

Edited by **FRED HARRIS** *and* **ALAN CURTIS**

AN EISENHOWER FOUNDATION BOOK

HEALING OUR DIVIDED SOCIETY

Investing in America Fifty Years
after the Kerner Report

TEMPLE UNIVERSITY PRESS
Philadelphia | Rome | Tokyo

TEMPLE UNIVERSITY PRESS
Philadelphia, Pennsylvania 19122
www.temple.edu/tempress

Library of Congress Cataloging-in-Publication Data

Names: Harris, Fred R., 1930– editor. | Curtis, Lynn A., editor.
Title: Healing our divided society : investing in America fifty years after the Kerner
    Report / edited by Fred Harris and Alan Curtis.
Description: Philadelphia : Temple University Press, 2018. | Includes index.
Identifiers: LCCN 2017050961 (print) | LCCN 2017054053 (ebook) |
    ISBN 9781439916049 (E-book) | ISBN 9781439916025 (cloth : alk. paper) |
    ISBN 9781439916032 (pbk. : alk. paper)
Subjects: LCSH: United States—Race relations. | African Americans—Social
    conditions. | Urban poor—United States. | Equality—United States. |
    United States. National Advisory Commission on Civil Disorders. Report.
Classification: LCC E184.A1 (ebook) | LCC E184.A1 H4155 2018 (print) |
    DDC 305.800973—dc23
LC record available at https://lccn.loc.gov/2017050961

Printed in the United States of America

9 8 7 6 5 4 3

To Marg Elliston, my ideal, and John Lewis, everybody's
—FRED HARRIS

To Ying, Miranda, and His Holiness the Dalai Lama
—ALAN CURTIS

Everybody does better when everybody does better.
—JIM HIGHTOWER

Our economy does not have to be a zero-sum game.
—BARACK OBAMA

When it's better for everyone, it's better for everyone.
—ELEANOR ROOSEVELT

Contents

New Will and the Media

About the Eisenhower Foundation

THE EISENHOWER FOUNDATION is the private-sector continuation of the 1967–1968 National Advisory Commission on Civil Disorders (the Kerner Commission, after many of the urban protests of the 1960s) and the 1968–1969 National Commission on the Causes and Prevention of Violence (after the assassination of Senator Robert F. Kennedy).

The Kerner Commission concluded in its 1968 report, "Our nation is moving toward two societies, one black, one white—separate and unequal." The Violence Commission concluded in its 1969 final report, "When . . . other great civilizations fell, it was less often from external assault than from internal decay. . . . Ours will be no exception."

Founded in 1981, the Eisenhower Foundation periodically updates the findings of the Kerner Commission and the Violence Commission.

The foundation's mission is to identify, financially support, technically assist, replicate, evaluate, and communicate evidence-based models that invest in high-risk minority youth and truly disadvantaged urban communities.

The foundation has worked in thirty-five states, Puerto Rico, the United Kingdom, France, Japan, and China.

On the basis of a national randomized control trial evaluation, the foundation's Quantum Opportunities Program has been peer reviewed as an evidence-based model by the Blueprints for Healthy Youth Development, Department of Justice Crime Solutions, and National Mentoring Resource Center online registries, as well as by the White House My Brother's Keeper initiative.

Deep mentoring, tutoring, life-skills training, college preparation, youth leadership training, and modest stipends mutually reinforce one another in the Quantum Opportunities Program, which invests in minority youth over all four years of high school. Outcomes include significantly higher grades, high school completion rates, and college admission rates for Quantum youth versus control youth.

The foundation's evidence-based Safe Haven model is a junior version of Quantum Opportunities, designed for middle school youth. Nonprofit organizations and police mentors collaborate to improve grades and to reduce crime in the impoverished Safe Haven neighborhoods.

As models like Quantum Opportunities and Safe Haven are evaluated as successful in local communities, the foundation communicates the need to replicate them at "a scale equal to the dimension of the problems," to quote the Kerner Commission report.

For more on the foundation, see www.eisenhowerfoundation.org.

The Eisenhower Foundation is nonpartisan. The views expressed by contributors to this book are not necessarily the position of the trustees of the foundation.

HEALING OUR DIVIDED SOCIETY

Introduction and the History of the Kerner Report

AMERICA'S SUMMER OF 1967 was, indeed, a ferociously long, hot summer. Riots, looting, and burning devastated the black sections of many of America's cities. Police and the National Guard—virtually all white, mostly poorly trained, and tragically overreacting and deadly—struggled to contain the violence in the urban neighborhoods where it began, but for a frighteningly long time, they were unable to do so.

The worst disorders occurred in Newark and Detroit. These were not finally quelled until, in each city, President Lyndon Johnson finally sent in U.S. Army soldiers to replace state National Guard troops. By the time order was restored in Newark, twenty-six people had been killed there—twenty-one of them civilians, including six women and several children, all African Americans.[1] A total of 1,324 persons were charged with crimes growing out of the Newark riot. There were whole blocks of burned-out ruins, and estimates of property damage ran into the multiple millions.

By the end of the disorders in Detroit, thirty-three African Americans and ten whites had been killed, seventeen of whom—fifteen African Americans and two white men—were looters. Two of the Detroit deaths resulted from a fallen power line. Seventeen people were shot by accident or were murdered. One police officer was accidentally killed during a scuffle with a looter by a shot from a gun held by another officer. One white man was killed by a looter. Two hundred seventy-nine persons were injured, including eighty-five police officers. Property damage was horrendous—682 buildings burned, 412 of them completely destroyed—and 7,231 persons were arrested.

But that was only part of what happened during that summer. Major riots—with numbers of deaths, injuries, and arrests and great property damage—also occurred during that time in Plainfield, New Jersey; Atlanta; Buffalo; Cambridge, Maryland; Cincinnati; Grand Rapids, Michigan; Milwaukee; Minneapolis; and Tampa. Twenty-eight more cities had serious disorders, lasting one or two days, and ninety-two cities had smaller outbreaks of violence that lasted a day or less.

All this terrible disorder caused enormous shock, fear, alarm, outrage, bewilderment, and anxiety throughout the country. Reacting to this and to restore calm, a solemn President Lyndon Johnson went on national television on the evening of July 27, 1967, in an address to the nation, and announced, partly at the suggestion of Senator Fred Harris of Oklahoma, the appointment of a blue-ribbon citizens commission, the President's National Advisory Commission on Civil Disorders (soon to be called the Kerner Commission, after its chairman, Governor Otto Kerner of Illinois), the purpose of which was not only to investigate and report concerning the riots from a law-and-order standpoint but also to deal with basic causes, the president declaring, "The only genuine, long-range solution for what has happened lies in an attack—mounted at every level— upon the conditions that breed despair and violence. All of us know what those conditions are: ignorance, discrimination, slums, poverty, disease, not enough jobs. We should attack those problems—not because we are fired by conscience. We should attack them because there is simply no other way to achieve a decent and orderly society in America."[2]

The eleven members appointed to the commission by the president were a kind of two-by-two Noah's ark of diversity: a Democrat, Kerner, as chairman, and a Republican, New York City mayor John Lindsay as vice chair; two U.S. senators as members, a Democrat, Fred Harris of Oklahoma, and a Republican, Edward Brooke of Massachusetts; two House representatives, a Democrat, James Corman of California, and a Republican, William McCulloch of Ohio; two African American leaders, Senator Brooke and Roy Wilkins, executive director of the NAACP; two public officials, Herbert Jenkins, Atlanta chief of police, and Katherine Peden, Kentucky secretary of state; and, finally, a labor leader, I. W. Abel, president of the United Steelworkers of America, and a business leader, Charles Thornton, chairman of the board and chief executive officer of Litton Industries. (A few years later, of course, there surely would have been a stronger level of gender and racial diversity in the appointments.)

A couple of progressive white leaders, as well as certain young African American activists, criticized the appointments as being a middle-of-the-road and bland group whose findings and recommendations would never amount to much. (Later, when the commission's report, dated March 1, 1968, was issued, these early critics seemed to be as surprised and pleased to have been wrong as President Johnson seemed as surprised and *dis*pleased that they had not been right.)

The mood was unusually somber in the Cabinet Room in the White House, where President Johnson had urgently called together, by telegram, the members of the new commission for the first time—on a Saturday morning, July 29, 1968. Underscoring the seriousness and importance of the task that was to be undertaken, there were also present at the meeting Vice President Hubert Humphrey, Attorney General Ramsey Clark, Budget Director Charles Schultze, Cyrus Vance, whom the president had earlier named as a special consultant to supervise federal riot-control efforts in Newark and Detroit, and several senior White House staff members.

After calling the meeting to order and making brief opening remarks, President Johnson introduced Cyrus Vance to report on the still-continuing Detroit disorders. Then, the president read aloud his executive order creating the commission and charging it to answer three basic questions about the riots: What happened? Why did it happen? What can be done to prevent it from happening again and again?

That same day, commission members alone met briefly again, and in that short session and in two later, longer organizational meetings with its new, presidentially appointed executive director, David Ginsberg, a caring, sensitive, distinguished Washington attorney with a background of government service, the Kerner Commission began its work.[3] A large staff was hired. Contracts were entered into for studies by academic and other experts.

The commission then commenced twenty days, from August to December 1967, of formal Washington hearings, held in the Treaty Room of the Executive Office Building, adjacent to the White House, and involving 130 witnesses ranging from civil rights leader Dr. Martin Luther King, Jr., to Federal Bureau of Investigation director J. Edgar Hoover.

Staff members and consultants conducted field surveys for the commission in twenty-three cities, including more than twelve hundred interviews, attitude or opinion surveys, and other serious studies of conditions and causes. Commission members divided up into teams for site visits to eight riot cities and personally observed there, close up, the human cost of wretched poverty and harsh racism. (One of these teams, made up of Senator Fred Harris, today the only living member of the Kerner Commission, and Mayor John Lindsay, walked the streets of Cincinnati and Milwaukee, spontaneously engaging there with groups of teenage and young-adult black men, typical of the rioters, whose uniform cry was always something like "Jobs, man; get us a job, baby!")[4]

THE REPORT

Returning to Washington, sobered and moved, commission members met, in room S. 211 on the Senate side of the Capitol, for forty-four days—

from December 1967 until near the end of February 1968—to actually write the Kerner Report, every paragraph of which was read aloud, then discussed and revised, before being approved by majority vote of commission members. If there was division on the harder questions, sometimes decisions would turn on a vote of six to five.

In these deliberations, the commission concentrated on the three questions the president had asked them to answer, having first decided, early on, to answer each question in order before moving on to the next one:

What Happened?

The commission was convinced that the riots had not been the result of a conspiracy, as President Johnson and some others believed—and they decided to say so, straight out: "The Urban Disorders of the summer of 1967 were not caused by, nor were they the consequence of, any organized plan or 'conspiracy.'"[5]

The commission detailed how, for two decades following World War II, roughly 1945 to 1965, African Americans began to migrate into the nation's cities, many being refugees from the desperate poverty and terrible degradation of the rural and small-town South. They came to places like Newark, Detroit, and Milwaukee looking for jobs—just when the better jobs were moving outside the city limits or to foreign countries or disappearing altogether because of automation. These new residents found northern-city segregation that was as rigid as in the southern states they had left. Three and four families might move into the rented rooms of what had once been an old single-family house, maybe turned away from already packed housing projects—as white flight began to rapidly turn the central city black. There were unresolved conflicts with nearly all-white police departments. Hostilities grew to the extent that almost any spark could set off an explosion.

The commission then truthfully laid out the facts in detail about the riots and about the way they had been handled, and mishandled, by the police and National Guard.

Why Did It Happen?

The commission condemned violence in strong terms: "Violence cannot build a better society. Disruption and disorder nourish repression, not justice. The community cannot—it will not—tolerate coercion and mob rule. . . . Violence and destruction must be ended."[6]

The commission, after all its hearings and studies, could not say for sure why violence occurred in once place and not another—why there had been a riot in the Watts section of Los Angeles in 1965, for example, but not in 1967, or why no 1967 riots occurred in Washington, D.C., or Baltimore. But the commission could, and did, describe with particularity the conditions that existed in the places where riots had occurred, and they declared that those conditions and "white racism" were the root causes of the riots.[7]

The commission report's basic conclusion was that "our Nation is moving toward two societies, one black, one white—separate and unequal."[8] "Segregation and poverty," the report continued, "have created in the racial ghetto a destructive environment totally unknown to most white Americans. What white Americans have never fully understood—but what the Negro can never forget—is that white society is deeply implicated in the ghetto. White institutions created it, white institutions maintain it, and white society condones it."[9]

What Can Be Done to Prevent It from Happening Again and Again?

When the commission arrived at this last question, it was clear to its members, including the more conservative ones, that the answers to the first two questions had already locked them into the answer to the third and final question: great and sustained national efforts were required, not only to combat racism but also to greatly expand social programs, including those against unemployment and low wages, poverty, inferior or inadequate education and training, lack of health care, and bad or nonexistent housing.

The commission was honest in saying, "These programs will require unprecedented levels of funding."[10]

The report also made strong recommendations to improve the conduct of the media and the police, as well as the hostile, toxic police-community relations that existed throughout the country.

While the commission understood that just dealing with economic-class issues, without special attention to the problems of racism and discrimination (and today, we would add women's rights), would be fundamentally inadequate, the commission also knew that their recommended solutions would not apply only to black people or city people. Instead, the report declared, quite broadly, "It is time to make good the promises of American democracy to all citizens—urban and rural, white and black, Spanish-surname, American Indian and every minority group."[11]

THE RELEASE OF THE REPORT

The commission met for the last time in a large ceremonial room, S. 201, on the Senate side of the Capitol Building. There was a last-minute flare-up around a discussion, led by a conservative member, about the possibility of minority reports by individual commissioners. But after this unsettling disruption was quickly squelched, the commission confirmed its earlier adoption of the report by unanimous vote, and all the commission members then affixed their signatures to the official federal document.

March 1, 1968, was set as the official date for the report's release, Members and staff shook hands all around, congratulated one another, and left, expecting to see each other soon at the White House, where they expected to formally deliver the report to President Johnson and ask him, as they had earlier agreed to do, for an additional six months of life for the commission, so that members and principal staff could lobby and advocate for the report's recommendations.

And they all knew that a great deal of lobbying and advocacy was going to be necessary. The commission had made a mistake in not opening its extensive hearings to the media and the public and in not working to foster media coverage of its field trips and riot-city visits. So no way had been provided for the media and the public to see the great racial problems and terrible living conditions that existed in the country in the same way and in the same depth as commission members had seen them. Members and staff of the commission had become worried that the long and expectedly sensational report—using the term "white racism" and calling for great new federal spending—would suddenly burst on the national consciousness with little context and with inadequate explanation and justification. So arrangements had already been made for the entire and lengthy report to be published in paperback by Bantam Books simultaneously with the March 1 release of the report's U.S. Printing Office version. (The Bantam Books edition proved to be a huge and sustained best seller, which bookstores could barely keep on the shelves as it was rushed through twenty-one separate printings.)

Careful arrangements were also made to get advance, embargoed copies of the report into the hands of reporters, columnists, television and radio commentators, and other selected writers in the fields of urban affairs, poverty, and race relations, so they would have the opportunity, with backgrounding by commission members and staff, to study the entire report and fully understand the bases for its findings and recommendations.

But it turned out that not enough of the right kind of early and late, complete backgrounding about the commission's work and report had been done with President Johnson himself. In fact, the president, it was learned, had been getting frequent, fragmentary, and often slanted backdoor reports from inside the commission, reports that made him increasingly apprehensive that the commission, particularly, as he was told, led by Senator Harris and Mayor Lindsay, was going "too far and too fast"—

and the president had complained to commission members and others about this from time to time.[12]

Then, commission staff learned from White House staff that a congressman friend of President Johnson, who was acting on the word of a conservative member of the Kerner Commission, had told the president that the Kerner Report was going to be a "disaster" for him because it "condoned and encouraged riots" and had "not one good thing" to say about all the president had already done for civil rights and against poverty.[13]

This was totally untrue, but President Johnson believed it. He cancelled the formal meeting with the commission, rejected its report, and summarily discarded the congratulatory thank-you letters that had already been prepared for signature and mailing to the individual commission members—actions especially sad because, on the basis of false information, they came from a president who had achieved greater progress in the fight against racism and poverty than any of his predecessors or successors to date.

But there was more. Someone, most likely a White House staff member,[14] hoping to greatly lessen the report's impact, leaked a copy of the full Kerner Report to the *Washington Post*, whose editor called the commission's executive director, David Ginsberg, to tell him that the *Post* would run a front-page story about the report in its next-morning, February 29, issue—before sufficient planned backgrounding had been done with the media people who had been given embargoed copies of the report. The *Post* editor could not be dissuaded from this course, even after Ginsberg told him that if the newspaper would not relent, Ginsberg would himself immediately release the full report to all media at once—which Ginsberg then did. (This is the reason that, while the official date on the Kerner Report is March 1, 1968, the actual release date is recorded as February 29.)

Chaos reigned in the commission's office that evening, as swarms of reporters with thirty-minute deadlines frantically sought capsulizations of the six-hundred-plus-page report. Newspaper headlines the next morning were mostly something like "White Racism Cause of Black Riots, Commission Says." Many people never learned the rest of the story.

There was considerable backlash in the country. The comment of one white farmer—who viewed the report as saying that he, out of the goodness of his heart, should pay more taxes to help poor black people rioting in Detroit—was typical of many: "To hell with that! I've got enough troubles of my own. I'm barely making a living, and I'm already paying too much tax."[15] He and a lot of others were never to believe that the Kerner Commission was on their side, too, or fully understand the way so many of their fellow citizens had to live.

But a lot of leaders supported the Kerner Report—leaders like Vice President Hubert Humphrey; Senator Robert Kennedy of New York;

Dr. Martin Luther King, Jr., who called the report "a physician's warning of approaching death, with a prescription for life"[16]; Secretary of Health, Education, and Welfare John Gardner, who said, "We are in deep trouble as a people, and history will not deal kindly with any nation which will not tax itself to cure its miseries"[17]; and Secretary of Labor Willard Wirtz, who said, "The Kerner Report can be summarized in the words of that great American philosopher, Pogo, who said, 'We have met the enemy, and he is us!'"[18]

And despite the opposition, following the Kerner Report, America made progress on virtually every aspect of race and poverty for nearly ten years. Then, with burgeoning globalization, increasing automation, conservative political change, and eventually, unfriendly Supreme Court decisions, progress was slowed or stopped and, finally, reversed. With some improvement during each of the Bill Clinton and Barack Obama administrations, regression has been the trend since about the mid-1970s—and that is true today.

This is why we, Fred Harris and Alan Curtis, and the Milton S. Eisenhower Foundation, the private-sector follow-on and keeper of the flame for both the Kerner Commission and the Milton S. Eisenhower Violence Commission, have joined, as we have done before,[19] to organize and produce a fiftieth-anniversary *Kerner Report* update, the most important of all, with the hope that the issues of racism and poverty, income inequality, jobs, wages, education, housing, health, women's and children's rights, and police-community relations can be put back on the public agenda and that a broad coalition—urban and rural, men and women, white, black, Hispanic,[20] and other—can be mobilized for action on their common problems, because everybody does better when everybody does better.

This is not another study. It is a call to action. We know what works. Now, we must build the will to do it.

PART I

Evidence-Based Policy

1

Policy That Works

> I'm not a nigger. I'm a man. . . . If I'm not the nigger here and . . . you, the white people, invented him, then you've got to find out why. And the future of the country depends on . . . whether or not it is able to ask that question.
>
> —JAMES BALDWIN, *I Am Not Your Negro*

THE KERNER COMMISSION BELIEVED it was "time to make good the promises of American democracy to all citizens—urban and rural, white and black, Spanish-surname, American Indian and every minority group." The commission concluded that the federal government was the only institution with the moral authority and resources to create change and replicate what works "at a scale equal to the dimension of the problems."[1] To carry out its recommendations and scale up, the commission cautioned that new attitudes, new understanding, and above all "new will" would be necessary among the American people.[2]

Since release of the Kerner Report, there has been progress, some of it remarkable. A substantial African American and Hispanic middle class has emerged, minority entrepreneurship has greatly expanded, minorities have been selected as chief executive officers of major corporations, minority celebrities earn millions of dollars, minority journalists write for leading newspapers and are major figures on newscasts, minority authors have achieved recognition for their literary works, minority athletes have a commanding presence in many professional sports, large numbers of minority local and state officials have been elected, the number of minorities in the Congress has increased substantially, and an African American president has been elected for two terms (see Chapter 7 in Part II).

Yet on many fronts there has been lack of or reversal of progress. In an interview, former First Lady Michelle Obama has recalled how a county government official referred to her as an "ape in heels" and how some people did not take her seriously because of her race.[3] The Kerner Commission pointed to "white terrorism directed against nonviolent protest," and that is what happened in 2017 when a white neo-Nazi supremacist killed and injured protesters he drove into at a rally at the University of Virginia.[4] In his 2015 book, *Between the World and Me*, Ta-Nehisi Coates observes that whites "have forgotten the scale of theft that enriched them in slavery; the terror that allowed them, for a century, to pilfer the vote; the segregationist policy that gave them their suburbs. They have forgotten, because to remember would tumble them out of the beautiful Dream and force them to live down here with us, down here in the world."[5]

In response, Table 1.1 summarizes the policies that in our view have *not* worked since the Kerner Report and the policies that *have* worked. Those that have worked are the basis for our recommendations, here, in Part I. We have drawn on the chapters by our contributors (in Part II), as well as on information from many other sources.

Too much policy in America's present political environment is based on sensationalized anecdotes and easily exploited fears rather than on the

TABLE 1.1 WHAT WORKS AND WHAT DOES NOT: A SUMMARY OF THE KERNER FIFTIETH

What works	What does not work
Policy based on evidence	Policy based on ideology
"We're in this together" policy	"You're on your own" policy
Expansion of responsible government and increased funding	Privatization and less funding
Demand-side, full-employment Keynesian economics	Supply-side, trickle-down economics
New tax credits and child allowances	No new tax credits or child allowances
Job training first	Work first and "welfare reform"
Substantial increases in the minimum wage	Minimal increases in the minimum wage
More labor union power	Less labor union power
Insured health care through a single-payer system	Reduced health care for workers and low-income Americans
Globalization within a framework of worker rights	Unrestrained corporate globalization
Racial integration in schools and neighborhoods	Racial segregation in schools and neighborhoods
Investments in public school equity, quality teachers, early childhood education, community schools, Quantum Opportunities, YouthBuild, Career Academies, and Bottom Line	Vouchers, choice, and charter schools
Subsidized housing for all eligible low-income citizens	Subsidized housing for only one-quarter of all eligible citizens
Rigorous enforcement of fair-housing laws	Continued minimal enforcement of fair-housing laws
Investments in neighborhood place-based multiple solutions to multiple problems	Uncoordinated place-based policy and rhetoric on empowerment
Community-based, problem-oriented policing	Zero-tolerance policing and excessive use of force
De-incarceration	Mass incarceration
Investment in proven ex-offender reintegration initiatives	Lack of investment

most rigorous evidence from peer-reviewed evaluations. One former director of the federal Office of Management and Budget has estimated that less than 1 percent of government spending goes to evidence-based initiatives (see Chapter 13 in Part II).

Nonetheless, the quantity and sophistication of scientific information available today far exceeds what was available to the Kerner Commission when it called for "new initiatives and experiments that can change the system of failure and frustration" (see Chapter 8 in Part II).

Public and governmental support for evidence-based interventions has grown. In 2002, the White House encouraged all federal agencies to support evidence-based programs and to discontinue programs without proof of effectiveness. In 2014, the White House endorsed the use of rigorous scientific evaluations for improving federal programs. In 2017, the bipartisan Commission on Evidence-Based Policymaking recommended that federal agencies seek "continuous improvement" by "supporting a cycle of first pilot testing a new program . . . then conducting research to learn from the pilot test, and finally, adopting the program . . . based on what was learned through the research."[6] It is now common practice that federal funding for prevention programs calls for evidence-based models (see Chapter 13 in Part II).

There currently are several online registries of evidence-based programs, practices, and policies. The exact definition of "evidence based" continues to be debated. Nonetheless, we are confident about moving in the right direction by grounding our recommendations, whenever possible, on programs that have been evaluated using randomized controlled trials, quasi-experimental comparison group designs, or both.[7] As we recommend the scaling up of programs so evaluated, we are aware that knowledge of exactly how to replicate on a wide scale remains limited. But we must try—and mature our understanding as we move forward.

The following review of trends since the Kerner Report, what does not work and what does work, covers economic and employment policy, education policy, housing and neighborhood investment policy, and criminal justice policy. We conclude with observations on Kerner-based soft power in foreign policy, recommendations for how to finance the scale-up of what works, and encouragement for how to generate new will to create change in America.

2

Economic and Employment Policy

SINCE THE KERNER COMMISSION, child poverty has increased in America. There are continuing high levels of wage, income, and wealth inequality. Trickle-down, supply-side economics has failed. We set forth a demand-side Keynesian economic policy focused on job creation, job training, tax credits, an increased minimum wage, the strengthening of labor unions, single-payer health care, and reformed trade policy to benefit workers.

TRENDS

Child Poverty

A look at the child poverty rate of any country is the quickest and surest way to measure that country's level of economic justice. How does America measure up? Not well, as shown by Figure 2.1.

The percentage of American children living in poverty has increased from the time of the 1968 Kerner Report to 2016 (from 15.6 percent in 1968 to 18.0 percent in 2016).[1] The percentage had been declining sharply in the 1960s, during the John F. Kennedy and Lyndon Johnson administrations. It was relatively flat, then gradually rose between 1969 and 1979, during the Richard Nixon, Gerald Ford, and Jimmy Carter administrations. The child poverty rate rose sharply from the early 1980s to the early 1990s during the Ronald Reagan and George H. W. Bush administrations, and it declined sharply between 1993 and 2000 during the Bill Clinton administration. The rate gradually rose through 2007, during the George

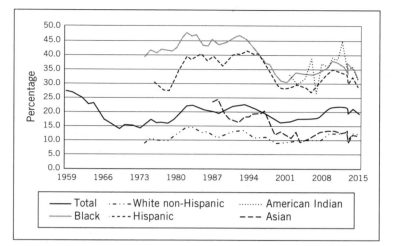

Figure 2.1 Children under eighteen living below the poverty line, United States, 1959–2015

Source: U.S. Census Bureau, "Historical Poverty Tables: People and Families, 1959 to 2015," September 8, 2017, available at https://www.census.gov/data/tables/time-series/demo/income-poverty/historical-poverty-people.html; U.S. Census Bureau, "CPS Table Creator," available at http://www.census.gov/cps/data/cpstablecreator.html.

Note: American Indian data may be unreliable in comparison to other races. Data for black children are retrieved from "Black" data prior to 2002 and "Black Alone or in Combination" data for 2002 and after. Data for Asian children are retrieved from "Asian Alone or in Combination" data prior to 2002 and "Asian and Pacific Islander" data for 2002 and after.

W. Bush administration; rose sharply during the Great Recession, beginning in 2007–2008; and started declining in 2013, as the economic recovery eventually began to reach some of the hardest-hit locales, including racial minority communities. In 2016, 31 percent of African American children, 27 percent of Hispanic children, and 11 percent of white children lived in poverty.[2]

How does the United States stack up against other countries in regard to child poverty? Not too well (see Figure 2.2). America's child poverty rate is among the highest reported by the Organization for Economic Cooperation and Development (OECD).[3]

Overall, poverty in the United States is about the same today as it was in 1968. Then, 25.4 million Americans were living in poverty, 12.8 percent of the population. By 2016, 40.6 million Americans were living in poverty, 12.7 percent of our people.[4]

Deep Poverty

The percentage of people living in deep or extreme poverty—that is, less than half the poverty threshold—has increased since 1975. (See

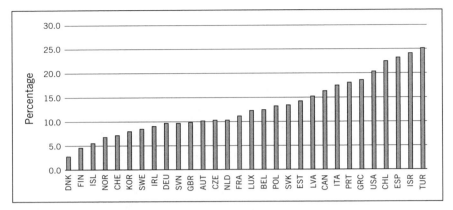

Figure 2.2 Child poverty rates in OECD countries, 2013
Source: Organisation for Economic Co-operation and Development, "Poverty Rate," available at http://www.oecd-ilibrary.org/social-issues-migration-health/poverty-rate/indicator/english_0fe1315d-en (accessed October 2, 2017).

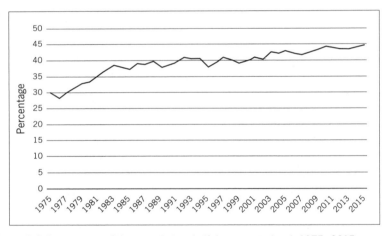

Figure 2.3 Percentage of the poor below half the poverty level, 1975–2015
Source: U.S. Census Bureau, "Historical Poverty Tables: People and Families, 1959 to 2015," September 8, 2017, table 3, table 22, available at https://www.census.gov/data/tables/time-series/demo/income-poverty/historical-poverty-people.html.

Figure 2.3.) By 2016, 46 percent of people living in poverty had incomes of less than half the poverty threshold.[5]

The rise in deep poverty stems in part from the lack of wage growth among lower earners. A key explanation has been the failure of the U.S. Congress to raise the minimum wage enough to keep pace with inflation. The current federal minimum wage of $7.25 is 25 percent lower, adjusted for inflation, than its peak value in 1968.[6]

As Figure 2.4 shows, the deep poverty rate for poor whites is higher than for poor African Americans and Hispanic Americans.

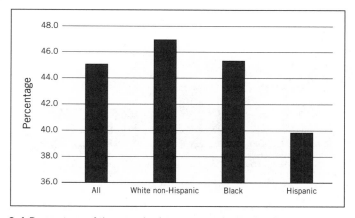

Figure 2.4 Percentage of the poor in deep poverty by race and ethnicity, 2015
Source: U.S. Census Bureau, *Current Population Survey: 2016 Annual Social and Economic Supplement* (Washington, DC: U.S. Census Bureau, 2016), available at https://www2 .census.gov/programs-surveys/cps/techdocs/cpsmar16.pdf.

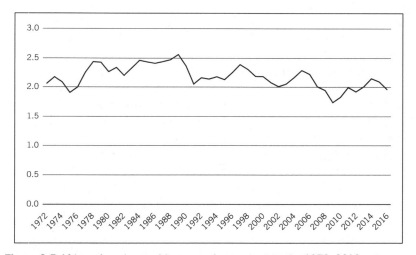

Figure 2.5 African American–white unemployment rate ratio, 1972–2016
Source: Bureau of Labor Statistics, "Labor Force Characteristics by Race and Ethnicity, 2016," October 2017, available at https://www.bls.gov/opub/reports/race-and-ethnicity/2016/home .htm.

Unemployment

From the early 1970s to the present, the African American unemployment rate has been almost always twice or more that of the white unemployment rate, as shown by Figure 2.5.

In 2016, African American unemployment was higher than white unemployment at all education levels, as Figure 2.6 shows.

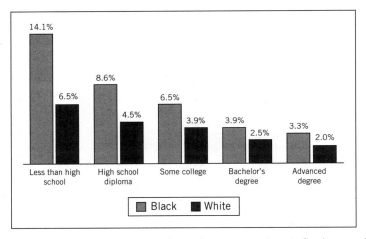

Figure 2.6 Annual unemployment rate for workers over age twenty-five by race, 2016
Source: Bureau of Labor Statistics, "Labor Force Statistics from the Current Population Survey," February 8, 2017, available at https://www.bls.gov/cps/cpsaat07.htm.

Wages and CEO Pay

For those who were employed in 2016, 33 percent of African American workers earned poverty-level wages, 34 percent of Hispanic workers, and 19 percent of white workers.[7]

As demonstrated by productivity growth—that is, the value of what workers produce in an hour—the American economy has been expanding and becoming more productive over time. This means that there has been plenty of room for wages of all workers to grow over the last four decades. However, pay for the vast majority of workers has been stagnant, as shown in Figure 2.7. That is because most of the economic gains from rising productivity have gone to the wealthiest 1 percent and to corporate profits. Corporate America shared little with workers.

Had all workers' wages risen in line with productivity, as they did in the three decades following World War II, an American earning around $40,000 today would instead be making close to $61,000.

The growing productivity-pay gap has also affected our ability to close long-standing racial wage gaps. While wages for the vast majority of all workers, regardless of race or gender, have been nearly stagnant since 1979, real wages for African Americans have grown more slowly than for whites and in some cases have even declined.

But something very different has happened to chief executive officer (CEO) compensation. From 1967 to 2015, inflation-adjusted CEO compensation increased over 940 percent, 73 percent faster than stock market growth and substantially greater than the painfully slow 10 percent growth in a typical worker's annual compensation over the same period. In 1967, the ratio of CEO pay to worker pay was about 25 to 1. In 2015, the ratio of CEO pay to worker pay was about 276 to 1, as shown in Figure 2.8.

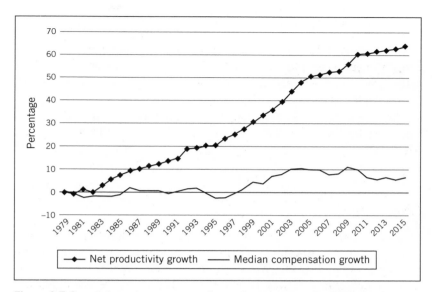

Figure 2.7 Growth in worker compensation and net productivity, 1979–2015
Source: Josh Bivens and Lawrence Mishel, "Understanding the Historic Divergence between Productivity and a Typical Worker's Pay," Economic Policy Institute, September 2, 2015, available at http://www.epi.org/publication/understanding-the-historic-divergence-between-produc tivity-and-a-typical-workers-pay-why-it-matters-and-why-its-real.

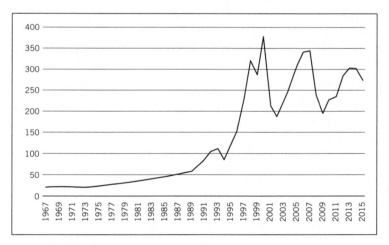

Figure 2.8 CEO-to-Worker compensation ratio, 1967–2015
Source: Lawrence Mishel and Alyssa Davis, "Top CEOs Make 300 Times More than Typical Workers," Economic Policy Institute, June 21, 2015, available at http://www.epi.org/publication/ top-ceos-make-300-times-more-than-workers-pay-growth-surpasses-market-gains-and-the -rest-of-the-0-1-percent.
Note: Chief executive officer annual compensation includes salary, bonus, restricted stock grants, options exercised, and long-term incentive payouts for CEOs at the top 350 U.S. firms ranked by sales.

Labor Union Membership

Since the Kerner Report was issued, labor union membership has declined precipitously. (See Figure 2.9.) The decline has weakened the bargaining power of workers, contributing to the suppression of wages for the vast majority of workers.

The recent expansion of so-called right-to-work laws to several states has been a key feature of the attack on labor unions. Historically, African American workers have had higher rates of union membership than whites, which continues to be true despite the decline in membership.

Income Inequality

Income inequality has grown dramatically over the last four decades in America. Between 1947 and 1979, incomes of low- and moderate-income families grew slightly faster than those of higher-income families. This trend in income growth was then dramatically reversed between 1979 and 2007—when higher-earning families experienced faster income growth than lower-earning families. See Figure 2.10.

In the 1970s, the richest 1 percent of Americans took home less than 9 percent of our national income. By 2016, they took home 24 percent.[8] The Great Recession, which began in 2007–2008, further exacerbated the trend of growing income inequality. Between 2007 and 2013, income for low- to moderate-income families declined faster than for higher-earning families. During the last years of the recovery, lower-income families finally started to recover some of the lost income of the past forty years.[9]

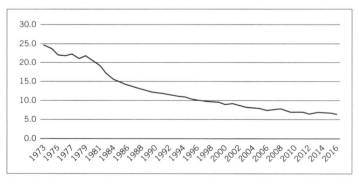

Figure 2.9 Private-sector union membership in the United States, 1973–2016
Source: Barry Hirsch and David Macpherson, "Union Membership, Coverage, Density, and Employment among Private Sector Nonagricultural Workers, 1973–2016," *Union Membership and Coverage Database from the CPS*, available at http://unionstats.gsu.edu (accessed December 6, 2017).
Note: There are no data for 1982 because there were no union questions in the 1982 Current Population Survey. The sample includes wage and salary workers, ages sixteen and over.

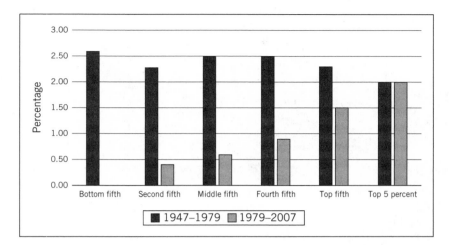

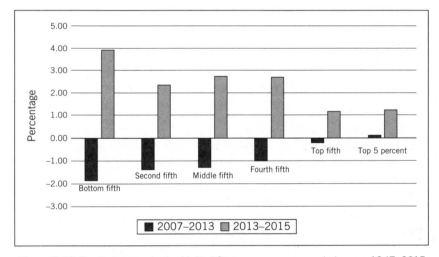

Figure 2.10 Family income in the United States, average annual change, 1947–2015
Source: U.S. Census Bureau, *Current Population Survey Annual Social and Economic Supplement*, table FINC-03, available at https://www.census.gov/data/tables/time-series/demo/income-poverty/cps-finc/finc-03.2015.html.
Note: Data are for money income.

Today, 52 percent of all new income in America goes to the top 1 percent.[10] It is as if, rather than expanding the seats in the theater of opportunity, the economy has been using its income to make the existing seats more luxurious and adding bars, restaurants, and other amenities for the people already there (see Chapter 3 in Part II).

Median African American income has averaged 59 percent of white income from 1972 to the present (see Chapter 2 in Part II). See Figure 2.11. In 2016, the median African American household earned $39,490, the

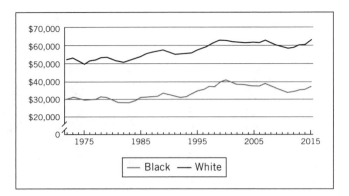

Figure 2.11 Real median income by race in 2015 dollars, 1972–2015
Source: Bernadette D. Proctor, Jessica L. Semega, and Melissa A. Kollar, "Income and Poverty in the United States: 2015," September 2016, available at https://www.census.gov/content/dam/Census/library/publications/2016/demo/p60-256.pdf.

median Hispanic American household earned $47,675, and the median white household earned $65,051.[11]

Wealth

Given the above trends, it is not surprising that the wealthiest 1 percent of Americans own almost as much wealth as the bottom 90 percent.[12]

Median white wealth was twelve times that of median African American wealth as of 2013 (see Chapter 2 in Part II). See Figure 2.12. The wealth gap for Hispanic Americans is comparable.[13]

Communities of color are much less likely than whites to be homeowners and to have a retirement plan from their employers. Racial minorities thus often do not have access to the various tax and other benefits that come with those savings.[14]

African Americans and Hispanic Americans are also less likely to inherit money. When they do, the amounts inherited are lower than for whites. Racial minorities tend to be good savers, but they fall behind in their wealth because they receive less help than whites do from the government, employers, and inheritances.[15]

Communities of color tend to pay higher fees for savings accounts and face higher interest rates on their debts than whites do, reducing the money they earn on their savings and slowing wealth growth. The wealth gap also increases with age as communities of color fall further and further behind whites over time.[16]

Notably, the racial wealth gap grew immediately after the Great Recession. Racial minorities lost their homes and jobs, and thus, their retirement plans, at a faster rate than whites did. When the housing and stock

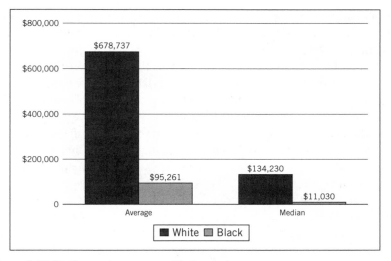

Figure 2.12 Median and average wealth, by race
Source: Janelle Jones, "The Racial Wealth Gap: How African-Americans Have Been Short-changed Out of the Materials to Build Wealth," Economic Policy Institute, February 13, 2017, available at http://www.epi.org/blog/the-racial-wealth-gap-how-african-americans-have-been-shortchanged-out-of-the-materials-to-build-wealth.

markets recovered, communities of color had less access to these markets and could make fewer contributions to their wealth than whites.[17]

WHAT DOES NOT WORK: THE FAILURE OF SUPPLY-SIDE ECONOMICS

Since the 1968 Kerner Commission, poverty, unemployment, and inequality have for the most part risen when federal macroeconomic policy has been supply side and trickle down.

Supply-side economics claims that cutting taxes on the rich and corporations will make the economy grow—and that the resulting economic boost will trickle down to the not rich. Tax reductions are accompanied by deregulation—for example, of financial and labor markets. If taxes are increased on the rich, the claim is that the economy will decline. In 1980, future president George H. W. Bush called this "voodoo economic policy."[18]

Since 1980, there is little evidence that trickle-down, supply-side economics works (except for the rich and for corporations). As the Nobel Prize–winning economist Paul Krugman has documented, the best national example of the failure of supply-side economics came in the early part of the new millennium, when taxes on the rich were reduced and many markets were deregulated. The result? The financial crisis and Great Recession, which most significantly affected minorities and the poor.[19]

The Great Recession was the result of the biggest federal economic policy failure that has occurred since the Kerner Report was issued.[20]

Another national illustration of the failure of trickle-down economics was when taxes were raised on the rich in the 1990s. Yet the economy boomed.[21] The most rigorous studies over extended periods provide more supporting evidence on the failure of trickle-down, supply-side economics nationally. One assessment examined the years 1949 to 2006. It found that when federal supply-side policies were pursued most aggressively, the economic results were least impressive compared to other years when these policies were not pursued, especially in terms of the income of the typical American family.[22]

At the state level, the failure of trickle-down economics has perhaps best been illustrated in Kansas. In recent years, the governor of that state brought about steep tax cuts and deregulation, promising that a high rate of economic growth would result. Instead, in what has been described as "fiscal self-evisceration," the promised business revitalization and job growth did not materialize. The Kansas economy remained sluggish. State spending on public education declined. The state's highest court concluded that minority and poor students were hurt. The state's bond ratings were downgraded. In 2017, the state legislature overrode the governor's veto and increased taxes.[23] Contrast the Kansas case with the example of California, where, in recent years, taxes were raised, and the state enjoyed impressive employment and economic growth.[24]

In spite of the lack of evidence in support of trickle-down economics, many continue to promote supply-side ideology. They are encouraged by lobbyists for the corporations and the rich.[25]

The Supply-Side Failure of "Welfare Reform"

While supply-side economics has been justifiably criticized as welfare for the rich, in the 1980s in some quarters criticizing welfare for the poor became popular. There was widespread agreement that the federal program Aid to Families with Dependent Children (AFDC), should be made more effective. Eventually, in 1996, AFDC was replaced with a supply-side program, Temporary Assistance for Needy Families (TANF). Under TANF, each state receives a block grant for its own customized welfare system.[26] State matching funds are required.

The most comprehensive evaluation of TANF assessed its effectiveness from 1996 to the second decade of the new millennium. The evaluation concluded that:

- TANF plays much less of a role in reducing poverty than AFDC did. The provision of less cash assistance by TANF has contributed to the increase in deep poverty documented in Figure 2.3.

- There was a 50 percent increase in deep poverty from 1996 to 2011, an increase of seven hundred thousand children living in poverty.
- Over time, TANF has provided basic cash assistance to fewer and fewer needy families, even when need increased.
- During the Great Recession and then in the slow recovery, TANF served few families in need.
- The amount of cash assistance provided to families has eroded in almost every state, leaving families without sufficient funds to meet their most basic needs.
- Although a key focus of "welfare reform" was on increasing employment, states spend little of their TANF funds on job training and helping recipients improve their employability.
- State governments have found ways to divert funds from work programs and childcare into other nonassistance uses. The result is that many poor families cannot cover their basic needs, like clothes for their children. They cannot live predictable lives that allow them to care for their families and to find decent jobs with upward mobility.[27]

The Modest Track Record of Work First

Since the Kerner Report, continuing high rates of unemployment of minorities, especially of young men in impoverished neighborhoods, has generated decades of federal initiatives focused on these populations. Ideally, such targeted workforce development programs are meant to complement overall macroeconomic policy.

The Manpower Development and Training Act (MDTA), launched in 1962, gave priority to minorities and the poor during the War on Poverty. In 1973, MDTA was replaced by the Comprehensive Employment and Training Act (CETA). In 1982, CETA was replaced by the Job Training Partnership Act (JTPA). In 1998, JTPA was replaced by the Workforce Investment Act (WIA).[28]

There have been some evidence-based successes, like Job Corps, discussed later, that undertake significant job training. However, overall, decades of rigorous evaluations have found that MDTA, CETA, JTPA, and WIA generated only modest positive impacts on the earnings of disadvantaged adults, with those for women often larger than those for men. Most earning increases were attributable to increases in hours worked rather than higher wages.[29]

Importantly, JTPA and WIA, like the failed TANF program, have been supply-side experiments that stress work-first placement in jobs, rather than significant job training before entering the workforce.[30]

WHAT WORKS: DEMAND-SIDE KEYNESIAN ECONOMIC POLICY

As Nobel Prize–winning economist Joseph Stiglitz writes in Chapter 1 of Part II, the Kerner Report had a "remarkable vision" of the Keynesian demand-side policy that the nation needed:

> In addition to the obvious proposals (more jobs and removal of the clear race-based barriers), the authors proposed job training (both public and private), behavioral counseling (ranging from motivation, personal dress, and hygiene to social relationships and job performance), transportation to and from work, appropriate medical and social services, flexible work schedules and patterns that fit the needs and abilities of the potential laborers (they recognized that many people have innate intelligence and skills that are unquantifiable), on-the-job training, a computerized (!) system for matching workers with jobs, work tryouts, and moving people out of the ghetto for work.

Today, on the basis of what has and has not worked, we support demand-side Keynesian policy that reduces poverty, inequality, and racial injustice and that respects the working and middle classes, as well as the truly disadvantaged.

Our policy embraces full employment, direct job creation, job training first, tax credits, child allowances, a significantly increased minimum wage, single-payer health insurance for all Americans, and trade agreements that increase benefits to American workers.

Full Employment and Direct Job Creation

At the same time as he began to evolve the civil rights movement into an economic justice movement, Dr. Martin Luther King endorsed "employment for everyone in need of a job."[31] The Kerner Commission agreed, concluding, "Employment . . . controls the present for the Negro American but, in a most profound way, it is creating the future as well" (see Chapter 2 in Part II).

The Kerner Commission observed that the unemployment rate for African Americans in 1967 was double the rate for whites. Figure 2.5 shows that this two-to-one gap has persisted over the last fifty years.

Skills deficits are not the sole explanation for why there are always millions of African American, Hispanic American, and Native American workers who want but cannot find gainful employment. The long-term absence of robust labor demand is a key factor and suggests the need for direct job creation. If the market fails to create enough jobs to meet the needs of this population, then such market failure must be corrected. The assumption that labor demand is adequate to meet the needs of the potential workforce is simply untenable on the basis of available evidence (see Chapter 2 in Part II).

Once one accepts the presence of market failure in terms of job creation, the role of government becomes paramount. After all, most economists and policy makers have no trouble accepting the role of the Federal Reserve as the lender of last resort when credit markets fail, as was the case in the financial crisis and Great Recession that began in 2007–2008. If that is the standard for credit markets, the same standard should apply to the job market (see Chapter 2 in Part II).

What is the policy process for maintaining full employment? The most commonly invoked Keynesian policy levers are monetary and fiscal policy. On the monetary side, the Federal Reserve must be willing to truly balance its dual mandate of full employment at stable prices. Too often, the Fed's actions have been weighted toward protecting against faster inflation, even when inflation was nowhere to be seen, at the expense of full employment. This disproportionately harms poor minorities and working-class people of all races (see Chapter 2 in Part II).

Direct job creation can take various forms. At the more interventionist end of the continuum, the federal government provides a public service job for which it pays a salary and benefits.

A less interventionist approach is for the government to subsidize someone's wages in a private-sector job (including work at nonprofit organizations). In fact, as Jared Bernstein, senior fellow at the Center for Budget and Policy Priorities discusses in Chapter 2 of Part II, the federal government took this approach in response to the Great Recession. The best evidence shows that the policy was quite successful, creating around 250,000 jobs. One careful evaluation of Florida's version of the initiative found that, relative to a control group, participants' work and earnings went up, not just during the program but after it as well, suggesting lasting benefits. A broader review of such interventions shows that government has done a lot more of this sort of direct job creation than is commonly realized, and well-designed programs generate a big job-creation bang for the buck.

Whether through public-sector jobs, subsidized jobs, or some combination, direct job creation to maintain full employment should concentrate on American infrastructure development. Along with a tremendous need today for investment in human capital, there is a need for investment in physical capital—just as President Franklin Roosevelt invested in the Civilian Conservation Corps and President Dwight Eisenhower invested in the Interstate Highway System.

Well-designed infrastructure-development blueprints already are in place, in accordance with which the federal government could invest more than $2 trillion over ten years, employing 2.5 million Americans in the first year.[32] As part of these blueprints, investments in education, affordable housing, roads, transit systems, and energy all reinforce the priorities set out in the Kerner Report:

- *Education:* Investments in more equitable school funding, more and better-trained teachers, and evidence-based early childhood and K–12 models of public school success (and documented in the section "Education Policy" in Part II) will help narrow the achievement gaps between low- and higher-income children and can significantly boost national productivity. One estimate is that complete elimination of the achievement gaps between children of different income groups would boost national income by about $70 billion annually.[33] In addition, the physical infrastructure of public school buildings influences learning—and the American Society of Civil Engineers has given a D+ to existing public school infrastructure.
- *Affordable housing:* Even working forty hours a week, a minimum-wage worker in the United States cannot afford the cost of a one-bedroom apartment at fair-market rent anywhere in the nation. Extremely low-income families face an affordable housing shortage of 7.4 million apartments or houses.[34]
- *Roads, bridges, public transit:* Employment is facilitated by efficient transportation. Yet the American Society of Civil Engineers estimates that one-third of our roads are in poor or mediocre condition. And America has fallen behind much of the industrialized world in pathbreaking innovations in public transit systems and high-speed passenger rail.[35]
- *Energy:* As Hurricane Maria illustrated by its devastation of Puerto Rico in 2017, the global rise in temperatures has caused, and may continue to cause, billions of dollars in damages annually, concentrating its impacts on low-income and working-class communities, which are most afflicted by the health and economic problems associated with our present fossil fuel economy. An overhaul of America's antiquated electricity-generation and transmission grid and the accelerated development of alternative green technologies will generate hundreds of thousands of new jobs. The public-sector need for accelerating the development of infrastructure in renewable alternative energy technologies has been estimated at $6 trillion by 2030. Already, in the last ten years, for example, employment in the solar industry has increased over tenfold—from 24,000 jobs to 260,000 jobs. Solar and other alternative technologies continue to improve.[36]

A comprehensive new American infrastructure policy also must address Department of Veterans Affairs facilities, clean drinking water, high-speed broadband, and airport facilities, among other priorities.[37]

Job Training First

As part of a full-employment economy, job creation needs to be linked to job training, so that workers have a base of skills to better ensure long-term employability and upward mobility. The present supply-side Workforce Innovation and Opportunity Act, which replaced the WIA in 2014, with its priority on work first, needs to be replaced with a new strategy that scales up the principles underlying proven, evidence-based job training models. Four illustrative models are YouthBuild, Year Up, Job Corps, and Argus:

YouthBuild. As its founder, Dorothy Stoneman, tells us in Chapter 4 of Part II, YouthBuild has created a network of 250 job training programs in the nation's most hard-pressed urban and rural communities. Low-income students who have left high school without a diploma enroll full time for about ten months. They spend half their time learning construction skills and getting paid a wage for building affordable housing for homeless and low-income people in their communities. They spend the other half working toward their high school equivalency diploma in highly supportive and individualized classrooms. YouthBuild is woven together with personal and peer counseling, deeply caring adults, and a major emphasis on leadership development and the internalization of positive values. At graduation, youth are ready for college and employment. Staff offer follow-up support for at least one year.

A randomized, controlled evaluation of four thousand young people at seventy-five YouthBuild sites around the nation from 2011 to 2013 found that, among other outcomes, YouthBuild increased the rate at which participants earned high school equivalency credentials, enrolled in college, and participated in vocational training. YouthBuild also led to a small increase in wages and earnings after thirty months of evaluation.[38]

Year Up. Year Up is an innovative and intensive program that combines skill acquisition and work experience for young adults. The Year Up model includes occupational skills training, apprenticeships that build experience and networks, stipends for students, college credits for training participation, and development of relationships with supportive adults, including program advisors and workplace mentors. A randomized, controlled evaluation found that participation in Year Up was associated with a 30 percent boost in annual earnings on average.[39]

Job Corps. Job Corps is one of the original War on Poverty programs. Residential Job Corps centers around the United States are run by private contractors, the Department of Agriculture, or the Department of the Interior. The majority of participants live at residential Job Corps centers while in the program. Some live outside, in the community. Job Corps interventions include academic education, health education, health care, vocational training, job placement, and mentoring. There is no set duration, but participants enroll for eight months on average.

A long-term randomized, controlled evaluation of Job Corps found several positive effects for participants, including reduced arrests and conviction rates, reduced reliance on public assistance, increased levels of educational attainment, higher levels of employment, and higher-paying jobs.[40]

Argus. The Argus Learning for Living model incorporates remedial education, high school equivalency education, life-management training, conflict resolution training, economic self-sufficiency skills, job training, job placement, and follow-up to ensure job retention. Since its inception in the Bronx in 1967, Argus has invested in severely disadvantaged young people and their families. Argus participants often have entered the program with substance abuse issues, criminal records, housing challenges, educational deficits, and financial instability.

A randomized, controlled evaluation of Argus and several comparison-group evaluations showed Argus participants to be associated with greater likelihood of completing high school equivalency courses and of securing employment. The assessments also documented decreased contact with police and reduced involvement in crime.[41]

For Argus and each of the other illustrative evidence-based job training models, workforce development includes life-skills training. Such training is especially important for poor minority young men. With globalization and the decline in American manufacturing, new jobs for workers with limited skills increasingly are in service industries. However, as Harvard Kennedy School professor William Julius Wilson has observed, employers often are less likely to hire young minority men because they are perceived as not having the interpersonal skills needed for service jobs.[42] This is blatantly discriminatory. Life-skills training teaches minority youth ways to navigate around such discrimination, while youth development programs like the job training models identified here offer pathways to more education, including college, so minority youth are not necessarily forced into a lifetime of service sector employment.

Tax Credits

In addition to demand-side, full-employment fiscal and monetary policy linked to job training that has proved to work, a large and growing body of evidence indicates that expanding the Earned Income Tax Credit (EITC) and creating a child allowance system will help significantly reduce the income and wealth gaps between racial minorities and whites in America.

The EITC is a wage subsidy for all low-income workers, claimed by more than five million African American workers with nearly seven million children. It is a refundable tax credit—meaning that recipients with no (or low) tax liability can receive it as a cash refund.

The EITC has received some bipartisan support and should be expanded. One recent analysis determined that a $1 trillion expansion of the EITC over the next decade would offset the damage done to low- and moderate-wage earners by the forces of inequality since 1979. A low-income working family with one child would see its credit almost double—from $3,400 to $6,500. A working-class family of four making $40,000 would receive an EITC boost of about $4,000 (from $2,000 to $6,000). African American and Hispanic American workers would disproportionately gain from such an expansion (see Chapter 2 in Part II).

One reason that child poverty in America is higher than in most other industrialized democracies (see Figure 2.2) is that other nations provide regular payments to families with children, because they recognize that investing in kids is an essential public good. Though we have the Child Tax Credit here in the United States, which like the EITC benefits millions of people, the lowest-income children, who are disproportionately children of color, receive no income support.[43]

We recommend that the Child Tax Credit be expanded into a monthly stipend for *all* families with children. A child allowance of $250 per month ($3,000 per year) would cost about $190 billion per year, though half the cost could be offset by consolidating existing policies that deliver cash to children but that are less well targeted. This reform would cut child poverty by about 40 percent and deep child poverty by half while providing middle-income families raising children with a baseline level of stable income (see Chapter 2 in Part II). Because the expanded Child Tax Credit would embrace poor families, working families, *and* the middle class, enactment would provide common ground to help generate the new will the Kerner Commission concluded was essential to achieving its priorities (see Chapter 8 in Part I).

The Minimum Wage and Labor Unions

Because African American, Hispanic American, and Native American workers disproportionately earn low wages, a higher minimum wage will help them more than other groups of workers. We endorse a new proposal to raise the federal minimum wage to $15 by 2024. African Americans make up 12 percent of the workforce but 17 percent of those who earn minimum wage. Forty percent of African American workers and 34 percent of Hispanic American workers would directly or indirectly receive a raise.[44]

As labor unions have fought for a higher minimum wage, trickle-down, supply-side policy has fought unions as it has also encouraged higher CEO pay. Unionization has declined steadily over the last four decades and now is at only about 9 percent of American workers. (See Figure 2.9.) The United States now has one of the lowest unionization rates among advanced industrialized democracies.[45]

It is not surprising, then, that America leads advanced industrial democracies in low-paying jobs, with over 20 percent of American jobs paying less than two-thirds of the median wage. As the International Monetary Fund has documented, another consequence of the decline of American unions is rising inequality. Unions reduce inequality by bringing up the wages of middle-income and lowest-paid workers. In addition, unionized workers are 28 percent more likely to be covered by employer-provided health insurance and 34 percent more likely to have a pension.[46]

As Harvard economist Lawrence Summers reminds us, the basic function of unions in our democracy has been to balance the power between employees and employers. Yet today the system is more and more rigged in favor of the highest corporate bidders.[47]

To reverse the decline of unions, we need to:

- Fight for legislation, like that in Germany, that requires union representation on corporate boards and worker profit sharing.[48]
- Encourage more direct action by unions, following the models of the Service Employees International Union and the United Food and Commercial Workers Union.[49]
- Press for labor law reforms ensuring that organized workers can bargain with the companies that profit from their work. The legal definition of employment should be expanded to cover more categories of workers. For example, Uber and Lyft drivers, who currently are "independent contractors," should be designated as employees.[50]
- Encourage unions to speak out more strongly against racism, as the AFL-CIO has begun to do, to secure more solidarity among minority and white workers.[51]
- Encourage labor to be part of the broader economic justice movement that we recommend in Chapter 8 of Part I as essential in creating the new will that the Kerner Commission concluded was essential for reform. Labor has a good case to make: when union wages increase, nonunion employers respond by also raising pay, to attract workers.[52]

- Encourage unions to advocate more for the individual rights that Americans hold dear and against the power of large employers and government. Just as Dr. King fought for individual civil rights as a fulfillment of the Declaration of Independence's promise of equal opportunity, so the labor movement must fight for individuals' First Amendment right to engage in the freedom of association, including the right to form a union.[53]
- Advocate for amendment of the Civil Rights Act of 1964 to outlaw employment discrimination not only on the basis of race and sex but also employment discrimination against joining a union. Doing so would allow employees to sue in federal court and to receive compensatory and punitive damages from employers. Without employers trying to block union organization, polls suggest that many American workers would join unions if given a free choice.[54]

In addition, we recommend passage of the Workplace Action for a Growing Economy (WAGE) bill. WAGE would amend the National Labor Relations Act (NLRA) to strengthen protections for working people who organize to promote change through collective action. The law would increase workers' rights and protections by:

- Doubling the back pay that employers must give to workers who are fired or retaliated against because they engaged in collective action, regardless of immigration status
- Providing workers whose rights are violated with the right to sue for monetary damages, just as they can under civil rights laws
- Providing for federal court injunctions to immediately return fired workers to their jobs[55]

If Congress is too gridlocked to consider such reforms, forward-looking states like California and New York should take the lead and then become models for other states.

Single-Payer Health Insurance Coverage for All Americans

Health policy is economic policy. Workers who have good health care insurance, and therefore better health, are more productive and live longer. The racial gaps in life expectancy in America are unconscionable. In addition, in recent years, life expectancy has fallen for working-class whites—reflecting, for example, the ravages of alcoholism, drug overdoses, and suicide brought on by the same lack of economic and employment opportunity faced for decades by poor minorities.[56] We believe health care is a basic human and moral right. It should not be a privilege.

The details of health care reform are beyond the scope of this Kerner Report update. But given the evidence that America spends more on health care than any other wealthy country and has some of the worst health outcomes, we believe the debate needs to become focused on a single-payer plan for the United States. It should build on a 2016 Pew study that showed that 60 percent of Americans felt it was the government's job to guarantee health care coverage for all Americans.[57]

"Single payer" has many meanings. From the perspective of not just the truly disadvantaged and workers but also the middle class, the single-payer plan ideally should be more generous than traditional Medicare and most private plans. It should eliminate all copays and deductibles and include coverage of long-term care.[58]

In Chapter 5 of Part II, Herbert Smitherman, Anil Aranha, and Lamar Johnson provide a broader view of public health policy in the context of the Kerner Commission's work.

Trade Policy and Globalization

As with health care, comprehensive assessment of trade policy is beyond the scope of this update. However, the evidence is clear that trickle-down, supply-side policy on globalization and trade has:

- Failed to secure reasonable compensation for those on the losing end of globalization, especially the poor and the working class
- Failed with trade agreements that have consistently aimed to undercut workers' economic leverage while carving out ample protections for corporate profits
- Failed to address currency misalignments that have led to large trade deficits and to loss of manufacturing employment[59]

The overriding principle of reform policy on globalization and trade is to stop pursuing new omnibus trade agreements that protect returns on capital and undercut wages. Policy needs to benefit workers in America and other countries—by addressing currency realignments, enabling countries to tax capital income, clamping down on abusive tax havens, instituting an international financial-transaction tax, and creating cooperative international agreements to better combat global climate change.[60]

A constructive first step is for America to begin on our own continent. The North American Free Trade Agreement (NAFTA) has reinforced inequality and insecurity in the United States, Mexico, and Canada. A new social contract should include:

- An enforceable bill of rights for all citizens of North America that would reassert the primacy of civil protection of individuals

and democratic government over the extraordinary privileges that NAFTA gives to corporate investors
- A new continental deal, in which Canada and the United States commit substantial long-term aid while Mexico commits to policies (independent trade unions, minimum wages, equitable taxes) that assure a wider distribution of the benefits of growth
- A continental development strategy that shifts the economic policy objectives of all three countries from subsidizing pursuit of global profits by corporate investors to support of green technology and increased investment in health and education[61]

The Most Vulnerable

It may be true, as President Kennedy said, that "a rising tide lifts all boats." But all boats cannot rise to the same level. There are too many people in our country in a boat that does not rise as high as others because it is full of water and needs bailing out. That is why, for example, Congress long ago rightly passed the Child Labor Laws and, in modern times, was right to adopt the Americans with Disabilities Act, as well as laws for special support for military veterans, returning after absence to society and the economy, many with serious physical or emotional wounds.

Of course, that is why, too, America must, as we do in this Kerner update, give special attention to the problems of African Americans (throughout and especially in Chapters 12 and 16 in Part II), Hispanic Americans (throughout and especially in Chapter 17 in Part II), children (throughout and especially in Chapters 8 and 9 in Part II), and Native Americans (in various parts and especially in Chapter 18 in Part II).

But more should be said about two groups that still need special or more attention: women and undocumented immigrants.

Women

Women constitute a majority of the American population.[62] That is a well-known fact, but many do not take it seriously enough. The feminist movement had considerable effect toward improving women's lives, employment, health, education, and well-being, generally, from 1970 to 2009. Still, there is much that very much needs to be done.

By 2015, women were still receiving only 80 percent of what men were paid, and the situation is not getting any better. Even women who are medical doctors make an average of approximately $20,000 a year less than male doctors. Unlike in other countries surveyed by the OECD, there is no federal paid family and medical leave in the United States (for men or women), and that hurts low-income women and women of color especially hard. There is a great lack of affordable, quality childcare, and this is a special and serious problem for women that shuts many of them out of the workforce. Women's reproductive health care is under severe attack, and a woman's right to choose, under *Roe v. Wade*, has suffered from numerous and serious state restrictions. The passage of the Violence against Women Act, with reauthorizations, is a welcome advance for women, but too much violence against women continues.

America needs more women in government and public office at all levels, on corporate boards, and in the private sector, generally. Their special experiences and perspective make a difference. We need to join other nations in enacting a paid family leave.

The 2017 Women's March on Washington and the widespread support for it, then and now, is a factor in helping create the new will necessary to improve the lives of women and, therefore, of all of America.

Undocumented Immigrants

Best estimates are that there are 11.7 million undocumented immigrants now in the United States, the great majority of them from Latin America, particularly Mexico. Most have been here for some time, working, paying taxes, raising and educating their children, and obeying the laws. And there is no way—virtually nobody really believes otherwise—that these millions will be, or could be, rounded up and deported.

According to former San Antonio mayor and former U.S. Secretary of Housing and Urban Development Henry Cisneros, attacks on these undocumented immigrants tend to conflate them with U.S. citizens who look like them and often go beyond opposition to immigration policies— to prejudices about language and heritage (see Chapter 17 in Part II). Cisneros adds that the undocumented are people "with whom Latinos go to church, collaborate in the workplace, [and] shop in neighborhood stores," and Latinos now more than ever perceive attacks on the undocumented as attacks on the entire Hispanic community.

Undocumented immigrants in the United States believe in all the American values of hard work and achieving the American Dream that citizens do, only more so. They are a boost for America's economy, their reported crime rate is lower than that for the general population, and with the declining fertility rate of U.S. citizens, they improve the worker-elderly ratio in this country and help shore up Social Security.[63]

We recommend legislation like that passed by the Senate in 2012 (which died in the House of Representatives) to bring longtime undocumented immigrants in this country out of the shadows, grant them permanent residence and work permits, and provide them a path to citizenship (though a somewhat easier one than that Senate bill would have provided). Not only will those 11.7 million hardworking people benefit by our support, but so will America and its economy.

We then should change our immigration laws to raise the number of people who can come to the United States, with documents, on the basis of scientific estimates of the new immigrants we will need here in the future, as our economy and new jobs continue to grow.

3

Education Policy

SINCE THE KERNER COMMISSION, American public schools have been inadequately and inequitably financed. School segregation has increased. Market-driven supply-side vouchers, Leave No Child Behind, Race to the Top, and School Improvement Grants have failed. Charter schools have a limited track record. Today, governments at all levels need to scale up proven, evidence-based models like high-quality early childhood education, community schools, Youth Safe Havens, Quantum Opportunities, YouthBuild, Career Academies, and Bottom Line. Scaling up needs to proceed within a strategic framework that substantially reinvests in America's public schools, allocates funds equitably among schools, hires and supports highly qualified teachers, closes achievement gaps, and renews the desegregation that was successful in the years immediately following release of the Kerner Report.

TRENDS

The Kerner Commission emphasized that most urban American neighborhoods were "rigidly segregated" and that, because children usually attend public schools in their neighborhoods, most schools also were rigidly segregated. The commission found that, in poor minority neighborhood schools, "children are processed instead of educated." Citing the findings of the Coleman Report on equal educational opportunity, the Kerner Commission observed that "the predominant socioeconomic background of the students in a school exerts a powerful impact upon achievement."[1]

Consequently, the Kerner commissioners' central recommendation on education was, "We support integration as the priority education strategy; it is essential to the future of American society."[2]

Yet since release of the Kerner Report, segregation has been increasing steadily, creating a growing number of apartheid schools that serve almost exclusively students of color, most of whom live in poverty. Racial achievement gaps in education have remained. Apartheid schools often are severely under-resourced, and they struggle to close academic gaps while underwriting the greater costs of addressing the effects of poverty—like hunger, homelessness, and other traumas experienced by children and families in low-income communities. For all these reasons, the most respected research has found that the extent to which students attend schools with other low-income students is one of the strongest predictors of their achievement.[3]

Today, gaps in educational opportunity and attainment in impoverished and working-class communities remain at a time when those without education are locked out of our knowledge-based economy.

Growing Poverty, Segregation, and Inequality in Public School Funding

As Stanford professor Linda Darling-Hammond concludes in Chapter 6 of Part II, since the Kerner Report, the roots of inequality in educational outcomes in the United States are growing poverty and resegregation, along with inequality in school financing and resources.

Chapter 2 of Part I documents that American child-poverty rates increased from the time of the Kerner Commission to the present. Among children attending American public schools, more than half now qualify for free or reduced-price lunch—the highest percentage since the National Center for Education Statistics began tracking this figure decades ago. American children living in poverty have a much weaker safety net than their peers in other industrialized countries, where universal health care, housing subsidies, and high-quality, universally available childcare are the norm.

A growing share of poor American children attend public school in districts where poverty is concentrated. (See Figure 3.1.) This creates huge challenges for their education. In 2007, of the 8.5 million low-income students in the country, about one in five lived in districts with a poverty rate of over 30 percent. By 2012, over one in three low-income children lived in districts with a poverty rate over 30 percent. The growing poverty caused by the Great Recession, which began in 2007–2008, contributed to this concentration. The growing disparity in incomes and wealth—now wider than it has been since 1929—has reinforced it.

In most major American cities, a majority of African American and Hispanic students attend public schools where at least 75 percent of

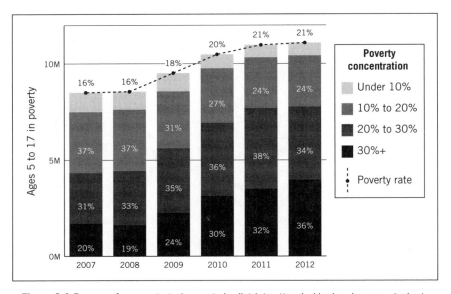

Figure 3.1 Degree of concentrated poverty in districts attended by low-income students
Source: Bruce D. Baker, David G. Sciarra, and Danielle Farrie, *Is School Funding Fair? A National Report Card* (Newark, NJ: Education Law Center, 2015).

students are poor. Increasingly, these schools are segregated by both race and class. For example, in Chicago and New York City, more than 95 percent of African American and Hispanic students attend majority-poverty schools. High-poverty schools are almost entirely populated by African American and Hispanic students. Low-poverty schools have very few such students. (See Figure 3.2.)

In the two decades immediately after the 1968 Kerner Report, there was a dramatic decline in segregation, especially in the South. Then, federal support and court orders for desegregation were discontinued. The result was increased residential segregation, which has led to a steady climb in school segregation. In 1968, about 60 percent of African American students nationwide—and about 80 percent in the South—attended intensely segregated schools (where minority students constitute 90 percent or more of the total). (See Figure 3.3.) In 1988, just over a third of African American students (and just over 20 percent in the South) attended intensely segregated schools. But by 2010, the proportion exceeded 40 percent nationwide and more than 50 percent in the Northeast, where segregation has increased steadily for the last fifty years.

In 1988, about 44 percent of African Americans attended majority-white schools nationally. Today, only about 20 percent of African American students attend majority-white schools nationally. (See Figure 3.4.)

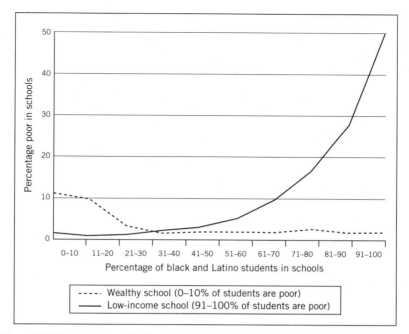

Figure 3.2 Proportion of African American and Hispanic students in schools by poverty concentration

Source: Jason M. Breslow, Evan Wexler, and Robert Collins, "The Return of School Segregation in Eight Charts," *Frontline*, July 15, 2014, available at https://www.pbs.org/wgbh/frontline/article/the-return-of-school-segregation-in-eight-charts.

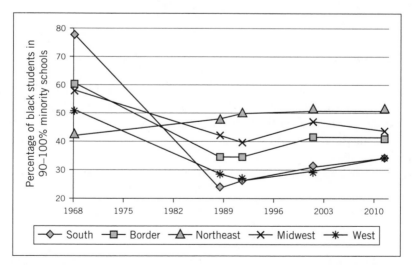

Figure 3.3 Percentage of African American students in increasingly segregated minority schools by region, 2012

Source: National Center for Education Statistics *Public Elementary/Secondary School Universe Survey Data*, available at https://nces.ed.gov/ccd/pubschuniv.asp; Gary Orfield, *Public School Desegregation in the United States, 1968–1980* (Washington, DC: Joint Center for Political Studies, 1983).

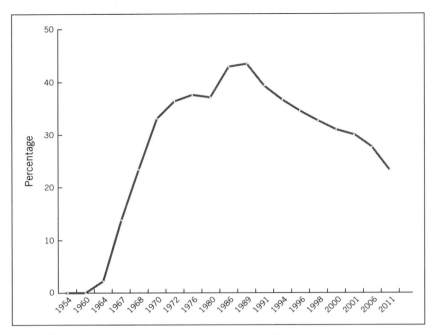

Figure 3.4 Percentage of African American students attending majority white student schools
Source: National Center for Education Statistics *Public Elementary/Secondary School Universe Survey Data*, available at https://nces.ed.gov/ccd/pubschuniv.asp; Gary Orfield, *Public School Desegregation in the United States, 1968–1980* (Washington, DC: Joint Center for Political Studies, 1983).

Together, high rates of poverty, housing segregation, and economic polarization have left most African American and Hispanic students marooned in schools where economic struggle is the rule and financial stability is the exception. Meanwhile, white students are the least likely group to go to school with students of other races.

Among the reasons for this growing resegregation is the abandonment of desegregation orders in many cities. Segregation declined significantly in districts under court oversight. When that oversight was terminated, segregation rapidly climbed back up. (See Figure 3.5.)

Continuation of Educational Achievement Gaps

Where children go to school matters greatly for their success, as Darling-Hammond shows in Chapter 6. Unequal opportunity is related to lower achievement. As one influential investigation concluded, "The large volume of research conducted since *Brown* . . . has shown that segregated, predominantly minority schools offer students unequal and inferior educational opportunities. . . . Educational inequalities in racially isolated

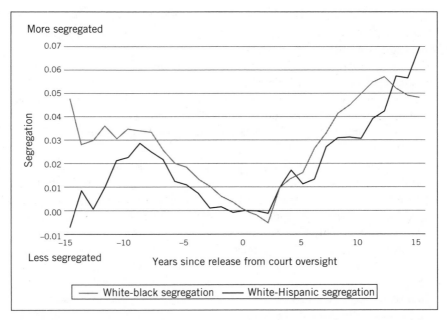

Figure 3.5 Degree of segregation in relation to years since release from court oversight
Source: Data from Sean F. Reardon, Elena Grewel, Demetra Kalogrides, and Erica Greenberg, "Brown Fades: The End of Court-Ordered School Desegregation and the Resegregation of American Public Schools," *Journal of Policy Analysis and Management* 31, no. 4 (2012): 876–904.

schools arise in several ways, such as limited educational resources (whether measured by class size, facilities, or per-pupil spending), fewer qualified teachers, and inadequate access to peers who can help improve achievement. . . . Not surprisingly, measures of educational outcomes, such as scores on standardized tests and high school graduation rates, are lower in predominantly minority schools."[4]

Similarly, an evaluation of court-ordered desegregation of students born between 1945 and 1970 found that graduation rates climbed by two percentage points for every year an African American student attended an integrated school. An African American student exposed to court-ordered desegregation for five years experienced a 15 percent increase in wages and an eleven percentage point decline in poverty. The difference was tied to schools under court supervision benefiting from higher per-pupil spending and smaller student-teacher ratios, among other resources. *Importantly, while there were positive outcomes for African Americans, court-ordered desegregation caused no statistically significant harm for whites.*

Desegregation was pursued by many communities during the 1960s and 1970s. As a result, there was a noticeable reduction in educational inequality in the decade after the 1968 Kerner Report, when desegregation and school finance reform efforts were launched and when the Great

Society's War on Poverty increased investments in urban and poor rural schools. At that time, substantial gains were made in equalizing both educational interventions and outcomes.

The Elementary and Secondary Education Act of 1965 targeted resources to communities with the most need, recognizing that where children grow up should not determine where they end up. Employment initiatives and welfare supports reduced child poverty to levels about 60 percent of what they are today and greatly improved children's access to health care.

The Elementary and Secondary Education Act also advanced desegregation, the development of magnet schools, and other strategies to improve both urban and poor rural schools. These efforts to level the playing field for children were supported by intensive investments in employing and retaining talented teachers, as well as in improving teacher education.

The investments paid off in measurable ways. By the mid-1970s, urban public schools spent as much as suburban public schools and paid their teachers as well as suburban public schools. Perennial teacher shortages had nearly ended. Gaps in educational attainment had closed substantially. Federally funded curriculum investments transformed teaching in many schools. Innovative public schools flourished in a number of cities. Financial aid for higher education was sharply increased, especially for need-based scholarships and loans. For a brief period in the mid-1970s, African American and Hispanic students attended college at the same rate as whites, the only time this has occurred, before or since.

Improvements in educational achievement for students of color followed. In reading, large gains in African American student performance throughout the 1970s and early 1980s reduced the achievement gap considerably, cutting it by more than half for thirteen-year-olds (from thirty-nine points on the National Assessment of Educational Progress to just eighteen points) between 1971 and 1988. The achievement gap in mathematics also narrowed by twenty points (about a third) over the same general period.

However, the gains from the Great Society programs were pushed back during the Reagan administration, when most targeted federal programs supporting investments in college access and K–12 schools in urban and poor rural areas were reduced or eliminated. Federal aid to schools was cut from 12 percent to 6 percent of a shrinking total. Meanwhile, childhood poverty rates, homelessness, and lack of access to health care grew with cuts in other federal programs supporting housing, subsidies, health care, and child welfare.

By 1991, stark differences had reemerged between segregated public urban schools and their suburban counterparts, which generally spent twice as much. Achievement gaps began to grow once again. While there have been small gains in the thirty years since, the gaps in achievement between African American and white students are larger today than they were then. For example, African American thirteen-year-olds have gained only four points in reading since 1988, while white students have gained nine points, leaving a gap that is nearly 30 percent larger today than it was three decades ago. Similarly, in mathematics today, African American thirteen-year-olds actually score a point lower than they did when the gap was smallest in 1990. White same-age students now score five points higher, so the gap has increased by 30 percent in mathematics as well as reading.

While national high school completion rates have steadily risen for all students since 2003, there still are significant gaps in high school graduation for non-Asian students of color and white students. White and Asian students graduate within four years at rates of 88 percent and 90 percent, respectively, whereas African American, Hispanic American, and Native American students graduate at rates of 75 percent, 78 percent, and 72 percent, respectively. This means that about one in four historically underserved minority students still fail to graduate high school within four years.

The gaps are much greater within specific states and cities, especially those that are strongly segregated. For example, only 64 percent of African American students graduate in four years in Wisconsin, compared to 93 percent of white students, and only 56 percent of African American students graduate in four years in Nevada, compared to 78 percent of white students. And African American–white achievement gaps of more than three grade levels exist in cities ranging from the District of Columbia to Seattle.

Educational shortcomings plus lack of family resources and cuts in federal funding for financial aid extend these disparities into higher education. At a time when more than 70 percent of American jobs require postsecondary education, only about a third of African American and Hispanic young people ages eighteen to twenty-four are enrolled in two-year and four-year colleges, compared to 42 percent of white youth. (See Figure 3.6.) In the population as a whole, disparities in access to college are obvious. Among whites, about 33 percent have at least four years of college, as do 54 percent of Asians. But the proportions of African Americans and Hispanics are about 22 percent and 16 percent, respectively. The gaps in college attainment between whites and African Americans and Hispanic Americans have grown since the Kerner Report.

The Opportunity Gap and Unequal School Funding

As Darling-Hammond concludes in Chapter 6, investments in the education of students of color that characterized the school desegregation and finance reforms of the 1960s and 1970s have never been fully reestablished

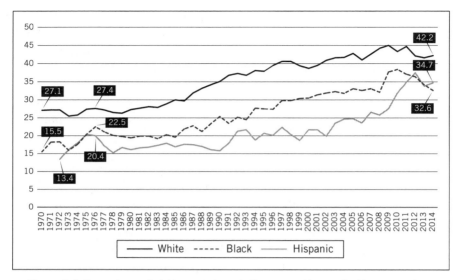

Figure 3.6 Percentage of eighteen- to twenty-four-year-olds enrolled in two- or four-year college

Source: National Center for Education Statistics, *Digest of Education Statistics: 2015*, table 302.60, available at https://nces.ed.gov/programs/digest/d16/tables/dt16_302.60.asp.

in the years since. Had the rate of progress achieved in the 1970s and early 1980s been continued, the achievement gap would have been fully closed by the beginning of the twenty-first century. Unfortunately, that did not occur.

Nations like Canada, Finland, and Singapore are now high achieving and equitable after the progressive reforms they launched in the 1970s. But the United States has reversed much of the progress it made during the 1970s. Although some federal support for high-need schools and districts was restored during the 1990s, it was not enough to fully recoup the earlier losses. After 2000, inequality grew once again.

These inequities reflect how public education is funded in the United States. In most cases, education costs are supported primarily by local property taxes, along with state grants-in-aid that are somewhat equalizing but typically not sufficient to close the gaps caused by differences in local property values. The wealthiest districts in most states spend at least three times what the poorest districts can spend per pupil. These differentials translate into dramatically different salaries for educators and different learning conditions for students. Within large districts, there are, as well, disparities in how funds are allocated to schools serving different kinds of students, usually favoring those with more political clout.

To further increase inequality, the wealthiest states spend about three times what the poorer states spend. So the advantages available to children in the wealthiest communities of high-spending and high-achieving states like Massachusetts, Connecticut, and New Jersey are dramatically different from those in the poorest communities of low-spending states like Arizona, Mississippi, and North Carolina, where buildings are crumbling, classes are overcrowded, instructional materials are inadequate, and staff are often transient and underprepared.

These inequalities result in disparities in the number and quality of teachers and other educators available to students and in unequal access to high-quality curricula. As segregation and school funding differentials grew worse after the 1980s, the practice of lowering or waiving credentialing standards to fill classrooms in high-minority, low-income schools became commonplace in many states, especially those with large minority and immigrant populations, like California, Texas, Florida, and New York. This practice is unheard of in high-achieving nations and in other professions.

There is evidence that teachers in high-need schools have, on average, lower levels of experience and education, are less likely to be credentialed for the field they teach, and have lower scores on certification tests and other measures of academic achievement. A growing body of research has shown that these kinds of qualifications matter for student achievement. Studies at the state, district, school, and individual-student level have found that teachers' academic background, preparation for teaching, certification status, and experience significantly affect their students' learning gains.

In combination, teachers' qualifications can have substantial effects. For example, a large-scale study of high school student achievement in North Carolina found that students' achievement growth was significantly higher if they were taught by a teacher who was certified in his or her teaching field, was fully prepared upon entry, had higher scores on the teacher licensing test, graduated from a competitive college, had taught for more than two years, or had National Board certification. Taken individually, each of these qualifications was associated with greater teacher effectiveness. In addition, the combined influence on achievement growth of having a teacher with most of these qualifications was larger than the effects of race and the effect of parent education combined. While achievement from one year to the next is still largely dependent on prior achievement, this finding suggests that the achievement gap might be reduced over time if minority students were more routinely assigned highly qualified teachers rather than the poorly qualified teachers they most often encounter.

The experience of other nations supports the importance of qualified teachers. For example, one leading investigation found that the most significant predictors of mathematics achievement across forty-six nations included teacher's certification, a college major in mathematics or mathematics education, and at least three years of teaching experience. This study also found that, although the national level of teacher quality in the

United States is similar to the international average, the opportunity gap in students' access to qualified teachers between students of high and low socioeconomic status in America is among the largest in the world.

Such disparities have come to appear inevitable in the United States. But they are *not* the norm in developed nations around the world, which typically fund their education systems *centrally and equally*, with additional resources often going to the schools where students' needs are greater. Investments of this kind made by high-achieving nations are steadier than in America and more focused on critical elements of the system. The critical elements include the quality of teachers and teaching, the development of curricula and assessments that encourage ambitious learning by both students and teachers, and the design of schools as learning organizations that support continuous reflection and improvement. With the exception of a few states with enlightened long-term leadership, the United States, by contrast, has failed to maintain such focused investments.

WHAT DOES NOT WORK

In sum, federal, state, and local executive-branch policy and court decisions reversing desegregation did not work, and reducing funding to public schools increased inequality. *Government decisions and court rulings reversed success.*

This abandonment of progress was combined with other federal and state policies that did not work, according to randomized, controlled evaluations and other rigorous assessments. Such failed or flawed policies and programs have included market-driven supply-side vouchers, charter schools, Leave No Child Behind, Race to the Top, and School Improvement Grants, which we now briefly review.

Vouchers, Choice, and Charter Schools

Vouchers are coupons that let parents use their tax dollars for private schools, including religious schools. Vouchers are based on market-driven ideology, just as supply-side, trickle-down economics policies are based on market-driven ideology. Vouchers are advocated under the banner of school choice. The free-market notion is that, in using vouchers, parents will choose good schools over bad ones.

However, evaluations of voucher programs in several American cities, the District of Columbia, and the states of Florida, Indiana, and Louisiana have found limited improvements at best in student achievement and school district performance. In the few cases in which test scores increased, other factors, especially increased public accountability and lack of private school competition, appeared most responsible. There have been high rates of attrition from private schools among voucher users in several studies. The longest-standing American voucher program, in Milwaukee, has yielded no solid evidence of student gains in either private or public schools.[5] Other evaluations of vouchers have documented that increased school segregation can result. School choice was the strategy used by southern governors and legislators in the 1950s and 1960s to evade desegregation.[6]

Charter schools are considered public schools. But charters operate with autonomy from local school systems. Charters are run by nonprofit or for-profit organizations. They are guided by a contract, or charter, with their state that specifies the conditions under which a school can operate. Ideally, the contract effectively holds a charter school accountable for achieving outcomes like improved student performance. Today, there are more than six thousand charter schools across forty-two states and the District of Columbia.[7]

There is evidence that some charter schools perform well. Some have suggested that perhaps 20 percent of charter schools outperform traditional public schools.[8] A good example is in Boston. A rigorous randomized, controlled evaluation examined Boston's "high expectations, high support" charter schools. Boston charter schools devote more of their resources to classroom teaching than traditional public schools and less to almost everything else. Students are kept in class for longer hours. The evaluation showed that high school students in Boston charter schools scored much higher on SAT math and reading tests and attended four-year colleges at much higher rates than students not in Boston charter schools.[9]

However, the Boston experience is not the national norm. In the most significant national randomized, controlled evaluation of charter schools, by Mathematica, thirty-six charter middle schools were selected from fifteen states, covering a broad geographic area. Applicants were randomly assigned to either a group that was admitted to the school or to a control group not admitted. The major finding was that, on average, charter schools had no significant effect on student achievement in math and reading. Effects varied widely across schools, being most positive among schools in large, urban areas and among those serving the most disadvantaged students.[10]

In addition, as UCLA professor Gary Orfield points out in Chapter 10 of Part II and elsewhere, there is substantial evidence from a number of assessments that charter schools do not serve an equitable share of special education and English-language-learner students, have failed students and sent them back to public schools, and have been even more segregated than regular public schools. For example, a study in Minnesota showed that, overwhelmingly, white charter schools were developing in that state—the first to enact charter legislation.[11]

The most sophisticated evaluations to date, then, suggest that market-driven vouchers do not work and that charter schools may work at times, especially in places with struggling public school systems, but at the cost of draining still more money from those systems.

On the basis of such evidence, a new organization, Journey for Justice, composed of civil rights and grassroots organizations in twenty-one cities, has advocated for "community-driven alternatives to the privatization and dismantling of public school systems." Its member cities include Atlanta, Baltimore, Boston, Detroit, Los Angeles, Minneapolis, New Orleans, Newark, New York City, Philadelphia, and Pittsburgh and Washington, D.C. The organization argues that "the policies of the last fifteen years, driven more by private interests than by concern for our children's education, are devastating our neighborhoods and our democratic rights. . . . Journey for Justice is intentionally creating a space for organized low-income and working-class communities [that] are directly impacted by top-down privatization and school closing efforts."[12]

No Child Left Behind, Race to the Top, and School Improvement Grants

The No Child Left Behind Act, passed in 2001, required that all schools reach 100 percent proficiency, as measured by standardized tests. States spent billions of dollars on the tests. The program encouraged the firing of thousands of teachers and the closing of thousands of low-scoring public schools—mostly in poor African American and Hispanic neighborhoods. No Child Left Behind was not formulated to deal with the evidence that, as measured by test scores, the best predictor of student achievement is family income. (That is, well-off students usually score in the top half of test results and students from poor homes in the bottom half.)[13]

No Child Left Behind advocates asserted that the creation of a national curriculum—the Common Core—would at least promote equity, because all students would study the same things and take the same tests. It was argued that Common Core standards would reduce the gaps between rich and poor, minority and white. However, after more than eight years of the first national standards, racial achievement gaps persisted.[14]

In 2009, the $4 billion Race to the Top initiative was launched as an extension of the No Child Left Behind law. A competition was begun in which winning states would agree to adopt programs that might raise test scores. To be eligible, states had to agree to open more charter schools, adopt Common Core standards in English and math, evaluate teachers on the basis of the rise or fall of their students' test scores, and close schools that persistently produced low test scores. The national evaluation of Race to the Top was inconclusive. For example, the evaluation concluded that trends in student outcomes in the states that implemented awards could be interpreted as providing evidence that Race to the Top had a positive effect, a negative effect, or no effect.[15]

At about the same time, the $7 billion competitive School Improvement Grants program was begun. Federal funds were granted for state distribution to the poorest-performing schools—those with exceedingly low graduation rates or poor math or reading scores. Individual schools were required to implement one of four interventions—replacing the principal and at least half the teachers, converting to a charter school, closing altogether, or undergoing a transformation. The transformation included hiring a new principal, adapting new instructional strategies, undertaking new teacher evaluations, and implementing a longer school day. However, the national evaluation concluded that test scores, graduation rates, and college enrollment were no different in schools that received the funding than in schools that did not.[16]

EDUCATION POLICY BASED ON WHAT WORKS

To learn from what has and has not worked since the Kerner Report, the American education system needs to turn away from market-driven policies that decrease equality, return to the strategies that increased equal opportunity in the 1960s and 1970s, and scale up evidence-based models that have demonstrated success in randomized controlled or quasi-experimental design evaluations.

Federal, State, and Local Policies to Achieve Equal Education Opportunity

Federal funding to states should be tied to each state's movement toward equitable access to education resources and continued progress toward school integration. A number of components under the Every Student Succeeds Act of 2015 would support this progress, *but they need to be enforced.* The substantial evidence that schools alone are not responsible for student achievement also should propel attention to the provision of adequate health care and nutrition, safe and secure housing, and universal health care for all low-income children and youth.[17]

In addition, the federal government should:

- Equalize allocations from the Every Student Succeeds Act across states so that high-poverty states receive a greater share. Allocation formulas should use indicators of student need, with adjustments for cost-of-living differentials, rather than rely on measures of spending that disadvantage poor states.
- Enforce integrative student-assignment policies and comparability provisions for ensuring equally qualified teachers for schools

serving different populations of students. The law requires that school districts minimize segregation in their decisions about student assignments to schools. The law also requires that states develop policies to balance the qualifications of teachers across schools serving more and less advantaged students. But these aspects of the law have been weakly enforced, and that policy needs to be reversed.

- Encourage states to report on opportunity indicators to accompany their reports of academic progress for each school. States should report on dollars spent; availability of well-qualified teachers; strong curriculum opportunities; books, materials, and equipment (such as science labs and computers); and adequate facilities. The federal government should evaluate progress on opportunity indicators in state plans, requiring states to meet opportunity-to-learn standards for schools identified as failing.

At the state level, the need is to complement federal policy by offsetting the inequality created by education that is tied to the wealth of communities. States need to:

- Establish weighted student-funding formulas. The formulas should allocate equal dollars to students adjusted, or weighted, for specific student needs—for example, low family income, limited English proficiency, foster-care status, or special education status—as Massachusetts and California have done.
- Focus funds on the investments that matter most. Such investments include high-quality, equitably distributed teachers and curriculum opportunities.

One of the best state models for replication is Connecticut. Connecticut ended shortages and boosted student achievement by equalizing the distribution of better-qualified teachers, raising and equalizing salaries, improving teacher education and standards, providing mentors, and supporting extensive professional development. This has led to strong gains for students of color, as well as for white students.

Local governments can:

- Allocate funds equitably to schools within their jurisdiction and create assignment zones and policies such as magnet schools in ways that reduce segregation.
- Hire, support, and retain highly qualified teachers and leaders for hard-to-staff schools and ensure they have the skills to work with diverse students successfully.
- Preserve and expand affordable housing in neighborhoods with

high-performing schools, enforce fair-housing laws, and dismantle exclusionary land-use policies. Here, a good model for replication is Montgomery County, Maryland, which has inclusionary zoning laws. (See Chapter 4 in Part I.)

Because the fates of individuals and nations are increasingly interdependent, the quest for access to an equitable education for all people has become a critical issue for America. No society can thrive in a technological, knowledge-based economy by starving large segments of its population of opportunities for learning.

Scaling Up Evidence-Based Education Models

Within an overall policy framework of significantly equalizing funding and opportunity among public schools, governments at all levels need to scale up models that have proved their success in randomized, controlled evaluations and related high-quality quasi-experimental design assessments. What follows are illustrations of proven successes at the early education, elementary school, middle school, and high school levels.

Early Childhood Education Models

Since the time of the Kerner Commission, and spurred by research on early brain development, rigorous evaluations of early education programs have documented positive annual rates of return from investments in high-quality early care and education programs, targeted to disadvantaged children. The positive returns include better educational, economic, and health outcomes along with reduced remedial education, health, and criminal justice costs.[18]

In terms of federal investments, Head Start is the best-known early childhood program. Established in 1965, Head Start promotes school readiness of children ages three to five from low-income families by enhancing their cognitive, social, and emotional development. Early Head Start, established in 1994, extended services to infants and toddlers. A recent well-regarded investigation, based on the National Longitudinal Survey of Youth, demonstrated that Head Start increases the probability of high school graduation, college attendance, and attainment of a post-secondary license or certification.[19]

For decades Head Start stood virtually alone in terms of federal investment in early childhood. Today, there are publicly funded prekindergarten programs in most states. Universal prekindergarten programs exist in Florida, Georgia, Oklahoma, Boston, New York City, and Washington, D.C. Most publicly funded prekindergarten programs serve primarily four-year-olds, but the proportion serving three-year-olds is increasing.

As Carol Emig, president of Child Trends, recommends in Chapter 8 of Part II, for America to catch up, every state should provide universal pre-kindergarten, with an emphasis on high-quality programs.

Promising as these investments are, preschool alone is not sufficient to prepare all children for school; nor is it enough to close racial and ethnic disparities in school readiness. African American children are more likely than white or Hispanic children to be enrolled in full-day preschool programs (39 percent versus 25 and 22 percent, respectively). Yet the United States remains far behind many other developed nations in the percentage of children participating in early education programs and in spending on early care and education as a share of gross domestic product.

Early care and education initiatives need highly qualified staff, yet early childhood professionals are poorly paid. Opportunities are limited for staff development, particularly in community-based programs serving low-income families. Building on the recommendations of Emig in Chapter 8, the early care and education infrastructure needs to be strengthened through higher compensation and more opportunity for staff professional development.

Elementary School, Middle School, High School, and College Models

Over the past two decades, community schools have developed as a holistic strategy, implemented by public elementary, middle, and high schools.

Most community schools have four basic kinds of interventions, though they vary in exactly how the interventions are carried out. The first intervention consists of integrated, wraparound student supports, such as dental and other health care, right in the school; counseling for children and families; conflict resolution training; and strategies to reduce bullying and punitive disciplinary actions, including suspensions. The second intervention is expanded learning time and opportunities, including after-school, weekend, and summer programs; individualized academic support and tutoring; and opportunities that emphasize real-world learning and community problem solving. The third intervention is active parental and community engagement. Parents and other community members are brought into schools, which are used as neighborhood hubs with adult educational opportunities. Such adult opportunities include English as a second language classes, permanent residency or citizenship preparation, and classes in computer skills. The final intervention consists of collaborative leadership, such as employment of a community school coordinator who manages the multiple, complex work of the school and community organizations.[20]

These four interventions create a synergy through which educators, families, nonprofits, community members, and others unite to create conditions in which all children learn and thrive.[21]

There is considerable evidence of the success of community schools. For example, the Tulsa Area Community Schools Initiative offered comprehensive supports to public school students, families, and communities and gave families and communities a voice in governance. The Tulsa evaluation compared outcomes in the model public schools to outcomes in carefully selected noncommunity public schools. By the third and fourth years, students at the fully implemented community schools scored significantly higher than their peers in noncommunity schools in standardized math and reading tests.[22]

Other good illustrations of positively evaluated community schools are in New York. At the Harlem Children's Zone, a random-assignment evaluation found that students in the community school (which also is a charter school) scored significantly higher on math and reading tests than students who attended other schools. A follow-up showed that the Harlem community school students had higher graduation rates, lower teen pregnancy rates, and lower incarceration rates.[23] In addition, two community schools in the Washington Heights neighborhood of Manhattan were evaluated against two comparison schools in similar neighborhoods over three years. Math and reading scores improved dramatically in the community schools versus the comparison schools, as did attitudes toward school.[24]

The Youth Safe Haven model is complementary to the community schools model. Evolved from the formative 1992 Carnegie Council on Adolescent Development report, *A Matter of Time*, the Youth Safe Haven initiative is implemented with elementary and middle school youth by indigenous nonprofit organizations on afternoons from about three o'clock to seven o'clock during weekdays and over summers. The primary interventions include individual and group mentoring, advocacy for youth, homework assistance, and tutoring. In a randomized, controlled evaluation in low-income African American and Hispanic neighborhoods in six cities, Youth Safe Haven participants had higher school attendance, school engagement, respect for teachers, and academic performance than did the control group. The outcomes were statistically significant.[25]

Solid evidence exists, as well, for the success of youth-development investments in minority high school youth at highest risk—in spite of naysayers who have claimed it is too late for young people by this age. For example, the Quantum Opportunities model, evolved from initial work by the Ford Foundation and developed over the last three decades, is implemented with high-risk high school youth by indigenous, nonprofit community-based organizations. Most Quantum initiatives have operated out of the facilities of the nonprofits, though there is very close coordination with the high schools attended by the youth. A youth investment and youth-development model, Quantum provides comprehensive, wraparound solutions: intense one-on-one and group mentoring, tutoring, life-skills training, college preparation, youth leadership training, and modest financial stipends over all four years of high school for at-risk youth. As with community school interventions, Quantum interventions are synergistic.[26]

A randomized, controlled evaluation from 2010 to 2014 of Quantum in five cities found that Quantum youth participants (called associates) were more likely than those in the control group to perform well academically, graduate from high school, gain acceptance into college, enroll in college, and persist in college. The findings were statistically significant at .001. The findings were particularly notable because Quantum is geared toward youth who are on the brink of dropping out. Quantum has been peer reviewed and accepted as an evidence-based model by the Blueprints for Healthy Youth Development registry, the U.S. Department of Justice Crime Solutions registry, and the National Mentoring Resource Center.[27] Quantum also has been recognized as an evidence-based model by the national My Brother's Keeper initiative. The model is being replicated by nonprofit community-based organizations on the South Side and West Side of Chicago.

Recommended in Chapter 1 of Part I as a job-training, evidence-based model, YouthBuild simultaneously is successful in securing high school equivalency and postsecondary education, on the basis of a randomized, controlled evaluation (see Chapter 4 in Part II).

While Quantum and YouthBuild are nonprofit community-based initiatives for high schoolers, the Career Academies model is a school-based initiative. Designed to help low-income youth stay engaged in high school and navigate the transition to either college or employment, Career Academies provide instruction in small learning communities and offer youth both academics and exposure to a particular occupation or sector. Career Academies partner with local employers to provide concrete work-based learning opportunities.[28]

About 85 percent of the participants in a randomized, controlled evaluation of Career Academies were African American or Hispanic American. Both young men and women participate in Career Academies, but the results have been particularly impressive for young men. For example, earnings for participating young men were nearly $30,000 higher than for control-group young men over the eight years following scheduled graduation from high school. Career Academies also improved the likelihood that young men would marry and live with their biological children. Spurred in part by the results of the evaluation, the Career Academies model has taken root in an estimated eight thousand high schools across the country, creating an impressive national infrastructure.[29]

High school, middle school, and elementary school minority youth at risk have increasingly been drawn into the school-to-prison pipeline. In the 2013–2014 school year, 2.8 million K–12 students received one or more out-of-school suspensions, with African American students almost four times as likely to be suspended from school as white students. And children with disabilities, were twice as likely to receive one or more out-of-school suspensions as their peers without disabilities. These suspensions often are for relatively mild forms of misconduct for which school officials have considerable discretion, not for violence or criminal activity (see Chapter 8 in Part II).

Discipline policies that exclude students from school can have lasting negative consequences. A longitudinal study of more than one million seventh- through twelfth-grade students found that those who were suspended from school were more than twice as likely to drop out compared to students who had no history of school removal. Suspended or expelled students were almost three times as likely as other students to become involved with the juvenile justice system within a year of leaving school. Yet considerable research has found that excluding students from school does not improve either individual behavior or school safety (see Chapter 8 in Part II).

As Carol Emig recommends in Chapter 8, keeping students in school and engaged in learning, therefore, should be part of a better solution. Some states and localities in America already are using alternative approaches to prevent and address disruptive behavior, such as social-emotional learning initiatives, positive behavioral interventions and supports, and early warning systems aimed at intervening proactively with students who have the potential to disrupt school or threaten school safety. Evaluations have suggested that such approaches are associated with reductions in school dropouts and increases in academic achievement. However, many of these interventions fail to include more immediate strategies to help educators respond to student behavior during an incident or administer appropriate consequences to prevent a recurrence. Here, more innovation is needed to provide teachers and other school personnel with actions other than suspensions and expulsions that hold young people accountable for their behavior, avoid disparities by race and disability, and keep offending students on track academically.

For youth who stay on track, benefiting we hope from scaled-up evidence-based models of success, one desired outcome after graduation is postsecondary education. Consistent with the recommendations of the Kerner Commission, governments at all levels need to provide more opportunities for high-risk youth to enter and remain in two- or four-year colleges. Improved support systems are needed to ensure that minority youth remain in college through graduation. An excellent evidence-based model is Bottom Line, which works with low-income students to ensure college graduation and prepare them for careers. Randomized, controlled evaluations have documented the effectiveness of Bottom Line.[30]

Such support needs to be complemented by significantly enhanced postsecondary financing for young people from low-income and working-class communities. Differences in college matriculation and completion rates by income and race are in large part driven by differences in opportunities for students before they even apply to college. But they are also a product of rising college costs and debt burdens for low-income, working-class, and middle-income people—costs that often fall particularly hard on racial minorities. In response, the nation needs to expand funding for Pell Grants, redesign tax-based aid for higher education to make it more progressive, and strengthen income-based repayment initiatives through which college loan liabilities are scaled to incomes (see Chapter 2 in Part II).

For all students, in conjunction with the states, a way must be found to make community college free and four-year college free or at least much more affordable. At the same time, the nation needs to find a way to forgive or ameliorate the present crushing student debt.

CONCLUSION

Combined with significantly increased funding of America's public schools, much more equitable allocation of resources among public schools, and greatly increased investments in teachers and training, scale-up of the evidence-based models discussed here will carry America a long way toward the education recommendations of the Kerner Commission. Other evidence-based models, archived in the Blueprints for Healthy Youth Development registry (http://www.blueprintsprograms.com), should be considered for widespread replication as well.

Scale-up of what works cannot wait. It needs to proceed on a parallel policy track with renewed racial integration of schools and neighborhoods.

4

Housing and Neighborhood Investment Policy

DRAMATIC REDUCTIONS IN FUNDING for low-income housing over recent decades are especially indefensible, given America's history of unconstitutional court rulings and federal, state, and local governmental policies promoting racial housing segregation. To realize the full potential of the nation's citizens and communities, we need to supply housing to all low-income families that qualify. We must expand the economic- and youth-development capacities of indigenous nonprofit organizations in low-income and working-class neighborhoods. Serious and faithful enforcement of the Fair Housing Act of 1968 should finally begin. A national policy that disengages the causal link between housing segregation and school segregation is essential.

TRENDS AND WHAT DOES NOT WORK

Created in 1934 as part of President Roosevelt's New Deal, the Federal Housing Administration (FHA) provides mortgage insurance on loans made by approved lenders throughout the United States. Fifteen years later, Congress passed the Housing Act of 1949, which established as a national goal "a decent home and suitable environment for every American family."[1]

FHA mortgage insurance gave incentives and protection to community-level lending institutions to furnish loans with low down payments, making homeownership affordable for millions of new home buyers. In 1938, Congress created the Federal National Mortgage Association (more popularly known as Fannie Mae), which provided a secondary mortgage market for the loans. This system helped enshrine the thirty-year, fixed-rate mortgage. The existence of mortgage insurance for loans and a secondary market for their purchase generated a tremendous volume of lending that lifted millions of families to the middle class.

Local community banks, credit unions, savings and loan associations, and other lenders had what they needed to finance housing. As droves of veterans returned from World War II, developers both large and small sprang forth to build homes, subdivisions, and entire suburbs. New communities and new wealth were created on a massive scale, transforming America into a nation of homeowners. The homeownership rate in the United States went from 44 percent in 1940, to 62 percent by 1960. A decent yet affordable home became more than just a stable place to raise a family; it became an asset—the largest asset for the average white household. Home equity provided access to capital to pay for higher education or a second car. It became capital invested among friends and family to start and grow small businesses. And it served as a cushion in unforeseen emergencies.

Redlining

But this was not the case for returning African American veterans or their families. As the mortgage machine kicked into gear over the 1940s and 1950s, most lenders were white, and they often refused to do business with African Americans. It was a time before credit scores. Private institutions and federal housing agencies that wrote mortgage underwriting guidelines judged risk on the basis of their prejudices—and on their beliefs that people of color and their neighborhoods were too risky for loans. (This even applied to Harlem at the height of the Harlem Renaissance.) Federal housing agencies marked minority neighborhoods with red lines or red shading—the source of the term "redlining." Federal policy makers and private lenders viewed racially mixed neighborhoods as risky and undesirable. FHA mortgage insurance guidelines encouraged banks and other home lenders to write mortgage agreements for white borrowers to purchase homes in all-white neighborhoods with covenants prohibiting the resale of those homes to buyers of other races.

With access to mortgages, many white households were able to move from crowded and in some cases racially integrated urban neighborhoods to homes in white-only suburbs, leaving most minority families no choice but to stay behind in neighborhoods that were being redlined for lending and capital investment. Residents and landlords had little to no access to the capital needed to acquire, maintain, or modernize buildings in minority neighborhoods. Policy makers then demolished large sections of redlined neighborhoods, using slum clearance programs authorized by the Housing Act of 1949. Many homes were bulldozed to make way for large-scale public housing complexes, interstate highways, or public works like the Lincoln Center for the Performing Arts in New York City.

Observing such trends and warning that the nation was heading "toward two societies, one black, one white—separate and unequal," the Kerner Commission recommended that "the supply of housing for low income families should be expanded on a massive basis."[2]

In 1968, President Lyndon Johnson's housing bill, which he dubbed the Magna Carta of housing, created new federal investments and a new FHA insurance program aimed at building affordable housing and supporting other development in low-income communities. The legislation said that millions of new and existing units of decent housing should be brought within reach of low- and moderate-income families over the next decade.

In the 1970s, Community Development Block Grants (CDBGs) came onto the scene, envisioned as a replacement for the slum clearance programs, which by that time had affected over two thousand communities across the country. CDBG funds were allocated to states and local governments. Cities above a certain population automatically qualified to receive an annual CDBG allocation according to their population and poverty. Each city then established its own local processes for determining how to use CDBG funding within broad guidelines. The grants served in part as a source of equity and gap financing—leveraging additional private and public capital for affordable housing production and other community development.

New Lenders

At the same time, a new cadre of lenders emerged that would come to specialize in financing housing for those living in redlined neighborhoods. They focused their efforts on smaller, community-level actors who took ownership of their neighborhoods. They created mostly rental housing, which therefore did not necessarily build individual wealth for tenants. But it was decent, affordable housing that opened opportunities for people and changed neighborhoods for the better.

In 1973, ShoreBank in Chicago became known as the nation's first community development bank, the inspiration for the creation of community development financial institutions. The ShoreBank model and legacy is a story of financing affordable housing. From its inception until it closed its doors in 2010, ShoreBank financed 59,000 units of housing, nearly all multifamily rental housing on the South Side of Chicago. By 2008, ShoreBank had more than $2.4 billion in assets. While keeping its focus on meeting the credit needs of historically redlined neighborhoods, ShoreBank routinely matched or exceeded the financial performance of similar-sized banks. As the founders learned in the first week after buying the bank, the only home-purchase loans available to the neighborhood were those insured by the FHA or the Veterans Administration. ShoreBank recruited a private mortgage insurer to work in the neighborhood, allowing the bank to keep interest rates affordable and down payments achievable. Those loans helped jumpstart and renew community self-confidence.

In New York, the Community Preservation Corporation started out in 1974, during New York City's fiscal crisis. Few wanted to build or preserve housing in New York City's formerly redlined neighborhoods—except for residents, community-based nonprofit developers, and entrepreneurs who often had grown up in those same neighborhoods. At the behest of Chase Manhattan Bank chair David Rockefeller, the city's large financial institutions formed the Community Preservation Corporation to serve as a one-stop shop to meet these smaller developers' needs, offering capital as well as technical assistance for those who wanted to pursue federal, state, and local subsidies. About half of Community Preservation Corporation borrowers were nonprofit community-based organizations, and half were small for-profit developers, many of them family-owned businesses. Since inception, the corporation has invested or loaned $9.7 billion, financing 170,660 units of affordable housing throughout New York State, of which 105,475 are in New York City.

Two large national social entrepreneurs emerged not much later to focus on historically underinvested neighborhoods: the Local Initiatives Support Corporation (LISC) and Enterprise Community Partners. Launched in 1980, LISC has since invested $17.3 billion in low- and moderate-income communities across the country, helping mostly community-based organizations build 365,922 units of affordable housing. Enterprise was founded in 1982 by James Rouse, a successful FHA mortgagor and developer. It has since made $28.9 billion in loans and investments, with its community-based borrowers producing 380,000 units of affordable housing.

The nation produced more than 200,000 new rent-subsidized units a year on average from 1975 to 1985. Lenders like ShoreBank, the Community Preservation Corporation, LISC, and Enterprise Community Partners focused on lending to community-level actors who could take advantage of the federal programs, creating positive impacts in their neighborhoods. Federal policy was working, partnering with community-level actors to build subsidized rental housing specifically for low-income households, mostly in urban areas, largely in formerly redlined neighborhoods. As a result, most subsidized affordable housing now is privately owned.

Reversal of Success

But in 1981 the pendulum swung hard in the opposite direction. President Ronald Reagan's policies eliminated new production of affordable housing, preferring to focus on housing vouchers. As a result, the gap between the availability of affordable housing and need widened dramatically. Federal funding for new rent-subsidized housing units has never again reached its pre-Reagan levels. From 2010 to 2015, the federal government provided funding for only twenty thousand new rent-subsidized units per year.

The Reagan changes stopped the housing-for-all machine in its tracks, leaving the country far short of what it might have produced in terms of providing sufficient affordable housing for households at every income level. The results of this dramatic change in policy are still being experienced today. According to nationwide estimates from the Urban Institute, there are only forty-six units of rental housing affordable for every one hundred renter households living at or below 30 percent of area median income in the United States. About half of those forty-six units are subsidized, and half are unsubsidized. Only 9 out of 3,143 counties have at least one affordable rental housing unit for every renter household at or below 30 percent of area median income. The shortage is worse in cities— metropolitan counties have forty-two adequate and affordable units available for every one hundred renters at or below 30 percent area median income, compared with sixty-nine units per one hundred in rural counties.

Homeownership and the Truly Disadvantaged

Today, homeownership remains much higher for whites than racial minorities. (See Figure 4.1.) The homeownership gap has narrowed somewhat for Hispanic Americans but has widened for African Americans. (See Figures 4.2 and 4.3.)

In particular, the Wall Street financial crisis and Great Recession of 2007–2009 was a disaster for African Americans. In 2004, the median net worth of white households was $134,280, roughly ten times the $13,450 median for African American households. After the crash, in 2009, median net worth for white households had fallen 24 percent, to $97,860, but median net worth for African American households had fallen 83 percent, to $2,170. In other words, the average African American household had between two and three cents for every dollar of wealth held by the average white household. Part of the reason the housing crisis exacerbated the gap was that African Americans were discriminated against by lenders. They were targeted for subprime loans that left them especially vulnerable to foreclosure. Banks were bailed out by taxpayers, and several financial institutions were penalized for illegal lending practices. But none of the compensation paid to the American government made its way back to African American families that were wiped out by the Great Recession (see Chapter 16 in Part II).

The wealth gap between whites and minorities in America continues to be explained by homeownership, gifts and inheritances from older generations, and a debt-free college education.

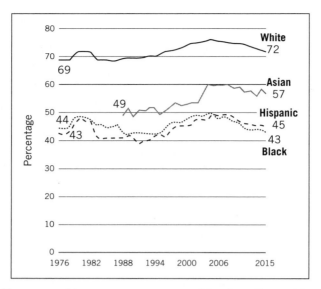

Figure 4.1 Homeownership more common among whites than other racial and ethnic groups
Source: Pew Research Center, "On Views of Race and Inequality, Blacks and Whites Are Worlds Apart," June 27, 2016, available at http://www.pewsocialtrends.org/2016/06/27/on-views-of -race-and-inequality-blacks-and-whites-are-worlds-apart.
Note: Race and ethnicity based on the race and ethnicity of the head of household. White, black, and Asian householders include only non-Hispanic Americans who reported a single race. Native Americans and mixed-race groups not shown. Data for Asians not available before 1988. Asians include Pacific Islanders. Hispanics are of any race.

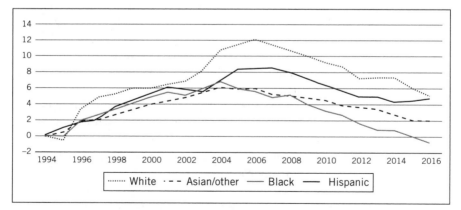

Figure 4.2 Cumulative change in homeownership rate (percentage points)
Source: Joint Center for Housing Studies, "The State of the Nation's Housing, 2017," 2017, p. 5, available at http://www.jchs.harvard.edu/sites/jchs.harvard.edu/files/harvard_jchs_state_of _the_nations_housing_2017.pdf.
Note: Hispanic households may be of any race. White, black, and Asian/other households are non-Hispanic households and include those reporting a second race until 2003. After 2003, Asian/other includes all other households and those reporting more than one race.

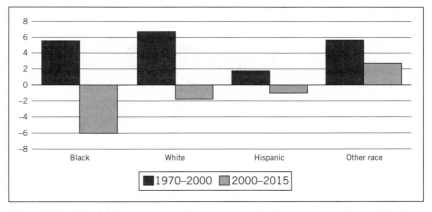

Figure 4.3 Percentage-point change in homeownership by homeowner's race/ethnicity
Source: Laurie Goodman, Jun Zhu, and Rolf Pendall, "Are Gains in Black Homeownership History?" *Urban Wire,* February 15, 2017, available at http://www.urban.org/urban-wire/ are-gains-black-homeownership-history.
Note: "Other" includes Asian Americans, Pacific Islanders, American Indians and Alaska Natives, people who identified as "other," and (starting 2000) people who chose more than one racial identity. Hispanics can be of any race; all other categories are non-Hispanic. Estimates for 1970 are based on Integrated Public Use Microdata Series imputation procedures (see https://ipums.org/).

Pointing out that the wealth gap exists does not fully convey the impact of racial segregation and minority poverty at the neighborhood level. The 1987 book by Harvard Kennedy School professor William Julius Wilson, *The Truly Disadvantaged,* captures the key differences between African American and white poverty in postindustrial American cities. Wilson demonstrates that poor African American neighborhoods were areas of concentrated poverty where over 40 percent of residents lived below the poverty line, a percentage far higher than the neighborhoods where poor whites lived (see Chapter 16 in Part II).

Concentrated poverty produces communal and multigenerational effects. People who live in poor African American neighborhoods are isolated both spatially and culturally. There are few decent schools, jobs, or health care facilities. Nor is there a critical mass of two-parent households or unmarried adults with steady employment who socialize young people and connect them to legitimate economic activities. Illicit economies sometimes fill this void, and such endeavors often rely on interpersonal (rather than economic and institutional) violence for regulation. These realities have been distorted and politicized to justify the further isolation and criminalization of minority people, who are falsely labeled by some whites as sharing a pathological culture. But Wilson has long since demonstrated that the root causes of urban violence are not cultural but fundamentally economic: extreme class and race segregation and joblessness lead to family disruption and antisocial behaviors (see Chapter 16 in Part II).

As Yale University professor Elijah Anderson discusses in Chapter 12 in Part II, racially isolated areas are not just physical locations in urban America. The ghetto has become an important source of symbolic racism. The iconography of the ghetto competes with the plantation system of the old South as a way to define African Americans. Given the pejorative connotation of the word "ghetto," most outsiders, including many whites from relatively homogeneous residential areas, have learned to be wary of the ghetto's inhabitants. As a result, when African Americans encounter others, they are burdened with a "deficit of credibility"—a powerful manifestation of what Anderson calls the "iconic ghetto," whereby the individual's race counts as a strike against his or her character. This wariness can dissipate in time, but only if the person so judged is willing to work for it, often before a distant and unreceptive audience.

Though waging a campaign for respect can leave middle-class African Americans feeling utterly spent and demoralized, they typically keep this side of themselves hidden from their white counterparts. But if the middle-class African American generally possesses the human capital to work for respect, the lower-class, ghetto-dwelling African American often does not. For such a person, the deficit of credibility often is much more consequential, affecting employment, health care, and daily life in ways that are little appreciated by the white public. Specifically, the deficit of credibility hinders poor minorities' ability to become employed, increases the likelihood that a police encounter will lead to arrest, and affects the quality of treatment they receive in hospital emergency departments, where illnesses may not be given the serious consideration they deserve (see Chapter 12 in Part II).

Both Anderson and Wilson warn that the combination of racial and class segregation present in America today makes it more difficult to sustain community-level institutions, including schools, churches, businesses, nonprofit organizations, and political organizations. And the lower the density and stability of such organizations, the more likely the development of illicit activities, like drug trafficking, crime, gangs, and prostitution.[3]

Fair Housing

Aware of how race and class reinforced one another in low-income neighborhoods, Dr. Martin Luther King, Jr., before his death, had become certain that a fair-housing policy that barred housing discrimination and integrated neighborhoods was critical. He was aware that governmental action, private prejudice, and suburbanite desire for homogeneous affluent environments contributed to segregation. Dr. King believed that racial discrimination in housing made it possible for city officials to create different levels of service, on everything from schools and hospitals to policing and recreation in minority and white neighborhoods.[4]

Today, we know that Dr. King was right to say that the most powerful cause of metropolitan segregation, nationwide, was federal, state, and local government policy.[5]

Many explicitly segregationist governmental actions ended in the late twentieth century. Yet they continue to determine today's racial segregation patterns. Such governmental policies have included zoning rules that classified white neighborhoods as residential and African American neighborhoods as commercial or industrial; segregated public housing projects that replaced integrated low-income areas; federal subsidies for suburban development conditioned on African American exclusion; federal and local requirements for property deeds and neighborhood agreements that prohibited resale of white-owned property to, or occupancy by, African Americans; tax favoritism for private institutions that practiced segregation; municipal boundary lines designed to separate African American neighborhoods from white neighborhoods so as to deny necessary services to the former; support for real estate, insurance, and banking regulators who tolerated and sometimes required racial segregation; and urban renewal plans whose purpose was to shift African American populations from central cities to inner-ring suburbs.[6]

For example, in New York, the government financed suburbs like Levittown with a federal requirement that no homes be sold to African Americans—and whites then moved into these federally financed suburbs. In Saint Louis and Los Angeles, neighborhoods that once had African American residents were rezoned to permit industrial and toxic uses. The rezonings turned the neighborhoods into slums. White families looked at such neighborhoods and labeled African Americans as slum dwellers. Whites concluded that African Americans would bring slum conditions with them if they moved into white neighborhoods.[7]

The sheer weight of the evidence that this occurred is overwhelming. In his powerful new book, *The Color of Law*, Richard Rothstein, research associate at the Economic Policy Institute and fellow at the Haas Institute at the University of California–Berkeley, demolishes the myth that government played a minor role in creating racial ghettos. He has uncovered conscious, purposeful policy of government segregation in metropolitan areas in the South, North, East, and West.[8]

White flight certainly existed, and racial prejudice was certainly behind it. But the cause was not racial prejudice alone. Governmental policies turned African American neighborhoods into overcrowded slums.[9]

A recent Brown University investigation has found that, today, the situation is so bad that 90 percent of African Americans and Hispanic Americans would need to move to create truly racially balanced communities.

And the average affluent African American or Hispanic family lives in a neighborhood where people and conditions are poorer than where the average low-income white family lives, a Stanford University study has found.[10]

Government racial housing policies were complemented by governmental actions in support of segregated labor markets—policies that prevented minorities from acquiring the economic strength to move to middle-class communities, even if they had been permitted to do so.[11]

As discussed in Chapter 2 of Part I, the same governmental racial housing-segregation policies created education segregation. Schools are segregated because the neighborhoods in which they are located are segregated. Some school segregation can be ameliorated—for example, by adjusting school attendance boundaries. But such devices are limited and mostly inapplicable to elementary school children, for whom long travel to school is neither feasible nor desirable.

The Kerner Commission emphasized that "areas outside of ghetto neighborhoods should be opened up to occupancy by racial minorities," and the Fair Housing Act of 1968 was designed to end racial discrimination in housing. But meeting fair-housing goals has been well down the priority list of most presidents and housing secretaries since 1968, and in vital ways, the law has not been enforced.[12]

Enterprise Zones and Buzz Words

At the same time that the federal government neglected fair housing and disinvested from housing and economic development in low-income neighborhoods in the 1980s and early 1990s, policy makers encouraged "enterprise zones." As part of trickle-down, supply-side economics, enterprise zones were premised on tax breaks to lure entrepreneurs and corporations into inner-city neighborhoods to generate jobs for the truly disadvantaged. Over five hundred enterprise zones were tried in almost forty states. Yet the Urban Institute concluded that extensive evaluations of state enterprise zone programs have found no evidence that incentives have contributed to employment or investment growth in designated areas. Few of the tax benefits directly accrued to the disadvantaged residents in enterprise zones. Many potential employers said they would not move into enterprise zones because potential employees were not trained.[13]

Investigations in the United States and the United Kingdom have shown that the hidden costs of enterprise-zone strategies in terms of lost tax revenues actually rendered them prohibitively expensive. "There is evidence," a writer stated in the *Economist*, "that they [enterprise zones] are often wasteful and tend to displace rather than create business activity."[14]

In the 1980s and 1990s, neighborhood disinvestment by the federal government was accompanied by words like "self-sufficiency," "self-reliance," "volunteerism," "partnership," "coalition building," and "empowerment."

During these and later years, the U.S. military was deploying large numbers of professional staff, large numbers of support staff, and an enormous amount of equipment to the Middle East and throughout the world. But when it came to investments in inner-city nonprofit organizations, federal funds were not available for professional staff, support staff, and equipment. Instead, grassroots nonprofit neighborhood organizations were encouraged to raise short-term start-up resources from the private and public sectors. Then, the nonprofits were urged to convert into "self-sufficient" operations by using (often poorly trained) volunteers. Volunteers were to be part of "partnerships" and "coalition building" among other financially competing and often penurious groups in impoverished neighborhoods—groups that were fighting for the same scarce grant dollars. This, the nonprofits were told, would somehow lead to the "empowerment" of the organizations and their neighborhoods.[15]

But there was little evidence to support such rhetoric, as anyone knows who runs a nonprofit organization in a poor minority neighborhood. The lesson was that political buzz words cannot be used as smokescreens for lack of funding.

Another political fashion of the time was to encourage grants to faith-based organizations in poor communities. Yet no evidence has been found that faith-based nonprofit organizations are any more effective than secular nonprofit organizations. Evaluations have shown that the key distinction is not faith versus secular. Rather, success depends on whether a nonprofit organization has sound institutional capacity—like competent financial management, an effective board, dedicated staff who do not burn out, ability to fund raise, and skill in communicating.[16]

POLICY BASED ON WHAT WORKS

We need housing assistance for all eligible low-income families, genuine enforcement of the Fair Housing Act of 1968, and an adequately financed federal Office of Neighborhoods that directly funds indigenous nonprofit organizations in poor and working-class communities.

Low-Income Housing for All Eligible Families

Figure 4.4 shows the large population of eligible Americans with worst-case housing needs who are not receiving low-income housing assistance. Today, only one of four eligible families receives federal rental assistance.

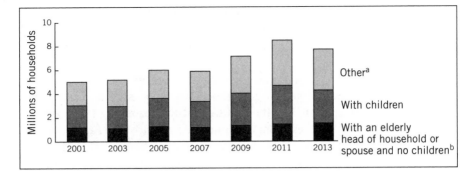

Figure 4.4 Eligible households that did not receive federal low-income housing assistance and met HUD's definition of "worst-case housing needs," 2001–2013
Source: Congressional Budget Office, "Federal Housing Assistance for Low-Income Households," September 2015, available at https://www.cbo.gov/sites/default/files/114th-congress-2015-2016/reports/50782-lowincomehousing-onecolumn.pdf.
Note: The Department of Housing and Urban Development (HUD) defines households with worst-case housing needs as those that have income of no more than 50 percent of area median income, are eligible for but do not receive federal housing assistance, and are paying more than half their income in rent (or live in severely substandard conditions). Only about 3 percent of households characterized as having worst-case needs are identified as such solely because of substandard conditions; in all, about 6 percent of households with worst-case needs live in substandard conditions.
ᵃ The category "Other" consists mostly of nonelderly people living alone.
ᵇ The head of the household, or his or her spouse, is age sixty-two or older.

Mindful of the Kerner Commission's conclusion that the supply of low-income housing should be significantly expanded, we recommend that all eligible American households receive rent-subsidized housing or other subsidies. This would add up to over eighteen million households.

Such inequality-reducing reform is all the more needed because the federal government today spends less on subsidizing housing for low-income Americans than on subsidizing housing for better-off Americans. The federal government spends $36 billion annually on housing assistance for households earning up to $40,000 a year while spending $43.9 billion annually on housing assistance for households earning $200,000 or more, including the mortgage-interest deduction, real estate tax deduction, and other deductions related to real estate. Annual federal housing spending per household is $1,529 for households making between $0 and $20,000 in annual income, compared with $6,076 per household earning $200,000 or more. The mortgage-interest or real estate tax deductions are pure entitlements: if you qualify, you get access to those deductions freely, without absolute limits. But rental assistance is severely limited. In a modern country as wealthy as ours, this inequity is indefensible.

There is no justifiable reason for an arbitrary limit on federally assisted rental housing other than need. Medicaid and the federal food stamp program kick in automatically for households earning below a certain income level. Social Security and Medicare begin automatically for persons who reach a certain age.

Presidents from both major parties have committed the federal government to expanding the nation's stock of affordable rent-assisted housing. To supply that housing, we need to return to the system that was developed before the 1980s, when community-level actors like Shore-Bank, the Community Restoration Corporation, the Local Initiatives Support Corporation, and Enterprise Community Partners coordinated with the federal government. Most of the private-sector actors are still present today, waiting to fulfill this potential.

The power grid to supply capital to build affordable housing needs to be turned back on, improved, and made universally available to all who qualify for it. The banking system needs to be held more accountable for its legal obligations while also gaining flexibility to be creative in how it meets those legal obligations—particularly when it comes to housing. Through government-sponsored entities like Fannie Mae, the secondary market must become much more of a factor in producing and preserving affordable rental housing, in addition to supporting affordable homeownership.

An adequately funded return to pre-1980s housing policy should be complemented by the Keynesian demand-side, full-employment policy set out in Chapter 2 of Part I. Households with solid employment and adequate wages are less in need of subsidies. Today, to afford a modest, two-bedroom rental home in America, renters need to earn over $21 an hour—much higher than the federal minimum wage of $7.25.

Other existing programs that need to be continued or reformed include the Low-Income Housing Tax Credit, the Community Reinvestment Act, and a Community Development Block Grant program that more effectively builds the capacity of neighborhood nonprofit organizations.

Fair Housing

The federal government needs to comprehensively enforce, for the first time, the Fair Housing Act of 1968. The potential for such enforcement was at least maintained in 2015, when the Supreme Court, in *Texas Department of Housing and Urban Affairs v. The Inclusive Communities Project*, preserved a well-established and critical tool in the battle to ensure a more integrated society. The ruling was that the law allows plaintiffs to challenge government or private-sector policies that have a discriminatory effect, without having to show evidence of intentional discrimination. This "results oriented," or outcome-based, language supports what the law calls "disparate-impact liability," which has been part of the accepted meaning of the Fair Housing Act for decades. In writing the majority opinion in the case, Justice Anthony Kennedy acknowledged that "much progress remains to be made in our Nation's continuing struggle against racial isolation."[17]

Moving forward, the federal government now should require state and local governments that receive federal money to direct more significant housing into healthier neighborhoods where residents are provided access to transportation, jobs, and decent schools. Enforcing the law and making sure that state and local governments actually pursue racial and economic integration will help poor whites as well as poor minorities. Low-income whites make up more than a third of the four million to six million poor families that receive federal housing assistance. They also will benefit from broader access to housing in healthier communities and consequent access to better schools and improved job opportunities.[18]

As Richard Kahlenberg, senior fellow at the Century Foundation, has proposed, the 1968 Fair Housing Act needs to be bolstered to bar exclusionary zoning laws that prohibit townhouses or apartments in single-family neighborhoods.[19] Incentives should be provided to communities. For example, in neighborhoods where housing exclusion is reduced, federal and local funds should be directed to community-based problem-oriented policing codirected by community-based nonprofit organizations, as we suggest in Chapter 5 of Part I. In addition, penalties might be considered when municipalities continue to engage in discriminatory zoning.

One excellent model is Montgomery County, Maryland, which requires developers to set aside units for low-income families. Disadvantaged students from those families are able to attend local schools. The math achievement gap between the lower-income youth and their middle-class peers was reduced by half between 2001 and 2007, based on a RAND Corporation evaluation.[20] The Montgomery County findings have been reinforced by Harvard University findings in other locations. Children whose families received federal assistance to move to better neighborhoods were more likely to attend college, attend better colleges, and earn higher incomes as adults than children whose families had not received the assistance.[21]

We now need to replicate the Montgomery County model nationally. The goals of the replications should be improved school performance for low-income youth who move with their families, more economic opportunities for their parents, no increase in crime and fear, and no decline in property values. The goals therefore require close coordination among housing, education, and police agencies.

Such replications should be carried out in locations with coalitions of supporters on both the right and the left. Advocates on the right might include libertarians who oppose government regulations on principle and developers who chafe at restrictions on building density. Advocates on the left could include civil rights organizations, public school systems, affordable housing advocates, community policing reformers, and antisprawl environmentalists.[22]

In addition, the federal government should:

- Widely replicate and greatly expand successfully evaluated mobility programs—like the Chicago Gautreaux program[23] and the federal Moving to Opportunity program—to encourage low-income and minority families to move into better neighborhoods.
- Provide financial incentives to much more widely replicate still other inclusionary zoning programs already in effect in over one hundred jurisdictions nationwide. In these jurisdictions, developers have been offered incentives to set aside a specific number of housing units for lower-income and minority families.
- Adjust existing housing subsidies so they are sufficient to allow low-income residents to rent housing in better neighborhoods.
- Reform the Community Reinvestment Act and the Home Mortgage Disclosure Act to subject private mortgage lenders and homeowner insurance companies to regulatory oversight—on issues like predatory lending and redlining.
- Adopt federal legislation that prevents use of federal funds (like Community Development Block Grants) to promote involuntary displacement of low-income households.
- Provide federal financial assistance in support of state and city litigation against predatory lenders.
- Deposit public funds in financial institutions that have demonstrated a commitment to community reinvestment and to diversity in their lending, investment, and service activities.
- Encourage construction of municipal buildings (like schools, police stations, and fire stations) in racially diverse communities.[24]

Neighborhood Development and Investment

Beyond supplying housing assistance to all eligible low-income families and seriously enforcing fair housing, the nation needs a new initiative that invests in nonprofit neighborhood development organizations. The initiative needs to re-create and expand the Office of Neighborhood Development that was launched by the late Monsignor Geno Baroni when he was a Department of Housing and Urban Development assistant secretary in the Carter administration in the late 1970s. The federal office we propose should directly fund indigenous nonprofit organizations.

The goal should be to strengthen the capacities of the nonprofits to undertake economic and youth development at the neighborhood level and to facilitate citizen participation and community organizing. The economic development should include housing rehabilitation and construction by nonprofit organizations like YouthBuild and Habitat for Humanity (see Chapter 1 of Part I). The youth development should include expansion of successes like Quantum Opportunities (see Chapter 3 of Part I). The crime prevention should include community-police partnerships in low-income neighborhoods (see Chapter 5 in Part I), as well as in wealthier neighborhoods where racial and class integration is being advanced.

The community organizing should build on Baroni's success in creating dialogue between poor and working-class minorities and white, urban, ethnic groups, as E. J. Dionne discusses in Chapter 21 in Part II.[25] The organizing needs to carry out the kind of bubble-up neighborhood-based citizen advocacy of the late Jane Jacobs, as she fought against Robert Moses and the top-down urban renewal and urban planning failures of the mid-twentieth century.[26]

The organizing we envision for the reconstructed Office of Neighborhoods would seek to integrate place-based programming in specific minority and working-class neighborhoods. Today, there are some place-based initiatives in some federal agencies—like the Departments of Education, Justice, and Housing and Urban Development. But the organizing potential of place-based innovation has barely been tapped.

The neighborhoods of most concern to the Kerner Commission require multiple solutions to multiple problems. In truly disadvantaged neighborhoods, the answers are not single, narrow, and categorical. The solutions are creative, comprehensive, and interdependent. For example, community-based, problem-oriented policing, in partnership with indigenous nonprofit organizations, can help secure a neighborhood. The security can help encourage community- based banking. Community-based banking can provide capital for community development corporations. Community development corporations can invest that capital in ways that help generate good jobs for local residents—jobs in housing repair and construction, public infrastructure repair and construction, school repair, health services, education, and transportation. High school dropouts can qualify for those jobs if they have been in successful job training, like that provided by YouthBuild, the Center for Employment Training, and Job Corps. Ex-offenders returning to the community can qualify for the jobs if they have been trained in programs that replicate the successes of the Safer Foundation, the Minnesota Comprehensive Offender Reentry Plan, and the Center for Employment Opportunities (as discussed in Chapter 5 of Part I). Teenage youth in the neighborhood can stay in high school and move on to postsecondary education if they have been involved in human capital investments like Quantum Opportunities. They can get that far if they have been in community schools and after-school Youth Safe Havens in the neighborhood. And they can get that far if they have been in early childhood education.

Coordinating existing federal, state, and local resources in specific locations, the new Office of Neighborhoods should facilitate such place-based multiple solutions.

Significant and sustained funding is essential. The Office of Neighborhoods should not be resourced by a false-rhetoric narrative on "self-sufficiency," "volunteerism," and "empowerment."

5

Criminal Justice Policy and Mass Incarceration

AFTER THE KERNER REPORT, a new Jim Crow prison-industrial complex developed, and zero-tolerance policing became fashionable. But mass incarceration failed, and zero tolerance proved ineffective. A reformed policy is needed that scales up evidence-based problem-oriented community policing, integrated with youth development by nonprofit organizations in disadvantaged minority neighborhoods. We recommend implementation of consent decrees for police departments designated in need of reform. Our policy builds on elimination of mandatory minimum sentences, support for the deincarceration movement, reduction of prison populations, pursuit of community-based substance abuse prevention and treatment, replication of evidence-based ex-offender reintegration models that have proved to work, incorporation of ex-offenders into the demand-side Keynesian job-creation and job-training policy set out in Chapter 2 of Part I, and elimination of all policies that contribute to racial inequality at every stage of the juvenile and criminal justice systems.

TRENDS

Crime reported to police was rising in the 1960s at the time of the Kerner Commission. Reported crime began to drop steadily in the 1990s. In some very recent years, crime reported to police began to rise again. Figure 5.1 illustrates this trend in America for murder, the most accurately reported and most serious crime. With the reported American murder rate at 5.3 per 100,000 in 2016,[1] the nation now is not far from the reported murder rates of the 1960s, even though there has been an enormous increase in the prison populations since the Kerner Report. And as Professor Elliott

Currie at the University of California–Irvine reminds us in Chapter 15 of Part II, today's murder rates would be higher—perhaps much higher—were it not for improvements in medical treatment of victims of violence, especially gun violence. In this sense, as is the case with the poverty rate discussed in Chapter 2 of Part I, can we claim much progress since the time of the Kerner Commission? While some celebrate "low" crime rates today, the reported homicide rate in America remains much higher than in most other industrialized democracies, as Figure 5.2 shows.

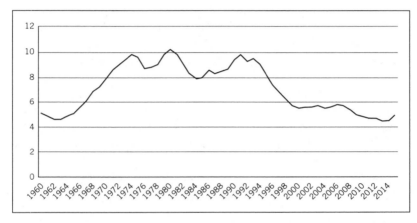

Figure 5.1 Reported murder rates per 100,000 population in the United States, 1960–2015

Source: Data from Federal Bureau of Investigation Uniform Crime Reporting data tool, at https://www.ucrdatatool.gov/Search/Crime/State/RunCrimeStatebyState.cfm.

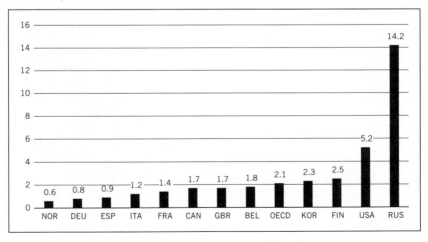

Figure 5.2 Reported intentional homicide rates per 100,000 population in selected OECD countries, 2008 or latest available year

Source: Organisation for Economic Co-operation and Development, *How's Life? Measuring Well-Being* (Paris: OECD, 2011), 246, figure 11.1.

The Kerner Commission spoke of "strikingly different" conditions in poor minority communities compared to white middle-class communities, including much higher crime rates. This continues today. For example, as measured by the Centers for Disease Control and Prevention of the Department of Health and Human Services, in 2015 the homicide rate was eighteen times as high for African American men ages fifteen to twenty-nine as for white, non-Hispanic men in the same group. As in the 1960s, the places most devastated by violence today are typically very poor and heavily populated by minorities (see Chapter 15 in Part II).

The disproportionate American response to rising reported crime after the Kerner Report was mass incarceration, as Figure 5.3 shows. At the time of the commission, the American state and federal prison population was near 200,000. In 2015, that population was close to 1.5 million. The United States has substantially higher reported incarceration rates than other industrialized nations, as Figure 5.4 shows.[2]

In effect, whereas the Kerner Report called for "massive and sustained" investments in economic, employment, and education initiatives, the United States pursued "massive and sustained" incarceration, framed as "law and order."[3] America still has the segregated, deteriorated urban areas and crime observed by the Kerner Commission, but now we also have resettled a substantial proportion of the minority poor into prison.

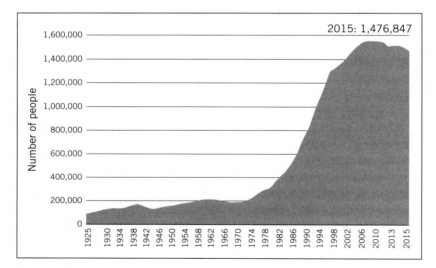

Figure 5.3 U.S. state and federal prison population, 1925–2015
Source: Sentencing Project, "U.S. State and Federal Prison Population, 1925–2015," available at http://www.sentencingproject.org/wp-content/uploads/2017/04/US-prison-popula tion-1925-2015.png (accessed November 28, 2017).

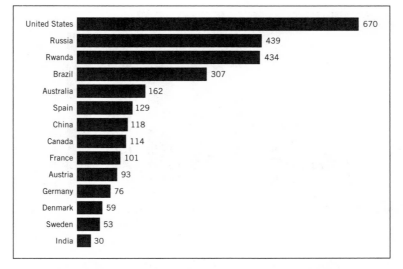

Figure 5.4 Rates of incarceration per 100,000 population in selected industrialized and developing countries in recent years
Source: Roy Walmsley, *World Prison Brief* (London: Institute for Criminal Policy Research, 2016), available at http://www.prisonstudies.org/world-prison-brief.

Mass incarceration was accompanied in some cities by aggressive policing that increased arrests. Tougher sentencing policies and punitive prosecuting then ensured that more convictions resulted.

In particular, sentencing policies in the federal War on Drugs resulted in dramatic growth of incarceration rates for drug offenses. The number of Americans incarcerated for drug offenses skyrocketed from 40,900 in 1980 to 469,545 in 2015. Harsh sentencing laws, such as those mandating minimum sentences, keep many people convicted of drug offenses in prison for long periods.[4]

This American law-and-order policy incorporated racial biases. For example, in spite of changes in the law in 2010, sentences for crack cocaine, used disproportionately by minorities, remain longer than sentences for powder cocaine, used disproportionately by whites.[5]

Youth of color have entered the system much more frequently than white youth and have been more likely to receive harsher punishment. Thousands of young people are transferred to the adult system each year, and many are sent to adult prisons and jails to serve their sentences.[6]

Led by federal administrations from both major parties and by state governments in the 1980s and 1990s, mass incarceration has been costly. For example, the states spent $6.7 billion on corrections in 1985 and $56.9 billion in 2015. (See Figure 5.5.) Prison expenditures have diverted state resources from evidence-based child and youth-development programs

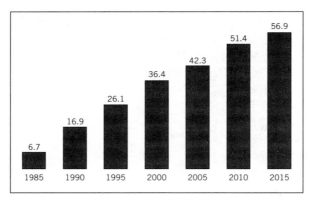

Figure 5.5 State expenditures on corrections in billions, 1985–2015
Source: National Association of State Budget Officers, *State Expenditure Report,* 1985–2015
(Washington, DC: National Association of State Budget Officers, 1987–2016).

that work, like early childhood education, Quantum Opportunities, and YouthBuild, discussed in previous chapters.[7]

Many new prisons are privatized and built in rural areas, away from public view. The prisons are disproportionately populated by minority men. Prison staff often are disproportionately white. In some ways, prison has become an economic development policy for rural whites and a housing policy for urban minorities. A racially biased prison-industrial complex has been created. For decades, well-paid lobbyists have urged legislators to further expand prison facilities—and keep them filled. The lobbyists have developed a constituency of seven hundred thousand prison and jail guards, administrators, service workers, and other personnel in America. This constituency has become a powerful opposition to significant reduction of the prison-industrial complex. Little has been done to educate prisoners or train them for employment when they are released. This has helped guarantee high recidivism rates after prisoners are released, with many returning to racially segregated, impoverished communities. The high recidivism rates help keep the prisons full and so help justify the prison-industrial complex and its profits.[8]

More than 60 percent of prison inmates today are people of color. (See Figure 5.6.) African American men are nearly 6 times as likely to be incarcerated as white men, and Hispanic men are 2.3 times as likely. For African American men in their thirties, one in every ten is in prison or jail on any given day.[9]

African American men have a 32 percent likelihood of serving time in prison at some point in their lives, and Hispanic men have a 17 percent likelihood.

In forty-eight states, a felony conviction can result in the loss of an individual's voting rights. The period of disenfranchisement varies by

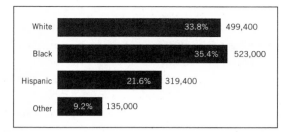

Figure 5.6 People in state and federal prisons, by race and ethnicity, 2013–2014
Source: E. Ann Carson and Elizabeth Anderson, "Prisoners in 2015," December 2016, available at https://www.bjs.gov/content/pub/pdf/p15.pdf.

Figure 5.7 Rate of disenfranchisement, by race, 2016
Source: Christopher Uggen, Ryan Larson, and Sarah Shannon, "6 Million Lost Voters: State-Level Estimates of Felon Disenfranchisement, 2016," October 6, 2016, available at http://www .sentencingproject.org/publications/6-million-lost-voters-state-level-estimates-felony-disenfran chisement-2016.

state. Some states restore the vote upon completion of a prison term, while others effectively disenfranchise for life. As a result of mass incarceration since the Kerner Report, felony disenfranchisement has lessened the political voice of many communities. Today, 6.1 million Americans are unable to vote because of state felony disenfranchisement policies. As seen in Figure 5.7, the rate of disenfranchisement is much higher for African Americans than non–African Americans.[10]

WHAT DOES NOT WORK

The Kerner Commission focused a great deal on the police but paid less attention to sentencing and incarceration.

Police

The Kerner Report concluded that police had often sparked the protests of the 1960s and overreacted after the protests began. The commission found that racial tensions frequently reflected low-income-community grievances with the police and the rest of the criminal justice system: "The police are not merely a 'spark' factor. To some Negroes police have come to symbolize white power, white racism and white repression. . . . The atmosphere of hostility and cynicism is reinforced by a widespread belief among Negroes in the existence of police brutality and in a 'double standard' of justice and protection—one for Negroes and one for whites."[11]

In a twenty-three-city survey of the causes of the disorders and protests in the 1960s, the Kerner Commission found "police practices" to be the most frequently cited grievance. "Police practices" also were rated at the highest "level of intensity" by residents. Yet the report made clear that "the blame must be shared by the total society." It stressed that "the policeman in the ghetto is a symbol, finally, of a society from which many ghetto Negroes are increasingly alienated." At the same time, the commission reported that residents in minority communities frequently demanded strong police protection, often leading to complaints if the response was too aggressive.[12]

Among other recommendations, the commission advised that police departments provide better protection to minority community residents, set up mechanisms for grievances against police and other city employees, eliminate abrasive practices, adopt guidelines to help officers make critical decisions at times when police conduct could create tension, innovate initiatives to ensure broad community support for police, recruit more minority officers, ensure fair promotion for minority officers, and create community service officer positions for young minority men.[13]

Nonetheless, after the Kerner Report, a policy of aggressive zero-tolerance policing developed in some police departments. In cities with such police departments, stop-and-frisk tactics and zero-tolerance arrests complemented the mass incarceration movement. In the early 1990s, zero tolerance was illustrated by the Los Angeles Police when officers beat an African American citizen, Rodney King, and were recorded on videotape. The 1992 disorders in South Central Los Angeles then erupted.[14]

Arguably, for a time, zero-tolerance policing may have affected some of the minority poor as negatively as supply-side economics and market-driven education vouchers.

Reported crime then began to fall in the late 1990s and into the new century, but evidence accumulated that zero-tolerance policing was not the primary cause of the decline. For example, reported crime fell in a number of cities that did not resort to heavy-handed policing but that, instead, improved relationships among youth, the police, and the community. Boston; Columbia, South Carolina; and San Diego were good examples. In addition, reported crime declined in some cities, like San Francisco, that did nothing new. The same was true in East Saint Louis, Illinois. From 1991 to 1996, reported murder declined rapidly in East Saint Louis—even though the police were so strapped for funds that police layoffs were common. Many police cars did not have functioning radios, and many vehicles were idle because there was no money for gas.[15]

Today, there is broad recognition that zero tolerance was ineffective. From 2014 to 2016, police brutality and excessive use of force by police against African Americans became more of a national issue. The police shooting of Michael Brown in Ferguson, Missouri, in 2014 was one of the first incidents to receive national media attention. National media also picked up on the police killings of Eric Garner in Staten Island in 2014, Tamir Rice in Cleveland in 2014, Walter Scott in North Charleston, South Carolina, in 2015, Freddie Gray in Baltimore in 2015, Alton Sterling in Baton Rouge in 2016, Philando Castile in Falcon Heights, Minnesota, in 2016, and Jordan Edwards in Dallas in 2017, among many other incidents.[16]

As Ta-Nehisi Coates wrote to his son in *Between the World and Me*, police "have been endowed with the authority to destroy your body" and have prerogatives that include "friskings, detainings, beatings and humiliations."[17]

There is no comprehensive government data source that tracks fatal shootings of citizens by police. But the *Washington Post* has created a database that suggests there were well over two hundred African Americans killed by police in each of 2015 and 2016. Research has found that African American teenage boys and men are twenty-one times more likely to be shot and killed by police than their white peers.[18]

In Ferguson, Missouri, where Michael Brown was killed, 60 percent of the residents were African American. Yet African Americans accounted for 92 percent of searches and 86 percent of vehicle stops by police. In the year before Brown was killed, 483 African Americans were arrested in Ferguson, compared to 36 whites. The police chief and the mayor of Ferguson were both white, as were fifty of the fifty-three officers on the Ferguson police force. A Department of Justice report on Ferguson found that African Americans were disproportionately penalized by the police and courts in Ferguson and that law enforcement was shaped by the need to generate revenue for the city.[19]

Ferguson and the nearby city of Jennings, Missouri, have jailed poor people for failing to pay municipal fines and fees. In litigation against such "wealth based detention," the nonprofit Civil Rights Corps has described the conditions in Jennings:

> Once locked in the Jennings jail, impoverished people owing debts to the City endure grotesque treatment. They are kept in overcrowded cells; they are denied toothbrushes, toothpaste, and soap; they are subjected to the stench of excrement and refuse in their congested cells; they are surrounded by walls smeared with mucus, blood, and feces; they are kept in the same clothes for days and weeks without access to laundry or clean undergarments; they step on top of other inmates, whose bodies cover nearly the

entire uncleaned cell floor, in order to access a single shared toilet that the City does not clean. . . . Perhaps worst of all, they do not know when they will be allowed to leave.[20]

Ultimately, the city of Jennings agreed to change its practices and compensate people who were jailed. But debtor jailing remains a problem in many other jurisdictions.

In Baltimore, after the death of Freddie Gray, a Department of Justice investigation found the police department's policing strategy, lack of training, and inattention to officer accountability had encouraged police to stop, search, or arrest African American residents with little or no legal justification. The Justice Department report concluded, "The relationship between the Baltimore Police Department and many of the communities it serves is broken."[21]

As with the videotaping of the Rodney King attack in Los Angeles in 1992, many of the police killings of minorities in recent years were exposed by citizens who captured the brutal evidence on their cell phones. The new technology helped lead to the emergence of the Black Lives Matter national protest movement after the Michael Brown killing in Ferguson. The movement, which we endorse, has argued that the lives of people of color matter as much as the lives of whites.[22] Wellesley professor Michael Jeffries points out in Chapter 16 of Part II that Black Lives Matter has sparked "the most serious public debate about policing and incarceration America has known since the 1960s." One poll has shown that 60 percent of whites under age thirty agree with the Black Lives Matter critique of law enforcement.[23]

Sentencing and Incarceration

The Kerner Commission did not anticipate the mass incarceration system that emerged after its work. The system often denies meaningful legal representation to poor minorities, who, after their arrests, then plead guilty. Once they are convicted, harsh sentencing laws as well as aggressive and punitive prosecution have ensured that offenders, especially drug offenders, spend long periods in jail, in prison, on probation, and on parole.[24]

After release, "invisible punishment" begins. Laws ensure that the great majority of ex-offenders are never integrated into mainstream American society. They are denied employment, education, housing, and other opportunities. This leads to high rates of recidivism. The majority of people coming out of prison are perpetually marginalized. They are denied basic rights and privileges of American citizenship.[25]

Importantly, the most comprehensive investigations have concluded that mass incarceration can explain relatively little of the crime drop since the 1990s. From about 2000 on, the crime reduction impact of adding more individuals to the prison population has been essentially zero. Incarceration has reached a point of diminishing returns—at enormous cost.[26]

The National Research Council has concluded that, while prison growth was a factor in reducing crime, "the magnitude of the crime reduction [due to mass incarceration] remains highly uncertain and the evidence suggests it was unlikely to have been large." Several factors explain why this impact was relatively modest. For example, incarceration is particularly ineffective at reducing certain kinds of crimes—in particular, youth crimes, many of which are committed in groups, and drug crimes. When people are locked up for these offenses, they are easily replaced on the streets by others seeking an income or struggling with addiction. In addition, people tend to age out of crime. Crime starts to peak in the mid- to late-teenage years and begins to decline when individuals are in their midtwenties. After that, crime drops sharply as adults reach their thirties and forties. The National Research Council has concluded, "Because recidivism rates decline markedly with age, lengthy prison sentences, unless they specifically target very high-rate or extremely dangerous offenders, are an inefficient approach to preventing crime by incapacitation."[27]

While mass incarceration has not been an effective system of crime prevention and control, it has been an extremely effective system of racial social control. Large numbers of people of color have been placed under the jurisdiction of the criminal justice system and saddled with criminal records for life.[28]

Mass incarceration also has destroyed many impoverished families. As of 2010, more than 50 percent of prisoners had children under eighteen years old when they were sent away. Incarcerated men are about four times more likely to attack their domestic partners than men who have never been imprisoned. Incarceration is positively linked to divorce and separation, in no small part because of the difficulty formerly incarcerated parents have when they attempt to seek employment after their release. As Jeffries discusses in Chapter 16, mass incarceration is not just a reflection of institutional racism. Nor is it only an acute setback limited to the person who is sent to prison. Incarceration also infects everyone in that person's social network. Like growing up in concentrated poverty, incarceration has a multigenerational impact on the life chances of the prisoner's family members.

Beyond the issue of incarceration, some of the drop in reported crime, starting in the 1990s, has been due to the waning of the crack epidemic, according to the most influential assessments.[29] The reasons for the waning of the epidemic appear to have been related in part to law enforcement strategies—but also in part to demand-side Keynesian economic policy in the 1990s and the consequent growth of realistic employment options for people who abandoned the drug trade.[30]

CRIMINAL JUSTICE POLICY BASED ON WHAT WORKS

The nation needs community policing that partners with nonprofit organizations in minority neighborhoods, sentencing reform, deincarceration, and a commitment to ex-offender reintegration that benefits from demand-side full-employment policy.

Police

A model more responsive to the Kerner Commission's calls for reform than zero-tolerance policing was community-based, problem-oriented policing, which began evolving in the 1970s and 1980s. A key theme underlying community policing is that law enforcement should not be just reactive, responding to calls, but also needs to be proactive, working with community nonprofit organizations and citizens to reduce crime, reduce fear, and increase trust. Other names for community-based, problem-oriented policing include guardian policing, trust policing, relationship-based policing, and partnership policing.[31]

Problem-oriented policing often is considered an element of community policing. It focuses on specific crimes and problems. Specific targeted solutions then are created. An early evidence-based success was in Newport News, Virginia, where burglaries were significantly reduced in a low-income housing complex by identifying the underlying circumstances that generated the crimes.[32]

Today, most police departments in large and medium American cities assert that they have some manner of community policing, problem-oriented policing, or both. There are many names and many initialisms for these initiatives across the nation. Some of the initiatives genuinely try to involve the community and to address the causes of crime in disadvantaged neighborhoods. Some are focused on high-risk individuals, while others are focused on high-risk, hot-spot locations. Most local initiatives are unevaluated. When they have been evaluated, findings from studies with quasi-experimental designs have been mixed, though some of these findings show reductions in violent crime, property crime, and fear.[33]

From the perspective of the Kerner Commission, we need to acknowledge that there are precious few evaluations of community-based, problem-oriented policing that addresses both individual and community-wide change in low-income minority neighborhoods where police partner with nonprofit youth-development organizations. However, at least one model, the Youth Safe Haven program, has a promising track record, as mentioned in Chapter 3 of Part I.

Evolving from the Japanese concept of community-based police mini-stations, the Youth Safe Haven model has facilitated partnerships between police and community-based nonprofit organizations in high-risk minority neighborhoods over the last thirty years. The police ministation concept has been merged with the youth-development and neighborhood organizing principles of nonprofit organizations like Centro Sister Isolina Ferre in Puerto Rico, which Charles Silberman, in a Ford Foundation book, *Criminal Violence and Criminal Justice,* called the "best example of community regeneration I have found anywhere in the United States."[34] Both civilian staff from nonprofit community organizations and police mentor elementary and middle school youth in Youth Safe Haven neighborhoods. They also help with homework. Police undertake foot patrols in the neighborhoods of the nonprofit organizations. There are meetings and other forms of community outreach. In a randomized, controlled evaluation from 2010 to 2014 in six cities in five regions of the United States, program youth received higher grades than control youth and demonstrated higher respect for teachers and better school attendance. The outcomes were statistically significant.[35]

In earlier years and at other locations (including Boston; Chicago; Columbia, South Carolina; Dover, New Hampshire; Philadelphia; and San Juan, Puerto Rico), reported serious crime rates in Youth Safe Haven neighborhoods were compared to reported rates in their cities as a whole. For the most part, declines in reported crime rates in the Youth Safe Haven neighborhoods were greater than in their cities as a whole. In one location, Columbia, South Carolina, the police chief established Youth Safe Havens in a number of public housing developments, deployed the kind of community service officers recommended by the Kerner Commission and opened a residential Safe Haven, where young police officers lived. Reported crime decreased and property values increased in the neighborhood with the residential program.[36]

The Youth Safe Haven model was further replicated with success in the Bayview Hunter's Point community of San Francisco in the late 1990s. Civilians managed the after-school Bayview Safe Haven, which invested in youth ages ten to seventeen. Two San Francisco foot-patrol officers interacted with program youth and monitored the area surrounding the program site, which was a recreation center provided by the Department of Recreation and Parks. Over a two-year period, the Bayview Safe Haven participants were evaluated in a quasi-experimental design with a matched comparison group. Bayview Safe Haven participants were significantly less likely to be suspended from school than comparison group members. Participants with a history of juvenile justice involvement were significantly less likely to recidivate. Participants with no juvenile justice history were significantly less likely to commit a first offense. The census tract within which the Bayview Safe Haven was located experienced reductions in juvenile crime over the evaluation period. Because of the positive outcomes, three more Youth Safe Havens were replicated in similar San Francisco low-income neighborhoods.[37]

Community-based, problem-oriented community policing needs to be refined and more extensively evaluated. But there is enough existing evidence, including from initiatives like the Youth Safe Haven program, in the poorest minority urban communities, to endorse the strategy as effective, successful, and in sync with the Kerner legacy. The principles underlying community-based, problem-oriented policing in low-income minority neighborhoods need to be applied more widely.

If police departments genuinely continue to move away from zero tolerance and toward community policing with real, not just rhetorical, minority community ownership, there is hope for reduction in excessive force by police. In the meantime, it is critical for the federal government to carry out court-mandated consent decrees to reform police departments.[38]

New governmental and foundation leadership is needed to create accident-proof policing across America. The federal government should establish an objective method for accurately collecting data on fatal shootings of citizens by police officers. Along with more accurate reporting, fatal incidents need to be investigated, following the model of aviation. After an airline crash, the National Transportation Safety Board sends out an independent team to investigate causes and uncover how often-hidden problems can spin into disaster. This has led to new procedures that have made flying safer. The country now needs an agency like the National Transportation Safety Board to do the same thing for police. This can lead to an overhaul in the ways that police and citizens interact at close range. At the state level, Wisconsin already has passed a law requiring independent investigation of police actions that result in civilian deaths.[39]

More fundamentally, there needs to be a change within policing culture. Minorities in low-income communities should not be viewed as the designated enemy. Those communities should not be treated as though they are occupied zones. The nation needs to move beyond the rhetoric of community policing to a method of engagement that promotes trust, healing, and genuine partnership. Such cultural change will not necessarily come easily to the nation's eighteen thousand state and local law enforcement agencies.

The 2015 White House Task Force on 21st Century Policing was a constructive step forward. In part, the task force was a response to the fatal shootings by police and the citizen protests that emerged in 2014 to 2016. Among other policies, the task force unanimously recommended that police embrace a guardian rather than a warrior mind-set, show citizens respect and give them a voice when encountered, be trained to reduce racial bias and bias toward immigrant status, and reduce actions that stig-

matize young people (like the criminalization of school disciplinary behavior that has created the school-to-prison pipeline discussed in Chapter
3 of Part I).

As George Mason University professor Laurie Robinson documents in
Chapter 14 of Part II, the White House task force recommendations have
been largely embraced by all the major leadership groups in law enforcement, including the International Association of Chiefs of Police (IACP),
Major Cities Chiefs Association, Major County Sheriffs Association, and
National Organization of Blacks in Law Enforcement. At a national conference, the IACP issued a formal apology for the role the policing profession has historically played in mistreating communities of color. The
IACP also set up a new Institute on Community-Police Relations to help
agencies implement the task force proposals.

A number of states have instituted training in line with the White
House task force recommendations. For example, Illinois passed legislation in 2015 requiring new police training in use of force. The Massachusetts Association of Police Chiefs requires all officers in the state to
undergo training on use of force and fair and impartial policing. Virginia's attorney general has begun a statewide program to train law enforcement in de-escalation, impartial policing, and use of force. In 2016, the
New Jersey attorney general required all five hundred police agencies in
the state to be trained on de-escalation techniques and implicit bias. The
Department of Justice has mandated implicit bias training for all U.S.
attorneys and federal law enforcement agents—more than twenty-five
thousand individuals. And thirty-four states and the District of Columbia
took legislative action on police reform during 2015–2016 on such topics
as use of force, profiling, body-worn cameras, and crisis intervention
training (see Chapter 14 in Part II).

While we have focused on police interventions, there are, of course,
many other models of reducing crime—and some have demonstrated that
they work, on the basis of peer-reviewed, randomized controlled or quasi-
experimental evaluations. In Chapter 13 of Part II, University of Colorado
professor Delbert Elliott reviews these evidence-based models, and we
recommend that the models most appropriate to the Kerner legacy be
scaled up. At the same time, we conclude that the most powerful interventions to reduce crime in the minority communities of highest priority
to the Kerner Commission are the economic, employment, and education
policies discussed in Chapters 2 and 3 of Part I.

Sentencing

Just as evidence-based strategies have had at least some impact on policing, more evidence-based policies have begun to exert a measured degree
of influence on the rest of the criminal justice system.

In terms of prison population, we need to remember that America's incarceration rate remains far higher than in other countries or in our own past. And a number of states—such as Ohio, Oklahoma, and Virginia—increased their prison populations in recent years.[40]

Nonetheless, as Figure 5.3 shows, the overall number of persons sentenced to prison began to decline in the twenty-first century. The number of minorities incarcerated also began to decline—even though incarceration rates for African Americans and Hispanic Americans remain much higher than for whites. The decline has not necessarily been because of moral and civil rights imperatives but probably more because of the excessive cost to state governments of prison building and maintenance.

Positive recent sentencing and prosecuting reforms can be identified. At the federal level, in 2010, Congress passed the Fair Sentencing Act, which reduced the disparity in sentencing between crack cocaine (used primarily by minorities) and powder cocaine (used disproportionately by whites). In 2014, the Sentencing Commission unanimously voted to reduce excessive sentences for up to forty-six thousand people serving time for federal drug offenses.[41]

At the state level, in 2009, New York reformed its Rockefeller drug laws, which imposed harsh mandatory minimum sentences for low-level drug offenses. In 2014, California voters passed a measure that reclassified low-level property and drug crimes from felonies to misdemeanors and reinvested some of the fiscal savings in prevention programs.[42] California also has made more prisoners convicted of nonviolent crimes eligible for parole and has given judges, not prosecutors, the power to determine when juveniles can be tried as adults.[43]

Some progress has evolved from local races for prosecutors. For decades, district attorney candidates have competed to prove they were tougher on crime than their opponents. But recently, more prosecutors around the country have been campaigning on promises to charge fewer juveniles as adults, stop prosecuting low-level marijuana possession, and seek the death penalty less often. They have done so even in some places with reputations for tough justice, including Chicago, Houston, and Tampa.[44]

Such state and local sentencing reforms need to be identified as models for replication across the nation.

These reforms move in positive, evidence-based directions, but the nation remains a long way from solving the crisis of mass incarceration. The way forward should begin by eliminating mandatory minimum sentences in all jurisdictions, cutting back on excessively lengthy sentences, and stopping all policies and practices that contribute to racial inequality at every stage of the juvenile and criminal justice systems.[45]

Drug dealers should be imprisoned. But American policy would do well to build on the policies of other democracies that frame drug use more as a public health issue. For instance, the experience in Portugal has been that many lives can be saved by a medical treatment strategy—at much lower cost than the American incarceration policy for users in our failed and racially unjust War on Drugs.[46]

Deincarceration

In terms of reducing prison populations, the National Council on Crime and Delinquency estimates that placing 80 percent of nonserious offenders currently serving time in prison into evidence-based community programs would save $9.7 billion across all states (see Chapter 13 in Part II).

A number of states have responded. As Marc Mauer, executive director of the Sentencing Project, and David Cole, professor of law at Georgetown University, have pointed out, California, New York, and New Jersey all have reduced their prison populations by about 25 percent in recent years—with no or little increase in crime.[47] On the basis of a report on the annual cost savings and reductions in crime generated by evidence-based alternatives to prison, the Washington State legislature cancelled plans to build a new prison. Using several evidence-based community alternatives to prison, Florida reduced its felon rearrest and conviction rate by 14 percent and saved over $193 million between 2004 and 2011 (see Chapter 13 in Part II).

Interestingly, one of the most promising state policy changes has come from Louisiana. The state has the highest per capita incarceration rate in the nation and is one of the poorest. Nonetheless, in 2017 Louisiana passed an ambitious criminal justice reform package. The new law projected to cut the prison population by 10 percent and keep it down—saving the state a projected quarter billion dollars over the next decade. The bulk of the savings will be used to reduce recidivism, support crime victims, and evaluate the outcomes of the new law. The legislation passed with overwhelming bipartisan majorities and was influenced by evidence of success in other states.[48]

We encourage the federal government and all state governments to follow the examples of California, New York, New Jersey, Washington State, Florida, and Louisiana.

Reducing prison populations will not be successful without reintegrating ex-offenders. Most people returning from prison have significant educational and employment deficits. Roughly half lack a high school degree or equivalent, more than half have been previously fired from a job, and many depended on illegal income before incarceration. After release, former prisoners have limited success finding employment. About half find work during the first postrelease year. Most former prisoners have financial debt, which few manage to pay during the year following their release. Former prisoners who held an in-prison job, participated in job training while incarcerated, earned a GED during imprisonment, or participated in an employment program soon after release work a greater percentage of time during their first year out of prison than those who did not. Former prisoners who are married or have marriage-like relationships have lower odds of recidivism, drug use, or alcohol use than those in more casual relationships.[49]

Reform needs to begin with education in prison. Decades of research have shown that inmates who participated in prison education programs are far less likely to recidivate than those who did not participate. A RAND Corporation evaluation concluded that every dollar spent on prison education translates into savings of four to five dollars further down the line. There is bipartisan movement in this direction in some states. New York is a leading model for replicating, with Cornell University, New York University, and Bard College among the schools teaching college courses in prison.[50]

Ex-offender reintegration models that have demonstrated success according to randomized, controlled evaluations include the Safer Foundation in Illinois, the Minnesota Comprehensive Offender Reentry Plan, and the Center for Employment Opportunities in New York.

The Safer program in Chicago provides case-management training in conflict resolution, life skills, and job skills and related interventions for previously incarcerated youth and adults. Safer's nonprofit arm runs a staffing agency. This allows Safer to offer temporary, temp-to-hire, and permanent staffing positions to local organizations. Safer handles all the human resources and paperwork. Employers are given the opportunity to try out previously incarcerated persons in positions before formally hiring them. Safer job managers are responsible for linking clients with employers and ensuring that clients meet employer standards. Safer retention specialists help keep clients on track and troubleshoot issues between employers and ex-offenders. Two recent randomized, controlled evaluations have demonstrated that Safer participants had significantly lower recidivism rates than control group members.[51]

The Minnesota Comprehensive Offender Reentry Plan provides education, job training, mentoring, housing, and income support. A recent randomized, controlled evaluation showed that participants recidivated significantly less than control group members.[52]

The Center for Employment Opportunities has operated as a nonprofit organization in New York City since 1996. The center's interventions include life- and parenting-skills training, paid transitional employment, part-time job placement, and long-term job placement. Each year, the Center works with an average of two thousand persons returning to the community from prison. In a randomized, controlled evaluation, participants were about 11 percent less likely to be reincarcerated three years after the program and about 8 percent less likely to be arrested, convicted, or incarcerated.[53]

While a number of promising ex-offender programs (like Delancey Street in San Francisco[54]) remain unevaluated, the three models just discussed provide a set of common evidence-based principles that need to be extensively replicated and scaled up around the nation—and funded in part by revenues saved by reducing prison populations.

More fundamentally, while these models can provide life-skills and job training, provision of actual public and private jobs to ex-offenders must be an essential part of the Keynesian demand-side, full-employment policy we recommend in Chapter 2 of Part I. The myriad laws that bar reentry for drug offenders for the rest of their economic, social, and political lives need to be eliminated. Federal and state reforms are needed to overturn decades-long practices that discriminate against hiring ex-offenders. For example, clean-slate laws should be enacted to expunge minor nonviolent crimes.[55]

Sustaining Progress and Encouraging New Leadership

To sustain the modest progress that recently has been made in criminal justice reform and to enhance it, we need to encourage more leadership from a new breed of change agents that has been emerging. Nonprofit reform groups now are tackling issues and adopting strategies that an earlier generation of reformers did not.

For example, directed by Alex Karakatsanis, a recent Harvard Law graduate, the Civil Rights Corps (CRC) was responsible for getting the city of Jennings, Missouri, to change its jailing practices, as discussed earlier in this chapter, and to compensate people who were jailed. In partnership with other nonprofits, like the Southern Law Policy Center, the CRC is filing lawsuits challenging such egregious forms of "human caging" and "wealth based detention" across the nation. With so much procedural injustice and with thousands of county-level fiefdoms in the balkanized American criminal justice system, this mission would seem to pit David against Goliath. However, as Michael Zuckerman writes, local jurisdictions are taking note of the CRC's success. The CRC has demonstrated to its clients that they can have power as citizens. And the CRC is motivating a new generation of lawyers to litigate against the injustices of the system.[56] The CRC model therefore deserves to be significantly scaled up.

Another example of new nonprofit leadership is Gideon's Promise, an Atlanta-based nonprofit organization. Gideon's Promise is addressing the reality that 80 percent of the people charged with crimes in this country cannot afford a defense attorney. Eighty percent of the people in court depend on a public defender to be their voice, tell their stories, and assert their humanity in a system that routinely denies it. Gideon's Promise asserts that the criminal justice system cannot significantly change without a dramatic increase in public defenders.[57]

Sympathetic to such advocacy, a number of nonprofit organizations now are led by formerly incarcerated people and their families. Examples of such groups advocating for sentencing and prison reform include JustLeadershipUSA, VOTE (New Orleans), A New Way of Life (Los Angeles), and Legal Services for Prisoners with Children (San Francisco). The public role of these activists may have a ripple effect. Each time a formerly incarcerated person appears before a legislature, speaks at a news conference, or writes about life in prison, others may find it easier to speak up.[58] We support the rapid development of such advocacy.

CONCLUSION: THE WHITE INSTITUTIONAL DOUBLE STANDARD

The Kerner Commission concluded that white institutions created conditions of inequality, poverty, and racial injustice in American minority communities. White mass incarceration institutions exacerbated these conditions, as did white financial institutions. Those financial institutions caused the Great Recession that began in 2007–2008 and that devastated so many American families, disproportionately poor and minority. Why were the top bankers not prosecuted? Why have the crimes of large white corporations not been high priority for prosecutors? Why are white financial corporations today being allowed to reestablish the alliances that caused the financial crisis? As Robert Morganthau, the crusading Manhattan prosecutor of the 1960s asked, "How do you justify prosecuting a 19-year-old who sells drugs on a street corner when you say it is too complicated to go after the people who move the money?"[59]

6

Domestic Reform, Global Impact

PROGRESS ON THE KERNER economic, employment, education, housing, neighborhood investment, criminal justice, and civil rights agenda will offer constructive opportunities for American foreign policy.

In Chapter 1 of Part II, Nobel Prize–winning economist Joseph Stiglitz reminds us that "[America's] greatness arises not so much from its military power but from its soft power and its economic power. In today's world, America's continued racism undermines that soft power and our overall economic performance."

Attainment of the Kerner domestic goals will enhance the nation's soft power abroad. The United States has alienated many of its traditional allies. A 2017 Pew Research Center poll in thirty-seven countries reported a substantial decline in favorable views of the United States.[1] Yet the world cannot afford an America that cedes foreign and economic policy to intolerant powers that are attempting to increase their influence.

Kerner reforms have the potential for generating new respect for the American values we profess but do not always carry out—values like life, freedom, diversity, rule of law, independence, and doing what is morally right.

In his Riverside Church speech in New York City a year before release of the Kerner Report, Dr. Martin Luther King, Jr., as winner of the Nobel Peace Prize in 1964, declared that the war in Vietnam was immoral. Dr. King argued that race, inequality, human rights, and American policy toward Asia were all pieces of the same fabric.[2] Today, much of that Asian fabric is woven into the relationship between America and China. China is now competing with the United States to be the world's leading economic power and is projecting its autocratic, hierarchical ideology globally. There is considerable debate over the book *Destined for War*, by Harvard Kennedy School professor Graham Allison, which warns of armed military conflict between America and China.[3]

In the already existing tension between America's democratic priority on freedom and China's authoritarian priority on order, China has criticized the failure of the United States to achieve racial justice and equality.[4] If the Kerner agenda is advanced, however, China's criticism will, of necessity, be diminished, and America can better project the importance of human values born of the Enlightenment.

Equally important, the United States will be in a much stronger moral and strategic position to criticize the racism, inequality, and lack of human rights in China—demonstrating to the world the internal vulnerabilities and corruption of the Chinese system. China can be put on the defensive, for example, for its state-sponsored terrorism against the racial minorities of Tibet and East Turkestan and for its treatment of political dissidents.

In 1950, China invaded Tibet and since then has brutally occupied and enslaved that nation. Tibetan citizens are Buddhists and bear allegiance to the Dalai Lama, who was awarded the Nobel Peace Prize in 1989 and lives in exile in India.[5]

North of Tibet, the vast East Turkestan Central Asia region, called Xinjiang by the Chinese, harbors an active separatist movement among Uyghurs, the indigenous population. The movement is responsible for waging low-level insurgency against China, which created a police state there after racial and ethnic violence erupted in 1990, 1997, and 2009. The Uyghur protests were over China's restrictions on economic opportunity, religious practices, and cultural traditions.[6]

Especially since the 1989 Chinese Army's Tiananmen Square massacre of students advocating democratic reform and rule of law, China has expanded its detention and torture of political prisoners. The United States has not sufficiently advocated for incarcerated dissidents. The Chinese have told their prisoners this demonstrates lack of American commitment to human rights. The winner of the Nobel Peace Prize in 2009, Lui Xiaobo, the democracy advocate and poet, was kept in prison by China even with cancer. There was little effort by the American government to grant his request for treatment in the West, and he died in 2017.[7]

With more American Kerner-created soft power, not only could the causes of Tibet, East Turkestan, and democracy be strengthened by America, but the movements for self-determination in Taiwan and Hong Kong could be reinforced.

Similarly, American racial injustice has been routinely criticized by Russia,[8] even though there is open contempt for minorities in that country.[9] As the United States combats Russian efforts to influence elections,[10] progress on the Kerner legacy will help show the world the value of American democracy. And increased soft power has the potential for reinforcing American leverage in other regions with authoritarian regimes, like those of the Middle East.

7

Financing Reform

MUCH OF WHAT we have proposed can be financed by eliminating policies and programs that do not work—like supply-side economics, work-first programming, Temporary Assistance for Needy Families "welfare reform," education vouchers, and mass incarceration and the prison-industrial complex.

Lobbyists will be deployed to defend what does not work. Over the long run, the evidence-based movement must demonstrate to taxpayers the commonsense need to eliminate programs and policies that have failed. Private foundations need to finance significant expansion of the evidence-based movement.

To finance the Kerner priorities we have set forth, additional revenues should be identified through reform of the federal tax system. To enable reform, what the Kerner Commission called "new will" is necessary, and this we turn to in the next chapter.[1] For now, and without attempting to be comprehensive, we illustrate just a few of the tax reforms that have been advocated in recent years.

Under President Dwight Eisenhower, the highest marginal income tax rate in the 1950s was over 90 percent. It was reduced in the 1960s to 70 percent and then to 50 percent in the 1980s. Today, the richest 1 percent of Americans pay 33 percent of their total income in taxes. If rates were changed so that they paid 40 percent, $170 billion of revenue would be generated in the first year, according to the nonpartisan Tax Policy Center.[2] Importantly, a 2017 report by the International Monetary Fund found no evidence for supply-side rhetoric that claims that making the rich pay more will result in lower economic growth.[3]

Tax rate increases should be accompanied by the elimination of tax-avoidance loopholes. For example, investment income currently is taxed at much lower levels than earned income. That motivates tax lawyers for wealthy individuals try to define income as deriving from investments, not earnings. We recommend that this tax-avoidance loophole be closed by equalizing tax rates on all types of income,[4] because in a country that believes in work, we should not tax money earned from work more than we tax money earned from money.

The tax base should be broadened by reducing the size of intergenerational wealth transfers. That is, we need to raise the estate tax. At present, the estate tax covers only 0.2 percent of estates—about two of every thousand people who die. As one observer has noted, "There are a lot of people out there who were born on third yet think they hit a triple."[5]

American corporations can defer tax on profits earned abroad and placed in overseas entities through accounting devices. Originally, this was intended to allow companies to more easily invest profits abroad. But the benefit has been abused and has become a tax shelter that shields $2.6 trillion. Many plans have been proposed to eliminate such tax avoidance. The simplest plan is a minimum tax that multinationals would pay on their foreign earnings at the time when they are earned.[6]

The trading of stocks, bonds, and derivatives has mushroomed in recent decades, generating enormous wealth for a very small percentage of the population. It has been estimated that a financial transaction tax of even 0.01 percent per trade ($10 on a $100,000 trade) could raise $185 billion over ten years—more than enough to pay for prekindergarten for three- and four-year-olds.[7]

Prominent former Republican and Democratic federal officials, such as George Shultz and Joseph Stiglitz, support a carbon tax imposed on emissions to reduce greenhouse gases.[8]

We agree with the late Secretary of Health, Education, and Welfare John Gardner, who famously once said after the urban protests in the summer of 1967, "History is not going to deal kindly with a rich nation that will not tax itself to cure its miseries."[9] We believe that taxes should be based on the ability to pay—should be progressive, in other words. One big reason for the worsening income inequality in America is that we have been making our tax system less and less progressive—cutting taxes for the rich and for big corporations. The kind of financing we are recommending here would importantly reverse that unfair trend.

8

___

New Will

THE KERNER REPORT concluded that "new will" was needed among the American citizenry before the policy it proposed could be enacted. Today, we know what needs to be done. We know what works based on evidence, not political ideology. But new will remains imperative.

We advocate for new will as patriots, devoted to the future of our country. Patriots as well, the members of the Kerner Commission were mostly moderate and mostly white men. They carried "the imprimatur of the political establishment," as one historian has noted (see Chapter 21 in Part II). Their recommendations attracted great public interest. The Kerner publication sold two million copies and reportedly was the best-selling federal report in American history (see Chapter 23 in Part II).

The Kerner Commission was bipartisan, and we base our strategy for the generation of new will on the traditions of two Republican presidents and two Democratic presidents: Abraham Lincoln, Theodore Roosevelt, Franklin Roosevelt, and John Kennedy. Abraham Lincoln crusaded for racial justice and invested in public infrastructure. Theodore Roosevelt regulated corporate greed to reduce inequality. Franklin Roosevelt generated jobs, broadened prosperity, created Social Security, and advanced "adequate health care." John Kennedy gave priority to "what we can do for our country" and "what together we can do."[1]

In the spirit of Kennedy, the American people can do a great deal to generate new will for the country. We will hold town meetings and forums on this Kerner update around the nation to identify and build grassroots consensus. We *can* create the new will, by reaching out to natural allies and making common cause with them. Those of us in such a coalition do not have to love one another—though that would be good. All we need to do is recognize that we share mutual goals that can be enacted if we get ourselves together.

Only the federal government has the resources to finance the Kerner legacy to scale. But we call on America's great foundations in the private sector to finance the ongoing generation of new will—through a significant increase of resources to existing and new nonprofit organizations, which need to advocate and organize for the new will we want to identify. Our measure of success will be whether the nation experiences a significant reduction in racial injustice, poverty, and inequality over coming years and decades.

In what follows, we present a framework within which to initiate dialogue at town hall meetings and forums. As we travel America, we will ask these questions: What are the key constituencies needed to generate new will? What is the vocabulary of the movement's narrative? How can citizens be better trained to run for office in support of those solutions? How can the media more accurately communicate the day-to-day realities that define the Kerner legacy and the long-run solutions? And how can we better ensure that average citizens get a fair vote, so the nation has a more representative, functional government than at present?

WHAT ARE THE KEY CONSTITUENCIES NEEDED TO GENERATE NEW WILL?

American democracy is a belief in governments created through free elections and universal suffrage; an independent judiciary; and guaranteed freedoms of speech, assembly, religion, and the press. We live in a time when these beliefs and freedoms are being threatened. The first step in creating new will, then, is vigilance in maintaining our founding principles.[2]

In the primaries and general election of 2016, there was little debate on how to reduce poverty and inequality. Many interpreted the election as a backlash after the first African American president.[3] Much of the ongoing policy debate threatens to move away from the Kerner legacy—by, for example, increasing inequality.

Yet, as University of California at Los Angeles professor Gary Orfield points out in Chapter 10 of Part II, the odds faced by Dr. Martin Luther King, Jr., and César Chávez in the 1950s and 1960s were more formidable. The Ku Klux Klan was powerful. Congress had not enacted a major civil rights law since the 1870s.

Within the scope of American history it therefore is credible and plausible to expect fresh leaders to emerge for a revitalized people's movement that organizes, advocates, and presses federal, state, and local authorities for legislation that advances the priorities of the Kerner Commission. If the present toxic atmosphere in Washington prevents national action, in the shorter run the movement needs to advance at the state and local levels—as, for example, California and New York are doing with criminal justice reform. Change can be created step by step, by building on models of success.

Constituencies needed for advocacy on Kerner priorities include organizations seeking multiracial economic justice for the poor and workers, groups focused on public morality, youth organizations, millennials, and the women's movement. Illustrative groups are as follows.

Dr. King's Coalition for Multiracial Economic Justice

In the mid-1960s, shortly before he was assassinated, Dr. Martin Luther King, Jr., began shifting from civil rights to a new movement for economic justice and human rights. This was his multiracial Poor People's Campaign. Dr. King realized that achieving justice for racial minorities could not be separated from achieving economic opportunities for all Americans. He sought fairer economic opportunity for poor and working-class people of all races, so they could see their interests aligned rather than in conflict. These racially transcending rights included employment, health care, education, childcare, housing, security against crime, and fairness by police and courts (see Chapter 21 in Part II).

A decade later, during the administration of President Jimmy Carter, Father Geno Baroni sought to build a multiracial movement among poor and working-class racial minorities and whites, as Brookings Institution senior fellow and Georgetown University professor E. J. Dionne discusses in Chapter 21 of Part II. The Catholic Church's coordinator for Dr. King's 1963 March on Washington, Baroni stimulated neighborhood-level festivals that brought together African Americans and white urban ethnic groups in celebrations of heritage. Many police chiefs predicted violence. But the festivals were peaceful—and were the first widespread gatherings of African Americans and white urban ethnics in many big cities since the protests of the 1960s that were the focus of the Kerner Commission. Baroni wanted to achieve more. But he thought the nation inevitably would recognize the need to work together.[4]

That did not happen. Many well-paying jobs began to disappear—in part through globalization, automation, and unfair trade deals. Well-financed campaigns weakened unions, and legal and other barriers to union organizing were thrown up. The minimum wage lagged behind the cost of living. Workers did not reap the rewards of increased productivity. Taxes were reduced for the rich and big corporations, substantially below the levels, for example, during the Dwight Eisenhower administration in the 1950s. Job-training and education spending were cut. Many white workers asked, "What about me?" Minorities and the poor felt the same way.

Today it is even more obvious that the interests of poor and working-class minorities and whites overlap. In 2017, reinforcing Dr. King and Father Baroni, Harvard Kennedy School professor William Julius Wilson emphasized:

> A new democratic vision must reject the commonly held view that race is so divisive that whites, blacks, Latinos, Asians, and Native Americans cannot work together in a common cause. Those articulating the new vision must realize that if a political message is tailored to a white audience, people of color draw back, just as whites draw back when a message is tailored to racial minority audiences. The challenge is to find issues and programs that concern the families of all racial and ethnic groups, so that individuals in these groups can honestly perceive mutual interests and join in a multiracial coalition to move America forward.[5]

Thinking in a similar way, but with some cautions, Wellesley College professor Michael Jeffries concludes, "At issue, I think, is the extent to which racial justice is an explicit tenet of the movement for economic justice, and whether a movement for economic justice can be successful without explicitly addressing institutional racism, and supporting black and brown self-determination."[6]

Neither Dr. King nor Father Baroni lived long enough to fulfill their dreams. But we do have their historical models, their precedent on which to build. Economic justice remains the key today for organizing the poor and working class, minority and white, into the core constituency of a new people's movement to enact the recommendations of the Kerner Commission.

The need is to convince poor and working-class white and racial minority Americans that the reduction of poverty and inequality requires a win-win mind-set. Not a mind-set that assumes we can win only when you lose. A revitalized movement to reduce poverty and inequality must be framed as "we are in this together," not "you are in this alone." We need new leaders with the charisma to bring the racial groups, the poor, the working class, and the middle class together. Shortly after the Kerner Commission's report was released in 1968, Senator Robert Kennedy demonstrated these qualities.

As we have seen earlier, the percentage of whites in poverty in America is lower than the percentage for minorities. But the number of whites in poverty is greater. As YouthBuild founder Dorothy Stoneman points out in Chapter 4 of Part II, eighteen million whites live in poverty, compared to twelve million Hispanics, ten million African Americans, one million Native Americans, and one million Asian Americans. That means poverty is the common ground for organizing forty-two million Americans of all races to create the new will to enact the Kerner legacy.

This alignment is reinforced by recent polling on inequality. More than two-thirds of Americans polled say reducing inequality is an urgent issue, as polling expert Celinda Lake tells us in Chapter 20 of Part II. There is a growing, evidence-based understanding that high levels of income and wealth inequality are socially corrosive, lower trust in society, increase mortality for particular groups, increase mental illness and substance abuse, and reduce worker productivity.

Just joining hands and singing "Solidarity Forever" will not make a multiracial, multiclass people's movement. What will? Standing up for job guarantees, the recognition that in a nation where there are so many jobs that need doing, everybody has a right to a job—at a living wage, a fifteen-dollar-an-hour wage, phased in with a ratchet clause to keep it current. Income for those who cannot work or who cannot find work. A good public education for all—from early childhood through college. Education and training, with special attention and special provision for jobs and income for those put out of work by circumstances beyond their control. Health care for all. The basic American principles of equal rights and equal opportunity for all—whatever a person's social standing, zip code, religion, gender, or color. Fair and progressive taxation. Getting the rich and the giant corporations off welfare.

E. J. Dionne, Thomas Mann, and Norman Ornstein have pointed out that there has been recent movement in America toward multi-issue King-like economic and racial justice coalition building and away from single-issue advocacy. For example, the NAACP, the Human Rights Campaign, Planned Parenthood, People for the American Way, and the Sierra Club have joined in support of the rights of immigrants. We need to build on this model.[7]

We encourage Indivisible, the largest new group of citizen activists promoting lasting multi-issue engagement, to play a lead role in linking economic and racial justice. Indivisible has amassed several thousand local chapters across the nation.[8] Its advocacy at the state and county level can potentially become a powerful force to advance civic culture and the Kerner legacy.

The Middle Class

Grounded in the need for economic justice, the people's movement must be strengthened by the middle class.

Recent presidential election campaigns have given priority to middle-class voters. We must demonstrate to these Americans the commonsense reality that their interests are closer to Kerner priorities than to the priorities of the very rich. Reducing inequality can be legislated to lessen the anxieties of the middle class, as can job training linked to job placement, investment in mass transit, significant improvement in airport and intercity rapid-rail infrastructure, a single-payer expansion of Medicare, improved public schools, and a reformed criminal justice system that reduces the tax burden through less prison building while it maintains public safety.

We must appeal to the new African American and Hispanic middle classes to help lead support for the Kerner legacy.

Though not necessarily limited to the middle class, one demographic trend that can potentially reinforce Kerner priorities is the increase in recent decades in interracial adoption, dating, and marriage. As of the 2010 census, 20 percent of cohabiting relationships and 17 percent of new marriages were interracial or interethnic. California now is a majority-minority state, and 25 percent of new marriages there in 2010 were interracial. Nationally, whites will cease to be a majority in thirty years.[9]

The Public Morality Constituency

In his televised speech to the nation on June 11, 1963, President Kennedy, announcing the integration of the University of Alabama, told the American people, "We are confronted primarily with a moral issue."[10] Similarly, Baroni believed "every economic and social issue is a moral issue."[11] Dr. King and Father Baroni gained credibility because they were religious leaders—and today an important emerging moral cohort is a mixture of African Americans, Hispanics, whites, and women. They include Catholics inspired by Pope Francis and Protestants, Jews, Muslims, Sikhs, Hindus, and Buddhists advocating social action on fundamental moral imperatives, like empowering the poor, welcoming strangers, and protecting the environment.[12]

One of the best examples is the Reverend William Barber, an African American minister from North Carolina, who is considered by some as "the closest person we have to Martin Luther King Jr. in our midst." With a combination of piety and politics, Reverend Barber preaches the immorality of inequality, poverty, and racial injustice. In his Moral Mondays movement in North Carolina, Reverend Barber has talked of politicians committing "the sin of taking health from the sick so that they can give tax cuts to the greedy, knowing that thousands will die unnecessarily." He talks of politicians denying "the God-given . . . human rights of individuals and then stack[ing] the courts to protect themselves."[13]

The Moral Mondays model now is being spread nationally by Reverend Barber, through the Repairers of the Breach organization and the new Poor People's Campaign. He is training activists in many states—an "army of moral defibrillators"—to put the issue of poverty front and center. In the words of the historian Tim Tyson, who has chronicled Reverend Barber for over a decade, Christianity, Judaism, Islam, and the other major faiths are all rooted in an ethos of love—an ethos Reverend Barber uses to speak to people who have an activist orientation. The activists are both believers and nonbelievers. This mixture helps broaden and strengthen the Moral Mondays movement.[14]

Carrying the message across the country, Reverend Barber is speaking in pulpits, presenting to audiences of union workers and millennial activists, and appearing as a regular on MSNBC. "We can't keep fighting in our silos," he told Service Employees International Union leaders at a health workers gathering. "No more separating issues—labor over here, voting rights over here. The same people fighting against one should have to fight against all of *us* together."[15]

A mission of doing what is morally right defines many other new organizations today, and they all are needed as part of the Kerner agenda. For example, Black Lives Matter, formed by three African American feminist social organizers—Alicia Garza, Opal Tometi, and Patrisse Cullors—has created a defining social movement. It has, in the words of Michael Jeffries, helped reinvigorate "participatory citizenship as the true source of people's power and the most essential ingredient of democracy" (see Chapter 16 in Part II).

Youth

A multiracial group of adults who were raised in urban and rural poverty and who overcame many barriers through youth development ventures like YouthBuild formed a new national organization, Opportunity Youth United. This organization is mobilizing younger Americans to, in effect, further much of the Kerner legacy and also to reach out to other constituencies, as Dorothy Stoneman explains in Chapter 4 of Part II.

One goal should be to better mobilize other younger Americans, not necessarily those raised in poverty, particularly the millennials, who have surpassed baby boomers as the nation's largest living generation. Polling has shown that millennials are more willing than many other Americans to accept the role of government, including government involvement in Kerner issues like redistribution of income and universal health care. Millennials were especially punished by the Great Recession, which began in 2007. They suffered higher unemployment rates than any other age group during the downturn, and their wages had fallen more than any other group when the downturn finally concluded.[16]

Millennials know that, while their wages are low, corporate profits are high and that, as we discuss in Chapter 4 of Part I, there has been little action by government against the Wall Street abuses that caused the recession. Millennials are the first generation worse off economically than their parents. Homeownership is more difficult. They are not optimistic about the future.[17]

This is the most educated generation in American history, as measured, for example, by proportion of college graduates (see Chapter 20 in Part II). Yet the rising costs of school have made it hard to pay off record student debt. If there is a sense among many millennials that America needs a rebirth in terms of jobs and education, echoing the Occupy Wall Street movement against corporate greed, there also is some sympathy for racial and moral rebirth. For example, about 60 percent of whites under age thirty agree with the Black Lives Matter critique of law enforcement.[18]

Millennials are the most diverse generation in American history. Some 40 percent of millennials come from racial minority groups.[19] These demographics help favor millennial commitment to a people's movement and the Kerner legacy.

Yet while millennials voted enthusiastically in the 2016 presidential primaries for candidates whose positions backed the Kerner legacy, in the November 2016 general election millennial turnout was down.[20] This trend needs to be reversed. In addition, the Kerner movement needs to acknowledge and respond to the small proportion of white millennials who have joined white supremacist organizations—in part protesting their perception that the Great Recession and increased economic inequality have hurt them more than racial minorities.[21]

Senior Citizens

Senior citizens have higher voter turnout rates than all other age groups. Their largest and most powerful nonprofit organization, the American Association of Retired Persons (AARP), has an affiliate, the AARP Foundation, that gives priority to the income, nutrition, housing, and safety needs of low-income citizens ages fifty and older.[22] A new people's movement needs to better mobilize these Americans.

Women

In 2017, the Women's March on Washington, as well as in hundreds of other American and foreign cities, drew millions of people. It was not a single-issue protest. The march brought together people taking a stand on economic justice, social justice, and human rights issues, including race, gender, sexual orientation, religion, immigration, and health care.[23] There were forests of homemade signs, some with quite pointed messages, some a little whimsical, but all serious, proclaiming what the great majority of Americans are for and what the great majority are against. Most of the message, was, in effect, supportive of the Kerner agenda. The march coordinated with many other movements—Indivisible, for example, whose vigorous gatherings at congressional town hall meetings have powerfully advanced the movement for better health care for all Americans and other policies consistent with the Kerner agenda.[24]

The initial organizers of the Women's March on Washington were a Chicana, a Palestinian American woman, and an African American woman. The march was a great success. At the same time, some African American women have pointed out that the women's rights movement has focused on occasion more on issues important to well-off white women, such as working outside the home and attaining the same high-powered positions that men hold. It has been suggested that minority women do not necessarily embrace all the same priorities. For example, African American women who have worked their lives as maids might care more about the minimum wage than about seeing a woman in the White House. And minority women who live in highly segregated impoverished neighborhoods might care most about reducing police brutality.[25]

We believe that the women's movement can become stronger still by embracing the way different women of different races and classes experience life. Just as Stoneman's movement of young people who have climbed out of poverty needs to influence millennials to embrace Kerner priorities, so the women's movement may need to better support Black Lives Matter.

A Multitude of Coordinating Constituencies

We have given only a few examples of the constituencies that need to coordinate with one another in a people's movement, complementary with the policies in this report and the Kerner legacy. But many other players and constituencies need to merge and support one another.

Labor and teacher unions need to better unify minority and white workers. Unions need to leverage the fact that a majority of Americans support increasing the minimum wage to fifteen dollars an hour, according to the Pew Research Center.[26]

The many organizations pushing for an increased Earned Income Tax Credit need to redouble their advocacy. And expansion of the Child Tax Credit, as we recommend in Chapter 2 of Part I, will benefit the poor, working class, and middle class and provide common ground for advocacy.

About 60 percent of Americans say the federal government is responsible for ensuring health care coverage for all Americans, and a growing number now support a single-payer plan according to Pew research.[27] The broad cross section of Americans who will benefit—including the poor, workers, the middle class, women and seniors—must use such polling information to advance their advocacy. Traditional civil rights organizations need to expand their missions to better embrace economic justice. New citizens must join in and press for the rights of immigrants.

Millennials need to advocate for increased early childhood education, join Journey for Justice in supporting public school systems and opposing privatization (see Chapter 3 in Part I), and organize for more affordable college education.

The solidarity of professional athletes in advocating for racial and economic justice potentially can have significant impact.

Affordable and fair-housing nonprofit groups need to more creatively work with school integration advocates and nonprofit organizations that facilitate genuine community-based policing to enact legislation that does not make the middle class defensive and that maintains property values.

Foundations need to increase support to nonprofits like the Sentencing Project, the Civil Rights Group, Gideon's Promise, Just Leadership USA, VOTE, and A New Way of Life (see Chapter 5 in Part I) to further criminal justice reform. Supporters of criminal justice reform need to make sure that advocates for Keynesian demand-side job training significantly expand the work opportunities of ex-offenders. Nonprofit organizations championing legislation based on Kerner reforms in employment, education, housing, neighborhood development, and criminal justice need to increase support to nonprofits fighting for campaign finance reform, voting rights reform, control of gerrymandering, and abolition of the Electoral College (as discussed later in this chapter). This will expand the base of citizens who can strengthen a people's movement at the ballot box. Advocates must build on Pew research findings that document how, among conservatives and liberals, Republicans and Democrats, large majorities favor limits on campaign spending.[28]

WHAT IS THE VOCABULARY OF THE MOVEMENT'S MESSAGE?

For all these constituencies, the narrative used by advocates for the people's movement should be along the lines suggested by one of us, Alan Curtis, in one of our earlier updates of the Kerner Report:

> You, the average citizen, are not alone in your search for a safe niche in the I-win-you-lose-world. The very rich have profited at the expense of the families of salaried and working people of America. It is not fair for the rich to get richer at the expense of the rest of us. Power has shifted so significantly toward those at the top of the income and wealth pyramid that the majority of Americans who are struggling must mobilize to force the rich and the elites back to the bargaining table. We must close the income, wage, job and wealth gaps.

The way to do this is to invest in education, training, and re-training, so that Americans have the opportunity for jobs—and for better jobs. Among the middle class, working class, and the truly disadvantaged, and among different racial and ethnic groups, this policy can be win-win. None of these groups needs to gain at the expense of the others. We can succeed with a full-employment pol-icy that eliminates the economic marginality of the poor and at the same time reduces the anxiety of the working and middle classes.[29]

We propose this narrative in one of our earlier Kerner updates, and it is even more relevant in the disarray of the present time. As one advocate for more commonsense policy has added:

Most people would prefer to live in a world in which everyone is treated with respect and decency, and in which we do not squan-der either our own lives or the natural gifts on which we and the rest of the living world depend. . . . But because we have failed to understand what is possible, and above all failed to replace our tired political stories with a compelling narrative of transforma-tion and restoration, we have failed to realize this potential. As we rekindle our imagination, we discover our power to act. And that is the point at which we become unstoppable.[30]

The people's movement narrative should expand on the Bill of Rights, making it clear that you're-on-your-own policy does not work and that, as Economic Policy Institute founder Jeff Faux writes in Chapter 3 of Part II, all citizens have these rights and obligations:

- A right to a job in which you share in the wealth you are creating and an obligation to work at it to the best of your ability
- A right to benefit from the investments previous generations have made in your productivity and an obligation to invest for the generations to come
- A right to protection against ill health and the infirmities of old age and an obligation to support social insurance
- A right to bargain collectively and an obligation to help create more productive workplaces
- A right to create a business and an obligation to support the community in which it prospers
- A right to consume the products of a global economy and the obligation to insist that they be produced in a way that does not exploit other workers

Celinda Lake makes clear in Chapter 20 of Part II that, while we need to ground the movement for Kerner priorities in the kind of evidence-based policy and programs set out in this update, our messaging should be framed by the common sense of David Letterman's mom—that is, by the shared values that are most important to Americans: family, community teamwork, respect, equality, dignity, opportunity, a reasonable reward for work, upward mobility, a secure retirement, safety, freedom, fairness, patriotism, and the American Dream.

Here are some illustrations of vetted messaging from Lake's chapter—the words we need to use on the basis of shared American values:

> Family Comes First: They may drive you crazy, but everyone knows family comes first. Whether it's for that newborn you swear already smiles, your elderly mom or your spouse who got laid off, providing for your family and being there when they need you isn't negotiable. Every working parent should get paid enough to care for their kids and set them off toward a great future. If politicians want to talk "family values," it's time they start valuing families—and that means making sure America's dedicated strivers and builders make ends meet. We work in order to make the future brighter for our kids and more secure for our families. Hard working Americans deserve to make more than a decent living—they deserve to have a decent life.
>
> Teamwork—Working Together: From sports stars to first responders, Americans deliver when we pull together as a team. It takes a team, where we have each other's backs, to get our country and economy moving forward. By working together, each of us get[s] where we need to go. That's why we need to come together for a fair return on work, which includes benefits and paid time to be home when our families need us. Today, a few powerful people get even richer from profits we produce, requiring the rest of us to do more with less. By acting as a team, we can change the rules so working Americans can win.
>
> Pro-freedom: In America, we value our freedom. And CEOs are free to negotiate their salaries, benefits, and bonuses. Working people deserve the very same freedom: to negotiate the return for the hard work we put in. When somebody can tell you how to do the job you've mastered and prevent any pay raises, no matter their profits or your accomplishments, there's no freedom in that. Standing together gives working people the leverage to help set the rules at work so we reclaim our freedom to prosper.

Furthermore, a people's movement should not allow itself to be misdirected by the self-serving epithets of naysayers. Words like "bleeding heart." (People are in fact bleeding to death because of lack of health care.) Words like "class warfare." (Sure, there is class warfare, by the 1 percent against the 99 percent.) Words like "political correctness." (You bet we are against the incorrect language that devalues and denigrates women or African Americans and other minorities.) Words like "Government isn't the solution; government is the problem." (That's not what heavily subsidized corporate farmers think.) Words like "Everything government does is wrong; everything they tried failed." (The truth is that much of what we tried worked; we just quit trying it, or we did not try it hard enough.)

A people's movement also must turn its back on what Joan Williams calls the "dumb politics of elite condescension."[31] For example, we need to reject words like "deplorables" and "trailer trash" as they have been applied to blue-collar workers without college degrees who live in rural areas, small towns of the heartland, and flyover states.

HOW CAN CITIZENS BE BETTER TRAINED FOR OFFICE?

Nonprofit organizations need to receive more support from foundations not only to organize for economic justice consistent with Kerner priorities but also to encourage and train citizens to run for office at the national, state, and local levels.

At this point in the nation's history, with gridlocked government in Washington, more and more significant decisions are made by state and local office holders. That means a people's movement can be advanced by training and electing citizens who then legislate local solutions complementing the Kerner agenda and make decisions that bring about higher minimum wages, more equity in public school finance, and genuine community-based policing.

The potential for progress was illustrated in 2016 in Baltimore when six city councilmembers were elected who had been trained by the national nonprofit Wellstone Action organization. Wellstone creates "leadership pipelines" by partnering with local nonprofit organizations to recruit community leaders to run for office. A high priority is placed on recruiting racial minorities, women, and young people and from among the LGBTQ community. Wellstone Action looks for people who are effective in building trust through the plain language of values. Via Camp Wellstone and other training, candidates and their teams are equipped with the skills, tactics, and confidence to run and win. The training combines grassroots organizing, public policy, and electoral strategy. Wellstone Action is on the cutting edge of teaching community organizers digital technology.[32] The curriculum includes learning to use social media and organizing through texting.

Wellstone Action recognizes that many Americans, especially younger citizens, treat the electoral process the way they treat Hollywood movies: they show up only for blockbusters. The message here is that the math of democracy is unyielding and is important not just every four years. The need is to vote again and again, in local, state, congressional, midterm, and presidential elections. The long-term goal is to maintain a constituent base around priority values and issues—especially, for us, Kerner issues—so that, when the next election comes along, the base can be rapidly mobilized for victory. Base voters form the year-in-year-out infrastructure for organizing independent and swing voters between elections.

At the grassroots level, Wellstone teaches the importance of reregistering voters whose information may be out of date, communicating citizens' rights in the electoral process, registering and helping new voters to vote without incident, training people in how to use ballots, and translating training materials into the native language of voters.

Expanding on the priorities of Wellstone, many other organizations that are part of a people's movement in sync with Kerner values must register many more people to vote—and then mobilize them to actually vote. For example, sixty-four million workers across the country make less than fifteen dollars an hour, and only half are registered to vote. Of those registered, only half actually voted in 2016. Forty-eight million of them did *not* vote.[33]

Over more than fifteen years, Wellstone Action has trained eighty-six thousand community leaders, guided 4,500 winning campaigns, and helped over a thousand alumni win office.[34] Those numbers now need to be significantly increased.

Another model to build on is Emily's List, which has priorities complementary to Kerner values and which trains and funds women running for office. Emily's List has more than eighteen thousand potential candidates interested in running for office, compared to fewer than a thousand candidates several years ago.[35]

Other important groups promoting and training candidates include Higher Heights (which is training more African American women to run for office), Run for Something (which is focusing on electing younger citizens to state and local offices), the Latino Victory Project, and Emerge.[36]

These efforts are being complemented by initiatives, like #KnockEveryDoor, to engage voters in civil dialogue on issues that complement the Kerner agenda. Similarly, the American Civil Liberties Union launched the People Power platform to train members in activism and connect them to events in their communities. And MoveOn.org is educating fresh cohorts of citizens in organizing and advocacy.[37]

HOW CAN THE MEDIA MORE ACCURATELY COMMUNICATE?

The Kerner Commission concluded that the media failed to report adequately on the causes and consequences of civil disorders and the underlying problems of race relations. The commission found that television and newspapers focused on how police controlled "rioters" rather than on police brutality and the economic and education inequalities in America that led to grievances.[38]

The commission observed that, for the most part, media coverage of the protests in the 1960s was not based on solid evidence. The commission pointed to "scare headlines." It concluded that reporters often were inexperienced. And few of the reporters were African American or other minorities. Accordingly, the commission called for media coverage that focused on underlying causes. It recommended more informed reporters and expansion of racial minorities in the media (see Chapter 22 in Part II).

Fifty years later, the Princeton professor and CNN analyst Julian Zelizer concludes in Chapter 22 of Part II, the media have made little progress in covering underlying causes. *Guardian* editor at large Gary Younge concurs in Chapter 23 of Part II. Younge writes movingly about how the media for the most part fail to report on the obvious. He reminds us of the journalistic aphorism that a dog biting a man is not news. But if a man bites a dog, that is news. In our culture, occurrences that are both commonplace and expected are not considered news, which our norms reserve for events that are relatively rare and unexpected.

From the perspective of the Kerner Commission, the realities of African American unemployment being consistently twice as high as white unemployment, public schools being underfunded, crime rates being high in the kinds of neighborhoods of greatest concern to Professors William Julius Wilson and Elijah Anderson (as discussed in Chapter 4), and segregation being institutionalized by the federal government are all commonplace and expected. So these realities are poorly covered by the media unless events are dramatic even by the low standards of the American media.

Zelizer and Younge illustrate such dramatic events with the criminal justice system. Zelizer documents in Chapter 22 how excessive police force has been poorly chronicled by the media. To the extent it has been covered, the reporting increasingly has been done, not by the media, but by citizens via new technology. This began in March 1991, when a citizen videotaped the brutal beating by Los Angeles police of Rodney King, an African American who had been stopped for speeding on the freeway while under the influence of drugs. Today, police brutality is often recorded first by citizens on cell phones during incidents like the killing of Michael Brown in Ferguson, Missouri, and the death of Freddie Gray in Baltimore.

In the case of Ferguson, one study has shown it took over ten days for media to start using the terms "race," "racism," and "racist" in coverage of what happened (see Chapter 22 in Part II). Media often have accepted the now-discredited ideology of zero-tolerance policing (see Chapter 5 in Part I) and have not sufficiently reported on the kind of community-oriented policing that we have found better addresses the underlying causes of disorder, like failed schools and lack of economic opportunity.

Reflecting on Ferguson, Younge observes in Chapter 23 that the Black Lives Matter movement was prompted not by an increase in the number of African Americans being killed by American police but rather by a growing political awareness that had "forced a reckoning with a preexisting condition. . . . The shootings were not news in the conventional sense, any more than 'the violence of the ghetto' had been in 1967." The shootings were "neither rare nor surprising. They were *made* to be news." He continues, "We were forced to recognize them, in no small part, because new technology enabled people with cell phones to do the job the established media had failed to do. The world had not changed; what had changed was our ability to pass off the grotesque as unremarkable simply because it is also commonplace."

Younge concludes that "the American media episodically discovers this daily reality in much the same way that teenagers discover sex— urgently, earnestly, voraciously, and carelessly, with great self-indulgence but precious little self-awareness. They have always been aware of it but somehow, when confronted with it, they are nonetheless taken by surprise. And then their surprise becomes the news." In effect, the media say, "Look what I've found out." Not, "Goodness, look what's been going on while I've been looking elsewhere."

In Chapter 22, Zelizer continues in noting that the media fail not only in their coverage of the police but in their coverage of the rest of the criminal justice system. The media have not sufficiently covered the everyday racism inherent in tougher sentencing laws, for example, and in the mass incarceration carried out by the prison-industrial complex.

These media failures have been compounded by the highly partisan media environment that has developed since the Kerner Commission. Studies have shown that more and more Americans have turned to news from sources that reflect their own biases. The Internet, with its echo chambers, especially on Facebook, has exacerbated these biases (see Chapter 22 in Part II).

Within such a partisan environment, people need to know what the facts are, and they cannot get them from fake news (which everyone, now more than ever, should counteract and knock down). Too many people think that government cannot really eliminate poverty and has no business trying. Remember the one where the old nester says, "We fought a war against poverty, and poverty won." Or about civil rights: "I thought we took care of all that." Or about so many working-class whites who are having a hard time: "It's their own fault." Too many Americans simply do not know that a majority of our people—minority and white—are having a hard time making it today. We have got to change that impression.

While there has been an increase in racial diversity among media reporters, gains have been limited. Minority reporters compose only

12 percent to 14 percent of all journalists. According to the American Society of News Editors, there has been a decline of over 50 percent in the number of African American journalists from 2000 to the present (see Chapter 22 in Part II).

To address and reverse this lack of progress, we intend to convene forums with representatives of the media and of media-reform-advocacy organizations. We will seek answers to the following kinds of questions:

- How can the media better cover the obvious Kerner "dog bites man" story? How can we stop writing large sections of society out of the news agenda? Why can't there be more stories on what works?
- How can examples of solid media coverage of past Kerner updates serve as models for better coverage in the future? (Some of the most professional past coverage of our twenty-five-, thirty-, and forty-year Kerner Commission updates has been on *Bill Moyers Journal*, *CBS Sunday Morning*, National Public Radio, and the *PBS News Hour* and in the *Guardian*, *Washington Post*, and *Los Angeles Times*.)
- To what extent can major media adopt rigorous and objective fact-checking systems to prevent fake news, as the BBC did?[39]
- How can Americans be better reminded that, in 1972, Watergate initially was called a "third-rate burglary" by the White House—before two young investigative reporters found that description to be fake news?
- How can journalism schools better prepare students to do in-depth investigative reporting of the facts and of the racial, inequality, and poverty underpinnings that explain much of America?
- How can we build on the philanthropic model of the Omidar Network, which has committed $100 million to support investigative journalism, fight misinformation, and counteract hate speech?[40]
- How can we address and reverse the proliferation of falsehoods and conspiracies on social media and the dissipation of our common basis for fact? Is this not intentionally blocking consensus on Kerner values?
- What action needs to be taken for how, in the words of Franklin Foer, "Facebook mines our data to keep giving us the news and information we crave, creating a feedback loop that pushes us deeper and deeper into our own amen corners"?[41] Do we need regulation of the big tech companies?
- How can the rights of citizens to record on smart phones be protected?

- How can the polling evidence that 70 percent of Americans believe that funding for public television is "well spent" and that public television is the most trusted media be converted into significantly higher public media financing?
- How can we better support the movement by the nonprofit Free Press organization to better engage local journalism with grassroots communities and to better serve civic needs? How can low-power FM radio stations that are outlets for nonprofit organizations be scaled up?[42]
- How can we reverse media-consolidating ownership by giant corporations focused on profits and increase ownership by minorities?

Leaders and politicians obviously have responsibility, here, too. Remember that poverty first got on the national agenda because John Kennedy, running for president and closely followed by the national press, walked among the poverty-stricken coal miners and other desperate hill people in West Virginia. And think about how Senator Robert Kennedy made Americans think about the wretched poverty of African Americans in the Mississippi delta by visiting them in their homes, with the press in tow. (That is how Senator Robert Kennedy met Mississippi lawyer and civil rights worker Marian Wright Edelman, who went on to form the Children's Defense Fund; see her Chapter 9 in Part II.)

Leaders and politicians should follow the examples of the two Kennedys today. People's movement groups should follow these examples, as well, making news to help the public see how things really are.

HOW CAN AVERAGE CITIZENS GET A FAIR VOTE?

American democracy needs to become more representative and fair. Majority rule must become a reality. If the votes of all Americans are truly given equal weight, a new people's movement has a better chance of reducing inequality, poverty, and racial injustice. Toward these ends, we need campaign finance reform, voting rights reform, control of gerrymandering, and abolition of the Electoral College.

Prospects for immediate change are dim. So it is of crucial importance that foundations increase funding to nonprofit advocacy organizations that press for reform. Such organizations include the Campaign Legal Center, Citizens for Responsibility and Ethics in Washington, and the Project on Government Oversight as well as the other nonprofits identified below.[43]

Campaign Finance Reform

Starting more than a century ago, Theodore Roosevelt and others pushed for reforms that would tame the great concentrations of power that were corrupting the nation. On the economic side, antitrust laws were passed and public utilities were regulated. On the political side, campaign finance regulations were passed and the Constitution was amended to allow Americans to elect senators directly. As Roosevelt wrote, "There can be no real political democracy unless there is something approaching an economic democracy."[44]

Today we have regressed to great concentrations of political and economic power. In 2016, candidates running for federal office spent a record $6.4 billion on their campaigns. Lobbyists spent $3.15 billion to influence the government in Washington. These amounts are much higher than in 2000 and dwarf spending in European countries. There, strict limits are placed on campaign spending and contributions, campaigns are kept short and paid political advertising on television is restricted or outright banned.[45]

America needs to reduce the corrupting influence of big donors and corporate money in day-to-day lobbying and political campaigns. Such reform is so difficult because the legislators and other public officials who need to enact it are dependent on the big money to win the elections that keep them in power.

One good model was the late Wisconsin senator William Proxmire. Especially during his later years in office, Proxmire's primary campaign expenditures were on stamps for letters he sent returning checks to campaign contributors.

We need to severely limit campaign contributions, publicly finance elections campaigns for all major offices, require broadcasters who use public airwaves to contribute free campaign advertising to candidates, prohibit lobbyists from soliciting and bundling big-check campaign donations from their business clients, severely limit corporate expenditures on lobbying and public relations intended to influence legislative outcomes, ban gifts to lawmakers by corporations or executives, prohibit privately financed junkets for legislators and aides, ban parties staged to "honor" politicians with corporate contributions, require lobbyists to disclose all lobbying expenditures, and mandate that all expert witnesses in legislative and regulatory hearings disclose financial relationships with economically interested parties. These reforms should be monitored and enforced by an independent inspector general with power to investigate abuses and impose stiff penalties on violators.

During the 1907 State of the Union Address, President Theodore Roosevelt stated "The need for collecting large campaign funds would vanish if Congress provided an appropriation for the proper and legitimate expenses of each of the great national parties." Public financing of elections, he believed, would ensure that no particular donor has an outsized influence on the outcome of any election, and would "work a substantial improvement in our system of conducting a campaign."[46]

Led by Arizona and Maine, thirteen states today provide some form of public financing options for campaigns.[47] But real progress on campaign finance needs to focus on the 2010 Supreme Court *Citizens United v. Federal Communications Commission* decision. The decision allowed corporations (including certain nonprofit corporations) and labor unions to expand their role in political campaigns.[48] The case did not affect contributions to a candidate's actual campaign. It is still illegal for companies and labor unions to give money directly to candidates for federal office. But the *Citizens United* decision did allow ostensibly outside, independent political action committees—super PACs—to spend unlimited amounts of money to support or oppose a candidate.[49]

Citizens United also paved the way for the creation of so-called dark-money nonprofit social welfare organizations, which can function the same way super PACs function as long as election activity is not their primary focus. But unlike super PACs, these "social welfare" groups do not have to report who funds them, allowing donors to avoid publicity. Neither the Internal Revenue Service nor the Federal Election Commission has shown much interest in investigating questionable practices.[50]

The unlimited money and the absence of disclosure obviously do not support an inequality-reducing Kerner agenda. And, importantly, a Bloomberg poll found that 80 percent of Republicans and Democrats surveyed oppose *Citizens United*. Yet our gridlocked system has not produced comprehensive reform.[51]

Some organizations, like Issue One and Democracy 21, are trying to bring a case before the Supreme Court that might prompt a reversal of *Citizens United* and reform of campaign financing.[52] But progress has been slow. A people's movement needs to help. Corporations are not people, and they should not be able to spend unlimited money in political campaigns.

Less comprehensive campaign finance reform has been proposed in the Government by the People Act. The legislation would do the following:

- Encourage the participation of everyday Americans in the funding of campaigns by providing a refundable twenty-five-dollar My Voice Tax Credit. This would bring the voices of the broader public into the funding side of campaigns and democratize the relationship between money and speech.
- Establish a Freedom from Influence Matching Fund to boost the power of small-dollar contributions. To be eligible for these matching funds, a candidate would have to agree to a limit on

large donations and demonstrate broad-based support from a network of small-dollar contributors. Amplified by the Freedom from Influence Matching Fund, the voices of everyday Americans would be as powerful as those of big donors.

- Provide candidates with an opportunity to earn additional resources in the homestretch of a campaign so that the voices of the people are not completely drowned out by super PACs and other dark-money interests. In the wake of *Citizens United*, this kind of support is critical to ensuring that citizen-backed candidates have staying power.[53]

We support the Government by the People Act but believe that Kerner priorities can never be fully achieved without much more fundamental campaign finance reform. This may not be possible without a change in the composition of the Supreme Court. Advocacy for the Kerner legacy can move the nation in that direction. In the meantime, we can at least take heart in the knowledge that, when a candidate is passionate on the issues and not afraid to say so, substantial amounts of money from a multitude of small donations can be raised on the Internet.

Voting Rights Reform

The Supreme Court's 2013 decision in *Shelby County v. Holder* struck down a core part of the 1965 Voting Rights Act. The Voting Rights Act had required jurisdictions with the most troubling histories of discrimination to allow Justice Department or federal court review before potentially discriminating legislation could be implemented. The *Shelby County* decision nullified this review process, leaving no preclearance at all. Discriminatory laws now can take effect without federal clearance.[54]

The nation's founders recognized the profound power of the franchise, as did the civil rights marchers near the time of the Kerner Commission. When we allow discrimination to infect our elections, we disrespect the sacrifices of those who came before us and threaten the progress they achieved. Today, we need to protect the rights of our fellow voters to make their choices, whatever those choices may be. In the long run, we believe this will strengthen resolve in favor of the Kerner legacy.

The Supreme Court invited Congress to enact new legislation to address the impact of *Shelby County*. It is well past time for Congress to take up the invitation to restore the Voting Rights Act to its full strength. State legislatures need to remove unjustified voting rules. Poll workers need to oversee fair elections. All eligible Americans need the opportunity to vote.

Beyond restoration of the original Voting Rights Act, we need to make voting easier by following the examples of many other democracies. Some states have begun to do so. For example, in 2015, Oregon became the first state to pass automatic voter registration. More than 272,000 people were registered in the law's first year. Of these, 116,000 were found to be unlikely to have registered otherwise, and 40,000 of that group voted in 2016, helping Oregon achieve the nation's largest turnout increase from 2012—over four points, to over 68 percent. Importantly for us, the new voters were more racially diverse than previously registered voters.[55]

By 2017, Illinois had become the tenth state, along with the District of Columbia, to enact automatic voter registration. All eligible Illinois voters now are registered when they visit the Department of Motor Vehicles or other state agencies. "The right to vote is foundational for the rights of Americans in our democracy," said Illinois governor Bruce Rauner, a Republican. "We as a people need to do everything we can to knock down barriers, remove hurdles for all those who are eligible to vote, to be able to vote."[56]

Yet the struggle for voters is far from over in America. For example, Texas has been pushing relentlessly in the opposite direction of Oregon and Illinois. In 2011, Texas legislators passed highly restrictive voter-ID laws, which then were challenged in court. In 2017, a federal judge struck down the laws on the grounds that they intentionally discriminated against African American and Hispanic voters, in violation of the Voting Rights Act and the Constitution. The ruling judge continues to ask the legislature for an unbiased plan.[57]

The Kerner legacy movement needs to advocate for Oregon and Illinois, not Texas.

Gerrymandering Reform

Gerrymandering, the long-standing practice of redrawing the lines of legislative districts to tip elections toward the party in power, is still another distortion of American democracy. Since the Kerner Commission, gerrymandering has become more extreme because increasingly powerful technology allows partisan mapmakers to distort with greater precision. Voters are packed into skewed districts, lessening their voice in the political process. The net result can make the Kerner legacy more difficult to fulfill. As bipartisan arguments have made clear, the broader implication is that gerrymandering undercuts democratic competition and weakens public faith in government, pushing lawmakers away from compromise, especially in the House of Representatives.[58]

The nation needs to establish standards for judicial oversight—to help deter lawmakers from cementing their hold on power and to reassure Americans that their votes matter. Algorithms now can detect outliers, or legislative maps that have been drawn so far outside the ordinary run of things that they must be for partisan purposes. These algorithms can be deployed to at least tell the difference between innocuous decision making on legislative districts and schemes unequivocally designed to protect one party from voters who might prefer the other.[59] We endorse using these algorithms and encourage Kerner advocates to press for widespread adoption. If election results suggest serious and enduring biases, courts can ask states to come up with a fairer process.[60]

Electoral College Abolition

By overwhelming majorities, Americans prefer to elect the president by popular vote, not by the antiquated Electoral College system, which is a vestige of the original constitutional counting of African Americans as three-fifths of a white person. The Electoral College gives more weight to smaller states—the vote of someone in Wyoming counts 3.6 times as much as someone in California. The Electoral College should be abolished completely. If it continues, it should be reformed to be a system in which all a state's electors vote for the winner of the national popular vote. Eleven states and the District of Columbia already have passed such legislation.[61] The National Popular Vote Interstate Compact is trying to move the nation toward the popular election of the president, and we support its advocacy.[62]

CONCLUSION

America could not have advanced in modern times without grassroots movements—the labor union movement, for example, or the civil rights movement, the women's movement, or the anti–Vietnam War movement.

We believe the people's movement for economic and racial justice that we advocate to create the Kerner Commission's "new will" can evolve from these earlier movements and enhance the needs of our time, restoring America's promise at home and abroad. As iconic civil rights leader and U.S. Representative John Lewis would say, let us do *something*, get involved.[63] Shake things up. Make common cause with people who are your natural allies and change things. Dolores Huerta, partner in agitation with César Chávez and the subject of a celebrated 2017 documentary film,[64] was right when she taught us to say *¡Sí se puede!* Yes, we can!

PART II

Perspectives from the Fiftieth-Anniversary
National Advisory Council

Economic and Employment Policy

1

Economic Justice

Fifty Years after the Kerner Report

Joseph E. Stiglitz

FIFTY YEARS AGO, the Kerner Report on the civil disorders that had broken out the previous year provided a stark description of the conditions in America that had led to the disorders. Their basic conclusion still rings true: "Our Nation is moving toward two societies, one black, one white—separate and unequal."[1] It featured a country in which African Americans faced systematic discrimination, with inadequate education and housing, and totally lacking economic opportunities—for them, there was no American dream. Underlying all this was a diagnosis of "the racial attitude and behavior of white Americans toward black Americans [as the cause]. Race prejudice has shaped our history decisively; it now threatens to affect our future."[2]

I have been asked to assess how things have changed in the subsequent half century. As I set about this, a passage from the report resonates:

> One of the first witnesses to be invited to appear before this Commission was Dr. Kenneth B. Clark, a distinguished and perceptive scholar. Referring to the reports of earlier riot commissions, he said: "I read that report . . . of the 1919 riot in Chicago, and it is as if I were reading the report of the investigating committee of the Harlem riot of '35, the report of the investigating committee on the Harlem riot of '43, the report of the McCone Commission of the Watts riot [of '65]. I must again in candor say to you members of this Commission—it is a kind of Alice in Wonderland—with the same moving pictures re-shown over and over again, the same analysis, the same recommendations and the same inaction." These words come to our minds as we conclude this report."[3]

And they come to my and everyone's mind as we review the nation's progress. These words are still true. Some problematic areas identified in the report have gotten better (participation in politics and government by black Americans—symbolized by the election of a black president), some have stayed the same (education and employment disparities), and some have gotten worse (wealth and income inequality).

The civil rights era did make a difference. It was not just that a variety of forms of discrimination were illegal. Societal norms changed. Many large corporations and most educational institutions believed in affirmative action; to be openly racist in many, if not most, quarters became unacceptable. Large corporate boards and major universities sought diversity as a policy. They believed in it and believed diversity would strengthen them.

But deep-seated and institutional racism continued. New tests of discrimination in hiring and housing revealed the extent: blind resumes were sent, with the only difference being the name of the individual, giving a suggestion of race. Callbacks were markedly different.[4]

And several countertrends impeded progress. Martin Luther King realized that achieving economic justice for African Americans could not be separated from achieving economic opportunities for all Americans. Five years before the release of the Kerner Report, King's March on Washington (which I attended, and the memories of which remain so vivid)[5] was called a march *for jobs and freedom.* Fifty-five years on from that march, America is a country more divided, with less economic opportunity. Thus, the struggle for opportunity for African Americans has been an uphill battle: it would have been difficult in any case, but all the more so as the economic environment was becoming harsher, especially for those without college degrees; 73 percent of African Americans did not have a bachelor's degree in 2016.[6] Moreover, while educational attainment has been on the rise, it has been rising faster for white Americans than for nonwhite Americans.

With the rungs of the ladder becoming further apart, middle-class families invested increasing amounts in ensuring that their children had an advantage. They worried that urban schools would not give their children the competitive edge they needed. White flight led to increased economic segregation;[7] and in a country where schools were local, both in control and in finance, it meant that the disparity increased in the quality of education between African Americans left behind in the urban areas and the children of the privileged living in suburban areas or sending their children to private schools. This meant that even in our needs-blind selective schools, the fraction of students from the economic bottom half remained appallingly low.[8] (Today, students from the bottom quartile make up only 3 percent of the total number of students in the most competitive postsecondary schools.)[9]

Moreover, while American politicians might speak forcefully about the role of American values, it seemed that there was increasing weight on materialism—what mattered was material success, no matter how achieved. In the aftermath of the financial crisis of 2007–2008, much attention was paid to the moral depravity of the bankers—exhibited, for example, in their predatory lending, abusive credit card practices, market manipulation, and insider trading. But the cheating of many automobile companies in their environmental testing showed that the bankers were not alone. With money the only object, anybody and anything was fair game—and the less well educated, including African Americans, were particularly the subject of exploitation.[10] The aspirations of African Americans wishing to live the American Dream were cruelly exploited by private universities offering promises of a higher living standard but delivering nothing but debts to be paid later, combined with bankers willing to take advantage of bankruptcy laws that made it almost impossible to discharge student debt. One of America's largest banks, Wells Fargo, had to pay a huge fine for discriminatory lending. They were caught. The question was only how many others got away with it.

In many quarters, too, there was a backlash. As poorly educated white Americans struggled to stay above water, they came to resent anyone who seemed to be making it. When hard-working African Americans got ahead, these whites wanted to believe that it was because they got some advantage. In a world of zero-sum thinking, if someone got ahead, it meant someone else was pushed further down; they thus viewed the notable successes of a few African Americans as coming at the expense of themselves and their children.

The backlash to the limited success in the first years after the Kerner Report manifested itself in politics as well, with America electing an openly racist president and with major campaigns at disenfranchisement. The politics of the culture wars meant that the agenda of equality of opportunity often got caught in the cross fire.

Fifty years ago, there was an ongoing debate over the relative role played by the historical legacy of slavery and oppression,[11] the absolute and relative deprivation faced by African Americans in their youth, the continued discrimination against African Americans in every aspect of American life, and the breakdown of the family. In some ways, parsing the relative role was impossible and irrelevant; the effects were intimately intertwined. What mattered were solutions: Where could we, as a society, intervene?

Economics as a discipline had little to contribute to this debate. The Kerner Report was written before the development of the subfield of the economics of discrimination and before more recent advances in behavioral economics.

Most importantly, the nation has unintentionally been conducting a field experiment: What happens if you deprive large numbers of white Americans of hope? If you create a divide within white America, perhaps not quite as large as that between black Americans and white but large nonetheless? Thus, we have come to a new understanding: if one deprives any group within the population of opportunity and hope, social and economic problems will appear. Of course, the deprivations facing African Americans are compounded by a historical legacy and ever-present discrimination. We now have better evidence of the pervasiveness of this discrimination and new understanding of what needs to be done to ameliorate it and its effects.

This chapter briefly describes the faltering progress we have made in each of these areas, the insights provided by changing perspectives in economics, and some suggestions about the way forward.

PROGRESS

Overall, as I have noted, progress in achieving equality and equality of opportunity for African Americans has been at best faltering. In some areas, things are worse. Though there are some remarkable successes at the top, *average* numbers are very disappointing, as the statistics below suggest. Part of the reason is the remarkable increase in inequality in the country as a whole, the evisceration of the middle class, and the lack of opportunity for those at the bottom:[12] America has among the lowest levels of equality of opportunity of any of the advanced countries, meaning that the life prospects of a young American are more dependent on the income and education of his or her parents than in other advanced countries.[13] Since today's African American parents are disproportionately poor, that means tomorrow's will be, too. And there is some evidence of a diminution of equality of opportunity.[14]

Institutional changes have also worked against the advancement of the goals set forth by the Kerner Commission. Industrial unions played an important role of compressing wage differences and opening industrial job opportunities for African Americans (as well as women). They also played an important political role, in advancing legislation to create a country with more equality and equality of opportunity. Unions have weakened, going from around 35 percent of private employment in the 1950s[15] to 6.4 percent now.[16] Part of the reason is the changing structure of the economy: manufacturing has declined from about 25 percent of the economy in 1968 to under 12 percent in 2016.[17] But there are other forces at play, including antiunion legislation and interpretations of existing legislation. Indeed, the latter alone can be closely linked with the increase in inequality in the country.[18]

A host of other institutional changes have played a role more broadly in the increase in inequality, such as a Federal Reserve policy focusing on inflation more than unemployment[19] and deregulation, including the elimination of usury laws, which provided greater scope for predatory lending.

Jobs

For African Americans, the glass ceiling has been broken, as they have taken on positions in boardrooms and as chief executive officers of major corporations. However, this gives a distorted picture of economic advancement. Incomes and wages, after improving slightly, going from 55 percent of that of whites in 1967 to about 65 percent in the late 1990s, have remained stuck at around 60 percent of that of whites in recent years.[20] Gaps exist at every educational level—and have in fact grown the most for the college educated, with whites now receiving an hourly wage that is 46 percent higher than what African Americans receive.[21] Unemployment rates remain as they were then, roughly twice that of whites. With youth unemployment roughly twice that of the national average, this has meant that youth black unemployment soared to almost 50 percent at the peak of the recession.[22] The only area in which relative performance may have improved is long-term unemployment, and this is because of the large increase in the number of white long-term unemployed, not a decrease in the number for African Americans; African Americans are still overrepresented among the long-term unemployed (constituting 23 percent of the long-term unemployed but only 11 percent of the employed).[23]

There was one period in which African Americans did well, and that was in the late 1990s, as the overall unemployment rate fell to record lows. At last, marginalized groups were drawn into the labor force.

This makes the recommendations of the Kerner Report truly prescient. The report, at least in parts, really has a remarkable vision of what sort of labor policy would be adequate to tackle the problem of un- and underemployment. In addition to the obvious proposals (more jobs and removal of the clear race-based barriers), the authors proposed job training (both public and private), behavioral counseling (ranging from motivation, personal dress, and hygiene to social relationships and job performance), transportation to and from work, appropriate medical and social services, flexible work schedules and patterns that fit the needs and abilities of the potential laborers (they recognized that many people have innate intelligence and skills that are unquantifiable), on-the-job training, a computerized (!) system for matching workers with jobs, work tryouts, and moving people out of the ghetto for work.

As I have noted, the changing structure of America's economy has disadvantaged African Americans because it has disadvantaged those with lower levels of educational attainment. But then, as now, America's discrimination in housing, dysfunctional health care system, and weak public transportation systems have had repercussions in the labor market. There is a mismatch between jobs and workers that disadvantages African Americans. If anything, matters may have become worse: as more jobs moved to largely white suburbs, the distance between African Americans and jobs may have increased. The Clinton administration tried some experimental programs to bring jobs to the cities, but these appear to have had limited success—partly because they received limited funding. As the Kerner Report recognized, the private sector on its own cannot be expected to create the requisite jobs. Strong macroeconomic policies are needed to ensure that the total number of jobs are sufficient to provide opportunities for all who wish to work; but structural policies are also required to ensure that there is an adequate supply of jobs accessible to African Americans with the skills that they have or that they could acquire through training programs.

Education

Lack of access to quality education was one of the most important impediments in economic advancement then and now. More broadly, education is one of the bases for the strong momentum for the perpetuation of poverty, whether white or African American: poor children of any race are likely to get a poorer education than the rich (of any race).

Again, if anything, the problem is worse today than it was then: the skill premium has increased (college graduates have an annual income that is 163 percent that of high school graduates now, compared to 123 percent then).[24] This is in spite of the increase in the overall fraction of those with a college education and reflects a move to a knowledge economy and that technological change has been skill biased—increasing the demand for skilled labor relative to unskilled—and thus depressing unskilled workers' wages at the same time that it has increased the value put on skills.

While there was some decrease in racial segregation—legislation reinforced changing norms—there was an increase in economic segregation.[25] Some of the white flight was in fact partially motivated by attempts to avoid integration (in the name of ensuring quality education for their children). While initially, in some locales, courts enforced busing to ensure integration, such forceful integration has fallen by the wayside. All of this has, as I have noted, disadvantaged those remaining in the urban centers.

The nation has repeatedly recognized these and other deficiencies in the quality of education. Americans scores in cross-country standardized tests are, in general, mediocre, with U.S. students performing just at or below OECD averages and having falling scores in reading and mathematics.[26] Yet a succession of programs have failed to improve not only the overall quality of education but especially that of those in our urban ghettos or our rural centers of poverty. Programs like No Child Left Behind, focusing on improving performance through standardized testing, have not been accompanied by the expenditure increases called for by the Kerner Commission.[27] The national consensus over the act's failures, from the left, right, and center, led to its replacement by the Every Student Succeeds Act. The titles of the acts say more about the ambitions than the commitments, especially of funds.

Again, the Kerner Report was prescient in calling for an "extension of quality early childhood education to every disadvantaged child in the country."[28] Fifty years later President Barack Obama was calling for the same things (as was candidate Hillary Clinton), and it still has not gotten done. In New York, while Mayor Bill de Blasio proposed making early childhood education available to all,[29] a conflict over funding between the mayor and New York's governor has stymied implementation.

Research by Nobel Prize–winning economist Jim Heckman has shown the disadvantaged position of African American children as they enter kindergarten[30] and how early childhood education can help remedy these deficiencies.

Fifty years ago, the focus was on equalizing educational opportunities. They are still not equal. But we now realize, far more clearly than then, that equalizing opportunities will require unequal expenditures. Disparities in expenditure persist, but they go in the wrong direction. The Kerner Commission recognized too that the additional resources required would have to come from the federal government. Fifty years ago, there were huge disparities between income per capita in different states, with income per capita in the richest state (Connecticut) twice that of the poorest state (Mississippi); now, those disparities are even larger.[31] Continued reliance on the states will mean continuing large disparities in expenditures per pupil.

Welfare

One of the most vivid quotes of the report is this: "Our present system of public welfare is designed to save money instead of people, and tragically ends up doing neither."[32] The welfare programs that existed at the time were inadequate and arguably contributed to the perpetuation of poverty. The Clinton administration enacted reforms, but unfortunately did not provide the funding needed for education, training, and childcare programs that would have really helped the poor (including African Americans) move from welfare to work. The reforms have had mixed effects, with some claiming they encouraged some movement into the labor force; but when they were tested by the financial crisis of 2008, they were found wanting. The food programs provided what safety net the country offered, with one out of seven Americans turning to the government. Still, almost a seventh of Americans went to bed hungry at least once a month, not because they were on a diet, but because they could not afford the food they needed. The Affordable Care Act (ACA) sought to ensure that all Americans, no matter how poor, were provided with health care. But a Supreme Court decision combined with extreme conservative views about the role of government meant that many states decided not to avail themselves of the opportunity afforded to provide health care to their very poor, even though the cost would be borne almost entirely by the federal government. Some 28.5 million (including 4.25 million African Americans) were left uncovered.[33] As this book goes to press, Republican efforts to roll back ACA in ways that would leave millions more uncovered have failed.

The most important program for helping the poor, enacted under Clinton, was the great expansion of the Earned Income Tax Credit (EITC). This is much aligned with what the report calls for. But the report asks for more. The EITC is limited to those with children. What the report calls for is effectively a universal basic income scheme (for families with dependent children, but it also uses similar language when speaking about the population as a whole), to provide a "minimum standard of decent living."[34]

ADVANCES IN THE SOCIAL SCIENCES

The Kerner Commission drew heavily on the findings of social scientists. Since then, race and racism have continued to be the object of intense study.[35] My remarks here draw on a few of the strands of work most important for understanding what has happened to the economic situation of African Americans over the past half century.

The first is the economics of discrimination, a subject formally explored by the Nobel Prize winner and Chicago economist Gary Becker in his book of that title. He argues that in a competitive market, there could not or would not be discrimination because nondiscriminatory employers would have an incentive to hire any workers that were underpriced as a result of discrimination.[36] That the theory was contradicted by the evidence shows that the assumptions of the model are deeply flawed.[37] There followed a rash of models explaining how discrimination could persist with rational individuals with rational expectations—that is, under all the simplifying assumptions used in economics. Particularly instructive were advances in game theory, which showed how systems of Jim Crow could persist, even when large numbers of the population did not have discriminatory attitudes: the system would punish those who deviated from the norm of segregation—and punish those who did not punish those who deviated.[38] While some social scientists talked about the importance of social capital and group identity,[39] it became clear that these constructs could lead to discriminatory equilibria, advantaging one group at the expense of another.[40] The notion of statistical discrimination was developed,[41] in which those who engaged in it did not even believe that they were unfair but were just using statistical information about differential productivity. It was shown how this could lead to an equilibrium with persistent differences in outcomes among races or ethnic groups, even if there were no innate differences or even differences in the provision of education but even more so if (as is the case) there were. Because they knew that they would have fewer job opportunities, it was rational for African Americans to invest less in education, in a self-fulfilling prophecy.[42]

But even more important were advances in behavioral economics, in which models of persistent racism were developed.[43] Perception—both of oneself and of others—affected performance;[44] and because of confirmatory bias, one's perceptions of reality were biased by one's prior beliefs. Thus, racist yet seemingly rational fictions—in which individuals' beliefs were in accord with reality *as they perceived it*—could persist, with again different groups being treated differently and leading to different behavior even when there were no intrinsic differences.[45] But of course, given differences in education and the host of other factors affecting productivity, these only amplified and further sustained the resulting differentials.

The increasing economic divide afflicting the country provided more opportunity to understand better the effects of poverty itself. Poverty was self-perpetuating, with those at the bottom, whether white or black, caught in a poverty trap. Mobility matrices—tracing out the likelihood of someone at the bottom making it up to the middle or top—showed how unlikely such transitions were for anyone of any race or color.[46] Those in poverty, focusing on survival, had less ability to think long term and thus were less likely to make the kinds of long-term investments that would help them get out of poverty.[47]

Contributing to this was the growth of single-parent families, which used to be thought of as the province of African Americans. Overall, 35 percent of children in the United States grow up in single-parent households, but the percentage is almost twice that—67 percent—for African American kids. Since almost half of all children with a single mother—47.6 percent—live in poverty, it is perhaps no surprise that the poverty rate among black children is 38.2 percent, more than twice as high as the rate among whites.[48] There was evidence that growing up in families without fathers was particularly hard on boys; and as the labor force was restructured to favor service sector jobs and jobs requiring higher levels of education, this mattered more and more.[49]

There was a growing consensus that inequality itself was bad for overall economic performance;[50] but some of the adverse effects related to how bad it was for those at the bottom. It was not just that those at the bottom were less likely to be able to live up to their opportunity. There were worries that attempts of those at the bottom to emulate the lifestyle of those higher up led to excessive debt—especially in the context of an economy rife with predatory lenders willing to take advantage of them and a bankruptcy law willing to impose what amounted to partial indentured servitude through the garnishing of wages.[51]

POLICY RESPONSES

The experience of the past half century has shown that an attack on racial disparities must be conducted on multiple fronts. First, there must be a broadside attack against inequality and poverty in the United States. The most important policy is to maintain a very tight job market: the only time that marginalized groups were brought into the economy was when the unemployment rate fell to record lows in the late 1990s under President Clinton. The benefits of this and the growth that it brings about far outweigh any deficits that might be experienced to support it or any inflation that might be engendered.

A range of expenditures would improve equality of opportunity. Earlier, I noted gaps in our education, employment, welfare, and health care programs. Most importantly, there is evidence that growing up in a family in poverty hurts future prospects, and not just in the ways described earlier, such as access to education. It affects learning and aspirations,[52] determines the experiences the individual is exposed to, and shapes the individual's sense of identity and worth.

Increasing taxes to finance investments in the country's future—including the kind of education, welfare, and jobs programs that the Kerner Commission called for—would simultaneously increase economic performance and reduce inequality. The evidence that reducing inequality would itself improve performance enhances the reasons for instituting such policies. Most important are (a) taxing "bads," like excessive financialization (through a set of taxes on the financial sector), or pollution (including the greenhouse gas emissions that contribute to global warming); (b) taxing inelastically supplied resources, like land and natural resources (land is there, whether it is taxed or not, and so too for oil and minerals),[53] which raises revenues without causing distortions; (c) taxing those at the very top at a rate at least the rate imposed on those less well off (the current tax system is regressive, with billionaires often paying a lower effective tax rate than those much poorer); and (d) increasing taxes on inheritances to reduce the intergenerational transmission of advantage.

But reducing inequality and poverty in general will not suffice. Racism and other forms of discrimination also have to be attacked. There is an important interplay between laws, norms, and politics. Changing laws may not necessarily on its own be as effective as we would like unless we change attitudes and norms. Racism, as we have learned, is often subtle. Sometimes, those acting in a discriminatory manner are hardly aware of it. As the Kerner Report emphasized, racism is deeply ingrained in the country. But changing laws can help, for they do affect what is expected and thus affect norms. Changing norms, though, is difficult, and there needs to be a concerted effort in early education and in public discourse, through television, the media, and films.[54] Perhaps there should be a nationally mandated course in civil rights. At the very least, the federal government should provide massive funding for summer schools and research programs advancing a broader understanding of racism in America and what can be done about it. Unfortunately, it will have to be a federal program, because not all states are committed to an agenda of full equality. And this is where politics matters. In many places across the country there is an active attempt to disenfranchise African Americans and Hispanics. Those in power realize that politics matters; and if more minorities (or as is the case in some places, more of the majority) vote, the policies will change.[55]

A large literature, both academic and popular, has identified the resentments of the large numbers of Americans who have not been doing well. They resent those who are doing better; they believe the system is rigged; they believe (in many cases wrongly) that they would do well in a fair game. Their zero-sum logic leads them to believe that the reason that others are getting ahead, including the few African Americans who are, is because they are getting an unfair boost. This makes it particularly hard to address historical legacies, but it makes it all the more imperative to undertake the broad-based policies to reduce the economic inequalities I have described.

CONCLUSION

The Kerner Commission was prescient in many ways in setting out an agenda for the country on how to achieve a more equal society, free from the racism that played such an important role in the riots, the cause of which had led to the commission's creation. A recent report of the Roosevelt Institute,[56] as well as a multitude of other studies, shows that the glass is far less than half full. While many of the reforms the Kerner Commission called for required significant increases in spending, the last fifty years have seen a squeezing of the overall budget of the federal government for expenditures other than the military and programs like Social Security and Medicare.[57] It is not that the country cannot afford these expenditures; it can, and as I suggest, there are ways of raising revenue that would actually enhance economic performance.

President Donald Trump ran on a platform of "Make America Great Again." A familiar retort was that America was still great. But it was not as great as it could be. Its greatness arises not so much from its military power but from its soft power and its economic power. In today's world, America's continued racism undermines that soft power and our overall economic performance. The warning of the Kerner Commission is as relevant today as it was then: "Our Nation is moving toward two societies, one black, one white—separate and unequal." That kind of society will not be a beacon to the world. And that kind of economy will not flourish. Everyone will lose if we continue in that direction. An alternative world is possible. But fifty years of struggle has shown us how difficult it is to achieve that alternative vision.

2

The Policy Agenda to Address Racial Injustice

Jared Bernstein

THOUGH IT IS DISPIRITING, I must start by recognizing that too little has changed since the release of the 1968 Kerner Report. Both active practices and vestiges of institutionalized racism remain glaringly evident in the criminal justice system, in policing, in residential segregation, and in economic opportunity.

Surely, some opportunity barriers have come down, as African Americans are significantly more represented in formerly segregated occupations, including government and public service (including public safety, something called for in the Kerner Report). African American educational achievement has also improved, and racial test score gaps have narrowed.[1]

But other barriers have been erected, particularly in areas of the criminal justice system. As a result, the extent of upward economic mobility by African American families is far too low to provide us with confidence that the sixtieth-anniversary Kerner Report will finally tell a more positive story than the fiftieth does.

This must change. Therefore, I conclude that it is not enough to present the evidence and suggest a set of policies that nibble around the edges. Those of us who believe that racial economic injustice has hardly been rectified since the 1960s must ask ourselves how and why we have failed to move an agenda we have been pushing for many decades. That diagnosis should inform our prescription of a policy agenda that I believe could make the next Kerner Report anniversary more uplifting than the present one.

DATA TRENDS

It is my strong sense that too many analyses of economic injustice spend more time on the problem than on the solutions. That is not surprising, given that persistent racial disparities are a lot easier to document than to solve. But here I want to flip this balance, providing only a set of bullet points that I think sufficiently tell the story of racial employment, income, wealth, education, and mobility gaps, with figures relegated to an appendix. I then use the bulk of this chapter to articulate the policy agenda with the potential to push back on these trends.

- Figure A2.1 in the appendix to this chapter shows black and white unemployment rates, along with their ratio (y axis, right side). Though both series show clear cyclical movements, the ratio is remarkably steady, with an average of 2.2 (meaning that black people have had about twice as much difficulty finding work as white people have had for as long as we have data) and standard deviation of 0.2.
- Similarly, the median income of black households has been consistently below that of whites (see Figure A2.2). The black-white average since 1972 is 59 percent, which notably was about the ratio's value at both the start and the end (2015) of the data series.
- Figure A2.3 shows that median white wealth was twelve times that of black wealth in the most recent data, and Figure A2.4 shows that large differentials persist by education levels. Time series data shown in Figure A2.5 on racial net-worth differences—income plus wealth minus debt—show that gaps of this magnitude have persisted for decades.
- While blacks have essentially closed the high school graduation gap with whites (see Figure A2.6), the gap in college completion persists (see Figure A2.7). Of course, the increase in the black college completion rate from about 5 percent in the mid-1960s to over 20 percent in the most recent data is extremely welcome. But a ten-percentage-point completion gap with whites has been a constant since the 1990s.
- Figure A2.8, from mobility experts Edward Rodrigue and Richard Reeves, shows that 78 percent of black children born into the bottom fifth of the income scale remained in the bottom 40 percent by the time they were forty years old, suggesting they experienced very little in the way of upward mobility. The comparable figure for white children born into the bottom fifth is 42 percent. Rodrigue and Reeves also find discouraging evidence of downward mobility (see Figure A2.9): almost 70 percent of black chil-

dren born into the middle fifth of the income scale end up in the bottom 40 percent as adults, compared to 34 percent for white children.[2]

There are, of course, many other racial disparities that could be shown here (some of which follow), such as in housing access or incarceration. But these few important, persistent differences provide ample motivation for the policy discussion that follows.

POLICY AGENDA

I recognize that our politics will have to change for the full policy agenda I discuss to be enacted. We need a movement that is both bottom up and top down, one that is carefully, thoughtfully, and persistently developed and nurtured. But I am confident that with a more functional, representative government—one well within the scope of contemporary American history—enactment of the following agenda is both politically credible and plausible.

Direct Job Creation

A half century ago, the Kerner Report contained this important observation: "Employment is a key problem. It not only controls the present for the Negro American but, in a most profound way, it is creating the future as well. Yet, despite continuing economic growth and declining national unemployment rates, the unemployment rate for Negroes in 1967 was more than double that for whites."[3]

In May 2017, the ratio of the black to the white unemployment rate was 2.0 (7.5:3.7 percent). This gap is often written off to educational differentials, because (a) those with higher educational attainment have lower unemployment rates and that (b) blacks have lower educational attainment. But as Figure 2.1 shows, black unemployment rates are higher at every level of educational attainment.

In fact, on the basis of a sample of non-Hispanic blacks and whites twenty-five years of age and over, the black unemployment rate in 2016 was 6.8 percent, compared to 3.3 percent for whites. If blacks had whites' educational attainment levels, their unemployment rate last year would have been 6 percent, still almost twice that of whites, which suggests that educational differences account only for 24 percent of the racial unemployment gap.[4]

The persistence of this unemployment gap, as well as education's limited contribution to it, tells us that skill deficits cannot be the sole explanation for why there are always millions of black workers who want, but cannot find, gainful employment. The long-term absence of robust labor

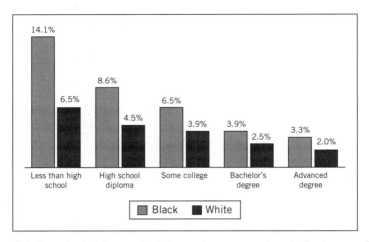

Figure 2.1 Annual unemployment rate for workers over age twenty-five by race, 2016
Source: Bureau of Labor Statistics, "Labor Force Statistics from the Current Population Survey," February 8, 2017, available at https://www.bls.gov/cps/cpsaat07.htm.

demand is a key factor and suggests the need for direct job creation. If the market fails to create enough jobs to meet the needs of this population, then such a market failure must be corrected. (This is especially the case given the extent to which antipoverty policy has increasingly shifted to a work-based approach; the assumption that labor demand is adequate to meet the needs of the potential workforce is simply untenable.)

Once you accept the presence of a market failure in terms of job creation, a role for government follows. After all, most economists and policy makers have no trouble accepting the role of the Federal Reserve as the lender of last resort when credit markets fail, as was the case in the financial crisis of 2008. If that is the standard for credit markets, the same type of standard should apply to the job market.

Direct job creation can take various formats. At the more interventionist end of the continuum, the federal government provides a public service job for which it pays salary and benefits. Such employment could exist in fields ranging from infrastructure to education to child and elder care. Recent proposals of this approach have been set out by Mark Paul, William Darity, and Darrick Hamilton[5] and by Jeff Spross.[6]

A less interventionist approach is for the government to subsidize someone's wage in a private-sector job (which could be at a nonprofit firm). In fact, the federal government took this approach in the Great Recession—through the Temporary Assistance for Needy Families emergency fund—and it was quite successful, creating around 250,000 jobs. One careful study from Florida's version of the program found that, relative to a control group, participants' work and earnings went up not just during the program, but after it as well, suggesting lasting benefits.[7]

A broader review of such programs shows we have done a lot more of this sort of direct job creation than is commonly realized, and well-designed programs in this space generate a big job-creation bang for the buck.[8]

In an effort to operationalize a direct job-creation program, Ben Spielberg and I recommend that policy makers provide a dedicated funding stream (an "employment fund") that can support job-creation efforts and expand when and where the economy is weak. We argue that such a program would provide job creation for those left behind even in good times (whether from discrimination, weak demand, or skill deficits) and play a countercyclical role during recessions.[9]

Maintaining Full Employment

It is worth recalling that the full name of the March on Washington organized by Dr. Martin Luther King, Jr., was the "March on Washington for Jobs and Freedom." Dr. King was fully aware of the benefits to African Americans from full employment, described above as a very tight matchup between job availability and job seekers. For reasons having to do with underlying changes in the macroeconomy,[10] it is increasingly challenging for economists to nail down an unemployment rate that is consistent with full employment, but using the Congressional Budget Office's estimates, Figure 2.2 shows that the U.S. labor market has been at full employment less than 30 percent of the time since 1980, compared to about 70 percent of the time in prior decades. Simply considering the 2-to-1 unemployment ratio stressed above, it should be clear that this persistent labor market slack has disproportionately hurt African Americans.

My own research has stressed numerous benefits of full employment for black workers.[11] The results of one simulation, based on the assumption that the Federal Reserve allows the jobless rate to fall a percentage point below its current estimate of the unemployment rate at full employment (about 4.7 percent), are shown in Figure 2.3. A lower overall jobless

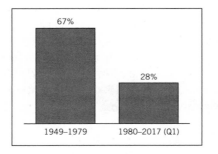

Figure 2.2 Percentage of quarters at full employment, 1949–2017 (Q1)
Source: Congressional Budget Office, "Budget and Economic Data," available at https://www.cbo.gov/about/products/budget-economic-data#4 (accessed December 5, 2017).

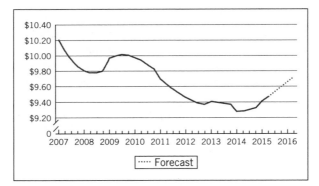

Figure 2.3 Real wages for low-wage black workers in 2015 dollars, 2007–2016 (Q2)
Source: Economic Policy Institute, "Wages by Percentile," February 13, 2017, available at http://www.epi.org/data/#?subject=wage-percentiles&r=*.

rate lowers the black unemployment rate to around 7 percent, which would be the lowest rate since the late 1990s, and increases the real twentieth-percentile wage for black workers by almost 3 percent.

In forthcoming work, I and coauthors Ben Spielberg and Keith Bentele highlight economically large responses of African American employment and earnings to the very tight job market that prevailed in the late 1990s. For example, the real annual earnings of the bottom fifth of African American working-age households doubled between 1994 and 2000, from about $4,600 in 1994 to about $9,600 in 2000 (2015 dollars). We estimate that two-thirds of the total earnings growth can be assigned to the tight labor market, the bulk of which is the result of that labor market pulling black workers into the labor market from the sidelines. In other words, millions more black workers would be expected to have jobs at full employment, which is why the absence of full employment since the 1980s has been so devastating to low-income, black households.

What is the policy agenda to maintain full employment? The most commonly invoked policy levers are monetary and fiscal policy. On the monetary side, the Federal Reserve must be willing to truly balance its dual mandate of full employment at stable prices. Too often, its actions have been weighted toward protecting against faster inflation, even when it was nowhere to be seen, at the expense of full employment. For example, the Fed has been proceeding (slowly, to be fair) with a rate-hike campaign that began at the end of 2015, despite inflation and, importantly, inflationary expectations, remaining well below the Fed's target 2 percent rate.[12]

Were the Fed to upweight the needs of less advantaged black workers and the disproportionate benefits I show above, they would be more cautious about raising rates and slowing economic and job growth. Fed officials note that their mandates involve the macroeconomy, not the fortunes of any specific group, but the Fed could consider these racial dynamics without violating its mandate.

I have already suggested one important fiscal intervention that could help fill out labor demand that is all too often missing from black communities: direct job creation. But other fiscal policies can also help achieve full employment, including job training programs, better educational access (yes, as shown above, racial unemployment differentials persist across education groups, but there is still a steep negative correlation for all races between educational attainment and unemployment), and infrastructure investment.

In this regard, much as the Fed has arguably tilted against inflation at the cost of tapping the benefits of full employment—a cost borne more heavily by minorities—the fiscal authorities have too often argued for austerity budgets when fiscal help was needed. In fact, such a comparison is unfair to the Fed, which until fairly recently was quite aggressive in applying monetary stimulus, whereas Congress endorsed austere fiscal policy in 2010, well before the recovery was reaching most people.

The economist Jason Furman endorses a "new view" of fiscal policy, one that pushes back against austerity.[13] He argues that, in slack labor markets, fiscal policy can complement monetary policy by generating demand for investors to take advantage of low interest rates. In this regard, government spending, formerly thought to crowd out private borrowing, can instead "crowd in" such activity. To the extent that such spending, say, on a direct jobs program, draws workers into the labor force—recall African Americans' large labor supply elasticity shown in Figure 2.3—it can expand aggregate supply and support stronger growth. Though Furman was not writing from the perspective of helping workers of color by creation of less job market slack, that would be the result of taking this approach to fiscal policy.

Wages, Incomes, and Public Goods

Following the above monetary and fiscal policy recommendations would raise the quantity of jobs, and, through pressures of full employment, would help with job quality (wages and benefits) as well, but given the long history of wage and income gaps shown in the first section of this chapter, more is needed. A large and growing body of research also indicates that the policy interventions outlined below, which would raise the incomes and provide needed benefits to black families, would be expected to improve long-term outcomes for the children in those families.[14]

Raising the Minimum Wage

Since African American workers disproportionately earn low wages, a higher minimum wage would help them more than other groups of workers. David Cooper of the Economic Policy Institute analyzed a new proposal to raise the federal minimum wage to fifteen dollars by 2024. He finds that the increase "would disproportionately raise wages for people of color—for example, blacks make up 12.2 percent of the workforce but 16.7 percent of affected workers. This disproportionate impact means large shares of black and Hispanic workers would be affected: 40.1 percent of black workers and 33.5 percent of Hispanic workers would directly or indirectly get a raise."[15]

The proposal would make the minimum wage higher than it has ever been before and thus must be viewed as out of sample. While the bulk of the research shows that moderate minimum-wage increases have their intended effects, we cannot be sure that an increase of this size will not bring unintended consequences for some low-wage workers. But the benefits to low-wage workers as a whole will very likely be positive: more will get raises than will lose jobs. In addition, as forthcoming research by David Cooper, Larry Mishel, and Ben Zipperer explains, job losses must be considered within the context of high rates of turnover in the low-wage labor market. Even if some workers have to look for jobs for longer, they could still end up with higher annual earnings when the jobs they eventually get pay a higher wage.

The need for bold ideas with the potential to decrease racial disparities identified fifty years ago by the Kerner Commission means that we should take a chance with an out-of-sample increase in the minimum wage. In fact, even with a fifteen-dollar minimum wage, many low-wage African American households will still have great trouble meeting their needs, much less building any kind of wealth. This is one reason a higher minimum wage and an increased Earned Income Tax Credit, discussed next, are such important complements.[16]

The Earned Income Tax Credit

The EITC is a wage subsidy for low-income workers claimed by more than five million African American workers with nearly seven million children.[17] Importantly, it is a *refundable* tax credit, meaning recipients with no (or low) tax liability can still receive it as a cash refund.

These credits, which receive some bipartisan support, should be expanded. One recent analysis determined that a $1 trillion expansion of the EITC over the next decade would offset the damage done to low- and moderate-wage earners by the forces of inequality since 1979.[18] A low-income working family with one child, maxing out on the current EITC, would see their credit almost double, from $3,400 to $6,500. Working-class families, say, a family of four making $40,000, would get an EITC boost of about $4,000 (from $2,000 to $6,000). Black workers would disproportionately gain from this ambitious expansion.

A Child Allowance

The childhood poverty rate in the United States is 21 percent, but for black children that rate rises to 36 percent, three times white children's rate of 12 percent. Though our antipoverty efforts have been somewhat effective in reducing market-driven rates of economic privation, international data show that after taxes and after public-cash and near-cash transfers, child poverty remains uniquely high in the United States, twice the German rate and seven times the rate in Denmark.[19]

One reason for the difference is that these countries, and most other advanced economies, provide regular payments to families with kids, recognizing that investing in children is an essential public good. Though we have the Child Tax Credit here in the United States, which like the EITC benefits millions of people (about 3.5 million African American working families with children claimed refunds averaging about $1,300 through the refundable portion of the Child Tax Credit in 2013), the lowest-income children, who are disproportionately children of color, get no income support.

The Child Tax Credit should thus be expanded into a monthly stipend for *all* families with children. A child allowance of $250 per month ($3,000 per year) would cost about $190 billion per year, though half the cost could be offset by consolidating existing policies that deliver cash to children but are less well targeted.[20] It would cut child poverty by 40 percent and deep child poverty by half while providing middle-income families raising children with a baseline level of stable income.

Health Care

As of this writing, the Affordable Care Act is under aggressive attack from congressional conservatives. At the heart of this attack is a proposal to roll back the ACA's expansion of Medicaid and to then turn the program into a block grant or per capita cap, both of which would undermine its ability to ramp up to meet needs and likely lead to states restricting eligibility, cutting benefits, or both. These changes would harm African Americans; both the expansion of Medicaid and the subsidization of premiums in the nongroup market have helped reduce the uninsured rate of African Americans by more than a third between 2013 and 2016,[21] from about 19 percent to about 12 percent. Such coverage is particularly valuable to low-income African Americans, because they suffer disproportionately from chronic illnesses such as diabetes, heart disease, and HIV/AIDS.

Instead of harming black Americans by repealing the ACA, we should be helping them by encouraging states that have not yet done so to adopt the Medicaid expansion. The uninsured rates for African

Americans are generally much lower in states that have already taken this step.

Housing

In his masterful book *The Color of Law*, Richard Rothstein presents extensive and meticulous research showing how the federal government and city and state governments have long employed racially discriminatory policies to deny blacks the opportunity to live in neighborhoods with good jobs, schools, and opportunities for upward mobility.[22] The creation of "racial ghettos," to use the language of the Kerner Report,[23] was neither an accident nor, as the courts to this day wrongly assert, a function of de facto discrimination, meaning that, for complicated reasons, it just turned out that way. Nor is it a *former* problem, one that has been solved by affirmative, corrective policy measures. Rothstein writes, "Today's residential segregation . . . is not the unintended consequence of individual choices and of otherwise well-meaning law or regulation but of unhidden public policy that explicitly segregated every metropolitan area in the United States."[24]

Raj Chetty, Nathaniel Hendren, and Lawrence Katz have developed a robust research agenda showing the connection between disadvantaged neighborhoods and reduced upward mobility for children who grow up in those neighborhoods. They stress "moving to opportunity" as a policy solution (i.e., relocating families with young children—exposure to factors that dampen mobility are particularly damaging for the young—to areas with higher rates of upward mobility).[25] In this regard, ideas discussed above, including more generous housing vouchers and banning racially motivated zoning rules, make sense.

We should strengthen programs such as Housing Choice Vouchers (HCV). The housing expert Barbara Sard notes that the HCV program has a strong track record in reducing homelessness, foster-care placements, and frequent disruptive moves and has been associated with lower rates of "alcohol dependence, psychological distress, and domestic violence victimization among the adults with whom . . . children live."[26] The HCV program "has an important, positive impact on minority families' access to opportunities," but too few families are able to use vouchers to find housing in low-poverty areas with access to better educational opportunities. Sard suggests improvements that would enable more such moves, including increased incentives for state and local agencies to focus on higher-opportunity locations; setting subsidy caps and jurisdictional rules that facilitate moving to opportunity; and direct assistance and encouragement both to landlords in low-poverty areas and to families who would benefit from moving to such areas.

Rothstein suggests providing historically large subsidies that would enable African Americans to "purchase homes in suburbs that have been racially exclusive," though he quickly admits that "such assistance is both politically and judicially inconceivable."[27] He also suggests a ban on zoning rules, such as those prohibiting multifamily housing, that he shows have long been used to keep lower-income families out of more affluent suburbs. An interesting idea by Rothstein in this space is to use the tax code to integrate neighborhoods by denying the mortgage-interest deduction to property owners in suburbs that fail to take steps to address the shortage of affordable housing in their area.

Schooling

Though it is not the cure-all some advocates suggest—recall the education-adjusted unemployment rate analysis in Figure 2.1—clearly, education is critically important. Racial gaps in schooling persist and have long-term impacts. At least three policy interventions can help in this space.

First, quality preschool—virtually a birthright among affluent families—is associated with improved outcomes for children in later years; it boosts not just educational attainment but health and employment as well, and it also reduces exposure to the criminal justice system.[28] Nuanced research reveals that many Head Start programs are effective, though often their positive impact does not show up until later in life. According to one study, these effects are particularly germane among African American participants: along with the other benefits noted earlier, Head Start "causes social, emotional, and behavioral development that becomes evident in adulthood measures of self-control, self-esteem, and positive parenting practices."[29]

Second, we need to adequately and equitably fund K–12 education at the state and local levels. While money is not a sufficient condition for improving school quality, it is a necessary one. That is true in both the charter school and the traditional public school sectors, and as Spielberg and I have argued, will help students most if those sectors work more in collaboration to learn from each other's best practices and ensure an efficient allocation of resources across the entire school system.[30]

Third, we must make higher education more affordable. Differences in college matriculation and completion rates by income and race are in large part driven by differences in opportunities for students before they even apply to college, but they are also a product of rising college costs and debt burdens for low- and middle-income people, costs that often fall particularly hard on people of color.[31] Increasing Pell Grants, redesigning tax-based aid for higher education to make it more progressive, and strengthening income-based repayment programs (in which college loan liabilities are scaled to incomes) would help with these problems.

Other Discretionary Programs

Much of what the federal government does in terms of investing in children and families is in the discretionary side of the federal budget, in areas like childcare, job training, college access, Head Start, housing assistance, aid to poor school districts, and funds that support community development. This funding is already heading for its lowest levels, as a share of gross domestic product, on record, and budgets put forth by the conservative majority double down on these sorts of cuts.[32] For example, 60 percent of the spending cuts proposed in the Trump administration's first budget come from low-income programs (though many of these proposed cuts are to mandatory programs, like nutritional support and Medicaid, as well).[33] These cuts are totally inconsistent with providing opportunity to low-income African American families and should be opposed.

Criminal Justice

Since well before the Kerner Commission elevated its importance, racial inequities embedded in our criminal justice system have been a major obstacle for black Americans, one with deep, generational implications. The issue deserves its own chapter; here, I raise only a few policy ideas related to reducing employment barriers for the millions of African Americans with criminal records.

To reduce the negative mobility impacts of incarceration rates, states and the federal government need to reduce penalties for low-level felonies, many of which fall disproportionately on minorities, and we must reexamine sentencing laws and reduce sentences. Congress could accelerate progress toward this with legislation allowing federal judges to impose sentences below mandatory minimums when warranted.

Maurice Emsellem and Jason Ziedenberg have also written about the need for expanding fair-chance hiring practices such as removing the question regarding a criminal record from employment applications, and they find positive results in many places that are trying these interventions.[34] They also underscore the importance of making background checks more reliable and accurate and recommend clean slate, or expungement, laws for minor, nonviolent felonies.

Reparations

This policy section would be incomplete without a discussion of reparations, or compensation to the current generation of African Americans for the lasting economic impacts of slavery, oppression, and violence against their forebears. I should be clear that I consider reparations to be even less likely to get through our current political system than some of the ideas noted earlier. However, the argument for reparations is strong, particularly regarding existing disadvantages in wealth accumulation, educational access (and the lasting consequences of restricted access in that space), and neighborhood segregation, and it cannot be ignored.

That argument was made most forcefully by Ta-Nehisi Coates.[35] Many of Coates's themes show up in the data and policy discussion above; he discusses wealth disparities, education differences, and especially racial segregation and the government-backed creation of black ghettos. The theme of economic immobility is especially key to Coates's argument, as he meticulously traces historical connections between discrimination and the broken ladder out of poverty faced by too many African American families today.

Coates also links these themes to the motivating impulse behind this chapter: that fifty years after the Kerner Report, the conditions facing black families would be far too easily recognized by the report's authors. He notes, for example, that among children born between 1955 and through 1970, "4 percent of whites and 62 percent of blacks across America had been raised in poor neighborhoods. A generation later . . . virtually nothing had changed."[36]

Interestingly, Coates does not elaborate a reparations program. Instead, he endorses passage of a bill that would set up a commission to study the issue and recommend action. The Black Lives Matter movement also endorses this approach and argues that "reparations . . . include cash, land, . . . economic development, scholarship funds . . . , and educational materials that accurately depict the history of Black people . . . all of which could begin to amend past and persistent injustice and exploitation."[37]

In this spirit, many of the policies above share the goal of enhancing African Americans' economic conditions and mobility through geographic desegregation, educational policies from preschool through college, income and wage policies, health care, housing, other work supports, and more.

CONCLUSION

The policy agenda I describe is admittedly ambitious, but that is as it must be given the depth to which racial injustice is embedded in our economy. It is also an agenda that invokes considerable budgetary costs. But as the Kerner Report noted in its opening, "The vital needs of the Nation must be met; hard choices must be made, and, if necessary, *new taxes enacted*."[38] Let us not raise the false cry of fiscal austerity to yet again avoid making the substantial investments we must make if we are to realize the vision set forth five decades ago by the Kerner Commission.

APPENDIX

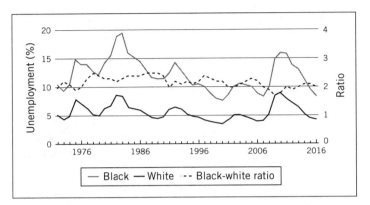

Figure A2.1 Unemployment by race (left axis) and black-white ratio, 1972–2016 (right axis)
Source: Bureau of Labor Statistics Current Population Survey data, available at https://data.bls.gov/cgi-bin/surveymost?ln.

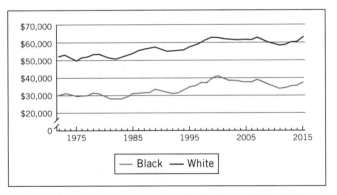

Figure A2.2 Real median income by race in 2015 dollars, 1972–2015
Source: Bernadette D. Proctor, Jessica L. Semega, and Melissa A. Kollar, "Income and Poverty in the United States: 2015," September 2016, available at https://www.census.gov/content/dam/Census/library/publications/2016/demo/p60-256.pdf.

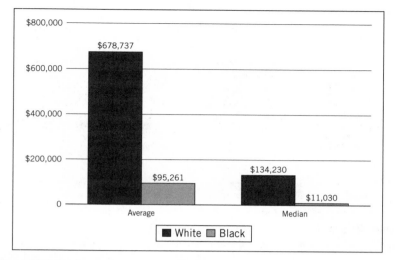

Figure A2.3 Median and average wealth, by race
Source: Janelle Jones, "The Racial Wealth Gap: How African-Americans Have Been Short-changed Out of the Materials to Build Wealth," Economic Policy Institute, February 13, 2017, available at http://www.epi.org/blog/the-racial-wealth-gap-how-african-americans-have-been-shortchanged-out-of-the-materials-to-build-wealth.

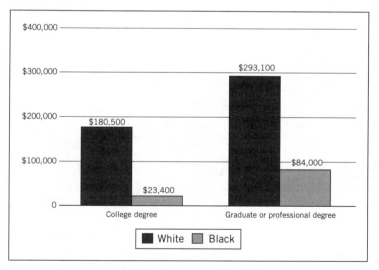

Figure A2.4 Median wealth, by educational degree and race
Source: Janelle Jones, "The Racial Wealth Gap: How African-Americans Have Been Short-changed out of the Materials to Build Wealth," February 13, 2017, available at http://www.epi.org/blog/the-racial-wealth-gap-how-african-americans-have-been-shortchanged-out-of-the-materials-to-build-wealth.

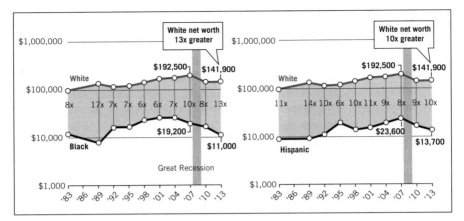

Figure A2.5 Median net worth of households, in 2013 dollars
Source: Rakesh Kochhar and Richard Fry, "Wealth Inequality Has Widened along Racial, Ethnic Lines since End of Great Recession," Pew Research Center, December 12, 2014, available at http://www.pewresearch.org/fact-tank/2014/12/12/racial-wealth-gaps-great-recession.
Note: Blacks and whites include only non-Hispanic Americans. Hispanic Americans are of any race. Chart scale is logarithmic; each gridline is ten times greater than the gridline below it. The Great Recession began December 2007 and ended June 2009.

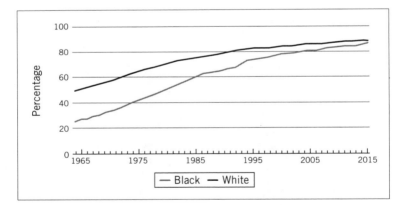

Figure A2.6 High school completion rates by race, 1964–2015
Source: U.S. Census Bureau, "Table A-2: Percent of People 25 Years and Over Who Have Completed High School or College, by Race, Hispanic Origin and Sex: Selected Years, 1940–2015," November 29, 2016, available at https://www.census.gov/data/tables/time-series/demo/educational-attainment/cps-historical-time-series.html.

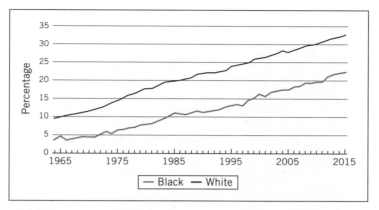

Figure A2.7 College completion rates by race, 1964–2015
Source: U.S. Census Bureau, "Table A-2: Percent of People 25 Years and Over Who Have Completed High School or College, by Race, Hispanic Origin and Sex: Selected Years, 1940–2015," November 29, 2016, available at https://www.census.gov/data/tables/time-series/demo/educational-attainment/cps-historical-time-series.html.

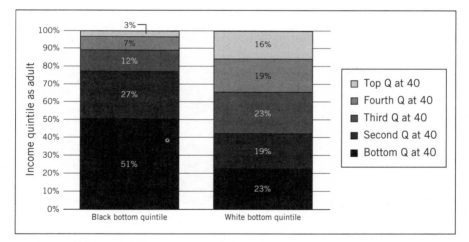

Figure A2.8 Half of black Americans born poor stay poor
Source: Edward Rodrigue and Richard V. Reeves, "Five Bleak Facts on Black Opportunity," Brookings Institution, January 15, 2015, available at https://www.brookings.edu/blog/social-mobility-memos/2015/01/15/five-bleak-facts-on-black-opportunity.

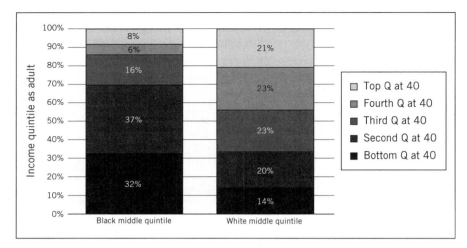

Figure A2.9 Most black middle-class kids are downwardly mobile
Source: Edward Rodrigue and Richard V. Reeves, "Five Bleak Facts on Black Opportunity," Brookings Institution, January 15, 2015, available at https://www.brookings.edu/blog/social -mobility-memos/2015/01/15/five-bleak-facts-on-black-opportunity.

3

The Case for Solidarity

JEFF FAUX

U NDERLYING THE KERNER COMMISSION'S warning of a divided America are two seemingly separate cracks in the foundation of American democracy. One is white racism, specifically aimed at denying the humanity of African Americans. The other is economic class inequality.

Public debate over the issues of poverty and race is often confused by an urge to prove that their roots lie in either one or the other. But the evidence of the last fifty years suggests that both these sources of oppression are closely connected and reinforce each other. And that we will never resolve the issues raised by the Kerner Commission unless we deal with them together.

The historic 1963 March on Washington was a demonstration for both "jobs and freedom," as the march was titled. As Martin Luther King, Jr.— the iconic symbol of the struggle against racism—said in his last sermon before he was killed, "But if a man doesn't have a job or an income, he has neither life nor liberty nor the possibility for the pursuit of happiness."[1]

FIFTY YEARS SINCE THE KERNER REPORT: THE GOOD NEWS

Think of economic opportunity in America today as a theater with not enough seats for all who are waiting in the line outside. The manager has various ways to decide who comes in. First come, first served is one way. Auctioning the tickets to the highest bidder is another. Still another is rationing access according to some characteristic—like race.

For most of the history of the United States, African Americans were not even allowed to get in the line.

Moreover, stirring up segregationist feelings was a way for economic elites to divert the anger of poor and working-class whites—who spent their lives in line but never got in—from the rich and powerful who excluded them. As President Lyndon Johnson remarked in 1965, all that white voters in the South ever heard from their politicians was "Negro, Negro, Negro!"[2]

The Civil Rights Act of 1964, as well as the antidiscrimination legislation that followed, in effect told the managers of the economic theater that they had to let African Americans in the line. It was not an easy struggle: lives were lost, communities torn apart, and American politics was permanently altered.[3]

Fifty years later, white bigotry has certainly not been eliminated from the American psyche. But for anyone who remembers the United States before the Civil Rights Act, much has changed.

Civil rights legislation forced whites to change the way they had behaved—that is, to accept integration as the law. But over time it also changed the way many white people thought and felt. The personal experience of sharing a lunch counter, a classroom, and a workplace with African Americans provided the space for white Americans to see their black fellow citizens—who, in the phrase of writer Ralph Ellison, had been largely "invisible"—as full human beings, like themselves.

The result was a steady erosion of what had been assumed to be white people's permanent visceral resistance to integration. Changes in the law brought changes in the heart.

In-depth studies of polls by the National Opinion Research Center at the University of Chicago show a clear and substantial drop in segregationist sentiments among whites on issues of education, housing, and a wide array of social attitudes since the early 1970s. As younger generations of whites increasingly experienced integration as a normal part of life, acceptance of blacks as equals spread from the realm of public policy to the realm of personal beliefs.

Thus, between 1990 and 2008, the percentage of whites who thought whites were harder working than blacks fell from 65 percent to 42 percent. The proportion who thought whites were more intelligent than blacks dropped from 57 percent to 25 percent. The share of whites who would object to a close relative marrying a black person dropped from 57 percent in 1990 to 25 percent in 2008.[4]

In his May 2016 commencement speech at Howard University, President Barack Obama noted that, sixty years before, his father would not have been served in many restaurants in Washington, D.C. He then ticked off a list of improvements in the lives of black Americans during his lifetime: "We're no longer only entertainers, we're producers, studio executives. No longer small business owners, we're CEOs, we're mayors, representatives, Presidents of the United States."[5]

Still, said the president, there was "much more work to do." Amen to that.

AND THE BAD NEWS

The gap between the real wages of white and African American workers actually widened between 1979 and 2015—from 22 percent to 31 percent for men and from 6 to 19 percent for women.[6] The wealth gap is even wider. White households have on average fifteen times more wealth than African American households.[7] Black men, as President Obama noted, are six times as likely to be in prison as white men. And housing segregation, with its attendant impact on education, seems to be getting worse. As one study noted, "The typical black student now [in 2014] attends a school where only 29 percent of his or her fellow students are white, down from 36 percent in 1980."[8]

Some claim these numbers are evidence that government programs aimed at helping African Americans get into the theater of opportunity did not work. But the evidence does not show that. For example, poverty rates for black Americans dropped by almost 50 percent in the decade after the antipoverty programs began in the mid-1960s. Rather, something happened in the overall economy at the end of the 1970s that undercut the effect of civil rights and antipoverty programs for African American families: economic opportunities began to shrink for working people of *both* races.

The moral engine of the civil rights movement of the 1960s was driven largely by an organized demand for justice by African Americans and, in response, compassion and guilt among many whites—although probably not a majority. White resistance was strong and in many places violent. But the worst was overcome because of the decadelong economic boom that expanded the number of available seats in the economic theater. Generally rising wages and increased financial security reduced the threat that economic opportunities for blacks would come at the expense of working-class whites.

At the beginning of that decade, Democratic president John Kennedy said, "A rising tide lifts all boats."[9] And by the end of the decade, the active management of the economy was accepted by both parties. As Republican Richard Nixon said in 1971, "I am now a Keynesian."[10] It followed, therefore, that poverty and the violence and national dysfunction that it engendered could be reduced, if not eliminated, by making sure that once African Americans had access to the line, they could get into the economic opportunity theater. Thus, the programs for the poor that followed the Civil Rights Act emphasized training and education that would lead to the upward-mobility jobs that were the path to the American Dream.

Central to this optimism was what seemed at the time to be an immutable economic law: that workers' incomes were a function of their productivity. Show up for work and do a good job, and you will get ahead. For the three decades following World War II, the real wages of American workers had, in fact, roughly matched their productivity—that is, the average increase in wealth that the average worker produced. Between 1948 and 1973 worker productivity rose by 97 percent and real compensation (wages plus benefits) rose by 91 percent. The ticket to a better future was a steady job.

But after the 1970s, the economic law of wages became less immutable. Workers continued to produce more per hour of work, but their compensation (wages plus benefits) flattened out. Between 1973 and 2016, worker productivity rose by 73 percent, but their compensation rose by only 11 percent. In other words, the typical American worker, of whatever race, was not sharing in the wealth he or she was producing.

Inasmuch as most Americans must work for a living, the growing gap between the wealth that workers produced and their paycheck is the primary cause of the extraordinary upward redistribution of income and wealth over the last several decades. The share of total income claimed by the richest 1 percent of the population rose from 9 percent in the late 1970s to 21 percent in 2014.[11] It is as if, rather than expanding the number of the opportunity seats, the economy has been putting its wealth into making the existing seats more luxurious and adding bars and restaurants and other amenities for the people already there.

RACE AND INEQUALITY

Those who speak for the people with good seats inside the opportunity theater would have us believe that inequality is the result of natural forces beyond our control. Thus, for example, they claim that inequality is caused by workers not being able or willing to keep up with the educational demands of the new age of technology. According to this story, African Americans as a group have failed to close the black-white income gap because they have less education and training. In other words, the problem is them, not us.

It is a widely held opinion. But it is wrong! If the problem were automation, we would expect to see a dramatic increase in labor productivity, capital investment, and the wages of people who were still employed—especially young people with advanced education. Instead, labor productivity since the 1970s has slowed down, capital investment has decelerated,[12] and in 2016, average real wages of young college graduates were just about where they had been sixteen years earlier.[13]

The root cause of the growth of inequality lies not in some inevitable and mysterious economic force but rather in deliberate policy choices that undercut the bargaining position of labor vis-à-vis investors. These include the following:

- *The decline in unions.* Overall, unions have been a vehicle for advancement for African American workers, whose rates of union membership are higher than their share of the workforce.[14]
- *Trade policies that increased import competition from countries where wages are deliberately suppressed.* This has dramatically shrunk the number of U.S. manufacturing jobs, a traditional ladder for upward mobility for working-class males.
- *The deregulation of financial markets that has shifted investment from domestic production to financial speculation.* This is another policy that closed off opportunities for the disadvantaged.
- *The deregulation of labor markets, which reduced the rewards of work for those at the bottom.* For example, if the federal minimum wage had continued to rise with productivity, by 2016 it would have been $18.85, rather than $7.25.[15]

Moreover, most of the jobs the U.S. economy is producing require less, not more, training. Of the ten occupations projected by the Bureau of Labor Statistics to add the most jobs to the U.S. economy between 2012 and 2022, *none require a four-year college degree.* Two—registered nurses and nursing assistants—require some education and training beyond high school. Six do not even require a high school diploma.[16]

Today, graduates of four-year colleges are taking jobs that previously went to graduates of two-year colleges, who, in turn, are taking jobs of high school graduates—and so forth, down the line. Moreover, in a desperate effort to get ahead, more people are going deeper into debt to further their education and training, only to find that they cannot earn enough to pay off their loans.

As the economist William Spriggs notes, "The media sees the victory of the civil rights movement in terms of viable black professionals like me. But the real accomplishment was in getting black working class good-paying union jobs. And just as we made that breakthrough, those jobs began to disappear."[17]

The decline of opportunities is of course felt the most by the people with the least training, family connections, or luck. So it should be no surprise that the poverty rate was 15 percent higher in 2015 than it was in 1979.[18]

THE POLITICAL CONSEQUENCES

The erosion of opportunities for the working class in general has weakened support for programs aimed at helping African Americans in particular.

When there was a general expectation that the expansion of jobs at rising wages would continue, the case for special programs for people historically disadvantaged could be more easily made to whites on the basis of simple justice and fairness. They could see a future in which there would be enough for everyone. But now that these expectations have changed, the case for race-based programs—while morally justified—is politically harder to make.

Imagine people working at dead-end jobs at Burger King for $10 an hour. One is an African American from a poor neighborhood whose family has been in America for three hundred years—in slavery or slavery-like conditions—and whose last job also paid $10 per hour. A second is an older white man whose family has been here for a hundred years and who used to work in a factory for $22 an hour but who cannot retire because his promised pension disappeared when the company filed for bankruptcy and relocated overseas. Another is a recent undocumented immigrant from El Salvador, worried that immigration agents may walk in and deport him at any moment. Add a fourth: the white college graduate who owes $40,000 in student debt and cannot find a job that will allow her to pay it off.

All now feel they have a grievance. The African American whose forebears did not voluntarily immigrate to American for a better life but were kidnapped and brought here in chains may still have a stronger moral claim for compensatory help than the white or Latino coworker, but this will not make much of an impression on his or her fellow workers who have their own struggle for survival in a dog-eat-dog labor market.

Today, the majority of American millennials, generally defined as those born in the decades of the 1980s and 1990s, will do worse than their parents. Seventy-six percent of all workers believe they will retire on less than their parents did. Again, black Americans do worse, but they share a disappointing future with the others. One study concludes that the effect of the Great Recession that began in 2008 will have reduced the wealth of black Americans in fourteen years by 40 percent. The number for white Americans is 30 percent.[19]

Moreover, as public budgets are squeezed, eligibility rules for programs for the poor have been tightened. Since African Americans have lower incomes, they appear to make up more of such programs' beneficiaries, and this increases the perception among whites that these programs are not for them.

Thus, fertile conditions have been created for the recent rise of demagogues, ready to channel the disappointment and anger of the white majority into scapegoating African Americans and other minorities—just as they did in President Lyndon Johnson's time. So it is no accident that, over the last decade of rising inequality and the slow recovery from the Great Recession, polls show that both black and white Americans think that race relations have gotten worse—the share of blacks who say that race relations are good having dropped from 61 percent to 49 percent between 2008 and 2015; the share of whites who say that, from 70 percent to 55 percent.

SOLIDARITY: THE WAY FORWARD

James Baldwin wrote, "Not everything that is faced can be changed; but nothing can be changed until it is faced."[20] It is time for all of us to face the fact that under the present distribution of bargaining power, there will be no natural return to the circumstances of the 1960s that led to the civil rights breakthrough of that era. The U.S. economy no longer dominates the world as it did. Economic growth is essential, and we could arguably have grown faster since the crash of 2008, but there is little prospect now of a sustained economic boom strong enough to overcome the maldistribution of income and wealth that currently characterizes our society.

This certainly does not mean that we do not need stronger and more vigorous programs that strike at the special barriers that African Americans face. But the political support needed to return to the historic task of creating a truly integrated society also requires a return to a more fair and equal distribution of income and wealth for all. The African American poor and working class will not prosper unless the nonblack poor and working class prosper as well. If it does not, the social disintegration the Kerner Commission warned about will surely accelerate. Our future may well see an America divided in more than just two ways, to wit: a super-rich of 1 percent; an upwardly mobile group of integrated professional elites of perhaps 10 percent; and a vast splintered group of whites and blacks and other minorities in a bitter—and increasingly racist—struggle for the crumbs from the tables of the well off.

Facing these new divisions of both race and class requires that whites and blacks see themselves as being in the same boat, although they might have gotten there in different ways. The essential task is a political movement that can forge a new social contact. The elements needed to revive that contract are not a mystery. They are built on the easy-to-understand idea that by virtue of being a citizen—not by virtue of your race, gender, or special talent or the wealth of your parents—you have certain rights and obligations:

- A right to a job in which you share in the wealth you are creating and an obligation to work at it to the best of your ability
- A right to benefit from the investments previous generations have made in your productivity and an obligation to invest for the generations to come

- A right to protection against ill health and the infirmities of old age and an obligation to support social insurance
- A right to bargain collectively and an obligation to help create more productive workplaces
- A right to create a business and an obligation to support the community in which it prospers
- A right to consume the products of a global economy and the obligation to insist that they be produced in a way that does not exploit other workers

We do not lack an understanding of at least some of the ways of getting from here to there. Popular support for movement to raise the national minimum wage to fifteen dollars an hour suggests the possibilities. Raising the minimum wage will apply to all workers, whatever their race or ethnicity—and it is popular with the general public, for whom redistribution of income makes sense if it is connected to the notion of a fair day's pay for a fair day's work.[21]

We need to build on these and other efforts that lay out practical steps that can involve the vast majority of Americans who must work for a living. In this regard it may be time to revive an effort that started in American communities in the 1970s around the bicentennial celebration of U.S. independence. In cities and towns across the nation, open forums, town meetings, and commissions were set up to discuss and debate the simple question of what our community should look like twenty-five years from now. People discussed everything from land-use planning to racial integration and produced some remarkable, forward-looking plans. But after 1980, the notion of planning for a common future was set aside by a political philosophy of radical individualism, in which it was each person for him- or herself in a brutally competitive world.

Returning to the idea of citizen participation in planning the future of our communities is a way to truly take back our government from the rich and powerful. And the progress in decreasing racial polarization in the several decades after the Kerner Report gives some confidence that bringing people together in forging a joint vision for the future in neighborhoods, towns, and cities could be a major step in turning the country's attention to the still-unfinished work.

4

The Power of Love Coupled with Opportunity

DOROTHY STONEMAN

THE KERNER REPORT states that "a sure method for motivating the hard-core unemployed has not yet been devised" but that the unemployed fifteen- to twenty-four-year-olds represent "a great reservoir of under-used human resources which are vital to the Nation."[1] In the last fifty years, I believe we have learned a reasonably sure method of tapping into this great reservoir. But we still lack the political will to fund effective approaches at the scale required.

The power of love coupled with opportunity is transformational when offered to young people who have endured poverty. It unleashes their positive energy, unlocks their many talents, and inspires them to build a successful life and help others. No matter how lost they have been, if they find a caring community that respects their intelligence and illuminates the way to build a productive life, their ability to learn and love is awakened. This poem by a YouthBuild student captures it movingly:

> Imagine a child captured in his rage;
> Anger, violence, it seems to be the only way.
> When he feels down . . . it's as if no one's around.
> When the world closes in on him,
> He only breaks down.
> To live in a world where ignorance nourishes a baby,
> Death is given by the handful,
> And sanity seems to be crazy,
> Searching and searching.
> It seems to never end.

For what, no one knows until it's found, my friends.
That's why I'm glad YouthBuild is made of family and friends.
In an unstable world it gives me stability.
YouthBuild, my extended family,
I'll love you until infinity.

This infinite love—the exact opposite of violence and despair—is waiting in the streets of Harlem and Roxbury, in the backwoods of West Virginia and Mississippi, and in every community where young people are struggling. It rises with awesome predictability and passion whenever caring, respect, and opportunity replace the emptiness and terror so many youth face.

Liberating this infinite love takes more than just minimally preparing young people for jobs. It occurs when we create a respectful, inclusive, sharing community of peers doing good works in their neighborhood while participating in governance and civic engagement. When we do it well, they almost always call it their family. When they get to belong to a family-like community that fosters responsibility and invites them to become leaders and change agents, it turns out they have the deepest passion for changing the conditions from which they and their loved ones have suffered. They become a powerful force for good that, if supported over time, can transform their communities, in addition to their own lives.

I witnessed this awakening process for thirty-eight years as the founder and chief executive officer of the nonprofit organization YouthBuild USA. With thousands of colleagues, we built a network of 250 YouthBuild programs, sponsored by local nonprofit and public entities, in the nation's most hard-pressed urban and rural communities. In these programs, low-income students who have left high school without a diploma enroll full time for about ten months. They spend half their time learning construction skills and getting paid a wage building affordable housing for homeless and low-income people in their communities; they spend the other half of their time working toward their high school equivalency or diploma in highly supportive and individualized classrooms. It is all knit together with personal and peer counseling, deeply caring adults, and a major emphasis on leadership development and the internalization of positive values. At graduation, they are ready for college and employment. Staff offer follow-up supports for at least one year.

Participant Carmen Williams describes her experience:

Being a young woman from the streets of Philadelphia I never thought I would achieve anything. Drug and alcohol abuse to cope with wasn't anything compared to the sexual, mental, physical, and emotional abuse I also experienced. It was only two options for the life I was living: to be an addict like my mother, or to die like both of my parents. I didn't want to die, but I didn't have a reason to live, either, until I found YouthBuild. There was always something inside of me waiting to have the opportunity to become great. YouthBuild gave me that opportunity. It gave me the chance to heal. Here is where I am able to have the family I always wanted. The people here believe in me, even when I did not believe in myself. I aspire to be what YouthBuild has been to me, to another young person. I do not think there are words to express my gratitude. I will continue the march towards change using the core values I have learned from YouthBuild.[2]

It is this passion we can liberate through all the effective youth programs across the nation. With this energy we can build the movement needed to generate the political will to dedicate the resources needed for this most important societal goal of securing our nation's economic and social stability for the coming generations. Young black Americans and all young people emerging from poverty can and want to be the core of that movement.

WHAT DO YOUNG PEOPLE NEED AND WANT?

In 2012, a multiracial group of young adults raised in both urban and rural poverty who had overcome many barriers with the support of sixteen different comprehensive youth engagement programs (such as YouthBuild, Year Up, Service and Conservation Corps, and others) formed the National Council of Young Leaders. They immediately developed "Recommendations to Increase Opportunity and Decrease Poverty in America."[3] This document calls for the expansion of six important pathways out of poverty for young adults who have fallen off track: access to higher education, internships, mentoring, national service, reentry programs, and comprehensive full-time programs. It then offers the details of change needed in five basic social systems that affect everyone in their communities: education, criminal justice, upward mobility, community development, and family supports. Thus, while calling for clear and structured opportunities for young adults to climb out of poverty in the short term, the members of the National Council of Young Leaders also call for changes in the fundamental conditions in their communities to improve the lives of all who reside there. Most of the system changes they call for have enormous overlap with those recommended by the Kerner Commission. I focus here on the pathways out of poverty and the role young people could play in building the political will to enact these changes.

OPPORTUNITY YOUTH

The Kerner Commission reported that the majority of the young people who rioted in the sixties were young black men who were high school dropouts and unemployed.[4] It recommended the creation of two million public and private jobs to empower young people of all races to join the economy as contributing members.[5] Sadly, this was not done.

Most young people who leave high school without a diploma become stuck on the margins, are often incarcerated, and are rarely employed. They are not only black men. There are 4.9 million sixteen- to twenty-four-year-olds who are not employed or in school in the United States. They include all races, men and women, gay and straight, urban and rural, all faith traditions, documented and undocumented, able and disabled. Two million, or 41 percent of them, live in low-income households.[6] They will birth and raise the next generation in poverty if education and jobs are not available to them. This is a manageable challenge. If we were to address their needs and aspirations, we could end poverty in a generation. We could rejoice in the humanity of our nation.

We now call this group "Opportunity Youth" because they are both seeking opportunity and offering opportunity to our nation if we invest in them. They are coming of age, making real decisions as young adults about what kind of life they will live. In destitute communities, many of them have not seen any welcoming path they could choose that would lead to productive adulthood. By their own accounts, many expect to be dead or in jail before they reach twenty-five years of age.[7] But if we embrace them and offer real opportunity at this critical inflexion point in their lives, they will deliberately pivot toward hope. They have the agency to choose, but that agency means something only if good choices are available.

Just as recommended by the Kerner Commission, two million good choices should be provided. In a caring context, these young people should be offered everything they are seeking: a visible and important role in the community that brings them respect from their neighbors and families, skills that can lead to a decent-paying job, a fresh start on their education, personal counseling from respected role models supporting deep healing from past and present trauma, consistent respect for their intelligence from caring adults in authority who include them in key decision making, a positive and supportive peer group with whom they can share their common pain and admit that they want to change their lives, a set of positive values strong enough to compete with the negative values of the streets, a stipend or wage to live on while they are learning, a path to college or a career, and something to belong to that they can believe in. They need to be part of a minicommunity in which people genuinely care about each other, embrace positive values, and share a vision of a better world.

All these elements were deliberately built into YouthBuild and have demonstrated their efficacy. They exist with varying emphases in the many other successful youth programs that have emerged over the decades as local innovations and national networks. It is past time to expand all these programs to full scale—with "full scale" being defined as reaching either the limit of demand or the limit of capacity to deliver high-quality programs.

Achieving this requires four immediate steps that national leaders and advocates are working to implement. If the political will could be generated to produce the resources, we could implement these four steps and produce the two million jobs and career pathways needed by low-income Opportunity Youth. The four steps are the following:

Step 1: Expand Existing Federally Funded Programs

Congress could fund the expansion of federally authorized programs to welcome one million Opportunity Youth each year as laid out in "A Bridge to Reconnection," a study done by Civic Enterprises in 2012 and updated in 2016.[8] The size and scope of existing programs were studied, along with the growth that existing demand and capacity would allow. The programs recommended for expansion include short-term part-time and longer-term full-time comprehensive job training, adult education, internships, apprenticeships, national service opportunities, and reentry programs.

The best known of these programs are Service and Conservation Corps (118 sites engaging 13,000 youth annually),[9] National Guard Youth ChalleNGe program (40 sites that have graduated 145,000 youth),[10] Job Corps (126 sites engaging 52,500 youth),[11] YouthBuild (260 sites engaging 9,000 youth),[12] AmeriCorps (about 6,000 Opportunity Youth),[13] and Workforce Innovation Opportunities Act grantees (about 95,000 Opportunity Youth).[14] These national programs have been evaluated using strong research designs and have been shown to produce positive impacts on some outcomes.[15] Of course, the moment new resources become available, wonderful new initiatives will crop up at the local level, created by committed leaders.

These federally funded programs are described in greater detail in the "Bridge to Reconnection" study. The study identifies 339,712 current opportunities and lays out how to expand this to one million each year with total annual federal expenditures of just $6.5 billion.[16] The study shows in detail that $170.9 billion in net fiscal gains would be produced by this investment through decreased crime, welfare, and health expenses and through increased taxes paid by the young people throughout their lives.

Another study reported that the lifetime direct cost to taxpayers for each twenty-year-old Opportunity Youth *not* reconnected to education or employment is $235,680.[17] The programs to reconnect them already exist, with proven results, at modest costs, with delivery systems already authorized in public law, with dedicated staff, strong demand from young people, and ample capacity at the local level to expand. These programs would produce an enormous return on investment (see Table 4.1). A Reconnecting Youth Campaign has been mobilized by a group of coalitions around this plan to produce one million program opportunities each year, initiated by the Forum for Youth Investment, YouthBuild USA, Jobs for the Future, the Aspen Institute, and the Center for Law and Social Policy.

Step 2: Reestablish Previously Successful Federal Programs

A government commission could assess the benefits of reinstating highly successful federal programs from the past such as the Civilian Conservation Corps (CCC) (1933–1942); the Comprehensive Employment and Training Act (CETA) program (1973–1982); and Youth Opportunity Grants (YOG) (1998–2005).

The CCC, as one example, provided direct training and employment to more than three million young men who in ten years built eight hundred parks and planted over one billion trees.[18] The CCC was responsible for over half the reforestation, public and private, done in the nation's history. (Sadly, the CCC was segregated, discriminated against black men, and was closed entirely to women, and even after an effort was undertaken to correct the racial discrimination, by 1936 black participation was up to only 10 percent.) Imagine what a new CCC could do in the present, absent discrimination and exclusion, and supporting the nonprofit organizations that have emerged to fill this space. The Corps Network, the national association of service and conservation corps across the country that grew out of the CCC and are now supported by a combination of local, state, federal, and private funding, has long advocated for the reestablishment of a CCC-like program to support the current network of nonprofits and engage thousands more diverse young adults, including Opportunity Youth and veterans.

Step 3: Collaborate with the Private Sector

Corporations report over five million unfilled jobs for which they cannot find qualified candidates, especially in the areas of health, information technology, advanced manufacturing, retail, and construction.[19] *Fortune* magazine estimated two hundred thousand unfilled construction jobs in 2016.[20] In 2015 Starbucks launched the 100,000 Opportunities Initiative, now involving over fifty corporations that have collectively committed to hiring one million Opportunity Youth.[21] Starbucks also wisely created a

TABLE 4.1 HOW TO REACH ONE MILLION OPPORTUNITY YOUTH

Program	Agency	Number of OY served	Target for growth	Projected federal cost per OY	Cost at estimate for growth	Estimated lifetime fiscal savings, by savings type				
						Taxes	Crime	Health	Welfare	Total
Comprehensive education and employment programs										
Job Corps	Labor	52,415	65,000	$30,106	$1,956,890,000	$6,857,500,000	$890,500,000	$2,721,550,000	$627,900,000	$11,097,450,000
YouthBuild	Labor	7,560	50,000	$15,000	$750,000,000	$5,275,000,000	$685,000,000	$2,093,500,000	$483,000,000	$8,536,500,000
Service and Conservation Corps	Various	14,780	65,000	$10,000	$650,000,000	$6,857,500,000	$890,500,000	$2,721,550,000	$627,900,000	$11,097,450,000
National Guard Youth ChalleNGe	Defense	9,000	20,000	$13,890	$277,800,000	$2,110,000,000	$274,000,000	$837,400,000	$193,200,000	$3,414,600,00
Reentry Employment Opportunities	Labor	6,130	18,000	$7,300	$131,400,000	$1,899,000,000	$246,600,000	$753,660,000	$173,880,000	$3,073,140,000
AmeriCorps National and Civilian Community Corps	CNCS	138	1,400	$29,674	$41,543,600	$147,700,000	$19,180,000	$58,618,000	$13,524,000	$239,022,000
AmeriCorps State and National	CNCS	6,260	50,000	$11,063	$553,150,000	$5,275,000,000	$685,000,000	$2,093,500,000	$483,000,000	$8,536,500,000
Subtotals		96,283	269,400		$4,360,783,600	$28,421,700,000	$3,690,780,000	$11,279,778,000	$2,602,404,000	$45,994,662,000
Short-term education programs										
Adult Secondary Education	Education	132,500	248,700	$300	$74,610,000	$26,237,850,000	$3,407,190,000	$10,413,069,000	$2,402,442,000	$42,460,551,000
Chafee Education and Training Vouchers	Health and Human Services	16,548	26,000	$2,555	$66,430,000	$2,743,000,000	$356,200,000	$1,088,620,000	$251,160,000	$4,438,980,000
Subtotals		149,048	274,700		$141,040,000	$28,980,850,000	$3,763,390,000	$11,501,689,000	$2,653,062,000	$46,899,531,000
Short-term employment programs										
WYIO Youth Activities	Labor	94,390	456,801	$4,424	$2,020,887,624	$48,192,505,500	$6,258,173,700	$19,126,257,870	$4,412,697,660	$77,989,634,730
Subtotals		94,390	456,801		$2,020,887,624	$48,192,505,500	$6,258,173,700	$19,126,257,870	$4,412,697,660	$77,989,634,730
Totals		339,721	1,000,901		$6,522,711,224	$105,595,055,500	$13,712,343,700	$41,907,724,870	$9,668,703,660	$170,883,827,730

Source: John M. Bridgeland, Erin S. Ingram, and Matthew Atwell, "A Bridge to Reconnection: A Plan for Reconnecting One Million Opportunity Youth Each Year through Federal Funding Streams," September 2016, p. 15, available at http://aspencommunitysolutions.org/wp-content/uploads/2017/06/BridgetoReconnection.2016.pdf.

Note: OY = opportunity youth; CNCS = Corporation for National and Community Service.

Youth Advisory Council for input on the supports needed for Opportunity Youth to become successful employees; and GAP has documented that the Opportunity Youth it employs have higher retention rates than other employees.[22] Expansion of the federal training programs described in "A Bridge to Reconnection" would prepare more youth for all these jobs and strengthen their success rates once they are hired by corporations. These programs would also prepare them for the union jobs that are now open in the construction industry.

Step 4: Mobilize for Investment at the Local Level

Each state, city, and county could create a study similar to "A Bridge to Reconnection" that identifies the number of young adults not employed or in school, the existing points of reconnection, and the new investments needed to invite Opportunity Youth into programs of education, job training, apprenticeships, community service, and leadership development that would prepare them for productive adulthood. Local public funds could expand existing options in those communities, create new ones to fill gaps, and work with local coalitions promoting collective strategies.

Following these four steps would fulfill the Kerner Commission's recommendation to create training and non-dead-end jobs as a solution to violence stemming from racism, poverty, and resentment, and it would reconnect all the Opportunity Youth.

WHO IS LEFT OUT AND NEEDS ATTENTION?

In addition to the two million low-income Opportunity Youth, another 166,900 young people ages eighteen to twenty-four are in federal and state prisons.[23] Despite having available the newly positive language of the term "Opportunity Youth," which signals the potential value to society of young people who are not employed or in school, unacceptable and inaccurate language is still being used to describe a different subset of American youth. The terms "thugs," "drug dealers," and "gangbangers" are used to dismiss them as having no value, deserving nothing except punishment and contempt. Leaders in both political parties do not hesitate to use these terms to discount a whole category of people. This is a serious mistake made from ignorance and bias. It has contributed to and grown out of the policies from the War on Drugs and mass incarceration that have been well documented in the book *The New Jim Crow*, by Michelle Alexander.[24] Many young people raised in poverty face a set of conditions that draw them down what seems to be the only lane open to them on a seemingly irreversible road to trouble. Sadly, society stands ready to punish them for the rest of their lives. Yet they are just as eager for opportunity as those who never committed a crime, joined a gang, or sold any drugs or who did so but were never caught. Or if caught, were not charged with a crime, as occurs often in upper-middle-class white communities when teenagers commit youthful errors.

Through my work in YouthBuild, I have gotten to know many individuals who had previously been involved in gangs or drug dealing. Among them, I have never met one who did not prefer to be a successful, contributing parent and leader. Given the distorted opportunity structure flowing from racism and classism, it also turns out that the leaders of gangs, who have risen in the street culture, are often highly intelligent and creative, resilient and resourceful. Their talents, when harnessed for good, informed by newly internalized positive values, are very powerful.

To illustrate this point, Mike Dean wrote a book about his own journey from drug dealer to pastor and nonprofit leader.[25] As director of Youth-Build Franklin County in Ohio, he now offers youth the same opportunities that helped him leave the streets. Ely Flores, now founding director of a nonprofit called LEAD in Los Angeles, testified before the Judiciary Committee of the House of Representatives in 2008 about his experiences in a gang lifestyle before finding his way out.[26] Robert Clark, once incarcerated, now advises the Newark, New Jersey, public school system on education policy. Antonio Ramirez, once active in a gang, is now the founding director of United at Peace, helping young people end violence in Rockford, Illinois. James Mackey, whose father and brothers had been incarcerated, leads a movement in Boston called Stuck on Replay to amend the Thirteenth Amendment of the Constitution, which ended slavery "except as a punishment for crime." Michael Donnelly, once gang involved, advises the police department in Bloomington, Illinois, on how to build positive relationships with youth. Antoine Bennett, who served eighteen months for a violent crime, later came to chair the homeowners association in Sandtown, Baltimore. He says, "I used to be a menace to my community; now I am a minister to it."[27]

These stories, and thousands of others, are books and films waiting to be written and filmed. Behind them is an enormous force for good waiting to be liberated. Most Americans are unaware of this untapped talent and goodness. Most are equally unaware of the pain and despair in poverty-stricken urban and rural communities. Most have never gotten to know a young person who grew up hungry, who was periodically and unpredictably homeless because of his parents' eviction for inability to pay the rent. They have not mentored a teenager whose father was incarcerated and whose stepfather abused him while his mother was at work at very low wages. They have not talked with teenagers who were invited by adults to carry bags of drugs here and there to get the fifty dollars that would enable them to bring some money and food home for their younger siblings. They do not know young people who moved through fifteen different foster-care families, being abused in some, and going to ten different schools during their vulnerable adolescence.

Until the heartbreaking stories of pain and the incredible stories of resilience and goodness of the young people who transcend these conditions are widely known, it is unlikely that we can build the political will to offer the opportunities needed for all. Some media efforts are under way. Grads of Life is a media campaign from Year Up, another fine program for Opportunity Youth, to persuade employers that young people who have been through hardships have learned valuable life skills. To win the hearts and minds of the public, we need daily stories on every channel about people who have emerged from poverty and are giving their lives to bettering their communities.

THE CORE CHALLENGE: BUILDING THE POLITICAL WILL TO INVEST IN OPPORTUNITY FOR ALL

The commission named the necessary condition: "to generate new will—the will to tax ourselves to the extent necessary to meet the vital needs of the nation."[28] But how do we generate that will? Regardless of their unlimited commitment and skill, the efforts of a generation of nonprofit leaders to spread their marvelous programs to full scale, to meet the enormous demand and the heart-wrenching needs in their communities, have been stymied by lack of political will.

My own steady efforts since 1984 to build political support for Youth-Build as a publicly funded approach to breaking the cycle of poverty resulted in the authorization of YouthBuild in federal law in 1992 and a cumulative federal expenditure since then of $1.7 billion; this allowed over 160,000 low-income young people to produce more than 35,000 units of affordable housing in over 250 urban and rural communities while working toward a high school diploma or its equivalent. Many emerged as superb local leaders.[29] It was clearly worth the investment. The affordable housing that students produced would have been sufficient impact, but the additional ripple effects from their personal transformations have been immeasurable.

The thirty-month 2016 interim report of a random-assignment evaluation done by MDRC on seventy-five YouthBuild programs shows meaningful gains for participants in GED acquisition, college access, wages, civic volunteering, and independence from public benefits.[30] Nonetheless, the public investment has neither met the demand nor tapped the full capacity: over 2,000 distinct local nonprofit and public entities have applied to the government since 1993 for funds to bring YouthBuild to their communities, but only about 145 are funded in 2017. The steady demand from youth and from local organizations warrants about ten times the annual investment, which in fiscal year 2017 was just $84 million. Unfortunately, real antipoverty investment seems to be distinctly against the grain of our political reality.

Even the modest scaling achieved would never have occurred had very rare elected officials not stepped forward as champions. Back in the early nineties, Senator John Kerry (D-MA) and Representative Major Owens (D-NY-Brooklyn) stepped forward, recruited bipartisan support, and got legislation passed. They served as champions for the annual appropriation as long as they served in Congress; then Senator Kirsten Gillibrand (D-NY) and Representative John Lewis (D-GA-Atlanta) took over, joined most recently by Senator Dean Heller (R-NV) and Representative Scott Perry (R-PA-York). Bipartisan support through four presidential administrations sustained the funding, and it was continued in the budget put forward by the federal Office of Management and Budget for the Trump administration in May 2017.

What was achieved over these decades was decidedly against the political trend. In 1991 when the YouthBuild legislation was first introduced, senior staff on the authorizing committee said to me, "Don't get your hopes up. Senators introduce thousands of bills for their constituents that never pass. Congress is not going in the direction of helping low-income communities. Unless John Kerry cares more about poor people than any senator has ever cared about poor people, this is dead in the water." Three weeks later the staffer called me and said, "You're in luck. John Kerry cares. He told me it was my job to get this passed." And so it did pass.

Later, in 1996, a staff member for House Speaker Newt Gingrich said to us, "You can forget about federal funding. Congress is not going to appropriate any more federal funds for programs that benefit poor people. It's all going to the states." (The federal appropriation for YouthBuild programs did survive through steadfast advocacy and bipartisan support.) Both of these statements were seared in my memory as unforgettable lessons.

Every year for twenty-five years, when lobbying for resources to benefit low-income youth and communities, I have been told on the Hill, "This is not a good year to ask for more. You are lucky and should be grateful for level funding." This resistance to adequate investment must change if we are ever to reverse the conditions in America that predictably produce poverty, despair, hate, rage, and violence.

I am not alone. Many people working at the grassroots level have created beautiful little oases of caring and opportunity. Some have created national networks of oases. We have learned how to empower individuals and neighborhoods to transform themselves and overcome enormous obstacles. We know how to transform depressed communities into thriving communities fired up by hope. But we are weary of oases. We need to unite all our separate ingenious efforts into one great torrent of powerful change that will bring the world closer to the vision we hold deep in our hearts. We are sick of witnessing poverty and despair and violence as if it cannot be changed. We are sad to be improving things for just a few thousand people when the conditions of poverty are damaging millions. *We need a breakthrough!* We have been caught in a paralyzing web of incremental struggle for small gains on too many separate and isolated single-issue fronts without overall vision or direction. I believe in patience and perseverance. I admire all the people who act from the bone-deep lifelong commitment to never giving up, never stopping, always doing the next task that could possibly contribute to a better world. I believe in being willing to take one small step at a time. It is a good way to live.

But we need a breakthrough! We need to break through our own willingness to settle for so little. We need to break out of our separate beautiful pieces of the work and weave them together into a more powerful whole. We need a larger movement, with higher expectations, broader goals, a more fleshed-out and coordinated set of goals that, taken together, would eliminate poverty and racism. I am aching for the breakthrough where we decide as a nation, a united nation, not to tolerate the ongoing slow and steady murder through poverty, despair, and criminalization of our own people. If America persists in neglecting our most impoverished citizens and assuming they are incapable of learning, working, contributing, and leading, we are doomed to the racism, violence, crime, poverty, divisions, and despair that our bad policies perpetuate.

The young leaders who developed the "Recommendations to Increase Opportunity and Decrease Poverty in America" in 2012 decided they needed a larger movement to achieve their goals. In 2015 they launched Opportunity Youth United to harness the passion for change among their peers by building a robust grassroots movement guided by principles of love and inclusion. They saw the need for unity among all affected groups plus allies.

Although poverty is disproportionately experienced by black Americans and other people of color as a result of the long-term structural racism in America, it is also importantly true that the largest single group of poor people in America is white. The percentage is lower among whites, but the absolute numbers are higher. According to census reports, 27 percent of Native Americans, 24 percent of black people, 21 percent of Latinos/as, 11 percent of Asian Americans, and 9 percent of white people in the United States lived in poverty in 2015.[31] Rounded off, this amounts to eighteen million white people, twelve million Latinos/as, ten million black people, one million Asian Americans, and one million Native Americans. The interests of all people living in poverty are similar. This fact must be understood and integrated into our analyses, our solutions, our organizing, and our politics. United and engaged, supported by allies, forty-two million poor people could build the political will to end poverty.

The perpetual neglect of poor people of all races seems founded both on a widespread assumption of their inferiority and on the private interests of a small minority that controls the flow of resources. Those who control the resources also control much of the narrative and many of the laws. We do not yet know how to persuade them that it is actually in their interest as humans to end poverty. But even if we fail to persuade them, they are a very small minority that should not control this democratic nation.

Martin Luther King, Jr., was building a multiracial, nonviolent, united movement for economic justice called the Poor People's Campaign at the time of his assassination two months after the release of the Kerner Report. Such a campaign is needed today. Racial equity, racial unity, and racial healing are all essential to our future together. Let us move to end poverty and racism. Let us build a fair and prosperous economy.

To do this we will need to tap into the infinite love that lies below the surface in our nation, listen to the hearts and minds of young leaders who have suffered from poverty and have a better vision, and build a dynamic movement that is a magnet to the best in all of us and together build a nation that is more wise, loving, respectful, and united and that produces a reasonable distribution of resources so that all people have the opportunities to fulfill their highest potential and their noblest aspirations within caring communities that offer respect and responsibility for all.

5

Fifty Years since the 1967 Rebellion, Have Health and Health Care Services Improved?

HERBERT C. SMITHERMAN, JR., LAMAR K. JOHNSON, AND ANIL N. F. ARANHA

> Of all the forms of inequality, injustice in health care is the most shocking and inhumane.
>
> —MARTIN LUTHER KING, JR., speech to the Medical Committee for Human Rights, 1966

DR. MARTIN LUTHER KING, JR., witnessed and experienced significant injustice in his life but characterized inequality and injustice in health care as the most shocking. This is because Dr. King understood that health is a precondition for achievement in any society, and therefore, it cannot be used as a reward for achievement. No real social or economic advancement of a people can occur with inequities in health. Children cannot learn appropriately in school if they are not healthy. One cannot be effective on a job if one is not healthy. One cannot fully and appropriately contribute to society if one is not healthy. Therefore, health is the prerequisite for a person to effectively participate and advance in any society. Also, distribution of resources for supporting a person's health in a just democracy must accordingly be fair and present to all. In this section, we discuss the progress of health and health care over the last fifty years since Detroit's 1967 rebellion and whether equity of the distribution of health resources, including fair opportunities needed to achieve well-being, have occurred.

To discuss health, it must first be defined. In this chapter, we use a modified version of the World Health Organization's definition of "health," expressed as "the state of physical, mental, spiritual and socioeconomic well-being of the individual and thus their community, not simply the absence of disease or infirmity."[1] This definition is important because it expands the definition of health to include social, behavioral, and environmental determinants of health and emphasizes the impact of community conditions of living on an individual's health status.

The interaction between individual and community and the health effects of socioeconomic and environmental factors were highlighted in a

2016 study, which showed that life expectancy increases continuously with income in the United States.[2] More interesting, however, was the large variation in life expectancy across geographic areas, which the study attributed to differences in health behaviors, including smoking, obesity, and exercise. Despite relative poverty, individuals in the lowest-income percentiles exhibited healthier behaviors and lived longer when they resided in areas with higher home prices and more college graduates. Concentrating poverty is detrimental. The study also noted that individuals of the lowest-income percentile living in cities like New York and San Francisco, which had higher overall levels of education and wealth, lived about five years longer than those of comparable income percentiles living in less affluent communities, such as Detroit. Other studies in Detroit, conducted in the 1960s, demonstrated that people in poor inner-city neighborhoods, with higher concentrations of African American residents, paid about 20 percent higher prices for food and prescription drugs than people in suburban communities while simultaneously being provided inferior quality food.[3] A more recent study, in 2008, observed higher rates of food safety violations by stores in poorer neighborhoods and those with higher concentrations of African American residents.[4] So, even after fifty years, predatory higher pricing for basic consumer goods and at times disproportionate poorer food quality in poor inner-city communities still exists; and nutritional health is obviously critical to overall health. These studies confirm and highlight what has been proved by multiple studies: that conditions of life linked to socioeconomic status and geographic location are strong predictors of variations in health.[5] Thus, with these community and socioeconomic factors playing such a vital factor in health, it is important to examine a few successful and significant social programs and policies implemented in the United States that provided safety net services in the realms of education, food security, and income and thus health.

One such policy is the Head Start program. Founded in 1965 as a comprehensive child development program, it was established to help communities meet the needs of disadvantaged children and has been recognized as one of the most successful social programs in U.S. history.[6] The goal was to promote school readiness of disadvantaged children under age five to ensure that they entered kindergarten on par with peers who had access to more resources. Children who had early childhood education and services, including health care and healthy meals, were shown to have a higher likelihood of graduating from high school, completing postsecondary education, and obtaining employment, thereby earning higher wages.[7] These children were also less likely to be in poor health than their counterparts who did not participate.[8]

Food insecurity is another major problem in the United States. Approximately one in eight households do not have enough food for all the household members. This lack of sufficient nourishment negatively impacts the opportunity for each family member to live a healthy and active lifestyle.[9] The Supplemental Nutrition Assistance Program (SNAP, formerly known as the food stamp program) became a permanent program in 1964 and now helps more than forty-five million low-income families maintain adequate nutrition.[10] SNAP not only has had a proven impact on reducing food insecurity but also has led to an increasing number of working households with less reliance on cash welfare assistance, a good indicator of economic advancement.[11]

The Earned Income Tax Credit (EITC) program benefits working low- and middle-income households and has become the largest federal aid program targeted to the working poor. The EITC provides a refundable income tax credit that can also be an additional source of income for those in need. The program has been directly associated with improved health outcomes for mothers and infants and reduces infant mortality. Additionally, EITC assists in lifting five million children out of poverty, and children out of poverty are proved to more likely perform better in school and have a higher educational attainment.[12]

Twenty percent of all U.S. children are currently living in poverty, and 11 percent of all children in the United States go hungry every day.[13] Despite these statistics, federal programs such as SNAP, Head Start, and EITC meant to protect families with low and moderate incomes have been constantly part of congressional budget cuts since their inception, undermining their effectiveness.[14] We must stop believing this policy ideology that says the wealthy need incentives, and so we give them money (tax breaks), and says the poor need incentives, and so we take money away from them (funding cuts).

Four hundred years of institutionalized health disparities, "inequality, [and] injustice in health care" will not be solved with federal public policies that increase effective individual taxes on the middle class and make cuts in Medicaid and Medicare, cuts in care to the disabled, cuts to mental health care services, cuts to nursing home care, cuts to community health centers, cuts to medical research, cuts to women's health, cuts to Planned Parenthood, cuts to SNAP, cuts in subsidies for mass transit, cuts in school lunch programs for inner-city children, cuts to funding for job training in urban areas, cuts to school loan programs for minority students, cuts to college aid and Pell Grants for disadvantaged students, cuts in after-school programs for inner-city children, cuts to public education by 20 percent, cuts in the Social Security program, cuts in housing resources to poor families in the Department of Housing and Urban Development, cuts to state funding for colleges so college education is no longer affordable for low- and middle-income families, cuts in corporate taxes and individual taxes on the wealthy, cuts in popular tax credits and tax deductions for the poor and middle class, and so on, to support trillions of dollars in tax cuts to the wealthiest 1 percent.

The poor and middle class also face an inadequate minimum wage, bank home foreclosures, and no effective wage increases for the middle class in the last thirty years. How can our country be serious about U.S. debt and deficit reduction and at the same time consent to tax cuts for the wealthy to the tune of $4 trillion to $6 trillion at the expense of social programs? U.S. debt and deficit reduction discussions in Congress are simply a congressional political gimmick to hide the true intention of cutting safety net spending for low- and middle-class families to provide tax breaks for the wealthy. With the continuous starting and stopping of programs for low- and moderate-income families, along with cutting and financially undermining safety net programs, it is no wonder that health, social and economic inequalities, inequities, and disparities continue fifty years since release of the 1968 Kerner Report. Hence, there continue to be "two societies, one black, one white—separate and unequal."[15] By cutting away the basic fabric of the social safety net, the United States will only continue to widen health disparities, reduce health care resources, and perpetuate social inequities between blacks and whites, creating a permanent underclass that will ultimately undermine the very foundation of our democracy and America itself. This country's current health care disparities and social inequities are in large part due to health and social policies, legislation, and choices on funding to low- and moderate-income safety net programs, because health and social policies, legislation, and funding drive health and social outcomes.

Some would argue that these disparities in health are the result of health behaviors driven simply by a conscious choice of an individual. Data and evidence do not support this argument. The social determinants of health and the effect of these policies on the vulnerable segments of the population are not addressed by this theory. The health and social disparities resulting from public policy funding and social engineering are the result of health behaviors as expressed by the social, cultural, and environmental determinants that condition and constrain behavior. Individuals do have responsibilities for themselves; however, a child born into abject poverty, living in a poor school district, whose family's heat and water are repeatedly turned off, and who is subject to food insecurity will experience involuntary behavioral effects and have limited choices in life.

THE KERNER COMMISSION LINKS RACE
AND SOCIOECONOMIC DISPARITIES

The Kerner Report was presented to President Lyndon Johnson in 1968 to explain why racial tensions in the United States had come to a head in the form of violent uprisings across the country in the summer of 1967. The report helped demonstrate how racial discrimination negatively affected many aspects of the lives of African Americans in the country. The overarching theme was that the violence that erupted was not a riot but rather a rebellion in response to systematic and systemic oppression of black and Latino people in the United States, which had led historically to poorer employment, education, housing, and health care and ultimately decreased social mobility in comparison to the dominant society.[16]

Health disparities are defined as "population-specific differences in the presence of disease, health outcomes, or access to healthcare."[17] Addressing these disparities is important, because estimates indicate that by 2050, one in two Americans will be a member of a minority group and, historically, evidence has demonstrated that minorities often receive inferior health care.[18]

HOW HEALTH STATISTICS HAVE CHANGED SINCE 1967

Overall health status in the United States has improved in measurable ways in this country since the Kerner Report. As of 2015, the average American lives about 8 years longer than in 1967, with the average male living about 76 years and the average female living about 81 years according to the Centers for Disease Control and Prevention's *Health, United States, 2016* study.[19] Furthermore, overall infant mortality has since decreased during the same time period.[20]

Has this improvement in health been reflected across all segments of the society? The answer is no. Although rates for infant mortality, death, and life expectancy have improved, gaps in these metrics have widened between blacks and whites in the last 50 years.[21] In 1967, life expectancy for whites was 6.5 years higher than that of nonwhites (blacks were not separately accounted for in 1967 but composed greater than 95 percent of the nonwhite population in the study). Compared to the more recent data of 2015, the life expectancy of blacks has increased by 16 percent, or 4.6 years, but is still lower than that for whites.[22] Thus, almost fifty years later, in 2015, the life expectancy of whites is 7 years higher than for blacks (compared to 6.5 years higher in 1967).

Infant mortality rate (the death of a baby before his or her first birthday) is another important measure of health in a population. This rate is often used as an indicator to measure the health and well-being of a nation. In 1967, the infant mortality rate was 19.7 deaths per 1,000 births for whites versus 37.5 per 1,000 births among blacks.[23] Fifty years later, infant mortality rates are down about 75 percent for whites (4.9 per 1,000) and about 71 percent for blacks (10.9 per 1,000 births), yet proportionally the gap has widened—the infant mortality rate of blacks in 1967 was 47.5 percent higher than whites and has subsequently risen to 55.1 percent in

2014—with an overall infant mortality rate in blacks being more than twice that of whites.[24]

Maternal mortality is defined as death related to or aggravated by pregnancy or pregnancy management that occurs within forty-two days after the end of pregnancy. It is another metric that, despite showing a dramatic decline overall in the last fifty years, continues to show significant

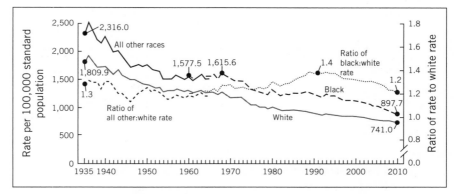

Figure 5.1 Age-adjusted rates and ratio of rates by race, 1935–2010
Source: Adapted from Donna L. Hoyert, "75 Years of Mortality in the United States, 1935–2010," *NCHS Data Brief,* no 88 (2012): 1.
Note: 2010 data are preliminary. Age-adjusted rates are per 100,000 standard U.S. population. Rates for 2001–2009 are revised and may differ from rates previously published.

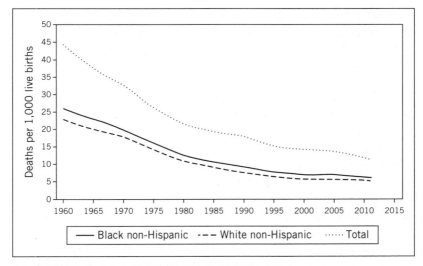

Figure 5.2 U.S. infant mortality rates by race, 1960–2015
Source: Adapted from Marian F. MacDorman and T. J. Mathews, "Understanding Racial and Ethnic Disparities in U.S. Infant Mortality Rates," *NCHS Data Brief,* no. 74 (2011), available at http://www.cdc.gov/nchs/data/databriefs/db74.htm.

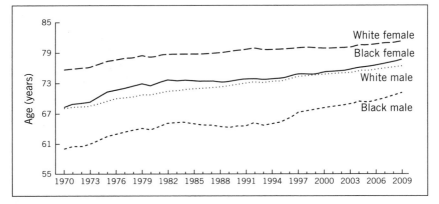

Figure 5.3 Life expectancy at birth by race and sex, 1970–2009
Source: Adapted from Elizabeth Arias, "United States Life Tables, 2009," *National Vital Statistics Reports* 62, no 7 (2014), available at https://www.cdc.gov/nchs/data/nvsr/nvsr62/nvsr62_07.pdf.

disparity between blacks and whites. The risk of maternal mortality has remained between three and four times higher in black women compared with white women over the last sixty years. Higher poverty rates were associated with higher maternal mortality risks for all women, though disparities persisted when adjusted for a given rate of poverty. These disparities surfaced when rates were compared to other countries, notably showing that the U.S. maternal mortality status is significantly higher in comparison to other countries. In fact, according to a 2009 World Health Organization study of 2005 statistics, at 15 maternal deaths per 100,000 live births, the United States has higher maternal mortality than forty-one other countries, including Canada, Australia, Japan, and all the Western and Northern European countries.[25] Because of the association of higher poverty rates with maternal mortality, it may be to our advantage to evaluate our policies and social and health investments and compare them to the countries that are ahead of the United States in these and other indicators of health and health and social outcomes.

Since records have been kept, gaps have existed in all-cause mortality between whites and blacks. In 1967, the all-cause mortality rate for nonwhites (blacks) was 15 percent higher than for whites. This gap between blacks and whites widened to 40 percent for all-cause mortality in all age groups younger than sixty-five in 2015. Furthermore, at all ages younger than sixty-five, blacks also had higher rates of chronic illnesses such as heart disease, cancer, cerebrovascular disease, diabetes, and HIV than whites. This difference was even more evident in the age group of eighteen to thirty-four, with blacks having higher death rates than whites for homicide and pregnancy, as well as childbirth-related conditions.[26]

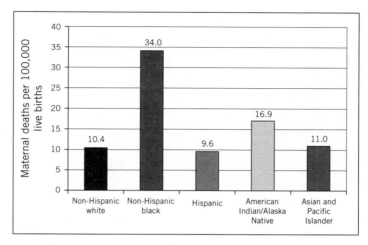

Figure 5.4 Maternal mortality rate by race/ethnicity, 2005
Source: Adapted from Gopal K. Singh, "Maternal Mortality in the United States, 1935–2007,"
2010, available at https://www.hrsa.gov/ourstories/mchb75th/mchb75maternalmortality.pdf.

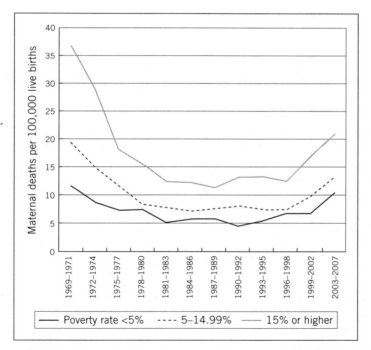

Figure 5.5 Maternal mortality rate by county-level family poverty rate, 1969–2007
Source: Adapted from Gopal K. Singh, "Maternal Mortality in the United States, 1935–2007,"
2010, available at https://www.hrsa.gov/ourstories/mchb75th/mchb75maternalmortality.pdf.

These health metrics illustrate that even though the health of blacks in this country has improved, the gaps in health status between blacks and whites is worsening. Why? The literature shows a direct relationship between income, wealth, and life expectancy whether comparing nations to one another, states to one another, local municipalities to one another, city suburbs to one another, or communities to one another. As the income and wealth of a community rises, so does the life expectancy of its population. As the economy of a community or a country improves, so does its health status indicators. Even more important, as income inequities within a society decline, so do its death rates.[27] Over the past twenty-five years, the wealth gap between blacks and whites has tripled, according to research by Brandeis University and others, with median household wealth of whites at $134,230, Hispanics at $13,730, and blacks at $11,030.[28] Poverty and lack of resources in large segments of U.S. society with associated joblessness creates extremely vulnerable and fragile communities, leading to low levels of social structure and organization and ultimately making mutually dependent institutions such as family, economy, education, community, health, politics, and so on, unsustainable. Families dissolve and community disorganization becomes the norm, resulting in cumulative cycles of reinforced poverty and poor health.[29] In essence, lifestyle is a composite expression of the social and cultural circumstances that condition and constrain behavior, not just the personal decisions that individuals might make in choosing one behavior over another. The objective therefore should be to fight poverty, not people in poverty.

Assessment of the British National Health System in the Whitehall I Study done in the 1970s also showed a failure to decrease class differences in health outcomes based on income gaps in its society. Despite having national health care, the poor in Great Britain saw class and income gaps in their health outcomes. Summing up the British Whitehall Studies, the researchers concluded, regarding the health outcomes of Britain, that "more attention should be paid to the social environments, job design, and the consequences of income inequality."[30]

Can poverty or large income inequalities be eradicated in the United States? Given that this country put a man on the moon, put a rover on Mars, and found over $40 billion for the city of New York forty-eight hours after the 9/11 attack on the World Trade Center, it is plausible that this country can solve whatever problem it puts its mind and will toward.

Historical Improvement of Health Disparities

In two periods of U.S. health reforms, efforts specifically sought to correct race-based health disparities and resulted in dramatically positive effects on African American health.

The first period occurred from 1865 to 1872, during the nation's post–Civil War Reconstruction. During this era, federal legislation and policy led to the establishment of black medical schools, hospitals, and clinics throughout the South. These improvements reduced to some extent the alarmingly high death rates among African Americans and improved many health status indicators and outcome parameters.

The second period of improvement in African American health status, which lasted from 1965 to 1975, was an outgrowth of the civil rights movement. During this time, the modern health system made its first real move toward solving the racial health disparities via judicial and legislative measures. The 1964 Civil Rights Act outlawed discrimination in government-funded health programs to improve access to health care for all people. Hospital desegregation also occurred, integrating both the medical staff and the patient populations. Medicare and Medicaid were established, which gave a large number of African Americans access to health care for the first time in their lives. Last, a movement toward community and neighborhood health centers increased access to basic primary care in African American communities. African American health status improved dramatically in virtually every measurable parameter during this ten-year period. However, after 1975, the gains halted and African Americans experienced a continuous decline in health status compared to whites.[31] As discussed above, federal and state funding cuts began to accelerate in 1975, slowly reversing the policy and funding gains of the previous decade.[32]

Strategies for Eliminating Health Disparities

Healthy People, 2010, an end-of-decade assessment of health performed by the Department of Health and Human Services, recommended strategies to reduce health disparities that built on the *2005 National Healthcare Disparities Report*.[33] The following is a summary of the proposed interventions at the state and local levels.

- Developing comprehensive surveillance instruments to enhance data collection that would improve measures of education, income, and socioeconomic status to better understand the problem
- Developing needed policies and funding for appropriate health and social interventions that achieve better care
- Combining and coordinating the allocation of health and social resources with a common focus to achieve healthy people and healthy communities
- Making care affordable

Ultimately, the *2005 National Healthcare Disparities Report* identified that disparities in health care could be interpreted only within the context of disparities in health and that eliminating disparities in health care is a logical method for eliminating associated disparities in health. This requires consistent and sustained policy, legislation, and funding for safety net programs, not the cyclical increase and decrease in funding of the past fifty years.

National Issues in Health and Health Care

The United States spends over $3 trillion a year on health care, more than any other developed nation, and in spite of this has worse health outcomes.[34] This is because although the United States delivers some of the best medical care in the world, we have the worst way of paying for it, and not everyone has equal access to it. Chronic disease, such as heart disease, cancer, stroke, chronic obstructive pulmonary disease, and diabetes, has become an epidemic in this country and is now responsible for more than three out of every four deaths each year (1.8 million deaths in all) and carries an annual financial burden of $350 billion. In addition, approximately one hundred million Americans, almost one-third of the population, experience disability or severe limitation of their daily activities because of chronic disease.[35] This is unfortunate, because while chronic diseases, fueled by unhealthy lifestyle and behavior, deteriorating social conditions, and reduced access to quality health care, are among the most common and costly diseases, they are also among the most preventable.

The major coverage provisions of the Affordable Care Act (ACA) went into effect in January 2014 and have led to significant coverage gains. The percentage of nonelderly population that lacked insurance was approximately 18 percent in 2010 but fell to 10.5 percent at the end of 2015. Coverage gains from 2013 to 2015 affected all of the population but were most notably felt among African Americans, Latinos, and Native Americans, who had higher uninsured rates historically than whites. Therefore, this law greatly benefited the poor and middle class.[36]

In its first two years of full implementation, the ACA significantly reduced socioeconomic disparities in health care access for low-income American families. The gains in insurance coverage were twice as large in Medicaid expansion states as compared to nonexpansion states.[37] Despite this improvement in health care access, multiple ACA repeal attempts were made in 2017. The American Health Care Act (AHCA) and the Senate's bills, the Better Care Reconciliation Act (BCRA) and the Graham-Cassidy bill, were recently presented before Congress and voted on, with no debate, no hearings, and hasty Congressional Budget Office analyses, with many congressional members admitting not to have read the bills.[38] None of these bills made it out of Congress. Under these bills, health insurance would have been cut for as many as twenty-four million people, and large companies would no longer have had to provide health insurance coverage to their employees, undercutting where most families in the United States receive their health insurance coverage. Additionally, these bills proposed large cuts to Medicaid spending, which covers care for seventy million people in the United States, primarily poor seniors and the disabled. Medicaid would have been cut by $880 billion dollars over ten years, hurting many of the most vulnerable Americans in the country.[39] The bills also allowed health insurance companies to opt out of covering any basic services they choose, such as hospitalization, pregnancy, emergency department care, gynecological services, cancer care, and behavioral health and drug treatment coverage (including mental health) and eliminated the Prevention and Public Health Fund, which focuses on preventing the chronic diseases that are becoming so prevalent. The bills went well beyond trying to reverse the gains of the ACA to making additional and significant cuts in the traditional 1965 Medicaid program.[40] If this legislation had passed, it would have completely undermined any progress that was made regarding health and health disparities over the last fifty years, again highlighting this country's cyclical up and down social and health policy funding.

Many studies have proved that there is a link between poorer health outcomes and poverty, social determinants of health, and environment, such as poor access to housing, education, food, and health care. In large part because of the effects of institutionalized racism in policy and practice, there have historically been socioeconomic disparities, which have also led in many ways to the health disparities that we continue to see today. We can predict in the aggregate how long a person will live in the United States on the basis of whether that individual graduates from high school, where that individual lives, and his or her household income. Life expectancy should not be based on the resources one has access to in the United States.

These and other studies have also demonstrated the measurable positive effect that sustained social programs have on improving the basic aspects and quality of life and, accordingly, overall health. Logically, then, improving health and eliminating health disparities can occur through sustained and coordinated bipartisan policies, legislation, and funding of programs to create a baseline safety net in this country below which no citizen should fall. Much of the debate since 1967 is about where the baseline should be drawn. Some policy makers believe there should be no safety net and care for the poor and indigent should be provided through charity care in the private sector alone. The argument could then be made that other public goods that all citizens share, including clean air, clean water, national defense, public education, public parks, public roads, and tax collection, should be provided by the private sector alone. Health is also a public good. Immunizing everyone, for example, prevents the spread of disease. Protecting individuals protects us all. Government has a role in maintaining and monitoring the public goods enjoyed by all citizens. The question of where the baseline safety net should be has been debated for the last fifty years. Without a consensus to the answer, the safety net eligibility line moves up and down (mostly down), creating an erratic, confusing, and often unpredictable system of care and support for low- and middle-income people and resulting in disparities and inequities in health and social outcomes in our country.

CONCLUSION

Over the course of the last half century (1967–2017), our country has witnessed numerous wars, stock market booms and busts, and dramatic transformation of the sociodemographics of the United States, a nation of over 325 million.[41] How we use our resources and how we invest in our society as it relates to human development is the question this country has not come to consensus on. Breaking the tight linkages between income, wealth, and health is about social and economic policy—that is, investing in education, housing, transportation, police (security), jobs and employment, childcare, recreation, public health, and the private sector, the primary wealth-creating segments of a society. A person in the lower economic stratum of society with heart disease and who smokes dies earlier than a person in a higher economic stratum with the same risk factors. Why? Social determinants of disease.[42] How does social policy drive health? Social policies drive income inequalities, which drive health inequalities. For people to flourish in their lives, they must live in a more just society. We must invest early and set good social and health trajectories in our society, or we will engage in perpetual late-life damage control, ultimately leading to poorer national health, higher national health costs, and less national health care access—all resulting in a poorer economy.[43] In the fifty years since the 1967 rebellion, have health and health care services improved? Yes; however, the gaps between blacks and whites continue to widen in this country, largely because of varying public policy, inconsistent public safety net funding, and public- and private-sector institutional injustice.

But we are hopeful. In the words of the late Reverend Martin Luther King, Jr., we "have a dream" that someday in the United States of America health care will be a right and not a privilege, and it will be enjoyed by all citizens.[44] If we continue on the path of the progress achieved in the last decade, we could get there—life, liberty, and the pursuit of happiness, including justice, food, housing, and health care for all—well within the next half century. We must though come together as a nation with a bipartisan-coordinated, comprehensive, collaborative, consensus-based social and health policy agenda to achieve this goal. If any country can do it, America can.

Education Policy

6

Education and the Path to One Nation, Indivisible

LINDA DARLING-HAMMOND

N 1968, the Kerner Report concluded that the nation was "moving toward two societies, one black, one white—separate and unequal."[1] Without major social changes, the Kerner Commission warned, the country faced a "kind of urban apartheid" in its major cities.[2] Today, fifty years after the report was issued, that prediction characterizes most of our large urban areas, where intensifying segregation and concentrated poverty have collided with disparities in school funding to reinforce educational inequality.

While racial achievement gaps in education have remained stubbornly large, segregation has been increasing steadily, creating a growing number of apartheid schools that serve almost exclusively students of color, most of whom live in poverty. These schools are often severely under-resourced, and they struggle to close academic gaps while underwriting the greater costs of addressing the effects of poverty—hunger, homelessness, and other traumas experienced by children and families in low-income communities.[3] For all these reasons, research has found, the extent to which students attend schools with other low-income students is one of the strongest predictors of their achievement.[4]

These trends once again threaten the very fabric of our nation, as gaps in educational opportunity and attainment continue at a time when those without education are locked out of the knowledge-based economy we live in.

GROWING SEGREGATION AND POVERTY

The root of inequality in educational outcomes in the United States is the combination of growing poverty and resegregation, along with inequality in schools' funding and resources. U.S. childhood poverty rates have grown by more than 50 percent since the 1970s and are now by far the highest among Organization for Economic Cooperation and Development nations, reaching 22 percent in the last published statistics.[5] Among children attending U.S. public schools, more than half now qualify for free or reduced-price lunch—the highest percentage since the National Center for Education Statistics began tracking this figure decades ago.[6] Further, American children living in poverty have a much weaker safety net than their peers in other industrialized countries, where universal health care, housing subsidies, and high-quality universally available childcare are the norm.

In addition, a growing share of poor children attends school in districts where poverty is concentrated, which creates more profound challenges for their education. (See Figure 6.1.) In 2007, of the 8.5 million low-income students in the country, about one in five lived in districts with a poverty rate of over 30 percent. Only five years later, by 2012, more than one-third (36 percent) of low-income children lived in high-poverty districts.[7] The growing poverty caused by the Great Recession, which began in 2007–2008, contributed to this concentration, and the growing disparity in incomes and wealth—now wider than it has been since 1929—has reinforced it.

The top 1 percent of families controlled less than 10 percent of national income in the late 1970s, when income distribution was at its most equitable point in the last century; this rose to more than 20 percent by the end of

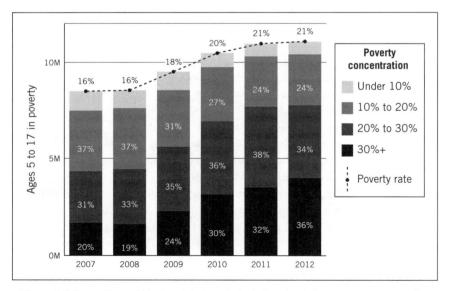

Figure 6.1 Proportions of black and Latino students in schools by poverty concentration
Source: Bruce D. Baker, David G. Sciarra, and Danielle Farrie, *Is School Funding Fair? A National Report Card* (Newark, NJ: Education Law Center, 2015).

2012. Even more alarming, the share of household wealth owned by the top one-tenth of 1 percent of the U.S. population has increased from 7 to 22 percent in the same period. The top 0.1 percent includes 160,000 families with total net assets greater than those of 145 million families at the bottom of the income distribution.[8]

At the same time, the middle class is shrinking. The proportion of Americans living in middle-income neighborhoods decreased from 65 percent to 42 percent between 1970 and 2009.[9] Meanwhile, the proportion living in affluent neighborhoods more than doubled—from 7 percent to 15 percent—as did the share living in poor neighborhoods—from 8 to 18 percent. Economic segregation of upper- and lower-income households increased in twenty-seven of America's thirty largest urban areas.[10] As middle-class neighborhoods have declined, America's economic landscape is increasingly polarized.[11]

The most recent federal data show that in most major American cities, a majority of African American and Latino students attend public schools where at least 75 percent of students are poor.[12] Increasingly, these schools are segregated by both race and class because racial segregation has also been increasing. For example, in Chicago and New York City, more than 95 percent of both black and Latino students attend majority-poverty schools, most of which are also majority minority.[13] As the UCLA Civil Rights project data show, high-poverty schools are almost entirely populated by black and Latino students, and low-poverty schools have very few such students. (See Figure 6.2.)

After a dramatic decline in segregation, especially in the South, in the two decades after 1968, the discontinuation of desegregation assistance and court orders in many districts, coupled with increasing residential segregation has led to a steady climb. In 1968, about 60 percent of black students nationwide—and about 80 percent in the South—attended intensely segregated schools (where minority students constitute 90 percent or more of the total).[14] At the low point of segregation, in 1988, just over a third of black students (and just over 20 percent in the South) attended intensely segregated schools. By 2010, the proportion exceeded 40 percent nationwide and more than 50 percent in the Northeast, where segregation has increased steadily for the last fifty years. (See Figure 6.3.)

Today, about half as many black students attend majority-white schools (just over 20 percent) as did so in 1988, when about 44 percent did so.[15] (See Figure 6.4.) A 2016 study by Janie Boschma and Ronald Brownstein showed that high rates of poverty, housing segregation, and economic polarization "have left most African American and Hispanic students marooned in schools where economic struggle is the rule and financial stability—and all the social and educational benefits that flow from that—is very much the exception." Meanwhile, white students are the least likely group to go to school with students of other races.[16]

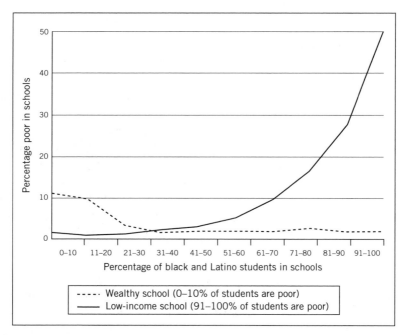

Figure 6.2 School poverty rates by percentage of black and Latino students in schools
Source: Jason M. Breslow, Evan Wexler, and Robert Collins, "The Return of School Segregation in Eight Charts," *Frontline*, July 15, 2014, available at https://www.pbs.org/wgbh/frontline/arti cle/the-return-of-school-segregation-in-eight-charts.

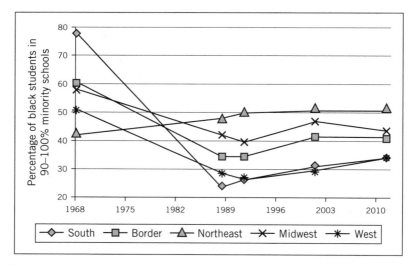

Figure 6.3 Percentage of black students in intensely segregated minority schools by region, 2012
Source: National Center for Education Statistics *Public Elementary/Secondary School Universe Survey Data*, available at https://nces.ed.gov/ccd/pubschuniv.asp; Gary Orfield, *Public School Desegregation in the United States, 1968–1980* (Washington, DC: Joint Center for Political Studies, 1983).

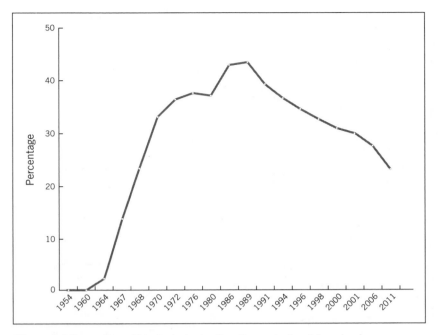

Figure 6.4 Proportion of black students attending majority white schools
Source: National Center for Education Statistics *Public Elementary/Secondary School Universe Survey Data*, available at https://nces.ed.gov/ccd/pubschuniv.asp; Gary Orfield, *Public School Desegregation in the United States, 1968–1980* (Washington, DC: Joint Center for Political Studies, 1983).

Among the reasons for this growing resegregation is the abandonment of desegregation orders that have been fought in many cities. The degree of integration has declined significantly in districts when court oversight is terminated. (See Figure 6.5.)

EDUCATIONAL ACHIEVEMENT GAPS CONTINUE

Where children go to school matters greatly for their success. In a case brought to challenge school desegregation efforts in Jefferson County, Kentucky, and Seattle, Washington, more than 550 scholars signed on to a social science report filed as an amicus brief that summarized an extensive body of research showing the persisting inequalities of segregated minority schools. The scholars concluded that "the large volume of research conducted since *Brown* . . . has shown that segregated, predominantly minority schools offer students unequal and inferior educational opportunities. . . . Educational inequalities in racially isolated schools arise in several ways, such as limited educational resources (whether measured by class size, facilities, or per-pupil spending), fewer qualified teachers, and inadequate access to peers who can help improve achievement. . . . Not surprisingly, measures of educational outcomes, such as scores on standardized tests and high school graduation rates, are lower in predominantly minority schools."[17]

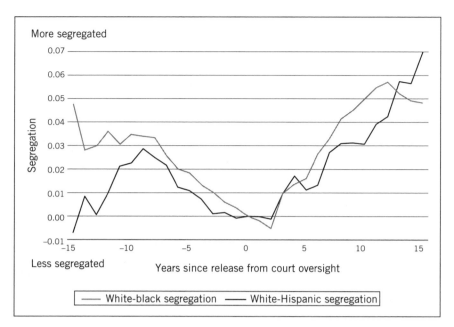

Figure 6.5 Degree of segregation relative to years since release from court oversight
Source: Data from Sean F. Reardon, Elena Grewel, Demetra Kalogrides, and Erica Greenberg, "Brown Fades: The End of Court-Ordered School Desegregation and the Resegregation of American Public Schools," *Journal of Policy Analysis and Management* 31, no. 4 (2012): 876–904.

Results from Desegregation and Equity Investments

In a study of the effects of court-ordered desegregation on students born between 1945 and 1970, economist Rucker Johnson found that graduation rates climbed by two percentage points for every year a black student attended an integrated school.[18] Black students exposed to court-ordered desegregation for five years experienced a 15 percent increase in wages and an eleven-percentage-point decline in annual poverty rates. The difference was tied to the fact that schools under court supervision offered higher per-pupil spending and smaller student-teacher ratios, among other resources. While there were positive outcomes for blacks, court-ordered desegregation caused no statistically significant harm for whites.

Efforts like these were taken up in many communities during the 1960s and 1970s. As a result, there was a noticeable reduction in educational inequality in the decade after the original Kerner Report, when desegregation and school finance reform efforts were launched and when the Great Society's War on Poverty increased investments in poor urban and rural schools. At that time, substantial gains were made in equalizing both educational inputs and outcomes. The Elementary and Secondary Education Act of 1965 targeted resources to communities with the most need, recognizing that where children grow up should not determine where they end up. Employment and welfare supports reduced childhood poverty to levels about 60 percent of what they are today[19] and greatly improved children's access to health care.

The Elementary and Secondary Assistance Act promoted desegregation, the development of magnet schools, and other strategies to improve urban and poor rural schools. This effort to level the playing field for children was supported by intensive investments in bringing and keeping talented individuals in teaching, improving teacher education, and investing in research and development—investments that paid off in measurable ways.[20]

By the mid-1970s, urban schools spent as much as suburban schools and paid their teachers well; perennial teacher shortages had nearly ended; and gaps in educational attainment had closed substantially. Federally funded curriculum investments transformed teaching in many schools. Innovative schools flourished in many cities. Financial aid for higher education was sharply increased, especially for need-based scholarships and loans. For a brief period in the mid-1970s, black and Hispanic high school graduates attended college at the same rate as whites, the only time this has occurred, before or since.

Improvements in educational achievement for students of color followed. In reading, large gains in black students' performance throughout the 1970s and early 1980s reduced the achievement gap considerably, cutting it by more than half for thirteen-year-olds (from thirty-nine points on the National Assessment of Educational Progress to just eighteen points) between 1971 and 1988.[21] The achievement gap in mathematics also narrowed by twenty points (about a third) over the same general period.[22]

Gains Reversed

Unfortunately, the gains from the Great Society programs were lost during the Reagan administration, when most targeted federal programs supporting investments in college access and K–12 schools in urban and poor rural areas were reduced or eliminated, and federal aid to schools was cut from 12 percent to 6 percent of a shrinking total. Meanwhile, childhood poverty rates, homelessness, and lack of access to health care also grew with cuts in other federal programs that supported housing subsidies, health care, and child welfare.

By 1991, when Jonathan Kozol wrote *Savage Inequalities*, which vividly describes the dramatic differences in resources among schools serving different groups of children,[23] stark differences had reemerged between segregated urban schools and their suburban counterparts, which generally spent twice as much as urban schools. Achievement gaps began to grow once again, and while there have been small gains in the thirty years since, the gaps in achievement between black and white students are larger today than they were then. For example, black thirteen-year-olds have gained only four points in reading since 1988, while white students have gained nine points, leaving a gap that is nearly 30 percent larger today than it was three decades ago. Similarly, in mathematics, black thirteen-year-olds actually score one point lower than they did when the gap was smallest in 1990, while white students now score five points higher; so the gap has increased by 30 percent in that subject as well.

While high school completion rates have steadily risen for all students since 2003,[24] there are still significant gaps in high school graduation for non-Asian students of color and white students.[25] White and Asian students graduate within four years of starting high school at rates of 88 percent and 90 percent, respectively, whereas black, Hispanic, and Native American students graduate at rates of 75 percent, 78 percent, and 72 percent, respectively. This means that about one in four historically underserved minority students still fails to graduate high school within four years.

The gaps are much greater within states and cities, especially those that are strongly segregated. For example, only 64 percent of black students graduate in four years in Wisconsin, compared to 93 percent of white students, and only 56 percent of black students graduate in four years in Nevada, compared to 78 percent of white students.

Educational shortcomings plus lack of family resources and cuts in federal funding for financial aid extend these disparities into higher education. At a time when more than 70 percent of jobs require postsecondary education, only about a third of black and Hispanic young people ages eighteen to twenty-four are enrolled in two- or four-year colleges, compared to 42 percent of white youth.[26] (See Figure 6.6.) In the population as a whole, disparities in access to college are obvious: among whites, about 33 percent have at least four years of college (as 54 percent of Asians do), whereas the proportions of blacks and Hispanics are just 22.5 percent and 15.5 percent, respectively. And while there are gains to be applauded, the gaps in college attainment have grown between whites compared with blacks and Hispanics since 1968.[27]

THE OPPORTUNITY GAP

Despite a single-minded focus on raising achievement and closing gaps during the era of No Child Left Behind (from 2002 until 2015), many states focused on testing without investing in the resources needed to achieve higher standards. Investments in the education of students of color that characterized the school desegregation and finance reforms of the 1960s and 1970s have never been fully reestablished in the years since. Had the rate of progress achieved in the 1970s and early 1980s been con-

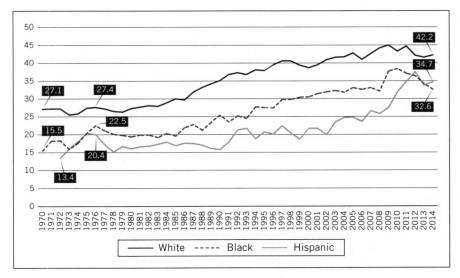

Figure 6.6 Percentage of eighteen- to twenty-four-year-olds enrolled in two- or four-year college
Source: National Center for Education Statistics, *Digest of Education Statistics: 2015*, table 302.60, available at https://nces.ed.gov/programs/digest/d16/tables/dt16_302.60.asp.

tinued, the achievement gap would have been fully closed by the beginning of the twenty-first century. Unfortunately, that did not occur.

While nations like Canada, Finland, and Singapore, which are now high achieving and equitable, built on the progressive reforms they launched in the 1970s,[28] the United States sought to reverse the progress it made during the 1970s for much of the next three decades and actually undid much of it. Although some federal support to high-need schools and districts was restored during the 1990s, it was not enough to fully recoup the earlier losses, and after 2000, inequality grew once again.

Unequal Funding

These inequities are in part a function of how public education is funded in the United States. In most cases, education costs are supported primarily by local property taxes, along with state grants-in-aid that are somewhat equalizing but typically not sufficient to close the gaps caused by differences in local property values. In most states, the wealthiest districts spend at least three times what the poorest districts can spend per pupil, differentials that translate into dramatically different salaries for educators, as well as inequitable learning conditions for students.[29] Within large districts, there are also disparities in how funds are allocated to schools serving different kinds of students, usually favoring those with more political clout.

Further, the wealthiest states spend about three times what the poorer states spend.[30] So the advantages available to children in the wealthiest communities of high-spending and high-achieving states like Massachusetts, Connecticut, and New Jersey are dramatically different from the schooling experiences of those in the poorest communities of low-spending states like Arizona, Mississippi, and North Carolina, where buildings are crumbling, classes are overcrowded, instructional materials are inadequate, and staff are often transient and underprepared.

Effects of Unequal Funding

These inequalities translate into disparities in the number and quality of teachers and other educators available to students and into unequal access to high-quality curriculum. As segregation and school funding disparities grew worse after the 1980s, the practice of lowering or waiving credentialing standards to fill classrooms in high-minority, low-income schools—a practice that is unheard of in high-achieving nations and in other professions—became commonplace in many U.S. states, especially those with large minority and immigrant populations, like California, Texas, Florida, and New York.

In many states where school funding schemes have been litigated, plaintiffs have documented that teachers in high-need schools have, on average, lower levels of experience and education, are less likely to be prepared and certified for the field they teach, and have lower scores on both certification tests and other measures of academic achievement. Further, a growing body of research has shown that these kinds of qualifications matter for student achievement. Studies at the state, district, school, and individual-student level have found that teachers' academic background, preparation for teaching, certification status, and experience significantly affect their students' learning gains.[31]

In combination, teachers' qualifications can have substantial effects. For example, a large-scale study of high school student achievement in North Carolina found that students' achievement growth was significantly higher if they were taught by a teacher who was certified in his or her teaching field, fully prepared upon entry (rather than entering through the state's alternative lateral-entry route), had higher scores on the teacher licensing test, graduated from a competitive college, had taught for more than two years, or had National Board certification.[32] Taken individually, each of these qualifications was associated with greater teacher effectiveness.

Moreover, the researchers found that the combined influence on achievement growth of having a teacher with most of these qualifications, compared to one with few of them, was larger than the effects of race and parent education combined or larger than the average difference in achievement between a typical white student with college-educated parents and a typical black student with high school educated parents. While achievement from one year to the next is still largely dependent on prior achievement, this finding suggests that the achievement gap might be reduced over time if minority students were more routinely assigned highly qualified teachers rather than the poorly qualified teachers they most often encounter.

These findings appear to extend around the world. A 2007 study by Motoko Akiba, Gerald LeTendre, and Jay Scribner,[33] for example, found that the most significant predictors of mathematics achievement across forty-six nations included teachers holding full certification, having a college major in mathematics or mathematics education, and having at least three years of teaching experience. The researchers also found that, although the national level of teacher quality in the United States is similar to the international average, the opportunity gap in U.S. students' access to qualified teachers between students of high and low socioeconomic status is among the largest in the world.

But such disparities, which have come to appear inevitable in the United States, are *not* the norm in developed nations around the world, which typically fund their education systems centrally and equally, with additional resources often going to the schools where students' needs are greater.[34] The more equitable investments made by high-achieving nations are also steadier and more focused on critical elements of the system: the quality of teachers and teaching, the development of curriculum and assessments that encourage ambitious learning by both students and teachers, and the design of schools as learning organizations that support continuous reflection and improvement. With the exception of a few states with enlightened long-term leadership, the United States, by contrast, has failed to maintain focused investments on these essential elements.

States like Connecticut, Massachusetts, New Jersey, and North Carolina have made these investments at different moments in time with payoffs in higher achievement and greater equity.[35] However, there is often eventually political pushback against these investments that can cause them to lose ground, at least partially.

Effects of Privatization

Meanwhile, in recent years, there has been a focused effort to turn public schools in many cities over to private managers, often for-profit organizations, which has been stimulated by fiscal crises and reinforced by federal incentives under No Child Left Behind to close district-run schools and replace them with charter schools. For example, in the last two years, a fiscal crisis in Detroit led to the installation of an emergency manager who aimed to replace the entire school district with charter schools. In Pennsylvania, Governor Tom Corbett cut Philadelphia's budget by $500 million, throwing the city into fiscal distress overnight. The local school board was eliminated, hundreds of educators were fired, and a newly installed city manager carved up the school district and gave large sections of it to private operators. After Hurricane Katrina, all seven thousand district educators were fired and most schools (eventually all) were turned into charters. More than twenty cities have experienced widespread public school closures coupled with charter expansion, with the breakup of public school districts into segments given to private organizations to run.

A new organization called Journey for Justice, comprising civil rights and grassroots organizations and community members in twenty-one cities, has set out to halt this progression, demanding "community-driven alternatives to the privatization of and dismantling of public school systems."[36] In addition to New Orleans, its members represent Atlanta, Baltimore, Boston, Detroit, Los Angeles, Minneapolis, Newark, New York City, Philadelphia, Pittsburgh, and Washington, D.C. The organization explains, "The policies of the last twenty years, driven more by private interests than by concern for our children's education, are devastating our neighborhoods and our democratic rights. . . . Journey for Justice is intentionally carving a space for organized low-income and working class communities who are directly impacted by top-down corporate education interventions."[37]

The coalition notes that in every one of its districts, school closings disproportionately affect African American and Latino students, schools, and communities. As a consequence, a number of organizations have filed complaints under Title VI of the Civil Rights Act with the Department of Education's Office of Civil Rights, demanding that the department investigate the racial impact of public school closings in their cities. The experiences of students in these cities suggest that, without a strong public education system that creates strong schools and manages choice, developing systems of schools worth choosing proves to be an elusive goal.

POLICIES NEEDED TO ACHIEVE EQUAL EDUCATION OPPORTUNITY

To survive and prosper, our society must finally renounce its obstinate commitment to educational inequality and embrace full and ambitious opportunities to learn for all our children. Although education is a state responsibility, federal policy is also needed to ensure that every child has access to adequate school resources, adequate facilities, and quality teachers.

Federal Strategies

Federal education funding to states should be tied to each state's movement toward equitable access to education resources and continued progress toward school integration. A number of components under the Every

Student Succeeds Act (ESSA) would support this progress, but they need to be enforced. Further, the obvious truth—that schools alone are not responsible for student achievement—should propel attention to the provision of adequate health care and nutrition, safe and secure housing, and healthy communities for children. In addition to investing in universal health care and high-quality preschool for all low-income children, the federal government could do the following:

- *Equalize allocations of ESSA resources* across states so that high-poverty states receive a greater share. Allocation formulas should use indicators of student need, with adjustments for cost-of-living differentials, rather than relying on measures of spending that disadvantage poor states.
- *Enforce integrative student assignment policies and comparability provisions for ensuring equally qualified teachers* to schools serving different populations of students. The law requires that districts minimize segregation in their decisions about student assignments to schools and that states develop policies to balance the qualifications of teachers across schools serving more and less advantaged students, but this aspect of the law has been weakly enforced, and wide disparities continue.
- *Encourage states to include opportunity indicators* in their reports of academic progress for each school that reflect the dollars spent: availability of well-qualified teachers; strong curriculum opportunities; books, materials, and equipment (such as science labs and computers); and adequate facilities. The federal government should evaluate progress on opportunity measures in state plans and evaluations under the law and require states to meet a set of opportunity-to-learn standards for schools identified as failing.

State-Level Strategies to Equalize Opportunity

In the past, a common state-level strategy has been to offer state aid to offset some of the core inequality resulting from locally funded education that is tied to the wealth of communities and add a variety of categorical programs that give additional money for specific purposes to local districts, often with extensive strings attached and not usable for students' most pressing needs. States could also do the following:

- *Establish weighted student funding formulas* that allocate equal dollars to students, adjusted or weighted for specific student needs, such as poverty, limited English proficiency, foster-care status, or special education status, as Massachusetts and California have done

- *Focus funding on the investments that matter most,* such as high-quality, equitably distributed teachers and curriculum opportunities

State efforts to rationalize resource allocations can leverage productive investments. As the Public Policy Institute of California observed:

> Equalization policies should do more than alter growth in overall budget levels. We believe they should target the area of greatest inequality: teacher preparation. . . . Traditional redistributive policies aimed at reducing variations in revenues per pupil across districts are unlikely to equalize student achievement across all schools. . . . [R]esource inequality is restricted primarily to teacher training and curriculum, so that redistribution must focus on these specific characteristics of schools rather than on revenues per pupil alone.

This analysis and other studies on the importance of well-prepared, committed, and culturally responsive teachers underscores the importance of a strategy like Connecticut's that ended shortages and boosted student achievement by equalizing the distribution of better-qualified teachers, raising and equalizing salaries, improving teacher education and standards, providing mentors, and supporting extensive professional development.[38] The strategy led to strong gains for students of color, as well as for white students.

Local Strategies

Local governments and school districts can also make a difference. They can:

- *Allocate funds equitably* to schools within their jurisdiction and create assignment zones and policies, such as magnet schools, that reduce segregation
- *Create community schools* that support children who attend high-poverty schools with wraparound services, extended time, and community partnerships that equip them with the educational, health, and social supports they need to succeed[39]
- *Hire, support, and retain highly qualified teachers and leaders* for hard-to-staff schools and ensure they have the skills to successfully work with diverse students[40]
- *Preserve and expand affordable housing* in neighborhoods with high-performing schools through proactive policies (such as the kind of inclusionary zoning Montgomery County, Maryland has

developed), enforcing fair-housing laws, and dismantling exclusionary land-use policies[41]

Because the fate of individuals and nations is increasingly interdependent, the quest for access to an equitable, empowering education for all people has become a critical issue for the American nation as a whole. As a country, we must enter a new era. No society can thrive in a technological, knowledge-based economy by starving large segments of its population of learning. The path to our mutual well-being is built on educational opportunity. Central to our collective future is the recognition that our capacity to survive and thrive ultimately depends on ensuring all our people receive what should be an unquestioned entitlement—a rich and inalienable right to learn.

7

Education

Racial and Social Justice

Diane Ravitch

THE REPORT ISSUED by the Kerner Commission focused primarily on the causes of violent civil disorders, pointing to racism, segregation, police brutality, conditions of life in racial ghettos, unemployment, and the hopelessness among African Americans in cities following the passage of civil rights legislation. Education was not a central issue, but the commission did not overlook it. In its identification of basic causes of civil disorders, the commission referred to "schools where children are processed instead of educated."[1]

In its recommendations for action, the Kerner Commission devoted several pages to analyzing the inadequacies of the public schools attended by urban black children. Black parents and children alike, the report said, viewed the schools with hostility. Black children entered first grade behind their white peers (though not in the same schools with them) and fell further behind with each passing grade. The black dropout rate was three times the white dropout rate. Even those black students who graduated high school had difficulty securing good jobs and were likely to be engaged in low-skill, low-wage jobs.

The report stated:

> The vast majority of inner-city schools are rigidly segregated. In seventy-five major central cities surveyed by the U.S. Commission on Civil Rights in its study "Racial Isolation in the Public Schools," 75 percent of all Negro students in elementary grades attended schools with enrollments that were 90 percent or more Negro. Almost 90 percent of all Negro students attended schools which

had a majority of Negro students. In the same cities, 83 percent of all white students in those grades attended schools with 90 to 100 percent white enrollments.[2]

This racial isolation was a direct result of residential segregation, "which transfers segregation from housing to education," the report said. And to worsen matters, the report continued, some 40 percent of white students in America's twenty largest cities were enrolled in private schools, intensifying segregation and reducing the possibilities for integration. The report then forecast that segregation would intensify if left undisturbed, stating:

> Segregation has operated to reduce the quality of education provided in schools serving disadvantaged Negro neighborhoods.
>
> Most of the residents of these areas are poor. Many of the adults, the products of the inadequate, rural school systems of the South, have low levels of educational attainment. Their children have smaller vocabularies and are not as well equipped to learn rapidly in school—particularly with respect to basic literary skills—as children from more advantaged homes.
>
> When disadvantaged children are racially isolated in the schools, they are deprived of one of the more significant ingredients of quality education: exposure to other children with strong educational backgrounds.[3]

The report cited the work of the Coleman Report on equal educational opportunity and the Civil Rights Commission to make the point that "the predominant socioeconomic background of the students in a school exerts a powerful impact upon achievement."[4]

The Kerner Report included a discussion of the negative attitudes of teachers, administrators, parents, and students toward segregated schools and of such schools being likely to have teachers with less experience and lower qualifications. The public schools attended by black students in the cities were typically overcrowded, poorly equipped, and housed in older buildings. Meanwhile, the states spent more on suburban schools, which were likely to be overwhelmingly white and well maintained, with experienced teachers and administrators. Suburban schools were better funded and newer than ghetto schools. Parents felt a sense of control because they elected their school boards. In big cities, black parents faced large bureaucracies and felt powerless and disrespected.

The most important recommendation of the Kerner Commission was to increase "efforts to eliminate de facto segregation." Nothing less than its elimination would provide equality of educational opportunity. The report said, "We have cited the extent of racial isolation in our urban schools. It is great and it is growing. It will not be easily overcome. Nonetheless, we believe school integration to be vital to the well-being of this country."[5]

The Kerner Commission stated as its central conclusion regarding education, "We support integration as the priority education strategy because it is essential to the future of American society."[6] The report proposed that the federal government create a funding mechanism through Title IV of the Civil Rights Act of 1964 to promote "comprehensive aid" to states and localities to desegregate their schools via magnet schools designed to foster integration by attracting white families back to city schools, educational parks, school pairings, rezoning for integration, and other strategies.

While funding efforts to increase integration, the Kerner Commission said, officials should pursue every opportunity to improve the quality of education in ghetto schools and to improve relations between the schools and the communities they serve.

AFTER FIFTY YEARS, WHAT HAVE WE DONE?
WHAT HAVE WE LEARNED?

As to the central concern of the Kerner Report—the persistence of racism—there have been some remarkable changes. An African American man was twice elected to the presidency, in 2008 and in 2012, a development that was unimaginable fifty years ago. Black men have been selected as chief executive officers of major corporations, such as American Express and the Dime Savings Bank. Black men and women are celebrities, earning millions of dollars for their work on television and in the movies. Black journalists write for major newspapers and are regulars on television newscasts. Black authors have achieved great recognition and honors for their literary works. Black patrons cannot be excluded from any hotel, restaurant, beach, or other place of public accommodation. Progress on many fronts has exceeded most people's dreams. The United States has changed dramatically in the past half century.

And yet that progress has not occurred in every sector, most especially not in education or housing. In central cities, many neighborhoods and schools continue to be highly segregated. Because housing is segregated, schools are segregated.

Major changes appeared to be possible in education after the passage of the Civil Rights Act of 1964. Title VI of the new law forbade discrimination in any federally funded program. Since there was no general federal aid to public schools in 1964, white southerners did not feel threatened. The following year, however, Congress passed the Elementary and Secondary Education Act, which established a major funding mechanism for schools enrolling poor children. The Office of Education in the Department of Health, Education, and Welfare (there was not yet a Department of Education) issued guidelines that required districts to demonstrate their progress in eliminating segregation in student and faculty assignments. Districts were expected to report the racial distribution of students and faculty in their schools and to show annual progress toward desegregation.

In the first year of implementing Title VI, the proportion of black children attending schools with whites rose from 2 percent to 6 percent. More than 1,500 school districts started the process of desegregation, more in one year than in the previous decade following the 1954 *Brown v. Board of Education* decision. Districts in the Deep South submitted plans for "freedom of choice," allowing students to choose their schools, with the intention of maintaining the segregated status quo. The Civil Rights Commission identified 102 "free choice" districts where not a single black student attended schools with whites. These plans did not satisfy the Office of Education, which wanted actual desegregation, not empty gestures. A year later, the new guidelines virtually prohibited school-choice plans. Every district was expected to make steady, incremental progress toward real desegregation of students and faculties.[7]

Whether and how to desegregate was settled by federal courts, which forcefully supported the Office of Education and blocked school-choice programs, the clear intent of which was to evade desegregation. The courts and the federal government acted in coordinated fashion in the late 1960s and early 1970s to insist on actual desegregation in southern districts. Even Denver, which had never been subject to laws requiring racial segregation of the public schools, was required to submit a desegregation plan because of existing segregation. By 1968, 32 percent of African Americans in the South attended schools with whites, and by 1972, the proportion had increased to 91 percent. As a result of the strategic use of federal funds and federal court orders to achieve the goal of ending racial isolation, the South became the most desegregated region in the nation.[8]

However, districts outside the South received mixed signals from the courts, which struggled to distinguish between de jure and de facto segregation. Where the state or district had imposed racial segregation as a matter of law, as in the southern states, the courts had clear direction. Where segregated neighborhoods produced segregated schools, the courts produced conflicting orders. Busing was one way to end segregation, but it provoked intense white opposition, demonstrations, protests, and even white flight.

Elected in 1968, President Richard Nixon opposed court-ordered busing, but in 1971, the Supreme Court, in *Milliken v. Bradley*, whose ruling was written by Chief Justice Warren Burger, a Nixon appointee, unanimously approved a metropolitan reassignment plan for the Charlotte-Mecklenburg,

North Carolina, schools that overturned the neighborhood school policy. Local officials were ordered to use any means necessary to eliminate one-race schools. Later, in 1973, in the *Keyes* decision, the court declared that the policies of the Denver school district had improperly created segregated schools. It appeared that the Supreme Court was on the verge of wiping out the distinction between de jure and de facto segregation.

Instead, the steady judicial march toward ending racial segregation was halted in 1974 in a case involving Detroit, where a federal district judge had ordered the creation of a metropolitan school district to include the suburbs, like the metropolitan district approved for Charlotte-Mecklenburg. But on appeal in the Detroit case, the Supreme Court ruled in a five–four decision that the fifty-three Detroit suburbs, where, as in many cities, white flight had hindered integration, could not be held responsible for racial segregation in their schools.

So the public schools in many of the nation's central cities became majority black, as whites retreated to the suburbs. Districts across the South were under federal court order and were monitored for compliance, although the quality of the monitoring became uncertain as time went by. The federal courts had been the strongest protectors of the right of black students to attend desegregated schools. But in 1991, the courts retreated from that duty, influenced by the increasingly conservative cast of the federal judiciary.

Nikole Hannah-Jones writes in *ProPublica* about the federal judiciary's abandonment of its role as guarantor of desegregation efforts, saying, "At the height of the country's desegregation efforts, there were some 750 school districts across the country known to be under desegregation orders."[9] By 2014, when she wrote, there were active court orders in more than three hundred districts. "But some federal courts don't even know how many desegregation orders still exist on their dockets. With increasing frequency, federal judges are releasing districts from court oversight even where segregation prevails, at times taking the lack of action in cases as evidence that the problems have been resolved."[10] *ProPublica* tried to assemble a comprehensive and accurate database of districts still subject to court-ordered monitoring. The Department of Education would not allow its officials to be interviewed by *ProPublica*, and the records it provided were inaccurate. Some districts that were still under federal mandate had forgotten or thought that the order had been lifted years earlier. The superintendent of a school district in North Carolina insisted that his district had never been subject to a court order, but Hannah-Jones found the court order in a federal archive in Atlanta, and it was still in force. The district's lawyer said the matter had not been mentioned "in 45 to 50 years."[11]

Neither the Department of Education nor the federal courts seemed to care about overseeing and enforcing racial integration of the nation's schools. In the spring of 2017, a federal judge in Birmingham, Alabama, took the extraordinary step of allowing Gardendale, a mostly white city, to secede from its racially diverse school district. The judge acknowledged that the purpose of the secession was racial, but she permitted the mostly white city to secede anyway.

Concerning this case, the *Washington Post* reports:

> Judge Madeline Haikala of the U.S. District Court in Birmingham ruled that the city of Gardendale's effort to break away was motivated by race and sent messages of racial inferiority and exclusion that "assail the dignity of black schoolchildren."
>
> She also found that Gardendale failed to meet its legal burden to prove that its separation would not hinder desegregation in Jefferson County, which has been struggling to integrate its schools since black parents first sued for an equal education for their children in the 1960s.
>
> Still, Haikala ruled Monday that Gardendale may move forward with the secession, basing her decision in part on sympathy for some parents who want local control over schools and in part on concern for black students caught in the middle. The judge wrote that she feared they would bear the blame if she blocked the city's bid.[12]

Could there be any clearer signal that the era of enforcement of desegregation by federal courts is over?

Gary Orfield and the Civil Rights Project at the University of California at Los Angeles have tracked trends in segregation and desegregation for many years. He and his colleagues reported in 2016 that public school enrollment had grown from 1990 to 2013 in size and diversity from 41.2 million to 49.9 million. The proportion of white students declined from 69 percent to 50 percent. The proportion of Latino students grew from 11 percent to 25 percent. The proportion of black students was steady at about 15 percent, and the proportion of Asian students increased from 3 percent to 5 percent. In the not-distant future, nonwhite students will be the majority.[13]

The high point for desegregation was 1988, Orfield writes, when only 5.7 percent of black students were in intensely segregated schools. By 2013, the proportion of black students in schools where 90–100 percent of students were nonwhite had tripled to 18.6 percent. At the same time, the proportion of schools where white students were 90–100 percent of the enrollment dropped from 42.6 percent in 1993 to 18.6 percent in 2013. Paradoxically, white students were increasingly likely to be in school with others of different racial and ethnic origins at the same time that the number of black students in nearly all-minority schools tripled.

The schools of the United States are resegregating because of the inaction of the Department of Education and the federal judiciary and the persistence of housing segregation. Orfield reminds us that this matters. It matters because "segregation creates unequal opportunities and helps perpetuate stratification in the society." It matters because diverse schools where children from different backgrounds meet on equal terms prepare young people "to live and work successfully in a complex society which will have no racial majority."[14]

Rucker Johnson of the University of California at Berkeley has also demonstrated in his studies that integration matters. He has found that blacks who attend desegregated schools are likelier to graduate high school, enroll in college, graduate from college, and lead healthier, more successful lives than their peers who attended segregated schools. Furthermore, they pass these advantages on to their children.[15]

What are the greatest obstacles to taking concerted public action to integrate our schools and our society? First is the belief that we tried it in 1965–1990 and it failed. As Orfield and others have shown, it did not fail. We abandoned it. Conservative elected officials and their judicial appointees turned their backs on this great project of civic reconciliation and racial justice.

Second is the belief that the era of ending de jure segregation is over, and nothing can be done about de facto segregation. Richard Rothstein's 2017 book, *The Color of Law: A Forgotten History of How Our Government Segregated America*, shows that this is a false distinction. Residential segregation did not happen because blacks and whites chose to live in different neighborhoods. Residential segregation was not the accidental by-product of personal choices. It happened because federal, state, and local laws and policies imposed racial segregation. Rothstein describes how federal mortgage programs were strictly segregated. The first federal housing programs, after World War I, excluded African Americans. Federal mortgage insurance for middle-income housing was available only for housing for whites. Federal public housing projects built in the 1930s and for many years afterward were racially segregated. Local zoning laws established segregated neighborhoods. On the rare occasions when black families, no matter what their income and education, bought a house in a white neighborhood, they often encountered mob violence, and the police did nothing to protect them. Residential segregation in the United States today is a direct consequence of laws and policies that required racial segregation for many decades. Our government segregated America.[16]

Given that the African Americans make up only 13 percent of the U.S. population, the segregation of so many African American students must be viewed as extraordinary and unacceptable. For one brief moment, when Barack Obama was elected president, there was an opportunity to create a meaningful federal program that would have reversed the reseg-regation of the public schools. In the wake of the financial crisis of 2008, Congress allocated $100 billion for the nation's schools; $95 billion was used to help them meet their basic expenses as tax revenues fell. But $5 billion was set aside as discretionary funding for education reform. Never before had federal education officials had this kind of discretionary money and the freedom to do with it what they wanted. President Obama's secretary of education, Arne Duncan, chose to create a competition for the states called Race to the Top, in which the winning states would agree to adopt programs that might raise test scores. To be eligible for the funds, states had to agree to open more privately managed charter schools, to adopt the Common Core standards in English and math (not yet com-plete at the time the contest began and thus untested), to evaluate teachers on the basis of the rise or fall of their students' test scores (although most teachers did not teach the tested subjects of reading and mathematics in grades three–eight), and to close or privatize schools that persistently pro-duced low test scores. The entire program was an extension and refine-ment of President George W. Bush's No Child Left Behind program, which also prioritized test scores as the goal of American education. Stan-dardized tests exist to differentiate among students, from the best to the worst. The scores are highly correlated with family income. The tests do not help children learn more; they are not tools for equity. They stigmatize children who are poor.

Providing $5 billion in discretionary money for reform by testing and privately managed charter schools was a lost opportunity. What if the same $5 billion had been turned into a competition for the states and districts that proposed the best plans with specific steps for desegregating their schools? What if, instead of the Duncan requirements for Race to the Top, the program had been a race to desegregate our schools by direct policy interventions?

The Obama administration's emphasis on charter schools and school choice as a remedy for low test scores (which they are not) set the stage for the reactionary choice-focused school policies of the Trump administra-tion. President Donald Trump and his secretary of education, Betsy DeVos, came into office with only one policy goal: school choice. They encouraged the use of public funds for charter schools and for vouchers for private and religious schools, despite clear evidence that these alterna-tive schools do not improve the education of the neediest students. School choice in the 1950s and 1960s was well understood as the favored ap-proach of southern governors and legislators who wanted to evade the duty to desegregate their schools. School choice is associated with social stratification, because families choose schools composed of others like themselves. Sweden and Chile, the only nations to endorse a free-market approach to schooling, allowing students to take public funds to private, religious, and for-profit schools, have both seen increased social stratification by income, religion, social class, and other criteria.

School choice will promote the trend toward resegregation. Since the Department of Education in the Trump administration has de-emphasized civil rights enforcement, the outlook for racial integration in the schools is probably the worst that it has been in the last fifty years. The Kerner Commission's hopes for integrated schools seem less likely than ever. The outlook for civil rights enforcement in 2018 is dim. But those who read the Kerner Report again and see its fundamental wisdom cannot afford to lose faith in the ideas of racial and social justice. The racism that the commission identified remains, though not so pervasive and virulent as in 1968. Presidents come and go. The future belongs to those who continue the long struggle for equality and justice in every part of American life. Regardless of setbacks, we cannot afford to abandon our will to advocate for and fight for a better future for all Americans of all racial groups.

8

Kerner and Kids

Work Remains

CAROL EMIG

I N 1968, the Kerner Commission called for "the realization of common opportunities for all within a single society."[1] When it comes to children and youth of color, much remains to be done to secure that common opportunity. Broadly speaking, the lives of many children of all races are better today than the lives of children fifty years ago, yet serious racial and ethnic inequities persist. Black, Hispanic, and American Indian children are still more likely to live in poverty. They lag behind their white and Asian peers on important well-being indicators that often predict long-term success. Even as legislative, judicial, and regulatory actions target inequities, work remains to address discriminatory policies and practices that often have deep and overlooked historical roots.

This work is unfolding today in a demographic, economic, and policy landscape greatly different from fifty years ago. This chapter briefly reviews the major changes in the child and youth field since 1968 and suggests future directions for policy and research.

THE CHANGING LANDSCAPE FOR CHILDREN AND YOUTH

Today's population of children and adolescents is racially and ethnically more diverse than ever before. In 1974, white[2] youth constituted 77 percent of the population under age eighteen but only 51 percent by 2015. As illustrated in Figure 8.1, the percentage of children who are black rose from 14 to 18 percent between 1974 and 2015, while the Hispanic child population more than tripled, from 7 percent in 1976[3] to almost 25 percent in 2015. Hispanics today are the largest group of minority children in the country, as well as the fastest-growing group of children. Demographers project that by 2050 Hispanics will be one-third of the child population, about the same proportion as white children.[4] The population of Asian children has also grown rapidly between 1988[5] and 2015, though they account for only about 6 percent of the child population. American Indian children have remained about 1 percent of the child population; while they are among the most disadvantaged children in the nation, their small numbers make it difficult to produce reliable data on their health and well-being, and as a result, their needs are often overlooked by the public and policy makers.

In addition to living in a more diverse nation, many of today's children experience family life differently from children in past decades. Children today are more likely to live with a single parent (typically a mother). In 1960, 85 percent of children lived with two parents, compared to 69 percent in 2016.[6] Over the same period, the percentage of children living with only one parent tripled, from 9 percent to 27 percent. Single-parent families, on average, have lower incomes than two-parent families, meaning they have fewer resources available to meet their children's needs and

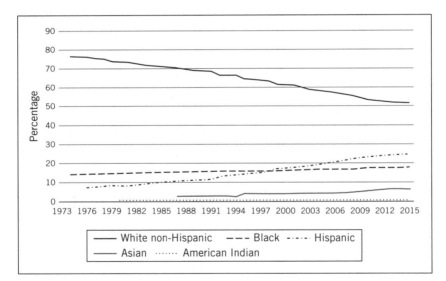

Figure 8.1 Racial/ethnic composition of children under eighteen, 1973–2015
Source: U.S. Census Bureau, "Historical Poverty Tables: People and Families, 1959 to 2015," September 8, 2017, available at https://www.census.gov/data/tables/time-series/demo/income-poverty/historical-poverty-people.html; Child Trends, "Racial and Ethnic Composition of the Child Population," July 2016, available at https://www.childtrends.org/?indicators=racial-and-ethnic-composition-of-the-child-population.
Note: Data for Black children are retrieved from "Black" data before 2002 and "Black Alone or in Combination" data for 2002 and after. Data for Asian children are retrieved from "Asian Alone or in Combination" data before 2002 and "Asian and Pacific Islander" data for 2002 and after.

support their aspirations. Moreover, when compared to children raised by two married biological or adoptive parents, children with single parents on average are in poorer health and are more likely to experience emotional or behavioral problems.[7]

Family structure varies by race and ethnicity. Black children in the United States are more likely than white or Hispanic children to live with only one parent, usually their mothers. For all three groups, the percentage of children living with one parent has increased over the decades, with the sharpest rate of increase among white children and lowest among Hispanic children. In 1960, 7 percent of white children lived with one parent; in 2015, 22 percent did, a more than threefold increase. For black children, the rate of increase was more than double, from 22 percent in 1960 to 54 percent in 2015. Among Hispanic children, 21 percent lived with one parent in 1980, rising to 29 percent by 2015.[8]

Today's children and youth are also more likely to live in families in which the only parent or both parents are employed; specifically, they are more likely to have a mother in the workforce. In 1974, fewer than half of all mothers with children under the age of eighteen were in the labor force, compared to 70 percent in 2015.[9] Maternal employment rates also vary by race/ethnicity: in 2015, 76 percent of black mothers were in the labor force compared to 70 percent of white mothers and 62 percent of both Hispanic and Asian mothers.[10] Changing parental employment patterns have affected a wide swath of American families; parental leave, early care and education, and after-school and summer care barely registered on the policy radar in the 1960s but are prominent concerns today.

Children continue to be the poorest age group in the United States. As Figure 8.2 illustrates, poverty rates for all racial and ethnic groups have fluctuated between 1975 and 2015 but have been consistently higher for black, Hispanic, and American Indian children than for white and Asian children. In 2015, poverty rates for black children were 33 percent, 31 percent for American Indian children, 29 percent for Hispanic children, and 12 percent for white children. Our knowledge of the damage that poverty inflicts on children has deepened in recent decades, underscoring further the urgent need for action.

CHILDREN AND YOUTH TODAY

Against this demographic and economic backdrop, how are children and youth faring? For many indicators of well-being, trends in recent decades are positive: school readiness has improved, high school graduation and college enrollment rates are up, teen birth rates have fallen, and placements in juvenile facilities are down. However, for each of these indicators, and others, large racial and ethnic disparities remain. For example:

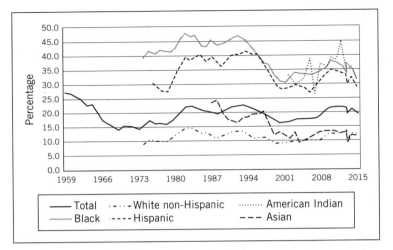

Figure 8.2 Children under eighteen living below the poverty line, 1959–2015

Source: U.S. Census Bureau, "Historical Poverty Tables: People and Families, 1959 to 2015," September 8, 2017, available at https://www.census.gov/data/tables/time-series/demo/income-poverty/historical-poverty-people.html; U.S. Census Bureau, "CPS Table Creator," available at http://www.census.gov/cps/data/cpstablecreator.html.

Note: American Indian data may be unreliable in comparison to other races. Data for Black children are retrieved from "Black" data before 2002 and "Black Alone or in Combination" data for 2002 and after. Data for Asian children are retrieved from "Asian Alone or in Combination" data before 2002 and "Asian and Pacific Islander" data for 2002 and after.

- All children have demonstrated improvement on a variety of early school readiness measures within the past twenty-five years, including letter recognition,[11] counting to twenty,[12] writing their name,[13] and reading words in a book;[14] but Hispanic children have lagged behind their white and black peers on the indicators for which we have data from 1993 to 2012.
- In 2015, 91 percent of all twenty-five- to twenty-nine-year-olds had earned at least a high school diploma. By race/ethnicity, the rates of diploma attainment were 95 percent for whites; 92 percent for blacks, and 77 percent for Hispanics.
- For college completion, white/nonwhite disparities are even more pronounced: 43 percent of white twenty-five- to twenty-nine-year-olds held a bachelor's degree or higher, compared to 21 percent of blacks and 16 percent of Hispanics.[15]
- While teen birth rates have fallen for all racial and ethnic groups, the rates for black (35 per 1,000) and Hispanic (38 per 1,000) females ages fifteen to nineteen remain higher than those for white females (17 per 1,000).[16]
- Juvenile detention rates have fallen by half in the past twenty years (from 356 per 100,000 youth in 1997 to 173 in 2013), but

the percentage of black youth in residential placements has remained steady (at 40 percent), and the percentage of Hispanic youth has increased (from 18 to 23 percent).[17] As discussed later in the chapter, these disparities are evident earlier in young people's lives—for example, in unequal administration of school discipline practices.

- Disparities in incarceration rates are even more glaring for young adults: black males between the ages of eighteen and twenty-nine far outnumber whites and Hispanics in state or federal prisons and local jails. In 2010, 9.7 percent of black men between the ages of eighteen and twenty-nine were in federal or state prison or local jails, compared to 3.9 percent of Hispanic and 1.5 percent of white men.[18]

PROMISING DIRECTIONS FOR PUBLIC POLICY

As the data above suggest, we have a long way to go to reduce and ultimately eliminate race-based disparities in child and youth outcomes. There are many possible policy avenues to pursue. Here, I briefly highlight three areas where past gains provide a springboard for future progress or where there is an opportunity to reach large numbers of children: universal health insurance for children and youth, early care and education, and school discipline policies. In these cases, the principles underlying the Kerner Report's recommendations still apply: "to mount programs on a scale equal to the dimension of the problems; to aim these programs for high impact in the immediate future, in order to close the gap between promise and performance; and to undertake new initiatives and experiments."[19]

Health

Health insurance coverage for children and youth has expanded, albeit in fits and starts, since the creation of Medicaid in 1965. Medicaid provided health insurance to low-income individuals, including those in families receiving Aid to Families with Dependent Children. Beginning in the mid-1980s and continuing to 2002, incremental changes in income and age eligibility, phased in over time, culminated in the extension of Medicaid coverage to all children through age eighteen in families with incomes below the federal poverty line and to children up to age six in families with incomes at or below 133 percent of the federal poverty line. In 1997, the Children's Health Insurance Program provided federal funds to states to cover children in families with incomes too high for Medicaid but too low to afford private insurance. Nearly every state had implemented the program within two years of the funding becoming available, and all states had implemented a program by early 2000.[20] Passage of the Patient Protection and Affordable Care Act in 2010 expanded eligibility even further, to include all Americans at or below 138 percent of the federal poverty line. A 2012 Supreme Court decision made states' adoption of this expansion optional and, consequently, not all states did so. But as of January 2017, thirty-two states (including the District of Columbia) had exercised this option.[21]

Research examining the effectiveness of Medicaid expansion in these states found significant reductions in uninsured rates (particularly among the most vulnerable populations, including children) and positive impacts on access to care, use of services, affordability of care, and financial security among low-income Americans.[22] By 2015, a record 95 percent of U.S. children had health insurance. Coverage for Hispanic children, whose levels had lagged behind those of black and white children, reached a record high of 93 percent. Nevertheless, research suggests that as many as a quarter of low-income Hispanic families with children are not aware that they could apply for Medicaid and other forms of public assistance. Additionally, fears of revealing the undocumented status of household members may prevent some parents from applying for Medicaid for their children. For some families, language and cultural factors may also be impediments.[23]

As of June 2017, Congress was considering health care legislation that would, among other things, limit the availability of Medicaid, which provides health insurance to 43 percent of the nation's children. Yet research attests to the value of health insurance to children's short- and long-term well-being. Children who have health insurance are more likely to get health care, more likely to be healthy, and more likely to have better educational and long-term economic outcomes[24]—compelling reasons for health care policy in the United States, whatever its form or financing, to include universal coverage for children.

Early Childhood

Perhaps the biggest shift in the public's and policy makers' thinking when it comes to children is the widespread recognition of the value of investments in early childhood,[25] spurred by research on early brain development,[26] rigorous evaluations of early education programs,[27] and projections of positive returns on such investments.[28] Head Start, established in 1965, stood virtually alone for decades in terms of federal investment in early childhood. Today, there are publicly funded prekindergarten programs in most states. In the 2015–2016 school year, Florida, Oklahoma, Wisconsin, and the District of Columbia each served more than 70 percent of the four-year-olds in their jurisdictions.[29] Universal prekindergarten programs exist in Florida, Georgia, Oklahoma, Boston, New York City, and Washington, D.C.[30] Most publicly funded prekindergarten programs serve primarily four-year-olds, but the proportion serving three-year-olds is increasing. Looking at younger children, the federal Early Head Start program, established in 1994, and the federal Maternal, Infant, and Early Childhood Home Visiting initiative, established in 2010, are notable examples of programs focused on infants and toddlers.

Promising as these investments are, they are not sufficient to prepare all children for school, nor are they enough to close racial and ethnic disparities in school readiness. Black children are more likely than white or Hispanic children to be enrolled in full-day preschool programs (39 percent versus 25 and 22 percent, respectively),[31] but overall, the United States is far behind many other developed nations in the percentage of children participating in early education programs and in spending (as a share of gross domestic product) on early care and education.[32] Increasing enrollment for all groups could be done by following the lead of the jurisdictions noted above that provide universal prekindergarten, or it could be done via programs targeted specifically at young children from disadvantaged families and communities.

Expanding access to early care and education programs is only part of the puzzle, though. The programs themselves must be high-quality, attending to not just cognitive development but also the multiple developmental domains that contribute to school readiness, including physical health and safety and social and emotional development. Research has established the association between high-quality early care and education programs and better child outcomes across multiple domains; poor-quality programs, on the other hand, are associated with negative ones.[33] Moreover, children who begin kindergarten with strong school readiness skills tend to continue to thrive, while those who are less prepared on average continue to lag behind.[34] Unfortunately, there is wide variation in preschool quality nationwide, and investments in quality have not kept pace with our growing knowledge of many of the elements that contribute to quality care.[35]

Staff are key to the quality of early care and education programs, yet the early childhood workforce is characterized by low compensation and limited opportunities for professional development, especially in community-based childcare programs, including family childcare, whose participants are more likely to be low-income families.[36] Education, training, and ongoing professional development for the early care and education workforce, as well as better compensation, are essential to creating and sustaining a high-quality early care and education infrastructure. Recent research also points to the need for an equity focus here. Black children are suspended from preschool at almost four times the rate of white children. Seeking to understand why, researchers at Yale identified implicit bias against black children by both white and black teachers.[37]

Racial and ethnic disparities in child outcomes emerge early. Analyses by Child Trends found that disparities in child outcomes associated with race exist as early as nine months of age, with black, Hispanic, Asian, and American Indian children lagging behind white children in cognitive, social, behavioral, and health outcomes. Worse still, these gaps widened between nine and twenty-four months.[38] The Child Trends researchers found a similar pattern of widening disparities when outcomes were analyzed by family income. So ensuring children a path to success also requires more attention to infants and toddlers.

The evidence base in this regard is growing. Findings from the Early Head Start Research and Evaluation Project show statistically significant positive improvements in children's cognition and levels of aggressive behavior.[39] Early evaluation findings from Educare, a comprehensive birth-to-five program operating in more than twenty disadvantaged communities across the country, showed impressive gains in kindergarten readiness, including among children with limited English proficiency.[40]

The economist and Nobel laureate James Heckman found positive annual rates of return from investments in high-quality early care and education programs targeted to disadvantaged children. The returns on investment took the form of better educational, economic, health, and social outcomes and reduced costs in remedial education, health, and criminal justice. Heckman concludes that "the highest rate of return in early childhood development comes from investing as early as possible, from birth through age five, in disadvantaged families."[41]

School Discipline

As promising as early childhood investments appear to be, they alone will not overcome the effects of poverty, discrimination, and other factors that disadvantage many children. To sustain the gains of high-quality early childhood investments, we need to continue to invest in proven interventions to promote quality and access from preschool through high school.

One notable area of reform focuses on shifting away from school discipline policies and practices that disproportionately exclude students of color and students with disabilities from school. In the 2013–2014 school year, 2.8 million K–12 students received one or more out-of-school suspensions, with black students almost four times as likely to be suspended from school as white students. (Hispanic and American Indian students were also more likely to be suspended than white students, but the practice is more pronounced for black students.) Children with disabilities, meanwhile, were twice as likely to receive one or more out-of-school suspensions as their peers without disabilities.[42] The data indicate that these suspensions are often for relatively mild forms of misconduct for which school officials have considerable discretion, not for violence or criminal activity.[43]

Discipline policies that exclude students from school can have lasting negative consequences for the suspended students. For instance, a longitudinal study of more than one million seventh- through twelfth-grade students found that those who are suspended from school even once in their first year of high school are more than twice as likely to drop out as students who have no history of school removal.[44] Additionally, suspended or expelled students are almost three times as likely as other similarly situated students to become involved with the juvenile justice system within a year of leaving school.[45] To make matters worse, a strong body of research concludes that excluding students from school does not improve either individual behavior or school safety.[46]

While certainly not the only path to more equitable educational outcomes, keeping students in school and engaged in learning has to be part of the solution.

States and communities across the country are using alternative approaches to prevent and address disruptive behavior, such as social-emotional learning initiatives,[47] positive behavioral interventions and supports,[48] restorative justice practices,[49] and early warning systems aimed at intervening proactively with students who have the potential to disrupt school or threaten school safety.[50] Evidence indicates that these approaches are associated with reductions in school dropout rates and with increased academic achievement.[51]

Most of these approaches are preventive and may not include ready strategies to help educators respond to student behavior during an incident or administer appropriate consequences to prevent a recurrence. There is more work to be done here to provide teachers and other school personnel with interventions, other than suspensions and expulsions, that hold young people accountable for their behavior, keep offending students on track academically, and avoid disparities by race and disability. This area is ripe for the kind of innovation that the Kerner Commission called for fifty years ago.

THE ESSENTIAL ROLES OF DATA AND EVIDENCE

This chapter relies on data to substantiate the racial and ethnic disparities in children's opportunities to exercise their right to life, liberty, and the pursuit of happiness. Reliable data can shine a light on groups of children who are overlooked and underserved and dispel harmful myths and misconceptions. The quantity and sophistication of data on children and youth available today far exceed what was available to the Kerner Commission. Most of the data cited in this chapter are from federal government sources, so their continued availability depends on maintaining adequate funding for the various federal statistical agencies. This data infrastructure underpins our understanding of whether the benefits of our society accrue equally to all children, regardless of race, ethnicity, or creed. Thus, this is also bedrock information for assessing a wide range of efforts to eliminate disparities.

This chapter also cites evidence of effective policies and programs in the areas of health, education, and early childhood. Again, when compared to fifty years ago, the evidence is plentiful for how to advance the health and well-being of children, yet we still have much to learn. We need more (and more rigorous) evidence of how to protect and promote child and youth well-being, and we need to know how to scale up evidence-based policies and programs to reach larger numbers of children.

Finally, we need better and more sophisticated ways to develop and use evidence that reveals disparate outcomes for different racial and ethnic groups. It is not sufficient simply to report disparities; we need to understand what drives them. Both cultural competence and a racial-equity lens are needed to inform research and evaluation, lest we overlook important contextual, historical, and cultural factors that might provide insight into disparate outcomes and suggest adaptations that would allow all children to reap the benefits of a program or policy. This is ultimately how we will fulfill the Kerner Commission's call for "new initiatives and experiments that can change the system of failure and frustration" in the twenty-first century.[52]

Achieving the vision of the Kerner Commission remains a work in progress. It may be that each generation of Americans will struggle anew with the challenge of creating a more perfect union. On the Kerner Report's fiftieth anniversary, looking at America's children and youth, we can say with pride that we have made progress. We must also admit, with dismay, that we have much further to go.

9

Still Struggling to Change the Odds for America's Poor Children and Children of Color

MARIAN WRIGHT EDELMAN

THE 1968 KERNER REPORT focused primarily on young African American adults, but it made clear that the discrimination, segregation, and lack of opportunity constricting those eighteen- to twenty-five-year-olds' lives had started in childhood. Fifty years later, how close have we come to making good on the promises of American democracy to all of America's children?

We have made great gains in protecting the civil rights of minorities, women, children, the elderly, those with disabilities, and those who are lesbian, gay, bisexual, and transgender. We have made important progress in alleviating poverty, extending health care, and creating other essential protections. Tens of billions of dollars have been invested in children's Head Start, health care, education, and childcare programs. Yet despite significant strides forward so much more remains to be done with urgency. The United States is still not a fair playing field for tens of millions of children afflicted by preventable poverty, hunger, homelessness, sickness, poor education, and violence in the world's biggest economy, and many of America's children, particularly children of color and poor children, continue to have the odds stacked against their early development and later academic and economic success.

Even as our nation becomes much more racially and ethnically diverse, children of color, especially black children, remain far behind their white peers. Growing inequality exacerbates the racial divide as very large disparities in family median income, wages, and family wealth stunt opportunity for children. Children are the poorest age group. Nearly one in five children is poor, and nearly 70 percent of the more than 13.2 million poor children are children of color.[1] The younger children are, the poorer they are, and black children remain the poorest—most likely to be trapped in what the Kerner Report calls the "prison of poverty."[2] Closing this inequality gap and racial divide remain the major unfinished business of our nation and, I believe, the greatest threat to our national security and economic future.

On March 31, 1968, a few days after the Kerner Commission released its report and recommendations, Dr. Martin Luther King, Jr., said in his last Sunday sermon before he was assassinated, "There is nothing new about poverty. What is new is that we now have the techniques and the resources to get rid of poverty. The real question is whether we have the will."[3] Fifty years later the answer to that question is clear. We have never found the will to fully respond to the Kerner Commission's urgent call for "massive and sustained" action.[4]

Children have only one childhood, and it is right now for today's children. We are failing millions because our nation's doors of economic and educational opportunity still have not fully opened to all God's children who are black, white, Latino, Native American, and Asian American and poor. We know much more today about what works, making it deeply shameful that we continue to tolerate political leaders in any party who choose not to invest adequately in critical services and just policies for all children and who refuse to end child poverty and illiteracy in order to give tax breaks to millionaires, billionaires, and powerful corporations. We must *finally* find the will to ease the burden of poverty and racial disparities and fling open the doors of opportunity so that every child has an equal chance of reaching his or her potential.

The need for action fifty years later has become even more urgent as children of color will become the majority of all children in America in two years.[5] In 2016, children under five crossed that threshold. But key statistics show a persistent, unjust portrait of widespread inequality for children of color and poor children in America today.

PORTRAIT OF INEQUALITY

We must help everybody in America—all of us—see what a true picture of inequality in our country looks like.

Poverty

Every third black child is poor compared to every ninth white child. Almost every sixth black child lives in extreme poverty compared to every twentieth white child.[6] Poverty hurts children, and the toxic stress of early childhood poverty stunts emotional and physical development during years of rapid brain development.[7] The harm of early poverty can last a lifetime and increase the odds stacked against success in school and later in life. The price tag for America's continuing failure to adequately act to end child poverty is estimated at half a trillion dollars a year from lost productivity, poorer health, and increased crime.[8] But there is no way to estimate the incalculable loss of denying millions of American children, particularly children of color, the opportunity to reach their full potential.

Hunger

While important progress has been made, critical programs fall short of meeting children's basic needs. One of the most successful government antipoverty programs is the Supplemental Nutrition Assistance Program (SNAP), formerly the food stamp program, which keeps the wolves of hunger outside the door for one in four American children and lifted more than 1.5 million children out of poverty in 2016, more than any other federal government program.[9] For the 4.9 million households (1.3 million with children) with *no* cash income, SNAP is their only protection against hunger.[10] The benefits of food stamps are long lasting: research shows children with access to them are nearly 20 percent more likely to graduate from high school.[11] No child in rich America should face hunger. Yet black and Latino children are twice as likely as white children to go to bed hungry.[12] Since SNAP benefits average less than two dollars a meal per person, more than half the families with this support still struggle to put food on the table. During the school year, many rely on free and reduced-priced breakfast and lunch programs to keep their children fed and ready to learn. But hunger never takes a vacation, and summer is often the most difficult time of the year for these families.

These are children like Linda Ransom, who was born into a poor, black family in Columbus, Ohio. Her mother became a single parent after fleeing an abusive marriage to create a healthy family for her five children. Despite a good job, she struggled. When Linda was six, her mother was diagnosed with stage-four breast cancer: "The only thing I knew was that my mother was sick. I didn't know that one prescription cost a million dollars. I didn't know that everything was going to change after it happened."[13] She remembers when the electricity and heat would be cut off. The times without hot water. She was grateful for food stamps, but at the end of the month, she says, "It was hard to get twenty dollars just to get food. . . . I was happy to have dinner because sometimes we just couldn't afford it; sometimes we couldn't go to the store." Although her mother has been cancer-free more than a decade and often worked multiple jobs, the family has never been able to regain their financial health. The summer before Linda's sophomore year in high school, they lost their home. After sleeping on a chair in an aunt's house for six months, Linda and her family moved into an apartment but soon got evicted again. This time they stayed with a friend and slept on the floor in an empty room.

Homelessness

Having a safe, stable home should not be a luxury that only some Americans can afford. But in the aftermath of the housing crisis that precipitated the Great Recession, affordable housing is harder to find. There is no state in the country where a person working full time year round and earning the minimum wage can afford the monthly fair-market rent for a two-bedroom unit and still have money for food, utilities, and other necessities.[14] Federal rental subsidies can make all the difference, but the current level of investment enables federal subsidies to serve only one in four of those eligible, despite those subsidies reducing homelessness and lifting families out of poverty.[15] The benefits for families with children include keeping families together, reducing foster-care placements, and sometimes providing an opportunity to move from a high-poverty neighborhood and school to a lower-poverty neighborhood with better schools. Homeless children are less likely to have access to medical care and are twice as likely to repeat a grade in school, be expelled, be suspended, or drop out.[16] We can and must invest more to meet the basic need for shelter for all of America's children.

Uninsured Children

The plight of black families in America has improved most dramatically in their access to health care over the past fifty years. Thanks in large part to Medicaid, the Children's Health Insurance Program, and the Affordable Care Act, 95 percent of children in America have health coverage.[17] This is the moment to ensure every child in America comprehensive and affordable health coverage.

Lack of Quality Early Childhood Investments

The odds are steeply stacked against the nearly four million children under five who are living in poverty, nearly two million of them living in extreme poverty during their years of rapid brain development.[18] The foundation for future success depends on what happens during the first five years.[19] High-quality early childhood development and learning opportunities from birth to age five have been proved to buffer the negative impacts of poverty and have lasting, lifelong benefits. Studies show children who experience high-quality early childhood programs are more likely to graduate from high school, hold a job, make more money, and pay more taxes and are less likely to commit a crime than children who do not.[20]

The federally financed Early Head Start and Head Start programs have been beacons of hope for millions of our most disadvantaged families with children. They are high-quality programs that provide comprehensive services, which include childcare, mental health, healthy meals, and other developmental services for the children, and connect families as needed to other resources in the community. Yet fifty years after the Kerner Commission first recommended early childhood learning opportunities to help close the racial and poverty divide, only 5 percent of eligible infants and toddlers are being served by Early Head Start, and 46 percent of eligible three- and four-year-olds are served by Head Start.[21] The economic case is clear. For every dollar invested in these high-quality programs, the Nobel Prize–winning economist James Heckman estimates a 13 percent per year return.[22] Every child should have the opportunity to be ready for school so as to thrive and succeed, but less than half of America's poor children enter school ready to learn.[23] We can and must do better with urgency.

Poor-Quality Education

Children who begin school behind their peers fall further behind as they struggle to climb the academic ladder to success. Poor African American and Latino students who most need the crucial pathway out of poverty that a good education provides are too often segregated in high-poverty schools, starved for resources and experienced teachers, and denied the opportunity to take the most challenging courses. Too many poor children of color attend schools that are still segregated and unequal. More than sixty years after the Supreme Court ruled school segregation unconstitutional in *Brown v. Board of Education*, black and Latino students are isolated by race and poverty. As the population of students becomes more diverse, schools have grown more segregated, creating unequal opportunities for African American and Latino children. From 2000 to 2014, the number of black and Latino students attending high-poverty schools more than doubled, increasing from more than four million to nearly eight and a half million.[24] As dramatic as the progress has been in increasing high school and college graduation rates, only one in four black children graduates from high school in four years.[25] High-poverty schools are more likely to employ exclusionary school discipline practices that start early, contribute to achievement gaps, and feed a school-to-prison pipeline. Black children constitute only 19 percent of the preschool population but are almost half of those suspended nationally. From kindergarten through twelfth grade, African American students are four times more likely to be suspended than white children.[26] Children who are pushed out of school for offenses that used to be handled in the principal's office fall further behind in school and often drop out and into a cradle-to-school-to-prison pipeline that begins before or at birth with inadequate prenatal and maternal health care. The beginning and end of the prison pipeline are located at the intersection of race and poverty in America, and the effects often get worse as children struggle to get through school. God did not make two classes of children, and America continues to do so at her peril.

Violence

Like so many, I have been deeply disturbed by the loss of black male lives at the hands of law enforcement. I was particularly affected by the senseless death of Tamir Rice—a twelve-year-old sixth grader who loved drawing, basketball, playing the drums, and performing in his school's drumline. Shot and killed by a trigger-happy white police officer in Cleveland, Ohio, his life was snuffed out in a public park in a few minutes. Our children deserve to grow up. That is what Tamir Rice's mother said at a rally shortly after her son died. Standing with Trayvon Martin's mother and the families of Eric Garner, Michael Brown, and other unnamed African American boys and men killed by police, she told the crowd, "I have one thing to say to the police force. Don't shoot. Our children want to grow up."[27] The violence of guns and poverty stalks our children in the streets of their neighborhoods, in the hallways and classrooms of their schools, in their churches and playgrounds, and in their homes and communities. No place in America is safe. Gun violence has become the number-one killer of black children.[28] A black child is killed by a gun every seven hours and twenty-five minutes in America.[29] More black children and teens have been killed by guns since 1968 than all the black people killed by lynching from 1877 to 1950.[30]

In Nashville, Tennessee, AJ Morris defied the odds and graduated from high school. His violence-ridden neighborhood had taken the lives of his friends by the time he began his senior year. He told it this way: "I have no friends that I grew up with. I have lost five this year, and I have lost three to prison. . . . From my freshman year to now, I have been to twelve to thirteen funerals."[31] A star athlete in middle school, AJ was sidelined with an injury in high school. "I lost hope. I stopped going to school." His family was struggling too. "I was homeless. I didn't have anything to wear to school. . . . I didn't even know where I was going to get my next meal." His high school peer E'Darrius Smith echoed his concerns: "We live in the worst condition where nobody helps you. And we live in a condition where you've got to watch your back every thirty seconds. You know, you don't know when you're going to get robbed; you don't [know] when you're going to get shot."[32] Children in America are seventeen times more likely to be killed by guns than children in twenty-five other industrialized countries combined.[33] This violent war on the young at home must stop.

Wealth and Income Inequality

Growing family-wage, income, and wealth inequality stunt opportunity for children and are the result of generations of systemic racial discrimination and denied opportunity for marginalized groups. The lack of opportunity for black children reflects the centuries of slavery and discrimination their ancestors endured in the United States over hundreds of years. The result is a much lower accumulation of wealth among black families—due to historical barriers of home ownership—that strongly dictates where black families can live and the educational opportunities available to their children. The wage gap between black men and their white counterparts remains unchanged since 1980. A black man earns 73 percent of a white man's earnings. The median income of black families with children is less than half the median income of white families with children.[34] The income gap is dwarfed by the wealth gap, which has widened since the Great Recession. The net worth of white families is thirteen times greater than that of black families.[35]

WE CANNOT BE TURNED BACK

Dr. Martin Luther King, Jr., guides us if we are willing to take the next step and use his voice as a road map for action. In *Where Do We Go from Here?* he reflects on what direction the struggle for civil rights and social justice would take next and shares a story about the need to recommit to difficult struggles for the long haul. Dr. King describes a flight he had taken from New York to London years earlier in an old, propeller airplane. The trip took nine and a half hours, but on the way home, the crew announced that the flight home from London to New York would take twelve and a half hours. When the pilot came out of the cabin, Dr. King asked him why. "You must understand the winds," the pilot said. "When we leave New York, a strong tail wind is in our favor, when we return, a strong head wind is against us."[36]

Dr. King concludes, "In any social revolution there are times when the tail winds of triumph and fulfillment favor us, and other times when strong head winds of disappointment and setbacks beat against us relentlessly. We must not permit adverse winds to overwhelm us as we journey across life's mighty Atlantic; we must be sustained by our engines of courage in spite of the winds. This refusal to be stopped, this 'courage to be,' this determination to go on 'in spite of' is the hallmark of any great movement."[37]

Today, we need to rev up our engines of courage, battle the fierce head-winds of greed that threaten to undo the progress of the last fifty years, and finally find the will to end child poverty, hunger, and homelessness and change the odds and open wide the vaults of opportunity to all America's children regardless of the color of their skin or immigration status.

CHANGE THE ODDS FOR AMERICA'S CHILDREN AND CLOSE OPPORTUNITY GAPS

To help ensure all children the opportunity for success in childhood and later in life, we must invest in their futures today and eliminate the disparate access to opportunity for black children and other children of color. We must preserve the gains that have been made (see Table 9.1) and persist in changing the odds for America's children. To do so, we must at a minimum make the following progress:

- *Commit to ending costly child poverty and its disproportionate negative impact on black children and other children of color in America through policies to help families work and make work pay and to better provide basic needs for food and housing.* The modest investments recommended in the Children's Defense Fund's *Ending Child Poverty Now* report would reduce overall child poverty by 60 percent, improve the economic circumstances of another four million poor children, and reduce black child poverty by 72 percent.[38] Increased investments in housing subsidies and food stamps, minimum-wage increases, and increased public support for subsidized jobs must be given high priority.
- *Ensure all children access to affordable, comprehensive health coverage that recognizes their unique needs, is easy to get and easy to keep, and will help increase opportunity by ensuring healthy children.* Strengthen and extend funding for the Children's Health Insurance Program, which covers nearly nine million children, and ensure that all eligible children, regardless of immigration status, can get and keep affordable health coverage without interruption. Protect Medicaid, the cornerstone of health coverage for more than thirty-seven million poor and low-income children and children with disabilities, and expand the extension of Medicaid to very low-income parents and other adults in all states.
- *Provide opportunities throughout the early years, from birth through age five, with a full continuum of quality supports—developmental, physical, social, emotional, and educational—to*

TABLE 9.1 OVERALL CHILD WELL-BEING AND BLACK-WHITE GAP, 1964–2014

	1964	2014	Change	Black-white gap
Poverty				
Child poverty	23%	21.8%	5.5% decrease	1964: 4.2:1
				2014: 3.4:1
Inequality				
Income share of top 1%	10.5%	21.4%	104% increase	
Unemployment				
Unemployment rate (age 16+)	5.2%	6.2%	19% increase	2014: 2.1:1
Education				
3- and 4-year-olds enrolled in preschool and kindergarten	9.5%	54.2%	470% increase	1964: 1.1:1
				2014: 1.07:1
High school graduates, ages 18–24	68.1%	86.8%	27.4% increase	1964: 0.6:1
				2014: 0.95:1
College graduates, ages 25–29	12.8%	34.0%	165% increase	1964: 0.4:1
				2014: 0.6:1
Health				
Infant mortality (per 1,000 live births)	24.8	5.82	326% decrease	1964: 2:1
				2014: 2.2:1
Child and teen gun deaths (per 100,000 children and teens)	2.47	3.1	25.5% increase	1964: 2.3:1
				2014: 3.5:1

Sources: U.S. Census Bureau, "Table 3: Poverty Status of People, by Age, Race, and Hispanic Origin: 1959–2015," September 8, 2017, available at https://www.census.gov/data/tables/time-series/demo/income-poverty/historical -poverty-people.html; Thomas Piketty and Emmanuel Saez, "Income Inequality in the United States, 1913–1998," *Quarterly Journal of Economics* 118, no. 1 (2003): 1–39 (see also the updated tables through 2015, available at https://eml.berkeley.edu/~saez); Bureau of Labor Statistics, "Employment Status of the Civilian Noninstitutional Population, 1944 to Date," February 12, 2015, available at https://www.bls.gov/cps/aa2014/cpsaat01.htm; U.S. Census Bureau, "Table A-2: Percentage of the Population 3 Years Old and Over Enrolled in School, by Age, Sex, Race and Hispanic Origin: October 1947 to 2016," August 28, 2017, available at https://www.census.gov/data/ tables/time-series/demo/school-enrollment/cps-historical-time-series.html; U.S. Census Bureau, "Table A-5a: Pop- ulation 14 to 24 Years Old by High School Graduate Status, College Enrollment, Attainment, Sex, Race, and His- panic Origin: October 1967 to 2016," August 28, 2017, available at https://www.census.gov/data/tables/time -series/demo/school-enrollment/cps-historical-time-series.html; U.S. Census Bureau, "Table A-2: Percent of People 25 Years and Over Who Have Completed High School or College, by Race, Hispanic Origin and Sex: Selected Years, 1940 to 2015," November 29, 2016, available at https://www.census.gov/data/tables/time-series/demo/educational -attainment/cps-historical-time-series.html; Kenneth D. Kochanek, Sherry L. Murphy, Jiaquan Xu, and Betzaida Tejada-Vera, "Deaths: Final Data for 2014," *National Vital Statistics Reports*, June 30, 2016, available at https:// www.cdc.gov/nchs/data/nvsr/nvsr65/nvsr65_04.pdf; Centers for Disease Control and Prevention, "Compressed Mortality File," available at https://wonder.cdc.gov/mortSQL.html (accessed September 20, 2017).
Note: The black-white gap is the ratio for each indicator as it occurs for black children relative to white children.

ensure that all children enter school ready to learn. Offer parents twelve weeks of paid family leave to welcome new children into their lives. Extend and expand funding for the Maternal, Infant, and Early Childhood Home Visiting Program. Expand funding for the successful Early Head Start and Head Start programs. Increase funding for the Child Care and Development Fund to help states improve quality, strengthen the childcare workforce, and ensure low-income families access to safe, affordable, and high-quality care. Invest in state efforts to implement high-quality preschool programs for three- and four-year-olds, beginning first with the poorest and most vulnerable children, who benefit most from these investments. And ensure full-day kindergarten is available for children in every state.

• *Address barriers that deny equal educational opportunities to children of color, poor children, English-language-learner students, children with disabilities, and children who are homeless, in foster care, or in the juvenile justice system. Make special efforts to curb summer learning loss and help close achievement gaps.* The federal government must continue its important role in ensuring progress in reducing the achievement gap, as state departments of education and local education agencies implement the enhanced protections for children in the Every Student Succeeds Act (ESSA). Promote policies that rectify discriminatory discipline, improve school climate, and enhance educational success for especially vulnerable students, including homeless children or those in foster care or the juvenile justice system to help close achievement gaps for children of color. Significant new investments are needed to provide summer and after-school reading enrichment for children who might otherwise not have access to books and suffer summer learning loss. As our own Children's Defense Fund Freedom Schools Program has demonstrated, developmentally appropriate and culturally relevant books accompanied by quality programming and a culturally diverse teaching staff can help boost students' motivation to read, generate more positive attitudes toward learning, increase self-esteem, connect the needs of children and families to resources in the community, and curb summer learning loss to close achievement gaps.

• *Keep children safe in their families and communities.* Ensure all children safe families and communities by investing in family violence prevention, enhanced mental health and substance abuse prevention and treatment, and other trauma-informed services and by providing alternatives to out-of-home placements in both the child welfare and juvenile justice systems. When placement is necessary, keep children in community programs that engage their families. Keep guns out of the hands of children, those who use them against children, and perpetrators of domestic violence through sensible gun-safety measures. Promote constructive police-community relations by engaging children, youths, and adults in meaningful interactions. Epidemic gun violence in America is a major public health issue that must be addressed with urgency and resolve.

We *must* finally find the will to act and to change the odds for all America's children to keep them safe, healthy, housed, fed, and prepared for school and ensure them an equally good public education that prepares them for successful futures. To return to the words of the Kerner Report: "There can be no higher priority for national action and no higher claim on the nation's conscience."[39]

10

A New Civil Rights Agenda

GARY ORFIELD

T IS NOW A HALF CENTURY since the end of the civil rights revolution. Though the movement transformed the South in lasting ways, many of its goals were not fully achieved. In some critical ways we have been moving backward for a third of a century. The killing of Dr. Martin Luther King, Jr., the split of the movement, the new conservative coalition embracing the segregationist South, and a changed Supreme Court majority ended the expansion of civil rights law; billions were spent on mass incarceration of young men of color; and major social-policy retreats combined to push the country backward. In spite of many intense and sometimes brilliant battles to protect and preserve civil rights initiatives and three Democratic presidents who offered hopeful interludes, there have been no serious new civil rights laws since the 1960s, the force of the existing laws has been diminished by negative Supreme Court decisions, and more often than not the civil rights agencies have been in the hands of civil rights opponents. There have been no major urban or housing policies or antipoverty initiatives to address the urban decay that was already evident by the 1960s. Many of the efforts of the Great Society and the War on Poverty period have been abandoned. Huge tax cuts by the federal government and many state governments, as well as the costs of a series of wars, have drained the resources for social policies. The development of globalized trade, antiunion policies, long freezes on minimum wages, a massive redistribution of economic gains from workers to owners, and a decline in general social mobility—all these have been very hard on families of color and have perpetuated racial inequality.

The social justice imperative of the civil rights era gave way to a long period of conservative domination in which liberals withdrew into a defensive posture with a much narrower agenda, while conservatives continually attacked civil rights and social policies. People of color, whose position was weakened by white mobilization by leaders of reaction and a severe weakening of voting rights by the courts and conservative takeover of most state governments, were left with a choice between an actively hostile party, which made almost no appeal for their support and created obstacles to their voting, and a centrist party, which expressed sympathy, wanted their support, but was afraid to alienate white voters in what had become a suburban society. The Donald Trump presidency is something that could not have been imagined fifty years ago—one of the great national parties in the hands of a demagogue, obviously mobilizing on the basis of racial and ethnic stereotypes.

At the current nadir, it is time to look up and look forward as the NAACP did in the dreadful period of President Woodrow Wilson. A century ago, the NAACP attacked the basic structure of racial segregation, even as Wilson, the first Southern-born president after the Civil War, was celebrating the KKK, showing the racist *Birth of a Nation* at the White House, and segregating federal agencies. Long decades of struggle against huge odds opened great new possibilities in the 1960s.

The civil rights struggle is never over. Victories won can be undone. Sometimes the same battle must be won again in another generation. There are many signs in recent years that we are moving backward. School segregation is now the most intense it has been in a half century. Although more black and Latino students are going to college, the racial gaps are actually growing. The gaps in family wealth are massive, perpetuating inequality. Incarceration reaches a larger share of nonwhite families than could have been imagined a half century ago. In many states, most families are too poor to pay for a school lunch. We had a black president, but he was followed by a presidential election in which the victor exploited racial stereotypes and deepened racial divisions. We now have to choose between fear of change and figuring out how to make a changing society fair.

We need civil rights, education, and social policies that make sense in a society in which most of the children being born now are nonwhite, a society with four major racial groups and American Indian tribes that continue to be neglected and excluded. We need a policy that addresses the problems of raising a very large share of our population that is in or near poverty and changing a metropolitan society with no metropolitan policies and increasingly intense isolation of both the poor and the rich within our predominantly suburban society. We need a set of policies that work in a setting of extreme economic inequality and declining social and economic mobility. We have a society in which the main key to the middle class is college, but in this society college is increasingly allocated on the basis of family resources, understanding of the system, and wealth enough to buy access to strong public schools through the housing market, and in an extremely unequal society in which conservatives insist that we follow color-blind policies that assume everyone has an equal chance and blame people of color when they do not make it.

A POLICY FRAMEWORK

After decades of experience, it is clear that the color-blind policies have failed by ignoring the obvious differences in opportunity—for example, between high-poverty minority schools and middle-class schools. When researchers look at data showing the distribution of what is most strongly related to student success, they see things that are provided very unequally by race. Black and Latino kids still come to school far behind, from families with much more limited resources, and weaker schools cannot close the gap. We need a new civil rights policy and a series of social and economic policies that expand opportunities and increase the resources and capacity of nonwhite families to take advantage of opportunities. It should start with a few basic assumptions:

- Segregation is inherently unequal in American society.
- Racial inequality is powerfully self-perpetuating.
- The failure to solve problems of housing and school boundaries create deeply unequal schools for students of color.
- Problems of immigrant status and language create exclusion, polarization, and unequal schooling.
- Race-conscious policies are essential if we are to move toward genuinely equal opportunity.
- Educators and officials need training to understand and relate effectively to different cultures and to manage multiracial classes.
- School choice and college markets will stratify schools and children without appropriate civil rights policies.
- In a metropolitan society, metropolitan collaboration is needed for social justice.
- Colleges must be genuinely affordable for low-income families and must support talented students of color from inferior segregated high schools.
- Housing integrated by race and income across metros is needed to foster equal opportunity.

Discrimination is still serious, and violators must face a clear risk of administrative or judicial sanctions. When school districts gerrymander assignment zones or choice policies in ways that systematically advantage some racial groups and harm others, they should be investigated and prosecuted. If there is discrimination in the hiring or assignment of employees by race and ethnicity, it should be prosecuted. When young men of color are placed on suspension or assigned to special education far more than is reasonable, that is a civil rights violation. If choice systems systematically disadvantage and isolate groups of students, they should be investigated and changed. If Latinos face harassment, that must be addressed. In recent decades, there have been harsh consequences for failure by schools to meet test-score goals but very few for civil rights violations, which have spread. This needs to be corrected, and local civil rights groups, scholars, and journalists should give serious attention to these issues. The Trump administration's announced policies and appointments in civil rights agencies promise to deepen the problems.

A BROADER VIEW

To expand opportunity, schools are not enough. Education policy must be supported by policies that improve opportunity in homes and communities. Housing policy is school policy. If children have to move often, it disrupts their learning. If the family cannot live in a safe neighborhood with a decent school and positive peer groups, the children will learn less. If families are homeless, education becomes chaotic.

Food policy is education policy. Students' health and vision care have an obvious and strong relationship to their ability to learn. Preschool and childcare policies strongly affect school opportunity. All these policies, if they distribute opportunities on racial and ethnic lines, are civil rights challenges and must be addressed in civil rights policy.

A good first step would be to stop policies that are unintentionally making things worse, such as driving good teachers out of low-achieving schools by punishing them for unequal achievement of students who come to school years behind rather than by rewarding the difference they make in closing gaps. We should stop building new subsidized housing for families in areas with segregated, dropout-factory schools, gangs, and very few jobs. We should fund no more intentionally segregated charter schools. Schools should stop suspending large fractions of their young men of color or placing them in special education. Research shows better alternatives. We should not eliminate transportation for poor kids to better schools in the name of budgeting. Denial of health care leaves many students unable to learn. We should not expand graduation requirements and test complexity until we are prepared to effectively teach the students what they are going to be tested on. We should not take young people released from juvenile detention and send them to a dead-end continuation school or let their records prevent them from getting a job. When every sentence becomes, in effect, a life sentence, we create people who can only survive by preying on our society. We have to create pathways into real jobs and second chances at education. We must solve as many problems as possible before incarceration or through alternatives to incarceration, which ruins lives.

Research has clearly shown that most of the difference in test scores among schools is not related to features of the school but to differences among families and in students' earlier schooling. Policies that seriously punish schools branded as failing on the basis of scores or abolish schools with low test scores have undermined public support for public schools and led to a major commitment to nonpublic schools in spite of the lack of evidence that they provide significant gains. We are dismantling public school systems whose problems are basically the problems of racial and economic polarization without providing anything significantly better. Picking apart schools and districts that serve the most disadvantaged students, removing many experienced teachers of color, and turning the students over to a maze of private operators who have political power and are rarely held accountable is a path filled with risks. Similarly, we must avoid college accountability policies that unintentionally punish the colleges that offer a chance to students ill prepared by inferior public schools but with talent that could be developed.

The central idea of the civil rights era was that fundamental racial injustice in American society must be addressed by conscious changes in education policy, specifically designed to bring down racial barriers and empower people from historically excluded groups to participate in stronger schools and colleges they had been excluded from. The idea was that there should be not only strong action to stop and remedy discrimination but also an array of programs and supports to make it possible for minority students who start from behind to succeed.

Post-Reagan education reforms have basically assumed that the schools can do it by themselves in an increasingly unequal and impoverished society and that the states can be trusted to do this fairly, in spite of a long history of state neglect and abuses. These ideas are the consequence of a color-blind set of beliefs and policies in a society severely stratified by color but with no consensus about the cause and remedies. Obviously, we need a set of policies that understand how race and class work in our society and that embrace a research-based strategy for overcoming those effects to the extent that schools can. There are important ideas for reforms already being implemented and promising experiments that can be expanded. To the extent that the problems are rooted in conditions outside the schools, it is imperative that educators understand those root causes, join with those from other fields to explore solutions, and claim a voice in the policy debates. Since many problems in learning relate to developmental deficiencies before birth and to untreated chronic health problems, for instance, a good education policy depends in part on a good health policy for children and mothers. When children are physically separated from good schools and successful communities, their education suffers and their future is limited. A massive national 2013 study of intergenerational mobility whose authors included two leading young U.S. economists (recipients of the renowned John Bates Clark Medal for the most outstanding young economists) found that segregation and weak school systems were directly related to low economic mobility not only for minorities but for all residents.[1] Economic failure in turn means the family does not have the means to buy access to good schooling in the housing market; so the long chain of inequality gets another link. Local boundaries set generations ago for other purposes often become walls of separation for education opportunity. The Obama administration until its final year failed to respond to the suggestions of twenty civil rights organizations and research centers to create significant incentives for integrated schools, and then it was too late to get anything enacted.[2] Developing these policies must become a long-term priority.

School choice programs are large and growing. The basic policy need is for the government to subject all funding for voucher, charter, and magnet schools to civil rights criteria, including diversity goals and recruitment processes, no admissions requirements, welcoming policies for English-learner students, a lottery selection method, and excellent parent information. Although the *Parents Involved* decision has created obstacles, there are still several legal means of pursuing racial diversity, and school districts need help.[3] With such changes, charter schools could become a building block for a diverse society rather than a force for separation. If there is to be real choice and students are to escape neighborhood segregation, free transportation for students' choosing is essential.

THE POLICY VACUUM

Only three major education reform laws have been enacted by Congress since the 1960s: Goals 2000 and No Child Left Behind, both of which failed miserably in equalizing education success. The third was 2015's Every Student Succeeds Act (ESSA). ESSA simply gave up on federal policy and transferred power over federal education funds to the states, which, with few exceptions, have little history of positive civil rights policies. The Trump administration and Congress quickly discarded the Obama regulations under this law and have pressed to transfer federal funds to private schools. No major urban policies have been enacted in more than four decades. The social safety net for the poor has been drastically reduced in terms of welfare payments, and there are proposals to reduce it more. Eligibility for food aid expanded greatly as the share of families unable to pay for a healthy diet or school lunches grew to more than half in substantial parts of the United States, but this aid, while essential, does nothing to change the underlying inequalities. The Obama administration expanded health insurance to millions of families and prevented exclusion on the basis of preexisting conditions, but the law was subjected to relentless political attack by opposition committed to radically rolling back coverage and is still unsettled. Despite it being impossible in many areas for a very large share of families to afford decent housing in a decent location and homelessness surging,[4] all the major affordable housing programs for poor families have been eliminated, and current construction reinforces the concentration of students from low-income, nonwhite families in weak, segregated schools.

Higher education has become both an essential need and an impossible, unaffordable reality for millions of families of color with low incomes and little wealth. The financial barriers and competitive pressures for strong public higher education have considerably lowered access to many colleges and forced millions of students to make the only choice the family can afford, usually a local community college with a low completion and transfer rate. We have had a major disinvestment in higher education by states, which has shifted the cost burden to families and students for decades and left what are often insuperable gaps in available aid. Weak students from high-income families have a substantially better chance of finishing college than strong students from low-income families.

We lack family and childcare benefits that virtually all other advanced nations provide, and much of our politics is about how to cut back social services further, in a nation where the only secure parts of government have become programs caring for the elderly, defense, and tax cuts and subsidies through the tax system for those with enough income and skill to take advantage of them. In this society courts and legislatures cut back on voting rights in ways that harm minorities and the poor while giving virtually unlimited power to the rich to buy political influence and distort our electoral process.[5] Some state governments have been employing multiple methods to limit eligibility, and many electoral districts have been gerrymandered in ways that increase the number of seats controlled by opponents of civil rights. Since one party seeks to polarize the white vote, voters of color have only one option and, with gerrymandering, limited leverage.

The dead end of policies that ignore racial and economic segregation can be seen in cities like Detroit. Detroit children were denied access to suburban schools by the Supreme Court four decades ago, the year after the court said poor schools had no constitutional right to fair funding in the *Rodriguez* decision.[6] The school district tried special reading programs, an Afrocentric curriculum, and many other strategies as middle-class families of all races continued to leave the city and its schools. The schools have been lashed by No Child Left Behind policies and picked apart by charter and transfer policies. There is now only a skeleton of a Detroit public school system. With the city in virtual bankruptcy, the state government took control and slashed expenditures. Moreover, when one looks at the devastation in Philadelphia, the massive school closings in black Chicago, and crises in many other cities and old suburbs it is obvious that we are beyond the point where marginal policies can work. It may be that we are now beyond the point at which school districts in the very poor, virtually all nonwhite cities are viable, and we must think about them becoming part of a larger, more viable entity on the model of what happened in North Carolina metropolitan areas or in Wilmington, Delaware.

BUILDING A NEW AGENDA

It is very important to protect the civil rights policies that have survived hard times, because we face much larger problems that need a new policy framework with new ways of conceptualizing and explaining the realities. We need a variety of small and large policy changes to increase opportunity and mobility for nonwhite children and their families. There are many things that could make a difference in moving toward the goal of equal opportunity in an integrated society. In terms of coordination of school and housing policy, for example, we could try to catch up to where we were at the end of the Carter administration, thirty-seven years ago, which began to take serious steps to coordinate education policy with Department of Housing and Urban Development programs and policies so that the department would not pay for housing that resegregated schools and communities. The Carter administration also combined housing and school litigation at the Justice Department in the search for coordinated policies. The administration used housing and regional planning funds to incentivize regional fair-share subsidized housing programs and supported experiments with Section 8 certificates and counseling to give some public housing tenants access to suburban neighborhoods and schools. Pending federal regulation on these issues and pending civil rights litigation in Houston, Phoenix, and elsewhere were quickly reversed under President Reagan. We need plans and incentives to spark interest. The largest affordable housing construction program, the Low-Income Housing Tax Credit, locks in poor minority families needing housing to weak schools.[7]

We need housing and land-use planning, which makes an entire metro area healthier economically and socially by offering a broader range of housing prices to permit more access to jobs and schools for households with a much wider range of incomes. One principal reason for this lack of permits is tax-payer resistance to property taxes sufficient to cover school costs. An equalization formula would aid communities to create more diversified housing stocks with, for example, housing that teachers and other public servants could afford to live in. Part of such a policy would be aggressive testing of housing markets and prosecution of discrimination and steering by real estate and rental agents of white clients to white areas and of nonwhite clients to minority or racially changing areas.

In education policy, high-stakes testing must follow the equalizing of education opportunity. It is worse than irrational to hold students responsible for things competent teachers never taught them. The authorities must be held accountable for providing equal education before the students are punished for the results of inequality. Since most of the segregation and inequality are among school districts, not within individual districts, there should be strong incentives and support for regional collaborations to devise regional magnet schools and transfer policies that have civil rights standards, something that has been found to be successful and popular in Connecticut metropolitan areas.

If there were a new civil rights movement, what would be the large goals? After a half century of neglect and painful reverses, we need a movement that turns the spotlight on racial inequality, a movement against poverty and income inequality and for the creation of fair and integrated communities, schools, and workplaces. We need to consider major changes in the structure of local government through creation of metropolitan collaboration and institutions, so that we do not let poor cities and suburbs die one by one as others consolidate their riches and build more gated communities. We need to admit that our War on Drugs and mass incarcerations have had immense costs, both economically and socially, and are a failure, and we need to learn lessons from our more successful states and our peer nations. For those who are incarcerated, we must have a path back into society that includes education.

We need a sensible immigration policy to replace the vast investment in a militarized border, a policy that welcomes and legalizes long-settled families and a reasonable number of young, hardworking immigrants, since we are headed toward demographic decline in many parts of our country. Without such a policy, we will age out, something many countries in Europe and some in Asia are already experiencing. We need to invent ways to see and use our diversity as a source of wealth, not as a problem. We need to have courts and administrative agencies staffed with people who understand how our nation is changing, not with those imagining that it can go back to their idealized version of the past. At all levels of government and in the private and nonprofit sectors we need leaders who acknowledge that problems of inequality and segregation have not been solved and who have the courage to support facing reality and solving the problems.

IS ANY OF THIS FEASIBLE?

When we look back at the period of great reforms a half century ago, there is a tendency to think that something on that scale can never be repeated. The truth is, however, that we confront much less formidable odds than the leaders of the civil rights movement then confronted, in many respects. They faced seventeen states, home to most blacks, where apartheid was totally locked into state law and history, and a situation in which almost no lawyers in the region would represent civil rights against a powerful establishment, most defending the status quo as well as the KKK and violent fringe groups willing to use terror.

They faced a Congress that had not enacted a major civil rights law since the 1870s and a Supreme Court that had passively accepted racial subordination. They faced extreme racial stereotypes and fears that were deeply rooted in American culture, which they overcame with persistence, courage, and dignity. Yet they initiated a social revolution that changed the South irrevocably in some key dimensions. We have many community leaders, some educators, researchers and intellectuals, lawyers, and others willing to help. We must take risks, face defeats, and work very hard to produce new language and a flood of information about what is destructive and what could be done. The racist wedge-issue politics of a failing, bitterly resistant movement of older white people, fearing the changes that are coming in our society, does not represent a viable future. The United States has wasted decades on hostile social policy and civil rights changes that have diminished and divided our society. It is time to reclaim and update the dream, linking the issues of racial justice to the widely shared values of country and faith.

It is, in the end, about us, about who we want to be, about how we go through the great transitions in our society, about how whites join with others to imagine and create a new society enriched by the contributions of all. It is about our major institutions recognizing that these problems are not solving themselves, that things have gotten significantly worse on some key dimensions, and that our leaders and our major organizations have engaged in endless wishful thinking because they do not want to call the situation as it is and name the realities that must be faced.

But there are many small and large ways to move forward. Now it is important for communities and organizations and leaders to show the way, first in small things and then to courageously talk about changing structures that are undermining our common future. We have to find a new language of true integration and mutual respect and, in the absence of one great leader, each try to be a leader and broaden the discussion in his or her own sphere.

It is an immense challenge, but also the great opportunity of our time. A movement begins when people decide that injustice is unacceptable and challenge the conscience of their community. It asks people to replace fears with dreams, to reach across lines, and to commit their talents to a fairer society. The civil rights movement a half century ago made the American South a much better and more successful region. A new civil rights strategy could do the same for our metropolitan society, which faces severe threats but has transformative potential.

Housing and Neighborhood Investment Policy

11

Housing

A National Anthem

Oscar Perry Abello, with Ron Grzywinski
and Marilyn Melkonian

IN HIS SECOND INAUGURAL ADDRESS, President Franklin Delano Roosevelt talked about government as "the instrument of our united purpose to solve . . . the ever-rising problems of a complex civilization."[1] It was not just a high-minded statement; it was an operational strategy. FDR's New Deal–era housing policies embodied government as a partner, putting tools and resources into the hands of thousands upon thousands of community-level actors. Working together, they launched America's middle class by creating affordable homeownership and housing for millions of families, though not for everyone.

The 1968 Kerner Report revealed deep racial disparities and inequities in our society, touching many aspects and elements. These elements include employment, education, health, housing, safety, and civility. The disparities and inequities cross racial lines. This chapter is about housing. It discusses our national housing policies from the New Deal to today. It shows great progress and many setbacks, as well as hope that we can meet the nation's aspiration of "a decent home and suitable living environment for every American."[2]

In 1932, the year FDR was elected, Congress created the Federal Home Loan Banks system, whose banks provide liquidity to member financial institutions—banks, credit unions, savings and loan associations, and others—giving them access to cheaper capital to make loans. Created in 1934, Federal Housing Administration mortgage insurance gave incentive and risk protection to lending institutions to make loans with low down payments, making homeownership affordable for millions of new home buyers. In 1938, the Congress created the Federal National Mortgage

Association, more popularly known as Fannie Mae, which provided a secondary mortgage market for these loans. Lenders could make loans and sell them to Fannie Mae, instantly getting back their principal, plus a share of the interest that they would have earned if they had kept the loans on their books for their entire terms. The secondary market reduced risk dramatically for financial institutions extending mortgages to millions of first-time homebuyers.

With these components in place, community banks and credit unions, savings and loan associations, and other lenders had what they needed to finance affordable homeownership for millions of families. It was a mortgage machine. The homeownership rate in the United States went from 44 percent in 1940 to 62 percent by 1960.[3] A decent affordable home became more than just a stable place to raise a family; it became an asset, the largest asset for the average household. Home equity provided access to capital to pay for higher education or a second car, it became capital invested among friends and family to start and grow small businesses, it served as a cushion in unforeseen emergencies.

But it did not work for everyone. As the mortgage machine really kicked into gear over the 1940s and 1950s, most lenders were white and often refused to do business with black households or in black neighborhoods. It was also an era before credit scores, so that private lenders and federal housing agencies who wrote mortgage underwriting guidelines judged risk according to their prejudice, by their belief that people of color and their neighborhoods (even Harlem at the height of the Harlem Renaissance) were too risky for them. Federal housing agencies marked neighborhoods of color with red lines or red shading—the source of the term "redlining." Federal policy and private lenders both viewed racially mixed neighborhoods as risky and undesirable. FHA mortgage insurance guidelines were written to encourage banks and other home lenders to write mortgage agreements for white borrowers to purchase homes in all-white neighborhoods with covenants prohibiting the resale of those homes to buyers of other races. Federal policy stopped encouraging racial covenants, thanks to lawsuits brought by the attorney Thurgood Marshall and others that received favorable decisions from the Supreme Court. Private lenders continued to practice biased lending and racially restrictive covenants explicitly and widely until finally outlawed by the Fair Housing Act of 1968.

One of the starkest statistics representing the decades of white-only access to the mortgage machine is that median net worth for white non-Hispanic households today ($132,483) is 14.6 times the median net worth of black households ($9,211).[4] About 80 percent of the absolute difference comes from real estate ownership.

Most families of color were left no choice but to stay in neighborhoods that were redlined. Residents and landlords had little or no access to the capital needed to acquire, maintain, or modernize buildings in neighbor-hoods of color. The condition of the housing stock in redlined neighbor-hoods became so bad that policy makers saw fit to demolish large sections, using Title I Slum Clearance programs authorized by the Housing Act of 1949. Racist policies and segregation trapped families of color in redlined neighborhoods, and many of their homes were subsequently bulldozed to make way for large-scale public housing complexes, interstate highways, or public works—like the Lincoln Center for the Performing Arts. At the same time that federal housing policy helped create white-picket-fence suburbs for white households, public housing for both blacks and whites, segregated by race, was being built around the country and subsequently neglected and under-resourced. With the aid of federal programs and policies, community-level actors, including lenders, developers, local housing authorities, and zoning and planning commissions, played lead-ing roles in shaping the reality of segregation. The Kerner Commission rang the alarm bell in its 1968 report that these forces were pushing the nation "toward two societies, one black, one white—separate and un-equal."[5]

The true costs of this history are only just beginning to be understood and measured. There is the moral cost of a debased national culture that cannot be measured in dollars. Yet it is captured almost daily in cell phone videos and underpins the urgent plea that Black Lives Matter. We now witness these incidents with mind-numbing regularity.

The story of the mortgage machine also shows how public policy can create action on a massive scale when it puts tools and resources into the hands of community-level actors. It built housing and wealth for millions, though it left millions behind solely on the basis of skin color. The chal-lenge today is figuring out how public policy can harness those same com-munity-level forces to build housing and opportunity for everyone, in every community, regardless of race.

A NEW HOPE

In the 1970s, a cadre of lenders emerged that would come to specialize in financing housing for those living in redlined neighborhoods. They, too, focused their efforts on financing smaller, community-level actors who would take ownership of their neighborhoods through family businesses or community-based organizations. They focused on rental housing, so while this did not necessarily build individual wealth for tenants, it was decent affordable housing that opened opportunities for people and changed neighborhoods for the better.

In 1973, there was ShoreBank, in Chicago. From its inception in 1973 until it closed its doors in 2010, ShoreBank financed fifty-nine thousand units of housing, nearly all of it multifamily rental housing on the South

Side of Chicago, centered on the South Shore neighborhood from which the bank took its name (it was previously called South Shore Bank). By 2008, ShoreBank had more than $2.4 billion in assets and earned more than $4.2 million in net income that year. While keeping its focus on meeting the credit needs of historically redlined neighborhoods, it routinely matched or exceeded the financial performance of similar-sized banks.

In New York, the Community Preservation Corporation (CPC) started out in 1974, during the time of New York City's fiscal crisis. These were the days of President Gerald Ford's October 1975 dismissal of the city that resulted in the infamous banner headline on the front page of the *New York Daily News*, "Ford to City: DROP DEAD."[6] At that time, few wanted to build or preserve housing in the city's formerly redlined neighborhoods except for residents, community-based nonprofit developers, and entrepreneurs who had often grown up themselves in those same neighborhoods. At the behest of Chase Manhattan Bank chair David Rockefeller, the city's large financial institutions formed CPC to serve as a one-stop shop to meet these smaller developers' needs, including capital as well as technical assistance for those who want to pursue local, state, and federal subsidies. About half of CPC borrowers are nonprofit community-based organizations and half are small for-profit developers, many of them small family-owned businesses or those that started out as such. Since its inception, CPC has invested or loaned $9.7 billion, financing 170,660 units of affordable housing throughout New York State, of which 105,475 are in New York City.

Two large national social entrepreneurs emerged not much later to focus on historically underinvested neighborhoods. The Local Initiatives Support Corporation (LISC) and Enterprise Community Partners. LISC, born in 1980, has since invested $17.3 billion dollars in low- to moderate-income communities all over the country, helping mostly community-based organizations build 365,922 units of affordable housing. Enterprise was founded in 1982 by Jim Rouse, a successful FHA mortgagor and developer. Enterprise has since made $28.9 billion in loans and investments, with its community-based borrowers producing 380,000 units of affordable housing.

Federal policy, too, played a key role in the work of these lenders, starting with the Housing Act of 1959, passed under the Eisenhower administration, and the Housing Act of 1961, passed under the Kennedy administration. These two acts created and expanded federal programs to provide and insure below-market-interest-rate loans for private developers, nonprofit and for-profit, to build or rehab multifamily rental housing for seniors and families of lower income. At the time of Kennedy's bill, the famous black comic and human rights leader Dick Gregory quipped, "With President Kennedy's new housing bill, I might be your neighbor now."[7]

The Housing Act of 1965, under President Lyndon Johnson, created the Department of Housing and Urban Development (HUD). It also included the first mechanism for federal rental assistance for tenants of lower income. Project-based rental assistance eventually became part of the Section 8 program in 1974. Under the terms of project-based Section 8 contracts, developers receive subsidies that make up the difference between tenants' 30 percent of income paid as rent and the fair-market rent, which is calculated by HUD for each metropolitan area. For lenders like CPC, LISC, or Enterprise, subsidies from project-based rental assistance helped support their borrowers' income streams, making it safer to finance the expansion of the developers' affordable-housing portfolios. Project-based rental assistance thus helped catalyze the expansion of affordable rental housing.

In 1968, President Johnson's housing bill, which he dubbed the Magna Carta of housing, created federal investments and an FHA insurance program aimed at building affordable housing and supporting other development in lower-income communities and elsewhere. The bill adopted as its vision one of the Kerner Commission's recommendations almost word for word, to bring millions of new and existing units of decent housing within reach of low- and moderate-income families over the next decade.

It fell to a president of the opposite party, Richard Nixon, to help carry out that vision. To the surprise of many, Nixon embraced affordable housing. The Nixon administration created 1.3 million units of low-income rental housing in its first four years.[8] Nixon introduced project-based Section 8 rental assistance as well as mobile Section 8 subsidies for residents who could take them to other locations. This reflected the issues argued in the Chicago *Gautreaux* decision.[9] Community Development Block Grants (CDBGs), came into existence in 1974. They helped counter the effects of the Title I Slum Clearance programs, which by that time had bulldozed over two thousand communities across the country.[10] CDBGs go directly to states and local government and were designed to allow maximum local flexibility and encourage local participation in determining their use. CDBGs became a vital source of equity and gap financing, leveraging additional private and public capital for affordable-housing production and other community development. Since 1977, HUD has disbursed nearly $150 billion in CDBGs to states and localities.

With these policies in place, the nation produced more than two hundred thousand new rent-subsidized units a year on average from 1975 to 1985. Lenders like ShoreBank, CPC, LISC, and Enterprise focused on lending to community-level actors who could take advantage of these federal programs, creating positive impacts in their neighborhoods.[11] Federal policy was working again, this time partnering at the community level to build affordable rental housing specifically for low-income households, mostly in urban areas, largely in former redlined neighborhoods. Most subsidized affordable housing today is privately owned. Project-based Section 8 rental assistance today supports 1.2 million households, while Section 8 vouchers support 2.1 million households. Public housing reaches 1.3 million households.

Moreover, all the federal funding streams and programs coming out of HUD were also supposed to serve as a lever for state and local governments to enforce the Fair Housing Act—an essential and critical recommendation of the Kerner Commission. The act passed in 1968, in the aftermath of both the assassination of Martin Luther King, Jr., and the same kind of civil disorders that had sparked the creation of the Kerner Commission. The act outlawed racially restrictive covenants and discrimination in the private housing market. The law also directed HUD's program participants (such as state and local governments that receive CDBG funding) "to take significant actions to overcome historic patterns of segregation, achieve truly balanced and integrated living patterns, promote fair-housing choice, and foster inclusive communities that are free from discrimination." The law gave HUD the authority to withhold funding or deny funding applications on the basis of failure to show such action. But when Nixon's first HUD secretary, George Romney, began using this authority to deny applications, Nixon promptly overrode Romney. HUD's authority to enforce the Fair Housing Act has never been used to its full potential. While the agency has built up a track record of enforcing cases of individual discrimination, an investigation in 2015 found only two occasions since Romney's tenure that HUD withheld money from communities for violating the Fair Housing Act.[12] In so doing, while continuing the bipartisan tradition since Eisenhower to build affordable housing across racial lines, Nixon sought to maintain segregation.

The worst was yet to come.

THE EMPIRE STRIKES BACK

In 1981, the bipartisan commitment to build housing for all (segregated or not) came to a screeching halt as President Ronald Reagan rode a wave of antigovernment sentiment into office. In his inaugural address, he proclaimed, despite decades of evidence to the contrary, "Government is not the solution to our problem; government is the problem."[13]

Once this ideology took hold, Reagan's policies shifted away from new production of affordable housing, preferring to focus on vouchers. In 1976, HUD's annual Section 8 program commitments peaked at 345,000 newly developed or renovated units and 172,000 vouchers. Seven years later, Reagan's administration proposed funding 132,000 vouchers and just 10,000 new and renovated units.[14] Federal funding for new rent-subsidized housing units has never again come close to its pre-Reagan levels. From 2010 to 2015, HUD provided funding for only 20,000 new rent-subsidized units per year.

Under these new priorities, the gap between availability of affordable housing and need widened dramatically. Today there are only 46 units of rental housing affordable for every 100 renter households living at or below 30 percent of area median income (AMI) in the United States.[15] About half those 46 units are subsidized and half are unsubsidized. Only 9 of 3,143 counties have at least one affordable rental housing unit for every renter household at or below 30 percent AMI. The shortage is worse in cities—rural counties have 69 adequate and affordable units available for every 100 renters at or below 30 percent AMI, compared with 42 units per 100 in metropolitan counties. Another measure of the afford-able-housing crisis is that an estimated 11.1 million households in 2017 pay more than 50 percent of their income in rent, an increase of about four million households from 2001.[16] Alarmingly, among the poorest quartile of families with children, households with severe housing cost burdens spend 53 percent less on food, health care, and transportation compared with similar households that are not overburdened.

THE RETURN OF THE COMMUNITY-BASED HOUSING DEVELOPERS

In 1987, Low-Income Housing Tax Credits (LIHTCs) came on the scene as part of the 1986 Tax Reform Act. LIHTCs provide federal income tax credits to private investors in exchange for equity investments in afford-able housing serving households with income below 60 percent of AMI. Tax credits are allocated by state housing finance agencies, which can mandate lower income levels. LIHTCs helped LISC and Enterprise Community Partners kick into high gear in the 1990s. CPC would add it to its toolbox as well, supporting its cadre of locally based nonprofit and for-profit developers. Since 1986, LIHTCs have facilitated production or rehab of an annual average of about one hundred thousand privately owned affordable-housing units. A total of over three million units have been built through 2016.

In 1994, the Riegle Community Development and Regulatory Im-provement Act established federal certification for community-develop-ment financial institutions (CDFIs), as well as the CDFI Fund, an arm of the U.S. Treasury to support the burgeoning CDFI field. Federally certi-fied CDFIs must target at least 60 percent of their lending or financial services to low- and moderate-income census tracts or households. Most exceed that number every year, some by a wide margin. Every federal dollar spent on CDFIs leverages another $10 from other funding sources, according to the Treasury.[17] While many of them predated the legislation, today there are more than one thousand federally certified CDFIs with more than $108 billion in assets. CPC, LISC, and Enterprise are CDFIs, as was ShoreBank. Programs administered by the Treasury's CDFI Fund, such as New Markets Tax Credits or the CDFI Bond Guarantee Program, have helped drive capital to comprehensive community development, not just housing, in low- and moderate-income areas. Since the first round of allocations in 2002, New Markets Tax Credits have directed more than $75 billion in capital to distressed areas and leveraged considerably more. New Markets Tax Credits are revenue neutral, and they generate over $1.88 billion in additional tax revenue. They accomplish this by leveraging employment in businesses that pay taxes. Since its first round of authorizations in 2013, the CDFI Bond Guarantee Program has authorized more than $1 billion in long-term, fixed-rate capital for community development in low- and moderate-income areas. An evaluation of CDFIs released in 2015 showed that they leveraged the preservation or construction of 17,749 affordable-housing units each year from 2003 to 2012.

Yet the combined LIHTC and CDFI affordable-housing production since 1988 is still far below the production levels that added subsidized housing in the pre-Reagan era. Before 1981, multiple presidents from both parties committed the federal government to a more robust expansion of the nation's stock of rent-assisted housing, enabling community-level actors to deliver housing to people in neighborhoods they serve.

The power grid built by federal, state, local, and community-level actors—a mix of mortgage insurance, rent subsidies, CDBGs, CDFIs, the secondary market, and below-market financing tools, to name a few—is today woefully underfunded and undercapitalized.

Funding for CDBGs has fallen 80 percent (in real terms) since 1979 and today is at only $3 billion nationally to serve fifty states.[18] Limits on vouchers and rental subsidies mean only one in four families eligible for rental assistance actually receives it.[19] One of the results of such low funding for affordable housing is that the bottom has fallen out. According to the National Alliance to End Homelessness, 565,000 individuals were homeless in the survey month of January 2015,[20] and millions cycle in and out of shelter systems throughout the year.[21]

Federal spending on different forms of rental assistance and other housing support has been steady at around $50 billion a year since 2003, or about 4 percent of the federal budget. Meanwhile, in 2014, the federal government spent $130 billion on housing assistance not targeted at low-income households, mostly through tax deductions for mortgage interest and other deductions related to real estate.[22] More than 80 percent of the value of mortgage interest deductions goes to households earning more than $100,000.[23]

It seems that some cap on mortgage interest deductions would be helpful to pay for expanded federal spending on rental assistance to low-income households, boost CDBG funding, provide more support for CDFIs, and increase significantly annual LIHTC funding. The mortgage interest and real estate tax deductions are offered without limits to those eligible, while other federal housing and community development assistance is severely limited. In a modern country as wealthy as ours, this inequality and inequity is indefensible.

INVESTING IN AFFORDABLE HOUSING STRENGTHENS COMMUNITIES

According to a study published by the Stanford researchers Rebecca Diamond and Jim McQuade in 2017, neighborhoods with a median income less than $26,000 saw a rise in property values after the construction of LIHTC-financed housing units. Even more intense effects appear in these neighborhoods within a tenth-of-a-mile radius of the new units, such that property values appreciate 6.5 percent after the affordable housing is built. The study also found that racial segregation decreased in both rich and poor neighborhoods when affordable housing was introduced.[24]

These findings affirm the prior experiences of lenders like ShoreBank and CPC. The development of larger, subsidized developments like those financed by LIHTC or with project-based Section 8 assistance often spurred others in the neighborhood to step forward and get into the neighborhood housing development business. Housing policy could give priority to locating subsidized housing in neighborhoods where each development is most likely to encourage other developers from the neighborhood to step forward to invest in smaller properties nearby. Every subsidized unit could spur one or more unsubsidized units of affordable housing.

Besides multiplying the units produced per subsidy dollar, another benefit of encouraging smaller, local developers is local hiring. From ShoreBank's borrowers to CPC's borrowers to many of LISC's and Enterprise's borrowers, local hiring is an underappreciated but important staple of their work. Neighborhood-based developers take pride in putting people to work on projects in their own neighborhoods—and these developers also often hire people from the neighborhood. The visibility of local workers rehabbing or building affordable housing has consequences beyond the specific project they are building. It cultivates a feeling of community ownership and economic self-determination, sentiments long denied to communities of color and other communities too. Affordable-housing development can help create jobs and careers in construction, maintenance, management, and elsewhere along the way.

DO NOT FORGET THE ROLE OF BANKS, BIG AND SMALL

The Community Reinvestment Act (CRA) of 1977 says that banks have a continuing and affirmative obligation to meet the credit needs of the communities where they do business. Should they fail to meet those needs, the law gives federal regulators the authority to deny bank expansion or bank merger applications. The CRA has grown to become an incentive that drives $77 billion a year in community development lending and investments by banks,[25] but banks can and must do more.

Out of $16.2 trillion in total assets at commercial banks in the United States, over $7 trillion consists of various securities or other financial instruments that are mere derivatives of other transactions. The genius of the CRA was not to outlaw other kinds of investments but to say to banks that they have to meet local needs first. In the United States, an estimated 93 percent of people over the age of fifteen have a bank account.[26] Even among the poorest 40 percent of the population, an estimated 87 percent of people over the age of fifteen have a bank account.[27] Nearly everyone in the United States has a bank account, meaning banks are doing business in every community—even those considered banking deserts because they are distant from a bank branch. At the same time, every community has some local capacity for affordable-housing development and restoration—developers of the kind that ShoreBank, CPC, LISC, and Enterprise have worked with for decades. And yet these communities and developers have difficulty accessing the capital needed to build enough housing that is affordable for all. CRA examiners should extend their analysis, looking more deeply at affordable-housing needs to determine whether banks are actually meeting those needs. Cities or large institutions like universities or foundations could make a point of depositing dollars or contracting banking services with banks that show a higher commitment of meeting the credit needs of the most vulnerable, including greater access to capital for affordable-housing developers.

CRA regulations can also do more to support more integrated communities. Under their current interpretation of the law, CRA examiners evaluate banks largely on the basis of how much capital they have driven into lower-income census tracts (80 percent of AMI or less). These areas certainly need capital, and it still makes sense to keep the criteria for CRA examiners' evaluation. But banks have fallen into the habit of making CRA-motivated loans in the same neighborhoods time and time again, as opposed to, say, financing the construction or provision of affordable housing to more affluent areas as well. Tweaking CRA regulations could expand greatly where CRA-motivated capital goes, helping counter the historic inertia of segregation. Banks should get CRA credit, for example, by financing the construction or preservation of housing that is affordable for low- and extremely low-income households outside low- and moderate-income areas. It does not need to be a zero-sum game; both markets can be served. Banks have the capital as well as a legal obligation to finance affordable housing and community development in both high-opportunity and underserved markets.

BACK WHERE WE STARTED

Fannie Mae and Freddie Mac (the Federal Home Loan Mortgage Corporation, created by Congress in 1970 to enlarge the secondary market for mortgages) could also create or expand measures to support both deseg-regation and housing affordability. Since 1992, HUD has had the author-ity over Fannie and Freddie to set affordable-housing goals and monitor compliance with fair-lending principles.[28] In 2016, Freddie Mac financing touched around 410,000 housing units with rents affordable for low-in-come (up to 50 percent AMI) or very low-income (up to 30 percent AMI) households—preserving them as affordable or adding some improve-ments like energy-efficient windows or other small changes that help re-duce the cost of living. Over 80 percent of Fannie Mae's $55 billion in multifamily rental financing in 2016 was for buildings with rents afford-able to low- or very low-income households.

Fannie and Freddie, also known as government-sponsored enterprises, still have an important role to play; they are important, in part, because of their unique standing to reflect both the public interest and the inter-ests of their stockholders and not what some might call Wall Street values, which led the agencies into the subprime quagmire. Some say it is impos-sible for people to weigh these interests together fairly. Others remark that the special ability to balance public and private interests was embodied in David Maxwell, the architect of the modern Fannie Mae from 1981 to 1991.

Fannie and Freddie could reach smaller developers with smaller aver-age building sizes. There are many smaller affordable-housing developers at the neighborhood level who build or preserve under 150 units and have small portfolios. Freddie Mac began a Small Balance Loan program in 2014. Under this program, Freddie Mac serves as a secondary buyer for loans on multifamily properties with five units or more, ranging from $1 million to $5 million. In its first three years, this program has financed 73,000 units of housing affordable for low- and very low-income house-holds. CPC is one of the participating lenders in this program.

The government-sponsored enterprises are also exploring how to work with state and local governments on financing housing that is subject to inclusionary zoning requirements—creating an incentive for more lend-ers to compete to finance such projects. These enterprises could also serve as a vehicle to finance reduced-cost home mortgages for families (of all colors) to make integrative moves. The government-sponsored enterprises have more potential to help finance affordable rental housing and home-ownership that reduces racial and economic segregation.

SCALE EQUAL TO THE DIMENSION OF THE PROBLEMS

The Kerner Commission called for solutions with the scale to meet the dimension of the problems. For a challenge on the scale of building "a decent home and suitable living environment for every American," put-ting community-level actors in a leading role has been the way this country has worked best. Policy makers need to remember that government spending more on housing does not necessarily mean government making all the decisions about where and what to build. As it has done for the single-family home market, and as it was doing for the multifamily rental market before the Reagan administration, federal policies and dollars can put tools and resources into the hands of community-level actors to meet the needs of each and every household in each and every community—renters and homeowners, white and black, urban or not.

The power grid to supply capital to build and preserve more affordable housing needs to be turned back on to end the affordable-housing crisis. To afford a modest, two-bedroom rental in the United States, renters need to earn $21.21 per hour—that is $13.96 higher than the federal minimum wage. In only twelve counties in the United States can a full-time minimum-wage worker afford a modest one-bedroom rental.[29] Housing assistance should be made available to all who qualify. The promise of "a decent home and a suitable living environment" needs to be fulfilled.

Housing policy is only a part of the answer to creating a just economy that works for everyone. Many pieces—health, education, and employment—are parts of that economy. What is clear is that the remarkable Kerner Commission got it right. The work that it called on America to do is not yet done.

A FEW LAST WORDS

The Kerner Commission held up a mirror to America. The revelation was the undeniable evidence of the nation's deep and destructive racism. The report made the bold statement, echoing Abraham Lincoln, that a house divided, a society so divided, could not remain so. The divide needed to be bridged. We have spent too much time under the cloud of racism—twisting our lives and slowing the progress of our common cause. Even today, nooses appear in public places and, once again, the encouragement of racism is heard from the highest levels. FDR quoted the poet O'Shaughnessy in his second inaugural: "Each age is a dream that is dying, or one that is coming to birth."[30] It is time to leave behind the fantasy of racial superiority underpinned by the pleasure of oppression and finally walk into the sunlight of "one Nation, under God, indivisible, with liberty and justice for all."

12

Race Relations since the Ghetto Riots of the 1960s

Elijah Anderson

THE CIVIL RIGHTS MOVEMENT culminated in riots and civil disorders in major cities around the United States. Tensions were high in ghetto communities, and city after American city burned. In these circumstances, almost any incident of police transgression or brutality could set off rioting, and in many cases a simple spark did; urban ghettos were likened to tinderboxes. The nation learned to dread long hot summers of rioting and civil disorders.

In late July 1967, during one of the worst of these conflagrations, in Detroit, Michigan, President Lyndon Johnson appointed the Kerner Commission to investigate these civil disorders and to make recommendations for alleviating their causes and preventing their recurrence. The commission's eventual 1968 report essentially concluded that the disorders were attributable to one central cause: white racism.

This finding was not well received by all, to say the least, and in fact many prominent white U.S. leaders rejected it. Indeed, the dominant ideology in the country at the time was one of egalitarianism, equality, freedom, equal opportunity, and fair play, and many in the establishment were simply unable to think of the system as racist. Yet the truth of this finding was well known and undeniable: since the days of slavery, black people had been lynched, ghettoized, marginalized, generally treated as second-class citizens, and excluded from American institutions largely on the basis of race, and the country had a long way to go to treat black people as full citizens. Thus, while President Johnson appeared to ignore the report and some members of the Congress repudiated it, many political, academic, and business leaders began in their own way to try to make America more consistent with its professed values and ideology.

RACIAL INCORPORATION—AND ITS FADING

These developments signaled in American society the advent of what I call the racial incorporation process, which set the stage for an ethos of inclusion that encouraged the mobility of black Americans and, ultimately, that of Hispanics, white women, Asians, and other underrepresented minorities.

At the heart of this process was the idea of affirmative action. This process was widely regarded as something of a second Reconstruction in the making, and President Johnson, who had himself emerged from a segregationist past, nevertheless led this significant social change. And he did so even though he and others in the establishment—in government, academia, and corporate America—did not address the process directly. However, powerful white people everywhere knew that if they were going to save the country, dominant white-controlled institutions needed to change: they needed to incorporate black people, to give them a stake in American society.

Initially, the incorporation process could be observed in small, informal ways: black employees in a shoe store transitioned from stock boys to salesmen, grocery stores hired black clerks, and black people now were suddenly viewed getting Excedrin headaches on television. To cool things down after civic unrest, window-dressing and tokenism became ever more prevalent, particularly in ghetto communities.

Later, the more formal, and consequential, aspects of this incorporation process included civil rights legislation, equal-employment policies, voting rights, fair-housing policies, school integration, set-asides, and nondiscrimination regulations for restaurants and other public accommodations. To placate the activists, these measures sometimes functioned as though akin to quotas, specifying how many blacks had to be in an institution, and were roundly criticized partly for this reason.

While diverse groups of white people supported these efforts, many others complained that these efforts against racial exclusion were based on race, and not explicitly on merit, and such policies, therefore, particularly affirmative action, were unsuited to an egalitarian country. What could have been a fuller incorporation process was stymied, as the white masses, consumed by deeply held prejudices, perceived that their own rights and assumed privileges were being abrogated by the advancement of blacks. For these reasons, a powerful conservative backlash formed. With the apparent rise in the mobility of black Americans, others began to inspect their relationship with black people as well as their own relationship with the extant system of social stratification. In doing so, many members of these groups, some of whom were erstwhile supporters of the civil rights movement, petitioned their political representatives to challenge affirmative-action policies or racial preferences for black people.

These actions encouraged political debate and court cases that effectively challenged affirmative action as a public policy.

Eventually, "affirmative action" became a pejorative term for someone who was utterly unqualified but hired as a token. "Diversity," on the other hand, was a politically more acceptable concept, since it was more inclusive. Essentially, diversity as a public policy became the political price that affirmative action was required to pay in order to exist at all. In effect, affirmative action became diversity. With diversity, there was a rising sense of inclusion by many others, but the policy would no longer address the special issues of black people and thus limited their incorporation.

Now, across the nation, the social programs that once aided so many and gave them hope for the future have had their funding slashed, with many subsequently being abolished. The public schools that serve the black poor and working class have been allowed to deteriorate to the point that they fail to educate children for the demands of today's society and economy. Widespread joblessness and the lack of a social safety net make it difficult for stable families to form, and many poor children grow up without effective parenting. Nonetheless, the incorporation process has been highly consequential for the nation, and for black people in particular, as it has resulted in the formation of the largest black middle class in history.

DEINDUSTRIALIZATION AND GLOBALIZATION

Another important development has emerged since the Kerner Commission wrote its report—deindustrialization and the increasingly globalized economy. Since the 1950s, the economy has been changing from one based largely on manufacturing to one based increasingly on service and high technology. As these changes occurred, great numbers of people became dislocated, as manufacturing jobs literally disappeared, or they were required to work at the lowest levels of the service economy in jobs that failed to pay them a living wage. To adjust to this new economy, people need skills and education, or human capital.

During the transition, great numbers of factory jobs left urban areas for the suburbs and then, in search of cheaper labor, for nonmetropolitan areas, then for Mexico, and then for China, India, and other developing countries—places where the work could be done at a fraction of the cost in the United States. In effect, U.S. manufacturing workers had to compete for jobs with the working poor in developing countries. With the decline in U.S. manufacturing and the emergence of the service and high-tech economy, workers needed more in the way of human capital to thrive, but many people—black and white alike—failed to adjust to the new economy, and many became mired in a new kind of structural poverty.

Of course, black people have a special problem here. Their poverty has become effectively racialized; as they seek employment, they carry the extra burden of racial prejudice. This burden allows those with whom they might compete for place and position to enjoy an upper hand, if only because they are not black and thus not implicitly associated with the social ills of the inner-city ghetto. Thus, black poverty is different in this fundamental respect.[1] Moreover, if black people fall through the cracks, more government assistance is required, but for accepting this, they are then blamed. With little hope for the future, many of the most enterprising young people then turn to the underground economy, for which there is more blame, exacerbating what has become an enduring cycle of debilitating events that negatively define the inner-city black community.

THE GHETTO

The institution of slavery established the black body at the bottom of society. When slavery was abolished and black people migrated to cities, North and South, they gravitated to black communities where they became concentrated, and the larger white society then worked to contain them there. In the past, the black ghetto was a haven from white racism, a place of refuge where black people could feel at home among their own kind. These neighborhoods developed as segregated communities, replete with their own infrastructures and social organization. But in time, they took on a more sinister definition and purpose, essentially reinforcing the lowly place of black people that slavery had previously established.

Today, in virtually every city in America, there is a black side of town, an area where the black people live or are concentrated—the so-called black ghetto. The urban ghettos of America continue to struggle with their legacy of racial caste. Buffeted by the winds of deindustrialization and a global economy that has left many of their residents disfranchised and socially excluded, these poor black communities are typically characterized by high rates of structural poverty, joblessness, crime, and violence.

A typical ghetto is a neighborhood in Philadelphia known as Southwest. Before the blacks, there were the WASPs, the Irish Catholics, and the Jews, but now the people living in Southwest are predominantly African American and poor, with a relatively small number of Latinos, Asians, and Africans. It is a neighborhood just to the southwest of West Philadelphia, near the University of Pennsylvania. The university community is racially mixed and, to a degree, gentrified; politically, it is moderately progressive. It suffers a significant amount of crime, in part because of the poor and desperate people who live so close to it. Such issues are prevalent in similarly situated edge areas around the United States, where the white and black well-to-do live side by side with poverty and desperation. In this edge area, whites often confuse their black middle-class neighbors with the poor blacks they fear.

When blacks first began to move into Southwest, whites gradually moved out; in turn, poorer blacks began to take their place. The consequences are visible not simply demographically but also in terms of institutional engagement with the neighborhood. Today, blight is everywhere: the police are rarely seen and drive by rapidly when they are, while municipal services from garbage pickup to building-code enforcement have become substandard in comparison with those at the core of downtown. Accompanied by redlining on the part of banks and insurance companies, these developments have worked to seal the neighborhood's fate as a ghetto.

Now, dilapidated and well-kept houses sit side by side in this area. The fully employed live right next door to the unemployed, who in many cases have given up on trying to find work. There is a great deal of demoralization. At times the most desperate people prey on those "with something." Residents observe the buying habits of others and, given the level of poverty and desperation of the community, those with resources become suspicious and guarded toward their neighbors—for instance, being careful about putting out telltale appliance boxes for trash removal, because they do not want their neighbors to know their business. When the police are summoned, they are likely to arrive late or not at all. Thus, in matters of personal defense, residents often feel they are on their own.

The main drag in Southwest is called Kingsessing Street. The street caters to the needs and desires of ghetto residents, offering everything from restaurants to convenience stores to taverns to delis. Sometimes Kingsessing is referred to simply as "the block," or "the street"—that street-corner scene where everyone hangs out or eventually passes by.

To walk down this street as an outsider is to witness the effects of the area's profound isolation. While the police presence is intermittent, the local businesses are open. People stand around in front of the carryout, the dime store, or the corner barbershop. Most stores have riot gates. Certain stores have a pane of Plexiglas separating the customers from the clerk. All the goods are behind the Plexiglas. The people being served are not to be trusted.

The inhabitants understand that they should take the same precautions as the storeowners. They realize that they are responsible for their own safety. They understand the police officer's position of disengagement, because they know he or she wants to get home safely at night. They can understand the need for riot gates: without them, break-ins would occur incessantly. They know that they should not let their guard down. They must never give the stickup boy the opportunity to rob them. Every person has to be vigilant about his or her own safety.

As this situation is manifested on the streets, as the civil authorities abdicate their responsibilities, the civil law is often regarded as weak or nonexistent, and street justice fills the void. This means that the threat of physical retribution is very close to the surface in matters of everyday life and is necessary for street credibility—an invaluable coin in the local community, and one that is not established once and for all, but is high maintenance and must be reasserted daily.

The incessant search for street credibility has turned the community on itself, and as a result, the homicide rate has increased by leaps and bounds: Philadelphia as a whole has one of the highest murder rates in the country, and this community has one of the worst rates in the city. With each published report of a crime or murder, the area's negative reputation increases. All communities that are predominantly black gradually become associated with this image, especially in the minds of outsiders, regardless of their particular crime rates. It is almost as though the identity and status of Southwest has been indiscriminately applied to every black community in America: if you have seen one ghetto, you have seen them all.

THE GHETTO AS ICON

But the ghetto is not solely a physical location; especially since the urban riots of the 1960s, it has become a major icon in American society and culture and has become an important source of stereotype and symbolic racism.[2] The iconography of the ghetto competes with the plantation system of the old South as a means to define black people. Given the pejorative connotations of "ghetto," most outsiders, including many whites from relatively homogeneous residential areas, have learned to be wary of the ghetto's inhabitants. Thus, when black people encounter others, they are burdened with a deficit of credibility—a powerful manifestation of the iconic ghetto, whereby the individual's race counts as a strike against his or her character. This wariness can dissipate in time but only if the person so judged is willing to work for it, often before a distant and unreceptive audience.

Because of his association with the iconic ghetto, the moment a black person enters an overwhelmingly white neighborhood, workplace, restaurant, or other public setting—which blacks refer to as the white space—he is placed in what amounts to a proverbial social hole. And he is put on notice that, to climb from that hole, he must work to disabuse his audience of its negative presumptions. Depending on his attitude, the black person may rise to the occasion with a host of presentation rituals, including dressing well, speaking well, and behaving properly—that is, with an acute sense of propriety.

Once a black person is able to pass inspection, the deficit of credibility may lessen, as others begin to view her more and more as a credible, law-abiding member of society. And while reaching this milestone is important, it is not the end of the story or the close of her campaign for trust and credibility. In a sense, her work has only just begun. Now that she has convinced a few whites and others of her credibility, chiefly by becoming better known, she must work diligently to continue to behave in ways that put her audience at ease. In essence, the black person graduates from the immediate deficit of credibility to a provisional status in which she still has something more to prove.

Though waging a campaign for respect can leave middle-class blacks feeling utterly spent and demoralized, they typically keep this side of themselves hidden from their white counterparts. But if the middle-class black person generally possesses the human capital to work for respect, the lower-class, ghetto-dwelling black person often does not. For such a person, the ghetto icon and the deficit of credibility are often much more consequential, affecting employment, health care, and daily life in ways that are little appreciated by both the lay public and social scientists. Specifically, the icon hinders poor blacks' ability to become employed, increases the likelihood that a police encounter will lead to arrest, and affects the quality of treatment they receive in hospital emergency departments, where illnesses may not be given the serious consideration they deserve.

In this fundamental respect, the impact of the iconic ghetto is likely to be highly consequential for the ghetto-dwelling black person. For unlike the middle-class black people living in the suburbs, ghetto-dwelling black people are unable to deny their residence and its heritage; they really do come from the ghetto. And no matter how hard they may try, they cannot shake off this association.

In 1903, W.E.B. DuBois presciently wrote that the "problem of the Twentieth Century is the problem of the color line."[3] In the twenty-first century, with the disappearance of institutional and government-supported racial segregation and the election of the nation's first black president, some claim that we now live in a postracial America. But if the recent political campaigns are any indication, this proposition is highly questionable.

Today, a complex racial configuration is emerging—one in which a new and powerful demarcation between the races is drawn out of the blue or at any minute. If the line separating blacks and whites was once rigid and sharp, it is now more ambiguous and arbitrary. It appears when others perceive black people as being out of their place, at times to the shock and dismay of those who thought that we were over that.

To be sure, the ongoing process of incorporation that began with the civil rights struggles and urban riots of the 1960s has made undeniable progress toward racial parity. But in the shadows lurks the specter of the urban ghetto. The iconic ghetto is always in the background, an anachronism, an artifact of state-sponsored segregation, having everything to do with the historical circumstances that blacks have been forced to endure: ghetto poverty, disenfranchisement, crime-ridden neighborhoods, and a host of other social ills. These social ills are now promoted by the images of the icon and in turn fuel the prejudices that are centered on the ghetto as a den of iniquity. In this special respect, the iconic ghetto deeply influences Americans' conception of the anonymous black person as well as the circumstances of blacks in all walks of life: America is far from being a color-blind society.

Although racial differences in economic status remain a negative feature of American society, blacks now work in a wider range of occupations than ever. Many black people are thriving in professional positions in which they rarely appeared before—as doctors, lawyers, professors, corporate executives, respected entertainers, professional athletes, and elected officials. Many of these people also live in racially mixed neighborhoods from which they were once excluded; they attend some of the best schools and universities in the country, places that only recently excluded them.

But this class of black people is generally obscured in the minds of many whites by the omnipresence and salience of the iconic ghetto. As Everett Hughes has written, a "master status" refers to a facet of identity that serves as the primary identifying characteristic of a person.[4] In American society, the iconic ghetto acts as a "master status," superseding whatever else a black person might claim to be. This stereotypical image of the ghetto works to define the black body as a powerful symbol in American culture—the iconic Negro.

Educated and well-off black people are generally considered the exception and not the rule. Thus, typically, when black people venture into the larger society—into the areas blacks generally perceive as white space, including corporations, universities, suburbs—the ghetto icon both follows and precedes their presence, hovering overhead and negatively affecting their relations with their fellow citizens.

White Americans typically regard these spaces as normal, everyday reflections of civil society and may even regard them as diverse. But what others see as diverse, black people may perceive as homogeneously white and relatively privileged. While the respective white and black spaces may appear to be racially homogeneous, typically they can be subclassified in terms of ethnicity and social class. White spaces, for instance, often include not only traditional Americans of European descent but also recently arrived European immigrants and visitors as well as others who may be perceived as phenotypically white. Comparatively lighter-complexioned blacks, and members of some other ethnic groups, such as Asians, may be granted a pass. Meanwhile, the people inhabiting black space are not always simply traditional African Americans but on closer inspection may be subclassified as African, Latino, Haitian, Caribbean, Cape Verdean, and so on.

The urban environment today can be conceptualized as consisting of white space, black space, and racially mixed space, spaces that are typically in flux. The racially mixed urban space, a version of which I have referred to elsewhere as "the cosmopolitan canopy,"[5] exists as a diverse island of civility located in a virtual sea of racial segregation.

While white people usually avoid black space, black people are required to navigate the white space as a condition of their existence.[6] By definition, white people predominate in white spaces, and by implication blacks and other people of color are often absent there or, when present, made to feel uneasy. In the white space, the most acceptable black person is one who is either in his place, working as a janitor or as a service person, or one who is otherwise being vouched for by white people in good standing. Such a black person is less likely to be disturbing to the perceived racial order of the typical white setting. When the black person does not appear in a subordinate role, dissonance may occur.

In many such spaces, black persons can expect to be racially profiled or to encounter acute disrespect on the basis of their blackness.[7] Thus, blacks may be highly self-conscious in such settings and may sense that they are in hostile territory even when this is not the case. The closer the ghetto, the more self-conscious the black person may feel, its proximity complicating his or her presence; on the outskirts of a ghetto, white people become more defensive and scrutinize the anonymous black person more thoroughly, wondering whether he or she may mean them harm. Hence, black people, as they commonly report, in these settings are often profiled and charged for driving while black, walking while black, or simply existing while black.

Blacks are now generally allowed to venture into spaces that are absolutely lily-white and expect to be present there uneventfully, often as the only black person present. But they may be mistaken for someone of menial position. Polite company may not overtly declare this as white space, which would draw unwanted attention to the observation, but some of the most marginal whites might do so, effectively drawing the color line, typically to put the black person in his or her place.

Among their friends, black people sometimes refer to such incidents as the "nigger moment," a moment of acute disrespect based on their blackness. Such moments vary in intensity, ranging from incidents they consider to be minor to those they know to be major. Black people generally try to ignore minor incidents, but they understand that major incidents can change their lives or even get them killed. When such a moment occurs, the black person may be so affected that his or her orientation toward the white space can be altered, at times profoundly.

Given these difficulties, many blacks may approach the white space ambivalently and often for instrumental reasons. When possible, they may avoid it altogether or leave it as soon as possible. In exiting the white space, however, a black person can feel both relief and regret—relief for departing a stressful environment and regret for perhaps leaving prematurely. Because the white space is where many social rewards originate, whether the brief pleasures of an elegant night on the town or life-course-affecting sources of cultural capital: education, employment, privilege, prestige, money, and the promise of general acceptance among the successful.

To obtain these rewards, blacks must venture into the white space and explore its possibilities. To prevail, they must manage themselves within this space. But all too frequently, prejudiced actors pervade the white space and are singly or collectively interested in marginalizing the black person, actively reminding him or her of his or her outsider status. The existence of racial segregation is a pervasive feature of American life, rooted in the assumption that whites and blacks belong in different physical spaces—with white spaces offering vastly more opportunities, amenities, and privileges than black ones.[8]

CONCLUSION

Large numbers of black people and white people alike have been unable to acquire the human capital necessary to make a decent living in the modern economy. Black people, particularly those residing in the nation's iconic ghettos, have a special burden, based solely on their historic, and compounded, exclusion on the basis of color. Until now, special efforts to directly address this problem have been effectively countered and dismissed as "racism in reverse," as others have come to feel that their own rights and privileges are being abrogated by any attention to the special plight of people of color. But these efforts must now be redoubled. In particular, police departments need to be refocused toward understanding and protecting black neighborhoods, instead of occupying them military style; black schools need to be drastically upgraded, physically and intellectually; decent, affordable housing needs to be built in black neighborhoods; meaningful job training and jobs need to be made available for lower-class and working-class blacks; health care must be made available to impoverished black families; local and national legal practices need to be developed to avoid, among many other problems, jailing blacks for (in effect) being poor or for minor offenses committed on the school yard or the street corner. Achieving these goals would require a long and expensive effort. But bringing millions of our fellow citizens into full citizenship and real participation in the economy would enrich us all, socially and economically.

Crime Prevention and Criminal Justice Policy

13

Evidence-Based Programs, Policies, and Practices

DELBERT S. ELLIOTT

THE KERNER COMMISSION'S RECOMMENDATION in 1968 was that the nation stop doing what does not work and replicate what does work at a scale equal to the dimensions of our problems. Subsequent updates of the commission's report have noted some progress in the identification and implementation of evidence-based interventions but conclude that implementations were relatively rare, local, underfunded, and had little impact on the ongoing operation of our major institutions.[1] The overall finding in the fortieth-anniversary update was that the prevention and control goals of the original report had not been met.

To what extent are current American prevention programs, practices, and policies evidence based and implemented at a scale sufficient to ensure a positive course of development for all children and youth? This is the question addressed in this chapter. As in the initial report, the focus in this fiftieth-anniversary update is on crime and violence[2] prevention, treatment interventions, and to the extent they are implicated in the causes of criminal behavior, interventions targeting health, education, and economic risk and protective factors.

ADVANCES IN PREVENTION SCIENCE

Without question, there have been major advances in prevention-science research over the past fifty years. Interpersonal violence and other forms of criminal and antisocial behavior have come to be viewed as public health, as well as justice system, problems, leading to a wider set of targeted prevention outcomes than identified in the original and updated reports, outcomes that include both risk and protective factors that facilitate a positive course of child and youth development. A new life-course developmental paradigm has become accepted, focusing attention on the timing of critical life events and their interaction with changing social and cultural contexts across different stages of development, calling attention to events and social and physical environments in childhood and early adolescence that put children at risk for later crime and violence.

Large-scale longitudinal studies have provided stronger evidence for the major risk and protective factors predicting violence, drug use, and criminal behavior; those factors' differences across cultural and environmental settings; and their patterns of change over the life course. This information has guided the development of new evidence-based prevention programs and practices. And new types of evaluation methods and statistical analysis have been developed to address many of the technical problems frequently encountered in earlier evaluation studies.

Public and governmental support for evidence-based interventions also has grown substantially. In 2002, the White House encouraged all federal agencies to support evidence-based programs and to discontinue programs without evidence of effectiveness,[3] and in 2014, the White House endorsed the use of rigorous scientific evaluations, particularly randomized, controlled trials, for improving federal programs.[4] It is now common practice that federal funding for prevention programs calls for evidence-based programs and practices.[5]

ONLINE REGISTRIES OF EVIDENCE-BASED INTERVENTIONS

In 2018, we have far better knowledge of what works and have identified far more evidence-based programs and practices than were known and identified in 1968 or even at the time of the fortieth-year update of the Kerner Report. A number of online registries of evidence-based programs, practices, and policies are now online.[6] The Justice Department alone currently lists 425 specific prevention programs and practices identified as evidence based (effective or promising) for violence, drugs, or crime.

Despite this large number of programs, there are concerns about the practical utility of this information for a nationally coordinated violence and crime prevention initiative such as that called for by the Kerner Commission.[7] There are several reasons for this concern. First, there is no consensus in the research, practitioner, or policy-making communities regarding the scientific standard for certifying a program, practice, or policy as evidence based. The types and levels of scientific evidence required for certification on existing registries varies from a single quasi-experimental design (QED) study to a single randomized, controlled trial (RCT), to multiple QEDs and RCTs, to requiring replication, and to requiring sustainability of effects for some designated time postintervention. Second, standards often are applied inconsistently by evaluators, and reviews of evaluations often lack scientific rigor and involve the judgment of a single reviewer. The concern is that evidence-based registries are failing to meet clients', practitioners', and funders' needs for current, trustworthy information about an intervention's effectiveness.[8]

Multiple lists with different standards and an uneven application of standards present a confusing picture to both public and private agencies looking for guidance in selecting an evidence-based program or practice. A federal scientific standard for certifying programs as evidence based has been proposed.[9] The Working Group of the Federal Collaboration on What Works[10] was created in 2004 to establish a scientific standard for identifying and classifying prevention programs. The report of the Federal Collaboration was published in 2005 and recommended that prevention programs be classified as (1) effective, (2) effective with reservation, (3) promising, (4) inconclusive evidence, (5) insufficient evidence, or (6) ineffective.[11] Only those programs and practices classified as effective were recommended for scale-up. These are the interventions with the minimum required evidence of effectiveness necessary for implementation in a national or state-wide prevention initiative with confidence of success. The standard for certification as an effective program requires statistically significant positive behavioral effects in a well-conducted[12] RCT,[13] evidence that these effects are sustained for at least one year following the intervention, and at least one external (independent evaluator) replication with a well-conducted RCT. The standard for effective with reservation is the same except that the replication need not be conducted by an independent evaluation team.

Although the goal of the Federal Collaboration was to create uniform standards to be adopted by all federal agencies serving children and youth, the criteria and classification were never formally adopted by any of the federal agencies represented in the Federal Collaboration. There was reluctance to do so because the standard is considered to be very high, given the limited number of RCT evaluations, and enforcement of these criteria would severely limit the number of interventions that could be recommended by these agencies.

WHAT WORKS: CURRENT EVIDENCE-BASED PROGRAMS

The only regularly maintained online registry that uses a standard close to that recommended by the Federal Collaboration is the Blueprints for Healthy Youth Development's registry.[14] The highest program rating on the Blueprints registry (model plus) is identical to the federal working group standard for effective programs except that the minimum of two experimental studies can include one QED and one RCT rather than requiring two RCTs. A model rating involves the same standard except that the replication need not involve an independent evaluation team. Model-plus and model programs come close to meeting the Federal Collaboration standard for programs that are effective and effective with reservation. Both also require that there be no evidence of iatrogenic effects in the evaluations, a condition not mentioned in the Federal Collaboration recommendation.

Table 13.1 lists current model and model-plus programs on the Blueprints registry that have demonstrated effectiveness in preventing violence, substance use or abuse, other crimes, or antisocial or externalizing behavior. Many of these programs target protective factors as well as risk factors and are effective in promoting positive behavior, but only those programs that proved effective in preventing forms of antisocial and criminal behavior are included in Table 13.1, and the specific types of behavior prevented are indicated in the last column.

The scientific standard used by the Blueprints registry for certifying the evidence-based programs ready for scale-up in Table 13.1 is indeed high, and only fourteen programs currently meet this standard. Table 13.2 provides a list of programs meeting a slightly lower standard, which I consider to be evidence-based programs that also can be considered for scale-up but with a somewhat lower level of confidence. These are programs on the Department of Justice Crime Solutions registry[15] that are rated as effective and involve at least one RCT, and replication with a QED study or RCT, target antisocial or criminal behavior, and have no evidence of iatrogenic effects. Of the ninety-two programs listed as effective on the Crime Solutions registry, only one-fourth meet this lower standard (the minimum for an effective rating, as in most registries, requires only a single QED study).

A number of programs rated as promising on the Blueprints registry also meet this lower standard and are included in Table 13.2. There is some overlap in the ratings of these two registries. Nine of the fourteen Blueprint model and model-plus programs are also rated as effective on the Crime Solutions registry. However, none of the Crime Solutions effective programs listed in Table 13.2 are rated as a model program by Blueprints. All programs listed in Tables 13.1 and 13.2 meet the minimum standard of having at least one RCT, a replication RCT or QED study, and no evidence of a harmful effect.

Tables 13.1 and 13.2 provide information on each program's target population, type of program, benefit-cost ratio (if known), length of the sustained effect (if known), and the type of effect found. The target population refers to the intervention's intended population.

The type of program also refers to the target population but with respect to variation in its exposure or involvement in the program's behavioral outcome. Program types are classified as universal, selective, indicated, or treatment.[16] Universal programs are delivered to all persons

TABLE 13.1 BLUEPRINT MODEL EVIDENCE-BASED PREVENTION PROGRAMS

Project	Target population	Type of program	Benefit/cost	Sustained effect	Evidence of effect
Nurse-Family Partnership*	At-risk pregnant women	Prenatal and postpartum nurse home visitation (S)	$1.88	Through age 15	Reductions in child abuse, neglect, and injuries and in youth arrests and adjudications
Blues Program	Depressed, substance-using high school age youth	Cognitive-behavioral training (S, I)	$0.24	2 years postintervention	Reductions in depressive symptoms and disorders, less substance use
Maryland Ignition Interlock Program*	Drivers with multiple alcohol-related traffic offenses	Alcohol recidivism prevention (I)	N/A	2 years postintervention	Lower rates of recidivism for alcohol-related offenses
Positive Action*	Early adolescence, middle school	Alcohol, drug abuse, delinquency prevention (U)	N/A	1 year postintervention	Reductions in substance abuse, violence, bullying, depression, and anxiety
New Beginnings	Divorced mothers with children	Cognitive behavioral parent training (S)	N/A	6 years postintervention	Reductions in child problem behavior, number sexual partners, and mental health disorders
Parent Management Training	Divorced, single, at-risk parents; parents of at-risk children	Parent training (S, I)	$9.50	9 years postintervention	Less child delinquency and aggression; more positive parenting
Brief Alcohol Screening and Intervention for College Students*	College students at high risk for alcohol abuse	Cognitive behavioral training (S, I)	$17.34	4 years postintervention	Reduction in drinking and problem behavior rates
Multisystemic therapy*	Violent, drug abusing juvenile offenders and families	Family ecological systems approach (I)	$2.42	4 years post-treatment	Reductions in rearrests, self-reported criminal behavior, and mental health problems
Functional Family Therapy*	At-risk, disadvantaged, adjudicated youth	Behavioral systems family therapy (S, I)	$8.87	30 months post-treatment	Reductions in rearrests and out-of-home placements, better family communication
Promoting Alternative Thinking Strategies*	Late childhood (5–11) elementary school	Social emotional and cognitive behavioral learning (U)	$20.80	3 years postintervention	Less aggression and depression, better self-regulation and social competence
Lifeskills Training*	Middle, junior school (6th, 7th grade)	Drug use prevention and general life skills training (U)	$17.35	4 years postintervention	Lower rates of tobacco, alcohol, and marijuana abuse; reductions in polydrug use

(continued)

TABLE 13.1 *(continued)*

Project	Target population	Type of program	Benefit/cost	Sustained effect	Evidence of effect
Treatment Foster Care*	Adjudicated serious and chronic delinquents	Temporary foster care with treatment (I)	$2.08	1 year post-treatment	Fewer arrests, fewer days incarcerated, less hard drug use
Multisystemic therapy for youth with problem sexual behavior	Youth at risk for sexual assault	Family ecological systems approach (I)	N/A	9 years post-treatment	Fewer arrests for sexual crimes, fewer crimes, and fewer days in detention
Toward No Drug Abuse	High school age youth	Self-control social competency instruction (U, S)	$7.93	2 years post-treatment	Reductions in alcohol and drug use; reductions in violent victimizations

Sources: Blueprints registry, at http://www.blueprintsprograms.com. Benefit-to-cost ratios are from Washington State Institute for Public Policy, "Benefit-Cost Results," May 2017, available at http://www.wsipp.wa.gov/BenefitCost.

Note: I = indicated; S = selective; T = treatment; U = universal.

*Listed as effective on the Crime Solutions registry, at https://www.crimesolutions.gov/programs.aspx.

in a general setting or demographic group, without respect to exposure or involvement in the outcome—for example, all students in a given school or grade level in a set of schools. Selective programs are those delivered to persons, groups, or settings known to have experienced specific risk factors. Indicated programs are delivered to persons or groups already involved in the program's behavioral outcome, and treatment programs are those delivered to persons with a clinical diagnosis related to the outcome, like oppositional defiant disorder or opiate use disorder.

Benefit-cost estimates are also provided for each program when available.[17] The length of each program's postintervention sustained effect on the outcome is given in the next-to-last column, and the type of effect from the program outcome is described in the last column.

DISCUSSION: EVIDENCE-BASED PROGRAMS

Slightly over half the programs listed in Table 13.1 and almost one-third in Table 13.2 are indicated programs. Nearly all are delivered in the community, and with few exceptions they target children, adolescents and their families, not adults. Relatively few evidence-based programs are delivered in the justice system or for adults. The Kerner Report specifically encouraged the development of these types of early interventions, and this is the direction prevention science has gone in the past fifty years.

Blueprint model programs with benefit-cost information have positive estimates ranging from $2 to $20 of savings per dollar invested. Less than half the effective programs listed in Table 13.2 have benefit-cost estimates, and those that do range from essentially $0 to $65 with a third of them being close to $0. It is clear that not all evidence-based programs are cost

TABLE 13.2 EFFECTIVE PROGRAMS: CRIME SOLUTIONS AND BLUEPRINTS

Project	Target population	Type of program	Benefit/cost	Sustained effect	Evidence of effect
Adolescent Community Reinforcement	Youth and adults ages 13–25 with substance addiction	Inpatient/outpatient behavioral intervention (I)	N/A	9 months postintervention	Greater sustained abstinence from marijuana, less reported substance use and depression
Adolescent Diversion Project	Young offenders	Conflict resolution, diversion, mentoring, skill development (I)	N/A	1 year postintervention	Lower official delinquency rates; no differences in self-report rates
Aggression Replacement Therapy	Serious violent offenders, young offenders	Cognitive behavioral therapy, group therapy, skill development (I)	$14.26	18 months postintervention	Lower rates of felony recidivism and parent/teacher reports of problem behavior
Behavioral Couples Therapy for Substance Abuse	Substance use offenders and families	CBT, group and individual therapy (I)	N/A	1 year postintervention	Higher rates of abstinence days, lower rates of alcohol use
Buprenorphine Maintenance Treatment	Alcohol and other drug offenders	Alcohol and drug therapy, individual therapy (I)	$1.75	9 months postintervention	Reductions in self-reported drug use and opiate use based on urine tests
Cognitive Behavioral Intervention for Trauma in Schools	Victims of crime, children exposed to violence	CBT, group/individual therapy, school and classroom environment (S, I)	N/A	3 months postintervention	Lower self-report PTSD/depression symptoms
Coping Power	Parents and at-risk children 5th and 6th grades	CBT, drug prevention/treatment, parent training (U, S)	$1.56	3 years postintervention	Lower teacher-rated aggression and delinquency, improved academics
EFFEKT	School-based (middle school) parent-focused intervention	Alcohol prevention/treatment, parent training (U)	N/A	34 months post-treatment	Reductions in drunkenness, drinking, and delinquency.
Familias Unidas	Immigrant Hispanic families with at-risk teens	Group parent training, skill development (S)	$0.18	9 months postintervention	Reductions in drug use/dependence, initiation of sex, unprotected sex
Family Checkup–Toddlers	At-risk parents with toddlers (ages 0–1)	Parent training, positive health promotion (U, S)	N/A	5 years postintervention	Lower parent and teacher reports of problem behavior; fewer depression symptoms at ages 7–8
First Step to Success	Kindergartners at risk for antisocial behavior	Classroom skill-building, class environment, parent training (S)	$3.89	4 years postintervention	Less aggressive behavior, parent-rated problem behavior

(continued)

TABLE 13.2 *(continued)*

Project	Target population	Type of program	Benefit/cost	Sustained effect	Evidence of effect
Good Behavior Game	K–elementary students	Classroom behavior modification strategy (U)	$65.47	14 years postintervention	Reduced teacher-rated aggression, alcohol abuse/dependence, drug use
Guiding Good Choices	Families with children in grades 4–8	Conflict resolution, skill development, parent training (U)	$2.77	10 years postintervention	Lower onset and progression of drug use
Head Start–REDI	Preschool children and families	Skills training, social-emotional learning, teacher training (U)	N/A	4 years postintervention	Reductions in antisocial behavior/aggression, better academic skills
Incredible Years: Child, Parent and Teacher Programs	Preschool children and parents	Classroom management, social emotional learning, teacher training (U, S)	$0.18	1 year postintervention	Reductions in conduct problems at home and school
INSIGHTS into Children's Temperaments	Urban elementary school children and parents	Classroom management, temperament-based strategies, parent training (U)	N/A	3 months postintervention	Lower problem behavior at home; improved math and reading
KIVA Antibullying Program	K–elementary school students (grades 2–6); victims of bullying	Bullying prevention, environmental change strategies (U, I)	N/A	3 months postintervention	Lower peer- and self-reported victimization; lower self-reported bullying
Methadone Maintenance Treatment	Inpatient/outpatient opiate dependent persons ages 18+	Alcohol/drug therapy/treatment, individual therapy (T)	$2.19	6 months postintervention	Less needle use, fewer positive urine tests, less HIV-risk behavior, less heroin use
Midwestern Prevention Project	6th- and 7th-grade students	Classroom curricula, drug use prevention, community mobilization (U)	N/A	1.5 years postintervention	Reductions in cigarette and alcohol use
Multidimensional Family Therapy	Families/teens with drug and behavior problems/delinquency	Alcohol/drug therapy/treatment, family therapy, parent training (S, I)	$0.28	1 year postintervention	Reduced drug use, lower onset of drug use
Multisystemic Therapy–Substance Abuse	Alcohol, other drug and status offenders	CBT, drug therapy/treatment, family/parent training (S, I)	N/A	1 year postintervention	Fewer crimes against persons, lower alcohol and marijuana use
Parent-Child Interaction Therapy	Children ages 2–11 with serious behavioral problems	Parent training (S, I)	$2.21	No postintervention follow-up	Fewer behavioral problems in children with oppositional defiant disorder, attention deficit hyperactivity disorder, reduced classifications of ODD

(continued)

TABLE 13.2 *(continued)*

Project	Target population	Type of program	Benefit/cost	Sustained effect	Evidence of effect
Perry Preschool Program/High Scope	Children ages 3–4 and their parents	Early educational curriculum-based, parent training (S)	N/A	36 months postintervention	Higher standardized test scores, teacher ratings; less delinquency, fewer arrests
Positive Family Support/Family Checkup	At-risk children/youth ages 12–14 and their parents, 3 levels	Family resource center, family management and communication (U, S)	$0.20	3 years postintervention	Lower substance onset/use, less antisocial behavior, arrests, and depression
Price-Based Incentive Contingency Management for Substance Abusers	Adult substance abusers in community treatment	Prize-based contingent management system (T)	N/A	No postintervention follow-up	Longer duration of abstinence; higher quality of life scores
Prolonged Exposure Therapy	Youth and adults with PTSD and subdiagnosis of PTSD	CBT; individual treatment (S, T)	N/A	12 months postintervention	Reduced severity of PTSD symptoms, depression, and anxiety
SNAP under 12 Outreach Project	Boys under 12 with aggressive and antisocial behavior	CBT, family therapy/training, mentoring (S)	$0.05	15 months post intervention	Lower Child Behavior Checklist delinquency/aggression scores, fewer convictions by age 18
Steps to Respect	Students grades 3–6	Bullying prevention; social emotional skills, class curriculum (U)	N/A	2 years postintervention	Lower rates of bullying and nonbullying aggression, lower bullying victimization
Strengthening Families Program: Youth 10–14	Families with children 10–14, middle school	Parent skills training, conflict resolution, family therapy, alcohol and drug prevention (U)	$6.45	9 years postintervention	Lower onset of alcohol and drug use; lower frequency of substance use; lower rates of antisocial behavior
Strong African American Families	African American families with children 10–14, middle school	Parent skills training, class curriculum, family therapy, alcohol and drug prevention (U)	N/A	5 years postintervention	Lower rate of alcohol use and risk behavior
Trauma Affect Regulation: Guide for Education and Therapy	Females 13–45 experiencing PTSD	Manualized trauma-focused psychotherapy, skill development, group therapy (S, T)	N/A	6 months postintervention	Fewer PTSD symptoms, less depression and anxiety
Trauma-Focused Cognitive Behavioral Therapy	Children 3–14 with behavioral problems following traumatic events	CBT, family therapy, parent training (S, T)	N/A	2 years postintervention	Fewer PTSD symptoms, less externalizing behavior and depression

Sources: Blueprints registry, at http://www.blueprintsprograms.com; Crime Solutions registry, at https://www.crimesolutions.gov/programs.aspx. Benefit-to-cost ratios are from Washington State Institute for Public Policy, "Benefit-Cost Results," May 2017, available at http://www.wsipp.wa.gov/BenefitCost.

Note: CBT = cognitive behavioral therapy; I = indicated; PTSD = post-traumatic stress disorder; S = selective; T = treatment; U = universal.

effective, one important consideration when selecting a program. At the same time, even relatively small benefits, when applied to the numbers of persons at risk for and involved in violence, substance abuse, and criminal behavior or processed in our health and justice systems, would return huge savings to American taxpayers.

One of the critical issues raised by the Kerner Commission was the disproportionate number of minority and disadvantaged persons involved in the justice system and served by our mental health system. While the evidence of effectiveness for these programs when delivered to diverse populations and settings is limited, it indicates that in most cases they are effective across racial/ethnic and social-class groups and for both males and females.[18] There are exceptions, and these are noted in the program description or summary of findings reported by the registries. The wide utility of evidence-based programs in their application to diverse population groups, when combined with their cost effectiveness, render them ideal programs for a broad, coordinated national initiative for the prevention of violence, substance abuse, and criminal behavior.

EVIDENCE-BASED PRACTICES AND POLICIES

In addition to programs, a number of generic intervention practices and a few policies have been certified as evidence based. A "prevention practice" refers to a generic intervention strategy shared by a set of programs or treatments allowing for variation in specific program logic models, components, number of sessions or treatments, intervention settings, or other details that are specified in a program. Examples include mentoring, group counseling, hot-spot policing, and family therapy. "Policies" refer to formal guidelines and procedures regulating behavior, often mandated by law.

Currently, the type of evidence used to certify effective practices and policies involves carefully conducted systematic reviews of available evaluation studies of the set of programs using a given practice or policy.[19] The available evidence for effective practices includes some RCTs but more typically involves nonexperimental and QED studies, often with small sample sizes. Meta-analysis[20] is ideally suited to summarizing this type of evidence, providing an estimate of an average effect size for each practice. The prevention practices and policies reviewed for the Crime Solutions registry, each with a minimum of four independent studies including one RCT and having statistically significant average positive effects on antisocial behavior, violence, substance abuse, or other forms of criminal behavior, are listed in Table 13.3.

These evidence-based practices include both individual-level and place-based or contextual-change strategies. Hot-spot policing, therapeutic communities, and classroom management are all strategies for improving social contexts or physical environments in which individuals

TABLE 13.3 EVIDENCE-BASED PREVENTION PRACTICES AND POLICIES

Justice and law enforcement	School
Electronic monitoring	Bullying prevention programs
Hot-spot policing	Classroom management programs
Ignition interlock policies	Dropout prevention programs
Incarceration-based therapeutic community for adults	Interventions to reduce dating and sexual violence
Intensive supervision	Prevention and intervention programs for aggressive and disruptive behavior
Intervention for domestic violence offenders– Duluth model	Social emotional learning programs
Mental health courts	Truancy interventions
Risk, need, and responsivity approach	**Community**
Legislation	Advocacy interviews for women who experience intimate partner violence
Increased minimum drinking age	Cognitive behavioral therapy
Per se laws; blood alcohol concentration	Drug treatment programs
Raising taxes on alcohol	Mentoring programs
Random breath testing	Motivational interviewing
Selective breath testing	Psychotherapies for victims of sexual assault
	Nurse examiners in cases of sexual assault/rape

Source: Crime Solutions registry, at https://www.crimesolutions.gov/programs.aspx. See also Delbert Elliott and Abigail Fagan, *The Prevention of Crime* (Chichester, UK: Wiley-Blackwell, 2017).

interact. Few evidence-based programs target contextual characteristics. Most of the interventions in Table 13.3 are practices; there are relatively few qualifying policies. Quality research on the effectiveness of policies is rare, in large part because of the difficulties in designing and conducting strong evaluations. Drunk-driving deterrence policies and practices have proved effective, but we have seen little advance in our knowledge of other effective policies since the original Kerner Report.

A number of justice system practices have proved effective: electronic monitoring, hot-spot policing, intensive supervision, therapeutic community programs in prisons, mental health courts, a type of domestic violence intervention, and interventions based on a risk, need, and responsivity approach. A number of school-based practices are effective on average—for example, school bullying prevention, dropout and truancy prevention, and social-emotional learning programs. And community-based practices involving cognitive behavioral therapy, mentoring, motivational interviewing, and drug treatment have proved effective.[21] Knowledge of the effectiveness of these general strategies represents an important advance in our understanding of what works, but its practical utility for mounting a comprehensive national violence and crime prevention initiative is limited. This type of information does not provide specific guidance for practitioners or policy makers seeking evidence-based interventions to implement.[22]

INEFFECTIVE AND HARMFUL INTERVENTIONS

The increased use of RCTs and high-quality QED studies over the past two decades also has revealed programs and practices that do not work, some of which are high-profile, heavily financed government programs. Ineffective programs are identified in Table 13.4. In certifying programs as ineffective, the same scientific standard of evidence used to identify effective programs in Table 13.2 is used. Those listed in italics have demonstrated harmful effects—that is, participants in these interventions are at *increased* risk of initiating or continuing involvement in antisocial behavior, violence, substance abuse, or criminal behavior.

Many of these programs and practices, including those known to be harmful, are still being implemented on a fairly wide scale. For example, Scared Straight, known for close to a decade to have harmful effects, has been heavily promoted in a current A&E Network program, *Beyond Scared Straight*. Judicial waivers that transfer juveniles into the adult criminal court, a practice known to involve a disproportionate number of minority youth, higher rates of victimization while in prison, and higher rates of reoffending upon release, continue in some states.

Other popular programs that are ineffective are still being implemented, like Drug Abuse Resistance Education (DARE). Media campaigns designed to reduce substance abuse among youth have little or no effect. Basic justice system interventions like incarceration, boot camps, shock probation, formal system processing for juveniles, arresting misdemeanor domestic violence offenders, noncustodial employment programs for offenders, and treatment strategies such as therapeutic community, narcotics maintenance, motivational interviewing, and cognitive behavioral therapy are not effective for some types of offenders. What is most

TABLE 13.4 INEFFECTIVE PREVENTION PROGRAMS AND PRACTICES

Adolescent Transitions Program	Interventions for domestic violence offenders, cognitive behavioral therapy
After-school programs	Interventions targeting street-connected youth
Arresting perpetrators of misdemeanor domestic violence offenses	License plate recognition technology
Boot camps	Media campaigns regarding illicit drug use by youth
California Repeat Offender Prevention Program	Motivational interviewing for juvenile substance abuse
CASASTART	Noncustodial employment programs for ex-offenders
School-Based Child Sexual Abuse Prevention Program	Parents as teachers
Comers School Development Program	Project alert
Corporate crime deterrence	Reconnecting youth
Deviance training programs	SafERteens
DARE	*Scared Straight*
Formal system processing for juveniles	Second responder programs
Incarceration	Sexual Assault Risk Reduction Program
Incarceration-based narcotics maintenance treatment	*Shock probation*
Incarceration-based therapeutic communities for juveniles	STARS
	Waivers, transfers of juveniles to adult court

Source: Crime Solutions registry, at https://www.crimesolutions.gov/programs.aspx. See also Delbert Elliott and Abigail Fagan, *The Prevention of Crime* (Chichester, UK: Wiley-Blackwell, 2017).
Note: Programs and practices in italics have harmful effects.

troubling is that, collectively, these practices are being used for the vast number of offenders in the justice system.

Many major federal initiatives remain untested or have mixed or inconclusive evidence for their effectiveness. Examples include restorative justice practices, educational programming for inmates, job training for inmates, weapons bans, gun buyback programs, Moving to Opportunity–type programs, three-strike laws, mandatory background checks, target hardening, incapacitation, antigang programs, monetary fines, work-release programs, halfway houses, and teen courts.[23] Many school-based and community programs and practices also are untested or have mixed or inconclusive evidence of effectiveness. Examples include school discipline policies, zero-tolerance policies, police officers in schools, community mobilization programs, neighborhood watch, and wilderness camps.

We cannot conclude that these programs, practices, and policies do not work; we simply do not know yet whether they work. But given the finding that many well-intended interventions do not work and that some have proved harmful, unevaluated programs, practices, and policies pose some risk. To continue to place individuals, particularly our children and youth, in these programs year after year, without investing in further research to determine their effectiveness, seems unethical. It is clearly unethical to place persons in programs known to be ineffective or harmful.

DISSEMINATION AND IMPLEMENTATION OF EVIDENCE-BASED INTERVENTIONS

The above review clearly demonstrates a much improved knowledge about interventions than was available when the original Kerner Report was written. But knowing which programs, practices, and policies have proved effective or ineffective is only half of what is needed to successfully meet the commission's call. Unfortunately, the effective interventions identified above are not being widely disseminated and implemented, ineffective interventions are continuing to be implemented, and current prospects for a comprehensive national initiative using evidence-based interventions are not encouraging.

Two former directors of the Office of Management and Budget estimate that less than 1 percent of government spending is used on evidence-based initiatives.[24] A review of use of the evidence-based-program registries found that agency decision makers when selecting interventions found the registries confusing, offering conflicting advice about which programs were evidence-based, and largely ignored the registries.[25] Dissemination of these proven interventions is limited and inconsistent, and their implementation is rarely at scale, often lacks fidelity, and is funded by short-term grants that are subject to competitive renewal and are thus unsustainable in the long run.[26] Most critically, these evidence-based programs are not being embedded in existing systems of care or the justice system.

There are some hopeful signs that this situation is changing. LifeSkills Training is the most widely implemented Blueprint model program, currently in over 20 percent of middle schools in the United States. Multisystemic Therapy and Functional Family Therapy are increasingly being adopted in states as alternative placements for adjudicated offenders and yielding huge savings to taxpayers.[27] The Nurse Family Partnership is being implemented statewide in several states, and legislation to fund the partnership on a national level was approved by Congress in FY 2008.

The potential impact of implementing evidence-based programs at scale is demonstrated in two specific initiatives. The Washington State Institute for Public Policy estimated the reductions in recidivism from investing in a moderate portfolio of evidence-based programs, primarily those listed in Table 13.1. Projected savings for taxpayers by 2030 was estimated to be more than $350 million annually. Given these projected crime reductions and cost savings, the Washington State legislature cancelled plans to build a new prison in the state.[28] Florida's Redirection Program, operating in eighteen circuits in the state, offers three evidence-based community treatment alternatives to commitment to a residential facility. Redirection cost $22,000 less per offender than commitment to a residential facility, reduced the rearrest and conviction rate by 19 percent, and saved over $93 million between 2007 and 2012.[29]

On a national level, the National Council on Crime and Delinquency estimates that placing 80 percent of nonserious offenders currently serving time in prison into evidence-based community programs would save $9.7 billion.[30] The council also estimates this would save California $1.4 billion, Florida $271 million, New York $1.1 billion, and Texas $2.4 billion.

CONCLUSION

Do we have sufficient number and kinds of proven evidence-based programs and practices to mount a comprehensive, coordinated national violence- and crime-prevention initiative? Is the goal in the 1968 Kerner Report of stopping doing what does not work and replicating what does work at a scale equal to the dimensions of our problems within reach? It is clear we do not yet have the political will to stop funding programs and practices known to be ineffective or harmful. The current set of evidence-based programs that meet a high enough scientific standard to take to scale is small and, with few exceptions, their expected effect sizes and benefit-to-cost ratios in real-world settings will be modest. Still, while the scope of a coordinated national initiative using these programs would be limited, the potential for such an initiative is now present. The programs in Tables 13.1 and 13.2 could form the nucleus of a comprehensive national crime, violence, and substance abuse prevention initiative.

Further progress toward the Kerner Commission's goal regarding evidence-based interventions requires several critical actions. First, funding priority must be given to *replicating* evaluations of promising programs and practices. The major limitation in our existing body of knowledge about what works is the limited number and quality of replication studies. Given the high proportion of replications that fail, relying on a single evaluation as evidence of proven effectiveness is problematic.[31]

Second, as recommended by the Institute of Medicine,[32] there needs to be a single agency with the authority to set and monitor the *standards and certification* of evidence-based interventions.

Third, additional research is needed to understand how to *disseminate and implement* evidence-based interventions effectively.[33] This is the new frontier of research and critical to achieving the Kerner Commission's goal. Finally, the *political will* to abandon ineffective and harmful programs and embed evidence-based programs, practices, and policies in our educational, health, and justice systems must be found. This was the critical obstacle identified in the original Kerner Commission report. It remains the critical obstacle.

14

Policing in the United States

From the Kerner Legacy Looking Forward

Laurie O. Robinson

POLICING TODAY is probably as great a topic of public debate as at any time since the Kerner Commission issued its report five decades ago. Few would dispute that in the interim years law enforcement has become far more professional. Yet the tensions that the commission described between police and minority communities too often still remain. What should be recognized—as the commission[1] and later bodies[2] have noted—is that these strains reflect wounds in the society that often extend far beyond law enforcement and, therefore, that police alone, no matter how well trained and skilled, do not have the capacity on their own to fully resolve. And unless addressed, that legacy threatens our ability to secure safe and equal justice in this country.[3]

THE COMMISSION REPORT: WHAT ABOUT POLICING?

The role of police was a major focus for the Kerner Commission. The report criticized law enforcement not only for its role in responding to the riots but also as a central factor in triggering the disorders. And from Detroit to Harlem to Watts, the commission found, racial tensions reflected community grievances with not only the police but also the broader criminal justice system. In fact, the commission wrote, "the policeman in the ghetto is the symbol not only of law, but of the entire system of law enforcement and criminal justice."[4]

The commission did not find a single or simple answer to the racial disorders that it studied. But it was clear that police played a central role, as a trigger for the riots and in their response to them. As the commission report noted, "The police are not merely a 'spark' factor. To some Negroes police have come to symbolize white power, white racism and white repression. . . . The atmosphere of hostility and cynicism is reinforced by a widespread belief among Negroes in the existence of police brutality and in a 'double standard' of justice and protection—one for Negroes and one for whites."[5]

In its assessment of the factors leading to the disorders—based on a survey of the twenty-three cities in which riots had occurred—"police practices" stood out as the most frequently cited grievance and was also the one rated at the highest "level of intensity" by residents.[6] Yet the commission also made clear that "the blame must be shared by the total society."[7] It pointed to the fact that "the policeman in the ghetto is a symbol, finally, of a society from which many ghetto Negroes are increasingly alienated."[8] However, residents in minority communities frequently demand strong police protection, the report said, which can often lead to grievances if the response is too aggressive.[9]

To remedy these problems, the commission came forward with a host of recommendations. They included the following:

- Provide better police protection to minority community residents
- Set up a mechanism for grievances against the police and other city employees
- Review law enforcement operations in the inner city to ensure proper police conduct and eliminate abrasive practices
- Adopt policy guidelines to help officers make critical decisions in areas where conduct can create tension
- Use innovative programs to ensure broad community support for police
- "Recruit more Negroes"[10] onto the police force, and review promotion policies to "ensure fair promotion for Negro officers"
- Create "community service officer" positions for young black youth to interest them in police work[11]

In developing its policing recommendations, the commission leaned heavily on the highly regarded work of the President's Commission on Law Enforcement and the Administration of Justice (the Crime Commission),[12] which had issued its report in 1967.[13] That report's in-depth treatment of issues, such as citizen grievance procedures and minority officer recruitment, proved invaluable as the Kerner Commission developed its recommendations.[14]

While the scope of this chapter does not allow a full recitation of the Kerner Commission's policing proposals, an important area to flag relates to funding. It was clear to the commission—wisely—that local governments could not alone bear the burden of supporting reform measures. It therefore called on the federal government to help provide monetary backing.[15] This funding, it suggested, could support such initiatives as community service officers and nonlethal weapon development—or, more broadly, improvements in the overall criminal justice system, as espoused by the Crime Commission.[16] While this did not mean local governments could or should avoid their responsibilities, the commission said, the importance of the issues involved required a federal commitment. In 1968, Congress passed the Omnibus Crime Control and Safe Streets Act,[17] creating a federal agency, the Law Enforcement Assistance Administration (LEAA), that over the following decade would provide billions of dollars in criminal justice assistance to states and localities.[18]

THE EVOLUTION OF POLICING: CHANGES OVER THE DECADES

In the fifty years since the Kerner Commission Report, policing in the United States has changed dramatically. Overall, the profession today is far more professional and more data driven, and the growth of a substantial research "industry" on policing has helped in some measure to keep it more accountable.[19] These developments have occurred despite the profession being very decentralized, with some eighteen thousand state and local law enforcement agencies around the country.[20]

In thinking about policing today, it is helpful to look back at its past. Scholars have described the history of U.S. policing as comprising three periods—the political era, the reform era, and the era of community problem solving. The first of these, which lasted from the 1840s through the early 1900s, was characterized by deep involvement of police with the political structure. The reform era, starting in the 1930s, was in reaction to the period of the political ward boss that preceded it.[21] During that time, police focused their attention on better management, efficiency, and addressing serious crime. Close ties to the community were frowned on because of worries of police corruption.[22]

But it was clear by the 1960s and 1970s that this approach—police detachment from communities—was no longer working.[23] This was a lesson drawn from the country's urban disorders and also from the United States, by the 1960s and 1970s, facing rising crime and experiencing sweeping social changes.[24]

With this came a third shift in the focus of policing toward what has been called the era of community problem solving. Experiments with foot patrol, already under way, proved popular, and research showed patrols to also reduce fear of crime.[25] Some scholars describe the goal of community policing as an "intimate relationship" with the community, with outcomes focused on the lofty goals of crime prevention, resident satisfaction, legal methods, and justice.[26] At the same time, communities such as

Madison, Wisconsin, and Newport News, Virginia, were experimenting with problem-oriented policing, a related law enforcement strategy that involves officers identifying and addressing crime and disorder problems.[27]

In the 1980s, community policing began to take root. It became established in cities like Houston, under police chief Lee Brown's leadership, and gained a philosophical foothold with the Harvard Kennedy School Executive Sessions on Policing, sponsored by the Department of Justice's National Institute of Justice.[28] Many facets of community policing—with its focus on problem solving, engagement with the community, and decentralization of authority to patrol officers—were in stark contrast to the reform model of policing[29] and would also lay the basis for the criminal justice system's later embrace of innovations such as drug courts, community prosecution, and the whole range of problem-solving initiatives that exist in the justice system today.

Community policing was given a significant boost in the 1990s when presidential candidate Bill Clinton campaigned on the promise of putting one hundred thousand community police officers on the street. Once elected, Clinton secured billions of dollars from Congress toward meeting that commitment. By the late 1990s—with funding from the Justice Department's Community Oriented Policing Services (COPS) Office—the numbers of community policing officers around the country had swelled. According to Bureau of Justice Statistics, 64 percent of local police agencies, serving 86 percent of U.S. citizens, had full-time community police officers, up from 34 percent of departments serving 62 percent of residents just two years earlier.[30]

But beyond the numbers, by the middle of the 1990s, with the organization changes, community partnerships, focus on accountability, and connections to minority communities, policing, as scholars George Kelling and Mary Ann Wycoff put it, "had pretty well recreated itself."[31]

One key facet of policing in the 1990s was its focus on data analysis in managing the response to crime. One city that tackled its crime problem successfully at that time used data tools as a significant part of its arsenal: the New York City Police Department, under Commissioner William J. Bratton, launched a revolutionary management system—dubbed CompStat—in 1994 to track crime statistics on a real-time basis, allowing the agency to make course corrections and adjust police deployment and strategies to aggressively address emerging crime problems.[32] Data analysis was central to this approach: "Crime analysts collect, analyze, and map crime statistics to spot trends and help precinct commanders identify underlying factors that explain crime incidents."[33]

CompStat transformed the NYPD, and the system spread rapidly across the country, with hundreds of police agencies nationwide adopting it.[34] As a partial result, crime analysis has now become an integral part of the fabric of modern policing, and it shapes how departments think about crime patterns, crime strategies, and crime solutions.

Meanwhile, during the 1990s, support for community policing and problem-oriented policing grew. But the tragic events of September 11, 2001, established different priorities, and with the creation of the Department of Homeland Security and requests for involvement of state and local law enforcement in antiterrorism enforcement, pressure grew on local police agencies to turn away from community policing initiatives. Despite that, however, many agencies tried to find a balance, meeting new homeland security responsibilities while still building on relationships they had forged during years of community policing.[35]

CRIMINAL JUSTICE TODAY: CHALLENGES AND A WAY FORWARD

While our country today is far safer than at the time of the Kerner Commission and in the 1990s, when we faced rising crime and rampant crack cocaine use,[36] far too many communities across our nation still struggle with gun violence, gang problems, and drug trafficking.[37] In addition, the opioid epidemic has hit American communities hard, with ninety-one citizens dying daily in 2015 from opioid overdoses (a number that has quadrupled since 1999),[38] and the latest Federal Bureau of Investigation Uniform Crime Reports reflect a disturbing uptick across all categories of violent crime.[39] Troubling questions continue to be raised, as well, about whether the criminal justice system in the United States treats racial and ethnic minorities fairly. The United States incarcerates a larger percentage of its citizens than any other country in the world.[40]

As the criminal justice field has moved to support evidence-based approaches in recent decades,[41] law enforcement has been part of that movement—for example, in embracing hot-spots policing, which focuses resources on the small number of places that generate a high percentage of crime in a jurisdiction.[42] Police today have gotten better at what has been called the "delicate balance" between strategies to fight crime and potential collateral consequences that can harm the communities these strategies are meant to serve,[43] and they are better at using data and analytics to drive crime control.

But numerous challenges remain, centered on bridging trust between police and communities. Those issues crystallized in 2014 with the death during a police encounter in Ferguson, Missouri, of young Michael Brown—followed by additional police shooting incidents that in turn attracted substantial national attention.[44]

In late 2014, in the aftermath of the Ferguson grand jury decision not to indict the police officer who shot Brown, President Barack Obama appointed a President's Task Force on 21st Century Policing and charged it with coming up with recommendations on how to build trust between communities and law enforcement while promoting effective crime reduction.[45] The eleven-member task force, which consisted of law enforcement leaders, civil rights lawyers, young activists, and academics, held hearings around the country. It received testimony from every sector of the field and from the public and produced a report with recommendations in a short ninety days.[46] I was privileged to cochair the task force with Philadelphia police commissioner Charles H. Ramsey.

The final task force report was issued in May 2015. Of note, despite the diversity of the task force membership, the group was able to come to consensus on every topic it addressed; there were no dissents. Many of the report's core themes—for example, its emphases on building stronger relations with communities, reducing abrasive practices that add to those tensions, and increasing minority recruitment of police officers—echoed recommendations from the Kerner Report.

Key principles in the task force report lay out a blueprint for policing in the twenty-first century:

- *Law enforcement agencies should build community trust through fair, impartial, and respectful policing.* A foundational element, the task force said, is for police to embrace a "guardian" rather than solely a "warrior" mind-set. There are clearly times when the warrior mind-set is needed—for example, in dealing with a drug trafficking gang or a hostage situation. But police should not be an occupying force in a community; instead, they should be its protectors and guardians.[47]
- *Procedural justice should be a guiding principle in how police interact with citizens.* Procedural justice consists of four key principles—treating individuals with dignity and respect, giving them voice during encounters, being neutral and transparent during any encounters, and conveying trustworthy motives. As Professor Tom Tyler of Yale told the task force, research has found that individuals treated in procedurally just ways are more likely to cooperate with authorities, helping to build trust across the police-community divide.[48]
- *Police agencies should think about the potential damage to public trust when they are contemplating crime-fighting strategies.* This is a real lesson learned from what has been seen in some jurisdictions with how stop and frisk has been implemented. While crime numbers might have been reduced, the question is, at what cost? Crime reduction alone is not self-justifying. Collateral consequences have to be considered because they can cause considerable damage to police-community relations—and undercut cooperation with the police by law-abiding neighborhood residents.[49]

- *Training on implicit bias should be given to all police officers.*[50] The task force heard compelling testimony from experts like Professor Jennifer Eberhardt of Stanford University on the question of implicit—or unconscious—bias. She told the task force, "Bias is not limited to so-called 'bad people.' . . . The problem is a widespread one that arises from history, from culture and from racial inequalities that still pervade our society."[51]
- *Police agencies should create a culture of transparency and accountability, collecting data and sharing it with citizens.* As examples, data should be collected and posted on agency websites on use of force generally, officer-involved shootings specifically, deaths in custody, stop and frisks, and agency demographics.[52] And—perhaps the most important recommendation— agencies should annually survey their communities for, in effect, customer feedback. How do citizens feel their police department is doing in serving them?[53]
- *Police agencies should adopt policies and implement training on use of force that emphasizes de-escalation and alternatives to arrest or summons when those approaches are appropriate.*[54] In the last several years, national law enforcement leadership and union groups have taken important steps to adopt thoughtful policies on use of force, putting an emphasis on de-escalation.[55]
- *Police agency policies should mandate independent and external criminal investigations when officer-involved shootings result in injury or death, and similarly, local district attorneys should turn to external and independent prosecutors in such cases.*[56] Restoring trust and credibility in the justice system is critical in these highly fraught cases. The appearance of justice therefore requires, and is best served by, a decision maker who is clearly unbiased.
- *Law enforcement agencies should adopt policies forbidding profiling based on race, ethnicity, national origin, religion, age, gender, gender identity/expression, sexual orientation, immigration status, disability, housing status, occupation, or language fluency.*[57] While most departments are already focused on the issue of racial profiling, the task force felt it was important to flag other areas—such as gender identity, language fluency, and disability— as well.
- *In the area of technology, police departments should take a comprehensive policy approach, involving the community, consulting with civil liberties groups on privacy and constitutional issues, and looking at national standards.*[58] The task force observed that technology can, of course, be a helpful tool to law enforcement, but it should not be viewed as a panacea. Today, the rush is to-

ward body-worn cameras; tomorrow, the focus may be on facial recognition technology; in the years after, it will likely be on something most of us cannot now envision. A carefully considered policy on technology will serve an agency well.

- *Building on community policing concepts, agencies' primary approach to addressing crime should be based on engagement with citizens to coproduce public safety.*[59] Community policing needs to be infused throughout the entire organization, and departments should be jointly identifying problems with the community and collaborating on implementing solutions. Agencies should seek out multiple settings for engagement in which to build collaborative partnerships with churches, schools, community groups, social service agencies, and other stakeholders.

- *Law enforcement agencies and communities should adopt policies to reduce aggressive policing tactics that unnecessarily stigmatize young people and result in marginalizing their participation in school and in their communities.*[60] The task force was struck by the testimony it heard regarding the "school-to-prison pipeline," in which behavior that in the past was dealt with as a school disciplinary matter has now been criminalized, even for young children.[61]

- *Police agencies should aim to hire a diverse workforce that reflects the communities they serve—both at entry levels and at every level of the department.*[62] As the task force noted, a workforce that includes a diversity of race and gender and a breadth of cultures, ethnicities, and backgrounds can "improve understanding and effectiveness in dealing with all communities."[63] At the same time, as experience in some cities has shown, hiring minority officers alone is not a solution to resolving police-community tensions.[64]

- *Police departments should ensure their officers receive training (both basic recruit and in-service training) in a host of areas—including procedural justice, de-escalation of incidents, implicit bias, interpersonal skills, and handling of the mentally ill.*[65] In preparing police officers for the challenges of the twenty-first century, substantial changes are needed in how education and training are conceptualized and implemented—not just for new officers but for all throughout their careers. A key priority should be on handling individuals with mental illness. According to the Virginia-based Treatment Advocacy Center, people with untreated serious mental illness are sixteen times more likely than others to be involved in fatal law enforcement encounters.[66] So this issue is clearly a critical one. As the task force urged, *every officer should receive the highly regarded Crisis Intervention Training for dealing with these individuals.*[67]

- *Because police officer safety and wellness is important not just for the officers but also for their departments and for public safety, every local agency should make this issue a high priority.*[68] Police officers face tremendous stress in their jobs, which affects their behavior. Research has found that life expectancy of law enforcement officers reflects these pressures and is shorter than for members of the general population,[69] and the rate at which police officers commit suicide is far greater than from line-of-duty deaths.[70]
- *Police leaders should implement internal procedural justice within their agencies to engage line officers in developing a shared vision for the department.* These kinds of partnerships, research shows, can encourage officers, in turn, to demonstrate external procedural justice.[71]

LOOKING AHEAD

So where are we now with the movement toward policing and broader criminal justice reform? Many have expressed pessimism about the future of this work—especially with the departure from Washington of an administration that aggressively advanced Smart on Crime policing, prosecution, and sentencing proposals[72] and the arrival of a new administration in 2017 espousing law-and-order remedies.[73]

There are several reasons, however, for optimism. First, as noted earlier, frontline criminal justice professionals across the country have been committed for several decades to data-driven approaches.[74] Law enforcement leaders remember well how the tough-on-crime edicts of the War on Drugs failed, and few believe now, as an example, that they can arrest their way out of the opioid crisis. Instead, there is a commitment to working in tandem with public health professionals to address these problems, using treatment and data tools.[75]

Second, while leadership from Washington is always helpful, criminal justice in the United States is largely, of course, a state and local enterprise. It was unusual to have a president as deeply involved as Barack Obama was in his personal engagement with the President's Task Force on 21st Century Policing. But with thousands of locally controlled law enforcement agencies in the United States, and with strong policing leaders—of which there are many across the country—reform work will continue with or without leadership from the bully pulpit in the nation's capital. And while it is not yet clear what role the Donald Trump Justice Department will play in its Civil Rights Division pattern-or-practice lawsuits challenging police practices, that involvement will likely continue in cities where federal judges are already engaged. Similarly, many police leaders nationally have vowed to press for reforms. As the executive director of the Police Executive Research Forum, Chuck Wexler, put it last year, it takes policing years to shift direction, and "once they change, it's hard to stop that direction."[76]

Third, despite stalled criminal justice reform legislation in Washington,[77] it is encouraging to see on numerous fronts continued bipartisan momentum toward criminal justice reform at the state level. In the area of drug enforcement, even Republican states do not appear to be following the Trump administration's call for a return to the War on Drugs of the 1980s and 1990s.[78] And on sentencing and corrections, there is considerable movement at the state level to adopt reforms, primarily working under the banner of the Justice Reinvestment Initiative.[79] For example, in North Dakota, Republican governor Doug Burgum signed legislation in April 2017 as part of broader justice reform to fund community-based drug treatment aimed at reducing both recidivism and the state's prison population.[80] Georgia's governor, Nathan Deal, also a Republican, signed legislation in May 2017 to implement evidence-based supervision strategies for probation to reduce recidivism and focus on the period after release when individuals are most likely to reoffend. The legislation waives fines and fees for individuals found to be indigent and allows them to pay their debt through community service.[81]

On the policing front, there has also been progress.[82] The task force recommendations have been largely embraced by all the major leadership groups in law enforcement, including the International Association of Chiefs of Police, Major Cities Chiefs Association, Major County Sheriffs Association, and the National Organization of Blacks in Law Enforcement. Significantly, at the 2016 conference of the twenty-three-thousand-member International Association of Chiefs of Police, Terrence M. Cunningham, its president, issued a formal apology for the role the policing profession had historically played in mistreating communities of color.[83] The organization has also set up an Institute for Community-Police Relations to help agencies (especially small and rural ones) implement the task force proposals.[84]

A number of states have instituted training in line with the task force recommendations. For example, Illinois passed legislation in 2015, in response to the task force report, requiring new police training in such areas as use of force and procedural justice.[85] The Massachusetts Association of Police Chiefs, also in response to the task force report, required all officers in the state to undergo training on use of force and fair and impartial policing.[86] In 2016, New Jersey's attorney general required all five hundred police agencies in the state to be trained on de-escalation techniques and implicit bias,[87] and the year before, Virginia's attorney general kicked off a statewide program to train law enforcement in de-escalation, impartial policing, and use of force.[88] In 2016, the Department of Justice mandated implicit bias training for all U.S. attorneys and federal law enforcement agents—more than twenty-five thousand individuals.[89] And thirty-four states and the District of Columbia, according to a 2017 Vera Institute of Justice report, took legislative action on police reform during 2015–2016 on such topics as use of force, profiling, body-worn cameras, data collection and reporting, and crisis intervention training.[90]

It is clear, however, despite these kinds of steps and the leadership of many police leaders across America, that much remains to be done. The support of line officers and unions will be critical to advancing real reform, and achieving culture change will not be easy.[91]

But we can look back fifty years to the Kerner Report to remind ourselves that it is critical to set out an ambitious blueprint for the future and then move toward it. For policing and criminal justice reform in America, we should ask for nothing less.

15

Race, Violence, and Criminal Justice

Elliott Currie

THE KERNER REPORT'S AUTHORS opened the chapter "Conditions of Life in the Racial Ghetto" with a section titled "Crime and Insecurity."[1] The placement of their analysis points to two things about the commission's view of crime in the ghetto: it was an issue of great importance and grave concern, and it was just one of a larger set of adverse circumstances that shaped the everyday experience of ghetto residents.

The report followed its discussion of the ravages of crime with a similar portrait of the effects of poverty and segregation on health and access to health care, including strikingly high rates of maternal and infant mortality and an average life expectancy seven years shorter than that of whites. It pointed to the causal role of ghetto poverty and also poor environmental and sanitary conditions, noting that in 1965 there were more than fourteen thousand reported cases of rat bites in the United States, mostly concentrated in ghetto neighborhoods. The chapter closed with a description of another defining feature of the racial ghetto—endemic commercial exploitation by local businesses, including shady credit practices and higher food prices.

The overarching message was that, in these and other ways, the conditions of life in these communities were "strikingly different from those to which most Americans [were] accustomed—especially white, middle-class Americans."[2] The racial ghetto was different—the lives people led there were simply worlds apart from those of other Americans. And the vulnerability to crime was preeminent in creating that profound and pervasive difference.

"Nothing is more fundamental to the quality of life in any area," the commission declared, "than the sense of personal security of its residents, and nothing affects this more than crime."[3] The report went on to detail the dimensions of this difference, noting that crime rates were consistently highest in the most disadvantaged areas of big cities. Indeed, the "difference between crime rates in these disadvantaged neighborhoods and in other parts of the city is usually startling."[4] The report presented statistics from five Chicago police districts in 1965 that showed, among other things, that rates of reported index crimes against persons were thirty-five times higher in one "very low income Negro district" than in a "high-income white district" in the same city.[5] This was true despite the highest-crime Negro district having three times as many police per hundred thousand population as the affluent, low-crime white district. Moreover, the commission suggested that the disparities in crime were most likely understated by official statistics, because most crimes in the ghetto were underreported.

The commission took care to insist that these high rates of crime did not mean that everyone who lived in the racial ghetto was a criminal: the majority of crime was committed by a relatively small proportion of ghetto residents. But that did not diminish the seriousness of the problem or its essential inequality: the burden of crime fell most heavily on other black residents. Like poor sanitation, inadequate garbage services, rats, and spotty medical care, crime was a fundamental fact of life in the ghetto. And because most Americans lived in places with relatively low rates of serious crime, they had "little comprehension of the sense of insecurity that characterizes the ghetto resident."[6]

VIOLENCE IN THE "TWO SOCIETIES" TODAY

The commission, moreover, was not optimistic about the future, barring very massive shifts in American social policy. They thought that crime would most likely rise in the future, partly because it had already been rising for several years (and rising much faster than the police resources to combat it), but also because of a projected increase in the proportion of black youth, who were the most crime-prone segment of the population.

Fifty years on, some things have changed—often in ways that the commission did not foresee. But the report's basic message remains strikingly on target. Serious violent crime continues to be a fundamental, inescapable fact of life in most racial ghettoes in America, on a level that sharply distinguishes those areas from other places—especially communities that are both affluent and white. In the hardest-hit urban ghettoes, violence in the twenty-first century remains at levels not seen outside the Third World. In some of those communities, violent crime is higher—sometimes much higher—than it was when the Kerner Report was published. Moreover, both the stunning levels of violence and the startling disparities between the racial ghetto and most of the rest of America have persisted in the face of a vast and unprecedented explosion of incarceration that was justified as the most realistic strategy to end that violence.

These assertions run counter to the popular narrative, dominant in much discussion of crime in America since the 1990s, that the country has enjoyed a long-term crime drop that has rendered many of our cities safe—even those that were the most dangerous. That narrative, to be sure, contains a kernel of truth, in that levels of serious violence have fallen from their worst peaks in the 1980s and 1990s. But it is a stunningly inadequate description of where we stand with race and crime in America today. And it breeds a kind of naïve complacency that has helped to push the continuing crisis of violence in the inner city off the table as an urgent subject of public debate and social action. As long as that remains true, the harsh existential difference in the experience of insecurity highlighted by the Kerner Commission half a century ago will persist.

The dimensions of this fundamental difference are most starkly apparent if we look closely at the numbers on racial disparities in violent death in recent years. As the commission pointed out in the 1960s, most crimes are underreported in official statistics, and that is likely to be especially true in areas where everyday crime is a routine fact of life. But homicide is a different story. Medical data on homicide deaths in particular, now collected annually by the Centers for Disease Control and Prevention, provide a generally reliable indicator of both the trends and the distribution of violent death in America. And they reveal the stubborn persistence of the startling racial differences in the risks of violence that the Kerner Commission highlighted fifty years ago.

From the start of the twenty-first century up through 2015, over 132,000 black Americans lost their lives to homicide.[7] Over the last *twenty* years, from 1996 through 2015, the figure rises to roughly 168, 000. To put that figure in some perspective, imagine that someone had lined up the entire population of the city of Jackson, Mississippi—men, women, and children—and mowed them down mercilessly. From another angle, consider that the number of African Americans who died by violence over this twenty-year period is roughly 150 times the total number of people who perished during Hurricane Katrina in New Orleans in 2005.

The figure of about 132,000 deaths since the start of the twenty-first century translates into a homicide death *rate* for the African American population as a whole of about 20 per 100,000 people. That number, by itself, means little until we compare it with the rate for whites. For white Americans—more precisely, for what the Census Bureau calls white non-Hispanic Americans—the rate is less than three per 100,000. Thus, during the course of the past decade and a half, the homicide death rate for white Americans has averaged about one-seventh that of black Americans.

As of 2015, the latest year for which we have CDC data, the homicide death rate for African Americans of both sexes exceeded that of their white non-Hispanic counterparts by 7.4 to 1. Among men specifically, the black-white disparity rises to nearly 10 to 1. And among young men ages fifteen to twenty-nine—the group singled out by the Kerner Commission—it rises to 18 to 1. The black-white disparity applies, though not as sharply, to women as well as men: at ages fifteen to twenty-nine, young black women are roughly four times as likely to meet a violent death as their white non-Hispanic counterparts.

The high level of homicide victimization among black women points to one of the most striking features of the continuing racial inequality in the risks of violent death: the racial disparity is sufficiently large that it overturns some of the usual demographic expectations about where violence is most likely to strike. One of the most consistent findings in criminology is that homicide usually strikes men far more often than women—especially in societies that, like the United States, have high overall rates of violence. But while that expectation remains true *within* different racial groups in America, it collapses when we compare the likelihood of violent death across the races.

Of the 132,000 black Americans who died by homicide during this century up through 2015, about 113,000—86 percent—were male. At last count, an African American man faced roughly six times the risk of dying by violence as an African American woman. And a similar, though less extreme, gender pattern holds among whites: a white man is twice as likely to die by violence as a white woman. But the overarching effect of race is so powerful that a black *woman* is more than half again as likely to be the victim of homicide as a white *man*. And that striking disadvantage is even worse for younger black women: at ages fifteen to twenty-nine, the homicide death rate for black women is nearly double that for white men.

Race also scrambles the usual connection between age and the likelihood of violent death. In the United States, as in other societies that suffer high levels of violence, it is the young who are most at risk. That risk predictably peaks from the late teens to the early thirties and declines more or less steadily thereafter. And, as with gender, that relationship does prevail *within* racial groups. More than half of all homicide deaths among black men in America take place among those ages eighteen to thirty. In 2015, the person with the greatest likelihood of dying by violence in the United States was a twenty-three-year-old black man, among whites, a thirty-two-year-old man. But race complicates this connection in very revealing ways. An older black man is indeed much less likely to be a homicide victim than a black youth in his twenties. But a *sixty-year-old* black man remains three times as likely to suffer a violent death as a white man of thirty-two—the age of highest risk for white men in America in 2015.

These realities become even more troubling when we consider that the likelihood of violent death among white men in America is itself quite high by comparison with those of men in other advanced industrial societies. Measured against Japanese, German, or English men, for example, white men in the United States are a distinctly vulnerable group—especially if they are young. They are several times more likely to meet a violent death than men of all races together in many countries at comparable levels of economic development. Non-Hispanic white men's current homicide death rate of roughly 3.7 per 100,000 is about six times the recent rate for all German men, and almost nine times the rate for men in Japan.[8] So when we say that a black man in America is ten times as likely to die by violence as his white counterpart, we are comparing him with people whose risk of being murdered is itself unusually high by the standards of the advanced industrial world.

If we put age and gender together, the power of race to eclipse other usually reliable predictors of violent death is even more evident. We have seen that the overall homicide death rate for African American women is higher than the rate for white men. Even more revealing is that the rate for black women of middle age is higher than that of the highest-risk young white men. During the first sixteen years of this century, it has not been until age forty-seven that a black woman's risk of dying by homicide falls below that of a white man of twenty-six—the age of highest risk for white men, on average, in this period.

Moreover, since these figures are averages for the United States as a whole, they mask that in many places in America, notably some especially hard-hit states and cities, the racialized character of violent death looms especially large.

In Missouri, the homicide death rate in 2015 for black males ages fifteen to twenty-nine was 189 per 100,000—thirty-five times the rate for young white men and higher by far than the overall homicide death rate of any country in the world. In the District of Columbia, it was nearly 200 per 100,000. Since the start of the twenty-first century, the homicide death rate for African American men ages fifteen to twenty-nine in Illinois has averaged 136 per 100,000, thirty-four times the rate for white non-Hispanic men the same age. Like most statistics, those numbers may sound technical and bloodless on the surface. But they reflect a stunning toll of youthful lives lost to violence. That death rate of 136 per 100,000 translates into nearly 5,000 young black men who have been lost to homicide in a single state in the course of sixteen years.

But even the state-level figures disguise, to some extent, the extraordinary concentration of violence within the most disadvantaged areas of some especially hard-hit cities—the areas pinpointed by the Kerner Commission. As in the 1960s, the places most devastated by violence are typically very poor and heavily African American. Among larger American cities in 2015, the "winner" in the grim contest of urban violent death was Saint Louis, with a homicide rate of 59 per 100,000. Saint Louis was closely followed by Baltimore, which achieved a homicide rate of 55 per 100,000. Of Baltimore's homicides in 2015, for which the victim's race was recorded, 93 percent of victims were black. Detroit, New Orleans, and Newark, New Jersey, all ended the year with homicide rates above 40 per 100,000. The smaller cities of Gary, Indiana (65 per 100,000), Flint, Michigan (48 per 100,000), and Camden, New Jersey (44 per 100,000), ranked near the top of the list, while the highest rates of all were suffered by the small and heavily African American cities of East Saint Louis, Illinois (71 per 100,000), and Chester, Pennsylvania (67 per 100,000).[9]

What is most troubling about this list is that it has been virtually unchanged for decades. Cities like Camden, Gary, and East Saint Louis have jockeyed for the top position in this grim ranking for years. In some cases, these high homicide rates represent declines from even worse rates in the recent past. In other cases, they represent a discouraging stability or even increase in the level of death by violence. In the years since 1985, East Saint Louis's 2015 homicide count was only exceeded during the peak years of the crack cocaine epidemic from 1991 through 1994. Baltimore's 2015 count was higher than at any year but one (1993) during this period.[10] And because there were roughly 100,000 more people living in the city in 1993, 2015 was, per capita, the deadliest in Baltimore's history.[11]

These numbers tell us that the experience of violent death in the black community in the United States remains very different from the experience among whites. That difference is not subtle, and it is not just a matter of degree. As in the 1960s, we are witnessing a fundamental divide in the risks of violence that profoundly affects the quality of life that people of different races can expect.

The extent of that divide becomes even clearer if we examine it through some other lenses.

For example, the huge difference in homicide death rates means that the pattern of causes of death between the two races looks remarkably different. And that difference reveals a great deal about the risks that different communities routinely face. In the United States, homicide is the seventh-biggest cause of death for blacks; for white non-Hispanics, it ranks nineteenth. Homicide becomes the leading cause of death for black males by age fifteen and continues as their number-one cause of death through age thirty-five. Homicide is never the leading cause of death for non-Hispanic white men at any age. Considerably fewer white men die of homicide than, for example, from aortic aneurisms. For black men overall, homicide ranks fifth among causes of death—exceeded only by heart disease, cancer, unintentional injuries, and stroke.[12]

Among young black men, violence simply overwhelms other causes of death. More twenty-one-year-old black men die of homicide than die of the next nineteen biggest causes of death combined. And once again, these racial disparities are so potent that they bend the usual expectations about gender and homicide. Only about one in twenty-four white males who die at age twenty-one dies by violence: but almost one in five black women who die at that age do. In Illinois, homicide is the number-one cause of death for young black women ages fifteen to twenty-four.

But even these numbers understate the impact of violent death in many black communities. One way to better appreciate that impact is to look at it through still another lens—what public health researchers call "years of potential life lost," or YPLL. YPLL is a measure of premature death. We choose an endpoint—say, sixty-five years of age—and ask how many years are lost before that age from some particular cause of death or from all causes put together. YPLL, then, allows us to combine two distinct factors: how many people die of a given cause and how old they are when they die.

In the United States today, heart disease is the leading single cause of death—that is, ultimately, more people die of it than of any other cause. But it is not the leading cause of YPLL—because people tend to die of heart disease at relatively older ages, thus losing fewer potential years of life when they do die. Instead, the biggest culprit for YPLL is what public health statisticians call unintentional injuries—a broad category that includes accidents (notably motor vehicle accidents) and poisoning (which includes drug overdose deaths), because those deaths typically occur at earlier ages.

YPLL is very important in understanding the social and personal burden of violence in the United States—because, like accidents, homicide strikes hardest at younger people. Homicide ranks sixteenth among causes of death in the United States today, but it is the sixth-biggest cause of years of life lost before age sixty-five. When we use this lens the impact of racial disparities in violence becomes most starkly apparent.

For black men as a whole, homicide is the leading cause of YPLL before age sixty-five. For white men, it is ninth. Almost one out of every five years of life that black men lose prematurely before age sixty-five is lost to violence. For white men, that figure is one in fifty. During the twenty-first century, homicide has taken more years of life from African American men than cancer, diabetes, and stroke combined. The difference between black and white men in this respect is so great that even though black men make up a far smaller proportion of the male population in the United States than white men do, they collectively lose far more years of life to homicide than white men. There are roughly five times as many white non-Hispanic men than black men in the American population, but black men as a group lose almost three times as many years of life to homicide as white men do.

And once again, the racial effect on YPLL bends the usual expectations about gender. As I have said, only about one in fifty years of life lost prematurely among white men is lost to violence. For black women, it is about one in twenty-five. Measured this way, by how many years of their lives it steals, violence looms much larger in the lives of black women than in the lives of white men. Black women lose considerably more years of life to homicide than to diabetes—a notorious killer of African American women. Among white women, the effects are reversed. And again, the national averages can mask an even more devastating presence of violence in especially hard-hit states. In Illinois, homicide is the leading source of YPLL before age sixty-five for the black population as a whole, not just for men—and has been throughout the twenty-first century.

What we observe through the lens of YPLL is nothing less than the massive eradication of human potential. These numbers tell us something more than that violent death strikes black Americans more often than white Americans. They tell us that, because it strikes so disproportionately at the young, it eliminates a substantial part of the future of an entire community. During the twenty-first century, the 132,000 violent deaths of black Americans have stolen an average of thirty-five years of life from their victims (almost nine more years than are lost on average by white victims, because blacks tend to lose their lives to violence at somewhat younger ages than whites).

A FATEFUL CHOICE

It is crucial to recognize, moreover, that this continuing public health crisis has persisted in spite of one of the most significant public policy interventions in the past half century: the explosive increase in incarceration.

It is noteworthy that the Kerner Commission did not discuss the role of state and federal prisons in shaping the conditions within African American communities. Indeed, there is no index reference for "prisons" in the Kerner Report—or for "penal system" or "correctional system." There is a reference for "jails," but only in the context of their "use during disorders." But beginning shortly after the report's publication, the nation embarked on an unprecedented experiment in attempting to contain crime, drugs, and disorder in the inner cities through massive prison building and increasingly harsh sentencing. As we have learned from a vast amount of careful research, that experiment transformed the conditions of life in disadvantaged black communities in ways that further deepened the existential divide between those communities and the rest of America.[13]

When the Kerner Report was published, in 1968, there were roughly 187,000 people in state and federal prisons in the United States. In 2015, there were over 1,500,000. More people were imprisoned in the states of Texas and Oklahoma alone in 2015 than in the entire country in 1968.

The prison incarceration rate—the number of inmates as a proportion of the overall population—was 94 per 100,000 when the Kerner Report was published. In 2015, it was 458 per 100,000. The racial dimension of this extraordinary shift is well known, but it is useful to recall its magnitude. In 1978, there were roughly 143,000 black Americans in state and federal prisons. In 2015, there were almost that many in just three states alone—California, Florida, and Texas. At the high point of U.S. incarceration in 2009, there were nearly 600,000 black Americans in state and federal prisons: by 2015, the number had declined somewhat, but well over half a million remained imprisoned across the country, resulting in a black prison incarceration rate of 1,745 per 100,000 adults—five and half times the rate for whites. For the group most likely to be behind bars in a state or federal prison—men ages thirty to thirty-four—the black rate was a startling 5,948 per 100,000, meaning that about 1 in every 17 black men that age were imprisoned (not even counting those in local jails), versus 1 in every 90 white men the same age.[14]

The Kerner Report famously set out three possible policy responses to the multiple crises that afflicted disadvantaged African American communities—the "present policies" choice, the "enrichment" choice, and the "integration" choice. The commission worried that the first strategy—essentially business as usual, in which "society would do little more than it is now doing against racial segregation, fundamental poverty, and deprivation"—might prevail. They argued that this choice was the one with "the most ominous consequences for society," because it "does nothing to raise the hopes, absorb the energies, or constructively challenge the talents of the rapidly growing number of young Negro men in the central cities." The level of unemployment and underemployment among those young men would accordingly "remain very high." And since young men in that situation had "contributed disproportionately" to crime and violence before, "there is a danger, obviously, that they will continue to do so."[15]

From the vantage point of half a century later, it seems troublingly clear that, if anything, the commission was overly optimistic. The "present policies" choice was not, in fact, the most ominous possibility. What we got in the decades following the report too often reflected a far worse choice: not a continuation of present policies but a backward movement—a rolling back of the limited efforts then in place.

The Kerner Commission worried that we might spend no more public resources to solve the problems of the inner cities than we were already spending. They did not explore the possibility that we might spend considerably less or that we would explicitly or tacitly abandon much of the minimal effort against poverty, joblessness, and blighted futures for the young we had made up through the late 1960s. The massive expansion of the penal system was arguably the shadow side of that more destructive choice. The security and social order that we would no longer try to achieve through massive and sustained investment in inner-city lives and communities would—in theory—be achieved instead through deterrence and incapacitation. Unless we believe that the 167,000 black lives lost to violence in the last two decades really do not matter, it is difficult to comprehend how this strategy can be deemed a success.

A recent survey of the neighborhood experiences of people of various races in Chicago, where homicides and gun violence generally have risen sharply in recent years, drives this point home. A stunning 86 percent of blacks, versus 50 percent of whites, said that it was "very likely" or "somewhat likely" that a young person in their neighborhood would be a victim of violent crime; 81 percent of blacks, versus 41 percent of whites, believed that it was either "very" or "somewhat" likely that a young person in their neighborhood would go to jail.[16] Fifty years after the Kerner Report, and forty-five years after we began our unprecedented experiment in mass incarceration, the "startling" differences in personal security the commission highlighted are still very much with us.

Equality and Inclusion

16

Suffering and Citizenship

Racism and Black Life

MICHAEL P. JEFFRIES

O N AUGUST 22, 2016, presidential hopeful Donald Trump stood before a crowd in Ohio and directly addressed black and Hispanic voters. He described Democrats' failures to address the issues that specifically plagued black Americans for so long, "poverty, rejection, horrible education, no housing," and brazenly asked black people, "What the hell do you have to lose? Give me a chance. I'll straighten it out."[1] Of course, people of color had already lost a great deal as a result of Trump's campaign. The candidate repeatedly primed white racism to rally support among his base. He trounced social norms in such a way that hate speech and hate crimes became commonplace during his rallies, a trend that continues after his election.[2]

Trump's policy agenda during the first few months of his presidency reflected this same animus, as his administration set to work crafting discriminatory immigration legislation and slashing education and health care funding desperately needed by vulnerable black people.

Yet there was a faint echo of truth in Trump's provocation: the government had either failed or purposefully penalized African Americans for decades, no matter who controlled the executive and legislative branches.

The politics of race in the early twenty-first century is dramatically different than it was in the 1960s. Demographics have shifted considerably, as Hispanics are now the largest nonwhite minority group in the country, and Asian Americans are the group with the fastest-growing population. Intersectional differences shaped by ethnicity, class, gender, and religion cut across all groups, especially as Muslims, Arabs, and South Asians are stereotyped as religious extremists and targeted by repulsive white nationalist and xenophobic attacks. For all these reasons, it can seem passé to focus solely on the lives and social conditions of black Americans when trying to understand racial politics. Yet Trump's campaign was grounded in the antiblack "tough on crime," "rule of law" rhetoric of the 1960s and 1980s—a language and logic of white nationalism that maps easily onto present day fears of "illegal" immigrants and foreign terrorists that attracted over sixty million voters.

We therefore cannot understand present or future permutations of the American racial order without close attention to the mechanics of black American oppression. The dire circumstances black Americans now face are a glimpse into the future for all vulnerable people in the United States, whether that vulnerability has its roots in poverty, ethnic- or gender-based bigotry, or any combination of these social forces.

AFRICAN AMERICANS TODAY

Black Americans live under a system of race-based inequality that is nakedly unjust, thickly woven, and multigenerational. The injustice is confirmed through the most rudimentary presentation of empirical evidence across four key dimensions: wealth and housing, education, policing, and incarceration and health. The codependence of these convening threads means that there is no single tear that will cause the tapestry of black oppression to unravel. American racism is deadly, adaptable, and resilient, and the government will not come to the rescue unprompted. But social movements for black liberation and justice have dramatized the current crisis such that it cannot be ignored. When citizens demand their rights, the government responds, and black dignity and justice for all become reasonable, if distant, hopes.

Wealth and Housing

The financial crisis of 2008 was a special disaster for black Americans. In 2004, the median net worth of white households was $134,280, roughly ten times the $13,450 median for black households. After the crash in 2009, median net worth for white households fell 24 percent, to $97,860, but median net worth for black households fell 83 percent, to $2,170. In other words, the average black household had two cents for every dollar of wealth held by the average white household.[3] We now know that part of the reason the gap was exacerbated by the housing crisis is that black people were discriminated against by lenders and targeted for subprime loans that left them especially vulnerable to foreclosure.[4] Banks were bailed out by taxpayers and several financial institutions were penalized for illegal lending practices,[5] but none of the compensation paid to the

American government made its way back to the black families who were completely wiped out by the recession.

Government-subsidized housing discrimination at the expense of black people is an American tradition. The formation of the Federal Housing Administration and the Home Owners Loan Corporation during the New Deal jump-started the American economy by creating wealth via homeownership for white Americans. Much attention is paid to the income gap between white and black people, and with good reason, as the gap persists across all education levels and has remained virtually unchanged over the last forty years.[6] But the root of the *wealth* gap is not income; there is no way for black people to simply educate and work themselves out of the hole they find themselves in. Rather, as the economists Darrick Hamilton and William Darity point out, "the largest factors explaining these differences are gifts and inheritances from older generations: a down payment on a first home, a debt-free college education, or a bequest from a parent."[7]

Merely showing that the wealth gap exists does not fully convey the impact of racial segregation and black poverty at the neighborhood level. William Julius Wilson's *The Truly Disadvantaged* captures the key differences between black and white poverty in postindustrial American cities. Wilson demonstrates that poor black neighborhoods were in fact areas of concentrated poverty where over 40 percent of residents lived below the poverty line, a percentage far higher than the neighborhoods where poor whites lived.[8]

Concentrated poverty produces communal and multigenerational effects, as people who live in poor black neighborhoods are isolated both spatially and culturally. There are no decent schools, jobs, or health care facilities in black ghettos, nor is there a critical mass of two-parent households or unmarried adults with steady employment who socialize young people and connect them to legitimate economic activities. Illicit economies fill this void, and these endeavors often rely on interpersonal (rather than economic and institutional) violence for regulation. These realities are distorted and politicized to justify the further isolation and criminalization of black and brown people, as fear of urban violence whips up moral panic about pathological culture in the ghetto.[9]

But Wilson and his colleague Robert Sampson have long since demonstrated that the root causes of urban violence are not cultural but fundamentally economic: extreme class and race segregation and joblessness lead to family disruption and antisocial behaviors.[10] Alarmingly, the problem is not eradicated even when families manage to leave such neighborhoods, as a mother's poor neighborhood experience a generation ago may have more of an impact on her child's school performance and life chances than the neighborhood the child grows up in.[11]

Education

Neighborhood is often a predictor of educational attainment because the U.S. public education system maintains its commitment to neighborhood schooling at the expense of integration and equal opportunity for all children. American schools are more segregated by race and class today than they were when the Kerner Report was published in 1968,[12] and African American students are almost completely isolated from predominantly white schools that benefit from superior resources. The average white student attends a school where 78 percent of students are white and less than 20 percent of students are impoverished. In contrast, roughly 90 percent of predominantly black and Latino schools suffer from concentrated poverty.[13] White Americans refuse to live near and send their children to school with people of color.

Again, merely describing the extent of segregation does not capture the lived experiences of black American students who attend underserved schools. The student population of these schools is prone to frequent student residential mobility because parents and guardians struggle to maintain steady employment and adequate housing. Frequent changes to class rosters in combination with attendance problems make it difficult for teachers to maintain consistency and teach at their own pace, as they are forced to adjust to students who fall behind or enter the class without requisite preparation.[14] Under these conditions, discipline in poor black and Latino/a schools differs markedly from discipline in predominantly white schools. Much has been written about the school-to-prison pipeline, a phrase that describes how zero-tolerance discipline policies and increased police presence in schools leads to increased arrest rates and involvement in juvenile court for students. As of 2013, black K–12 students were four times as likely to be suspended and two times as likely to be expelled as their white classmates. Importantly, these disparities begin in preschool; 20 percent of preschool students in the country are black, but these students account for roughly half of all preschool suspensions.[15]

Incarceration and Policing

The school-to-prison pipeline would not be culturally resonant were it not for mass incarceration in the late twentieth century. Michelle Alexander's 2010 landmark work, *The New Jim Crow*, is perhaps the most important of a slew of studies that make the case that the criminal justice complex has the most devastating impact on the life chances of African Americans of all forms of institutional racism. The American prison population rose from 350,000 in the 1970s to 2.3 million by 2008.[16] A white baby born in 2014 had a one-in-seventeen chance of spending time in jail over the course of their lives, but a Hispanic baby had a one-in-six chance, and black baby had a one-in-three chance.[17]

For many years it was fashionable for those on the left to blame the Ronald Reagan administration for the unjust expansion of the prison state. There is no doubt that President Reagan's updated version of Richard Nixon's War on Drugs promoted and incentivized the arrest and incarceration of low-level nonviolent offenders, which was a disaster for black and brown people and their communities. As Naomi Murakawa explains, the events that spurred the Kerner Commission's report also updated the defining discourse of racist criminality, as black civil rights were framed in opposition to public safety and white people's rights in mainstream political discourse.[18]

President Reagan's investment in policing and incarceration was complemented by the reorganization of urban economies during the 1980s, as the industrial sector disintegrated and President Reagan pulled federal money out of city and state budgets. Changes in criminal court, such as the rise of mandatory minimum sentencing and plea bargains, destroyed judicial discretion and provided a constant stream of new prisoners. But the Reagan administration was not solely responsible for the damage, as research demonstrates the catastrophic impact of the Bill Clinton administration and the 1994 Violent Crime Act, which doubled down on the rhetoric and false premises of the Reagan policies and pumped more money into racialized policing and incarceration.[19]

Mass incarceration has no positive impact on crime rates. It does, however, destroy impoverished families. As of 2010, more than 50 percent of prisoners had children under eighteen years of age when they were sent away, and men who were incarcerated are about four times more likely to attack their domestic partners than men who were never imprisoned. Not surprisingly, incarceration is positively linked to divorce and separation, in no small part because of the difficulty formerly incarcerated parents have when they attempt to seek employment after their release. Mass incarceration is not merely an outcome or reflection of institutional racism but an input and engine of disparate racial outcomes. It is not an acute setback limited to the person who is sent to jail; it is a contagion that affects everyone in that person's social network and, like growing up amid concentrated poverty, leaves a multigenerational impact on the life chances of the prisoner's family members.[20]

Surveillance and violent discipline at the hands of the state is a common experience among black people regardless of whether they are incarcerated, because twenty-first century policing remains devastatingly unjust. Racism in policing is both institutional and psychological. Ferguson, Missouri, the site of the Michael Brown killing, is a classic example of institutionalized racism in policing. At the time Brown was killed by police officer Darren Wilson, 60 percent of Ferguson residents were black, yet black people accounted for 92 percent of searches and 86 percent of vehicle stops by police. In the year before Brown was killed, 483 black people were arrested in Ferguson compared to 36 white people. The police chief and the mayor of Ferguson were both white, as were fifty of the fifty-three officers on the Ferguson police force.[21] A Department of Justice report on policing and court practices in Ferguson found that African Americans were disproportionately penalized by the police and courts in Ferguson and that law enforcement was shaped by the need to generate revenue for the city rather than the duty to protect and serve.[22]

At the psychological level, racial bias and fear of black people has a cataclysmic impact on the rate at which police detain and use deadly force against black Americans.[23] Research shows that black American teenage boys and men are 21 times more likely to be shot by and killed by police than their white peers,[24] and the probability of an unarmed black person being shot by police is 3.5 times higher than that of a white person.[25] The racially disparate crime rate has no explanatory impact on racial disparities in police use of force.[26] There was some hope that the adoption of body cameras would incentivize officers to behave differently, but the initial returns on the new technology are deeply disappointing. The first rigorous study of body camera footage shows that police officers speak to black residents less respectfully than white residents,[27] and the footage from body cameras, no matter how heinous, has not led to convictions of police officers for killing black civilians.

Health and Health Care

One of the reasons the criminal justice complex continues to gobble up government resources is that it serves a critical function beyond punishment: America's jails are, in many respects, warehouses to store the mentally infirm. Roughly 56 percent of state prisoners, 45 percent of federal prisoners, and 64 percent of jail inmates have mental health issues.[28] It would be too generous to refer to prisons as "mental asylums," because the word "asylum" might suggest that residents receive treatment with the hope of rehabilitation. This is not the case in prisons, as only one of three state prisoners and one of six jail prisoners receive mental health treatment after their admission.[29] A 2010 report found that roughly 1.5 million of the 2.3 million people in jail in the United States met the criteria for substance abuse or addiction.[30] The economic and human costs of this social-control mechanism are staggering, as states' spending on prisons outpaces their investment in public education, and incarcerating people who are mentally ill often exacerbates their illness and leads to misconduct and recidivism.[31]

The prison system is but one facet of an American public health crisis that results from and further calcifies black suffering. Black Americans receive inadequate health care in no small part because they cannot afford health insurance and live in neighborhoods without access to suitable health clinics and food required for a healthy diet.

Predominantly black neighborhoods are also more likely to feature a dizzying array of pollutants, as the devastation of environmental racism engendered by the overlay of class and race segregation results in disproportionate rates of pregnancy and childbirth complications and afflictions, as well as childhood illnesses like asthma and lead poisoning.[32]

When Barack Obama took office in 2008, black life expectancy was six to ten years shorter than that of whites, and the age-adjusted cancer rate was approximately 25 percent higher for black people than for white people.[33] Almost ten years later, many of these disparities persist even in areas where progress is being made. Take diabetes, for example: 13.2 percent of non-Hispanic blacks are diagnosed with the disease compared to only 7.6 percent of non-Hispanic whites.[34]

The Affordable Care Act (ACA) passed by the Obama administration was a step in the direction of securing health insurance for all Americans and reducing racial disparities in access to health care. A 2015 report showed that 7.4 million white Americans, 4 million Hispanics, and 2.6 million black Americans were added to health insurance rolls after the ACA became law in 2010. As a result, the uninsured rate among white Americans dropped from 14.3 percent to 8.3 percent; the Hispanic rate, from 41.8 percent to 30.3 percent; and the black rate, from 22.4 percent to 12.1 percent.[35] These gains could be short-lived, as the 2017 GOP-led Congress began what looked like a maniacal push to repeal the ACA and effectively cut access for over twenty million Americans from their health insurance plans within a decade, though poor people and people of color, especially, would be disproportionately victimized by such changes.

Citizenship Reconsidered

Black Americans have never fully enjoyed the rights of citizenship as prescribed in the Constitution, and this second-class status has cost us dearly, as outlined above. The struggle against racism and discrimination reveals citizenship for what it truly is. Citizenship is not a legal status granted once and for all by legislation or validated by a passport. Citizenship exists only to the extent it is practiced. Freedom of assembly, freedom of speech, the right to a fair trial, the right to privacy, and the right to vote are constantly contested whether most Americans realize it or not. Black Americans stand at the center of these contests, and our willingness to embody citizenship and dramatize its contingency calls others forward and makes justice possible.

Black Lives Matter is the defining social movement of the Obama and post-Obama era, and it demonstrates the power of citizenship as practice.

The movement began after the killing of sixteen-year-old Trayvon Martin, which went unpunished by the police and the criminal justice system. The ideology and organization of Black Lives Matter were conceived by the black feminist social organizers Alicia Garza, Opal Tometi, and Patrisse Cullors, who explicitly defined the movement as intersectional and antihierarchical. Tactically, the early stages of Black Lives Matter relied on civil disobedience and public protest, which dramatized and publicized dangerous conflicts with police and sparked the most serious public debate about policing and incarceration America has known since the 1960s.

Make note of the word "dramatized." Black Lives Matter did not lead to the police surveillance and repression that were broadcast on television and the Internet during the movement; surveillance, harassment, and repression by police were always part and parcel of black American life. Black Lives Matter activists embodied their citizenship, enacting free speech and free assembly and testing the right to privacy and the right to trial to make the truth of state surveillance and violence plain to everyone in the country.

Opponents cast Black Lives Matter as disorganized and politically unsophisticated even after the Movement for Black Lives coalition put forth an impeccably researched set of policy demands, including the eradication of privatized prisons and police; capital punishment; for-profit policing, including money bail and "defendant funded" court proceedings; and the consideration of past criminal history as a disqualifier for voting, obtaining a loan, and gaining employment.[36] The movement also makes a strong case for democratic civilian control of police through the creation of civilian oversight boards, which would improve police accountability by giving civilians the power to "hire and fire officers, determine disciplinary action, control budgets and policies, and subpoena relevant agencies for information."[37] The legacy of Black Lives Matter will not be dampened by these demands being essentially ignored by media and politicians, because two achievements are beyond question. First, Black Lives Matter forced legislators to think critically about mass incarceration and policing, and by the end of President Obama's presidency he was defending the validity of Black Lives Matter, and punishment reform was a mainstream political idea. Presidential candidates Hillary Clinton and Bernie Sanders both affirmed that black lives matter during the 2016 Democratic primaries. Attorney general Eric Holder instructed federal prosecutors to reduce the number of charges for nonviolent drug offenses, and 130 police chiefs and prosecutors formed a new organization in October 2015 that was designed to address mass incarceration. In one exemplary sound bite, Austin police chief Art Acevedo publicly disagreed with Texas lieutenant governor Dan Patrick's assertion that Black Lives Matter activism fueled a shooting in Dallas that targeted police and resulted in the deaths of five officers. Acevedo said, "Maybe [Patrick] needs to meet with our local Black Lives Matter. . . . I can tell you that the vast majority are good people [and] that all they want is good policing."[38] Considering Black Live Matter's humble beginnings and the degree of slander endured by activists, these are truly remarkable developments.

The second key achievement of Black Lives Matter may be even greater than the first. Black Lives Matter reinvigorated participatory citizenship as the true source of people's power and the most essential ingredient of democracy. The Higher Education Research Institute has been conducting surveys of incoming college freshmen for fifty years, and 9 percent of incoming students in 2015 said they had a "very good chance" of participating in protests while in college; it was the highest percentage ever recorded by the survey. In addition, 16 percent of black students said they planned to protest, suggesting that black Americans will continue to set the standard for participatory citizenship as the twenty-first century unfolds.[39]

Political organizing and protesting received another jolt when Trump was elected, especially among women. Three women of color—Linda Sarsour, Tamika Mallory, and Carmen Perez—organized the 2017 Women's March, which garnered the largest number of single-day protestors in the country's history; 2.6 million Americans took to the streets. Protest actions in defense of immigrants, the environment, and scientific research were also carried out during the early days of Trump's presidency.

THE FUTURE

This is the path forward. The research explaining institutional racism and the horrific damage it causes is unimpeachable. Solutions to problems like racist policing and criminal justice are so obvious that police chiefs, prosecutors, and legislators on both sides of the aisle have started to come together. But the catalyst of political consensus and redress when it comes to matters of racial injustice is not sound research or common sense. It is a widespread commitment among ordinary people to live citizenship out loud, even in the face of repression. This commitment is the fountain of black American political power in the twenty-first century and hope for the future. There will be no justice and no democracy without it.

17

New Dimensions of Equity

The Experience of American Latinos

HENRY G. CISNEROS

WHEN THE MARCH 1, 1968, Kerner Commission report was published, the sharpest tension among domestic priorities was the state of relations between African Americans and white Americans. The civil rights movement had drawn long-overdue national attention to entrenched segregation and continuing discrimination. In numerous American cities, civil disturbances, mass demonstrations, civil disobedience, and violence gave witness to the reality that black-white relations in the nation were at a crisis point. The nation could not know on March 1, 1968, that by the next month Dr. Martin Luther King would be assassinated in Memphis and the nation would be plunged deeper into mourning and anger, despair and loss.

In the prevailing black-white context, the national Latino community had not emerged in the consciousness of the nation as a major dimension of civil rights concerns. Some Americans knew that they depended on Latino farmworkers for agricultural labor. There was a scattering of high-profile Latino entertainers who had drawn attention to a Latino presence in movies, music, and television. Most Americans had no idea how many Latinos might live in the United States because the Hispanic population tended to be concentrated in specific states. Latinos were substantial percentages of the population and even the dominant population in some counties in parts of Texas, California, New Mexico, and Arizona; and Latino farmworkers and Cuban refugees were changing the demographics of Florida. But the American news media and even academic scholars had little familiarity with the true extent of Latinos in the United States or with their role in the national economy.

LATINOS AND THE KERNER REPORT

The principles and recommendations presented in the Kerner Report matched initiatives that were already addressing Latino concerns. The federal government had begun to focus on bilingual education for Spanish-speaking populations and had launched initiatives to address farmworker housing and health needs. Migration of refugees fleeing the Castro regime in Cuba had resulted in growth in the Cuban American population, first in South Florida and then in communities around the nation, and Congress had passed the 1966 Cuban Adjustment Act, which allowed Cuban refugees who had lived in this country for at least two years to become U.S. citizens.

Spontaneous community-based groups had begun to advocate for Latino civil rights. The formation of the United Farm Workers in 1965 and the creation of the Mexican American Legal Defense and Educational Fund in 1968 were examples of the drive for self-determination, which had its roots in the lessons of the civil rights movement but which was uniquely focused on the special needs of the American Latino population.

LATINOS IN THE YEARS AFTER THE KERNER REPORT

In the years immediately following the Kerner Report, the nation's attention was concentrated as never before on issues of inclusion and expanded participation in American public life, and Latinos were the beneficiaries of both local actions geared to self-determination and positive actions taken by the federal government to advance Latino progress.

The 1970s saw the continuation of Latino initiatives at the local and national levels. At the local level, organizations such as the Southwest Voter Registration Education Project focused on registering Latino voters. In 1974, the Supreme Court, in *Lau v. Nichols*, a case that arose in California, held that student access to public education programs could not be denied because of a student's inability to speak English. That same year, Congress passed the Equal Educational Opportunity Act, which provided for bilingual education in public schools all across the country and expanded the 1965 Voting Rights Act to require language assistance at all polling places.

It is fair to say that the Kerner Commission raised the consciousness of Americans about the importance of addressing the divisions in our society and helped create the setting in which the national administration and the Congress could act. It is also true to that the Kerner Commission framed the intellectual arguments and offered official recommendations that made it possible for Latino leaders to energize their constituencies of Latinos across the nation.

The focus of the Kerner Report thus helped shape the next fifty years of Latino progress.

LATINOS TODAY

America is now much more aware of the size of its Latino population, which today approaches 60 million people out of a total U.S. population of 320 million.[1] At 20 percent of national population, Latinos are our country's largest minority group and its fastest-growing minority group. It is estimated that over the next thirty years, the Latino population will grow to about 100 million people, while the national population is growing to about 400 million[2]—meaning that Latinos will be responsible for about half of all U.S. population growth during that period.

While many once thought that Latinos resided principally in the Southwest, New York, and Florida, we should today be aware that their population is now truly spread nationwide. The states with the fastest-growing percentages of Latinos include Arkansas, Georgia, and North Carolina. Latino populations are growing substantially in Illinois, Virginia, Kansas, Nebraska, Tennessee, Washington State, and Oregon and by substantial, if slower, rates in states not regarded as traditional Latino destinations, such as Maine, Connecticut, Pennsylvania, Michigan, and Ohio.

Latino newcomers in many of these states are rejuvenating older neighborhoods and small towns, while in what had earlier been traditional and homogeneous communities, new tensions arise about language and social customs. One of the major challenges facing the country is the integration of Latinos into the social and political life of the nation, especially as intense concerns about immigration have made public dialogue more acrimonious and reforms more difficult to enact.

Growing Latino Economic Power

In the arena of economic advancement, Latinos have made substantial progress in recent years, and they have become a major force in expanding the nation's economy by creating new businesses and by contributing to the growth of jobs for all Americans. The increase in the numbers of Latino consumers with rising incomes has expanded demand for the goods and services provided by mainstream U.S. companies. Latino purchasing power is projected to reach $1.7 trillion by 2020.[3] Because of the demographic reality that Latinos are, on average, younger than other Americans, Latino workers will play an important and growing role in replenishing the aging U.S. workforce with energetic and ambitious new workers. In all these ways, Latinos are a significant force in driving America's economic growth as their incomes increase, they become better educated, they capitalize more on their entrepreneurial abilities, and they contribute to tax bases locally and to the Social Security system nationally. Several of these points bear further examination. Latinos are active creators of new businesses: the Stanford Latino Entrepreneurship Initiative documents that American Latinos formed 86 percent of the total net new businesses in the nation between 2007 and 2012.[4] Thus, Latinos are contributing directly to the core of the American economy. Employment in Latino-owned firms between 2007 and 2012 grew by 22 percent at a time when employment in non-Latino owned firms declined by 2 percent.[5]

According to Pew Research Center projections, by 2035, 34 percent of the U.S. workforce will be immigrants and U.S.-born children of immigrants, many of whom will be Latino.[6] With the number of nonimmigrant working-age adults simultaneously decreasing, this influx of immigrants into the ranks of U.S. workers will be necessary to maintain a manageable ratio of retirees to workers—the significance of all this being that young Latino workers will be essential to keeping the Social Security system actuarially sound.

The Partnership for a New American Economy estimates that with a growing population and growing income, the state tax contributions of Latinos now total, for example, more than $17 billion in California and more than $11 billion in Texas.[7]

Growing Latino Influence

The last fifty years have seen dramatic progress in the strength of Latino advocacy organizations and in Latino leadership development. Today there are forty-four Latino members of the Congressional Hispanic Caucus and about five thousand Hispanic elected local officials across the United States. The largest Latino advocacy organizations are broad in their capacity to address concerns, composed of effective affiliates in virtually every state of the nation, and effective in their access to national decision-making forums. Prominent among them is the oldest of the Latino advocacy organizations, the League of United Latin American Citizens; equally effective are the National Council of La Raza (now UnidosUS), the Mexican American Legal Defense and Educational Fund, the National Association of Latino Elected and Appointed Officials, the Puerto Rican Legal Defense and Education Fund (now LatinoJustice), the Hispanic Association on Corporate Responsibility, the Latino Corporate Directors Association, the Cuban National Forum, the U.S. Hispanic Chamber of Commerce, the American GI Forum, the Latino Donor Collaborative, and multiple other organizations representing specialized Latino constituencies. The leaders of these organizations are important voices in the national public policy dialogue, and from the membership of these organizations come many national leaders who hold important positions, such as in the president's cabinet and on corporate boards and in business forums, and are increasingly elected to local, state, and national public offices.

Still another dimension of Latino progress over the last fifty years is the cultural presence of Latinos, adding to the richness of the American mosaic. Latinos have created pathbreaking innovations in such diverse fields as music, fashion, architecture, food, film and television, and literature. Latinos are winning audiences and broad recognition for enriching the creative life of the nation. Latino themes are merging into the American popular culture and responding to broad public interest in global creativity and panethnic identities.

THE ROAD AHEAD: THE NEXT FIFTY YEARS

While substantial progress has been made over the last fifty years, the challenges that the Latino population and the nation still face are immense. To the degree that America is able to create expanded opportunities for Latino progress in the economic, educational, and social realms, the nation itself will benefit mightily. The Latino population is now of such a scale that its progress will register as notable advances for the nation as a whole. On the other hand, if Latinos are marginalized and left behind, then Latino deficits will become large-scale national deficits.

Education: The Highest Priority

A critical priority for Latino progress is education at all levels. Most expert analyses of the Latino future pinpoint educational underperformance as a major liability for Latinos and for the country. Fortunately, in most surveys of how Latinos rank their public policy priorities, education ranks first.[8]

Recognizing the high proportion of Latino children of preschool and elementary school age, the nation's school districts must expand their preschool programs so that children can start elementary school ready to learn. Some cities are doing this. In San Antonio, Texas, for example, a bond issue was passed to fund a network of prekindertgarten campuses.

School districts with Latino populations must improve education in the K–12 years, too. Most analyses of Latino performance in education indicate that while substantial progress has been made over the last decades, gaps in Latino performance remain significant. Latino underperformance on state tests, isolation of Latino students in the poorest underperforming schools, high dropout rates, and low progression to college are all dimensions of the problematic Latino educational condition that underscores the need for specific educational policies.

In recent years, the National Assessment of Educational Progress, a congressionally mandated survey conducted by the Department of Education, showed that while almost 80 percent of white high school seniors scored at or above the basic level in reading, only about 60 percent of Latinos scored at basic levels. A similar gap exists in mathematics: whereas almost 70 percent of white seniors scored at or above basic levels on the NAEP math test, only 40 percent of Latinos achieved basic proficiency in mathematics.[9]

School districts with large Latino populations must focus on smaller school sizes, better school facilities, properly equipped laboratories, modern computer facilities, better training and compensation for teachers, preparation of principals and superintendents, improvements in school board governance, and responsible levels of school finance. All these strategies must be pursued together if the necessary progress is to be made. Innovative frameworks for education at the K–12 level should include all types of schools: traditional public schools, public magnet schools, charter schools and religious schools, and other private schools.

The inadequacy of the education of Latinos of the K–12 ages unfortunately ensures that rates of college attendance are below potential. Latino high school graduates often face insurmountable remediation at the point of entering college. Statistics indicate that the likelihood of successfully completing college is dramatically diminished for students who are not able to remediate their learning gaps before entering college.[10]

In addition to the traditional progression to college, there is also a need for improving the skills of the existing Latino workforce. Programs to provide enhanced skill training for noncollege-educated workers are critical to meet the demands of advanced industries for computer-literate and technically proficient employees. Quality training programs are essential to raising family incomes and to establishing family economic stability.

It is clear that America's failure to develop the immense asset that is its youthful and energetic population of Latino students and workers will result in a shortfall of national talent prepared for the technological requirements of the emerging economy. We risk relegating a high-potential Latino population to the margins of society where they will be underemployed and unable to pass along the benefits of the new economy to their children.

Income and Wealth: Building the Next American Middle Class

Also prioritized highly by Latinos are employment and economic opportunities, measured in income, wages, and wealth development. Latino household median income continues to trail the white non-Hispanic average in the United States, averaging about 65 percent of white non-Hispanic incomes.[11] The conditions in which many Latinos live can accurately be described as a Latino underclass. Many factors contribute to that reality, including population concentrations in regions where wages are lower, the mismatch between skills and higher-wage occupations, and structural factors that have created slow wage growth and segmented labor markets. Only about 14 percent of Hispanic households have incomes exceeding $100,000.[12] The effects of poverty undermine Latino goals to advance economic and social progress, and they perpetuate the debilitating and disheartening cycle of disadvantage into future generations.

The gap in Latino incomes is wide and slow to close, but it pales in comparison to the gap in wealth. Many Latino families have a net worth of essentially zero, and the average net worth of Latino families is less than 10 percent of the average white non-Hispanic net worth. Latinos lag in every measure of net worth: homeownership, insurance ownership, access to stock and bond investments, retirement and pension plans, 401(k) retirement plans, annuities, and other savings investments.

Numerous efforts are under way to address gaps in Latino incomes and Latino wealth. They include improvements in the quality of jobs through economic development, enhanced education and training to match skills with higher-paying jobs, minimum-wage strategies that place an effective floor under family incomes, the Earned Income Tax Credit, and savings incentives that make it possible for families to access tangible resources. Specific initiatives to encourage asset building in the Latino community are homeownership counseling, technical assistance in small business formation, access to credit, and financial literacy education, including in primary and secondary curricula.

Decent Housing: A Platform for Social Progress

Access to housing for Latinos must address the gap in homeownership, in which the disparity between Latinos and white non-Hispanics exceeds twenty-five points, 45.6 percent compared to 71.8 percent, respectively.[13] When one considers that homeownership has been defined as a step up on the ladder into the American middle class, a thirty-point gap in home-ownership illustrates the steepness of the steps of Latino progression to the middle class.

Apart from the economic aspects of homeownership, affordable and decent housing is the means toward establishing stability for Latino families as they pursue the personal goals for better education and job training, career promotion, and improved health, personal safety, and multi-generational support. The crisis of affordable rental housing in the United States has hit Latinos with particular force. When Latino families live in housing that is overcrowded and unsafe and spend as much as 50 percent or more of their monthly income for shelter, personal financial stress is inevitable, and there is simply not enough money left to pay for food, clothing, medicines, transportation, and the other requirements of daily life. The unaffordable cost of housing near centers of employment often forces Latino workers to drive long distances from home to the workplace, with a resulting high cost of transportation for workers and lower productivity for employers.

Accelerated programs to build affordable housing, involving both public-sector leaders and private-sector builders and financial institutions, are imperative in many metropolitan areas. Creating a mix of housing types and a mix of housing prices for the workforce is of immense importance to Latinos, who are now so essential to the functioning of metropolitan economies across the country.

Health and Wellness: Unacceptable Disparities for Latinos

Health morbidities are among the most serious problems confronting the Latino community. The intersection of poverty, language barriers, lack of education concerning nutrition, and impediments caused by gaps in the health care and health insurance systems creates massive problems for the Latino population with respect to health and wellness. Poverty creates Latino health disparities, for example, through diets of unhealthy foods. Often the cheapest foods are starchy foods that result in retained body fat, leading to epidemic levels of obesity and its attendant diseases, such as diabetes. Latino children are at higher risk for childhood obesity and juvenile diabetes than white non-Hispanic children.[14] When such health conditions are combined with the inability to access health care and the lack of health insurance, diseases go untreated for longer periods and become more severe.

Gaps in language proficiency undermine access to health care, and the vast disparity in access to health insurance makes it financially impossible for families to afford needed care. Throughout the last decade, uninsured rates for Hispanics were almost 50 percent, compared to about 13 percent for non-Hispanic whites—at a time when Hispanics made up 30 percent of the total U.S. uninsured population.[15]

Efforts to address the disparities in the Latino health indices and access to care must take into account the cultural nuances of Latino communities, of immigrant status, and of language proficiency. Latinos would be well served by the addition of Latino medical personnel in disadvantaged communities. That would mean increasing the number of Latino students in medical, dental, and nursing schools and increasing the presence of Latino medical professionals in positions of responsibility in public hospitals, in health organizations, and in private practice. The location of clinics, medical offices, and hospitals in cities and communities where Latinos represent large proportions of the population would also be decisive. Policy makers must understand the connections between health services and decent housing, education, literacy, access to transportation, and the devastation wrought by low incomes and poverty.

A Broken Immigration System

Of overarching importance to the Latino future is resolution of the problems generated by the nation's ineffective immigration system. The immigration system has immensely complex dimensions. On the one hand, there is the existence within the United States of an estimated twelve million undocumented persons, the majority of whom are immigrants from nations to the south, particularly Mexico. Their presence raises questions about the porousness of the border and of the adequacy of border security. But their presence is also a reminder that these people are an essential workforce, though they must live in the shadows of society where their potential contributions are diminished and where they exist outside the protection of the country's laws.

Immigration experts have generally held that corrections to the immigration system involve a three-part reform. Step one addresses border security and protections. A national political shouting match has centered on the efficacy of a wall, but many experts believe that the necessary corrective measures must be broader than a physical wall. There are more cost-effective ways to protect the border that use electronic systems at the border and e-verify measures at places of employment. Because a substantial percentage of undocumented persons in the country have overstayed visas, a more effective means of tracking visa overstays is a tighter system of verification at the workplace, which would eliminate the employment magnet that attracts foreign nationals to cross the border.

The second generally accepted element of immigration reform is the legalization of workers who are already in the country. In 2012, the Senate passed a bill that would have created a rigorous process by which undocumented workers with good records as residents in the United States could acquire legal status so that they could work here. The process would have involved paying a penalty, paying back taxes, verifying their record of living within the law, and documenting their stability of employment. The Senate bill did not advance, even though it presented a plausible structure for legalization of workers and would have addressed the presence of undocumented workers in a more practical manner than mass deportation of twelve million people.

The third leg of immigrant reform is that of an earned pathway to eventual citizenship for those among the newly legalized who demonstrate a desire to become U.S. citizens. The pathway envisioned in the Senate legislation included a rigorous thirteen-year process involving documentation of a demonstrated capacity to live within U.S. laws, learn English, and work in a meaningful job over a number of years. Another critical element of the proposed legislation was the requirement that legalized candidates for citizenship had to go to the back of the line of persons waiting to enter the country and not be allowed to jump ahead in the queue.

Reform of the immigration system is obviously important to the people directly involved, to their families, and to employers. But it has taken on an immense significance in the Latino community at large because the attacks of opponents tend to conflate undocumented workers with Latinos who may be long-standing U.S. citizens. Many Latinos are subjected to suspicions about their citizenship status because of their physical appearance, last name, accent, or other outward manifestations of their Hispanic heritage. The attacks go beyond concerns about immigration policies and slide into prejudices about language and heritage.

This unfortunate and baseless denigration of an entire population has had the effect of creating a sense of solidarity among American Latinos concerning the contributions that undocumented Latinos make within our nation. The undocumented are among the people with whom Latinos go to church, collaborate in the workplace, shop in neighborhood stores, and have daily relationships such as those related to childcare and homemaking duties. The attack on undocumented immigrants is now more than ever perceived as an attack on the entire Hispanic community.

Failure to reform the immigration system will increasingly touch multiple dimensions of American life. The current broken system decreases the availability of workers for key sectors; creates a sense of unease within communities; leaves unresolved the status of some twelve million people, their families, and workplace associations; and creates barriers for a youthful and energetic segment of our population who could be immensely productive and valuable in advancing the American economic future.

Civic Participation and Public Service

These priorities—education, incomes, housing, health, and immigration—have a common denominator: they require greater political participation and a stronger voice from the Latino community itself. The participation of American Latinos as citizens and voters and their representation by accountable leaders are important dimensions of America's political future. Strategies to register and educate voters, encourage voter participation, encourage qualified citizens to seek public office, and recognize the contributing talents of genuine leaders will serve the nation well. Contrastingly, efforts to suppress minority voters are damaging in their long-term effects for the country. America is best served by broadening access to full democratic participation and by engaging the youthful energies of an emergent American Latino community in its public life.

THE RESONANT MESSAGE OF THE KERNER REPORT

The central lesson of the last fifty years concerning Latinos is that the Latino potential in America is immense and that it is in the nation's interest to develop that potential. The Latino presence in the American story has been a long and rich narrative; now it takes on the dimensions of a shaping force for the American future. It is wise policy for America to undertake the full integration of this population. That means we must harness its economic capacities, uplift its educational potential, encourage its civic participation, and integrate it into the foundation of a durable middle class. These themes are obviously important to American Latinos themselves. It is for these reasons that Latinos study, work, organize, and strive.

These themes are also important to America as a whole. It is a basic reality of the law of numbers that, as this population grows in sheer magnitude, its potential to contribute grows in significance. But it is also true that if it is marginalized and its potential is wasted, the negative effects are grievously damaging to the nation. The swing between those choices will in great measure define alternative American futures.

Many Americans may not fully appreciate the extent to which Latinos live by values that have been considered prototypical American values. In fact, polling conducted by the *Washington Post*, the Kaiser Family Foundation, and the Harvard University Survey Project demonstrates that Latinos, as has been the case with previous generations of immigrants during America's history, fully embrace the values of hard work, of belief in America's promise and its being a nation of laws, of spiritual faith, and of sacrifice in the present generation to create opportunity for the next.[16] These are values that we think of as integral to the functioning of the American models of enterprise and democracy, and often, immigrants are the strongest adherents of these values, bringing with them the faith of converts.

The polling reflects that. When asked, the majority of Latinos embraced the idea that hard work leads to success.[17] And 72 percent of Latinos expressed optimism about the future in that they believe their children will be financially better off than they are.[18] Such polling evidence underscores what many Americans who live and work among Latinos understand: Latinos are grateful for the opportunity to be in this country; they are naturally predisposed to work hard; they strive for what they can achieve; they have faith that short-term sacrifice is the key to long-term family progress; they are devoted to a better life for their children; and they are willing to sacrifice today, pay taxes, work long hours, and play by the rules to make that future possible.

These assertions of Latino hope and ambition should make all Americans confident that the Latinos in their midst are positive additions to the cultural stock of America, the latest infusion of positive immigrant energies into the American story. And they should make it clear to Americans that despite the superficial differences—skin complexion, Spanish accent, and Latin surnames, and differences in food or music preferences—the ambitions and drive that Latinos bring to this country are positive qualities that can reenergize the nation as significant portions of the traditional population age beyond their working years and these and other populations express skepticism about the core American values.

The overarching message of the Kerner Report was that America works better when concepts of inclusion and fairness evolve beyond mere abstractions and actually become the working dynamic of daily life. Those principles were important to the members of the Kerner Commission, were vital in transcending the tragedies of the Jim Crow era, and over the last fifty years have guided the nation to our most inclusive time ever. They will be even more important going forward. In a hopeful vision of the American future, the American Latino community will most certainly rise to a larger significance. By its present scale and by its future potential it can be one of the forces that sustain America in its domestic ambitions and activate its hopes for the world. As we revisit the enduring lessons of the Kerner Report from the vantage point of fifty years of progress, we would be wise to renew our commitments to the universal principles the Kerner Commission so effectively presented as recommendations for achieving a more prosperous and more inclusive America.

Everybody Does Better in Indian Country When Tribes Are Empowered

Kevin K. Washburn

IN THE FIFTY YEARS since the publication of the Kerner Report, the cure for poverty has proved elusive for many of the poorest communities throughout the United States.[1] In the mostly rural areas of the United States defined by the federal government as "Indian country,"[2] economic development has proved especially difficult. Today, many American Indians endure living conditions that would shock ordinary middle-class Americans. Indeed, poor American citizens on some Indian reservations live without indoor plumbing and must transport water to their rural homes.[3] For others, water exists nearby, but it is not safe to drink.[4] Moreover, many impoverished households in Indian country are crowded with ten or more family members living in a one- or two-bedroom home.[5] In many instances, a single employed family member supports numerous members of his or her extended family, often under one roof. Native communities in urban areas also face challenges.

The time of social upheaval that brought attention to inner-city poverty by the Kerner Report also prompted critical thinking on the particular rural poverty that faces American Indian reservations. Tribal nations occupy a unique place in the United States. They predate the existence of the United States and occupy lands that, for some purposes, lie physically within the boundaries of the constituent states but remain legally separate and apart. The U.S. government is deemed to have a "trust responsibility" to Indian nations, a moral and legal principle derived from the United States existing entirely on land once occupied solely by self-governing Native Americans and taken from them, in many cases, with broken promises.

On the basis of the conditions of life on Indian reservations, educated observers often feel that the moral obligations underlying the trust responsibility are honored more in the breach than in the observance. While actions by the federal government over more than two hundred years have contributed substantially to the poverty, public health and safety, and other issues facing Indian tribes, it is no longer clear that the federal government will be the source of the solutions to these problems. One of the great insights of the War on Poverty was that impoverished communities themselves are more likely to develop the best solutions to the problems posed by poverty. Nowhere is this more true than in Indian country.

Increasingly, tribal governments are taking responsibility for solving the problems in Indian communities, and the federal government is empowering them to do so. Over the long term, this approach is expected to yield increasing dividends. It has already improved public-sector job growth in Indian country. Though progress measured by some key indicators has been slow, it is increasingly apparent that the social problems that have developed over more than two centuries may well take decades to address.

THE LAST FIFTY YEARS IN INDIAN COUNTRY

Since the time of the 1968 Kerner Commission report, major developments have occurred in Indian country. Beginning about that time, the federal government began to reconsider the role of tribal governments in providing services on Indian reservations.

Tribal governments by the 1960s had been marginalized for so many decades that they had become weak institutions. Federal policy makers realized, however, that tribal governments, if empowered, could be crucial allies in addressing the specific and persistent problems on Indian reservations. These views gave rise to support for policies known as "tribal self-determination" and "tribal self-governance."[6]

The first major congressional statute to implement the tribal self-determination policy was enacted in 1975. Under the Indian Self-Determination and Education Assistance Act of 1975, Indian tribes could contract to run certain federal Indian programs and receive the federal funding directly. For tribes that opted to contract federal functions, no longer would such programs be performed by Bureau of Indian Affairs (BIA) employees; the programs and services would be performed by tribal employees.

The contracting of federal functions on Indian reservations by Indian tribes has been widely regarded as an improvement in federal Indian policy and a meaningful step toward self-determination. Under the federal policies of tribal self-determination and eventually self-governance, the tribal government role in implementing federal trust responsibilities to tribes was eventually broadened beyond the BIA and the Indian Health Service (IHS) to the Environmental Protection Agency[7] and even to the Department of Housing and Urban Development.[8]

Today, a substantial portion of the annual federal appropriations for federal Indian programs, including more than half the budget for Interior Department programs and nearly half the budget of the IHS, is spent by tribes under the self-determination and self-governance programs.[9] Tribes are now running programs for law enforcement, health care, education, social services, land and resource management, and numerous other functions, including housing. For example, tribes operate more than 130 of 187 federal Indian school campuses.

Tribal self-determination is successful for a variety of reasons. A powerful practical explanation is fiscal prudence. Because of the effectiveness of tribal governments and the perceived ineffectiveness of the long-entrenched federal bureaucratic structure, it is widely believed that the federal taxpayer gets more value from each dollar spent when tribes are contracted to operate federal programs. A rural tribe, for example, may be able to hire one and a half or even two employees for the cost of a single federal employee, thereby increasing reservation employment. A tribe may also be more flexible than federal officials in developing local solutions to local problems. Of course, tribal employees may also be more accountable than federal employees to the Native American people served under federal or tribal programs.

Tribal governments were fairly modest organizations at the beginning of the self-determination era in the 1960s. At that time, a tribal government may have constituted a volunteer governmental structure with a single paid employee, such as an executive director or administrator. Since that time, tribal governments have developed strong institutional infrastructure, capacity, and expertise to address real problems facing Indian communities. Today, many tribes have dozens or hundreds of tribal governmental employees and some have thousands of gaming employees.

Fiscal resources vary dramatically across Indian country and, for most tribes, resources never seem to be adequate. Moreover, because of the same kinds of human frailty that are seen periodically in state and federal governmental entities, such as corruption or incompetence, tribal governments sometimes fail in meeting their obligations. On balance, however, tribal nations are capably running programs and demonstrating the ingenuity and flexibility to run federal programs more effectively than federal actors, even when those programs are underfunded.

In historical terms, the engagement of tribal governments is still a new development. Only in the 1990s and first decade of the twenty-first century did tribal governments begin to contract significantly with the federal government. One major impact has been an increase in the number of jobs based on Indian reservations. For perspective, in 1983, more than eight years after the Indian Self-Determination Act was enacted, the BIA still had more than fifteen thousand employees. Today, though federal appropriations have increased, the equivalent Indian affairs offices (now separated into the BIA and the Bureau of Indian Education) together have fewer than eight thousand employees. Since the 1990s, the number of BIA employees has dropped steadily as tribes contracted more and more federal programs. In contrast, tribal public employment across the country has grown. Tribes now cumulatively employ tens of thousands in public jobs. In sum, tribal governments have been rejuvenated by the federal contracting regime.

Some tribal governments have also benefited from Indian gaming, but only a minority of tribes have gaming operations and an even smaller minority have achieved significant revenues. Because of the unevenness of these opportunities, which depend on location near non-Indian populations, gaming has, to some degree, created a division within Indian country between the haves and have-nots. Neither federal contracting nor Indian gaming has fully addressed the serious economic conditions in Indian country.

POVERTY REMAINS A SERIOUS PROBLEM

For many tribal communities, poverty remains entrenched. Indian reservations partially or entirely encompass several of the nation's poorest counties.[10] The poverty rate for the American Indian and Alaska Native population across the United States averages 23 percent, according to data from the 2010 U.S. census. In some states, however, the figure is far higher. In South Dakota, for example, between 43 percent and 47 percent of Native American families live in poverty.[11] The average poverty rate for American Indian families in North Dakota, Montana, Nebraska, Arizona, Minnesota, and New Mexico is estimated with great confidence to exceed 30 percent.[12] The financial stress of poor communities in Indian country reflects high rates of joblessness and often brings other forms of misery, such as high rates of drug abuse, violence, and teen and adult suicide.

Urban poverty is also a problem for Native American communities. In the 1950s, the federal government developed the urban Indian relocation program, through which it encouraged Native Americans to sever ties with their home communities and move to cities to find work. Today, more than 70 percent of Native Americans live in cities.[13] One unfortunate outcome of the urban relocation program has been chronic high rates of alcoholism and homelessness in some of our nation's largest cities.

RECOMMENDATIONS

Federal Obstacles to Tribal Success Must Be Addressed

For many years, tribes have labored under the burden of a history of injustice that was never adequately addressed. Tribal communities must be empowered to look forward to a brighter future, rather than backward toward past injustices. While tribal self-determination policies will be an important investment over the long term, a significant obstacle to empowering tribes to address significant social problems has been the refusal of the federal government to address past injustices. For tribes, it has been maddening to hear federal officials describe the United States as a just nation when it largely ignored so many of its own past injustices against Indian nations and people.

In recent decades, tribes have been more empowered to recognize and fight for their legal rights. In some ways, the government-to-government relationship between the federal and tribal governments became characterized more by fighting and litigation than by close coordination and cooperation. Tribes have successfully used the federal government's own courts to seek redress for injustices committed by the United States. The federal courts, which constitute in some ways the legal conscience of the nation, have recognized the injustices asserted by Indian nations and then sought to remedy them.[14]

In the past ten years, the federal government has made real efforts to transform the government-to-government relationship from one of adversarial litigation to one reflecting cooperation and respect. Robust commitments by federal agencies for consultation with tribes about matters affecting Indian people have improved federal policy making in Indian country. More than one hundred significant lawsuits between the United States and tribes have been settled, many of them involving multiple tribes, facilitating a more productive and respectful government-to-government relationship. The U.S. government has begun to take greater responsibility for its role in developing the conditions on Indian reservations now faced by tribes. In the past ten years, the federal government has settled disputes collectively amounting to more than $10 billion to address just claims involving breach of trust, breach of contract, and land and water rights. To live up to its claims to being a just nation, the federal government must continue to admit its past mistakes and, where possible, rectify them. It must also maintain its commitment to tribal consultation on federal matters important to Indian country.

Economic Development Programs Must Be Supported

Economic development programs that provide jobs must continue. Jobs are no less important today than they were fifty years ago. A disproportionate number of Native Americans and Alaska Natives work in public jobs, for federal, state, tribal, or local governments. While tribal governmental jobs have created opportunities for some tribal citizens, a tribal employee frequently supports numerous members of an extended family, often under one roof.

Opponents have begun to question the legitimacy of federal economic development programs for tribes.[15] Special programs for tribes have been upheld by the Supreme Court in the past. In the context of tribal nations and Indian people, such governmental programs are justified not by race but by the sovereign political status of tribes and their citizens and the government-to-government relationship between tribes and the federal government.[16] Such programs are unambiguously consistent with constitutional law and should be supported vigorously by the federal government.

Appropriations Have a Strong Moral Basis and Must Continue

The moral basis for strong federal financial support for tribal governments is the occupation of Indian lands in North America, first by European nations to which the United States is a successor and, later, settlement of those Indian lands by Americans. American economic success has been driven by the richness of North American lands, once occupied exclusively by Native Americans.

In the past decade, the federal government has increased its appropriations for Indian tribes by more than $2 billion through the IHS, BIA, Bureau of Indian Education, Department of Justice, and other agencies, but much more is needed. Financial support must continue as long as the United States continues to occupy former Indian lands.

Tribal Self-Determination and Self-Governance Programs Must Be Consistently Supported

Tribal self-determination contracting of federal programs has been exceedingly successful in Indian country. One of the obstacles to success of the tribal self-determination contracting model, however, was the failure of the federal government, for years, to pay all the costs promised under the contracts, including administrative costs known as "contract support costs." Contract support costs were intended to cover administrative costs that would be borne by the federal government in its highly developed bureaucratic structure, such as personnel costs, worker compensation insurance, and other costs that would not come from program funds of a federal agency.

When tribes were not compensated for administrative costs to which they were entitled, tribes were forced to forgo some important administrative activities and also to cannibalize substantive program funds to cover administrative costs. This failure caused two general problems. First was a failure to develop tribal government properly, effectively stunting the growth of expertise and institutional capacities. Second, programs were not as successful as they would have been if program funds had been expended on the programmatic mission. In sum, appropriations must be adequate to the purpose of the task assigned by the federal government. The federal government must meet its own contractual obligations to tribes and break no more legal promises to tribes.

Tribes Must Be Supported in Addressing Public Safety on Indian Lands

Tribal nations continue to face high rates of violent crime, including, especially, sexual and domestic relations violence. Tribal nations have made important strides in expanding public safety infrastructure by, for example, developing and expanding tribal police forces. Congress has responded appropriately by restoring tribal jurisdictional authority. Tribal nations now have the option to define and prosecute limited felony offenses (of up to three years' imprisonment) over their own members and exercise limited criminal jurisdiction in Indian country over non-Indians for certain crimes of domestic or dating violence. Such powers are crucial to preventing Indian country from becoming a prosecution-free zone where offenses can be committed with impunity. Tribes must be supported and encouraged to develop their own culturally appropriate means of addressing criminal offenses.

Tribal Governments Must Be Able to Develop Tax Bases

Federal appropriations have a strong moral basis, but they remain crucial precisely because the federal government has handicapped the ability of tribal governments to develop adequate tax bases. All tribal economies are hampered by a lack of taxation infrastructure. Tribes lack the ability to impose property taxes on most Indian lands. While tribes have the authority to regulate and tax economic *activities* on such lands, state and local taxation authority is often coextensive with tribal authority. Because state and local taxing authority is usually being exercised already by state and local governments, tribes are loathe to levy their own taxes for fear that businesses will flee any community in which they must pay taxes to tribal and state authorities. Such dual taxation is deadly to economic development.

Tribal governments, like all governments, must have the authority to develop revenue to support their governmental programs. Tribal tax primacy must be established in Indian country, so that tribal governments can develop a healthy economic environment that can attract businesses and jobs, at least for those tribes who wish to pursue economic development.

CONCLUSION

In many respects, tribal nations can be characterized as developing nations. They face many of the same challenges faced by developing nations on other continents: poverty, lack of infrastructure, and lack of investment.

In light of these challenges, we cannot expect tribal governments to provide instantaneous solutions to problems that developed over centuries. Over the long term, however, empowering tribes to address reservation problems related to public health and poverty, and even economic development, will produce significant improvements in economic opportunities for Native American people living on Indian reservations. Such efforts should remain the central strategy in federal efforts to address Indian country poverty.

19

We Must Do Better

Fifty Years of Fitful Progress for Women

Martha F. Davis

A **WOMAN LIVING IN 1968**, using a crystal ball to look ahead to 2018, would see that progress toward women's economic equality has been slow, sporadic, or even nonexistent in many areas. To be sure, women's educational opportunities and engagement with athletics have expanded—a clear case of legal reform contributing to dramatic social change. These are areas of high visibility that often have a path-making effect, giving many women the skills and confidence needed to assume greater leadership in workplaces and political settings.

At the same time, even women at the highest levels of achievement continue to suffer from a wage gap that can be explained only by subtle sex discrimination. For women of color, this gap is compounded by multiple discriminatory -isms and structural barriers that affect their economic advancement. Further, local, state, and national policy makers have often been slow to address issues that have unique economic impacts on women, such as domestic violence and reproductive health. Indeed, in some instances, the crystal ball would show that women's lot in these areas has barely changed since 1968.

I cannot, here, fully survey fifty years' worth of economic progress for more than half the American population. But I do examine five key areas of critical concern to women's economic well-being: education, workplace policies, family support policies, health care access, and safety. I pay particular attention to the differences among women that may affect their experiences with each of these areas. And finally, I draw on the data to make recommendations for legal and policy changes to address the challenges that continue to impede women's progress toward economic equality.

EDUCATION

The second-wave feminist movement spanning the early 1960s to the 1980s had a profound impact on women's educational aspirations and opportunities over the past fifty years. From 1970 to 2009, the percentage of women with a high school education increased from 59 percent to 87 percent.[1] In 2015, men and women age twenty-five and older had equal rates of high school graduation.[2] The data for 2017 show that more women than men have completed bachelor's degrees,[3] and since 1996 more women than men, ages twenty-five to twenty-nine, have achieved a college education.[4] Black women's attainment of higher education is also rising rapidly, though they continue to have overall lower levels of education than white men and women.[5]

There is no doubt that the baseline provided by Title IX of the Education Act Amendments of 1972 played an important role in expanding educational opportunities for women and girls, including opportunities to participate in school sports.[6] However, many challenges remain. In particular, girls are still disproportionately targeted by sexual harassment in schools, with troubling negative impacts on their classroom engagement and emotional well-being.[7] Further, while women are increasingly obtaining educational training in STEM (science, technology, engineering, and math) fields, they are likely to encounter barriers when they seek employment in those fields. For example, a 2014 study showed that if a job required math skills, employers were twice as likely to hire a male candidate over an equally qualified female candidate.[8] To be fully effective, strides in women's educational opportunities must translate into expanded economic opportunities for women of all races.

WORKPLACE POLICIES

Women's workplace participation and employment experiences have also shifted dramatically since 1968, again spurred by law reform efforts that put teeth into calls for equal treatment and opportunity. When Title VII of the Civil Rights Act was enacted in 1964, a prohibition on sex discrimination was added in the final stage of the congressional debate.[9] The law's impact was gradual. In 1968, women were paid only 58.2 percent of what men earned for comparable work.[10] As late as 1973, employers still routinely advertised positions designated as "men only."[11]

As jobs that were once closed to women opened up, women's employment increased substantially, from 37.1 percent of the workforce in 1968 to 46.8 percent in 2015.[12] Also in 2015, the Pentagon—in a move of both symbolic and practical significance—opened all combat roles to women.[13] Still, women are far from reaching equality in the workplace. Strikingly, in 2015, women were paid 80 percent of what men were paid in the United States.[14] Women of color are particularly hard-hit; while a greater percentage of women of color than white women are in the workforce, women of color's median annual earnings fall below those of their white counterparts[15] and have actually declined in the past decade.[16] At the current rate, women in the aggregate will not achieve equal pay for comparable work until 2152![17]

This pay gap stretches across all sectors of the workforce. For example, female doctors earn approximately $20,000 less than male doctors, even when comparisons are adjusted for multiple factors.[18] Not surprisingly, women's lower wages affect other aspects of their lives and careers. Women are more likely to be in poverty than men at any age, with over a quarter of black and multiracial women living in poverty.[19] Even among the highest achievers, college-educated women are less likely than men to have paid off their college debt, affecting their economic stability and purchasing power during their early earning years.[20]

FAMILY SUPPORT

The nation's failure to close the pay gap between men and women and the racial disparities hidden within that gap compound the financial challenges faced by American women struggling to balance work and family obligations. It was not until 1994 that Congress enacted the Family and Medical Leave Act (FMLA), which provides up to twelve weeks of unpaid leave for covered workers to care for new children or ill family members or to recover from their own illnesses. A breakthrough in U.S. cultural expectations, the law is nevertheless woefully deficient as family support. It applies only to employers of fifty or more workers and can be used only by workers who have been employed for at least twelve months, working at least 1,250 hours in one year.[21] Because of these restrictions, 2012 data showed that the FMLA protects only 59 percent of all workers in the United States.[22] Further, because FMLA leave is unpaid, the lowest-income workers (disproportionately women of color) are often unable to take advantage of the law.[23]

Paid family leave is the norm around the world; in a survey of forty-two nations, the Organization for Economic Cooperation and Development found that the United States was the outlier, the only country that did not offer paid family leave.[24] In recent years, several states have adopted state-level paid-leave programs, beginning in 2002 with California.[25] Still, most employers have not responded to their employees' needs for greater work-life balance and support. As of 2014, only 13 percent of workers in the United States had access to paid family leave through their employers.[26] Similarly, while the Fair Labor Standards Act requires that employers provide a "reasonable break time" for nursing mothers to breastfeed, this break need not be compensated.[27]

Even as they have entered the workforce in greater numbers, women continue to shoulder a disproportionate responsibility for providing or arranging their families' childcare, a necessary support when parents work outside the home.[28] The costs of childcare can be staggering,[29] particularly for single-parent households headed by "breadwinner moms."[30] In a 2016 survey, 71 percent of parents who paid for childcare said that the costs posed a serious problem for their household.[31] In forty-eight of fifty states, the costs of childcare amount to more than 20 percent of black women's median earnings.[32]

At the same time, 40 percent of childcare workers are women of color, with wages typically at the rock bottom of American workers.[33] This arrangement highlights the economic challenges facing women. On one side, childcare work is poorly paid and offers few benefits to workers. On the other side, women who work outside the home—whose own pay is suppressed by the wage gap—need childcare to support their families. Women on both sides of the arrangement suffer from the policy failures that have not aggressively addressed women's economic needs.

HEALTH CARE ACCESS

In many respects, the past five decades have brought improved health outcomes to women. For example, female mortality from heart disease decreased by 36 percent between 2001 and 2013.[34] Women's health risks from illegal abortion have also declined dramatically. In 1967, experts estimated that eight hundred thousand illegally induced abortions occurred every year, posing great risks to women's health. Though its protections have been compromised in the intervening decades, the 1974 Supreme Court decision in *Roe v. Wade* continues to stand for a woman's right to a safe, legal procedure, resulting in a dramatic decrease in abortion-related deaths.[35]

However, the health data for women carrying pregnancies to term shows less positive trends. The United States has the highest rate of maternal mortality of all economic peer nations, and the rates are rising.[36] In 1987, there were 7.2 deaths per 100,000 live births; by 2011, the rate had increased to 17.8 deaths per 100,000 live births.[37]

Several factors may contribute to these distressing statistics. Maternal mortality was added as a check box on death certificates only in 2003, potentially resulting in an increase in reporting.[38] Women's rate of diabetes, a complicating factor for pregnancy, is rising; between 2001 and 2013, the rate of women diagnosed with diabetes increased by almost 50 percent.[39] Obesity—a society-wide threat—is a risk factor for pregnant women. These, and other health risks, such as HIV/AIDS, hypertension, and diabetes, are disproportionately faced by women of color.[40] Meanwhile, state-level restrictions on legal abortion have skyrocketed. Between

1980 and 2010, no more than thirty restrictions on abortion were enacted per year. In 2016, this increased to fifty restrictive measures,[41] and the first three months of 2017 saw 431 such measures introduced.[42]

The lack of policy-maker attention to women's health issues is reflected in policies affecting menstruation. The overwhelming majority of U.S. jurisdictions impose a sales tax on tampons and pads, though these are necessities that most women must purchase monthly throughout their reproductive lives.[43] Employers are not required to provide these items; women who are incarcerated or detained may be provided with inadequate supplies, if any. This natural process, experienced by almost all women, is treated as an aberrational experience because it is not shared by men.

SAFETY

All women make decisions—where to work, where to go after dark, where not to go alone—that are shaped by their concerns about violence against women. In 1968, there were few resources available to women experiencing domestic violence and little recognition of the discriminatory ways that violence against women impinged on women's full participation in society. The 1970s brought a sea change, with the first U.S. battered women's shelter opening in Saint Paul, Minnesota, in 1973; the first statewide domestic violence coalition forming in Pennsylvania in 1976; and in 1978, the National Coalition against Domestic Violence forming.[44] Beyond domestic violence, women's rights activists in the 1960s and 1970s raised awareness regarding sexual assault, sexual harassment, and other forms of sexual violence.

In 2018, that awareness is wide ranging. One important milestone is the Violence against Women Act, repeatedly reauthorized since 1994 to fund services for victims of rape and domestic violence and to provide training for law enforcement officers dealing with violence against women. In 2013, new provisions were added to address challenges facing Native American women, the LGBTQ community, and immigrants.[45]

Still, the violence persists. In 2010, Centers for Disease Control and Prevention data showed that one in four women have experienced "severe physical violence" from an intimate partner. For black and multiracial women, the rate is even higher, at 44 percent and 54 percent, respectively.[46] The CDC also reported that 44 percent of lesbian women and 61 percent of bisexual women experienced intimate partner violence during their lifetime, higher than the percentage of heterosexual women.[47] Rape is also astonishingly common, with one in five women experiencing an attempted or completed rape. Despite these high numbers, many researchers believe that sexual violence is underreported.[48]

In 1968, only the most prescient of crystal ball gazers could have foreseen the pervasiveness of the Internet. As social interactions increasingly move to virtual spaces, violence against women has followed, and in 2010, 36 percent of middle and high school girls reported experiencing online harassment.[49] Lawmakers have begun addressing these issues, amending the Violence against Women Act in 2005 to address online harassment,[50] but policy makers must be nimble to keep up with emerging technologies that are abused to perpetuate violence against women.

RECOMMENDATIONS

If we want to move beyond the fitful progress of women in the past fifty years, we cannot continue to rely on the same hands-off approaches to achieving women's equality. Here are five recommendations for action that would make a real difference to women across the board.

Increased Representation

Policy and legal reform can drive social change, but women's experiences have too often been treated as afterthoughts by lawmakers. It is no surprise that Representative Patsy Mink, a pioneering female legislator, was the force behind Title IX or that Barbara Boxer, then a member of the House of Representatives, shepherded the original Violence against Women Act through that body. Yet women's representation in government bodies is embarrassingly low.

Women are gaining ground in the halls of Congress, but oh so slowly. In 1968, the Senate had a single woman and the House of Representatives had 12 women. In 2017, 21 women served in the Senate and 109 in the House of Representatives.[51] At this rate of progress, women will not hold 50 percent of the seats in Congress until 2117.[52]

These deficiencies are important. Experiences and perspectives are lost when women are absent. What woman can forget the haunting 2017 photo of a roomful of smiling congressmen voting to strip mammogram coverage from health insurance because it is not "essential"?[53] Studies show that even the mere presence of a woman in such meetings can change the tone of the discussion,[54] and women with legislative power can dictate the terms of the debate.[55] In other countries, from Germany to India, governments and political parties have used quotas to assure that all perspectives are at the table.[56]

In the United States, there is deep antipathy to this proven approach to jumpstarting women's progress. Absent quotas, political parties and elected officials must be held accountable for ensuring that diverse perspectives are at the table by providing encouragement and material support to women seeking and holding office. In corporate settings, a "comply and explain" approach is gaining ground, requiring companies where women are underrepresented to provide justification for their lack of diversity.[57] A similar approach could move the needle in government settings.

Paid Family Leave

The absence of paid family leave in the United States harms both workers and employers, since it contributes to higher worker turnover, absenteeism, and stress. With some states already adopting such policies, it is past time for paid family leave to trickle up to the federal level. Congress should act immediately to extend FMLA to more employees and to mandate access to paid family leave and paid sick days. This move will help equalize opportunities across women's race and class lines and lead to a broader cultural shift in caregiving expectations.

Affordable, Quality Childcare

Few things sabotage women's workplace participation as much as the lack of affordable childcare options. Despite decades of discussion about egalitarian principles within families, women bear the disproportionate responsibility for providing and arranging childcare. Again, other countries provide far more support than does the United States. Quality, affordable childcare accessible to working parents of all income levels would boost worker productivity, provide children with stability and early education, and alleviate stress on families, particularly mothers. It is critical to women's equality. The federal government must make a major investment in childcare, at least doubling its current outlay to bring support into line with that provided in peer countries. With adequate government support, universal and affordable childcare access is an achievable goal.

Ending Violence against Women

Dramatic cultural change is required to eliminate gender-based violence and transform social norms so that violence against women is not tolerated in the United States. Clear changes in law and public policy, combined with public education and grassroots activism, can jumpstart such a shift. The national government and individual states should develop long-term, multiyear, coordinated antiviolence campaigns, with specific benchmarks, including penalties and incentives, to focus policy makers on this issue. These campaigns should include interventions in K–12 education to model gender equality and nonviolent behavior. Legal reforms such as redefining violence against women as a civil rights violation, expanding tort liability for creators and purveyors of violent media, and expanding culpability of gun sellers and manufacturers will build momentum for such cultural shifts.

Taking Women's Health Seriously

When mammograms are deemed inessential, when women's sanitary products are taxed, when women's personal reproductive health and autonomy can be negotiated away in political deals, women are being treated as dispensable. Women must speak out about these issues, but it is also true that policy makers must hear them. Even in 2018, gaining that foothold will require consistent pressure from women themselves and everyone who has a mother, wife, or daughter whose health is on the line. Seamless services that respect women's dignity and autonomy, focus on prevention, and make substantial investments in women-focused high-quality care are required to save women of all incomes and backgrounds from needless deaths and injury.

CONCLUSION

Women are everywhere, yet their progress toward equality over the past fifty years has been painfully slow. More than ever, society requires a new will to gain ground.

On January 21, 2017, the Women's March held in Washington, D.C., with sister marches around the world, drew an estimated five million participants worldwide. Denominated as a broad march for human rights, the trivialization of violence against women during the presidential election campaign was one of the triggering events for the gathering. Heightened activism and organizing has continued after the successful march. As set out on its website, the march was not just a one-day event but represents an ongoing effort "to harness the political power of diverse women and their communities to create transformative social change."[58]

There is hope, then, that this women-led movement, energized by the Women's March of 2017, will partner with other human rights movements to help push forward the "new will" called for by the Kerner Report that is still needed to create a more inclusive society. Surely it is not too much to expect that when a young woman in 2018 looks in a crystal ball to see life in 2068, she will see women fully and confidently participating in making the wide range of decisions that affect them, their families and communities, and society as a whole.

New Will and the Media

20

Messaging Strategy Needed to Combat Inequality Today

CELINDA LAKE

NCOME AND WEALTH INEQUALITY form the fundamental underpinning of most sources for civil disorders in America today. Unfortunately, since the 1980s, leaders have imposed economic rules that create and exacerbate income and wealth inequality.[1] We know it does not need to be this way. Following the Great Depression, our leaders made policy choices that reduced inequality and economic insecurity while vastly broadening prosperity.[2]

One could hardly be faulted for assuming that, following eight years of our nation's first African American president, African Americans and others would have made substantial gains and that the tensions that compelled the original Kerner Report would have lessened. The reality is more complicated. The impact of the Great Recession lasted longer than anticipated. Despite progress on some fronts, some of the conditions that foster civil disorder have heightened over the past decade.[3] From a strictly economic standpoint, the last decade saw new policies and rules that put barriers before working and middle-class people (especially people of color), inhibiting their economic progress and engendering inequality as part of the same destructive cycle of the prior three decades.

Further, the current leaders of our nation work to enact policies that favor top-income Americans and increase the barriers to prosperity for the rest of us. Lawmakers threaten to pull billions out of public education when we need, instead, to increase targeted public school funding to reach those youth longest denied. They are looking to gut housing assistance, economic development, and job training programs that break down the barriers to success for millions of Americans. They appoint justices who side with large corporate interests over working people while simultaneously cutting taxes for the richest Americans and corporations—depriving the government of revenue to fund programs to help the middle class and economically disadvantaged people. They threaten the crucial social safety net programs of Medicare and Social Security and insurance premium subsidies for tens of millions for whom coverage is needed to ward off bankruptcy or even to avoid (preventable) death.

INEQUALITY OF INCOME AND WEALTH

As noted commentators and researchers have documented, high levels of income and wealth inequality are immoral and socially corrosive and dramatically lower trust in society, increase mortality and morbidity for particular groups, increase crime and incarceration rates, increase mental illness and substance abuse, and *reduce* worker productivity and economic growth.[4] It is a tragic fact that if Americans today want their children to achieve the American Dream, they should send them to Denmark, where policies have been enacted to curb economic inequality.[5] That is because reducing inequality also has the direct effect of increasing social mobility. Across party lines, Americans are coming to realize that inequality has reached crisis levels. More than two-thirds of Americans say reducing inequality is an urgent issue.[6]

Inequality of income and wealth hurt African Americans and Latino Americans the most. We currently imprison at least 2.2 million people (over a third of whom are African American men and over seven in ten of whom are African American or Latino).[7] While 14 percent of all Americans and 21 percent of children currently live in abject poverty (excluding the working poor), the rate among African Americans is 24 percent and among Latinos it is 21 percent (well over double the 9 percent rate among whites). It is unconscionable that 37 percent of African American children and 32 percent of Latino children live in poverty—meaning that these children have nearly triple the poverty rate of white children.[8] African American household income is roughly 60 percent that of white households, and the net worth of white households is a staggering thirteen times the net worth of African American households.[9]

As Alan Curtis of the Eisenhower Foundation has noted, African American poverty spiked during periods of trickle-down economics, with huge tax cuts for the wealthy.[10] As we seemingly embark on a new era of proposed massive cuts to public health, education, and community programs to hand over more to the rich, we will exacerbate inequality and disproportionately hurt African Americans and Latinos. The low rate of social mobility also means that the children of African American and Latino families and low-income people will not escape the cycle of poverty. As social trust falls, racial animus has increased. It has led to greater levels of discrimination in employment, health care, housing, financialization, and criminal injustice for African American and Latino people alike.[11]

The same policies and choices that produce high levels of inequality also slow economic growth, hurting the poorest end of the income distribution (who are far more likely to be African American and Latino). This is especially true for unmarried women of color.

But We Are All in This Together

We would all be better off if those who are best off would pay their fair share and make a commitment not to undermine those worse off. Instead, public policy is rewarding the wealthiest while slashing support for the majority who benefit from public services and infrastructure. However, not even the very rich are better off in a society with high levels of income and wealth inequality.[12] Since supporting the policies and programs that work to alleviate inequality helps not just people of color but also all working-class and poor people, a broad coalition that includes blue-collar whites and rural people is absolutely possible. From the standpoint of moving these policies forward, it is absolutely necessary. This is all the more urgent given that the next generation is not sanguine about the future. Millennials are arguably the first American generation worse off than their baby boomer parents, despite being better educated.[13] On the eve of the 2016 election, three-quarters of voters reported believing that the next generation after them would be worse off.

None of the needed changes can happen without new political will. Generating political will is impossible without first creating public will and the sufficient energy to translate that into collective public action. Advocates should focus on shifting fundamental beliefs and ideas about economic issues to a new narrative by engaging the base, persuading the middle, and repudiating the false beliefs of immovable opponents.[14] So when fake news generates false stories that misstate the statistics or facts, a strong majority coalition can reject these stories because they do not fit our values.

Strategies and Tactics to Move Us toward a More Equitable Society

Before launching into fully formed messages, it is instructive to review some useful strategies that underpin those messages and all communications regarding inequality. Advocates need to escape the trap of speaking in passive abstractions that remove agency ("wages have stagnated," "wealth was lost") and, instead, employ a vocabulary that offers a clear origin story for our current problems ("big corporations rigged the game," "special interests lobbied," "bankers gave themselves bonuses," etc.).

Similarly, we should identify the beneficiaries of sound policies in a direct and inclusive fashion, identifying them as working people, middle-class Americans, and our families.

Make Clear That Economic Inequality Is Not Natural or Immutable. Inequality is generated from intentional policy choices. Different policy choices could dramatically reduce inequality, injustice, and the civil disorder that it generates. Make clear that the choices politicians and chief executive officers made have led to an economy that is out of balance, which implies that it could be fixed by empowering those who would make more equitable choices. Advocates should explain that a strong middle class does not appear by accident, but is, instead, the product of intentionally enacted smart policies. Conversely, policies enacted by lawmakers to help rich benefactors are ill conceived and harm the middle and working classes. Policy choices determine the rules of the game and thus the winners and losers.

Values-Based Messaging Is Key. Establishing the values-based frame in our advocacy is critical. We know that the side that sets the frame wins the debate. George Lakoff observes that when the facts do not fit our framework for understanding an issue, we reject the facts, not our framework.[15] Advocates should resist the temptation to lead with policies and programs, however effective they may be and, instead, lead with shared values—like family, community, interdependence, freedom, respect, equality, dignity, upward mobility, fairness, security, and prevention of poverty.[16]

Tie these values directly to universally desired outcomes like more time with family, a secure retirement, reward for work, and a decent life—the American Dream. Contrast this with the reality faced by millions of hardworking Americans who cannot succeed, no matter how hard they try, trapped by poverty and unable to get ahead. Demonstrate how inequality is a barrier to success at the individual and societal level. Stress that as citizens, we all have the ability and responsibility to shape the economy we need.

Powerful Metaphors Can Help. Using metaphors can build support for a robust role for government in overcoming obstacles to opportunity and prosperity. One such effective metaphor is inequality as a barrier during a person's life journey.[17] The work of Anat Shenker-Osorio, Topos and Demos, and Lake Research Partners shows that this metaphor's power derives from it deemphasizing any perceived lack of effort or intelligence of groups and, instead, posits a process-oriented challenge, making it about obstruction rather than the merit of the obstructed.

Cast government as an effective force in reducing inequality through its use of public structures that pave the way for innovation and shared prosperity: "Americans exposed to examples and descriptions of public structures' fundamental role quickly take on a new and much richer (and more accurate) perspective towards the workings of the economy. The idea shifts thinking away from the dominant view of individual actors as the prime shapers of the economy and toward an emphasis on constructive government action that produces broadly-shared economic prosperity."[18]

Make Data Understandable. Advocates would benefit by changing how they present data to avoid invoking statistics that lack meaning to ordinary people. Math should be made social by (1) breaking a number down by time (e.g., "Every eight minutes a baby is born to a teen," instead of "The number of babies born to teen mothers peaked at 70,322"); (2) breaking a number down by place (e.g., "If the 13.5 million poor children in America were gathered in one place, they would form a city bigger than New York City"); (3) localizing a number (e.g., "Experts estimate there are more than 100,000 obese children in the San Diego region. It would take two Qualcomm Stadiums to hold all of those children."); (4) comparing to familiar things (e.g., "There are at least six times as many licensed gun dealers in California as there are McDonald's restaurants"); and (5) employing an ironic comparison (e.g., "The average childcare teacher makes $15,430 each year—only half as much as correctional facility officers and jailers").[19] Thinking in numerical terms moves thinking away from the empathetic region of the brain to more analytical regions, making the targeted use of data and turning numbers to values all the more important.[20]

Messages to Generate the Will to Create a More Equitable Society

The research of Lake Research Partners, as well as that conducted by others, confirms that progressives lack a sustained social movement to address economic inequality because they do not speak in human terms about those struggling to make ends meet and the barriers erected that impede people's prosperity. Key to this effort are (1) operationalizing this language in campaigns with grassroots partners, (2) sharing what we learned with national allies, and (3) holding the media accountable to speak about people who are living on the financial brink.[21] The examples that follow provide vetted messaging and narrative guidance to both speak effectively about the policy choices that trap one-third of our nation in poverty and create real opportunities to join those most affected in a movement to dismantle them.

This first message taps into the value of family, and it does so in a personal and relatable way. It then transitions to the concept of working to support families with adequate pay. It finishes with the value of family security and a compelling quality-of-life argument.

> Family Comes First: They may drive you crazy, but everyone knows family comes first. Whether it's for that newborn you swear already smiles, your elderly mom or your spouse who got laid off, providing for your family and being there when they need you isn't negotiable. Every working parent should get paid enough to care for their kids and set them off toward a great future. If politicians want to talk "family values," it's time they start valuing families—and that means making sure America's dedicated strivers and builders make ends meet. We work in order to make the future brighter for our kids and more secure for our families. Hard working Americans deserve to make more than a decent living—they deserve to have a decent life.[22]

Another powerful message touts the value of working together to secure workplace benefits and builds on the notion of collective effort, which Alexis de Tocqueville noted was a critical part of the American experience:[23]

> Teamwork—Working Together: From sports stars to first responders, Americans deliver when we pull together as a team. It takes a team, where we have each other's backs, to get our country and economy moving forward. By working together, each of us get[s] where we need to go. That's why we need to come together for a fair return on work, which includes benefits and paid time to be home when our families need us. Today, a few powerful people get even richer from profits we produce requiring the rest of us to do more with less. By acting as a team, we can change the rules so working Americans can win.[24]

The message operationalizes progress through a journey metaphor—"moving forward"—using a vocabulary of teamwork. The goal of this concerted group effort is not merely workplace benefits but specifically a fair return on work, which includes wages and benefits. "Return on work" means that the money to pay people comes from their work. Contrast this with the pervasive—and lackluster—tropes about raising wages because we should. This relegates working people to the position of supplicant, asking the boss for more rather than claiming what is rightfully due: a fair portion of what the employee's efforts produce. It also positions working people's wages as making them more than mere consumers. It poses a strong contrast of the rich getting even richer while everyone else must get by with less—phrasing that exploits perceptions of a zero-sum game. The message concludes with working together to "change the rules" so that working Americans win (not just the rich).

The next tested message uses a reminder that Americans faced difficult circumstances in the past and overcame them by joining together to make smart policy choices. Americans like aspirational and positive messages even during tough times. Further, messages must lend credibility to the assertion that we can change deplorable conditions. Pointing to past progress in trying times helps make that case.

The message offers an explanation, or origin story, for our predicament: The "greedy few" have "rigged the game" so we no longer "do right" by those who "keep America working." It challenges those who claim to "value . . . freedom"—a core belief—to demand adequate pay and time off "to be with family" (another core value) as necessary for security (yet another core value).

> We Can Do It: America's gone through tough times before and came back to build a middle class the world envied. After the Great Depression, we banded together through government to build roads, open schools and guarantee work paid enough to live on, and retire in dignity. . . . But then a greedy few rigged the game in their favor. Today, many jobs don't cover our needs—let alone enable our dreams. It's time to do right by those who clock in and out everyday to keep America working. If we value everyone's freedom, we need adequate pay for our work, time to be with family and a secure foundation on which to build a good life.[25]

The following message evokes fairness by equating CEOs' unchallenged right to negotiate their salaries and bonuses (the last of which is a vulnerability of CEOs and Wall Street) with the ability of working people to negotiate a return for their own hard work. It then posits that fairness and freedom are precluded if a powerful few prevent working people from negotiating collectively. It finishes by invoking a rule to enable, not just freedom, but a positive conception of freedom (freedom to prosper).[26]

> Pro-freedom: In America, we value our freedom. And CEOs are free to negotiate their salaries, benefits, and bonuses. Working people deserve the very same freedom: to negotiate the return for the hard work we put in. When somebody can tell you how best to do the job you've mastered and prevent any raises, no matter their profits or your accomplishments, there's no freedom in that. Standing together gives working people the leverage to help set the rules at work so we reclaim our freedom to prosper.[27]

Another high-performing message taps into values of opportunity, upward mobility, and the American Dream but also contains solution-oriented language:

> Made in America: *The American Dream* used to mean something, that if you put in a hard day's work you could expect good American wages, benefits and a better life for your kids. And it meant we were a middle-class country, with middle class values, of hard work, *opportunity* and *fairness*. Now, we're in danger of losing the middle class, as big corporations, CEOs, and their lobbyists are writing all the rules. It's time we stopped rewarding companies that ship our jobs overseas. It's time we stopped giving tax breaks to billionaires and big corporations when working Americans are struggling to make ends meet. And it's time we stopped signing free trade agreements and started signing fair trade agreements that bring the pay and benefits of American workers up, not down to the level of Mexico and China. You can't have a vibrant economy without a vibrant middle class, because someone's got to build things and someone's got to buy them. Our economy doesn't work if Americans aren't working and earning a fair wage. That's the bottom line.[28]

This message works because it taps into the American Dream but also evokes the need to hold the wealthiest corporations and individuals accountable for paying their fair share. People are prone to think in zero-sum terms, and this message repositions the haves as wealthy corporations (not people receiving assistance). Thus, this is more effective than arguing everyone benefits when we take care of those who need help (despite the demonstrable truth of that).

Messaging and Narrative Strategies to Reduce Racial Inequality

It is critical to identify messages that increase desire for programs and resources to help people of color, who are disproportionately excluded from economic prosperity. This becomes even more complicated in the Trump era and beyond. At the same time, we have a moral and policy mandate to advance the dialogue and consciousness of our nation by being forthright on racial issues. Fortunately, messaging that refers to people of color has the potential to outperform race-neutral progressive messaging, which is why the Center for Social Inclusion concludes that "we must affirmatively include race in current and emerging policy debates."[29] Racial inequality messages should tap into the values of equality for all, shared goals, freedom, and the American Dream.[30] Next, call for removing the barriers of discrimination, tapping into ideas that unify us as a diverse people and make us stronger. Third, encourage everyone to speak out against discrimination when they see it.[31]

While advocates need to raise awareness of ongoing racial disparities and understand them as a product of past actions and structural constraints, it is important to refer to our progress so we can talk about how far we still must go. Recognize people's better angels and confront the conflict between conscious and unconscious values.[32] Appealing to conscious values is the path to effective persuasion. Start with shared values or the targeted policy area and then make explicit reference to racial groups. The charge of racism can lead to defensiveness among persuadable individuals, but the concept of unconscious prejudice lacks similar baggage and can be effective in gaining acceptance from white audiences. Acknowledge that some people might be uncomfortable with change when asserting the importance of diversity, which can lower defenses. Highlight the importance of getting to know and accepting people from different backgrounds as a solution. When talking about universal values of being American, explicitly say "no matter what someone looks like/where they come from/what their race is" to create common ground and experience."[33] Finally, employ priming techniques like saying "white" before "black and brown."

The following message is strong because it makes diversity indispensable to solving our problems and invokes the core value of opportunity. Instead of singling anyone out for reprisal, the message is an aspirational call to action, rooted in the shared values of strength and unity.

> Diversity as Strength: We are stronger when we work together and when we learn from each other's experiences, united as Americans. When people from different backgrounds join together we all benefit from the diversity of those perspectives. . . . If we embraced our diversity and valued the views of our fellow Americans, we'd be more likely to find solutions to our problems and better ensure that everyone has the opportunity to pursue their dreams. Whether white, Black, or Latino, whether Christian, Jew, or Muslim, we are all Americans. We need to embrace our different experiences, perspectives, and cultures because united we stand, and divided we fall.[34]

The next message tested by Lake Research Partners on behalf of the Opportunity Agenda is compelling because it uses "zip code" to create a spatial reference for opportunity. It creates a direct connection between policy decisions made (schools, housing, and transportation) and curtailed opportunities for communities of color. It finishes with a concrete call for laws that dismantle segregation and discrimination.

[Networks of Opportunity:] Every child deserves an equal opportunity regardless of the zip code they are born into. Our country has made great strides breaking down barriers of discrimination, but still today, too many people are kept out of networks of opportunity connected to where you live, like quality schools, good parks and recreation, jobs, and hospitals which help you make a better life for your family. Sometimes decisions on where to build schools, affordable housing and transportation keep minorities outside of these opportunities. We need strong laws that connect people, provide equal opportunity, and dismantle patterns of segregation and discrimination wherever they exist.[35]

Like the "Diversity as Strength" message cited earlier, the following message emphasizes that what ties us together as Americans is more important than forces that threaten to divide us. That commonality is rooted in the core values of family and community. The message then pivots to economic security and the need to end discrimination. We found that the last line is especially compelling—"everyone means everyone, no exceptions"—because it is universal and taps into the drive for fairness and equality.

Patriotism with Ending Discrimination: You wouldn't know it from politicians, but Americans stand largely united. We work for our families. We pitch in for our communities and we believe in America. We want to leave things better for our children. To get there, we have to create good stable jobs for anyone willing to work that provide benefits and pay you can sustain a family on and end racial and gender discrimination. We believe everyone means everyone, no exceptions.[36]

CONCLUSION

We stand at a crossroads. While inequality in America is extreme and rising, politicians risk making things much worse and undermining civil order itself. This is not the time to limit ourselves to rearguard defense of past programs; it is a time for compelling communications and activism to bring about the kind of broad and far-reaching positive changes we know are possible. With the right messaging, messengers, resources, and organization, we have the power to persuade Americans to act and elect new leaders who represent the interests of the vast majority rather than those of the elite few—with the ultimate goal of enacting policies that dramatically reduce the corrosive and pernicious inequality plaguing our country today.

21

The Kerner Commission and the Challenge of Politics

The "New Ethnicity," Class, and Racial Justice

E. J. Dionne, Jr.

T HE KERNER COMMISSION reached the right conclusion at an inconvenient time—even if there should not be a wrong time to remind Americans of our legacy of racial oppression, and even if we never seem quite ready as a nation to devote the resources required to move the excluded and the marginalized toward opportunity and equality.

The inconvenience of its report was about politics. Its official date was March 1, 1968, when the liberal coalition that reached its zenith in the 1964 election was falling apart. President Lyndon Johnson, who named the commission, was struggling merely to maintain funding for his Great Society programs even as the Vietnam War raged. The prospects of financing the massive project of social reconstruction the commission called for were negligible. That the report spoke far more about the dire problems facing the country than about LBJ's civil rights victories and the successes of his poverty initiative irked a president who also had little use for the radicalism of the commission's language. Johnson, who was no doubt also bothered by his political powerlessness to carry out the report's recommendations, declined to sign thank-you notes to the commission members he appointed.[1]

To call the Kerner Report right was controversial at the time it was issued, and it is controversial still among the dwindling number of our fellow citizens familiar with its history. Yet it deserves to be judged by the most basic standard: Was what it said true? Unless one is in denial about the country's racial history, the answer must be yes.

"White racism is essentially responsible for the explosive mixture which has been accumulating in our cities since the end of World War II," the report declared in a line that reverberated across the country. The authors pointed to "the most bitter fruits of white racial attitudes." These included "pervasive discrimination and segregation," "black migration and white exodus," and the rise of "black ghettos" where "segregation and poverty have intersected to destroy opportunity and hope and to enforce failure."[2]

"Segregation and poverty have created in the racial ghetto a destructive environment totally unknown to most white Americans," the commission said with deadly accuracy. "What white Americans have never fully understood—but what the Negro can never forget—is that white society is deeply implicated in the ghetto. White institutions created it, white institutions maintain it, and white society condones it."[3]

The report used a word particularly resonant in our time, pointing to "white terrorism directed against nonviolent protest, including instances of abuse and even murder of some civil rights workers in the South [and] by the open defiance of law and Federal authority by state and local officials resisting desegregation."[4]

Many, including President Johnson, were looking for something else: a much stronger condemnation of violence and perhaps even reference to a conspiracy that fomented it. The report's emphasis, instead, was on the social causes of discontent, and it came back to racism again and again. It is true that the authors did conclude the sentence on "white terrorism" with a bow toward those who wanted to ascribe some responsibility to the rioters. They thus also criticized "some protest groups engaging in civil disobedience who turn their backs on nonviolence, go beyond the constitutionally protected rights of petition and free assembly and resort to violence to attempt to compel alteration of laws and policies with which they disagree."[5] But this long phrase—carefully wrought and a bit plodding—did not ring out the way condemnations of the "white power structure" did.

The courage to name and condemn racism so explicitly and so forcefully is something for which the National Advisory Commission on Civil Disorders deserves praise, and it is a central reason why it has maintained its relevance many decades after the long hot summers that brought the commission into being. As the historian Sean Wilentz notes in his introduction to the 2016 Princeton University Press reissue of the report, that it came with "the imprimatur of members of the political establishment" gave it particular power. Wilentz also points to the observation of former *New York Times* columnist Tom Wicker: "Reading it is an ugly experience but one that brings, finally, something like the relief of beginning." Wicker added, "What had to be said has been said at last, and by representatives of that white, moderate, responsible America that, alone, needed to say it."[6]

The relief Wicker described was especially profound in the African American community, which had been making the case for the depth of the country's racism since the days of Reconstruction. In his compact and valuable history of the report written for the 2016 republication, the historian Julian Zelizer cited the response to it in the black press. The *Chicago Daily Defender*, for example, pointed to the commission's warning against the development of "two societies, one black, one white" and observed that "the Negro press and civil rights organizations have been pointing this out to the nation for more than a decade. While there is nothing new in the report, the commission, headed by Governor Otto Kerner, did emphasize in stern language the severity of the sickness with which American society is afflicted and prescribed the needed remedy." The *Los Angeles Sentinel* pointed to an obvious truth that was seldom stated so plainly. "It is extremely rare," the *Sentinel* wrote, "for whites to recognize and blame themselves for their own failures."[7]

Rare indeed, and in the sweltering political year of 1968, conservative politicians insisted that this blame had been misplaced. George Wallace, Alabama's segregationist governor who was waging a campaign tinged with racism and organized around promises of law and order, knew exactly how to respond. "The people know the way to stop a riot is to hit someone on the head," he said.[8]

In a speech at Madison Square Garden on October 24, 1968, Wallace summarized the document, as he saw it, for his largely white audience: "The Kerner Commission report, recently written by Republicans and Democrats, said that you are to blame for the breakdown of law and order, and that the police are to blame. Well, you know of course you aren't to blame. They said we have a sick society. Well, we don't have any sick society. We have a sick Supreme Court and some sick politicians in Washington, that's who's sick in our country."[9]

Richard Nixon, the ultimate victor of the 1968 election, was slightly more subtle but just as clear. The report, he said, "blames everybody for the riots except the perpetrators of the riots." Nixon urged "retaliation against the perpetrators of violence" that would be "swift and sure." The future president understood the power of the law-and-order issue. "I have found great audience response to this theme in all parts of the country," Nixon wrote to Dwight Eisenhower, "including areas like New Hampshire, where there is virtually no race problem and relatively little crime."[10]

Thus, one of the paradoxes of the Kerner Report: its bold determination to call out and defeat racism was used to strengthen the forces of racial backlash. The report itself was obviously not responsible for the broad shift in public opinion against further civil rights advances, which had already taken hold by 1966. In the midterm elections that year, opposition to the Great Society in general and liberal open-housing laws in particular helped Republicans post large gains in the House and in governorships and also pick up seats in the Senate. As a practical matter, the country being at the start of what would prove to be a historic crime wave gave law-and-order appeals bite far beyond the realm of backlash voters. If crime was used as a symbolic issue, it was also a real one.

But as Wallace and Nixon showed, the Kerner Report could be deployed (often with considerable distortion) to parody what an increasingly conservative white electorate saw as liberalism's flaws, particularly what the right charged were its inattentiveness to crime and its inclination to use arguments about society's responsibilities to undercut personal responsibility. (It is no accident that, many years later, British prime minister Tony Blair would coin the slogan "Tough on crime and tough on the causes of crime" to suggest one could be committed to both values.[11])

In retrospect, one of the most arresting sentences in the report, the "two societies" line that appeared on its very first page, may also have been one of its most problematic. Zelizer points out that the sentence was added by two of New York City mayor John V. Lindsay's aides, Peter Goldmark and Jay Kriegel. Lindsay was a very liberal Republican who in 1969 lost a GOP primary race in his campaign for reelection, an early instance of a purge of liberals from the party that would continue for decades. Lindsay ultimately won the general election on a third-party ticket, and he later became a Democrat.

On Lindsay's behalf, Goldmark and Kriegel were trying to frame a passage that would grab the media's attention, and they found it: "This is our basic conclusion," the report declared, "our Nation is moving toward two societies, one black, one white—separate and unequal."[12]

At the time, the line captured something important about the nature of the country's deep racial divide and the persistence of racism. But as a prediction, it was flawed. The country was in fact moving not toward two societies but toward three or four or more.

The commissioners certainly did not foresee the long-term effects of the 1965 Immigration and Naturalization Act, which would add to the nation's already substantial population of Latinos, then mainly Mexican and Puerto Rican in origin, and open the way for millions of new immigrants from Africa and Asia as well. Nor did they predict what would become a sharp class divide within the African American community itself. If blacks, regardless of class, all continued to confront persistent discrimination and exclusion, the circumstances in different parts of the African American community would come to vary sharply. Ten years after the appearance of the commission's report, William Julius Wilson would publish his landmark and at the time controversial book *The Declining Significance of Race*.[13] It pointed to the widening class gap within the African American community and the immiseration of the community's most disadvantaged members. His later works *The Truly Disadvantaged* and *When Work Disappears* highlighted the damage wrought when the injuries of class aggravated the wounds of racial marginalization.[14]

Finally, there were other divides in the country besides race, and these continue to bedevil struggles for racial and economic justice. America's white working class did not feel itself represented in the report, except as part of America's history of racism. It is true that the Kerner Commission was given a specific task: to explain the causes of riots and discontent in African American neighborhoods. It was not asked to solve all the nation's social and economic problems. But the less privileged parts of white society had grievances of their own. As the 1960s turned into the 1970s, new movements arose to give them expression.

THE NEW ETHNICITY MOVEMENT

The Black Power movement and the splintering of the old civil rights coalition had many social and political effects. One of the most surprising, given the dominance of an assimilation model of immigration at the time, was a reassertion of ethnic consciousness among whites, particularly in the working class in the cities and suburbs of the Northeast and Midwest.

The ideologists of the new ethnicity movement were open in saying that they were responding to various forms of black nationalism even as many in their ranks were sympathetic to the cause of African Americans and looked on Black Power with some sympathy. Their goal was to build bridges rather than barriers between discontented whites and the civil rights movement. But they also argued that many white liberals who sympathized with the cause of black America expressed little interest in the injustices faced by ethnic white America. Some of them put matters quite starkly. "It is all right for the blacks and the Chicanos and the American Indians to have some sort of racial consciousness," wrote Father Andrew Greeley, a sociologist who later became a popular novelist, in his 1971 book *Why Can't They Be like Us?* But, he continued, "for other American ethnic groups, ethnic consciousness is, somehow or other, immoral."[15]

The idea of using white ethnicity to expand rather than contract the coalition for civil rights was central to the argument of the political scientist Richard Krickus:

> With rising self-awareness, the appearance of vigorous leadership, and the evolution of organization structures, many black communities can meet the minimum requirement necessary for coalition. Because similar structures do not exist in most white ethnic communities, a coalition with blacks is not yet feasible. Until the white ethnics, through heightened group identity, generate new leaders and develop new organizational props, the precondition for coalition activities will not materialize in their communities.[16]

What is striking here is a kind of organization envy for the civil rights movement. While working-class whites had long had ways to influence politics through their unions, urban political machines, and in many communities, churches, those older forms seemed less relevant and effective at a time of rising racial and ethnic consciousness. If politics was being increasingly defined in ethnic and racial terms—the Kerner Report's focus on racism can be seen as part of that shift—then the white working class needed to speak in this language and organize along these lines.

The complexity of the politics behind the new ethnicity movement is reflected in many of its champions being authentic sympathizers with the civil rights movement. They were disturbed by white reaction against African American advances but also sensitive to white-working-class discontent around issues related to economic injustice. Their primary goal, as Krickus suggests, was to ally white ethnic communities with African American communities, not to drive them apart.

"If you want to live in the city and improve your neighborhoods, you have to learn to get along with the blacks and Chicanos," said Monsignor Geno Baroni, who founded the National Center for Urban Ethnic Affairs to give voice to white ethnic neighborhoods within a context of forging relationships with African Americans communities. "In fact, if you want to get anywhere you have to form political coalitions with them."[17]

Monsignor Baroni's civil rights credentials were legendary: as a young priest, he pressed Washington archbishop Patrick O'Boyle to throw the Catholic Church behind Dr. Martin Luther King's 1963 March on Washington, and Baroni became the church's coordinator for the march. He also founded the church's economic justice charity, the Campaign for Human Development (which many years later was to pay the salary of a young Chicago community organizer named Barack Obama). But Baroni, like others in the movement he helped lead, insisted that an undifferentiated narrative of white racism would render impossible the coalition building between the ethnic white working class and African Americans that he so devoutly advocated.

It is important to notice that the new ethnicity movement had far more to say to working-class whites in the Northeast, Midwest, and on the West Coast than in the South. The focus of its attention was almost entirely on the Irish, Italians, Poles, Croats, Serbs, Ukrainians, Greeks, French Canadians, and other groups that were predominantly Catholic or Christian Orthodox. Jews—themselves an ethnically diverse group—were usually included as part of this movement, but not always.

Indeed, the sociologist Irving Louis Horowitz noticed an incoherence in the new ethnicity literature's answer to the question What is an ethnic? Jews and Japanese were sometimes defined in and sometimes defined out because they were too upper class. The role of Latinos was also ambiguous. Horowitz argues that "ethnicity is at least as much a tactic as a definition" and that the new ethnicity movement could best be seen as "a statement of relatively deprived sectors seeking economic relief through political appeals."[18]

Nathan Glazer and Daniel Patrick Moynihan argued that ethnicity was a useful conceptual frame that had been too long ignored in the academy, but they were both too attuned to politics to ignore ethnicity's utility in struggles for power and benefits. In their introduction to *Ethnicity: Theory and Experience*, a useful gathering of scholarship and analysis published in 1975, they write of the competition between class and ethnic identities and "the strategic efficacy of ethnicity as a basis for asserting claims against government." They ask, "Why on earth would one wish to be a Pole when one could be a worker?" There might, of course, be the simple "desire to be Polish." But there was more—namely, "that being a Pole, or a Sikh, or a mestizo frequently involves a distinctive advantage or disadvantage, and that remaining a Pole or a Sikh or a mestizo is just as frequently a highly effective way either to defend the advantage or to overcome the disadvantage."[19]

The new ethnicity movement was thus at once an intellectual suggestion and a political initiative. It argued that social scientists had vastly underestimated the importance of ethnic group identification in American life and had overstated the extent to which American ethnic groups had assimilated. If the Bastille was the symbol of oppression for the French revolutionaries, the intellectual construct of the melting pot played that role for the new ethnicity movement. The title of the Catholic intellectual Michael Novak's 1971 book, *The Rise of the Unmeltable Ethnics*, made the point.[20]

And this is where the movement immediately fell into politics. At its core was a demand that attention be paid to a particular group of Americans whose interests, so its advocates insisted, had been ignored. The movement also paid attention to the vital role played by local communities, often organized around ethnic identification, in the lives of their residents. This had implications that could be drawn on from both the left and the right.

Community organizers working to preserve neighborhoods from large-scale redevelopment (or from destruction in the big urban road projects common in the 1960s and early 1970s) focused on community vitality in their arguments against what they saw as a false kind of progress. The sociologist Herbert Gans's *The Urban Villagers* (published in 1962, before the new ethnicity movement took off) was a brilliant example of this style of argument.[21]

But if the cultural and ethnic character of a neighborhood mattered to its residents for legitimate reasons, then opposition to racial integration was cast in a different light. For civil rights advocates, these arguments looked like a rationale for racism. The sociologist Gerald Suttles coined the term "the defended neighborhood" to describe how a variety of government policies and the behavior of real estate interests kept neighborhoods segregated, or from the point of view of residents who more or less liked things as they were, "defended."[22]

The difficulty, politically and morally, was that, on the one hand, tight-knit local communities *were* an asset for those who lived in them, and strong communities were a particularly important political resource for working-class citizens, including ethnic whites. But there was another side: that the defense of these enclaves often *did* involve outright racism, opposition to desegregation, and policies that left African Americans at a strong disadvantage. As the Kerner Commission wrote:

> Deliberate efforts are sometimes made to discourage Negro families from purchasing and renting homes in all-white neighborhoods. Intimidation and threats of violence have ranged from throwing garbage on lawns and making threatening phone calls to burning crosses in yards and even dynamiting property. More often, real estate agents simply refuse to show homes to Negro buyers.[23]

One politician who found himself caught between sympathy for white ethnics and his strongly professed support for civil rights was an insurgent Democratic presidential candidate named Jimmy Carter. During the 1976 Democratic primaries, Sam Roberts, a reporter for the New York *Daily News*, asked Carter where he stood on the construction of scatter-site, low-income housing in the suburbs. Carter's answer proved explosive when he questioned the need "to artificially inject another racial group in a community." Carter continued, "I see nothing wrong with ethnic purity being maintained. I would not force a racial integration of a neighborhood by government action. But I would not permit discrimination against a family moving into that neighborhood."[24]

Carter, not grasping the potentially insidious ring of the term "ethnic purity," thought he had threaded a political needle, supporting old ethnic neighborhoods but opposing outright discrimination, and his statement did not initially cause a stir. As the journalist Jules Witcover noted in his definitive account of the 1976 campaign, *Marathon*, the quotation "ran on page 134 of the Sunday edition, and might have remained buried there for all time" had not CBS News political editor Marty Plissner noticed it and urged Ed Rabel, his network's correspondent traveling with Carter, to press the candidate further.[25]

After again reiterating his opposition to outright discrimination, Carter dug himself in deeper: "I don't think the government ought to . . . try to break down deliberately an ethnically oriented neighborhood by artificially interjecting into it someone from another ethnic group just to create some sort of integration."[26]

Carter eventually backed off his statement when his leading black supporters—particularly Andrew Young, later Carter's United Nations ambassador—pointed out the damage it could do to him with African American voters, among whom he had run well, and also with white liberals, who were already skeptical of Carter but whose support he would eventually need.[27] The episode was instructive about the high-wire act that can be required of politicians trying to maintain support among African Americans on the alert for white racism and white working-class voters who assume that progressive elites will always view them as suspect on racial issues.

Looked at in retrospect, the new ethnicity movement made an important intellectual contribution by calling attention to how older loyalties of ethnicity (and religion as well) had not been obliterated in the sweep of secular modernity. Primordial attachments continued to matter and explained political conflicts that could simply not be understood purely in class or economic terms. "In a world in which Marxism competed with liberalism, the problems of ethnicity, as a source of conflict within nations and among nations, have generally appeared as simply a leftover, an embarrassment from the past," Glazer wrote in 1975. "It is my conviction that they must now be placed at the very center of our concern for the human condition."[28] Developments around the world in the four decades since Glazer wrote have only confirmed his intuition.

On the other hand, as Horowitz suspected, the new ethnicity movement was at least in part a method for defending the interests of the white working class in new circumstances. Writing in 1981 with some distance on the controversy, Stephen Steinberg argued in *The Ethnic Myth* that the movement had overstated its case and that the real dividing line was class.[29]

And some critics of the movement saw it as reactionary, despite the pedigree of so many of its advocates. The political scientist Martin Kilson charged that "neo-ethnicity," as he called it, was primarily a conservative project "carefully orchestrated at the national level by the Republican Party."[30] And the sociologist Orlando Patterson saw the movement as another form of "chauvinism," a dangerous retreat from universalistic norms, egalitarianism, and democracy.[31]

The experience of four decades ago should be instructive to us now. Many of the debates carried on in the name of the new ethnicity are being recapitulated in arguments now about whether white-working-class support for Donald Trump should be seen primarily as a form of economic protest against the costs to large numbers of Americans of globalization and technological change or as primarily a reaction to race culture and immigration. Now, as then, it would be mistaken to focus on one set of motivations to the exclusion of the other. The economic grievances are real, but so are the vocal expressions of racism and nativism within the Trump movement. The new ethnic advocates scolded affluent liberals for their distance from the struggles and the pain of the white working class, and they were right to do so. But civil rights advocates were right to ask them, in turn, to confront the persistence, the costs, and the power of racism.

THE NEED FOR COALITION

There are issues on which the Kerner Commission's insistence that race is central to our national dilemma, independent of class and economics, still rings true. The report's warnings about attitudes toward the police in many of the country's African American neighborhoods could be reissued today, with little change. "Negroes firmly believe that police brutality and harassment occur repeatedly in Negro neighborhoods," the Kerner Commission wrote. It minced no words in saying that the police themselves had come to represent "white power, white racism and white oppression." And it found that in several cities "the principal response" to violence "has been to train and equip the police with more sophisticated weapons."[32] These complaints almost exactly mirror those of the Black Lives Matter movement.

Yet precisely because the problem is so racially polarizing, policing is an area in which the search for common ground is especially urgent. It will not be found through the Trump administration's approach of casting the goals of better community-police relationships and safer neighborhoods as contradictory. On the contrary, fighting crime and building community support for the police go hand in hand with demands that the police respect the rights of the communities they serve. (Stronger gun laws would also benefit the police and high-crime communities alike.) That the Kerner Report sounds so familiar to us on these issues is a tragic commentary on our country's failure to discover a politics that would take seriously both the problem of crime and the demands of African American communities for just and fair treatment.

The response to the Kerner Report among white Americans and the rise of the new ethnic movement demonstrate that broad coalitions are never simple. The complexities of race, ethnicity, and class—and the ways these various categories overlap—create numerous tactical and strategic challenges in constructing alliances across lines of difference. But the experiences of the 1960s and 1970s also point to the importance of bridging social divides and creating diverse movements. The call for justice is louder and more powerful when many voices are raised at once.

Economic justice is one area in which coalition building should be easier than we have made it—as advocates of cross-racial and cross-ethnic working-class alliances such as Baroni insisted in the 1970s. If deindustrialization has created a crisis in once thriving industrial cities and towns in the heartland that are predominantly white, it had already created a comparable crisis in the nation's African American neighborhoods, as William J. Wilson documented in *When Work Disappears.* A shared problem requires a common approach to policy and politics, even as the particularities of different racial and ethnic groups can be respected and celebrated.

The Kerner Report paid considerable attention to unemployment and underemployment in the ghetto, and its members were struck during visits to the sites of the riots how often the demands they heard focused on employment opportunities. Former senator Fred Harris, a member of the commission, told Bill Moyers in 2008 of one such visit with Mayor Lindsay, the commission's cochair. "Jobs is what we heard everywhere," Harris said. "John Lindsay and I were walking down the streets of Cleveland, I believe it was, for example. And we'd see idle young black men on the streets, you know. And these guys get up, and they said, 'What we need is jobs, baby. Jobs. Get us a job, baby.' I remember that so—and that's what we heard all over."[33]

It is a demand that is heard today, across every line of racial and ethnic division.

The lesson from both the years after the Kerner Report and from the 2016 election is that if politics becomes an exercise in casting one group's pain against another's, the result will be division and inaction—and a repetition of the same cycle, again and again.

The National Advisory Commission on Civil Disorders—the Kerner Commission—described the appropriate goal for our nation: "the realization of common opportunities for all within a single society."[34] We are still seeking a politics that would allow us to fulfill this aspiration.

22

The Media and Race Relations

Julian E. Zelizer

N THE FIFTEENTH CHAPTER of the Kerner Report, the authors turned to the issue of race and the media. In their careful examination of the riots that shook the nation in the summer of 1967 and the roots of racial injustice, the commissioners and their staff realized that the main institution through which Americans learned about these issues had to come under scrutiny as well: the news media. The commission understood that the news media did not just report on race relations but that its coverage influenced how Americans thought about these issues.

As Americans watched and read about the riots throughout the hot summer months of 1967, it became apparent that the character of the coverage mattered greatly. During the investigative period, the Kerner Commission spent much time examining how the three major television networks, local news, commercial news radio, and a handful of the major big-city newspapers had covered the riots and in the process what reporters conveyed about race relations more broadly.

KERNER COMMISSION CRITICISM OF THE MEDIA

The Kerner Report was not *totally* critical of the press. In general, the report concluded that the media had made a serious and legitimate effort to provide a balanced and factual account of the riots. Despite the best intentions, however, the report stated, the coverage tended to be overly sensational, and it frequently exaggerated key elements of what had occurred—incorrectly labeling violence as "race riots," for instance, even though the incidents primarily involved black-on-black violence. As a result, the commissioners concluded, with disappointment, "We have found a significant imbalance between what actually happened in our cities and what the newspaper, radio and television coverage of the riots told us happened.... We found that the disorders, as serious as they were, were less destructive, less widespread, and less of a black-white confrontation than most people believed."[1]

The Kerner Commission blamed the newspapers for printing "scare headlines," which were not based on solid evidence and were reported on rumors, that sold newspapers and did not reflect what was happening on the ground. Reporters too often turned to inexperienced local sources— namely, the police themselves—to obtain assessments of the scale and scope of the damage caused by the riots.

Most of the commissioners and the staff were also in agreement that the media had "failed to report adequately on the causes and consequences of civil disorders and the underlying problems of race relations."[2] The media treated the riots as isolated events rather than being conditioned by what local residents had experienced during the past few decades. Like the rest of the commission's report, its analysis of the media emphasized the failure of American elites to deal with the institutional dimension of racism. Television newscasts, for instance, placed most of their emphasis on law enforcement, with images of National Guardsmen and police confronting the rioters, as opposed to discussions of the "underlying grievances" that were behind the flare-ups.[3]

In part, the commissioners believed that this resulted from the paucity of African American journalists, who would have had a better understanding of these issues: "The media report and write from the standpoint of a white man's world. The ills of the ghetto, the difficulties of life there, the Negro's burning sense of grievance, are seldom conveyed."[4] The failure also resulted from the larger blindness in American society to the real roots of racial injustice.

Through their treatment of the riots that unfolded in the summer of 1967, reporters and producers replicated the same systematic bias in their coverage of racism that had limited national discussions for years. It was not a surprise that so many policy makers in Washington, not to speak of many American citizens, were shocked by what they saw in Newark and Detroit. With so much coverage of race relations in those years having missed the kinds of institutional concerns that loomed large in the African American neighborhoods in the cities, the riots did not make sense. Most attention had been on the issue of segregation in the South and much less on how white racism manifested itself in *northern* urban life.

The riots were easily characterized by conservative opponents of President Lyndon Johnson's Great Society, as well as by disaffected liberals, as the violent actions of irresponsible misfits or "riff-raff."[5] The demands for law and order by Republicans, like candidate and later president Richard Nixon, resonated with a public that saw the social disorder as a case of the rioters ignoring criminal justice institutions and not the criminal justice system as frequently the cause of the social disorder.

The Kerner Report painted a very different picture from what the media had shown. This was very relevant. Once the riots were seen within a long trajectory of police harassment of African Americans, it made more sense that individual incidents could spark massive levels of disorder. While the Kerner commissioners hoped that their report would push back against the conventional arguments about the rioting of 1967, they were well-aware of limits to what they could achieve without changing the underlying bias of the information that most Americans received in their daily newspapers and news shows.

The Kerner Commission's report called on media outlets to change the way that they covered race relations and to increase the number of reporters who were covering these kinds of stories.

THE MEDIA RESPONSE

Five decades since the publication of the Kerner Report, it has become clear that the news media did not adequately follow through on the commission's recommendations regarding race. Concerning one of the big questions of our era, for example, the relationship of race and the criminal justice system, media coverage until the last couple of years has been utterly lacking. As a series of scandals unfolded centering on police brutality against African Americans in 2014, 2015, and 2016, the continued shortcomings in the way the news media covered these problems quickly became evident.

Most important, the driving force behind exposing the kinds of excessive force often used by police against African Americans did not emanate from reporters or producers but from citizens who captured the brutal images of the violence on their smart phones. New technology empowered the kind of documentary coverage that had generally eluded reporters.

The first breakthrough in coverage took place on March 3, 1991, and was accomplished with the technology of the day. A private citizen used a handheld video recorder to film the Los Angeles police brutally assaulting an African American named Rodney King, who had been stopped for speeding on the freeway while under the influence of drugs. This videotape of a group of white police officers surrounding King and beating him while he was on the ground shocked many citizens. Cable television stations such as CNN rebroadcast the images to dramatic effect, and this generated national outrage about what had happened.

But the news stories at the time were not usually coupled with substantive coverage of police discrimination or analysis of how police unions protected perpetrators of violent crimes from grand juries. The coverage, like that of the King story, tended to be sensationalistic—more interested in the riveting drama of the recordings than on the policy issues behind these kinds of incidents. When a jury decided that retired football player O. J. Simpson was not guilty of murdering his ex-wife and her friend in 1995, many white Americans could not understand why polls showed that African Americans were as suspicious of the police in Los Angeles as they were of Simpson.

Years later, smart phone technology greatly enhanced the ability of regular Americans to capture other moments of police violence. Most of the national conversation about how police handled African Americans emerged only because residents in cities like Staten Island were able to capture the violence of the police on their smart phones.

The press, however, was often slow to connect the issue of race to policing incidents when they emerged. The stories were initially treated as isolated incidents in which confrontations between bad cops and individuals with criminal records led to tragic outcomes. The sensationalism of the images continued to overwhelm the treatment of the context within which they occurred.

One of the first major scandals involving policing resulted from the police shooting of the African American Michael Brown in Ferguson, Missouri, on August 9, 2014, following which Brown's lifeless body was left callously exposed on the street for hours after he was killed. A study by Race Forward showed that it took over ten days after this terrible event for the press to start using the terms "race," "racism," or "racist" in their coverage of what had happened. Only 7 percent of the stories that did use any of these terms dealt with the violent acts committed by the police. The Race Forward study found that this media narrative had an impact on the way the criminal justice system handled the issues involved.[6] Another study revealed that between March and April of 2011, 73 percent of stories that were broadcast on television about African American men were either about sports or crime.[7] Study after study discovered a commonality in showing Africans as criminals. African Americans were rarely reported on in a sympathetic light, and the depictions of African Americans were often threatening.[8]

MEDIA AND POLICING

The press coverage of policing has also been remarkably disconnected from the economic circumstances of the communities in which many of the cases of police brutality and killings have taken place or on the relationship among economic conditions, policing, and the victims. One of the most important findings in the Kerner Report had to do with connecting the different facets through which white racism affected racial injustice. Economics was central in terms of understanding how this played out on the streets. The riots, the commission learned, grew out of the dire economic conditions that African Americans lived in—with high rates of unemployment and the depleted state of civic institutions. In their account of what happened in the summer of 1967, the commissioners made a connection between the lack of economic opportunities and the kinds of neighborhoods that were the most plagued by police misconduct related to race. Yet the media coverage in recent years is usually disconnected from these kinds of economic fundamentals. Reporters have often treated racial prejudice against African Americans as lacking any economic dimension, from the kinds of communities where this kind of brutality often occurs to the role of assumptions about the economic class of victims.

The news coverage about criminal justice policy devoted great attention to the drug epidemics of the 1980s and 1990s—from crack cocaine to heroin to methamphetamines—that were tearing apart the cities and suburbs. Much of the coverage did not do much to look at why rates of addiction were rising or the reasons that the illegal drug markets were thriving in impoverished areas. The coverage veered toward shocking images of abusers and dealers, differing only a little from reality shows such as *Cops*. Coverage biased in favor of a sensational outlook diverted attention from the kinds of policy questions that were more relevant, yet less dramatic, than endless loops of violence and confrontations aimed at attracting a greater audience. Coverage about crack cocaine particularly tended to focus on the high rates of addiction and the crimes that users and dealers committed. The violence that existed in the crack networks was a conventional theme.[9] The headlines about crack cocaine were usually something like "New Violence Seen in Users of Cocaine." This contrasted with headlines about opioid use in recent years—an addiction suffered in greater numbers by white Americans—which read something like "In Heroin Crisis, White Families Seek Gentler War on Drugs." Incidentally, both these headlines were in the *New York Times*.[10]

Importantly, there were some improvements in media coverage. In one examination of the coverage of the Los Angeles riots in 1992, it was clear that reporters did heed some of the Kerner recommendations. For example, in that case, the media did not rely on official sources for their information, and they often arrived at the scene before the police. Television news did not hesitate to convey images of the violence and tensions. Yet such improvements were limited. In the case of the LA riots, 61 percent of the national and local network stories focused on the riot and reaction to the violence, 43 percent featured ordinary citizens, 20 percent focused on political leaders, 9 percent revolved around the King case, and only 10 percent of the coverage was about issues like racial discrimination or poverty. Prevalent in media discussions of causal forces and public policy was attention to morality and character, individual responsibility, and the police response.[11]

This kind of press coverage is not totally surprising when you consider, as the historian Dan Rodgers argues, that media coverage about race relations has generally taken place in a national framework increasingly centered on individuals, markets, and autonomous units of society and culture as opposed to institutions, organizations, and structures of power. This trend, in the social sciences, in literature, and in popular culture, has permeated the media as well.[12] Nowhere is this more evident than in the way the subject of institutional racism that was featured in the Kerner Report has faded from news coverage. It seems to have become easier for the press to focus on the particulars of specific racial flare-ups—whether looking at rogue police who abused their authority, dramatic and violent instances of rioting, or the citizens who were the victims of this violence—than it is for reporters to find space or air time to discuss the deeper structures of society that perpetuate racism, including policing and criminal justice institutions.

THE CARCERAL STATE

So the press gave little attention before 2014 to one of the biggest policy developments to take place since the 1960s: the great establishment and expansion of a militarized criminal justice system that discriminated against African Americans. At the same time that a new generation of reporters came of age, leaning to the left in the wake of the Vietnam War and the Watergate scandal, news organizations continued to devote little attention to the problems that had taken form in the aftermath of the 1960s and that were becoming even worse in the lived experience of African Americans in their encounters with police, the courts, and prisons.

Numerous historians and social scientists have recently been writing about the policy changes that took place: starting in the mid-1960s there was an aggressive push toward vastly expanding the carceral state. Starting with President Lyndon Johnson, the federal government began to pour huge amounts of resources into militarized policing, larger prison systems, and more punitive sentencing. Neoconservative arguments about the need for the police to be much tougher, even with smaller crimes (the broken-windows theory), in their effort to change community norms led to more forceful interaction with police and higher imprisonment rates.

The Rockefeller drug laws resulted in a greater number of Americans, a disproportionate number being African Americans, going to prison for small infractions. The push for this carceral state, importantly, was bipartisan, because both sides converged on a law-and-order approach to handling the problems of the cities. The result was an explosion of the prison system and of local police forces with militarized power that exacerbated, rather than calmed, the problems found to be at the root of the 1967 rioting. Prisons expanded rapidly. The federal government started to pour more money into these institutions, and private organizations took on a bigger role in constructing and running them, as the government contracted out these obligations. Private companies had strong financial incentives to keep more people within the prison walls.[13]

THE RECORDINGS

Not only was much of the coverage that examined the police shootings since 2014 a product of citizens capturing abusive behavior digitally, but the recordings themselves became the focus rather than the underlying problems in policy and law. The recordings, though scandalous, played well on television especially, where each outlet was constantly in search of more eyeballs. Rather than the recordings being a foundation for offering hard-hitting analyses of what was wrong with the criminal justice system, they became more a mechanism for attracting additional viewers and readers in an age when the commercial pressures on news organizations had greatly intensified. The images were played over and over, more attention being devoted to the recordings themselves, as well as to left and right pundit battles over who was responsible, than to what changes were necessary to prevent such abuse in the future. Despite all the attention to these high-profile images, there was little press coverage of the police violence that takes place regularly but is not captured on videotape or a cell phone or does not stimulate protests.

In our visual media age, much of the coverage now depends on the existence of dramatic footage or photographs. While this has clearly helped gain attention for cases such as the death of African American Eric Garner in Staten Island, the premium on such material diminishes the appetite for the thousands of other cases that occur regularly but that lack evidentiary material. Coverage becomes contingent on these kinds of images, which is dangerous, since it creates ample opportunity for the press to move away from these sorts of questions when they do not exist.

As one reporter who had covered the LA riots in 1991 concluded when reflecting on race and journalism, "You know, I think that a lot of what the African American community in the greater St. Louis area would say was not that they necessarily had been voiceless but that they had been *unheard* [emphasis added] in cities like Ferguson, Baltimore, I mean, the cities didn't really register on our national conscious before these police-involved killings happened. And so while there may have been some kind of attention on the local level, nationally, reporters were parachuting in and really kind of uncovering these issues for the first time. . . . I know, you know, a lot of reporters who are really kind of astonished to learn about the level of racial tension in the heart of America."[14]

Media Partisanship and Ideological Bias

The difficulty of communicating substantive analysis is compounded by much of the media environment now being partisan or ideology based. Since the 1980s, the media has changed significantly with the emergence of news organizations that are openly partisan. There were many reasons for this development, including the end in 1987 of the Fairness Doctrine of the Federal Communications Commission and commercial changes in the industry. And they resulted in shows that reported on the news from specific partisan angles. The Internet has only exacerbated this dynamic. At the same time, studies have shown that more Americans turn to the news from sources that reflect their own biases. In a recent study, two social scientists found that conservative voters receive almost all their information about politics from conservative sources.[15] This affects the way the news is received by millions of Americans. In news institutions such as Breitbart and Newsmax, for example, the focus of the coverage of policing was on the criminal background of Staten Island's Eric Garner rather than on the actions of the police.[16]

Short Attention Span

The other pertinent characteristic of the media has been the short attention span of the industry and the audiences. Take, for example, how coverage of racial police incidents greatly diminished with the 2016 election and its aftermath. While it might be that some of this results from police changing their practices in response to heightened scrutiny, equally relevant, surely, is that the press does not provide sustained attention to questions like race and the criminal justice system, particularly the institutional dimensions of the subject, such as sentencing, juries, and police training. In an era when readers spend only a few seconds on an article and change channels with great rapidity, all while multitasking on numerous devices, it is not surprising that the press is reluctant to overload audiences with information. The news media must realistically contend with what experts have found to be the eight-second attention span of most Americans, down from twelve seconds in 2000.[17] With so much attention on President Donald Trump and his controversies, there has also not been much room left for these other kinds of issues.

DIVERSITY

The Kerner Commission argued that one of the best ways to address these matters was to bring more diversity into the newsroom. The scarcity of African American reporters, it said, undercut the kind of coverage that the press could provide about race. "Like most black boys, I was given 'the talk' when I was very young about how to survive an encounter with the police," recalled one African American journalist who covered the Los Angeles riots. "I was also given a version of it again from a female friend when I moved to L.A. in 1988. She called it 'The black man's guide to survival in L.A.' 'Rule #1: Do not mess with LAPD.'"[18] The sociologist Ronald Jacobs found that black press coverage provided the most social and historical context for the LA riots, much more than did the coverage by the rest of the press.[19]

While there has been some breakdown in the racial insularity of the newsroom, offering space for more diverse perspectives, these gains have been limited. Minority reporters continue to hover at 12 percent to 14 percent of all journalists, and there has been a 52.3 percent drop in the number of black journalists since 2000, according to the American Society of News Editors.

The news media, as the Kerner Commission realized, is a pivotal institution. Without a news media that takes seriously the institutional roots of white racism, public understanding of the tensions that continually flare into violence and discord will never be resolved.

When President Barack Obama took office, there was great hope that his election meant there would be improvement in race relations—Pew Research Center polls showed 70 percent of Americans believed that this was the case[20]—yet the years that followed produced great disappointment in that respect. Citizens holding up their smart phones exposed to all of us the deep foundation on which racial violence and injustice still rest, often with persons who wear the badge of law and order. While some parts of the media have responded by devoting more coverage to the forces that explain what was captured on the tapes, much of the coverage has remained as thin as the news stories of the 1960s. And even worse, parts of the audience understand the crisis only as they see it through partisan eyes.

Until the news media really responds to the challenge put down by the commission back in 1968, we will not as a nation be able to have the kinds of conversations that are essential to racial progress, and politicians who support criminal justice reform will perpetually be hamstrung by how Americans understand race.

WHAT NEEDS TO BE DONE?

The need to reform our journalistic coverage of race relations is urgent. Over the course of President Trump's first year in office, the fragility of our media commitment to these critical civil rights issues became clear. As President Trump's controversies and scandals came to Washington, the amount of attention paid to the racial crisis in criminal justice quickly faded. Rather than developing a more comprehensive look at what was going wrong and what needed to be done to achieve racial justice, the issue almost completely faded from the news.

Journalism schools must take the lead in responding to this vacuum. Although many young journalists never pass through these hallways, and the focus of news coverage comes from executives and producers who decide what stories will command the most attention, journalism schools still have the capacity to push the profession in new directions. There is a massive opportunity for the deans of the most prestigious programs to invest more heavily in courses and events that take a deep dive into the history of race relations and how these dynamics work today. These projects need to be cross-disciplinary, providing budding reporters with a full sense of the sociological, historical, institutional, and economic dimensions of this crisis.

Politicians also have a role to play. Members of Congress have often focused media attention on particular questions that are on the margins of reporters' interest. In 1968, for instance, Senator Robert Kennedy traveled to the Mississippi Delta and generated media attention on how race and class worked in that devastated area. Today, legislators who have been working with the Black Lives Matter Movement on these issues need to do the same. As members of both parties can see, the attention span of the media is often as limited as that of the public itself. One can imagine key representatives or senators taking publicized tours of neighborhoods afflicted by police violence against African Americans or conducting hearings with citizens who have lived with these challenges that have triggered renewed debate.

These efforts will be doubly important in an era of fake news and alternative facts circulated through social media and then increasingly spreading to the larger institutions of the media. It will be vital not only to keep attention on the way race works in our criminal justice institutions but also now to bat back incorrect information, easier than ever to be disseminated by opponents, with new technology. Even videos cannot be counted on to simply reveal the facts when those videos are so easy to manipulate and when partisan or ideologically biased media outlets can interpret them in politically specific ways.

As was the case in 1968, it will be vital that the institutions of journalism and government respond to our current civil rights crisis by taking substantive steps to throw greater light on the problems that we face and to make certain that we cover these stories in the right way, so as to move toward effective policy responses.

Sometimes, "Dog Bites Man" Really Is the Story

GARY YOUNGE

A **LANGUAGE STUDENT** during the dying days of the Soviet Union, I lived with a woman and her son in what was then still Leningrad. Every weekday evening at around the same time my hostess would get herself ready to take their dog, a cocker spaniel called Redek, for a walk. Since I am no lover of the cold and not a great lover of dogs, I would watch with bemusement as she readied herself and Redek for the trip to the local park. She would leave at almost the same time each night. You could set your watch by it.

Everybody has their routines, and I thought little of it until spring came and I decided, one night, to accompany her. I noted a slight urgency in her voice as she stood by the door, lead in hand, while I searched the flat for my hat. We made it out on time—though on time for what was not exactly clear—and arrived at the park to find scores of dog owners already there.

"What's this?" I asked. "It looks like a meeting."

"We call it the 'dog hour,' she explained. "It's when the state news, *Vremya*, is on. We don't want to listen to the propaganda, so we walk our dogs."

This collective, low-key act of civil disobedience against a political culture that had left information sources with so little relevance to peoples' daily lives that the news was no longer even worthy of decoding has long stayed with me.

Not because we live in a totalitarian state that dictates what the news should be but because we live in an ostensibly democratic state in which the fate of large sections of society are written out of the news agenda in ways that force a reckoning with the nature of the democracy that we live in.

So while riots of the kind that prompted the 1968 Kerner Report were deemed newsworthy, the brutal reality is that it took riots of that scale for the media and political classes to pay attention to the conditions highlighted in the report. This is by no means an issue limited to the United States. In Britain, where I am from, there were major inner-city uprisings during the early 1980s. Back then a Conservative cabinet minister, Michael Heseltine, produced a paper laying out what he believed to be the root cause of the disturbances. It was called "It Took a Riot."[1]

The Kerner Report could hardly have been more straightforward in drawing a link between the social and economic violence of daily life and the violence of the riots and in pointing out that both had to be understood within the context of America's racial inequality. "Violence and destruction must be ended—in the streets of the ghetto and in the lives of people," the report argued. "Segregation and poverty have created in the racial ghetto a destructive environment totally unknown to most white Americans. What white Americans have never fully understood but what the Negro can never forget—is that white society is deeply implicated in the ghetto. White institutions created it, white institutions maintain it, and white society condones it."[2]

But while the riots were news, the segregation and poverty that made them possible were not. The report sold two million copies and was reportedly the best-selling federal report in American history, suggesting there was no lack of public interest. But as long as news was framed as "things people didn't know," as opposed to "things that shouldn't be," the ghetto was never going to make the news just by being there. The ghetto's presence did not shock; its pain was not contagious; its problems were understood to be contained. America had established a moral, political, and economic threshold that had made almost all of its opinion formers and lawmakers—none of whom lived in the ghetto—inured to, but not unaware of, the obscenity of its existence.

While the nature of both poverty and segregation has changed a great deal over the last fifty years, the question of this dislocation between what we have all become used to and what is nonetheless a scandal remains. In a period in which black male life expectancy in Washington, D.C.,[3] is lower than male life expectancy on the Gaza Strip,[4] what is outrageous may also be understood, through the jaded lens of privilege, to be banal.

This dichotomy brings to mind the widely known aphorism, taught in most journalism colleges, about what constitutes a news story. Attributed to both Alfred Harmsworth, an early nineteenth-century British newspaper magnate, and the *New York Sun* editor John Bogart, of the same period, the aphorism states simply, "When a dog bites a man, that is not news. But if a man bites a dog, that *is* news." The logic here is clear.

Occurrences that are both commonplace and expected cannot be considered news, which is a category reserved for events that are relatively rare and unexpected.

But increasingly, as one covers America as a foreign correspondent, as I did for twelve years,[5] one is compelled to provide an addendum to that adage—a qualifying footnote to what seems like the obvious. For, sometimes, events derive their potential news value precisely because they happen so often. Indeed, there are things that happen with such regularity and predictability that journalists have simply ceased to recognize their news value, and politicians have ceased to acknowledge their import—not least if those things are least likely to happen to the people most likely to be journalists and politicians. Ultimately, to pursue the metaphor, there is often value in asking, "Why do dogs keep biting people?" "Who owns these dogs?" And "Why do the same people keep getting bitten?"

This first occurred to me in 2007 when I was writing a magazine article about all the children and teens who were shot dead on a random single day in America.[6] I chose November 25, 2006, a day on which nine children were shot somewhere in the United States, and I set about reporting on each case. With one child's story, I kept reaching a dead end. I knew he had been shot in Detroit and he was sixteen years old. But the city's two main newspapers never even saw fit to mention his name when they described how he had been shot dead outside National Wholesale Liquidators after a tussle with a security guard. When I contacted the police about this, it was clear that the newspapers barely rewrote the press release. It was news in brief.

Eventually, I found out that the boy's name was Brandon Martell Moore. Brandon, who was African American, was in the store with his cousins and their uncle. The store had a policy that children should be accompanied by an adult. But when the uncle went to pay, the kids stayed to look at some video games. A security guard told them to get out and ushered them out. They told him they were with their uncle. The guard ignored them and got physical. Brandon's older brother fought back. When they saw the guard's gun fly out of his pocket, they all started to run. "Then he picked it up, put one arm on top of the other arm and started aiming at us," Brandon's older brother, John Henry, recalled. "Brandon wasn't involved in anything. He was the last one to take off running, I guess."[7]

That in itself, I thought, was worth more than a paragraph. But then came what should have made banner headlines. The guard, it turned out, was an off-duty cop. In 1971, he was sacked from the force after he was involved in a fatal hit-and-run accident while under the influence of alcohol. He was reinstated on appeal in 1974. Five years later, he shot dead an armed and drunk thirty-one-year-old man involved in a neighborhood dispute. Five years after that, he shot his wife in the side during a domestic dispute in which he claimed she lunged at him with a pair of scissors.

This was the man who killed Brandon. This was the story not worth telling. The problem was not that the papers ignored it. They never even bothered to look. The fact of a black teen being shot in the city prompted no questions. It did not challenge how they understood the ghetto to work; it confirmed it. With no public scrutiny, there was no public pressure. The security guard/policeman was assigned to a traffic unit, pending an investigation. The investigation eventually judged the shooting justifiable homicide.

That the policeman in question was black was itself significant. Nobody can say that in a range of ways America has not changed in the last fifty years—we have had eight years of a black president, and African Americans can now be found in a range of powerful positions in commerce, politics, and public service that would not have been deemed possible in 1968. The trouble is that there are significant ways in which America has remained the same and some important ways in which it is getting worse.

The discrepancy between black and white unemployment is the same as it was in 1963;[8] incarceration disparities are higher.[9] According to the Institute on Assets and Social Policy at Brandeis University, between 1984 and 2007 the black-white wealth gap quadrupled.[10] Meanwhile, the Supreme Court is dismantling affirmative action and gutting voting rights.

As the radical professor and former Black Panther Angela Davis once told me, "When the inclusion of black people into the machine of oppression is designed to make that machine work more efficiently, then it does not represent progress at all. We have more black people in more visible and powerful positions. But then we have far more black people who have been pushed down to the bottom of the ladder. When people call for diversity and link it to justice and equality, that's fine. But there's a model of diversity as the difference that makes no difference, the change that brings about no change."[11]

This dialectic between looking different but acting the same was highlighted just a couple of weeks before Barack Obama ended his term when the U.S. Mint celebrated its 225th anniversary with plans to issue a twenty-four-carat commemorative coin depicting Lady Liberty as an African American woman. With full lips and braided hair tied back in a bun, her gold-embossed profile is framed by the words "LIBERTY" above and "In God We Trust" below. "As we as a nation continue to evolve," said Elisa Basnight, the Mint's chief of staff, "so does Liberty's representation."[12]

Sadly, the representation is evolving far faster than the nation. The coin is worth one hundred dollars; according to the Center for Community and Economic Development, in 2010 the median net wealth for women of color in their prime working years was calculated at just five dollars.[13] Black women now earn sixty-five cents for every dollar made by a white man,[14] which is the same gap as existed twenty years ago. So the Treasury has produced a coin in these women's image that most such women cannot afford—because the economy is producing low-wage jobs that leave them with liberty without equality.

Thus, all too often we end up celebrating great symbolic victories even as the material conditions of those in whose name those victories are claimed either stall or slide. Those symbols should not be dismissed as insubstantial, but they should not be mistaken for substance either.

This is what has made the explosion of the Black Lives Matter movement during Obama's presidency so resonant. At various moments, particularly when there were clashes with police or looting, the limits of what constitutes success in the post–civil rights era were laid bare. There was the first black president appealing for calm on one side of a split screen while on the other was the sight of alienated black youth smashing store windows or demonstrating.

It is particularly revealing that as far as anyone could make out, Black Lives Matter was prompted not by an increase in the number of black people being killed by police (amazingly, no official nationwide statistics exist on lethal police shootings)[15] but rather by a growing political awareness that had forced a reckoning with a preexisting condition. So these shootings of unarmed black people were not news in the conventional sense, any more than "the violence of the ghetto" had been in 1967. They are neither rare nor surprising. They were *made* to be news. We were forced to recognize them not because of the overwhelming statistical evidence suggesting wrongdoing, not by the testimony of thousands to ill treatment, and not by historical precedent of how certain inequities and injustices work. We were forced to recognize them, in no small part, because new technology enabled people with cell phones to do the job the established media had failed to do. The world had not changed; what had changed was our ability to pass off the grotesque as unremarkable simply because it is also commonplace.

The American media episodically discovers this daily reality in much the same way that teenagers discover sex—urgently, earnestly, voraciously, and carelessly, with great self-indulgence but precious little self-awareness. They have always been aware of it but somehow, when confronted with it, they are nonetheless taken by surprise. And then their surprise becomes the news, "Crikey, look what I've found out," instead of the news itself, "Goodness, look what's been going on while I've been looking elsewhere."

But those who live it do not have the luxury of discovery. When I interviewed the late Maya Angelou in 2002, she told me that the September 11 attacks of the previous year were understood differently by African Americans. "Living in a state of terror was new to many white people in America," she said. "But black people have been living in a state of terror in this country for more than 400 years."[16]

At the time, I thought this was an interesting thing to say. But it would take more than a decade before I really understood it. Only after I had reported from America for ten years and decided to repeat the exercise I had undertaken when I discovered the case of Brandon Moore did the enormity of what Maya Angelou had evoked become clear to me. Once again, I picked a day at random—this time November 23, 2013—and set out to write profiles of all the children and teens who were shot dead that day, only this time for a book.[17] Over the next two years, I sought out everyone who knew them—from their parents to their pastors and basketball coaches. Ten kids were shot dead that day in the United States. The youngest was nine; the eldest, just a few days shy of his twentieth birthday. Seven were black, two were Hispanic, and one was white.

One of the first things I noticed was that when I called the reporters who had written the original stories, I found that rarely had their news organizations followed the stories up. Clearly, I was the only one who had called the reporters to seek more information. They would generously rifle through their notes and tell me what they knew and, if they had been to the crime scene, what they had seen. Invariably, when I asked if they had any contact details for family members I could speak to or if there had been any developments in the investigation, they would explain, somewhat matter-of-factly, why they had moved on. "Unfortunately, homicides are not uncommon in that area," said one reporter. "Unless something unexpected happened, it just wouldn't be the kind of story we'd follow up on," said another.

These were, in other words, "dog bites man" stories. What soon became apparent, however, was how traumatized the bitten had become. Every parent of a black teen that I spoke to said they had, essentially, long factored in the possibility that their child might die in this way. Audry Smith, the mother of sixteen-year-old Samuel Brightmon, who was shot dead that day in Dallas, told me she did not think it would be him; she thought it would be his brother. Gary Anderson, whose eighteen-year-old son of the same name was shot dead in Newark just an hour after Samuel, told me, "You wouldn't really be doing your job as a parent here if you didn't think it could happen."[18] In between Samuel's shooting and Gary's, another eighteen-year-old, Tyshon Anderson, was shot dead in a stairwell on the Southside of Chicago. A mother who lived in the same building told a reporter the next day that "she was happy that her 14-year-old son was locked up because it was safer for him to be incarcerated than to live in the neighborhood."[19]

It was only after hearing these stories, told so consistently among such a random cohort, that it dawned on me what was the nature of the state of terror to which Maya Angelou had referred—a state that left parents in constant fear that they would have to bury their children and children assuming they might never live to be adults. This is the condition Jesmyn

Ward writes about in her book *Men We Reaped*, in which she tells about the deaths in just four years of five young men who were close to her. "By all official records," she writes, "here at the confluence of history, of racism, of poverty, and economic power, this is what our lives are worth: nothing."[20]

Doriane Miller, a primary-care physician in Chicago, told me about a kind of "learned hopelessness" that so many young people she sees have after living close to so many deaths and that prompts them to ask themselves existential questions, even if not always articulated in the most sophisticated way. A few years ago, Miller told me, she started seeing growing numbers of young patients with psychosomatic illnesses. She also noticed that many of them had "RIP" tattoos, dedicated to deceased loved ones. But when she tried to talk to these young people about all this, they clammed up, Miller said. "They think, 'What's the point? I don't care. There's nothing you can do about this. Many people I know at the age of twenty-five have passed on in my community, and the same thing might happen to me.' And so, in that late-adolescent mind frame in which you tend to do more risk taking and tend not to think about the consequences of your behavior on your future, you think, 'What the heck, I'm not going to be here anyhow. I might as well live fast, die young, and leave a pretty corpse.'"[21]

This, then, is the white noise, set sufficiently low as to allow the country to go about its business undisturbed while entire communities live in constant fear.

The reason this state of affairs has continued is, in part, because while segregation is no longer the law of the land, it remains no less the lived experience for many Americans now than when the Kerner Report came out. In their 1993 book *American Apartheid*, Douglas Massey and Nancy Denton present five "distinct dimensions" in which segregation might be measured, and they describe those metropolitan areas that scored highly on at least four of them as "hypersegregated."[22] Of the sixteen cities that fit that designation, four—Dallas, Chicago, Indianapolis, and Newark—were places where I had found that children and teens were shot dead on November 23, 2013, the day I had chosen to check out.

Massey and Denton write, "Black Americans in these metropolitan areas live within large, contiguous settlements of densely inhabited neighborhoods that are packed tightly around the urban core. In plain terms, they live in ghettos. . . . Ironically, within a large, diverse, and highly mobile post-industrial society such as the United States, blacks living in the heart of the ghetto are among the most isolated people on earth."[23]

Indeed, for all the commonalities in race and class of the young people who were killed that November 23 I checked out, Newark still stood out to me as being particularly impoverished. The area in Newark around the Kretchmer complex on Freilinghuysen Avenue, where Gary Anderson, Jr., was shot dead, is a warren of high-rise social housing, not far from the airport. A short walk away, another whole apartment complex stands uninhabited; windows that once offered a view of the cranes and freight on Newark Bay are now stuffed with hastily cemented breeze-blocks. According to the census tract for that general area, it was by far the poorest place where any young person had been shot dead that day. Median income in the tract was just $10,307. That is less than half the next-most-poor area where a child or teen was killed. More than three-quarters of the people who live in that census tract earned less than $30,000 a year.

The pathos in this vulnerability is summed up in a poem written two generations after the Kerner Report by a freshman, named Tyler, at Central High School in Newark. The teacher had written "hope" on the blackboard and had given the all-boy class a little while to think about it before penning their verses. Tyler wrote:

> We hope to live,
> Live long enough to have kids
> We hope to make it home every day
> We hope we're not the next target to get sprayed. . . .
> We hope never to end up in Newark's dead pool
> I hope, you hope, we all hope.[24]

"The way we see things is affected by what we know and what we believe," writes John Berger in *Ways of Seeing*. "The relation between what we see and what we know is never settled."[25] What is truly unsettling to me is that fifty years after the production of the Kerner Report, we cannot legitimately claim that we do not know what we see. We have been told. And yet every time we see it again there is a collective pretense that we have no idea where it came from.

After the suburb of Ferguson, Missouri, went up in flames a little over two years ago, following the shooting of Michael Brown, the Department of Justice conducted a study into how the city was being run. Their report, I believe, any enterprising journalist could have produced if he or she had not become inured to the kind of systemic discrimination that exists. Among other things, the Department of Justice found that, between 2007 and 2014, a particular black woman, for example, was arrested twice, spent six days in jail and had to pay a total fine of $550, all as a result of one instance of illegal parking for which she had originally been fined $151. She tried to pay in smaller installments—$25 or $50 at a time—but the court had refused to accept anything less than the full payment, which she could not afford. Seven years after the original infraction, she still owed $541. This was how the town raised its revenue. And this was not some glitch in the system, it was the system. It was how the city raised its funds.[26]

Then there was the Ferguson case of the fourteen-year-old boy found in an abandoned building who had been chased down by a police dog that bit his ankle and his left arm as he tried to protect his face. The boy said the officers kicked him in the head and then laughed about it afterward. Officers said they thought he was armed, He was not. Department of Justice investigators found that every time a police dog had bitten someone, the victim was black.[27]

It turns out that, sometimes, "dog bites man" really is the story. And we keep missing it.

Acknowledgments

WE ARE PROUD once again, as on earlier anniversaries, to have the Milton S. Eisenhower Foundation, the private-sector follow-on, the "keeper of the flame," for the National Commission on the Causes and Prevention of Violence (the National Violence Commission) and the National Advisory Commission on Civil Disorders, the Kerner Commission, as the sponsor of an update of the 1968 Kerner Report. On the occasion of the Kerner Report's fiftieth anniversary, this update is arguably the most important ever.

We express sincere gratitude to the Trustees of the Eisenhower Foundation for their great and continued encouragement. Our heartfelt thanks go to Tracey Felder, executive assistant to the president of the Eisenhower Foundation, for her vital work on the book and in follow-up forums, from start to finish, and to Tawana Bandy, vice president for programs and evaluation at the foundation, for her meticulous research on evidence-based models and commitment to replicating what works.

Patrick McCarthy, president of the Annie E. Casey Foundation, and Lisa Hamilton, executive vice president and chief program officer of the Casey Foundation, provided inspiring encouragement for and crucial financial investments in this Kerner Report fiftieth-anniversary update, as well as earlier support for the evaluation of the Quantum Opportunities evidence-based model—one of the examples in this update of what works for high-risk minority youth.

To Darren Walker, president of the Ford Foundation; Larry Kramer, president of the Hewlett Foundation; and Hilary Pennington, vice president for education, creativity, and free expression at the Ford Foundation, we convey our admiration for their priority on reducing inequality and our indebtedness for their help in funding the Kerner fiftieth update, the evaluation of the Quantum Opportunities model and the replication of Quantum.

Rip Rapson, president of the Kresge Foundation, and Ken Zimmerman, director of U.S. programs at the Open Society Foundations, were generous in their financial underwriting of the update. Their commitment motivated our work.

We are grateful to and deeply respect the Kerner Fiftieth Anniversary Advisory Council, the chapter authors, each highly qualified and widely recognized as a leading authority in his or her field, for taking on such an important task and coming through splendidly and influentially, despite the constraints of a very tight deadline.

Thanks go to Valerie Wilson, director of the Program on Race, Ethnicity and the Economy at the Economic Policy Institute, for her excellent research and for the outstanding charts and graphs she constructed for this undertaking.

Our editor, Ryan Mulligan, and the other great people at Temple University Press deserve their well-earned, superb reputation in the field of urban affairs. Ryan expertly guided the book through a time-constricted production schedule, keeping his sense of humor, conveying patient winks, and launching the Kerner fiftieth update into the light of national attention.

Notes

INTRODUCTION

Portions of this Introduction are taken from Fred R. Harris, *Alarms and Hopes: A Personal Journey, a Personal View* (New York: Harper and Row, 1968), and Fred R. Harris, foreword to *The Kerner Report* (New York: Basic Books, 1988).

1. For a recent historical article on the Newark riot, see Rick Rojas and Khorri Atkinson, "Fifty Years after the Uprising: Five Days of Unrest That Shaped, and Haunted, Newark," *New York Times*, July 11, 2017, available at https://www.nytimes.com/2017/07/11/nyregion/newark-riots-50-years.html.

2. See *Report of the National Advisory Commission on Civil Disorders* (New York: Bantam Books, 1968), xv.

3. For a new and definitive history of the Kerner Commission, its operations, and its report, see Steven M. Gillon, *Separate and Unequal: The Kerner Commission and the Unraveling of American Liberalism* (New York: Basic Books, forthcoming).

4. *Harris, Alarms and Hopes*, 11.

5. *Report of the National Advisory Commission on Civil Disorders*, 202.

6. Ibid., 3.

7. Ibid., 203.

8. Ibid., 1.

9. Ibid., 2.

10. Ibid.

11. Ibid.

12. See Fred Harris, *Does People Do It? A Memoir* (Norman: University of Oklahoma Press, 2008), 86.

13. Ibid.

14. For more on the possible sources of this leak, see Gillon, *Separate and Unequal*.

15. Quoted in Fred Harris, "Greatest US Challenge: Income Inequality," *New Mexico Mercury*, December 18, 2014, available at http://newmexicomercury.com/blog/comments/greatest_us_challenge_income_inequality.

16. James Ciment, ed., *Postwar America: An Encyclopedia of Social, Political, Cultural, and Economic History* (Abingdon, UK: Routledge, 2015), 753.

17. John Gardner, speech at the annual meeting of the American Statistical Association, December 1967.

18. Fred Harris, "Greatest US Challenge: Income Inequality," *New Mexico Mercury*, December 18, 2014, available at http://newmexicomercury.com/blog/comments/greatest_us _challenge_income_inequality.

19. See, for example, Fred R. Harris and Lynn A. Curtis, eds., *Locked in the Poorhouse: Cities, Race, and Poverty in the United States* (Boulder, CO: Rowman and Littlefield, 1998); and Milton S. Eisenhower Foundation and Corporation for What Works, *The Millennium Breach: Richer, Poorer and Racially Apart* (Washington, DC: Milton S. Eisenhower Foundation, 1998), available at http://www.eisenhowerfoundation.org/docs/millennium.pdf.

20. We use the term "Hispanic" in Part I for consistency with the research studies on which our recommendations are based. In Part II, we preserve the terminology of individual contributors, who use both "Hispanic" and "Latino."

PART I

Chapter 1

1. National Advisory Commission on Civil Disorders, *Final Report* (Washington, DC: U.S. Government Printing Office, 1968), 2.

2. Ibid., 11.

3. Nadia Khomami, "Michelle Obama Tells of Being Wounded by Racism as First Lady," *The Guardian*, July 27, 2017, available at https://www.theguardian.com/us-news/2017/jul/27/ michelle-obama-wounded-racism-first-lady.

4. National Advisory Commission on Civil Disorders, *Final Report*, 5; Joe Heim, Ellie Silverman, T. Rees Shapiro, and Emma Brown, "One Dead as Car Strikes Crowds amid Protests of White Nationalist Gathering in Charlottesville; Two Police Die in Helicopter Crash," *Washington Post*, August 13, 2017, available at https://www.washingtonpost.com/local/fights -in-advance-of-saturday-protest-in-charlottesville/2017/08/12/155fb636-7f13-11e7-83c7-5bd 5460f0d7e_story.html.

5. Ta-Nehisi Coates, *Between the World and Me* (New York: Spiegel and Grau, 2015), 143.

6. Susan E. Dudley, "Bipartisan Commission Offers Evidence-Based Reform Ideas," *Forbes*, September 8, 2017, available at https://www.forbes.com/sites/susandudley/2017/09/08/ bipartisan-commission-offers-evidence-based-reform-ideas.

7. Randomized trials randomly assign subjects to the experimental or control group. In quasi-experimental designs, the control and experimental groups have similar characteristics rather than being randomly assigned.

Chapter 2

1. Jessica L. Semega, Kayla R. Fontenot, and Melissa A. Kollar, "Income and Poverty in the United States: 2016," September 2017, available at https://www.census.gov/content/dam/ Census/library/publications/2017/demo/P60-259.pdf.

2. Valerie Wilson, "Updated Trends on Inequality, Poverty and Income," unpublished report submitted to the Eisenhower Foundation, June 2017.

3. Jared Bernstein, "Is There an Emerging Democratic Agenda?" *New York Times*, June 5, 2017, available at https://www.nytimes.com/2017/06/05/opinion/democratic-party-inequal ity-child-allowance.html.

4. Semega, Fontenot, and Kollar, "Income and Poverty in the United States: 2016."

5. Ibid.

6. Wilson, "Updated Trends on Inequality, Poverty and Income."

7. Ibid.

8. Ganesh Sitaraman, "Our Constitution Wasn't Built for This," *New York Times*, September 16, 2017, available at https://www.nytimes.com/2017/09/16/opinion/sunday/constitu tion-economy.html.

9. Wilson, "Updated Trends on Inequality, Poverty and Income."

10. Paul Krugman, "Build He Won't," *New York Times*, November 21, 2016, available at https://www.nytimes.com/2016/11/21/opinion/build-he-wont.html; Bernie Sanders, "How Democrats Can Stop Losing Elections," *New York Times*, June 13, 2017, available at https://www.nytimes.com/2017/06/13/opinion/bernie-sanders-how-democrats-can-stop-losing-elec tions.html.

11. Heather Long, "Paychecks Hit High for Middle Class," *Washington Post*, September 13, 2017, available at https://www.pressreader.com/usa/the-washington-post/20170913/281500751415818; Heather Long and Tracy Jan, "Inequality Gaps Persist despite Widespread Gains," *Washington Post*, September 28, 2017, available at https://www.pressreader.com/usa/the-washington-post/20170928/281509341380897.

12. Krugman, "Build He Won't"; Sanders, "How Democrats Can Stop Losing Elections."

13. "Not Yet Talking about the Poor," *New York Times*, September 14, 2016, p. A26.

14. Christian Weller, "The Racial Gap Widens and Policymakers Turn Their Backs," *Spotlight on Poverty and Opportunity*, May 3, 2017, available at https://spotlightonpoverty.org/spotlight-exclusives/racial-gap-widens-policymakers-turn-backs.

15. Ibid.

16. Ibid.

17. Ibid.

18. Paul Krugman, "Zombies of Voodoo Economics," *New York Times*, April 24, 2017, available at https://www.nytimes.com/2017/04/24/opinion/zombies-of-voodoo-economics.html.

19. Ibid.

20. Wilson, "Updated Trends in Inequality, Poverty and Income."

21. Krugman, "Zombies of Voodoo Economics."

22. Jared Bernstein, *All Together Now: Common Sense for a Fair Economy* (San Francisco: Berrett-Koehler, 2016).

23. "The Kansas Mirage Fades," *Washington Post*, June 10, 2017, available at http://archive.sltrib.com/article.php?id=5387840&itype=CMSID.

24. Krugman, "Zombies of Voodoo Economics."

25. Ibid.

26. Jordan Weissmann, "The Failure of Welfare Reform," *Slate*, June 1, 2016, available at http://www.slate.com/articles/news_and_politics/moneybox/2016/06/how_welfare_reform_failed.html.

27. Center on Budget and Policy Priorities, "Chart Book: TANF at 20," August 5, 2016, available at https://www.cbpp.org/sites/default/files/atoms/files/8-22-12tanf.pdf; Ife Floyd, Ladonna Pavetti, and Liz Schott, "Lessons from TANF: Initial Unequal State Block-Grant Funding Formula Grew More Unequal over Time," Center on Budget and Policy Priorities, July 20, 2017, available at https://www.cbpp.org/research/family-income-support/lessons-from-tanf-initial-unequal-state-block-grant-funding-formula.

28. Harry J. Holzer, "Going, Going . . . Gone? The Evolution of Workforce Development Programs for the Poor since the War on Poverty," paper presented at War on Poverty conference, Ann Arbor, MI, June 12–13, 2012.

29. Ibid.

30. Ibid.

31. David Dayen, "It's Time for the Government to Give Everyone a Job," *The Nation*, May 19, 2017, available at https://www.thenation.com/article/its-time-for-the-government-to-give-everyone-a-job.

32. Congressional Progressive Caucus, "21st Century New Deal for Jobs," May 25, 2017, available at https://cpc-grijalva.house.gov/21st-century-new-deal-for-jobs.

33. Josh Bivens and Hunter Blair, "A Public Investment Agenda That Delivers the Goods for American Workers Needs to Be Long-Lived, Broad, and Subject to Democratic Oversight," Economic Policy Institute, December 8, 2016, available at http://www.epi.org/files/pdf/117041.pdf.

34. Congressional Progressive Caucus, "21st Century New Deal for Jobs."

35. Ibid.

36. Ibid.

37. Ibid.

38. Cynthia Miller, Megan Millenky, Lisa Schwartz, Lisbeth Goble, and Jillian Stein, "Building a Future: Interim Impact Findings from the YouthBuild Evaluation," November 2016, available at https://www.mdrc.org/sites/default/files/YouthBuild_Interim_Report_2016_FR.pdf.

39. Anne Roder and Mark Elliott, "Sustained Gains: Year Up's Continued Impact on Young Adults' Earnings," May 2014, available at https://economicmobilitycorp.org/uploads/sustained-gains-economic-mobility-corp.pdf.

40. Peter Z. Schochet, John Burghardt, and Sheena McConnell, "National Job Corps Study and Longer-Term Follow-Up Study: Impact and Benefit-Cost Findings Using Survey and Summary Earnings Records Data," August 2006, available at https://wdr.doleta.gov/research/FullText_Documents/National%20Job%20Corps%20Study%20and%20Longer%20Term%20Follow-Up%20Study%20-%20Final%20Report.pdf.

41. Milton S. Eisenhower Foundation and Corporation for What Works, *The Millennium Breach: Richer, Poorer and Racially Apart* (Washington, DC: Milton S. Eisenhower Foundation, 1998), available at http://www.eisenhowerfoundation.org/docs/millennium.pdf; A. Curtis and T. Brandy, *The Quantum Opportunities Program: A Randomized Control Evaluation*, 3rd ed. (Washington, DC: Eisenhower Foundation, 2016).

42. William Julius Wilson, "Reflection on Race, Class and Cumulative Adversity," speech given at Wellesley College, April 4, 2017, available at https://www.youtube.com/watch?v=_TpQgHVxhlU.

43. Christopher Wimer, Jane Waldfogel, and Luke Shaefer, "A Universal Child Allowance to Combat Child Poverty," *Spotlight on Poverty and Opportunity*, June 21, 2017, available at https://spotlightonpoverty.org/spotlight-exclusives/universal-child-allowance-combat-child-poverty; see also Chapter 2 in Part II.

44. David Cooper, "Raising the Minimum Wage to $15 by 2024 Would Lift Wages for 41 Million American Workers," Economic Policy Institute, April 26, 2017, available at http://www.epi.org/publication/15-by-2024-would-lift-wages-for-41-million.

45. Teresa Ghilarducci, "Farewell to America's Middle Class: Unions Are Basically Dead," *The Atlantic*, October 28, 2015, available at https://www.theatlantic.com/business/archive/2015/10/unions-are-basically-dead/412831.

46. Ibid.

47. Lawrence H. Summers, "Why We Need Unions," *Salt Lake Tribune*, September 4, 2017, available at http://www.sltrib.com/opinion/commentary/2017/09/04/lawrence-summers-why-we-need-unions.

48. Ghilarducci, "Farewell to America's Middle Class."

49. David Moberg, "How to Revive the Labor Movement," *Moyers and Company*, October 20, 2014, available at http://billmoyers.com/2014/10/20/post-political-labor-movement.

50. William E. Forbath and Brishen Rogers, "New Workers, New Labor Laws," *New York Times*, September 4, 2017, p. A21.

51. Moberg, "How to Revive the Labor Movement."

52. Richard D. Kahlenberg and Moshe Z. Marvit, "Why the Right to Form a Union Should Be a Civil Right," *Washington Post*, August 31, 2012, available at https://www.washingtonpost.com/opinions/why-the-right-to-form-a-union-should-be-a-civil-right/2012/08/31/1a91e7fc-f302-11e1-a612-3cfc842a6d89_story.html.

53. Ibid.

54. Ibid.

55. Economic Policy Institute, "A Real Agenda for Working People: What Trump Would Do If He Were Serious about Creating Jobs, Raising Wages, and Fixing Our Rigged Economy," December 7, 2016, available at http://www.epi.org/workers-agenda.

56. Richard D. Kahlenberg, "Harvard's Class Gap," *Harvard Magazine*, May–June 2017, available at http://harvardmagazine.com/2017/05/harvards-class-gap.

57. Suzy Khimm, "Democrats' Big Idea," *New York Times*, July 16, 2017, p. SR2; Aaron Blake, "The Biggest Winner in the Current Health-Care Debate: Single-Payer," *Washington Post*, July 1, 2017, available at https://www.washingtonpost.com/news/the-fix/wp/2017/07/01/the-biggest-winner-in-the-current-health-care-debate-single-payer.

58. Khimm, "Democrats' Big Idea."

59. Josh Bivens, "Adding Insult to Injury: How Bad Policy Decisions Have Amplified Globalization's Costs for American Workers," Economic Policy Institute, July 11, 2017, available at http://www.epi.org/publication/adding-insult-to-injury-how-bad-policy-decisions-have-amplified-globalizations-costs-for-american-workers.

60. Ibid.

61. Jeff Faux, "The Politics of Recapturing the Future," unpublished paper submitted to the Eisenhower Foundation, September 2007.

62. Information in this section is taken from Chapter 19 in Part II.

63. See Daniel Costa, David Cooper, and Heidi Shierholz, "Facts about Immigration and the U.S. Economy," Economic Policy Institute, August 12, 2014, available at http://www.epi.org/publication/immigration-facts; Adam Davidson, "Do Illegal Immigrants Actually Hurt the U.S. Economy?" *New York Times*, February 17, 2013, p. MM17; Ruchir Sharma, "To Be Great Again, America Needs Immigrants," *New York Times*, May 6, 2017, available at https://www.nytimes.com/2017/05/06/opinion/sunday/to-be-great-again-america-needs-immigrants.html; Fred Harris and Demetría Martínez, *These People Want to Work: Immigration Reform* (Amazon Digital Services, 2013); Brady E. Hamilton, Joyce A. Martin, Michelle J. K. Osterman, Anne K. Driscoll, and Lauren M. Rossen, "Births: Provisional Data for 2016," June 2017, available at https://www.cdc.gov/nchs/data/vsrr/report002.pdf; and Fred R. Harris, ed., *The Baby Bust: Who Will Do the Work? Who Will Pay the Taxes?* (Boulder, CO: Rowman and Littlefield, 2006).

Chapter 3

1. National Advisory Commission on Civil Disorders, *The Kerner Report* (Princeton, NJ: Princeton University Press, 2016), 425, 426, 208; see also Chapter 7 in Part II.

2. National Advisory Commission on Civil Disorders, *The Kerner Report*, 26; see also Chapter 7 in Part II.

3. For the data in this section, including its subsections, see Chapter 6 in Part II.

4. American Educational Research Association, amicus curiae brief filed in Parents Involved in Community Schools v. Seattle School District No. 1, 127 S. Ct. 2738 (2007), available at http://www.aera.net/Portals/38/docs/News_Media/AERABriefings/RaceConsciousSchool/AERA_Amicus_Brief.pdf.

5. Martin Carnoy, "School Vouchers Are Not a Proven Strategy for Improving Student Achievement," Economic Policy Institute, February 28, 2017, available at http://www.epi.org/publication/school-vouchers-are-not-a-proven-strategy-for-improving-student-achievement.

6. Casey Quinlan, "Why the Racist History of Vouchers Matters Today," *Think Progress*, January 10, 2017, available at https://thinkprogress.org/why-the-racist-history-of-school-vouchers-matters-today-c972bec8a257.

7. Philip Gleason, Melissa Clark, and Christina Tuttle, "Charter Schools: Are They Effective?" Mathematica Policy Research, 2010, available at https://www.mathematica-mpr.com/our-publications-and-findings/projects/charter-schools-are-they-effective.

8. Jitu Brown, "Charter Schools and Civil Rights," *New York Times*, October 20, 2016, p. A26.

9. David Leonhardt, "Schools That Work," *New York Times*, November 4, 2016, available at https://www.nytimes.com/2016/11/06/opinion/sunday/schools-that-work.html.

10. Philip Gleason, Melissa Clark, Christina Clark Tuttle, Emily Dwoyer, and Marsha Silverberg, "The Evaluation of Charter School Impacts: Executive Summary," June 2010, available at https://ies.ed.gov/ncee/pubs/20104029/pdf/20104030.pdf.

11. Gary Orfield, "Tenth Annual 'Brown' Lecture in Education Research: A New Civil Rights Agenda for American Education," *Educational Researcher* 43, no. 6 (2014): 273–292.

12. Journey for Justice, "Who We Are: Journey for Justice Alliance," available at https://www.j4jalliance.com/aboutj4j (accessed September 7, 2017).

13. Diane Ravitch, "The Common Core Costs Billions and Hurts Students," *New York Times*, July 23, 2016, available at https://www.nytimes.com/2016/07/24/opinion/sunday/the-common-core-costs-billions-and-hurts-students.html.

14. Ibid.

15. Lisa Dragoset, Jaime Thomas, Mariesa Herrmann, John Deke, Susanne James-Burdumy, Cheryl Graczewski, Andrea Boyle, Courtney Tanenbaum, Jessica Giffin, and Rachel Upton, *Race to the Top: Implementation and Relationship to Student Outcomes* (Washington, DC: Institute of Education Sciences, 2016); Ravitch, "The Common Core." See also Chapter 7 in Part II.

16. Emma Brown, "Obama Administration Spent Billions to Fix Failing Schools, and It Didn't Work," *Washington Post*, January 19, 2017, available at https://www.washingtonpost.com/local/education/obama-administration-spent-billions-to-fix-failing-schools-and-it-didnt-work/2017/01/19/6d24ac1a-de6d-11e6-ad42-f3375f271c9c_story.html; Dragoset et al., *Race to the Top*. See also Chapter 7 in Part II.

17. The recommendations in this section are based on data in Chapter 6 of Part II.

18. For data in this section, see Chapter 8 of Part II.

19. Diane Whitmore Schanzenbach and Lauren Bauer, "The Long-Term Impact of the Head Start Program," Brookings Institution, August 19, 2016, available at https://www.brookings.edu/research/the-long-term-impact-of-the-head-start-program.

20. Jeannie Oakes, Anna Maier, and Julia Daniel, "Community Schools: An Evidence-Based Strategy for Equitable School Improvement," Learning Policy Institute, June 5, 2017, available at https://learningpolicyinstitute.org/product/community-schools-equitable-improvement-brief.

21. Ibid.

22. Ibid.

23. Ibid.

24. Helene Clark and Robert Engle, "The Children's Aid Society Community Schools: Summary of Research Findings, 1992–1999," unpublished report for the Children's Aid Society (in authors' possession).

25. Eisenhower Foundation, *Youth Investment and Police Mentoring: The Fourth Generation* (Washington, DC, forthcoming).

26. See Blueprints for Healthy Youth Development, "Eisenhower Quantum Opportunities Program," available at http://www.blueprintsprograms.com/factsheet/eisenhower-quantum-opportunities-program (accessed September 7, 2017); National Institute of Justice, "Program File: Eisenhower Quantum Opportunities," September 8, 2015, available at http://www.crimesolutions.gov/ProgramDetails.aspx?ID=426; and National Mentoring Resource Center, "Eisenhower Quantum Opportunities," available at http://www.nationalmentoringresourcecenter.org/index.php/insight-display/105 (accessed September 7, 2017).

27. Ibid.

28. Christopher Wimer and Dan Bloom, "Boosting the Life Chances of Young Men of Color: Evidence from Promising Programs," June 2014, available at http://www.mdrc.org/sites/default/files/Young_Men_of_Color.pdf.

29. Ibid.

30. Michael D. Shear and Julie Hirschfeld Davis, "Obama Defiantly Sets an Ambitious Agenda," *New York Times*, January 21, 2015, p. A1.

Chapter 4

1. For more on the information in this chapter, see Chapter 11 in Part II.

2. National Advisory Commission on Civil Disorders, *Final Report* (Washington, DC: U.S. Government Printing Office, 1968), 260.

3. See William Julius Wilson, "Reflections on Race, Class and Cumulative Adversity," speech given at Wellesley College, April 4, 2017, available at https://www.youtube.com/watch?v=_TpQgHVxhlU; and Chapter 12 in Part II.

4. Jannell Ross, "A Rundown of Just How Badly the Fair Housing Act Has Failed," *Washington Post*, July 10, 2015, available at https://www.washingtonpost.com/news/the-fix/wp/2015/07/10/a-look-at-just-how-badly-the-fair-housing-act-has-failed/?utm_term=.8879470ae66f.

5. Richard Rothstein, "The Making of Ferguson: Public Policies at the Root of Its Troubles," Economic Policy Institute, October 15, 2014, available at http://www.epi.org/publication/making-ferguson; Richard Rothstein, *The Color of Law: A Forgotten History of How Our Government Segregated America* (New York: Liveright, 2017).

6. Rothstein, *The Color of Law*.

7. Ibid.

8. Ibid.

9. Ibid.

10. Ross, "A Rundown of Just How Badly the Fair Housing Act Has Failed."

11. Rothstein, "The Making of Ferguson."

12. National Advisory Commission on Civil Disorders, *Final Report*, 260; "Ben Carson's Warped View of Housing," *New York Times*, December 19, 2016, available at https://www.nytimes.com/2016/12/19/opinion/ben-carsons-warped-view-of-housing.html.

13. Milton S. Eisenhower Foundation and Corporation for What Works, *The Millennium Breach: Richer, Poorer and Racially Apart* (Washington, DC: Milton S. Eisenhower Foundation, 1998), available at http://www.eisenhowerfoundation.org/docs/millennium.pdf.

14. Ibid., 31.

15. Ibid., 33–39.

16. Ram Cnaan, presentation at the Eisenhower Foundation Forum on Public Morality: In Celebration of the 75th Birthday of Father Geno Baroni, Washington DC, October 24–25, 2005, available at http://www.eisenhowerfoundation.org/docs/cnaan.pdf; Lynn A. Curtis, "Lessons from The Street: Capacity Building and Replication," *Journal for Nonprofit Management* 5, no. 1 (2001), available at http://eisenhowerfoundation.org/docs/JrnlNonprfitMngmnt_LessonsfrmStreet.pdf.

17. Texas Department of Housing and Urban Affairs v. The Inclusive Communities Project, 576 U.S. ___ (2015), available at https://www.supremecourt.gov/opinions/14pdf/13-1371_8m58.pdf.

18. "Ben Carson's Warped View of Housing"; "The Supreme Court Keeps the Fair Housing Law Effective," *New York Times*, June 25, 2017, available at https://www.nytimes.com/2015/06/26/opinion/the-supreme-court-keeps-the-fair-housing-law-effective.html.

19. Richard D. Kahlenberg, "The Walls We Won't Tear Down," *New York Times*, August 3, 2017, available at https://www.nytimes.com/2017/08/03/opinion/sunday/zoning-laws-segregation-income.html.

20. Ibid.

21. "Ben Carson's Warped View of Housing"; "The Supreme Court Keeps the Fair Housing Law Effective."

22. Kahlenberg, "The Walls We Won't Tear Down."

23. For information on the program, see Alexander Polikoff, *Waiting for Gautreaux* (Evanston, IL: Northwestern University Press, 1996).

24. Milton S. Eisenhower Foundation and Corporation for What Works, *The Millennium Breach*; Kahlenberg, "The Walls We Won't Tear Down."

25. Lawrence M. O'Rourke, *Geno: The Life and Mission of Geno Baroni* (Mahwah, NJ: Paulist Press, 1991); see also Chapter 21 in Part II.

26. Jane Jacobs, *The Death and Life of Great American Cities* (New York: Random House, 2011).

Chapter 5

1. Mark Berman, "Violent Crimes and Murders Increased in 2016 for a Second Consecutive Year, FBI Says," *Washington Post*, September 25, 2017, available at https://www.washingtonpost.com/news/post-nation/wp/2017/09/25/violent-crime-increased-in-2016-for-a-second-consecutive-year-fbi-says.

2. Sentencing Project, "Criminal Justice Facts," available at http://www.sentencingproj ect.org/criminal-justice-facts (accessed September 10, 2017).

3. *Report of the National Advisory Commission on Civil Disorders* (New York: Bantam Books, 1968), 2.

4. Sentencing Project, "Criminal Justice Facts."

5. Ibid.

6. Ibid.

7. Ibid.

8. Michelle Alexander, *The New Jim Crow: Mass Incarceration in the Age of Colorblindness* (New York: New Press, 2012).

9. Sentencing Project, "Criminal Justice Facts."

10. Ibid.

11. U.S. National Advisory Commission on Civil Disorders, *Report of the National Advisory Commission on Civil Disorders* (New York: Bantam Books, 1968), 10; see also Chapter 14 in Part II.

12. *Report of the National Advisory Commission on Civil Disorders*, 8, 17, 300; see also Chapter 14 in Part II.

13. *Report of the National Advisory Commission on Civil Disorders*.

14. Milton S. Eisenhower Foundation, *To Establish Justice, to Insure Domestic Tranquility* (Washington, DC: Milton S. Eisenhower Foundation, 1999).

15. Ibid.; Bruce E. Harcourt, *Illusion of Order* (Cambridge, MA: Harvard University Press, 2001); "Moving Past 'Broken Windows' Policing," *New York Times*, August 10, 2016, available at https://www.nytimes.com/2016/08/10/opinion/moving-past-broken-windows-policing.html; Barry Friedman, "We Spend $100 Billion on Policing: We Have No Idea What Works," *Washington Post*, March 10, 2017, available at https://www.washingtonpost.com/posteverything/wp/2017/03/10/we-spend-100-billion-on-policing-we-have-no-idea-what-works.

16. John Sullivan, Reis Thebault, Julie Tate, and Jennifer Jenkins, "No Letup in Police Killings," *Washington Post*, July 2, 2017, available at https://www.pressreader.com/usa/the-washington-post-sunday/20170702/281500751271709. See also Chapter 16 in Part II.

17. Ta-Nehisi Coates, *Between the World and Me* (New York: Spiegel and Grau, 2015), 143.

18. Tony Ortega, "Black Americans Killed by Police in 2014 Outnumbered Those Who Died on 9/11," *Raw Story*, April 8, 2015, available at http://www.rawstory.com/2015/04/black-americans-killed-by-police-in-2014-outnumbered-those-who-died-on-911; "The Counted: People Killed by Police in the US," *The Guardian*, available at https://www.theguardian.com/us-news/ng-interactive/2015/jun/01/the-counted-police-killings-us-database (accessed September 10, 2017); Sullivan et al., "No Letup in Police Killings."

19. Lynh Bui and Peter Hermann, "Baltimore Officials, Justice Department Promise Sweeping Overhaul of City Police," *Washington Post*, August 10, 2016, available at https://www.washingtonpost.com/local/public-safety/baltimore-officials-justice-department-prom ises-sweeping-overhaul-of-city-police/2016/08/10/f022ded2-5e72-11e6-8e45-477372e89d78 _story.html; see also Chapter 16 in Part II.

20. Michael Zuckerman, "Criminal Injustice," *Harvard Magazine*, September–October 2017, available at https://harvardmagazine.com/2017/09/karakatsanis-criminal-justice-reform.

21. Bui and Hermann, "Baltimore Officials."

22. Ibid.; Andrew Rosenthal, "The Real Story of Race and Police Killings," *New York Times*, September 4, 2015, available at https://takingnote.blogs.nytimes.com/2015/09/04/the-real-story-of-race-and-police-killings.

23. Rosenthal, "The Real Story of Race and Police Killings"; Sheryll Cashin, "How Interracial Love Is Saving America," *New York Times*, June 3, 2017, available at https://www.nytimes.com/2017/06/03/opinion/sunday/how-interracial-love-is-saving-america.html.

24. Alexander, *The New Jim Crow*.

25. Ibid., 186.

26. Oliver Roeder, Lauren-Brooke Eisen, and Julia Bowling, "What Caused the Crime Decline?" Brennan Center for Justice, February 12, 2015, available at https://www.brennancenter.org/publication/what-caused-crime-decline.

27. Marc Mauer and David Cole, "How to Lock Up Fewer People," *New York Times*, May 24, 2015, p. SR6; Sentencing Project, "Criminal Justice Facts," available at http://www.sentenc ingproject.org/criminal-justice-facts (accessed January 9, 2017).

28. Alexander, *The New Jim Crow.*

29. Alfred Blumstein and Joel Walman, *The Crime Drop in America* (Cambridge: Cambridge University Press, 2006); Franklin Zimring, *The Great American Crime Decline* (Oxford: Oxford University Press, 2007).

30. Eisenhower Foundation, *To Establish Justice, to Insure Domestic Tranquility.*

31. Charlie Beck and Connie Rice, "How Community Policing Can Work," *New York Times*, August 12, 2016, available at https://www.nytimes.com/2016/08/12/opinion/how-com munity-policing-can-work.html.

32. John E. Eck and William Spelman, *Problem Solving: Problem Oriented Policing in Newport News* (Washington, DC: U.S. Department of Justice, 1987).

33. National Institute of Justice, "Focused Deterrence Strategies," available at https://www.crimesolutions.gov/PracticeDetails.aspx?ID=11 (accessed September 11, 2017); National Institute of Justice, "Hot Spots Policing," available at https://crimesolutions.gov/Practice Details.aspx?ID=8 (accessed September 11, 2017); David Weisburd, David Farrington, and Charlotte Gill, eds., *What Works in Crime Prevention and Rehabilitation: Lessons from Systematic Review* (New York: Springer, 2016); Thomas Blomberg, Julie Mestre Brancale, Kevin Beaver, and Williams Bales, eds., *Advancing Criminology and Criminal Justice Policy* (Abingdon, UK: Routledge, 2016).

34. Charles E. Silberman, *Criminal Violence and Criminal Justice* (New York: Random House, 1978).

35. Eisenhower Foundation, *Youth Investment and Police Mentoring: The Fourth Generation* (Washington, DC: Eisenhower Foundation, forthcoming).

36. Eisenhower Foundation, *Youth Investment and Police Mentoring* (Washington, DC: Eisenhower Foundation, 1998), available at http://www.eisenhowerfoundation.org/docs/ YIPM_opt.pdf; Eisenhower Foundation, *Youth Investment and Police Mentoring: The Third Generation* (Washington, DC: Eisenhower Foundation, 2011), available at http://www.ei senhowerfoundation.org/docs/Bluebook,%20Gen3.pdf; Barry Hillenbrand, "Kobans and Robbers," *Time*, April 20, 2001, available at http://www.eisenhowerfoundation.org/docs/Ko bansandRobbers_TIME_April20-2001.pdf.

37. Steven LaFrance, Fay Twersky, Nancy Latham, Eileen Foley, Cynthia Bott, and Linda Lee, *A Safe Place for Healthy Youth Development: A Comprehensive Evaluation of the Bayview Safe Haven* (San Francisco: BTW Consultants and LaFrance Associates).

38. Richard A. Oppel, Jr., Sheryl Gay Stolberg, and Matt Apuzzo, "Justice Department to Release Blistering Report of Racial Bias by Baltimore Police," *New York Times*, August 9, 2016, available at https://www.nytimes.com/2016/08/10/us/justice-department-to-release-blister ing-report-of-racial-bias-by-baltimore-police.html.

39. Pagan Kennedy, "Accident-Proofing the Police," *New York Times*, August 13, 2017, p. SR1.

40. Elliott Currie, personal communication to Alan Curtis, August 1, 2017.

41. Sentencing Project, "Criminal Justice Facts."

42. Ibid.

43. James Forman, Jr., "Justice Springs Eternal," *New York Times*, March 25, 2017, available at https://www.nytimes.com/2017/03/25/opinion/sunday/justice-springs-eternal.html.

44. Ibid.

45. Sentencing Project, "Criminal Justice Facts."

46. Nicholas Kristoff, "How to Win a War on Drugs," *New York Times*, September 24, 2017, p. SR1.

47. Mauer and Cole, "How to Lock Up Fewer People."

48. "Louisiana's Big Step on Justice Reform," *New York Times*, July 19, 2017, available at https://www.nytimes.com/2017/07/19/opinion/louisiana-justice-prison-reform.html.

49. Lois M. Davis, Robert Bozick, Jennifer L. Steele, Jessica Saunders, and Jeremy N. V. Miles, *Evaluating the Effectiveness of Correctional Education: A Meta-analysis of Programs That*

Provide Education to Incarcerated Adults (Santa Monica, CA: RAND, 2013); Urban Institute Justice Policy Center, "Understanding the Challenges of Prisoner Reentry: Research Findings from the Urban Institute's Prisoner Reentry Portfolio," January 2006, available at https://www .urban.org/sites/default/files/publication/42981/411289-Understanding-the-Challenges-of -Prisoner-Reentry.PDF.

50. "Let Prisoners Learn While They Serve," *New York Times*, August 16, 2017, available at https://www.nytimes.com/2017/08/16/opinion/prison-education-programs-.html.

51. Jocelyn Fontaine, Samuel Taxy, Bryce Peterson, Justin Breaux, and Shelli Rossman, *Safer Return Demonstration: Impact Findings from a Research-Based Community Reentry Initiative* (Washington, DC: Urban Institute, 2015); Richard Allen Olson, "The Safer Foundation: An In-depth Program Evaluation and Recidivism Study," master's thesis, Loyola University Chicago, 2013.

52. G. Duwe, "A Randomized Experiment of a Prisoner Reentry Program: Updated Results from an Evaluation of the Minnesota Comprehensive Offender Reentry Plan (MCORP)," *Criminal Justice Studies* 27, no. 2 (2014): 172–190; Harry J. Holzer, Going, Going . . . Gone? The Evolution of Workforce Development Programs for the Poor Since the War on Poverty," paper presented at War on Poverty conference, Ann Arbor, MI, June 12–13, 2012; Cynthia Miller, Megan Millenky, Lisa Schwartz, Lisbeth Goble, and Jillian Stein, "Building a Future: Interim Impact Findings from the YouthBuild Evaluation," November 2016, available at https://www .mdrc.org/sites/default/files/YouthBuild_Interim_Report_2016_FR.pdf.

53. Cindy Redcross, Dan Bloom, Gilda Azurdia, Janine Zweig, and Nancy Pindus, "Transitional Jobs for Ex-Prisoners: Implementation, Two-Year Impacts, and Costs of the Center for Employment Opportunities (CEO) Prisoner Reentry Program," August 2009, available at https://www.acf.hhs.gov/sites/default/files/opre/ex_prisoners.pdf.

54. See Milton S. Eisenhower Foundation and Corporation for What Works, *The Millennium Breach: Richer, Poorer and Racially Apart* (Washington, DC: Milton S. Eisenhower Foundation, 1998), available at http://www.eisenhowerfoundation.org/docs/millennium.pdf.

55. Alexander, *The New Jim Crow.*

56. Zuckerman, "Criminal Injustice."

57. Forman, "Justice Springs Eternal."

58. Ibid.

59. Paul Butler, "Why Federal Prosecutors Often Wimp Out in Going After Financial Malfeasance," *Washington Post*, August 10, 2017, available at https://www.washingtonpost .com/outlook/why-federal-prosecutors-often-wimp-out-in-going-after-financial-malfeasance/ 2017/08/10/6e6421ee-6182-11e7-8adc-fea80e32bf47_story.html. See also "Letting Dodd-Frank Die of Neglect," *New York Times*, September 8, 2017, p. A26.

Chapter 6

1. Jacob Poushter and Kristen Bialik, "Around the World, Favorability of the U.S. and Confidence in Its President Decline," Pew Research Center, June 26, 2017, available at http:// www.pewresearchcenter.org/fact-tank/2017/06/26/around-the-world-favorability-of-u-s-and -confidence-in-its-president-decline; Margaret Vice, "In Global Popularity Contest, U.S. and China—Not Russia—Vie for First," Pew Research Center, August 23, 2017, available at http:// www.pewresearch.org/fact-tank/2017/08/23/in-global-popularity-contest-u-s-and-china-not -russia-vie-for-first.

2. David J. Garrow, "When Martin Luther King Came Out against Vietnam," *New York Times*, April 4, 2017, available at https://www.nytimes.com/2017/04/04/opinion/when-martin -luther-king-came-out-against-vietnam.html.

3. Graham Allison, *Destined for War* (Boston: Houghton Mifflin Harcourt, 2017).

4. "China Issues Report on U.S. Human Rights," *Xinhua*, April 14, 2016, available at http://news.xinhuanet.com/english/2016-04/14/c_135278381.htm.

5. William Meyers, Robert Thurman, and Michael Burbank, *Man of Peace* (New York: Tibet House, 2016).

6. Tom Phillips, "In China's Far West, the 'Perfect Police State' Is Emerging," *The Guardian*, June 22, 2017, available at https://www.theguardian.com/world/2017/jun/23/in-chinas -far-west-experts-fear-a-ticking-timebomb-religious.

7. Jared Genser and Yang Jianli, "Dear President Trump: Please Let Liu Xiaobo Die as a Free Man," *Washington Post*, June 27, 2017, available at https://www.washingtonpost.com/ news/democracy-post/wp/2017/06/27/dear-president-trump-please-let-liu-xiaobo-die-as-a -free-man.

8. Julian Pecquet, "State Dept. Scoffs at Russian Criticisms of US Human Rights Record," *The Hill*, October 23, 2012, available at http://thehill.com/policy/international/263591-us-to -russian-critics-bring-it-on.

9. Cody Boutilier, "Racism Runs Deep in Russia," *National Review*, February 1, 2014, available at http://www.nationalreview.com/article/370083/racism-runs-deep-russia-cody -boutilier.

10. David Smith and Sabrina Siddiqui, "New Details of Russia Election Hacking Raise Questions about Obama's Response," *The Guardian*, June 23, 2017, available at https://www .theguardian.com/us-news/2017/jun/23/obama-cia-warning-russia-election-hack-report.

Chapter 7

1. National Advisory Commission on Civil Disorders, *Final Report* (Washington, DC: U.S. Government Printing Office, 1968), 11.

2. "What Tax Reform Could Be," *New York Times*, August 8, 2017, p. A22; David Leonhardt, "When the Rich Said No to Getting Richer," *New York Times*, September 5, 2017, p. A19; Robert Reich, "A Super-High Tax for the Super Rich? Wouldn't Be the First Time," *Christian Science Monitor*, February 16, 2011, available at https://www.csmonitor.com/Business/Robert -Reich/2011/0216/A-super-high-tax-for-the-super-rich-Wouldn-t-be-the-first-time..

3. "Yes, Tax the Super-Rich," *The Guardian*, October 12, 2017, available at https://www .theguardian.com/commentisfree/2017/oct/12/the-guardian-view-on-the-imfs-message-yes -tax-the-super-rich.

4. Jared Bernstein, "We're Going to Need More Tax Revenue: Here's How to Raise It," *American Prospect*, June 13, 2016, available at http://prospect.org/article/were-going-need -more-tax-revenue-heres-how-raise-it.

5. Ibid. See also "What Tax Reform Could Be."

6. Ibid.

7. "What Tax Reform Could Be." See also Chapter 1 in Part II.

8. "What Tax Reform Could Be." See also Chapter 1 in Part II.

9. *District of Columbia Appropriations for 1973: Hearings Before a Subcommittee of the Committee on Appropriations*, 92nd Cong. (1972) (statement of Hugh Scoot, DC Superintendent of Schools), 905.

Chapter 8

1. Eisenhower Foundation, *What Together We Can Do: A Forty Year Update of the National Advisory Commission on Civil Disorders*, 4th ed. (Washington, DC: Eisenhower Foundation, 2008), available at http://www.eisenhowerfoundation.org/docs/Kerner%2040%20 Year%20Update,%20Executive%20Summary.pdf.

2. E. J. Dionne, Jr., "The Most Consequential Question Facing the World," *Washington Post*, August 23, 2017, available at https://www.washingtonpost.com/opinions/the-most-con sequential-question-facing-the-world/2017/08/23/3d2f5514-7eb3-11e7-83c7-5bd5460f0d7e _story.html.

3. Carol Anderson, "The Politics of White Resentment," *New York Times*, August 5, 2017, available at https://www.nytimes.com/2017/08/05/opinion/sunday/white-resentment-affirma tive-action.html.

4. Lawrence O'Rourke, *Geno: The Life and Mission of Geno Baroni* (Mahwah, NJ: Paulist Press, 1991).

5. William Julius Wilson, "Reflections on Race, Class and Cumulative Adversity," speech given at Wellesley College, April 4, 2017.

6. Michael Jeffries, personal communication to Alan Curtis, September 25, 2017.

7. E. J. Dionne, Jr., Thomas E. Mann, and Norman J. Ornstein, "How Trump Is Helping to Save Our Democracy," *Washington Post*, September 22, 2017, available at https://www.washing tonpost.com/outlook/how-trump-is-helping-to-save-our-democracy/2017/09/22/539b795e -9a1f-11e7-82e4-f1076f6d6152_story.html.

8. Ibid.

9. Sheryll Cashin, "How Interracial Love Is Saving America," *New York Times*, June 3, 2017, available at https://www.nytimes.com/2017/06/03/opinion/sunday/how-interracial -love-is-saving-america.html; Will Wilkinson, "The Devil in the Diverse City," *Washington Post*, March 19, 2017, available at https://blendle.com/i/the-washington-post/the-devil-in-the -diverse-city/bnl-washingtonpost-20170319-7d1d9e41ffd.

10. A clip of the speech is available at https://www.youtube.com/watch?v=2GmZ1a5hnxo.

11. Alan Curtis, "Geno's Principles," *Salt of the Earth*, November–December 1996, available at http://www.eisenhowerfoundation.org/aboutus/baroniprinciples.html.

12. Cleve R. Wootson, Jr., "Rev. William Barber Builds a Moral Movement," *Washington Post*, June 29, 2017, available at https://www.washingtonpost.com/news/acts-of-faith/ wp/2017/06/29/woe-unto-those-who-legislate-evil-rev-william-barber-builds-a-moral-move ment.

13. Ibid.

14. Ibid.

15. Ibid. (emphasis added).

16. Derek Thompson, "The Liberal Millennial Revolution," *The Atlantic*, February 29, 2016, available at https://www.theatlantic.com/politics/archive/2016/02/the-liberal-millenni al-revolution/470826; Richard Fry, "Millennials Overtake Baby Boomers as America's Largest Generation," Pew Research Center, April 25, 2016, available at http://www.pewresearch.org/ fact-tank/2016/04/25/millennials-overtake-baby-boomers.

17. Ibid.

18. Cashin, "How Interracial Love Is Saving America."

19. Thompson. "The Liberal Millennial Revolution."

20. Ibid.

21. Catherine Rampell, "Trump's Lasting Legacy Is to Embolden an Entirely New Generation of Racists," *Washington Post*, August 14, 2017, available at https://www.washingtonpost .com/opinions/racism-isnt-dying-out/2017/08/14/058cefc8-812d-11e7-b359-15a3617c767b _story.html.

22. See AARP Foundation, "Our Work," available at http://www.aarp.org/aarp-founda tion/our-work (accessed October 13, 2017).

23. Erica Chenoweth and Jeremy Pressman, "This Is What We Learned by Counting the Women's Marches," *Washington Post*, February 7, 2017, available at https://www.washington post.com/news/monkey-cage/wp/2017/02/07/this-is-what-we-learned-by-counting-the-wom ens-marches; Laura Graham, "Five Lessons the Women's March Movement Can Learn from Black Lives Matter," *Newsweek*, February 2, 2017, available at http://www.newsweek.com/wom ens-march-can-learn-black-lives-matter-551566.

24. Kate Aronoff, "Visible and Indivisible: The Birth of a Resistance Movement," *Moyers and Company*, August 22, 2017, available at http://billmoyers.com/story/visible-indivisible -birth-resistance-movement; Kurtis Lee, "Meet Indivisible, the Young Progressives Leading the Resistance to President Trump," *Los Angeles Times*, March 26, 2017, available at http://www .latimes.com/nation/la-na-indivisible-protests-20170325-story.html.

25. Lavanya Ramanathan, "Was the Women's March Just Another Display of White Privilege? Some Think So," *Washington Post*, January 24, 2017, available at https://www.wash ingtonpost.com/lifestyle/style/was-the-womens-march-just-another-display-of-white-privi lege-some-think-so/2017/01/24/00bbdcca-e1a0-11e6-a547-5fb9411d332c_story.html; Amanda Hess, "How a Fractious Women's Movement Came to Lead the Left," *New York Times Mag-*

azine, February 7, 2017, available at https://www.nytimes.com/2017/02/07/magazine/how-a -fractious-womens-movement-came-to-lead-the-left.html; Farah Stockman, "Women's March on Washington Opens Contentious Dialogues about Race," *New York Times*, January 9, 2017, available at https://www.nytimes.com/2017/01/09/us/womens-march-on-washington-opens -contentious-dialogues-about-race.html.

26. Pew Research Center, "Clinton, Trump Supporters Have Starkly Different Views of a Changing Nation," August 18, 2016, available at http://www.people-press.org/2016/08/18/ clinton-trump-supporters-have-starkly-different-views-of-a-changing-nation.

27. Pew Research Center, "Public Support for 'Single Payer' Health Coverage Grows, Driven by Democrats," June 23, 2017, available at http://www.pewresearch.org/fact -tank/2017/06/23/public-support-for-single-payer-health-coverage-grows-driven-by-demo crats/ft_17-06-23_healthcare_responsible.

28. Pew Research Center, "Beyond Distrust: How Americans View Their Government," November 23, 2015, available at http://www.people-press.org/2015/11/23/beyond-dis trust-how-americans-view-their-government.

29. Lynn A. Curtis, "Policy for the New Millennium," in *Locked in the Poorhouse: Cities, Race, and Poverty in the United States*, ed. Fred R. Harris and Lynn A. Curtis (Boulder, CO: Rowman and Littlefield, 1998), 148–149.

30. George Monbiot, "It's Time to Tell a New Story If We Want to Change the World," *Guardian Weekly*, September 22, 2017, available at https://www.pressreader.com/uk/the-guard ian-weekly/20170922/281977492797927.

31. Joan C. Williams, "The Dumb Politics of Elite Condescension," *New York Times*, May 27, 2017, p. SR4.

32. See the organization's website, at https://www.wellstoneaction.org.

33. Thomas B. Edsall, "Where Democrats Can Find New Voters," *New York Times*, June 15, 2017, available at https://www.nytimes.com/2017/06/15/opinion/can-the-democratic-party -find-new-voters.html.

34. Wellstone, "The Wellstone Impact," available at https://www.wellstoneaction.org (accessed October 13, 2017).

35. Dionne, Mann, and Ornstein, "How Trump Is Helping."

36. Ibid.

37. Ibid.

38. National Advisory Commission on Civil Disorders, *Final Report* (Washington, DC: U.S. Government Printing Office, 1968), available at http://www.eisenhowerfoundation.org/ docs/kerner/Kerner_C15.pdf.

39. Jasper Jackson, "BBC Sets Up Team to Debunk Fake News," *The Guardian*, January 12, 2017, available at https://www.theguardian.com/media/2017/jan/12/bbc-sets-up-team-to -debunk-fake-news.

40. Margaret Sullivan, "Omidyar Network Gives $100 Million to Boost Journalism and Fight Hate Speech," *Washington Post*, April 4, 2017, available at https://www.washingtonpost .com/lifestyle/style/omidyar-charity-gives-100-million-to-boost-journalism-and-fight-hate -speech/2017/04/04/aebb013c-193d-11e7-855e-4824bbb5d748_story.html.

41. Franklin Foer, "How Silicon Valley Is Erasing Your Individuality," *Washington Post*, September 8, 2017, available at https://www.washingtonpost.com/outlook/how-silicon-val ley-is-erasing-your-individuality/2017/09/08/a100010a-937c-11e7-aace-04b862b2b3f3_story .html.

42. See the Free Press website, at http://freepress.org.

43. Dionne, Mann, and Ornstein, "How Trump Is Helping."

44. Ganesh Sitaraman, "Our Constitution Wasn't Built for This," *New York Times*, September 16, 2017, available at https://www.nytimes.com/2017/09/16/opinion/sunday/constitu tion-economy.html.

45. Celestine Bohlen, "American Democracy Is Drowning in Money," *New York Times*, September 20, 2017, available at https://www.nytimes.com/2017/09/20/opinion/democ racy-drowning-cash.html.

46. National Conference of State Legislatures, "Overview of State Laws on Public Financing," available at http://www.ncsl.org/research/elections-and-campaigns/public-financing-of-campaigns-overview.aspx (accessed October 13, 2017).

47. Ibid.

48. National Conference of State Legislatures, "*Citizens United* and the States," July 21, 2016, available at http://www.ncsl.org/research/elections-and-campaigns/citizens-united-and-the-states.aspx.

49. John Dunbar, "Analysis: How Might the 'Citizens United' Decision Be Undone?" Center for Public Integrity, March 14, 2016, available at https://www.publicintegrity.org/2016/03/14/19420/analysis-how-might-citizens-united-decision-be-undone.

50. Ibid.

51. Ibid.

52. Ibid.

53. Nancy Pelosi and John Sarbanes, "Nancy Pelosi and John Sarbanes: Reversing the Grievous Error of Citizens United," *Washington Post*, February 4, 2014, available at https://www.washingtonpost.com/opinions/nancy-pelosi-and-john-sarbanes-reversing-the-grievous-error-of-citizens-united/2014/02/04/0f197d0a-8dba-11e3-98ab-fe5228217bd1_story.html.

54. Vanita Gupta, "Defend Democracy by Restoring the Voting Rights Act," *Washington Post*, August 1, 2016, available at https://www.washingtonpost.com/opinions/defend-democracy-by-restoring-the-voting-rights-act/2016/08/01/9be58996-5756-11e6-831d-0324760ca856_story.html.

55. "On Voting Reforms, Follow Illinois, Not Texas," *New York Times*, August 31, 2017, available at https://www.nytimes.com/2017/08/31/opinion/voting-reform-illinois-texas.html.

56. Ibid.

57. Ibid.

58. "A Call to Action against Gerrymandering," *Washington Post*, September 13, 2017, available at https://www.pressreader.com/usa/the-washington-post/20170913/281968902851082.

59. Jordan Ellenberg, "The Math of Gerrymandering," *New York Times*, October 8, 2017, p. SR6.

60. Emily Bazelon, "The New Front in the Gerrymandering Wars: Democracy vs. Math," *New York Times*, August 29, 2017, available at https://www.nytimes.com/2017/08/29/magazine/the-new-front-in-the-gerrymandering-wars-democracy-vs-math.html.

61. "Time to End the Electoral College," *New York Times*, December 19, 2016, available at https://www.nytimes.com/2016/12/19/opinion/time-to-end-the-electoral-college.html.

62. E. J. Dionne, Jr., Norman J. Ornstein, and Thomas E. Mann, "Why the Majority Doesn't Rule on Guns," *Washington Post*, October 6, 2107, available at https://www.newsday.com/opinion/commentary/why-the-majority-doesn-t-rule-on-guns-1.14357343.

63. See, for example, the graphic-book trilogy by John Lewis, Andrew Ayon, and Nate Powell: *March: Book One* (Marietta, GA: Top Shelf, 2013), *March: Book Two* (Marietta, GA: Top Shelf, 2015), and *March: Book Three* (Marietta, GA: Top Shelf, 2016).

64. For more on *¡Sí Se Puede!*, see http://www.sisepuedefilm.com/pages/filmmakers.html.

PART II

Chapter 1

Acknowledgment: I am indebted to Andrew Kosenko for research assistance, to Debarati Ghosh and Eamon Kircher-Allen for editorial assistance, and to the Ford Foundation, the Bernard and Irene Schwartz Foundation, and the John D. and Catherine T. MacArthur Foundation for financial support.

1. *The Kerner Report: The 1968 Report of the National Advisory Commission on Civil Disorders* (New York: Pantheon Books, 1988), 1.

2. Ibid., 203.

3. Ibid., 483.

4. Marianne Bertrand and Sendhil Mullainathan, "Are Emily and Greg More Employable than Lakisha and Jamal? A Field Experiment on Labor Market Discrimination," National Bureau of Economic Research Working Paper 9873, July 2003, available at http://www.nber.org/papers/w9873.pdf.

5. See Joseph E. Stiglitz, *The Great Divide: Unequal Societies and What We Can Do about Them* (New York: Norton, 2015), part II.

6. Camille L. Ryan and Kurt Bauman, "Educational Attainment in the United States: 2015," March 2016, available at https://www.census.gov/content/dam/Census/library/publications/2016/demo/p20-578.pdf.

7. It deserves noting that the Kerner Report emphasized the need to desegregate poor urban neighborhoods and create more communities that are mixed; what ended up happening was quite the contrary. And when trends reversed—with gentrification of urban areas—it often did not help. Housing prices soared, and talented African Americans sometimes found themselves being displaced in the magnet schools.

8. Caroline Hoxby and Christopher Avery, "The Missing 'One-Offs': The Hidden Supply of High-Achieving, Low-Income Students," *Brookings Papers on Economic Activity*, Spring 2013, available at https://www.brookings.edu/wp-content/uploads/2016/07/2013a_hoxby.pdf.

9. Jennifer Giancola and Richard D. Kahlenberg, "Fact Sheet: True Merit," January 2016, available at http://www.jkcf.org/assets/1/7/JKCF_True_Merit_Fact_Sheet.pdf.

10. See, e.g., George A. Akerlof and Robert J. Shiller, *Phishing for Phools: The Economics of Manipulation and Deception* (Princeton, NJ: Princeton University Press, 2015).

11. The consequences of this oppression have now been traced back to Africa itself. See Nathan Nunn, "The Long-Term Effects of Africa's Slave Trades," *Quarterly Journal of Economics* 123, no. 1 (2008): 139–176. See also Graziella Bertocchi and Arcangelo Dimico, "Slavery, Education, and Inequality," *European Economic Review* 70 (2014): 197–209; and Glenn C. Loury, "An American Tragedy: The Legacy of Slavery Lingers in Our Cities' Ghettos," *Brookings Review* 16, no. 2 (1998): 38.

12. For a brief review, see Joseph E. Stiglitz, *The Price of Inequality: How Today's Divided Society Endangers Our Future* (New York: Norton, 2013).

13. Gary Solon, "Intergenerational Mobility in the Labor Market," in *Handbook of Labor Economics*, ed. Orley Ashenfelter and David Card (Amsterdam: Elsevier, 1999), 3:1761–1800; Nathan D. Grawe and Casey B. Mulligan, "Economic Interpretations of Intergenerational Correlations," *Journal of Economic Perspectives* 16, no. 3 (2002): 45–58; Sandra E. Black and Paul J. Devereux, "Recent Developments in Intergenerational Mobility," in *Handbook of Labor Economics*, ed. Orley Ashenfelter and David Card (Amsterdam: Elsevier, 2011), 4:1487–1541; Raj Chetty, Nathaniel Hendren, Patrick Kline, and Emmanuel Saez, "Where Is the Land of Opportunity? The Geography of Intergenerational Mobility in the United States," National Bureau of Economic Research Working Paper 19843, January 2014, available at http://www.nber.org/papers/w19843.pdf.

14. Jonathan Davis and Bhashkar Mazumder, "The Decline in Intergenerational Mobility after 1980," Federal Reserve Bank of Chicago Working Paper 2017-05, March 2017, available at https://www.chicagofed.org/publications/working-papers/2017/wp2017-05; Julia Isaacs, "Economic Mobility of Families across Generations," 2007, available at https://www.brookings.edu/wp-content/uploads/2016/06/11_generations_isaacs.pdf.

15. Steven Greenhouse, "Share of the Workforce in a Union Falls to a 97-Year Low, 11.3%," *New York Times*, January 23, 2013, available at http://www.nytimes.com/2013/01/24/business/union-membership-drops-despite-job-growth.html.

16. Bureau of Labor Statistics, "Table 3: Union Affiliation of Employed Wage and Salary Workers by Occupation and Industry," January 26, 2017, available at https://www.bls.gov/news.release/union2.t03.htm.

17. See the United Nations *National Accounts Main Aggregates Database*, at https://unstats.un.org/unsd/snaama/dnllist.asp.

18. See Joseph E. Stiglitz, with Nell Abernathy, Adam Hersh, Susan Holmberg, and Mike Konczal, *Rewriting the Rules of the American Economy: An Agenda for Growth and Shared*

Prosperity (New York: Norton, 2015); Mark Stelzner, "The New American Way—How Changes in Labour Law Are Increasing Inequality," *Industrial Relations Journal* 48, no. 3 (2017): 231–255.

19. See Stiglitz, *The Price of Inequality*, chap. 9.

20. Pew Research Center, "On Views of Race and Inequality, Blacks and Whites Are Worlds Apart," June 27, 2016, available at http://www.pewsocialtrends.org/2016/06/27/on -views-of-race-and-inequality-blacks-and-whites-are-worlds-apart.

21. Valerie Wilson and William M. Rodgers III, "Black-White Wage Gaps Expand with Rising Wage Inequality," Economic Policy Institute, September 20, 2016, available at http:// www.epi.org/publication/black-white-wage-gaps-expand-with-rising-wage-inequality.

22. Bureau of Labor Statistics, "Unemployment Rate: 16 to 19 Years, Black or African American," September 1, 2017, available at https://fred.stlouisfed.org/series/LNS14000018.

23. Alan B. Krueger, Judd Cramer, and David Cho, "Are the Long-Term Unemployed on the Margins of the Labor Market?" *Brookings Papers on Economic Activity*, Spring 2014, pp. 229–280, available at https://www.brookings.edu/wp-content/uploads/2016/07/2014a_Krue ger.pdf.

24. Pew Research Center, "The Rising Cost of Not Going to College," February 11, 2014, available at http://www.pewsocialtrends.org/2014/02/11/the-rising-cost-of-not-going-to-col lege.

25. Sean F. Reardon and Kendra Bischoff, "Income Inequality and Income Segregation," *American Journal of Sociology* 116, no. 4 (2011): 1092–1153.

26. Organisation for Economic Co-operation and Development, "PISA 2015: Results in Focus," 2016, available at https://www.oecd.org/pisa/pisa-2015-results-in-focus.pdf.

27. The NCLB Act was preceded by the Academic Achievement for All Act of 1999.

28. *Kerner Report*, 26.

29. City of New York, "Mayor de Blasio Announces 3-K for All," April 24, 2017, available at http://www1.nyc.gov/office-of-the-mayor/news/258-17/mayor-de-blasio-3-k-all#/0.

30. See Heckman Equation, "Early Childhood Education: Research Summary," avail- able at https://heckmanequation.org/resource/early-childhood-education-quality-and-ac cess-pay-off (accessed September 14, 2017); Heckman Equation, "Invest in Early Childhood Development: Reduce Deficits, Strengthen the Economy," available at https://heckmanequation .org/resource/invest-in-early-childhood-development-reduce-deficits-strengthen-the-econ omy (accessed September 14, 2017); Jorge Luis García, James J. Heckman, Duncan Ermini Leaf, and María José Prados, "The Life-Cycle Benefits of an Influential Early Childhood Program," Human Capital and Economic Opportunity Working Paper 2016-035, December 2016, avail- able at https://heckmanequation.org/assets/2017/01/Garcia_Heckman_Leaf_etal_2016_life-cy cle-benefits-ecp_r1-p.pdf; and James J. Heckman, "The American Family in Black and White: A Post-racial Strategy for Improving Skills to Promote Equality," National Bureau of Economic Research Working Paper 16841, March 2011, available at http://www.nber.org/papers/w16841.

31. See Federal Reserve Bank of St. Louis, "State per Capita Personal Income," available at https://fred.stlouisfed.org/release?rid=151 (accessed September 14, 2017).

32. *Kerner Report*, 457.

33. Henry J. Kaiser Family Foundation, "Uninsured Rates for the Nonelderly by Race/ Ethnicity," available at http://www.kff.org/uninsured/state-indicator/rate-by-raceethnicity/? dataView=1 (accessed September 14, 2017).

34. *Kerner Report*, 27.

35. It is worth noting that the issues of race have continued to draw the attention of many of the world's leading scientists. Gunnar Myrdal, who published a classic study of racism in America, received the Nobel Prize in 1974. See Gunnar Myrdal, *An American Dilemma: The Negro Problem and Modern Democracy* (New York: Harper, 1944). This short chapter cites the work of six other Nobel-winning economists.

36. Gary S. Becker, *The Economics of Discrimination*, 2nd ed. (Chicago: University of Chicago Press, 1971).

37. Joseph E. Stiglitz, "Approaches to the Economics of Discrimination," *American Eco- nomic Review* 63, no. 2 (1973): 287–295; George Akerlof, "The Economics of Caste and of the Rat Race and Other Woeful Tales," *Quarterly Journal of Economics* 90, no. 4 (1976): 599–617;

Kenneth Arrow, "Models of Job Discrimination," in *Racial Discrimination in Economic Life*, ed. A. H. Pascal (Lexington, MA: D. C. Health, 1972), 83–102; Kenneth Arrow, "The Theory of Discrimination," in *Discrimination in Labor Markets*, ed. Orley Ashenfelter and Albert Rees (Princeton, NJ: Princeton University Press, 1973), 3–33.

38. Dilip Abreu and Rajiv Sethi, "Evolutionary Stability in a Reputational Model of Bargaining," *Games and Economic Behavior* 44, no. 2 (2003): 195–216; George A. Akerlof and Rachel E. Kranton, "Identity and the Economics of Organizations," *Journal of Economic Perspectives* 19, no. 1 (2005): 9–32.

39. Robert D. Putnam, *Bowling Alone: The Collapse and Revival of American Community* (New York: Simon and Schuster, 2000).

40. Nilanjana Dasgupta and Anthony G. Greenwald, "On the Malleability of Automatic Attitudes: Combating Automatic Prejudice with Images of Admired and Disliked Individuals," *Journal of Personality and Social Psychology* 81, no. 5 (2001): 800–814; Partha Dasgupta, "The Economics of Social Capital," *Economic Record* 81, no. S1 (2005): S2–S21; Partha Dasgupta, "Dark Matters: Exploitation as Cooperation," *Journal of Theoretical Biology* 299 (2012): 180–187.

41. Edmund S. Phelps, "The Statistical Theory of Racism and Sexism," *American Economic Review* 62 (1972): 659–661.

42. See Joseph E. Stiglitz, "Theories of Discrimination and Economic Policy," in *Patterns of Racial Discrimination*, ed. George M. von Furstenberg, Bennett Harrison, and Ann R. Horowitz (Lexington, MA: Lexington Books, 1974), 5–26; and Arrow, "The Theory of Discrimination."

43. This literature emphasized (1) the cultural determination of preferences and beliefs and (2) the role of identity. For the former, see, e.g., Paul DiMaggio, "Culture and Cognition," *Annual Review of Sociology* 23 (1997): 263–287; Ernst Fehr and Karla Hoff, "Tastes, Castes, and Culture: The Influence of Society on Preferences," Institute for the Study of Labor Discussion Paper 5919, August 2011, available at http://federation.ens.fr/ydepot/semin/texte1011/HOF2011TAS.pdf; Karla Hoff and Priyanka Pandey, "Making Up People: The Effect of Identity on Performance in a Modernizing Society," *Journal of Development Economics* 106 (2014): 118–131; and Karla Hoff and Joseph E. Stiglitz, "Striving for Balance in Economics: Towards a Theory of the Social Determination of Behavior," *Journal of Economic Behavior and Organization* 126, no. B (2016): 25–57. For the latter, see, e.g., Claude Steele, *Whistling Vivaldi and Other Clues to How Stereotypes Affect Us* (New York: Norton, 2011); and George Akerlof and Rachel Kranton, "Economics and Identity," *Quarterly Journal of Economics* 115, no. 3 (2003): 715–753.

44. Fehr and Hoff, "Tastes, Castes, and Culture."

45. Karla Hoff and Joseph E. Stiglitz, "Equilibrium Fictions: A Cognitive Approach to Societal Rigidity," *American Economic Review* 100, no. 2 (2010): 141–146.

46. Debopam Bhattacharya and Bhashkar Mazumder, "A Nonparametric Analysis of Black-White Differences in Intergenerational Income Mobility in the United States," *Quantitative Economics* 2 (2011): 335–379; S. M. Ravi Kanbur and Joseph E. Stiglitz, "Intergenerational Mobility and Dynastic Inequality," Economic Research Program Research Memorandum 324, April 1986, available at http://www.princeton.edu/~erp/ERParchives/archivepdfs/M324.pdf.

47. Anandi Mani, Sendhil Mullainathan, Eldar Shafir, and Jiaying Zhao, "Poverty Impedes Cognitive Function," *Science*, August 30, 2013, pp. 976–980.

48. Jason Breslow, "By the Numbers: Childhood Poverty in the U.S.," *Frontline*, November 20, 2012, available at http://www.pbs.org/wgbh/frontline/article/by-the-numbers-childhood-poverty-in-the-u-s; Suzanne Macartney, "Child Poverty in the United States, 2009 and 2010: Selected Race Groups and Hispanic Origin," November 2011, available at https://www.census.gov/prod/2011pubs/acsbr10-05.pdf; Kathleen Short, "The Research Supplemental Poverty Measure: 2011," November 2012, available at https://www.census.gov/prod/2012pubs/p60-244.pdf; Carmen DeNavas-Walt, Bernadette D. Proctor, and Jessica C. Smith, "Income, Poverty, and Health Insurance Coverage in the United States: 2011," September 2012, available at https://www.census.gov/prod/2012pubs/p60-243.pdf; Sarah Fass, Kinsey Alden Dinan, and Yumiko Aratani, "Child Poverty and Intergenerational Mobility," December 2009, available at http://www.nccp.org/publications/pdf/text_911.pdf.

49. Deborah A. Cobb-Clark and Erdal Tekin, "Fathers and Youths' Delinquent Behavior," *Review of Economics of the Household* 12, no. 2 (2014): 327–358; Karen Smith and Minghua Li, "Family Structure and Child Outcomes: A High Definition, Wide Angle "Snapshot," *Review of Economics of the Household* 10, no. 3 (2012): 345–374.

50. Jonathan David Ostry, Andrew Berg, Charalambos G. Tsangarides, "Redistribution, Inequality, and Growth," International Monetary Fund Staff Discussion Notes 14/02, February 17, 2014, available at https://www.imf.org/en/Publications/Staff-Discussion-Notes/Issues/2016/12/31/Redistribution-Inequality-and-Growth-41291; Stiglitz, *The Price of Inequality*; Organisation for Economic Co-operation and Development, *In It Together: Why Less Inequality Benefits All* (Paris: OECD, 2015).

51. See Joseph E. Stiglitz, *Freefall: America, Free Markets, and the Sinking of the World Economy* (New York: Norton, 2010); and Stiglitz, *The Price of Inequality*.

52. One of the insights of behavioral economics is showing how cognition is affected by poverty, as described earlier. See Mani et al., "Poverty Impedes Cognitive Function."

53. Obviously, the extraction of natural resources can be affected by taxation. I am calling for a tax on the *natural resource rents*, on the value of the resource in excess of the cost of extraction.

54. See, e.g., Robert Jensen and Emily Oster, "The Power of TV: Cable Television and Women's Status in India," *Quarterly Journal of Economics* 124, no. 3 (2009): 1057–1094.

55. The Census Bureau estimates that whites will become a minority by 2044. See Sandra L. Colby and Jennifer M. Ortman, "Projections of the Size and Composition of the U.S. Population: 2014 to 2060," March 2015, available at https://www.census.gov/content/dam/Census/library/publications/2015/demo/p25-1143.pdf.

56. Andrea Flynn, Susan Holmberg, Dorian Warren, and Felicia Wong, "Rewrite the Racial Rules: Building an Inclusive American Economy," June 2016, available at http://roosevelt institute.org/rewrite-racial-rules-building-inclusive-american-economy.

57. These are formally called "mandatory non-military" expenditures. See Center on Budget and Policy Priorities, "Policy Basics: Non-defense Discretionary Programs," August 14, 2017, available at https://www.cbpp.org/research/policy-basics-non-defense-discretion ary-programs.

Chapter 2

Acknowledgment: I thank Ben Spielberg, Ted Lee, and Christine Kim for help with this chapter. Any mistakes are my own.

1. Stanford Center for Education Policy Analysis, "Racial and Ethnic Achievement Gaps," available at http://cepa.stanford.edu/educational-opportunity-monitoring-project/achieve ment-gaps/race (accessed September 15, 2017).

2. Edward Rodrigue and Richard V. Reeves, "Five Bleak Facts on Black Opportunity," Brookings Institution, January 15, 2015, available at https://www.brookings.edu/blog/social -mobility-memos/2015/01/15/five-bleak-facts-on-black-opportunity.

3. National Advisory Commission on Civil Disorders, *The Kerner Report* (Princeton, NJ: Princeton University Press, 2016), 14.

4. This calculation uses white education shares and black unemployment rates for each educational group; Hispanics are excluded for the analysis. If Hispanics are included, as they are in the official Bureau of Labor Statistics data (a choice that likely biases the size of the racial unemployment gap downward), differences in educational attainment explain only 11 percent of the gap.

5. Mark Paul, William Darity, Jr., and Darrick Hamilton, "Why We Need a Federal Job Guarantee," *Jacobin*, February 4, 2017, available at https://www.jacobinmag.com/2017/02/fed eral-job-guarantee-universal-basic-income-investment-jobs-unemployment.

6. Jeff Spross, "You're Hired!" *Democracy*, no. 44 (2017), available at http://democracy journal.org/magazine/44/youre-hired.

7. LaDonna Pavetti, "Subsidized Jobs: Providing Paid Employment Opportunities When the Labor Market Fails," Center on Budget and Policy Priorities, April 2, 2014, available at http://www.cbpp.org/sites/default/files/atoms/files/4-2-14fe-pavetti.pdf.

8. Indivar Dutta-Gupta, Kali Grant, Matthew Eckel, and Peter Edelman, "Lessons Learned from 40 years of Subsidized Employment Programs," Spring 2016, available at https://www.law.georgetown.edu/academics/centers-institutes/poverty-inequality/current-projects/upload/GCPI-Subsidized-Employment-Paper-20160413.pdf.

9. Jared Bernstein and Ben Spielberg, "Preparing for the Next Recession: Lessons from the American Recovery and Reinvestment Act," Center on Budget and Policy Priorities, March 21, 2016, available at http://www.cbpp.org/research/economy/preparing-for-the-next-recession-lessons-from-the-american-recovery-and.

10. The problem is the flattening of the Phillips curve—that is, the diminished correlation between labor market slack and price pressures. See Jared Bernstein, "Important New Findings on Inflation and Unemployment from the New ERP," *On the Economy* (blog), February 22, 2016, available at http://jaredbernsteinblog.com/important-new-findings-on-inflation-and-unemployment-from-the-new-erp.

11. Jared Bernstein, "Connecting a Bunch of Dots in the Interest of Racial Economic Equality," *Washington Post*, February 25, 2016, available at https://www.washingtonpost.com/posteverything/wp/2016/02/25/connecting-a-bunch-of-dots-in-the-interest-of-racial-economic-equality.

12. Jared Bernstein, "Why the Federal Reserve Should Not Raise Rates in June," *Washington Post*, June 2, 2017, available at https://www.washingtonpost.com/posteverything/wp/2017/06/02/why-the-federal-reserve-should-not-raise-rates-in-june.

13. Jason Furman, "The New View of Fiscal Policy and Its Application," paper presented at Global Implications of Europe's Redesign conference, New York, October 5, 2016, available at https://obamawhitehouse.archives.gov/sites/default/files/page/files/20161005_furman_suerf_fiscal_policy_cea.pdf.

14. Jason Furman and Krista Ruffini, "Six Examples of the Long-Term Benefits of Anti-poverty Programs," White House, May 11, 2015, available at https://obamawhitehouse.archives.gov/blog/2015/05/11/six-examples-long-term-benefits-anti-poverty-programs.

15. David Cooper, "Raising the Minimum Wage to $15 by 2024 Would Lift Wages for 41 Million American Workers," Economic Policy Institute, April 26, 2017, available at http://www.epi.org/publication/15-by-2024-would-lift-wages-for-41-million.

16. Robert Greenstein, "Strengthen Minimum Wage—and EITC," Center on Budget and Policy Priorities, May 27, 2015, available at http://www.cbpp.org/blog/strengthen-minimum-wage-and-eitc.

17. Center on Budget and Policy Priorities, "The Earned Income Tax Credit, the Child Tax Credit, and African Americans," July 21, 2015, available at http://www.cbpp.org/sites/default/files/atoms/files/7-21-15tax-factsheet1.pdf.

18. Neil Irwin, "What Would It Take to Replace the Pay Working-Class Americans Have Lost?" *New York Times*, December 9, 2016, available at https://www.nytimes.com/2016/12/09/upshot/what-would-it-take-to-replace-the-pay-working-class-americans-have-lost.html.

19. Organisation for Economic Co-operation and Development, "OECD Income Distribution Database (IDD): Gini, Poverty, Income, Methods and Concepts," available at http://www.oecd.org/social/income-distribution-database.htm (accessed September 15, 2017).

20. Hirokazu Yoshikawa and Courtney Sale Ross, "A Universal Child Allowance to Reduce Poverty and Improve Child Development," presentation for US Partnership on Mobility from Poverty Webinar, November 22, 2016, available at https://www.urban.org/events/universal-child-allowance-reduce-poverty-and-improve-child-development.

21. Peggy Bailey, Matt Broaddus, Shelby Gonzales, and Kyle Hayes, "African American Uninsured Rate Dropped by More than a Third under Affordable Care Act," Center on Budget and Policy Priorities, June 1, 2017, available at http://www.cbpp.org/research/health/african-american-uninsured-rate-dropped-by-more-than-a-third-under-affordable-care.

22. Richard Rothstein, *The Color of Law: A Forgotten History of How Our Government Segregated America* (New York: Liveright, 2017).

23. National Advisory Commission on Civil Disorders, *The Kerner Report*, 14.

24. Rothstein, *The Color of Law*, vii–viii.

25. Raj Chetty, Nathaniel Hendren, and Lawrence Katz, "The Effects of Exposure to Better Neighborhoods on Children: New Evidence from the Moving to Opportunity Experiment,"

August 2015, available at https://scholar.harvard.edu/files/hendren/files/mto_paper.pdf.

26. Barbara Sard, "The Future of Housing in America: A Better Way to Increase Efficiencies for Housing Vouchers and Create Upward Economic Mobility," Center on Budget and Policy Priorities, September 21, 2016, available at http://www.cbpp.org/housing/the-future-of-housing-in-america-a-better-way-to-increase-efficiencies-for-housing-vouchers.

27. Rothstein, *The Color of Law*, 203–204.

28. "The Economics of Early Childhood Investments," January 2015, available at https://obamawhitehouse.archives.gov/sites/default/files/docs/early_childhood_report_update_final_non-embargo.pdf.

29. Lauren Bauer and Diane Whitmore Schanzenbach, "The Long-Term Impact of the Head Start Program," Hamilton Project, August 19, 2016, available at http://www.hamiltonproject.org/papers/the_long_term_impacts_of_head_start.

30. Ben Spielberg and Jared Bernstein, "A Vision for Charter Schools That Helps, Not Hurts, Non-charters," *Washington Post*, December 22, 2016, available at https://www.washingtonpost.com/posteverything/wp/2016/12/22/a-vision-for-charter-schools-that-helps-not-hurts-non-charters.

31. Marshall Steinbaum and Kavya Vaghul, "How the Student Debt Crisis Affects African Americans and Latinos," Washington Center for Equitable Growth, February 17, 2016, available at http://equitablegrowth.org/research-analysis/how-the-student-debt-crisis-affects-african-americans-and-latinos.

32. David Reich and Chloe Cho, "Unmet Needs and the Squeeze on Appropriations," Center on Budget and Policy Priorities, May 19, 2017, available at http://www.cbpp.org/research/federal-budget/unmet-needs-and-the-squeeze-on-appropriations.

33. Isaac Shapiro, Richard Kogan, and Chloe Cho, "Trump Budget Gets Three-Fifths of Its Cuts from Programs for Low- and Moderate-Income People," Center on Budget and Policy Priorities, May 30, 2017, available at http://www.cbpp.org/research/federal-budget/trump-budget-gets-three-fifths-of-its-cuts-from-programs-for-low-and.

34. Maurice Emsellem and Jason Ziedenberg, "Strategies for Full Employment through Reform of the Criminal Justice System," Center on Budget and Policy Priorities, March 30, 2015, available at http://www.cbpp.org/research/full-employment/strategies-for-full-employment-through-reform-of-the-criminal-justice.

35. Ta-Nehisi Coates, "The Case for Reparations," *The Atlantic*, June 2014, available at https://www.theatlantic.com/magazine/archive/2014/06/the-case-for-reparations/361631.

36. Ibid.

37. Black Youth Project 100, "Agenda to Build Black Futures: Solutions," available at http://agendatobuildblackfutures.org/our-agenda/solutions (accessed September 15, 2017).

38. National Advisory Commission on Civil Disorders, *The Kerner Report*, 1 (emphasis added).

Chapter 3

1. Carl Herman, "'Remaining Awake through a Great Revolution': Dr. King's Last Sermon to You," *Washington's Blog*, January 16, 2013, available at http://www.washingtonsblog.com/2013/01/remaining-awake-through-a-great-revolution-dr-kings-last-sermon-to-you.html.

2. Lyndon B. Johnson, "Remarks at a Fundraising Dinner in New Orleans," October 9, 1964, available at http://www.presidency.ucsb.edu/ws/?pid=26585.

3. Among other things, as Johnson predicted when he signed the Civil Rights Act, the Democratic Party lost its traditional base in the South.

4. John Wihbey, "White Racial Attitudes over Time: Data from the General Social Survey," *Journalist's Resource*, August 14, 2014, available at https://journalistsresource.org/studies/society/race-society/white-racial-attitudes-over-time-data-general-social-survey.

5. "Obama's Full Remarks at Howard University Commencement Ceremony," *Politico*, May 7, 2016, available at http://www.politico.com/story/2016/05/obamas-howard-commencement-transcript-222931.

6. Valerie Wilson and William M. Rodgers III, "Black-White Wage Gaps Expand with Rising Wage Inequality," Economic Policy Institute, September 20, 2016, available at http://www.epi.org/publication/black-white-wage-gaps-expand-with-rising-wage-inequality.

7. Rebecca Tippett, Avis Jones-DeWeever, Maya Rockeymoore, Darrick Hamilton, and William Darity, Jr., "Beyond Broke: Why Closing the Racial Wealth Gap Is a Priority for National Economic Security," May 2104, available at http://globalpolicysolutions.org/wp-content/uploads/2014/04/Beyond_Broke_FINAL.pdf.

8. Richard Rothstein, "Brown v. Board at 60," Economic Policy Institute, April 17, 2014, available at http://www.epi.org/publication/brown-at-60-why-have-we-been-so-disappointed-what-have-we-learned.

9. John F. Kennedy, "Remarks of Senator John F. Kennedy, Municipal Auditorium, Canton, Ohio," September 27, 1960, available at http://www.presidency.ucsb.edu/ws/?pid=74231.

10. Leonard S. Silk, "Nixon's Program: 'I Am Now a Keynesian,'" *New York Times*, January 10, 1971, p. E1.

11. Institute for Policy Studies, "Income Inequality in the United States," available at http://inequality.org/income-inequality (accessed September 15, 2017).

12. Lawrence Mishel and Heidi Shierholz, "Robots, or Automation, Are Not the Problem: Too Little Worker Power Is," Economic Policy Institute, February 21, 2017, available at http://www.epi.org/publication/robots-or-automation-are-not-the-problem-too-little-worker-power-is.

13. Teresa Kroeger, Tanyell Cooke, and Elise Gould, "The Class of 2016: The Labor Market Is Still Far from Ideal for Young Graduates," Economic Policy Institute, April 21, 2016, available at http://www.epi.org/publication/class-of-2016.

14. With some exceptions among the building trades, unions have been well ahead of business in supporting the civil rights movement. The 1963 March on Washington was led by two African American labor leaders and largely financed by the autoworkers and other industrial unions.

15. Economic Policy Institute, "The Top Charts of 2016," December 22, 2016, available at http://www.epi.org/publication/the-top-charts-of-2016-13-charts-that-show-the-difference-between-the-economy-we-have-now-and-the-economy-we-could-have.

16. Bureau of Labor Statistics, "Occupational Employment Projections to 2022," *Monthly Labor Review*, December 2013, available at https://www.bls.gov/opub/mlr/2013/article/occupational-employment-projections-to-2022.htm.

17. Jeff Faux, *The Party's Not Over* (New York, Basic Books, 1996), 215.

18. Federal Safety Net, "U.S. Poverty Statistics," available at http://federalsafetynet.com/us-poverty-statistics.html (accessed September 15, 2017).

19. Jen Wieczner, "Most Millennials Think They'll Be Worse Off than Their Parents," *Fortune*, March 1, 2016, available at http://fortune.com/2016/03/01/millennials-worse-parents-retirement.

20. James Baldwin, "As Much Truth as One Can Bear," in *The Cross of Redemption: Uncollected Writings*, ed. Randall Kenan (New York: Vintage, 2011), 42.

21. Bruce Drake, "Polls Show Strong Support for Minimum Wage Hike," Pew Research Center, March 4, 2014, available at http://www.pewresearch.org/fact-tank/2014/03/04/polls-show-strong-support-for-minimum-wage-hike/; Ariel Edwards-Levy, "Raising the Minimum Wage Is a Really, Really Popular Idea," *Huffington Post*, April 13, 2016, available at http://www.huffingtonpost.com/entry/minimum-wage-poll_us_570ead92e4b08a2d32b8e671.

Chapter 4

1. National Advisory Commission on Civil Disorders, *The Kerner Report* (Princeton, NJ: Princeton University Press, 2016), 416, 392.

2. Carmen Williams, e-mail to the author, May 30, 2014.

3. National Council of Young Leaders, "Recommendations to Increase Opportunity and Decrease Poverty in America," August 2016, available at https://oyunited.org/sites/default/files/download/Recommendations.final.August.2016.pdf.

4. National Advisory Commission on Civil Disorders, *Kerner Report*, 108.

5. Ibid., 25.

6. Sarah Burd-Sharps and Kristen Lewis, "Promising Gains, Persistent Gaps: Youth Disconnection in America," March 2017, available at https://ssrc-static.s3.amazonaws.com/moa/Promising%20Gains%20Final.pdf.

7. Andrew Hahn, Thomas D. Leavitt, Erin M. Horvat, and James E. Davis, *Life after YouthBuild: 900 YouthBuild Graduates Reflect on Their Lives, Dreams, and Experiences* (Somerville, MA: YouthBuild USA, 2004).

8. John M. Bridgeland, Erin S. Ingram, and Matthew Atwell, "A Bridge to Reconnection: A Plan for Reconnecting One Million Opportunity Youth Each Year through Federal Funding Streams," September 2016, available at http://aspencommunitysolutions.org/wp-content/uploads/2017/06/BridgetoReconnection.2016.pdf.

9. Corps Network, "FY16 Annual Report," 2017, available at http://www.corpsnetwork.org/sites/default/images/blog%20posts/2017/2-February/Annual%20Report_FY16_FINAL.pdf.

10. National Guard Youth Foundation, "About Challenge," available at http://www.ngyf.org/about-challenge-2 (accessed December 1, 2017).

11. Bridgeland, Ingram, and Atwell, "A Bridge to Reconnection," 18.

12. Ibid.

13. Ibid.

14. Ibid., 9.

15. Louisa Treskon, "What Works for Disconnected Young People: A Scan of the Evidence," MDRC Working Paper, February 2016, available at http://www.mdrc.org/sites/default/files/What_works_for-disconnected_young_people_WP.pdf.

16. Bridgeland, Ingram, and Atwell, "A Bridge to Reconnection," 12.

17. Clive R. Belfield, Henry M. Levin, and Rachel Rosen, "The Economic Value of Opportunity Youth," January 2012, available at http://www.civicenterprises.net/MediaLibrary/Docs/econ_value_opportunity_youth.pdf.

18. Eric Foner and John Arthur Garraty, *The Reader's Companion to American History* (New York: Houghton Mifflin, 1991).

19. Gary Halbert, "Almost Six Million Unfilled Jobs in America—Question Is Why?" *Advisor Perspectives*, September 14, 2016, available at https://www.advisorperspectives.com/commentaries/2016/09/14/almost-six-million-unfilled-jobs-in-america-question-is-why.

20. Reuters, "What's Holding Back the Housing Market? Not Enough Construction Workers," *Fortune*, September 5, 2016, available at https://fortune.com/2016/09/06/housing-construction-worker-shortage.

21. See the initiative's website, at https://www.100kopportunities.org.

22. John B. King, Jr., and Art Peck, "A Double Bottom Line Investment for Companies: Giving Young People Their First Jobs," *Linkedin*, March 10, 2016, available at https://www.linkedin.com/pulse/double-bottom-line-investment-companies-giving-young-people-john-king?published=t.

23. E. Ann Carson and Elizabeth Anderson, "Prisoners in 2015," December 2016, p. 13, available at https://www.bjs.gov/content/pub/pdf/p15.pdf.

24. Michelle Alexander, *The New Jim Crow: Mass Incarceration in the Age of Colorblindness* (New York: New Press, 2012).

25. See Mike Dean, *What If I Had A Father? The Man I Never Knew* (Columbus, OH: DeanBooks, 2015).

26. Ely Flores, "From a Gang Lifestyle to a Life of Community Activism," June 10, 2008, available at https://judiciary.house.gov/wp-content/uploads/2008/06/Flores080610.pdf.

27. Antoine Bennett, remarks at a meeting with the staff of congressman Newt Gingrich, Washington, DC, 1996.

28. National Advisory Commission on Civil Disorders, *Kerner Report*, 23.

29. Center for Information and Research on Civic Learning and Engagement, "Pathways into Leadership: A Study of YouthBuild Graduates," 2012, available at http://civicyouth.org/wp-content/uploads/2012/05/YouthBuild.pdf.

30. Cynthia Miller, Megan Millenky, Lisa Schwartz, Lisbeth Goble, and Jillian Stein, "Building a Future: Interim Impact Findings from the YouthBuild Evaluation," November 2016, available at https://www.mdrc.org/sites/default/files/YouthBuild_Interim_Report_2016_508 .pdf.

31. Bernadette D. Proctor, Jessica L. Semega, and Melissa A. Kollar, "Income and Poverty in the United States: 2015," September 2016, available at https://www.census.gov/content/dam/ Census/library/publications/2016/demo/p60-256.pdf.

Chapter 5

1. James D. Chesney, Herbert C. Smitherman, Cynthia Taueg, Jennifer Mach, and Lucille Smith, *Taking Care of the Uninsured* (Detroit, MI: Wayne State University, 2008), 36.

2. R. Chetty, M. Stepner, S. Abraham, S. Lin, B. Scuderi, N. Turner, A. Bergeron, and D. Cutler, "The Association between Income and Life Expectancy in the United States, 2001–2014," *JAMA* 315, no. 16 (2016): 1750–1766.

3. "Focus: HOPE Consumer Survey on Food and Drugs," September 1968, Focus: HOPE Collection: Records, Walter P. Reuther Library of Labor and Urban Affairs, Wayne State University, Detroit, MI; Gary Lonston, "Detroit Poor Charged More," *Detroit Free Press*, September 5, 1968, p. 2-A.

4. Kameshwari Pothukuchi, Rayman Mohamed, and David A. Gebben, "Explaining Disparities in Food Safety Compliance by Food Stores: Does Community Matter?" *Agriculture and Human Values* 25, no. 3 (2008): 319–332.

5. David R. Williams and Valerie Purdie-Vaughns, "Social and Behavioral Interventions to Improve Health and Reduce Disparities in Health," Agency for Healthcare Research and Quality, August 2015, available at http://www.ahrq.gov/professionals/education/curric ulum-tools/population-health/williams.html; J. E. Dalton, A. T. Perzynski, D. A. Zidar, M. B. Rothberg, C. J. Coulton, A. T. Milinovich, D. Einstadter, J. K. Karichu, and N. V. Dawson, "Accuracy of Cardiovascular Risk Prediction Varies by Neighborhood Socioeconomic Position: A Retrospective Cohort Study," *Annals of Internal Medicine* 167, no. 7 (2017): 456–464.

6. National Head Start Association, "About Us: Mission, Vision, History," available at https://www.nhsa.org/about-us/mission-vision-history (accessed July 29, 2017).

7. Frances Campbell, Gabriella Conti, James J. Heckman, Seong Hyeok Moon, Rodrigo Pinto, Elizabeth Pungello, and Yi Pan, "Early Childhood Investments Substantially Boost Adult Health," *Science* 343, no. 6178 (2014): 1478–1485.

8. National Head Start Association, "Head Start Facts and Impacts," available at https:// www.nhsa.org/facts-and-impacts# (accessed July 29, 2017).

9. U.S. Department of Agriculture, "Food Security in the U.S.: Overview," September 6, 2017, available at https://www.ers.usda.gov/topics/food-nutrition-assistance/food-security -in-the-us.

10. Center on Budget and Policy Priorities, "Policy Basics: Introduction to the Supplemental Nutrition Assistance Program (SNAP)," March 24, 2016, available at https://www.cbpp.org/ research/policy-basics-introduction-to-the-supplemental-nutrition-assistance-program-snap.

11. U.S. Department of Agriculture, "Measuring the Effect of Supplemental Nutrition Assistance Program (SNAP) Participation on Food Security (Summary)," August 2013, available at https://fns-prod.azureedge.net/sites/default/files/Measuring2013Sum.pdf; Dorothy Rosenbaum, "The Relationship between SNAP and Work among Low-Income Households," January 2013, available at https://www.cbpp.org/sites/default/files/atoms/files/1-29-13fa.pdf.

12. Centers for Disease Control and Prevention, "Earned Income Tax Credits," June 22, 2017, available at https://www.cdc.gov/policy/hst/hi5/taxcredits/index.html; Nicole L. Hair, Jamie L. Hanson, Barbara L. Wolfe, and Seth D. Pollak, "Association of Child Poverty, Brain Development, and Academic Achievement," *JAMA Pediatrics* 169, no. 9 (2015): 822–829, available at http://jamanetwork.com/journals/jamapediatrics/fullarticle/2381542.

13. National Center for Children in Poverty, "Child Poverty," available at http://nccp.org/ topics/childpoverty.html (accessed July 30, 2017).

14. Adrienne Lu, "Head Start Hit with Worst Cuts in Its History," *USA Today*, August 19, 2013, available at https://www.usatoday.com/story/news/nation/2013/08/19/stateline-head -start/2671309; Robert Greenstein, Richard Kogan, and Isaac Shapiro, "Low-Income Programs Not Driving Nation's Long-Term Fiscal Problem," Center on Budget and Policy Priorities, February 21, 2017, available at http://www.cbpp.org/cms/?fa=view&id=3772; Isaac Shapiro and Richard Kogan, "Congressional Budget Plans Get Two-Thirds of Cuts from Programs for People with Low or Moderate Incomes," Center on Budget and Policy Priorities, July 2, 2015, available at https://www.cbpp.org/research/federal-budget/congressional-budget-plans-get -two-thirds-of-cuts-from-programs-for-people.

15. Kerner Commission, *Report of the National Advisory Commission on Civil Disorders* (Washington, DC: U.S. Government Printing Office, 1968), 1; see also "'Our Nation Is Moving toward Two Societies, One Black, One White—Separate and Unequal': Excerpts from the Kerner Report," History Matters, available at http://historymatters.gmu.edu/d/6545 (accessed July 16, 2017).

16. Bill McGraw, "Riot or Rebellion? The Debate on What to Call Detroit '67," Detroit Free Press, July 4, 2017, available at http://www.freep.com/story/news/2017/07/05/50-years-later -riot-rebellion/370968001; H. Smitherman, presentation at the National Congressional Black Caucus, Washington DC, September 25, 2008.

17. Wayne J. Riley, "Health Disparities: Gaps in Access, Quality and Affordability of Medical Care," *Transactions of the American Clinical and Climatological Association* 123 (2012): 167–174, available at https://www.ncbi.nlm.nih.gov/pmc/articles/PMC3540621.

18. Sandra L. Colby and Jennifer M. Ortman, "Projections of the Size and Composition of the U.S. Population: 2014 to 2060 Population Estimates and Projections," March 2015, available at https://www.census.gov/content/dam/Census/library/publications/2015/demo/ p25-1143.pdf; U.S. Department of Health and Human Services, "Disparities in Healthcare Quality among Racial and Ethnic Minority Groups: Selected Findings from the 2010 National Healthcare Quality and Disparities Reports," October 2014, available at http://archive.ahrq .gov/research/findings/nhqrdr/nhqrdr10/minority.html.

19. U.S. Department of Health and Human Services, *Health, United States, 2016* (Washington, DC: U.S. Government Printing Office, 2017).

20. Federal Interagency Forum on Child and Family Statistics, "Infant Mortality: Death Rates among Infants by Detailed Race and Hispanic Origin of Mother, 1983–2014," available at https://www.childstats.gov/americaschildren/tables/health2.asp (accessed July 29, 2017).

21. S. Jay Olshansky, Toni Antonucci, Lisa Berkman, Robert H. Binstock, Axel Boersch-Supan, John T. Cacioppo, Bruce A. Carnes, Laura L. Carstensen, Linda P. Fried, Dana P. Goldman, James Jackson, Martin Kohli, John Rother, Yuhui Zheng, and John Rowe, "Differences in Life Expectancy due to Race and Educational Differences Are Widening, and Many May Not Catch Up," *Health Affairs* 31, no. 8 (2012): 1803–1813.

22. U.S. Department of Health, Education, and Welfare, *Vital Statistics of the United States, 1967*, vol. 2, *Mortality* (Washington, DC: U.S. Government Printing Office, 1969).

23. Ibid.

24. U.S. Department of Health, Education, and Welfare, "Section 5: Life Tables," in *Vital Statistics of the United States*, vol. 2, *Mortality* (Washington, DC: U.S. Government Printing Office, 1969), available at https://www.cdc.gov/nchs/products/life_tables.htm; D. L. Hoyert, "75 Years of Mortality in the United States, 1935–2010," *NCHS Data Brief*, no. 88 (2012): 1–8; Marian F. MacDorman and T. J. Mathews, "Understanding Racial and Ethnic Disparities in U.S. Infant Mortality Rates," *NCHS Data Brief*, no. 74 (2011), available at http://www.cdc.gov/ nchs/data/databriefs/db74.htm; Elizabeth Arias, "United States Life Tables, 2009," *National Vital Statistics Reports* 62, no. 7 (2014), available at https://www.cdc.gov/nchs/data/nvsr/nvsr62/ nvsr62_07.pdf.

25. Gopal K. Singh, "Maternal Mortality in the United States, 1935–2007: Substantial Racial/Ethnic, Socioeconomic, and Geographic Disparities Persist," 2010, available at https:// www.hrsa.gov/ourstories/mchb75th/mchb75maternalmortality.pdf.

26. Timothy J. Cunningham, Janet B. Croft, Yong Liu, Hua Lu, Paul I. Eke, Wayne H. Giles, "Vital Signs: Racial Disparities in Age-Specific Mortality among Blacks or African

Americans—United States, 1999–2015," *Morbidity and Mortality Weekly Report* 66, no. 17 (2017): 444–456.

27. Stephanie A. Bond Huie, Patrick M. Krueger, Richard G. Rogers, Robert A. Hummer, "Wealth, Race, and Mortality," *Social Science Quarterly* 84, no. 3 (2003): 667–684, available at https://www.researchgate.net/publication/229458604_Wealth_Race_and_Mortality.

28. Ryan *Very*, "Black Capitalism: An Economic Program for the Black American Ghetto," *International Journal of Humanities and Social Science* 2, no. 22 (2012): 53–63; Tami Luhby, "The Black-White Economic Divide in 5 Charts," *CNN Money*, November 25, 2015, available at http://money.cnn.com/2015/11/24/news/economy/blacks-whites-inequality; Jeffrey M. Humphreys, "The Multicultural Economy, 2008," 2008, available at http://media.terry.uga .edu/documents/selig/buying_power_2008.pdf.

29. Michael W. Byrd and Linda A. Clayton, "An American Health Dilemma: A History of Blacks in the Health System," *Journal of the National Medical Association* 84, no. 2 (1992): 189–200.

30. Michael Marmot, G. Rose, M. Shipley, and P. J. Hamilton, "Employment Grade and Coronary Heart Disease in British Civil Servants," *Journal of Epidemiology and Community Health* 32, no. 4 (1978): 244–249; M. G. Marmot, G. Davey Smith, S. Stansfeld, C. Patel, F. North, J. Head, I. White, E. Brunner, and A. Feeney, "Health Inequalities among British Civil Servants: The Whitehall II Study," *Lancet* 337, no. 8754 (1991): 1387–1393.

31. U.S. Department of Health, Education, and Welfare, "Section 5: Life Tables"; Hoyert, "75 Years of Mortality in the United States."

32. James L. Curtis, *Affirmative Action in Medicine: Improving Healthcare for Everyone* (Ann Arbor: University of Michigan Press, 2006).

33. U.S. Department of Health and Human Services, *Healthy People, 2010: Final Review* (Washington, DC: U.S. Government Printing Office, 2012); U.S. Department of Health and Human Services, *2005 National Healthcare Disparities Report* (Rockville, MD: Agency for Healthcare Research and Quality, 2005), available at https://archive.ahrq.gov/qual/nhdr05/ nhdr05.pdf. See also U.S. Department of Health and Human Services, "Disparities," *Healthy People, 2020*, November 21, 2017, available at https://www.healthypeople.gov/2020/about/foun dation-health-measures/disparities; and U.S. Department of Health and Human Services, *2016 National Healthcare Quality and Disparities Report* (Rockville, MD: Agency for Healthcare Research and Quality, 2017), available at https://www.ahrq.gov/sites/default/files/wysiwyg/ research/findings/nhqrdr/nhqdr16/final2016qdr.pdf.

34. Centers for Medicare and Medicaid Services, "NHE Fact Sheet," June 14, 2017, avail- able at https://www.cms.gov/research-statistics-data-and-systems/statistics-trends-and-re ports/nationalhealthexpenddata/nhe-fact-sheet.html; David Squires and Chloe Anderson, "U.S. Health Care from a Global Perspective: Spending, Use of Services, Prices, and Health in 13 Countries," Commonwealth Fund, October 8, 2015, available at http://www.common wealthfund.org/publications/issue-briefs/2015/oct/us-health-care-from-a-global-perspec tive.

35. Darrell J. Gaskin and Patrick Richard, "The Economic Costs of Pain in the United States," *Journal of Pain* 13, no. 8 (2012): 715–724.

36. Henry J. Kaiser Family Foundation, "Key Facts about the Uninsured Population," Sep- tember 19, 2017, available at http://www.kff.org/uninsured/fact-sheet/key-facts-about-the-un insured-population.

37. Kevin Griffith, Leigh Evans, and Jacob Bor, "The Affordable Care Act Reduced So- cioeconomic Disparities in Health Care Access," *Health Affairs* 36, no. 8 (2017): 1503–1510.

38. "Obamacare Repeal: Graham-Cassidy Health Care Bill Gains Traction," *Vox*, June 25, 2015, available at https://www.vox.com/2017/1/5/14179258/obamacare-repeal-republi can-votes-trump; Tami Luhby, "'Skinny Repeal' of Obamacare Would Wreck the Insurance Market," *CNN Money*, July 27, 2017, available at http://money.cnn.com/2017/07/26/news/econ omy/senate-obamacare-skinny-repeal/index.html.

39. Herbert C. Smitherman, Jr., "Congressional Cuts Harmful to Healthcare," *Michigan Chronicle*, May 24, 2017, available at https://michronicleonline.com/2017/05/24/congressio nal-cuts-harmful-to-healthcare.

40. Andrew Prokop, "Trump Promised Not to Cut Medicaid; His Health Bill Will Cut $880 Billion from It," *Vox*, March 13, 2017, available at https://www.vox.com/2017/3/13/14914812/trump-ahca-medicaid-cuts.

41. U.S. Census Bureau, "U.S. and World Population Clock," available at https://www.census.gov/popclock (accessed July 28, 2017).

42. See U.S. Department of Health and Human Services, "Determinants of Health," *Healthy People, 2020*, November 21, 2017, available at https://www.healthypeople.gov/2020/about/foundation-health-measures/determinants-of-health; Commission on Social Determinants of Health, "Health Equity through Action on the Social Determinants of Health," 2008, available at http://apps.who.int/iris/bitstream/10665/69832/1/WHO_IER_CSDH_08.1_eng.pdf; and Richard Wilkinson and Michael Marmot, eds., *Social Determinants of Health: The Solid Facts*, 2nd ed. (Copenhagen: World Health Organization, 2003), available at http://www.euro.who.int/__data/assets/pdf_file/0005/98438/e81384.pdf.

43. See Amy Gutman, "Failing Economy, Failing Health," *Harvard Public Health*, available at https://www.hsph.harvard.edu/magazine/magazine_article/failing-economy-failing-health (accessed November 12, 2017); John Irons, "Economic Scarring: The Long-Term Impacts of the Recession," Economic Policy Institute, September 30, 2009, available at http://www.epi.org/publication/bp243; and Claire Conway, "Poor Health: When Poverty Becomes Disease," January 06, 2016, available at https://www.ucsf.edu/news/2016/01/401251/poor-health.

44. Martin Luther King, Jr., *The Words of Martin Luther King Jr.*, ed. Coretta Scott King, 2nd ed. (New York: Newmarket Press, 2008).

Chapter 6

1. *Report of the National Advisory Commission on Civil Disorders* (New York: Bantam Books, 1968), 1.

2. Ibid., 398.

3. Linda Darling-Hammond, *The Flat World and Education: How America's Commitment to Equity Will Determine Our Future* (New York: Teachers College Press, 2010).

4. Sean F. Reardon, Joseph P. Robinson-Cimpian, and Ericka S. Weathers, "Patterns and Trends in Racial/Ethnic and Socioeconomic Academic Achievement Gaps," in *Handbook of Research in Education Finance and Policy*, 2nd ed., ed. Helen F. Ladd and Margaret E. Goertz (New York: Routledge, 2015), 491–509.

5. U.S. Department of Health and Human Services, "Information on Poverty and Income Statistics: A Summary of 2012 Current Population Survey Data," September 12, 2012, available at http://aspe.hhs.gov/hsp/12/PovertyAndIncomeEst/ib.cfm.

6. Southern Education Foundation, "A New Majority: Low Income Students Now a Majority in the Nation's Public Schools," January 2015, available at http://www.southerneducation.org/getattachment/4ac62e27-5260-47a5-9d02-14896ec3a531/A-New-Majority-2015-Update-Low-Income-Students-Now.aspx.

7. Bruce D. Baker, David G. Sciarra, and Danielle Farrie, *Is School Funding Fair? A National Report Card* (Newark, NJ: Education Law Center, 2015).

8. Emmanuel Saez and Gabriel Zucman, "Wealth Inequality in the United States since 1913: Evidence from Capitalized Income Tax Data," National Bureau of Economic Research Working Paper 20625, October 2014, available at http://socialprotectionet.org/sites/default/files/saezzucman2014.pdf.

9. Kendra Bischoff and Sean F. Reardon, "Residential Segregation by Income: 1970–2009," in *Diversity and Disparities: America Enters a New Century*, ed. John R. Logan (New York: Russell Sage Foundation, 2014), 208–234.

10. Richard Fry and Paul Taylor, "The Rise of Residential Segregation by Income," Pew Research Center, August 1, 2012, available at http://www.pewsocialtrends.org/2012/08/01/the-rise-of-residential-segregation-by-income.

11. Richard Florida, "The U.S. Cities with the Highest Levels of Income Segregation," *Citylab*, March 18, 2014, available at https://www.citylab.com/life/2014/03/us-cities-highest-levels-income-segregation/8632.

12. Janie Boschma and Ronald Brownstein, "The Concentration of Poverty in American Schools," *The Atlantic*, February 29, 2016, available at https://www.theatlantic.com/education/archive/2016/02/concentration-poverty-american-schools/471414.

13. Ibid.; National Equity Atlas, "Indicators: School Poverty, United States," available at http://nationalequityatlas.org/indicators/School_poverty/By_race~ethnicity%3A35576 (accessed September 19, 2017).

14. National Center for Education Statistics, "Public Elementary/Secondary School Universe Survey Data," available at https://nces.ed.gov/ccd/pubschuniv.asp (accessed September 19, 2017); Gary Orfield, *Public School Desegregation in the United States, 1968–1980* (Washington, DC: Joint Center for Political Studies, 1983).

15. Orfield, *Public School Desegregation.*

16. Boschma and Brownstein, "The Concentration of Poverty in American Schools."

17. American Educational Research Association, amicus curiae brief filed in Parents Involved in Community Schools v. Seattle School District No. 1, 127 S. Ct. 2738 (2007), available at http://www.aera.net/Portals/38/docs/News_Media/AERABriefings/RaceConsciousSchool/AERA_Amicus_Brief.pdf.

18. Rucker C. Johnson, "Long-Run Impacts of School Desegregation and School Quality on Adult Attainments," National Bureau of Economic Research Working Paper 16664, January 2011, available at http://www.nber.org/papers/w16664.pdf.

19. U.S. Census Bureau, "Population Characteristics (P-20)," in *Current Population Survey* (Washington, DC: U.S. Department of Commerce), available at https://www.census.gov/prod/www/population.html.

20. Jeannie Oakes, Anna Maier, and Julia Daniel, "Community Schools: An Evidence-Based Strategy for Equitable School Improvement," Learning Policy Institute, June 5, 2017, available at https://learningpolicyinstitute.org/product/community-schools-equitable-improvement-brief.

21. National Center for Education Statistics, "The Nation's Report Card: NAEP 2012; Trends in Academic Progress," 2013, available at https://nces.ed.gov/nationsreportcard/subject/publications/main2012/pdf/2013456.pdf. See also Thomas D. Snyder and Sally A. Dillow, *Digest of Education Statistics, 2013* (Washington, DC: National Center for Education Statistics, 2015), table 222.85.

22. National Center for Education Statistics, "The Nation's Report Card." See also Snyder and Dillow, *Digest of Education Statistics, 2013*, table 221.85.

23. Jonathan Kozol, *Savage Inequalities* (New York: Crown, 1991).

24. National Center for Education Statistics, "Trends in High School Dropout and Completion Rates in the United States," table 4.2, available at https//nces.ed.gov/programs/dropout/ind_04.asp (accessed September 19, 2017).

25. U.S. Department of Education, *Consolidated State Performance Report, 2014–2015* (Washington, DC: U.S. Department of Education), available at https://www2.ed.gov/admins/lead/account/consolidated/index.html#sy14-15. See also Thomas D. Snyder, Cristobal de Brey, and Sally A. Dillow, *Digest of Education Statistics, 2015* (Washington, DC: National Center for Education Statistics, 2016), table 219.46, available at https://nces.ed.gov/pubs2016/2016014.pdf.

26. Snyder, de Brey, and Dillow, *Digest of Education Statistics, 2015*, table 302.60.

27. U.S. Census Bureau, "Table A-2: Percent of People 25 Years and Over Who Have Completed High School or College, by Race, Hispanic Origin and Sex, Selected Years 1940 to 2015," November 29, 2016, available at https://www.census.gov/data/tables/time-series/demo/educational-attainment/cps-historical-time-series.html.

28. Linda Darling-Hammond, Dion Burns, Carol Campbell, A. Lin Goodwin, Karen Hammerness, Ee-Ling Low, Ann McIntyre, Mistilina Sato, and Kenneth Zeichner, *Empowered Educators: How High-Performing Systems Shape Teaching Quality around the World* (San Francisco, CA: Jossey-Bass, 2017).

29. Frank Adamson and Linda Darling-Hammond, "Funding Disparities and the Inequitable Distribution of Teachers: Evaluating Sources and Solutions," *Education Policy Analysis Archives* 20, no. 37 (2012), available at http://epaa.asu.edu/ojs/article/view/1053/1024.

30. Baker, Sciarra, and Farrie, *Is School Funding Fair?*

31. For a summary, see Darling-Hammond, *The Flat World and Education.*

32. Charles T. Clotfelter, Helen F. Ladd, and Jacob L. Vigdor, "How and Why Do Teacher Credentials Matter for Student Achievement?" National Bureau of Economic Research Working Paper 12828, January 2007, available at http://www.nber.org/papers/w12828.pdf.

33. Motoko Akiba, Gerald LeTendre, and Jay Scribner, "Teacher Quality, Opportunity Gap, and National Achievement in 46 Countries," *Educational Researcher* 36 (2007): 369–387.

34. Darling-Hammond et al., *Empowered Educators*.

35. See Darling-Hammond, *The Flat World and Education*; and Linda Darling-Hammond and Titilayo Tinubu Ali, "How School Investments Matter for Educational Outcomes: Insights from School Finance and Governance Reforms," *American Journal of Education*, forthcoming.

36. Journey for Justice, "Who We Are: Journey for Justice Alliance," available at https://www.j4jalliance.com/aboutj4j (accessed September 7, 2017).

37. Ibid.

38. See Darling-Hammond, *The Flat World and Education*.

39. See Oakes, Maier, and Daniel, *Community Schools*.

40. See Darling-Hammond, *The Flat World and Education*.

41. See National Equity Atlas, "Indicators."

Chapter 7

1. National Advisory Commission on Civil Disorders, *The Kerner Report* (Princeton, NJ: Princeton University Press, 2016), 208.

2. Ibid., 425.

3. Ibid., 426.

4. Ibid.

5. Ibid., 436.

6. Ibid., 26.

7. Diane Ravitch, *The Troubled Crusade: American Education, 1945–1980* (New York: Basic Books, 1983), 163–167.

8. Ibid., 176.

9. Nikole Hannah-Jones, "Lack of Order: The Erosion of a Once-Great Force for Integration," *ProPublica*, May 1, 2014, available at https://www.propublica.org/article/lack-of-order -the-erosion-of-a-once-great-force-for-integration.

10. Ibid.

11. Ibid.

12. Emma Brown, "Judge: Mostly White Southern City May Secede from School District Despite Racial Motive," *Washington Post*, April 27, 2017, available at https://www.washing tonpost.com/local/education/judge-says-mostly-white-southern-city-may-secede-from-its -school-district--even-though-the-effort-has-attacked-dignity-of-black-school-children/ 2017/04/26/4d654232-2a89-11e7-b605-33413c691853_story.html.

13. Gary Orfield, Jongyeon Ee, Erica Frankenburg, and Genevieve Siegel-Hawley, "*Brown* at 62: School Segregation by Race, Poverty and State," May 16, 2016, p. 2, available at https://www.civilrightsproject.ucla.edu/research/k-12-education/integration-and-diversity/brown -at-62-school-segregation-by-race-poverty-and-state/Brown-at-62-final-corrected-2.pdf.

14. Ibid., 1.

15. See a summary of Rucker Johnson's research in Diane Ravitch, *Reign of Error: The Hoax of the Privatization Movement and the Danger to America's Public Schools* (New York: Knopf, 2013), 295–296.

16. Richard Rothstein, *The Color of Law: A Forgotten History of How Our Government Segregated America* (New York: Liveright, 2017).

Chapter 8

Acknowledgments: I gratefully acknowledge the assistance of several colleagues at Child Trends: Maryjo Oster for her close collaboration and help in shaping the direction of this chapter; Tyler McDaniel and Heather Steed for gathering, analyzing, and checking data and sources; Kristen Harper for contributions to the discussion of school discipline; and David Murphey, Kristine Andrews, and Jody Franklin for their careful reviews.

1. National Advisory Commission on Civil Disorders, "Report of the National Advisory Commission on Civil Disorders: Summary of Report," available at http://www.eisenhower foundation.org/docs/kerner.pdf (accessed September 20, 2017).

2. The U.S. Census did not distinguish between Hispanic and non-Hispanic white children before 1974. The term "white" in this chapter refers specifically to non-Hispanic whites.

3. The first year for which data on Hispanic youth are available in the U.S. Census Historical Poverty Tables is 1976.

4. Federal Interagency Forum on Child and Family Statistics, "America's Children: Key National Indicators of Well-Being, 2017," table POP1, table POP3, available at http://www .childstats.gov/americaschildren/tables.asp (accessed September 20, 2017).

5. The first year for which data on Asian youth are available in the U.S. Census Historical Poverty Tables is 1988.

6. U.S. Census Bureau, "Historical Living Arrangements of Children," April 3, 2017, table CH-1, available at https://www.census.gov/data/tables/time-series/demo/families/children .html.

7. National Center for Health Statistics, *Family Structure and Children's Health in the United States: Findings from the National Health Interview Survey, 2001–2007* (Washington, DC: U.S. Government Printing Office, 2010).

8. Child Trends, "Family Structure," December 2015, appendix 1, available at https:// www.childtrends.org/?indicators=family-structure.

9. U.S. Bureau of Labor Statistics, "Women in the Labor Force: A Databook," April 2017, table 7, available at https://www.bls.gov/opub/reports/womens-databook/2016/home.htm.

10. Ibid., table 5.

11. Child Trends, "Early School Readiness," July 2015, appendix 1, available at https:// www.childtrends.org/?indicators=early-school-readiness.

12. Ibid., appendix 2.

13. Ibid., appendix 3.

14. Ibid., appendix 4.

15. Child Trends, "Educational Attainment," December 2016, appendix 1, available at https://www.childtrends.org/?indicators=educational-attainment.

16. Child Trends, "Teen Births," November 2016, appendix 1 available at https://www .childtrends.org/?indicators=teen-births.

17. Child Trends, "Juvenile Detention," December 2015, appendix 1, available at https:// www.childtrends.org/?indicators=juvenile-detention.

18. Child Trends, "Young Adults in Jail or Prison," April 2012, available at https://www .childtrends.org/?indicators=young-adults-in-jail-or-prison.

19. National Advisory Commission on Civil Disorders, "Report of the National Advisory Commission on Civil Disorders."

20. Henry J. Kaiser Family Foundation, "A Historical Review of How States Have Responded to the Availability of Federal Funds for Health Coverage," August 2012, available at https://kaiserfamilyfoundation.files.wordpress.com/2013/01/8349.pdf.

21. Henry J. Kaiser Family Foundation, "Current Status of State Medicaid Expansion Decisions," January 1, 2017, available at http://www.kff.org/health-reform/slide/current-sta tus-of-the-medicaid-expansion-decision.

22. Larisa Antonisse, Rachel Garfield, Robin Rudowitz, and Samantha Artiga, "The Effects of Medicaid Expansion under the ACA: Updated Findings from a Literature Review," Henry J. Kaiser Family Foundation, February 22, 2017, available at http://www.kff.org/ medicaid/issue-brief/the-effects-of-medicaid-expansion-under-the-aca-updated-findings -from-a-literature-review.

23. Child Trends, "Health Insurance Coverage Improves Child Well-Being," May 12, 2017, available at https://www.childtrends.org/publications/health-insurance-coverage-im proves-child-well.

24. David Murphey, "Health Insurance Coverage Improves Child Well-Being," May 2017, available at https://childtrends-ciw49tixgw5lbab.stackpathdns.com/wp-content/up loads/2017/05/2017-22HealthInsurance_finalupdate.pdf.

25. First Five Years Fund, "2017 National Poll: Research Summary," 2017, available at http://ffyf.org/resources/2017-national-poll-research-summary.

26. Jack P. Shonkoff and Deborah A. Phillips, eds., *From Neurons to Neighborhoods: The Science of Early Childhood Development* (Washington, DC: National Academies Press, 2000).

27. Hirokazu Yoshikawa, Christina Weiland, Jeanne Brooks-Gunn, Margaret R. Burchinal, Linda M. Espinosa, William T. Gormley, Jens Ludwig, Katherine A. Magnuson, Deborah Phillips, and Martha J. Zaslow, "Investing in Our Future: The Evidence Base on Preschool Education," October 2013, available at https://www.fcd-us.org/assets/2013/10/Evidence 20Base20on20Preschool20Education20FINAL.pdf.

28. Frances Campbell, Gabriella Conti, James J. Heckman, Seong Hyeok Moon, Rodrigo Pinto, Elizabeth Pungello, and Yi Pan, "Early Childhood Investments Substantially Boost Adult Health," *Science* 343, no. 6178 (2014): 1478–1485.

29. W. Steven Barnett, Allison H. Friedman-Krauss, G. G. Weisenfeld, Michelle Horowitz, Richard Kasmin, and James H. Squires, "The State of Preschool, 2016," 2017, available at http://nieer.org/wp-content/uploads/2017/05/YB2016_StateofPreschool2.pdf.

30. Daphna Bassok, Maria Fitzpatrick, and Susanna Loeb, "Does State Preschool Crowd-Out Private Provision? The Impact of Universal Preschool on the Childcare Sector in Oklahoma and Georgia," *Journal of Urban Economics* 83 (2014): 18–33; Christina Weiland and Hirokazu Yoshikawa, "Impacts of a Prekindergarten Program on Children's Mathematics, Language, Literacy, Executive Function, and Emotional Skills," *Child Development* 84, no. 6 (2013): 2112–2130; Taryn W. Morrissey, Kristi S. Lekies, and Moncrieff M. Cochran, "Implementing New York's Universal Pre-kindergarten Program: An Exploratory Study of Systemic Impacts," *Early Education and Development* 18, no. 4 (2007): 573–596; Simone Zhang, "A Portrait of Universal Pre-kindergarten in DC," Urban Institute, April 30, 2014, available at http://www.urban.org/urban-wire/portrait-universal-pre-kindergarten-dc.

31. Child Trends, "Preschool and Prekindergarten," February 2015, appendix 1, available at https://www.childtrends.org/?indicators=preschool-and-prekindergarten.

32. Organisation for Economic Co-operation and Development, *Education at a Glance, 2012: OECD Indicators* (Paris: OECD, 2012).

33. Kathryn Tout, Tamara Halle, Sarah Daily, Ladia Albertson-Junkans, Shannon Moodie, "The Research Base for a Birth through Age Eight State Policy Framework," 2013, available at https://childtrends-ciw49tixgw5lbab.stackpathdns.com/wp-content/uploads/2013/10/2013-42AllianceBirthto81.pdf.

34. A. Martin, M. Gardner, J. Brooks-Gunn, and Jennifer Hill, "Early Head Start Impacts over Time and by Level of Participation," Mathematica Policy Research Reference No. 6260-520, 2008; N. Yazejian and D. M. Bryant, "Educare Implementation Study Findings—August 2012," August 2012, available at http://fpg.unc.edu/node/5216.

35. Barnett et al., "The State of Preschool, 2016."

36. Ibid.

37. Walter S. Gilliam, Angela N. Maupin, Chin R. Reyes, Maria Accavitti, and Frederick Shic, "Do Early Educators' Implicit Biases Regarding Sex and Race Relate to Behavior Expectations and Recommendations of Preschool Expulsions and Suspensions?" September 2016, available at http://ziglercenter.yale.edu/publications/Preschool%20Implicit%20Bias%20Pol icy%20Brief_final_9_26_276766_5379.pdf.

38. Tamara Halle, Nicole Forry, Elizabeth Hair, Kate Perper, Laura Wandner, and Jessica Vick, "Disparities in Early Learning and Development: Lessons from the Early Childhood Longitudinal Study—Birth Cohort (ECLS-B)," June 2009, available at https://www.childtrends .org/wp-content/uploads/2013/05/2009-52DisparitiesELExecSumm.pdf.

39. Martin et al., "Early Head Start Impacts over Time and by Level of Participation."

40. Yazejian and Bryant, "Educare Implementation Study Findings."

41. Heckman Equation, "Invest in Early Childhood Development: Reduce Deficits, Strengthen the Economy," available at https://heckmanequation.org/resource/invest-in

-early-childhood-development-reduce-deficits-strengthen-the-economy (accessed September 20, 2017).

42. U.S. Department of Education Office for Civil Rights, "2013–2014 Civil Rights Data Collection: A First Look," October 28, 2016, available at http://www2.ed.gov/about/offices/list/ocr/docs/2013-14-first-look.pdf.

43. M. Karega Rausch and Russell Skiba, "Unplanned Outcomes: Suspensions and Expulsions in Indiana," *Education Policy Briefs* 2, no. 2 (2004): 1–7, available at http://files.eric.ed.gov/fulltext/ED488917.pdf.

44. Daniel J. Losen and Tia Elena Martinez, "Out of School and Off Track: The Overuse of Suspensions in American Middle and High Schools," April 8, 2013, available at https://www.civilrightsproject.ucla.edu/resources/projects/center-for-civil-rights-remedies/school-to-prison-folder/federal-reports/out-of-school-and-off-track-the-overuse-of-suspensions-in-american-middle-and-high-schools/OutofSchool-OffTrack_UCLA_4-8.pdf.

45. Tony Fabelo, Michael D. Thompson, Martha Plotkin, Dottie Carmichael, Miner P. Marchbanks, and Eric A. Booth, "Breaking Schools' Rules: A Statewide Study of How School Discipline Relates to Students' Success and Juvenile Justice Involvement," July 2011, available at https://csgjusticecenter.org/wp-content/uploads/2012/08/Breaking_Schools_Rules_Report_Final.pdf.

46. Michelle Massar, Kent McIntosh, and Bert M. Eliason, "Do Out-of-School Suspensions Prevent Future Exclusionary Discipline?" May 2015, available at https://www.pbis.org/Common/Cms/files/pbisresources/EvalBrief_May2015.pdf.

47. Roger P. Weissberg, Celene E. Domitrovich, and Thomas P. Gullotta, eds., *Handbook of Social and Emotional Learning* (New York: Guilford Press, 2015).

48. Catherine P. Bradshaw, Christine W. Koth, Leslie A. Thornton, and Philip J. Leaf, "Altering School Climate through School-Wide Positive Behavioral Interventions and Supports: Findings from a Group-Randomized Effectiveness Trial," *Prevention Science* 10, no. 2 (2009): 100–115.

49. Brenda Morrison, Peta Blood, and Margaret Thorsborne, "Practicing Restorative Justice in School Communities: Addressing the Challenge of Culture Change," *Public Organization Review* 5, no. 4 (2005): 335–357; Michael D. Sumner, Carol J. Silverman, and Mary Louise Frampton, "School-Based Restorative Justice as an Alternative to Zero-Tolerance Policies: Lessons from West Oakland," 2010, available at https://www.law.berkeley.edu/files/thcsj/10-2010_School-based_Restorative_Justice_As_an_Alternative_to_Zero-Tolerance_Policies.pdf.

50. Brittany Hecker, Ellie L. Young, and Paul Caldarella, "Teacher Perspectives on Behaviors of Middle and Junior High School Students at Risk for Emotional and Behavioral Disorders," *American Secondary Education* 42, no. 2 (2014): 20–32.

51. Carl J. Liaupsin, John Umbreit, Jolenea B. Ferro, Annmarie Urso, and Gita Upreti, "Improving Academic Engagement through Systematic, Function-Based Intervention," *Education and Treatment of Children* 29, no. 4 (2006): 573–591; Russell Skiba and Jeffrey Sprague, "Safety without Suspensions," *Educational Leadership* 66 (2008): 38–43; Matthew Theriot, Sarah W. Craun, and David R. Dupper, "Multilevel Evaluation of Factors Prediction School Exclusion among Middle and High School Students," *Children and Youth Services Review* 32, no. 1 (2010): 13–19.

52. National Advisory Commission on Civil Disorders, "Report of the National Advisory Commission on Civil Disorders."

Chapter 9

1. U.S. Census Bureau, "POV-01: Age and Sex of All People, Family Members and Unrelated Individuals Iterated by Income-to-Poverty Ratio and Race," August 9, 2017, available at https://www.census.gov/data/tables/time-series/demo/income-poverty/cps-pov/pov-01.html.

2. *Report of the National Advisory Commission on Civil Disorders* (Washington, DC: U.S. Government Printing Office, 1968), 12.

3. Martin Luther King, Jr., "Remaining Awake through a Great Revolution," speech delivered at the National Cathedral, Washington, DC, March 31, 1968.

4. *Report of the National Advisory Commission on Civil Disorders*, 1.

5. Sandra L. Colby and Jennifer M. Ortman, "Projections of the Size and Composition of the U.S. Population: 2014 to 2060," March 2015, available at https://www.census.gov/content/dam/Census/library/publications/2015/demo/p25-1143.pdf.

6. U.S. Census Bureau, "POV-01: Age and Sex of All People."

7. Children's Defense Fund, *Ending Child Poverty Now* (Washington, DC: Children's Defense Fund, 2017), chap. 1, available at http://www.childrensdefense.org/library/Poverty Report/EndingChildPovertyNow.html.

8. Harry Holzer, Diane Whitmore Schanzenbach, Greg J. Duncan, and Jens Ludwig, "The Economic Costs of Poverty: Subsequent Effects of Children Growing Up Poor," January 24, 2007, available at http://www.americanprogress.org/issues/2007/01/poverty_report.html.

9. U.S. Census Bureau, "Table A-7: Effect of Individual Elements on the Number of Individuals in Poverty: 2016 and 2015," September 21, 2017, available at https://www.census.gov/data/tables/2017/demo/income-poverty/p60-261.html.

10. Kelsey Farson Gray, Sarah Fisher, and Sarah Lauffer, "Characteristics of Supplemental Nutrition Assistance Program Households: Fiscal Year 2015," November 2016, table B.3, available at https://www.fns.usda.gov/snap/characteristics-supplemental-nutrition-assistance-households-fiscal-year-2015.

11. "Long-Term Benefits of the Supplemental Nutrition Assistance Program," December 2015, available at https://obamawhitehouse.archives.gov/sites/whitehouse.gov/files/documents/SNAP_report_final_nonembargo.pdf.

12. Feeding America, "Map the Meal Gap, 2017: A Report on County and Congressional District Food Insecurity and County Food Cost in the United States in 2015," 2017, available at http://www.feedingamerica.org/hunger-in-america/our-research/map-the-meal-gap/2015/2015-mapthemealgap-exec-summary.pdf.

13. Linda Ransom, interview by the author, Columbus, Ohio, 2016.

14. National Low Income Housing Coalition, *Out of Reach, 2016* (Washington, DC: National Low Income Housing Coalition, 2016), available at http://nlihc.org/sites/default/files/oor/OOR_2016.pdf; U.S. Department of Labor, "Minimum Wage Laws in the States," July 3, 2017, available at http://www.dol.gov/whd/minwage/america.htm.

15. Center on Budget and Policy Priorities, "Fact Sheet: Federal Rental Assistance," March 30, 2017, available at http://www.cbpp.org/sites/default/files/atoms/files/4-13-11hous-US.pdf.

16. Child Trends, "Homeless Children and Youth," October 2015, available at https://www.childtrends.org/indicators/homeless-children-and-youth.

17. U.S. Census Bureau, "HI-08: Health Insurance Coverage Status and Type of Coverage by Selected Characteristics for Children under 18: 2015," September 5, 2017, available at https://www.census.gov/data/tables/time-series/demo/income-poverty/cps-hi/hi-08.2015.html.

18. U.S. Census Bureau, "POV-01: Age and Sex of All People."

19. Jack P. Shonkoff and Deborah A. Phillips, eds., *From Neurons to Neighborhoods: The Science of Early Childhood Development* (Washington, DC: National Academies Press, 2000), available at http://www.nap.edu/read/9824.

20. Hirokazu Yoshikawa, Christina Weiland, Jeanne Brooks-Gunn, Margaret R. Burchinal, Linda M. Espinosa, William T. Gormley, Jens Ludwig, Katherine A. Magnuson, Deborah Philips, and Martha J. Zaslow, "Investing in Our Future: The Evidence Base on Preschool Education," October 2013, available at https://www.fcd-us.org/assets/2013/10/Evidence 20Base20on20Preschool20Education20FINAL.pdf.

21. U.S. Department of Health and Human Services, "Fiscal Year 2017: Administration for Children and Families Justification of Estimates for Appropriations Committees," p. 111, available at https://www.acf.hhs.gov/sites/default/files/olab/final_cj_2017_print.pdf (accessed September 20, 2017); Children's Defense Fund calculations using U.S. Census Bureau, Current Population Survey Table Creator, at https://www.census.gov/cps/data/cpstablecreator.html.

22. James J. Heckman, "There's More to Gain by Taking a Comprehensive Approach to Early Childhood Development," 2016, available at https://heckmanequation.org/assets/2017/01/F_Heckman_CBAOnePager_120516.pdf.

23. Julia B. Isaacs, "Starting School at a Disadvantage: The School Readiness of Poor Children," March 2012, available at https://www.brookings.edu/wp-content/uploads/2016/06/0319 _school_disadvantage_isaacs.pdf.

24. U.S. Government Accountability Office, "Better Use of Information Could Help Agencies Identify Disparities and Address Racial Discrimination," April 2016, available at http://www.gao.gov/assets/680/676745.pdf.

25. National Center for Education Statistics, "Table 1: Public High School 4-Year Adjusted Cohort Graduation Rate (ACGR), by Race/Ethnicity and Selected Demographics for the United States, the 50 States, and the District of Columbia: School Year 2014–15," September 15, 2016, available at https://nces.ed.gov/ccd/tables/ACGR_RE_and_characteristics_2014-15.asp.

26. U.S. Department of Education Office for Civil Rights, "2013–2014 Civil Rights Data Collection: A First Look," October 28, 2016, available at http://www2.ed.gov/about/offices/list/ocr/docs/2013-14-first-look.pdf.

27. Sabrina Eaton, "Thousands Join Al Sharpton and Tamir Rice's Mother, Samaria, at 'Justice for All' March against Police Violence," *Cleveland.com*, December 13, 2014, available at http://www.cleveland.com/metro/index.ssf/2014/12/thousands_join_al_sharpton_and.html.

28. Centers for Disease Control and Prevention, *Underlying Cause of Death, 1999–2015* database, available at http://wonder.cdc.gov/ucd-icd10.html (accessed September 20, 2017).

29. Children's Defense Fund calculation using data from Centers for Disease Control and Prevention, *Underlying Cause of Death, 1999–2015* database. Child and teen data are for birth through age nineteen and exclude deaths from interactions with law enforcement.

30. Centers for Disease Control and Prevention, "Compressed Mortality File, 1968–1998," available at https://www.cdc.gov/nchs/data_access/cmf.htm; Centers for Disease Control and Prevention, *Underlying Cause of Death, 1999–2015* database; Equal Justice Initiative, "Lynching in America: Confronting the Legacy of Racial Terror," 2015, available at https://eji.org/sites/default/files/lynching-in-america-second-edition-summary.pdf.

31. AJ Morris, "Word in the Street: Cradle to Prison Pipeline" plenary session, Clinton, TN, July 22, 2015.

32. E'Darrius Smith, "Word in the Street: Cradle to Prison Pipeline" plenary session, Clinton, TN, July 22, 2015.

33. Children's Defense Fund, "Protect Children, Not Guns, 2013," 2013, available at http://www.childrensdefense.org/library/protect-children-not-guns/protect-children-not-guns-2013.pdf.

34. Eileen Patten, "Racial, Gender Wage Gaps Persist in U.S. Despite Some Progress," Pew Research Center, July 1, 2016, available at http://www.pewresearch.org/fact-tank/2016/07/01/racial-gender-wage-gaps-persist-in-u-s-despite-some-progress.

35. Urban Institute, "Nine Charts about Wealth Inequality in America," February 2015, available at http://apps.urban.org/features/wealth-inequality-charts.

36. Martin Luther King, Jr., *Where Do We Go from Here: Chaos or Community?* (1967; repr., Boston: Beacon Press, 2010), 48.

37. Ibid.

38. Children's Defense Fund, *Ending Child Poverty Now.*

39. *Report of the National Advisory Commission on Civil Disorders*, 2.

Chapter 10

A version of this chapter was previously published as Gary Orfield, "Tenth Annual *Brown* Lecture in Education Research: A New Civil Rights Agenda for American Education," *Educational Researcher* 43, no. 6 (2014): 273–292. This version has been substantially revised for the Trump period.

1. David Leonhardt, "Geography Seen as Barrier to Climbing Class Ladder," *New York Times*, July 22, 2013, p. A1.

2. National Coalition on School Diversity, "Federal Support for School Integration: A Status Report," April 2014, available at http://www.school-diversity.org/pdf/DiversityIssue BriefNo4.pdf.

3. Anurima Bhargava, Erica Frankenberg, and Chinh Q. Le, *Still Looking to the Future: Voluntary K–12 School Integration* (New York: NAACP Legal Defense and Educational Fund and Civil Rights Project/Proyecto Derechos Civiles, 2008); Mexican American Legal Defense and Educational Fund and Civil Rights Project, "Preserving Integration Options for Latino Children: A Manual for Educators, Civil Rights Leaders, and the Community," February 2008, available at https://www.civilrightsproject.ucla.edu/research/k-12-education/integration-and -diversity/preserving-integration-options-for-latino-children/maldef-preserving-integration -latino-children-2008.pdf.

4. Joint Center for Housing Studies of Harvard University, "The State of the Nation's Housing, 2017," 2017, available at http://www.jchs.harvard.edu/sites/jchs.harvard.edu/files/ harvard_jchs_state_of_the_nations_housing_2017.pdf.

5. Citizens United v. Federal Election Commission, 558 U.S. 310 (2010).

6. San Antonio Independent School District v. Rodriguez, 411 U.S. 1 (1973).

7. Deidre Pfeiffer, "The Opportunity Illusion: Subsidized Housing and Failing Schools in California," December 2009, available at https://civilrightsproject.ucla.edu/research/ metro-and-regional-inequalities/housing/the-opportunity-illusion-subsidized-housing-and -failing-schools-in-california/pfeiffer-opportunity-illusion-2009.pdf.

Chapter 11

Acknowledgments: Special thanks go to Claire Alexander, Benny Docter, Peter Melkonian, and Ethan Tillman for their research, contributions to this writing, and spirited discussion.

1. Franklin D. Roosevelt, "Inaugural Address," January 20, 1937, available at http://www .presidency.ucsb.edu/ws/?pid=15349.

2. Harry S. Truman, "Statement by the President upon Signing the Housing Act of 1949," July 15, 1949, available at http://www.presidency.ucsb.edu/ws/?pid=13246.

3. Daniel K. Fetter, "The Twentieth-Century Increase in US Home Ownership: Facts and Hypotheses," in *Housing and Mortgage Markets in Historical Perspective*, ed. Eugene N. White, Kenneth Snowden, and Price Fishback (Chicago: University of Chicago Press, 2014), 329–350, available at http://www.nber.org/chapters/c12801.pdf.

4. U.S. Census Bureau, "Table 1: Median Value of Assets for Households, by Type of Asset Owned and Selected Characteristics, 2013," May 4, 2017, available at https://www.census.gov/ data/tables/2013/demo/wealth/wealth-asset-ownership.html.

5. *Report of the National Advisory Commission on Civil Disorders* (New York: Bantam Books, 1968), 1.

6. Frank Van Riper, "Ford to City: DROP DEAD," *New York Daily News*, October 30, 1975.

7. Camila Domonoske, "Comedian and Civil Rights Crusader Dick Gregory Dies at 84," *NPR*, August 21, 2017, available at https://www.npr.org/2017/08/21/544953031/comedian-and -civil-rights-crusader-dick-gregory-dies-at-84.

8. William Tucker, "The Source of America's Housing Problem: Look in Your Own Back Yard," February 6, 1990, available at https://object.cato.org/pubs/pas/pa127.pdf.

9. Hills v. Gautreaux, 425 U.S. 284 (1976). This case resulted in a unanimous Supreme Court decision expanding fair housing opportunities into the Chicago suburbs.

10. William J. Collins and Katharine L. Shester, "Slum Clearance and Urban Renewal in the United States, 1949–1974," January 2010, available at http://www.webmeets.com/files/ papers/ESWC/2010/613/Collins_Shester_January_2010.pdf.

11. Center on Budget and Policy Priorities, "Chart Book: Cuts in Federal Assistance Have Exacerbated Families' Struggles to Afford Housing," April 12, 2016, available at http://www .cbpp.org/research/housing/chart-book-cuts-in-federal-assistance-have-exacerbated-fami lies-struggles-to-afford#section03.

12. Nikole Hannah-Jones, "Living Apart: How the Government Betrayed a Landmark Civil Rights Law," *ProPublica*, June 25, 2015, available at https://www.propublica.org/article/ living-apart-how-the-government-betrayed-a-landmark-civil-rights-law.

13. Ronald Reagan, "Inaugural Address," January 20, 1981, available at http://www.pres idency.ucsb.edu/ws/?pid=43130.

14. Andre Shashaty, "U.S. Cuts Back and Shifts Course on Housing Aid," *New York Times*, October 18, 1981, available at http://www.nytimes.com/1981/10/18/realestate/us-cuts-back-and-shifts-course-on-housing-aid.html.

15. Urban Institute, "Mapping America's Rental Housing Crisis," April 27, 2017, available at http://apps.urban.org/features/rental-housing-crisis-map.

16. Joint Center for Housing Studies of Harvard University, "The State of the Nation's Housing, 2017," 2017, available at http://www.jchs.harvard.edu/sites/jchs.harvard.edu/files/harvard_jchs_state_of_the_nations_housing_2017.pdf.

17. U.S. Department of the Treasury, "U.S. Treasury Announces over $90 Million in Awards for Affordable Housing," September 22, 2016, available at https://www.treasury.gov/press-center/press-releases/Pages/jl0557.aspx.

18. Brett Theodos, Christina Plerhoples Stacy, and Helen Ho, "Taking Stock of the Community Development Block Grant," April 2017, available at http://www.urban.org/sites/default/files/publication/89551/cdbg_brief_finalized.pdf.

19. Erika C. Poethig, "One in Four: America's Housing Assistance Lottery," *Urban Wire*, May 28, 2014, available at http://www.urban.org/urban-wire/one-four-americas-housing-assistance-lottery.

20. National Alliance to End Homelessness, "The State of Homelessness in America, 2016," available at http://endhomelessness.org/wp-content/uploads/2016/10/2016-soh.pdf (accessed September 20, 2017).

21. "Facts and Figures: The Homeless," *PBS*, June 26, 2009, available at http://www.pbs.org/now/shows/526/homeless-facts.html.

22. Congressional Budget Office, "Federal Housing Assistance for Low-Income Households," September 2015, available at https://www.cbo.gov/sites/default/files/114th-congress-2015-2016/reports/50782-lowincomehousing-onecolumn.pdf.

23. Will Fischer and Barbara Sard, "Chart Book: Federal Housing Spending Is Poorly Matched to Need," March 8, 2017, available at http://www.cbpp.org/research/housing/chart-book-federal-housing-spending-is-poorly-matched-to-need.

24. Tracy Jan, "A Surprising Way to Increase Property Values: Build Affordable Housing," *Washington Post*, July 6, 2017, available at https://www.washingtonpost.com/news/wonk/wp/2017/07/06/a-surprising-way-to-increase-property-values.

25. Josh Silver, "The Community Reinvestment Act: Vital for Neighborhoods, the Country, and the Economy," June 2016, available at http://www.ncrc.org/images/ncrc_cra_affirmation_final.pdf.

26. World Bank, "Account at a Financial Institution (% Age 15+)," 2015, available at http://data.worldbank.org/indicator/WP_time_01.1?view=map.

27. World Bank, "Account at a Financial Institution, Income, Poorest 40% (% Ages 15+)," 2015, available at http://data.worldbank.org/indicator/WP_time_01.8?view=map.

28. This authority was granted by the Federal Housing Enterprises Financial Safety and Soundness Act of 1992.

29. National Low Income Housing Coalition, "How Much Do You Need to Earn to Afford a Modest Apartment in Your State?" available at http://nlihc.org/oor (accessed September 20, 2017).

30. Roosevelt, "Inaugural Address."

Chapter 12

1. See William Julius Wilson, *When Work Disappears: The World of the New Urban Poor* (New York: Random House, 1996).

2. See Elijah Anderson, "The Iconic Ghetto," *Annals of the American Academy of Political and Social Science* 642 (2012): 8–24.

3. W.E.B. DuBois, *The Souls of Black Folk* (New Haven, CT: Yale University Press, 2015).

4. See Everett C. Hughes, "Dilemmas and Contradictions of Status," *American Journal of Sociology* 50, no. 5 (March 1945): 353–359.

5. See Elijah Anderson, *The Cosmopolitan Canopy: Race and Civility in Everyday Life* (New York: W. W. Norton, 2011).

6. See Elijah Anderson, "The White Space," *Sociology of Race and Ethnicity*, no. 1 (2015): 10–21.

7. See Elijah Anderson, *Code of the Street: Decency, Violence, and the Moral Life of the Inner City* (New York: W. W. Norton, 1999).

8. For all this, generally, see Mitchell Dumeier, *Ghetto: The Invention of a Place, the History of an Idea* (New York: Farrar, Straus and Giroux, 2016); Anderson, *The Cosmopolitan Canopy*; and Hughes, "Dilemmas and Contradictions of Status."

Chapter 13

1. See Eisenhower Foundation, *Investing in Children and Youth* (Washington, DC: Milton S. Eisenhower Foundation, 1993); Eisenhower Foundation, *To Establish Justice, to Insure Domestic Tranquility: A Thirty-Year Update of the National Commission on the Causes and Prevention of Violence* (Washington, DC: Milton S. Eisenhower Foundation, 1999); Eisenhower Foundation, *What Together We Can Do: A Forty-Year Update of the National Advisory Commission on Civil Disorders* (Washington, DC: Milton S. Eisenhower Foundation, 2008).

2. The focus is on individual and group forms of crime and violence. State-level forms of violence such as terrorism, war, and armed conflicts are not addressed.

3. U.S. Office of Management and Budget, *The President's Management Agenda, FY 2002* (Washington, DC: Office of Management and Budget, 2001).

4. White House, *Economic Report of the President, Together with the Annual Report of the Council of Economic Advisors, 2014* (Washington, DC: U.S. Government Printing Office, 2014); National Science Foundation, *Common Guidelines for Education Research and Development* (Washington, DC: Institute of Education Sciences, U.S. Department of Education, and National Science Foundation, 2013).

5. Delbert Elliott and Abigail Fagan, *The Prevention of Crime* (New York: Wiley-Blackwell, 2017).

6. See, for example, the National Institute of Justice's CrimeSolutions.gov, at https://www.crimesolutions.gov; the Office of Juvenile Justice and Delinquency Prevention's "Model Programs Guide," at https://www.ojjdp.gov/mpg; the Department of Health and Human Services National Registry of Evidence-Based Programs and Practices, at http://www.healthdata.gov/dataset/national-registry-evidence-based-programs-and-practices-nrepp; the Community Guide website, at https://www.thecommunityguide.org; and the website of Blueprints for Healthy Youth Development, at http://www.blueprintsprograms.com.

7. Jill Eden, Ben Wheatley, Barbara McNeil, and Harold Sox, eds., *Knowing What Works in Health Care: A Roadmap for the Nation* (Washington, DC: National Academies Press, 2008); Anthony Biglan and Terje Ogden, "The Evolution of Evidence-Based Practices," *European Journal of Behavior Analysis* 9 (2008): 81–95.

8. Alex Neuhoff, Simon Axworthy, Sara Glazer, and Danielle Berfond, "The What Works Marketplace: Helping Leaders Use Evidence to Make Smarter Choices," April 2015, available at http://results4america.org/wp-content/uploads/2015/04/WhatWorksMarketplace-vF-1.pdf.

9. See Working Group of the Federal Collaboration on What Works, "The OJP What Works Repository," available at https://www.ncjrs.gov/pdffiles1/nij/220889.pdf (accessed September 23, 2017). The Society for Prevention Research has also proposed a standard that is much more complex than the federal working group standard reviewed in this chapter. See the society's website, at http://www.preventionresearch.org.

10. The working group included members from the Center for Substance Abuse Prevention, Substance Abuse and Mental Health Services Administration; National Institute of Drug Abuse, National Institutes of Health; National Center for Education Evaluation and Regional Assistance, Institute of Education Sciences, U.S. Department of Education; Office of Justice Programs; National Institute of Justice; and Office of Juvenile Justice and Delinquency Prevention.

11. See Working Group of the Federal Collaboration on What Works, "The OJP What Works Repository."

12. A well-conducted study is one that adequately addresses the potential threats to the internal validity of study findings. For example, see C. H. Brown, D. Berndt, J. M. Brinales, X. Zong, and D. Bhagwat, "Evaluating the Evidence of Effectiveness for Prevention Interventions: Using a Registry System to Influence Policy through Science," *Addictive Behaviors* 25 (2000): 955–964.

13. RCTs are widely recognized as the best evaluation design and when rigorously conducted provide the strongest evidence for the effects of the program on participants. Institute of Medicine, *Community Programs to Promote Youth Development* (Washington, DC: National Academies Press, 2002).

14. See the Blueprints website, at http://www.blueprintsprograms.com.

15. See the National Institute of Justice's list at https://www.crimesolutions.gov/pro grams.aspx.

16. Patricia J. Mrazek, and Robert J. Haggerty, eds., *Reducing Risks for Mental Disorders: Frontiers for Preventive Intervention Research* (Washington, DC: National Academies Press, 1994); Mary Ellen O'Connell, Thomas Boat, and Kenneth E. Warner, eds., *Preventing Mental, Emotional and Behavioral Disorders among Young People: Progress and Possibilities* (Washington, DC: National Academies Press, 2009).

17. See Washington State Institute for Public Policy, "Benefit-Cost Results," May 2017, available at http://www.wsipp.wa.gov/BenefitCost.

18. Elliott and Fagan, *The Prevention of Crime*; Delbert Elliott and Sharon Mihalic, "Issues in Disseminating and Replicating Effective Prevention Programs," *Prevention Science* 5 (2004): 47–53; Vangie A. Foshee, Karl E. Bauman, Susan T. Ennett, Chirayath Suchindran, Thad Benefield, and G. Fletcher Linder, "Assessing the Effects of Dating Violence Prevention Program 'Safe Dates' Using Random Coefficient Regression Modeling," *Prevention Science* 6, no. 3 (2005): 245–257; Stanley J. Huey, Jr., and Antonio J. Polo, "Evidence-Based Psychosocial Treatments for Ethnic Minority Youth," *Journal of Clinical Child and Adolescent Psychology* 37 (2008): 262–301; André B. Rosay, Denise C. Gottfredson, Todd A. Armstrong, and Michele A. Harmon, "Invariance of Measures of Prevention Program Effectiveness: A Replication," *Journal of Quantitative Criminology* 16 (2000): 341–367; Sandra Jo Wilson, Mark W. Lipsey, and Haluk Soydan, "Are Mainstream Programs for Juvenile Delinquency Less Effective with Minority Youth than Majority Youth? A Meta-analysis of Outcomes Research," *Research on Social Work Practice* 13 (2003): 3–26.

19. For more about systematic reviews for evidence-based policy and practice, see the Campbell Collaboration website, at https://www.campbellcollaboration.org.

20. Larry V. Hedges and Ingram Olkin, *Statistical Methods for Meta-analysis* (Orlando, FL: Academic Press, 1985).

21. Evidence-based practice effects are *average* effects for the set of evaluations and programs included in the meta-analysis; a positive average effect does not mean that all studies of a particular type of practice or strategy found positive effects or that any particular set of components, processes, protocols, or logic models characterizing individual programs are effective. The level of evidence for any specific program in the set is usually not sufficient to classify that program as evidence based.

22. David Weisburd, David P. Farrington, and Charlotte Gill, "What Works in Crime Prevention and Rehabilitation: An Assessment of Systematic Reviews," *Criminology and Public Policy* 16 (2017): 415–450.

23. Elliott and Fagan, *The Prevention of Crime*.

24. Jim Nussle and Peter Orszag, eds., *Moneyball for Government* (New York: Disruption Books, 2014).

25. Neuhoff et al., "The What Works Marketplace."

26. Mary Jane England, Adrienne Stith Butler, and Monica L. Gonzalez, eds., *Psychosocial Interventions for Mental and Substance Use Disorders: A Framework for Establishing Evidence-Based Standards* (Washington, DC: National Academy Press, 2015).

27. Peter W. Greenwood, Brandon C. Welsh, and Michael Rocque, "Implementing Proven Programs for Juvenile Offenders: Assessing State Progress," December 2012, available at http://

youthjusticenc.org/download/juvenile-justice/prevention-interventions-and-alternatives/Implementing%20Proven%20Programs%20for%20JuvenIle%20Offenders.pdf.

28. Steve Aos, Marna Miller, and Elizabeth Drake, "Evidence-Based Public Policy Options to Reduce Future Prison Construction, Criminal Justice Costs and Crime Rates," October 2006, available at http://www.wsipp.wa.gov/ReportFile/952/Wsipp_Evidence-Based-Public-Policy-Options-to-Reduce-Future-Prison-Construction-Criminal-Justice-Costs-and-Crime-Rates_Full-Report.pdf.

29. Justice Research Center, "Redirection Continues to Save Money and Reduce Recidivism," June 2012, available at http://www.evidencebasedassociates.com/wp-content/uploads/2016/09/JRCEval_12.pdf; Evidence-Based Associates, "Redirection: Florida's Commitment to Helping At-Risk Youth," January 2012, available at http://www.fftllc.com/documents/redirectionQ4_11.pdf.

30. Linh Vuong, Christopher Hartney, Barry Krisberg, and Susan Marchionna, "The Extravagance of Prison Revisited," 2010, available at http://scholarship.law.berkeley.edu/cgi/viewcontent.cgi?article=2720&context=facpubs.

31. John P. A. Ioannidis, "Why Most Published Research Findings Are False," *PLoS Medicine* 2, no. 8 (2005): e124; Open Science Collaboration, "Estimating the Reproducibility of Psychological Science," *Science* 349, no. 6251 (2015): aac4716-1–aac4716-8.

32. Eden et al., *Knowing What Works in Health Care.*

33. Dean L. Fixen, Sandra F. Naoom, Karen A. Blase, Robert M. Friedman, and Frances Wallace, *Implementation Research: A Synthesis of the Literature* (Tampa, FL: National Implementation Research Network, 2005).

Chapter 14

1. *Report of the National Advisory Commission on Civil Disorders* (New York: Bantam Books, 1968), 299.

2. See President's Task Force on 21st Century Policing, *Final Report of the President's Task Force on 21st Century Policing* (Washington, DC: Office of Community Oriented Policing Services, 2015), 7–8.

3. Delores Jones-Brown, Kevin Moran, Erica King-Toler, and Susruta Sudula, "The Significance of Race in Contemporary Urban Policing Policy," in *U.S. Criminal Justice Policy*, ed. Karim Ismaili (Burlington, MA: Jones and Bartlett Learning, 2017), 28.

4. *Report of the National Advisory Commission on Civil Disorders*, 299.

5. Ibid., 10.

6. Ibid., 8.

7. Ibid., 17.

8. Ibid., 300.

9. Ibid., 17.

10. The commission used the term "Negro" rather than "African American" or "black," reflecting language in use at that time.

11. *Report of the National Advisory Commission on Civil Disorders*, 17.

12. President's Commission on Law Enforcement and Administration of Justice, *The Challenge of Crime in a Free Society* (Washington, DC: U.S. Government Printing Office, 1967).

13. *Report of the National Advisory Commission on Civil Disorders*, 301.

14. Ibid., 311, 315.

15. Ibid., 335.

16. Ibid., 336.

17. P.L. 90-351, 82 Stat. 197.

18. William F. Powers, "The Law Enforcement Assistance Administration: An Administrative History," Ph.D. diss., Nova University, 1982, available at https://www.ncjrs.gov/pdffiles1/Photocopy/153696NCJRS.pdf.

19. National Research Council, *Fairness and Effectiveness in Policing: The Evidence* (Washington, DC: National Academies Press, 2004), 35.

20. Brian A. Reeves, "Census of State and Local Law Enforcement Agencies, 2008," July 2011, p. 2, available at https://www.bjs.gov/content/pub/pdf/csllea08.pdf.

21. George L. Kelling and Mark H. Moore, "The Evolving Strategy of Policing," *Perspectives on Policing*, November 1988, p. 2, available at https://www.ncjrs.gov/pdffiles1/Digitiza tion/114213NCJRS.pdf.

22. Jones-Brown et al., "The Significance of Race," 24.

23. Ibid.

24. Kelling and Moore, "The Evolving Strategy of Policing," 9.

25. Ibid., 10.

26. George Kelling and Mary Ann Wycoff, "Evolving Strategy of Policing: Case Studies of Strategic Change," May 2001, p. 126, available at https://www.ncjrs.gov/pdffiles1/nij/grants/198029.pdf.

27. Ibid.

28. See National Institute of Justice, "Past Executive Session on Policing," March 4, 2009, available at https://www.nij.gov/topics/law-enforcement/administration/executive-sessions/Pages/past.aspx.

29. Kelling and Moore, "The Evolving Strategy of Policing," 10–12.

30. Matthew J. Hickman and Brian A. Reeves, "Community Policing in Local Police Departments, 1997 and 1999," February 2001, p. 1, available at https://www.bjs.gov/content/pub/pdf/cplpd99.pdf.

31. Kelling and Wycoff, "Evolving Strategy of Policing," 129.

32. As William Bratton noted in 2008, the abbreviation stands for computerized statistics. See William J. Bratton and Sean W. Malinowski, "Police Performance Management in Practice: Taking COMPSTAT to the Next Level," *Policing* 2, no. 3 (2008): 259–265, available at http://assets.lapdonline.org/assets/pdf/WJB%20SWM%20Article%20Oxford%20Journal.pdf.

33. James Willis, Stephen Mastrofski, and David Weisburd, "Making Sense of COMPSTAT: A Theory-Based Analysis of Organizational Change in Three Police Departments," *Law and Society Review* 41, no. 1 (2007): 148.

34. Bureau of Justice Assistance and Police Executive Research Forum, *COMPSTAT: Its Origins, Evolution, and Future in Law Enforcement Agencies* (Washington, DC: Police Executive Research Forum, 2013), available at https://www.bja.gov/publications/perf-compstat.pdf.

35. Ben Brown, "Combative and Cooperative Law Enforcement in Post-September 11th America," in *U.S. Criminal Justice Policy*, ed. Karim Ismaili (Burlington, MA: Jones and Bartlett Learning, 2017), 73.

36. Richard Rosenfeld. "Changing Crime Rates," in *Crime and Public Policy*, ed. James Q. Wilson and Joan Peersilia (New York: Oxford University Press, 2011), 559–588.

37. U.S. Department of Justice, "Justice Department Expands Violence Reduction Network to Five New Sites," September 28, 2015, available at http://www.justice.gov/opa/pr/justice-department-expands-violence-reduction-network-five-new-sites; U.S. Department of Justice, "Attorney General Sessions Announces Creation of National Public Safety Partnership to Combat Violent Crime," June 20, 2017, available at https://www.justice.gov/opa/pr/attorney-general-sessions-announces-creation-national-public-safety-partnership-combat.

38. Centers for Disease Control and Prevention, "Understanding the Epidemic: Drug Overdose Deaths in the United States Continue to Increase in 2015," August 30, 2017, available at https://www.cdc.gov/drugoverdose/epidemic/index.html; Audrey J. Weiss, Molly K. Bailey, Lauren O'Malley, Marguerite L. Barrett, Anne Elixhauser, and Claudia A. Steiner, "Patient Characteristics of Opioid-Related Inpatient Stays and Emergency Department Visits Nationally and by State, 2014," June 2017, available at https://www.hcup-us.ahrq.gov/reports/statbriefs/sb224-Patient-Characteristics-Opioid-Hospital-Stays-ED-Visits-by-State.pdf.

39. Federal Bureau of Investigation, "Table 1: January to June, 2015–2016, Percent Change by Population Group," in *Preliminary Semiannual Uniform Crime Report, January–June 2016* (Washington, DC: FBI, 2016), available at https://ucr.fbi.gov/crime-in-the-u.s/2016/preliminary-semiannual-uniform-crime-report-januaryjune-2016/tables/table-1.

40. Michelle Ye Hee Lee, "Yes, U.S. Locks People Up at a Higher Rate than Any Other Country," *Washington Post*, July 7, 2015, available at https://www.washingtonpost.com/news/fact-checker/wp/2015/07/07/yes-u-s-locks-people-up-at-a-higher-rate-than-any-other-country.

41. Thomas Blomberg, Julie Mestre Brancale, Kevin Beaver, and William Bales, "Introduction: Evidence, Evaluation, and Strategies for Moving Criminal Justice Policy Forward," in *Advancing Criminology and Criminal Justice Policy*, ed. Thomas Blomberg, Julie Mestre Brancale, Kevin Beaver, and William Bales (Abingdon, UK: Routledge, 2016), 7.

42. Anthony A. Braga, "The Science and Practice of Hot-Spots Policing," in *Advancing Criminology and Criminal Justice Policy*, ed. Thomas Blomberg, Julie Mestre Brancale, Kevin Beaver, and William Bales (Abingdon, UK: Routledge, 2016), 139.

43. Anthony A. Braga, "Arrests, Harm Reduction, and Police Crime Prevention Policy," *Criminology and Public Policy* 16 (2017): 370.

44. Anna Stolley Persky, "Policing the Police," *Washington Lawyer*, January 2016, pp. 28–35, available at https://www.dcbar.org/bar-resources/publications/washington-lawyer/articles/january-2016-reviewing-law-enforcement.cfm. The *Washington Post* has tracked fatal police shootings over the past three years, with the number holding steady at just under 1,000. The *Post* noted in its latest tally that "police have continued to shoot a disproportionately large number of black males, who account for nearly a quarter of the deaths, yet are only 6 percent of the nation's population." John Sullivan, Reis Thebault, Julie Tate, and Jennifer Jenkins, "Number of Fatal Shootings by Police Is Nearly Identical to Last Year," *Washington Post*. July 1, 2017, available at https://www.washingtonpost.com/investigations/number-of-fatal-shootings-by-police-is-nearly-identical-to-last-year/2017/07/01/98726cc6-5b5f-11e7-9fc6-c7ef4bc58d13_story.html.

45. President's Task Force on 21st Century Policing, *Final Report*.

46. Ibid., iii.

47. Ibid., 11.

48. Ibid., 10.

49. Ibid., 16.

50. Ibid., 11.

51. Ibid., 10.

52. Ibid., 12–13, 16.

53. Ibid., 16.

54. Ibid., 20.

55. On January 29, 2016, the Police Executive Research Forum issued "Use of Force: Taking Policing to a Higher Standard," spelling out thirty guiding principles on use of force and de-escalation. See Police Executive Research Forum, "Use of Force: Taking Policing to a Higher Standard," January 29, 2016, available at https://www.themarshallproject.org/documents/2701999-30guidingprinciples. In January 2017, eleven police groups issued "National Consensus Policy on Use of Force." Those organizations are the International Association of Chiefs of Police, the Association of State Criminal Investigative Agencies, Fraternal Order of Police, Commission on Accreditation of Law Enforcement Agencies, Federal Law Enforcement Officers Association, Hispanic American Police Command Officers Association, International Association of Directors of Law Enforcement Standards and Training, National Association of Police Organizations, National Association of Women Law Enforcement Executives, National Organization of Black Law Enforcement Executives, and National Tactical Officers Association. See Sara Dziejma and Darryl De Sousa, "National Consensus Policy on Use of Force: How 11 Leading Law Enforcement Leadership and Labor Organizations Arrived at One Policy," *Police Chief*, April 2017, available at http://www.policechiefmagazine.org/wp-content/uploads/PoliceChief_April2017_F_WEB.pdf.

56. President's Task Force on 21st Century Policing, *Final Report*, 21.

57. Ibid., 28.

58. Ibid., 33.

59. Ibid., 45.

60. Ibid., 47.

61. Ibid.

62. Ibid., 16.

63. Ibid.

64. Former Philadelphia police commissioner Charles H. Ramsey notes that a majority African American police force does not guarantee that problems go away. Charles H. Ramsey, "Where to Go from the Anger in Charlotte," *New York Times*, September 24, 2016, available at https://www.nytimes.com/2016/09/25/opinion/sunday/where-to-go-from-the-anger-in-charlotte.html.

65. President's Task Force on 21st Century Policing, *Final Report*, 51.

66. Doris A. Fuller, H. Richard Lamb, Michael Biasotti, and John Snook, "Overlooked in the Undercounted: The Role of Mental Illness in Fatal Law Enforcement Encounters," December 2015, available at http://www.treatmentadvocacycenter.org/storage/documents/overlooked-in-the-undercounted.pdf.

67. President's Task Force on 21st Century Policing, *Final Report*, 56.

68. Ibid., 61.

69. Office of Community Oriented Policing Services and Bureau of Justice Assistance, "Improving Law Enforcement Resilience: Lessons and Recommendations," October 2016, p. 27, available at https://ric-zai-inc.com/Publications/cops-p362-pub.pdf.

70. James R. "Chip" Coldren, Jr., "Police Officer Safety and Wellness—New Directions," Office of Justice Programs Diagnostic Center, June 29, 2017, available at https://www.ojpdiagnosticcenter.org/blog/police-officer-safety-and-wellness%E2%80%94new-directions.

71. President's Task Force on 21st Century Policing, *Final Report*, 14.

72. Barack Obama, "The President's Role in Advancing Criminal Justice Reform," *Harvard Law Review* 130 (January 2017): 811–865.

73. See Attorney General Jeff Sessions's speech at the National Summit on Crime Reduction and Public Safety on June 20, 2017, available at https://www.justice.gov/opa/speech/attorney-general-jeff-sessions-delivers-remarks-opening-national-summit-crime-reduction.

74. Laurie O. Robinson and Thomas P. Abt, "Evidence-Informed Criminal Justice Policy: Looking Back, Moving Forward," in *Advancing Criminology and Criminal Justice Policy*, ed. Thomas Blomberg, Julie Mestre Brancale, Kevin Beaver, and William Bales (Abingdon, UK: Routledge, 2016), 13–14.

75. Al Baker, "When Opioid Addicts Find an Ally in Blue," *New York Times*, June 12, 2017, available at https://www.nytimes.com/2017/06/12/nyregion/when-opioid-addicts-find-an-ally-in-blue.html.

76. Tom Jackman and Mark Berman, "Some in Local Law Enforcement Pledge to Stick to Reform," *Washington Post*, April 5, 2017 available at http://www.standard.net/National/2017/04/05/Some-in-local-law-enforcement-pledge-to-stick-to-reform.

77. Justin George, "Can This Marriage Be Saved?" *Marshall Project*, June 6, 2017, available at https://www.themarshallproject.org/2017/06/06/can-this-marriage-be-saved.

78. Jon Schuppe, "Republican States Make the Case against Trump's Drug Policy," *NBC News*, May 19, 2017 available at http://www.nbcnews.com/news/us-news/republican-states-make-case-against-trump-s-drug-policy-n761651.

79. Obama, "The President's Role," 846.

80. Council of State Governments Justice Center, "North Dakota Allocates $7M for Addiction Treatment and Passes Bills to Help Reduce Prison Population Growth," April 24, 2017, available at https://csgjusticecenter.org/jr/north-dakota/posts/north-dakota-allocates-7m-for-addiction-treatment-and-passes-bills-to-help-reduce-prison-population-growth.

81. Council of State Governments Justice Center, "Georgia Governor Signs Bill to Strengthen Probation and Increase Public Safety," May 10, 2017, available at https://csgjusticecenter.org/jr/georgia/posts/georgia-governor-signs-bill-to-strengthen-probation-and-increase-public.

82. Tammy Felix, Laura Kunard, James "Chip" Coldren, and James "Chips" Stewart, "Forward Momentum: Examples from the Advancing 21st Century Policing Initiative," *Police Chief*, March 2017, pp. 20–23, available at http://www.policechiefmagazine.org/forward-momentum.

83. Tom Jackman, "U.S. Police Chiefs Group Apologizes for 'Historical Mistreatment' of Minorities," *Washington Post*, October 17, 2016, available at https://www.washingtonpost

.com/news/true-crime/wp/2016/10/17/head-of-u-s-police-chiefs-apologizes-for-historic-mis treatment-of-minorities.

84. Donald W. De Lucca, "The Institute for Community-Police Relations: Aiding Law Enforcement in Enhancing Community Trust," *Police Chief*, March 2017, p. 6, available at http://www.policechiefmagazine.org/presidents-message-the-institute-for-community-police-relations.

85. Hart M. Passman, "New Police Procedures Laws for Illinois Municipalities," *Lexology*, December 30, 2015, available at http://www.lexology.com/library/detail.aspx?g=d0c40b32 -3c91-40d8-82d6-656a74385b0c.

86. Massachusetts Chiefs of Police Association and the Massachusetts Major City Chiefs, "A Response to the Final Report of the President's Task Force on 21st Century Policing," September 2015, p. 23, available at https://www.masschiefs.org/files-downloads/news-1/866 -mcopa-mmcc-response-to-the-final-report-of-the-president-s-task-force-on-21st-century -police/file.

87. S. P. Sullivan, "N.J. Attorney General Orders Statewide Police Training on Racial Bias, Deadly Force," *NJ.com*, October 5, 2016, available at http://www.nj.com/politics/index .ssf/2016/10/nj_ag_creates_police_training_on_racial_bias_deadl.html.

88. "Herring Announces Initiatives to Promote Safe, Impartial 21st Century Policing in Virginia," September 29, 2015, available at http://www.oag.state.va.us/media-center/news -releases/626-september-29-2015-herring-announces-initiatives-to-promote-safe-impar tial-21-st-centry-policing-in-virginia.

89. "DOJ Requiring 28,000 Employees to Be Trained on Racial Bias," *Crime Report*, June 28, 2016, available at https://thecrimereport.org/2016/06/28/doj-requiring-28000-employees -to-be-trained-on-racial-bias.

90. Ram Subramanian and Leah Skrzypiec, "To Protect and Serve: New Trends in State-Level Policing Reform, 2015–2016," April 2017, available at https://storage.googleapis.com/ vera-web-assets/downloads/Publications/protect-and-serve-policing-trends-2015-2016/leg acy_downloads/041417-PolicingTrendsReport-web.pdf.

91. International City Managers Association, "Seeing the Red Flags of Organizational Cultures Gone Wrong," February 16, 2016, available at https://icma.org/node/18142.

Chapter 15

1. *Report of the National Advisory Commission on Civil Disorders* (New York: Bantam Books, 1968), 266.

2. Ibid.

3. Ibid., 267.

4. Ibid.

5. Ibid.

6. Ibid.

7. Unless otherwise noted, the following homicide death figures are from the Centers for Disease Control and Prevention Web-Based Inquiry Statistics Query and Reporting System (WISQARS) Fatal Injury Data, June 22, 2017, available at https://www.cdc.gov/injury/wisqars/ fatal.html.

8. Elliott Currie, *The Roots of Danger: Violent Crime in Global Perspective* (New York: Oxford University Press, 2015).

9. Figures on city homicide rates are calculated from Federal Bureau of Investigation, *Crime in the United States, 2015*, available at https://ucr.fbi.gov/crime-in-the-u.s/2015/crime -in-the-u.s.-2015 (accessed November 28, 2017).

10. Figures are calculated from the Federal Bureau of Investigation Uniform Crime Reporting data tool, at https://www.ucrdatatool.gov.

11. Kevin Rector, "In 2016, Baltimore's Second-Deadliest Year on Record, Bullets Claimed Targets and Bystanders Alike," *Baltimore Sun*, January 2, 2017, available at http://www.balti moresun.com/news/maryland/crime/bs-md-ci-homicides-2016-20170102-story.html.

12. Centers for Disease Control, WISQARS Fatal Injury Data.

13. See, among others, Todd Clear, *Imprisoning Communities: How Mass Incarceration Makes Disadvantaged Communities Worse* (New York: Oxford University Press, 2007); Elliott Currie, *Crime and Punishment in America*, rev. ed. (New York: Picador, 2013); Rucker Johnson, "Ever-Increasing Levels of Incarceration and the Consequences for Children," in *Do Prisons Make Us Safer?* ed. Steven Raphael and Michael A. Stoll (New York: Russell Sage Foundation, 2009), 177–206; and Sara Wakefield and Christopher Wideman, *Children of the Prison Boom* (New York: Oxford University Press, 2014).

14. Figures are calculated from U.S. Bureau of Justice Statistics, *State and Federal Prisoners, 1925–1985* (Washington, DC: U.S. Government Printing Office, 1986), and U.S. Bureau of Justice Statistics, *Prisoners in 2015* (Washington, DC: U.S. Government Printing Office, 2016).

15. *Report of the National Advisory Commission on Civil Disorders*, 397.

16. Monica Davey and Giovanni Russonello, "In Deeply Divided Chicago, Most Agree: City Is Off Course," *New York Times*, May 6, 2016, available at https://www.nytimes.com/2016/05/07/us/chicago-racial-divisions-survey.html.

Chapter 16

1. Jenna Johnson, "Donald Trump to African American and Hispanic Voters: 'What Do You Have to Lose?'" *Washington Post*, August 22, 2016, available at https://www.washingtonpost.com/news/post-politics/wp/2016/08/22/donald-trump-to-african-american-and-his-panic-voters-what-do-you-have-to-lose.

2. Mark Potok, "The Trump Effect," Southern Poverty Law Center, February 15, 2017, available at https://www.splcenter.org/fighting-hate/intelligence-report/2017/trump-effect.

3. Jesse Washington, "Black Economic Gains Reversed in Great Recession," Center for Social Inclusion, July 6, 2011, available at http://www.centerforsocialinclusion.org/black-economic-gains-reversed-in-great-recession.

4. Jacob S. Rugh and Douglas S. Massey, "Racial Segregation and the American Foreclosure Crisis," *American Sociological Review* 75 (October 2010): 629–651.

5. Nate Raymond and Sruthi Shankar, "Wells Fargo to Pay $1.2 Billion in U.S. Mortgage Fraud Settlement," Reuters, February 3, 2016, available at http://www.reuters.com/article/us-wellsfargo-housing-idUSKCN0VC1KO.

6. Pew Research Center, "On Views of Race and Inequality, Blacks and Whites Are Worlds Apart," June 27, 2016, available at http://www.pewsocialtrends.org/2016/06/27/on-views-of-race-and-inequality-blacks-and-whites-are-worlds-apart.

7. Darrick Hamilton, William Darity, Jr., Anne E. Price, Vishnu Sridharan, and Rebecca Tippett, "Umbrellas Don't Make It Rain: Why Studying and Working Hard Isn't Enough for Black Americans," April 2015, available at https://gallery.mailchimp.com/bf2b9b3cf3fdd8861943fca2f/files/Umbrellas_Dont_Make_It_Rain8.pdf.

8. William Julius Wilson, *The Truly Disadvantaged* (Chicago: University of Chicago Press, 1987).

9. Rick Pearson, "Trump Again Assails Chicago Gun Violence in Speech to Congress," *Chicago Tribune*, March 1, 2017, available at http://www.chicagotribune.com/news/local/politics/ct-donald-trump-congress-speech-chicago-met-20170228-story.html.

10. Robert J. Sampson and William Julius Wilson, "Toward a Theory of Race, Crime, and Urban Inequality," in *Crime and Inequality*, ed. John Hagan and Ruth D. Peterson (Stanford, CA: Stanford University Press, 1995), 37–56.

11. Patrick Sharkey, *Stuck in Place: Urban Neighborhoods and the End of Progress toward Racial Equality* (Chicago: University of Chicago Press, 2013).

12. Richard Rothstein, "For Public Schools, Segregation Then, Segregation Since: Education and the Unfinished March," Economic Policy Institute, August 27, 2013, available at http://www.epi.org/publication/unfinished-march-public-school-segregation.

13. Andrew Grant-Thomas and Gary Orfield, *Twenty-First Century Color Lines: Multiracial Change in Contemporary America* (Philadelphia: Temple University Press, 2009), 52–53.

14. Rothstein, "For Public Schools."

15. Julia Lurie and Edwin Rios, "Black Kids Are 4 Times More Likely to Be Suspended than White Kids," *Mother Jones*, June 8, 2016, available at http://www.motherjones.com/politics/2016/06/department-education-rights-data-inequality-suspension-preschool.

16. Michelle Alexander, *The New Jim Crow: Mass Incarceration in the Age of Colorblindness* (New York: New Press, 2010), 92.

17. Carrie Johnson, "20 Years Later, Parts of Major Crime Bill Viewed as Terrible Mistake," *NPR*, September 12, 2014, available at http://www.npr.org/2014/09/12/347736999/20-years-later-major-crime-bill-viewed-as-terrible-mistake.

18. Naomi Murakawa, *The First Civil Right: How Liberals Built Prison America* (Oxford: Oxford University Press, 2014).

19. Ibid.

20. Bruce Western and Becky Pettit, "Incarceration and Social Inequality," *Daedalus*, Summer 2010, pp. 8–19.

21. Hannah Levintova, Tasneem Raja, and A. J. Vincens, "Ferguson Is 60 Percent Black; Virtually All Its Cops Are White," *Mother Jones*, August 13, 2014, available at http://www.motherjones.com/politics/2014/08/10-insane-numbers-ferguson-killing.

22. Mark Berman and Wesley Lowery, "The 12 Key Highlights from the DOJ's Scathing Ferguson Report," *Washington Post*, March 4, 2015, available at https://www.washingtonpost.com/news/post-nation/wp/2015/03/04/the-12-key-highlights-from-the-dojs-scathing-ferguson-report.

23. One such study uses video game simulations of shootings to track officers' responses to racial stereotypes. See Melody Sadler, Joshua Correll, Bernadette Park, and Charles M. Judd, "The World Is Not Black and White: Racial Bias in the Decision to Shoot in a Multiethnic Context," *Social Issues*, June 2012, pp. 286–313. For an annotated bibliography of relevant research, see Kia Makarechi, "What the Data Really Says about Police and Racial Bias," *Vanity Fair*, July 14, 2016, available at http://www.vanityfair.com/news/2016/07/data-police-racial-bias.

24. Ryan Gabrielson, Eric Sagana, and Ryann Grochowski Jones, "Deadly Force, in Black and White," *ProPublica*, October 10, 2014, available at https://www.propublica.org/article/deadly-force-in-black-and-white.

25. Cody T. Ross, "A Multi-level Bayesian Analysis of Racial Bias in Police Shootings at the County-Level in the United States, 2011–2014," *PLoS One*, November 5, 2015, available at https://www.ncbi.nlm.nih.gov/pmc/articles/PMC4634878.

26. Phillip Atiba Goff, Tracey Lloyd, Amanda Geller, Steven Raphael, and Jack Glaser, "The Science of Justice: Race, Arrests, and Police Use of Force," July 2016, available at http://policingequity.org/wp-content/uploads/2016/07/CPE_SoJ_Race-Arrests-UoF_2016-07-08-1130.pdf.

27. Rob Voigt, Nicholas P. Camp, Vinodkumar Prabhakaran, William L. Hamilton, Rebecca C. Hetey, Camilla M. Griffiths, David Jurgens, Dan Jurafsky, and Jennifer L. Eberhardt, "Language from Police Body Camera Footage Shows Racial Disparities in Officer Respect," *Proceedings of the National Academy of Sciences of the United States of America* 114, no. 25 (2017): 6521–6526.

28. KiDeuk Kim, Miriam Becker-Cohen, and Maria Serakos, "The Processing and Treatment of Mentally Ill Persons in the Criminal Justice System," March 2015, available at http://www.urban.org/sites/default/files/publication/48981/2000173-The-Processing-and-Treatment-of-Mentally-Ill-Persons-in-the-Criminal-Justice-System.pdf.

29. Doris J. James and Lauren E. Glaze, "Mental Health Problems of Prison and Jail Inmates," September 2006, available at https://www.bjs.gov/content/pub/pdf/mhppji.pdf.

30. National Center on Addiction and Substance Abuse, "Behind Bars II: Substance Abuse and America's Prison Population," February 2010, available at https://www.centeronaddiction.org/addiction-research/reports/behind-bars-ii-substance-abuse-and-america%E2%80%99s-prison-population.

31. Kim, Becker-Cohen, and Serakos, "The Processing and Treatment of Mentally Ill Persons."

32. Elizabeth Dawes Gay, "Environmental and Health Justice Intersect for Healthy Black Futures," *Huffington Post*, February 17, 2017, available at http://www.huffingtonpost.com/entry/environmental-justice-intersect-black-futures_us_58a71552e4b037d17d27209a.

33. See United Nations Committee on the Elimination of Racial Discrimination, "Unequal Health Outcomes in the United States," January 2008 pp. 9–11, available at http://www.prrac.org/pdf/CERDhealthEnvironmentReport.pdf.

34. According to the American Diabetes Association, the overall rate of diabetes is roughly 9.3 percent. American Diabetes Association, "Statistics about Diabetes," July 19, 2017, available at http://www.diabetes.org/diabetes-basics/statistics.

35. Tierney Sneed, "More Whites Gain Obamacare Coverage than Blacks and Latinos Combined," *Talking Points Memo*, September 22, 2015, available at http://talkingpointsmemo.com/dc/obamacare-white-black-hispanic-numbers.

36. Movement for Black Lives, "End the War on Black People," available at https://policy.m4bl.org/end-war-on-black-people (accessed September 26, 2017).

37. Movement for Black Lives, "Community Control," available at https://policy.m4bl.org/community-control (accessed September 26, 2017).

38. John Wright, "'Shame on Him': Texas Police Chief Calls Out Race-Baiting Lt. Gov. Dan Patrick," *New Civil Rights Movement*, July 9, 2016, available at http://www.thenewcivilrightsmovement.com/johnwright/_shame_on_him_austin_police_chief_schools_texas_lt_gov_dan_patrick_on_black_lives_matter.

39. Jake New, "Get Ready for More Protests," *Inside Higher Ed*, February 11, 2016, available at https://www.insidehighered.com/news/2016/02/11/survey-finds-nearly-1-10-freshmen-plan-participating-campus-protests.

Chapter 17

1. U.S. Census Bureau, "United States Population Estimates, July 1, 2016," available at https://www.census.gov/quickfacts/fact/table/US/PST045216.

2. U.S. Census Bureau, "Population by Race and Hispanic Origin: 2012 and 2060," available at https://www.census.gov/newsroom/cspan/pop_proj/20121214_cspan_popproj_13.pdf (accessed November 28, 2017); U.S. Census Bureau, "Facts for Features: Hispanic Heritage Month, 2016," October 12, 2016, available at https://www.census.gov/newsroom/facts-for-features/2016/cb16-ff16.html.

3. Nielson, "Hispanic Influence Reaches New Heights in the U.S.," August 23, 2016, available at http://www.nielsen.com/us/en/insights/news/2016/hispanic-influence-reaches-new-heights-in-the-us.html.

4. Stanford Latino Entrepreneurship Initiative, "State of Latino Entrepreneurship: Research Report, 2015," November 2015, available at http://lban.us/wp-content/uploads/2015/11/Final-Report-.pdf; Jerry Porras and Remy Arteaga, "Latinos: The Force behind Small-Business Growth in America," *CNBC*, April 18, 2016, available at https://www.cnbc.com/2016/04/18/latinos-the-force-behind-small-business-growth-in-america.html.

5. U.S. Census Bureau, "Survey of Business Owners: Survey Results, 2012," February 23, 2016, available at https://www.census.gov/library/publications/2012/econ/2012-sbo.html.

6. Jeffery S. Passel and D'Vera Cohn, "Immigration Projected to Drive Growth in U.S. Working-Age Population through at Least 2035," March 8, 2017, available at http://www.pewresearch.org/fact-tank/2017/03/08/immigration-projected-to-drive-growth-in-u-s-working-age-population-through-at-least-2035.

7. Partnership for a New American Economy, "The Power of the Purse: The Contributions of Hispanics to America's Spending Power and Tax Revenues in 2013," 2014, available at http://newamericaneconomy.org/wp-content/uploads/2014/12/PNAE_hispanic_contributions.pdf.

8. Renee Stepler, "Hispanic, Black Parents See College Degree as Key for Children's Success," Pew Research Center, February 24, 2016, available at http://www.pewresearch.org/fact-tank/2016/02/24/Hispanic-black-parents-see-college-degree-as-key-for-childrens-success.

9. Sarita Brown, "Making the Next Generation Our Greatest Resource," in *Latinos and the Nation's Future*, ed. H. G. Cisneros (Houston, TX: Arte Publico Press, 2009), 88.

10. Ibid., 89.

11. Carmen DeNavas-Walt and Bernadette D. Proctor, "Income and Poverty in the United States: 2014," September 2015, available at https://www.census.gov/content/dam/Census/library/publications/2015/demo/p60-252.pdf.

12. Nielson, "Hispanic Influence."

13. Hispanic Wealth Project, "2016 State of Hispanic Homeownership Report," 2017, available at http://hispanicwealthproject.org/shhr/2016-state-of-hispanic-homeownership-re port.pdf.

14. Elena Rios, "A First-Order Need: Improving the Health of the Nation's Latinos," in *Latinos and the Nation's Future*, ed. H. G. Cisneros (Houston, TX: Arte Publico Press, 2009), 172.

15. Ibid., 171.

16. Washington Post, Kaiser Family Foundation, and Harvard University Survey Project, "National Survey on Latinos in America," May 2000, available at https://kaiserfamilyfounda tion.files.wordpress.com/2000/04/wph007-external-toplines.pdf. See also Amy Goldstein and Robert Suro, "A Journey in Stages," *Washington Post*, January 16, 2000, available at https:// www.washingtonpost.com/archive/politics/2000/01/16/a-journey-in-stages/177636bb-72c6 -492f-b443-5bb65d208d50.

17. Ibid.

18. Mark Hugo Lopez, Rich Morin, and Jens Manuel Krogstad, "Latinos Increasingly Confident in Personal Finances, See Better Economic Times Ahead," Pew Research Center, June 8, 2016, available at http://www.pewhispanic.org/2016/06/08/latinos-increasingly-confi dent-in-personal-finances-see-better-economic-times-ahead.

Chapter 18

1. Milton S. Eisenhower Foundation and Corporation for What Works, *The Millennium Breach: Richer, Poorer and Racially Apart* (Washington, DC: Milton S. Eisenhower Foundation, 1998), available at http://www.eisenhowerfoundation.org/docs/millennium.pdf.

2. 18 U.S.C. §1151.

3. Ethan Millman, "Navajo Nation Reservation in Need of Running Water," *U.S. News and World Report*, May 20, 2017, available at https://www.usnews.com/news/best-states/ari zona/articles/2017-05-20/navajo-nation-reservation-in-need-of-running-water.

4. See, generally, Environmental Protection Agency, "Five-Year Plan to Address Im pacts of Uranium Contamination," available at https://www.epa.gov/navajo-nation-uranium -cleanup/five-year-plan-address-impacts-uranium-contamination (accessed September 28, 2017).

5. U.S. Government Accountability Office, "Native American Housing: Tribes Generally View Block Grant Program as Effective, but Tracking of Infrastructure Plans and Investment Needs Improvement," February 25, 2010, available at https://www.gao.gov/assets/310/301163 .html.

6. Kevin K. Washburn, "Tribal Self-Determination at the Crossroads," *Connecticut Law Review* 38 (2006): 777–798.

7. See 42 U.S.C. §7601(d)(2)(1) (Clean Air Act), 33 U.S.C. §1377(e) (Clean Water Act), 42 U.S.C. §200j-11(b)(1) (Safe Drinking Water Act), and 42 U.S.C. §9626(a) (Comprehensive Environmental Response Compensation and Liability Act).

8. 25 U.S.C. §4101 et seq. (Native American Housing Assistance and Self-Determination Act of 1996). This act established a single federal flexible block grant for tribes or tribally des ignated housing entities to design and administer housing assistance to tribal members.

9. Geoffrey D. Strommer and Stephen D. Osbourne, "The History, Status, and Future of Tribal Self-Governance under the Indian Self-Determination and Education Assistance Act," *American Indian Law Review* 39, no. 1 (2015): 1–75.

10. Ryan Lengerich, "Nation's Top Three Poorest Counties in Western South Dakota," *Rapid City Journal*, January 22, 2012, available at http://rapidcityjournal.com/news/nation -s-top-three-poorest-counties-in-western-south-dakota/article_2d5bb0bc-44bf-11e1-bb c9-0019bb2963f4.html (citing the counties occupied by the Crow Creek, Cheyenne River, Oglala, and Rosebud Sioux tribes). See also U.S. Census Bureau, "Small Area Income and Pov erty Estimates," December 14, 2016, available at https://www.census.gov/did/www/saipe/data/ highlights/2015.html.

11. U.S. Department of the Interior, "2013 American Indian Population and Labor Force Report," January 16, 2014, p. 54, available at https://www.bia.gov/sites/bia.gov/files/assets/pub lic/pdf/idc1-024782.pdf.

12. Ibid., 57.

13. National Urban Indian Family Coalition, "Urban Indian America: The Status of American Indian and Alaska Native Children and Families Today," 2012, available at http://caseygrants.org/wp-content/uploads/2012/04/NUIFC_Report2.pdf.

14. See, e.g., Salazar v. Ramah Navajo Chapter, 132 S. Ct. 2181 (2012).

15. See Donald J. Trump, "Statement by President Donald J. Trump on Signing H.R. 244 into Law," May 5, 2017, available at https://www.whitehouse.gov/the-press-office/2017/05/05/statement-president-donald-j-trump-signing-hr-244-law. Trump's comments suggest that federal Indian Housing Block Grants may implicate the equal protection clause of the Constitution by allocating benefits on the basis of race.

16. See, e.g., Morton v. Mancari, 417 U.S. 535 (1974).

Chapter 19

Acknowledgment: I thank Anna Maria Annino for her research and editorial assistance and Jennifer True for her technical support.

1. U.S. Department of Commerce, "Women in America: Indicators of Social and Economic Well-Being," March 2011, p. 19, available at http://www.esa.doc.gov/sites/default/files/womeninamerica.pdf.

2. Camille L. Ryan and Kurt Bauman, "Educational Attainment in the United States: 2015," March 2016, p. 2, available at https://www.census.gov/content/dam/Census/library/pub lications/2016/demo/p20-578.pdf.

3. Teresa Kroeger and Elise Gould, "The Class of 2017," Economic Policy Institute, May 4, 2017, available at http://www.epi.org/publication/the-class-of-2017.

4. Ryan and Bauman, "Educational Attainment in the United States," 8–9.

5. Asha DuMonthier, Chandra Childers, and Jessica Milli, *The Status of Black Women in the United States* (Washington, DC: Institute for Women's Policy Research, 2017), 13, available at http://statusofwomendata.org/wp-content/uploads/2017/06/SOBW_report2017_com pressed.pdf.

6. "Before and after Title IX: Women in Sports," *New York Times*, June 16, 2012, available at http://www.nytimes.com/interactive/2012/06/17/opinion/sunday/sundayreview-titleix -timeline.html.

7. Catherine Hill and Holly Kearl, *Crossing the Line: Sexual Harassment at School* (Washington, DC: American Association of University Women, 2011), 2, available at http://www .aauw.org/files/2013/02/Crossing-the-Line-Sexual-Harassment-at-School.pdf.

8. Joan C. Williams, Katherine W. Phillips, and Erika V. Hall, "Double Jeopardy? Gender Bias against Women of Color in Science," 2014, p. 3, available at http://www.uchastings.edu/news/articles/2015/01/double-jeopardy-report.pdf.

9. Meritor Savings Bank v. Vinson, 477 U.S. 63–64 (1986).

10. Bernadette D. Proctor, Jessica L. Semega, and Melissa A. Kollar, "Income and Poverty in the United States: 2015," September 2016, p. 41, available at https://www.census.gov/library/publications/2016/demo/p60-256.html.

11. Pittsburgh Press Co. v. Pittsburgh Commission on Human Relations, 413 U.S. 376 (1973).

12. U.S. Department of Labor, "Facts over Time: Women in the Labor Force," July 2016, available at https://www.dol.gov/wb/stats/facts_over_time.htm.

13. Matthew Rosenberg and Dave Phillips, "All Combat Roles Now Open to Women, Defense Secretary Says," *New York Times*, December 3, 2015, available at https://www.nytimes .com/2015/12/04/us/politics/combat-military-women-ash-carter.html.

14. Proctor, Semega, and Kollar, "Income and Poverty in the United States," 10.

15. Catherine Hill, "The Simple Truth about the Gender Pay Gap," 2017, pp. 10–11, available at http://www.aauw.org/aauw_check/pdf_download/show_pdf.php?file=The -Simple-Truth.

16. Institute for Women's Policy Research, "Black Women Are among Those Who Saw the Largest Declines in Wages over the Last Decade," August 2016, available at https://iwpr.org/wp-content/uploads/wpallimport/files/iwpr-export/publications/Q053.pdf.

17. Hill, "The Simple Truth about the Gender Pay Gap," 4.

18. Anupam B. Jena, Andrew R. Olenski, and Daniel M. Blumenthal, "Sex Differences in Physician Salary in US Public Medical Schools," *JAMA Internal Medicine* 176, no. 9 (2016): 1294–1304, available at http://jamanetwork.com/journals/jamainternalmedicine/fullarticle/2532788.

19. Cynthia Hess, Jessica Milli, Jeff Hayes, and Ariane Hegewisch, *The Status of Women in the States: 2015* (Washington, DC: Institute for Women's Policy Research, 2015), 141, available at http://statusofwomendata.org/wp-content/uploads/2015/02/Status-of-Women-in-the-States-2015-Full-National-Report.pdf.

20. Catherine Hill, "Pay Gap Especially Harmful for Black and Hispanic Women Struggling with Student Debt," American Association of University Women, February 8, 2016, available at http://www.aauw.org/2016/02/08/pay-gap-especially-harmful-for-black-and-hispanic-women-struggling-with-student-debt.

21. Jane Waldfogel, "Family and Medical Leave: Evidence from the 2000 Surveys," *Monthly Labor Review*, September 2001, p. 17, available at https://www.bls.gov/opub/mlr/2001/09/art2full.pdf.

22. Jacob Alex Klerman, Kelly Daley, and Alyssa Pozniak, "Family and Medical Leave in 2012: Executive Summary," September 13, 2013, p. i, available at https://www.dol.gov/asp/evaluation/fmla/FMLA-2012-Executive-Summary.pdf.

23. Waldfogel, "Family and Medical Leave," 18.

24. Organization for Economic Cooperation and Development, "PF2.1: Key Characteristics of Parental Leave Systems," March 15, 2017, p. 13, available at http://www.oecd.org/els/soc/PF2_1_Parental_leave_systems.pdf.

25. Eileen Appelbaum and Ruth Milkman, "Leaves That Pay: Employer and Worker Experiences with Paid Family Leave in California," 2011, pp. 1–2, available at http://cepr.net/documents/publications/paid-family-leave-1-2011.pdf.

26. Bureau of Labor Statistics, "Table 32. Leave Benefits: Access, Civilian Workers," in *National Compensation Survey: Employee Benefits in the United States, March 2014* (Washington, DC: Bureau of Labor Statistics, 2014), 124, available at https://www.bls.gov/ncs/ebs/benefits/2014/ebbl0055.pdf.

27. U.S. Department of Labor, "Section 7(r) of the Fair Labor Standards Act—Break Time for Nursing Mothers Provision," available at https://www.dol.gov/whd/nursingmothers/Sec7rFLSA_btnm.htm (accessed June 16, 2017).

28. Bureau of Labor Statistics, "American Time Use Survey Summary," June 27, 2017, available at https://www.bls.gov/news.release/atus.nr0.htm.

29. National Public Radio, Robert Wood Johnson Foundation, and Harvard T. H. Chan School of Public Health, "Child Care and Health in America," October 2016, p. 8, available at http://www.npr.org/documents/2016/oct/Child-Care-and-Development-Report-2016.pdf.

30. Wendy Wang, Kim Parker, and Paul Taylor, "Breadwinner Moms," Pew Research Center, May 29, 2013, available at http://www.pewsocialtrends.org/2013/05/29/breadwinner-moms.

31. National Public Radio, Robert Wood Johnson Foundation, and Harvard T. H. Chan School of Public Health, "Child Care and Health in America," 8.

32. DuMonthier, Childers, and Milli, *The Status of Black Women in the United States*, xviii.

33. Julie Kashen, Halley Potter, and Andrew Stettner, "Quality Jobs, Quality Child Care," June 13, 2016, available at https://tcf.org/content/report/quality-jobs-quality-child-care.

34. Hess et al., *The Status of Women in the States*, 3.

35. Willard Cates, Jr., David A. Grimes, and Kenneth F. Schulz, "The Public Health Impact of Legal Abortion: 30 Years Later," *Perspectives on Sexual and Reproductive Health* 35, no. 1 (2004): 25–28, available at http://www.guttmacher.org/journals/psrh/2004/01/public-health-impact-legal-abortion-30-years-later.

36. "Global, Regional, and National Levels of Maternal Mortality, 1990–2015: A Systematic Analysis for the Global Burden of Disease Study 2015," *Lancet* 388 (2016): 1800, available at http://www.thelancet.com/pdfs/journals/lancet/PIIS0140-6736(16)31470-2.pdf.

37. Centers for Disease Control and Prevention, "Pregnancy Mortality Surveillance System," June 29, 2017, available at https://www.cdc.gov/reproductivehealth/maternalinfanthealth/pmss.html.

38. "Global, Regional, and National Levels of Maternal Mortality," 1784, 1800.

39. Hess et al., *The Status of Women in the States*, 4.

40. Ibid., 20.

41. Guttmacher Institute, "Assault on Abortion Access Continues," 2017, available at https://www.guttmacher.org/sites/default/files/images/071.yestatetrendline.png.

42. Elizabeth Nash, Rachel Benson Gold, Zohra Ansari-Thomas, Olivia Cappello, and Lizamarie Mohammed, "Laws Affecting Reproductive Health and Rights: State Policy Trends in the First Quarter of 2017," Guttmacher Institute, April 12, 2017, available at https://www.guttmacher.org/article/2017/04/laws-affecting-reproductive-health-and-rights-state-policy-trends-first-quarter-2017.

43. Sarah Larimer, "The 'Tampon Tax,' Explained," *Washington Post*, January 8, 2016, available at https://www.washingtonpost.com/news/wonk/wp/2016/01/08/the-tampon-tax-explained.

44. Saint Martha's Hall, "History of Battered Women's Movement," available at http://saintmarthas.org/resources/history-of-battered-womens-movement (accessed June 17, 2017).

45. The reauthorized act is available at https://www.gpo.gov/fdsys/pkg/BILLS-113s47enr/pdf/BILLS-113s47enr.pdf.

46. National Center for Injury Prevention and Control, "An Overview of Intimate Partner Violence in the United States: 2010 Findings," available at https://www.cdc.gov/violenceprevention/pdf/ipv-nisvs-factsheet-v5-a.pdf (accessed June 17, 2017). Intimate partner violence is defined as "rape, physical violence, or stalking by an intimate partner."

47. National Center for Injury Prevention and Control, "NISVS: An Overview of 2010 Findings on Victimization by Sexual Orientation," available at https://www.cdc.gov/violenceprevention/pdf/cdc_nisvs_victimization_final-a.pdf (accessed June 17, 2017).

48. Kathleen C. Basile, Sharon G. Smith, Matthew J. Breiding, Michele C. Black, and Reshma Mahendra, "Sexual Violence Surveillance: Uniform Definitions and Recommended Data Elements," 2014, p. 1, available at https://www.cdc.gov/violenceprevention/pdf/sv_surveillance_definitionsl-2009-a.pdf.

49. Hill and Kearl, *Crossing the Line*, 2.

50. The 2005 reauthorized act is available at https://www.congress.gov/bill/109th-congress/senate-bill/1197.

51. U.S. Senate, "Women in the Senate," available at https://www.senate.gov/artandhistory/history/common/briefing/women_senators.htm (accessed June 17, 2017); U.S. House of Representatives, "People Search," available at http://history.house.gov/People/Search?Term=Search&SearchIn=LastName&ShowNonMember=true&ShowNonMember=false&Office=&Leadership=&State=&Party=&ContinentalCongress=false&BlackAmericansInCongress=false&WomenInCongress=true&WomenInCongress=false&HispanicAmericansInCongress=false&CongressNumber=90&CurrentPage=1&SortOrder=LastName&ResultType=Grid&PreviousSearch=Search%2CLastName%2C%2C%2C%2C%2CFalse%2CFalse%2CTrue%2C84%2C85%2C86%2C87%2C88%2C89%2C90%2C91%2C92%2C93%2C94%2CLastName (accessed June 17, 2017).

52. Hess et al., *The Status of Women in the States*, 4.

53. Amanda Terkel, "Room Full of Men Decides Fate of Women's Health Care," *Huffington Post*, March 23, 2017, available at http://www.huffingtonpost.com/entry/room-men-maternity-coverage_us_58d416e6e4b02d33b749b713.

54. For example, see Jennifer L. Peresie, "Female Judges Matter: Gender and Collegial Decisionmaking in the Federal Appellate Courts," *Yale Law Journal* 114 (2005): 1786–1787, available at http://www.yalelawjournal.org/pdf/211_35ddrdm9.pdf.

55. Harvard Kennedy School Women and Public Policy Program, "Political Empowerment," available at https://wappp.hks.harvard.edu/politics (accessed June 17, 2017).

56. Drude Dahlerup and Lenita Freidenvall, "Electoral Gender Quota Systems and Their Implementation in Europe," September 2008, p. 29, available at http://www.europarl.europa.eu/document/activities/cont/200903/20090310ATT51390/20090310ATT51390EN.pdf.

57. Deborah L. Rhode, *Women and Leadership* (New York: Oxford University Press, 2016), 125–126.

58. Women's March, "Our Mission," https://www.womensmarch.com/mission (accessed October 1, 2017).

Chapter 20

Acknowledgment: I extend special thanks to Anat Shenker-Osorio (ASO Communications) for her invaluable role in developing much of the message language and strategy contained in this chapter and for her feedback. David Mermin, Josh Ulibarri, Jonathan Voss, and Daniel Gotoff of Lake Research Partners were heavily involved in the research in many of these messages in this chapter. Dan Spicer greatly assisted with the research for the chapter.

1. Chad Stone, Danilo Trisi, Arloc Sherman, and Emily Horton, "A Guide to Statistics on Historical Trends in Income Inequality," Center on Budget and Policy Priorities, September 25, 2017, available at https://www.cbpp.org/research/poverty-and-inequality/a-guide-to-statistics-on-historical-trends-in-income-inequality.

2. Thomas Piketty and Emmanuel Saez, "Income Inequality in the United States, 1913–2002," November 2004, available at https://eml.berkeley.edu/~saez/piketty-saezOUP04US.pdf.

3. Pew Research Center, "America's Shrinking Middle Class: A Close Look at Changes within Metropolitan Areas," May 11, 2016, available at http://www.pewsocialtrends.org/2016/05/11/americas-shrinking-middle-class-a-close-look-at-changes-within-metropolitan-areas.

4. Richard Wilkinson, *The Impact of Inequality* (New York: New Press, 2006).

5. Ali Meyer, "Fed Official: America No Longer Top Country to Achieve American Dream," *Washington Free Beacon*, April 11, 2016, available at http://freebeacon.com/issues/fed-official-u-s-no-longer-top-country-achieve-american-dream.

6. "Americans' Views on Income Inequality and Workers' Rights," *New York Times*, June 3, 2015, available at https://www.nytimes.com/interactive/2015/06/03/business/income-inequality-workers-rights-international-trade-poll.html.

7. Amber Pariona, "Incarceration Rates by Race, Ethnicity, and Gender in the U.S.," *World Atlas*, April 25, 2017, available at http://www.worldatlas.com/articles/incarceration-rates-by-race-ethnicity-and-gender-in-the-u-s.html.

8. Forum on Child and Family Statistics, "America's Children in Brief: Key National Indicators of Well-Being, 2016," 2016, available at https://www.childstats.gov/pdf/ac2016/ac_16.pdf.

9. Tanzina Vega, "Blacks Still Far behind Whites in Wealth and Income," *CNN*, June 27, 2016, available at http://money.cnn.com/2016/06/27/news/economy/racial-wealth-gap-blacks-whites/index.html.

10. Eisenhower Foundation, "What Together We Can Do: Forty Year Update of the National Advisory Commission on Civil Disorders," November 2008, available at http://www.eisenhowerfoundation.org/docs/Kerner%2040%20Year%20Update,%20Executive%20Summary.pdf.

11. Sandra Susan Smith, "Race and Trust," *Annual Review of Sociology* 36 (2010): 453–475, available at http://sociology.berkeley.edu/sites/default/files/faculty/Smith/RACE%20AND%20TRUST.pdf.

12. Nick Hanauer, "The Pitchforks Are Coming . . . for Us Plutocrats," *Politico*, July–August 2014, available at http://www.politico.com/magazine/story/2014/06/the-pitchforks-are-coming-for-us-plutocrats-108014.

13. Josh Boak and Carrie Antlfinger, "Millennials Are Falling Behind Their Boomer Parents," *Associated Press*, January 13, 2017, available at https://apnews.com/8b688578bf764d3998cca899a448aa33.

14. D. J. Flynn, Brendan Nyhan, and Jason Reifler, "The Nature and Origins of Misperceptions: Understanding False and Unsupported Beliefs about Politics," *Advances in Political Psychology* 38, suppl. S1 (2017): 127–150.

15. George Lakoff, *Don't Think of an Elephant: Know Your Values and Frame the Debate* (White River Junction, VT: Chelsea Green, 2004).

16. Leslie McCall, *The Undeserving Rich: American Beliefs about Inequality, Opportunity, and Redistribution* (Cambridge: Cambridge University Press, 2013).

17. Ibid.

18. Topos and Demos, "Government, the Economy and We, the People," October 2009, available at http://www.topospartnership.com/wp-content/uploads/2012/05/Government-The-Economy-and-We-The-People.pdf.

19. Berkeley Media Studies Group, "Using Social Math to Support Your Policy Issue," *BMSG Blog*, March 30, 2015, available at http://bmsg.org/blog/social-math-support-public-health-policy; Diane Benjamin, "Doing Social Math: Case Study in Framing Food and Fitness," *FrameWorks E-Zine*, July 20, 2007, available at http://www.frameworksinstitute.org/ezine40.html.

20. Anthony I. Jack, Philip Robbins, Jared P. Friedman, and Chris D. Meyers, "More than a Feeling: Counterintuitive Effects of Compassion on Moral Judgment," in *Advances in Experimental Philosophy of Mind*, ed. Justin Sytsma (London: Bloomsbury Academic, 2014), 125–180.

21. Center for Community Change, "Messaging for Economic Justice: Research Brief," 2014, available at http://www.communitychange.org/wp-content/uploads/2014/07/CCC-Research-Brief.pdf.

22. Ibid., 3.

23. Alexis de Tocqueville, *Democracy in America*, trans. George Lawrence (New York: Harper and Row, 1966).

24. Jobs with Justice, AFL-CIO, and National Education Association, "The Strength of Coming Together: Championing Working People," 2015 (in author's possession).

25. Center for Community Change, "Messaging for Economic Justice," 4.

26. The positive conception of freedom referred to here juxtaposes it against the negative conception of freedom in the very limited libertarian sense—i.e., the freedom to be left alone (from government and regulations).

27. Jobs with Justice, AFL-CIO, and National Education Association, "The Strength of Coming Together."

28. Ibid.

29. Center for Social Inclusion, "Talking about Race Right: How to Win by Addressing Race," 2010, available at http://www.centerforsocialinclusion.org/wp-content/uploads/2010/03/Talking-About-Race-Right-An-Introduction-1.pdf.

30. Ibid.

31. Opportunity Agenda, "Rise Above: Countering Fear-Based Messaging," 2017, available at https://opportunityagenda.org/explore/resources-publications/rise-above-countering-fear-based-messaging.

32. Opportunity Agenda, "Ten Lessons for Talking about Race, Racism and Racial Justice," 2017, available at https://opportunityagenda.org/explore/resources-publications/ten-lessons-talking-about-race-racism-and-racial-justice.

33. Opportunity Agenda, "Rise Above."

34. Ibid.

35. Opportunity Agenda, "Ten Lessons."

36. "Putting Families First: Good Jobs for All Research Brief," February 18, 2016, available at https://documents.tips/documents/putting-families-first-message-research-project.html.

Chapter 21

1. Nicholas Lemann, *The Promised Land: The Great Black Migration and How It Changed America* (New York: Knopf, 1991), 191. Lemann writes, "Johnson was furious about the report,

not least because it ruled out the possibility of a conspiracy behind the riots. He felt it put him in an impossible position—he couldn't respond to it in a way that matched the bits of angry language that had gotten the headlines, and he certainly couldn't get through Congress the billions of dollars' worth of new government programs for the ghettos that the report recommended" (191).

2. National Advisory Commission on Civil Disorders, *The Kerner Report* (Princeton, NJ: Princeton University Press, 2016), 207–208. Princeton University Press's James Madison Library in American Politics should be commended for republishing the report as part of its extraordinary series of historically important American books. The introduction to the book by Julian E. Zelizer is a superb compact history of the commission, the report, and its aftermath. I relied on it for this chapter and am grateful for it. The general editor's introduction by the historian Sean Wilentz is also very insightful.

3. Ibid., 2.

4. Ibid., 208.

5. Ibid., 208–209.

6. Ibid., x.

7. Ibid., xxxi.

8. Quoted in Julian E. Zelizer, "Is America Repeating the Mistakes of 1968?" *The Atlantic*, July 8, 2016, available at https://www.theatlantic.com/politics/archive/2016/07/is-america-re peating-the-mistakes-of-1968/490568.

9. George C. Wallace, speech at Madison Square Garden, October 24, 1968, in *History of Political Parties*, vol. 4, *1945–1972: The Politics of Change*, ed. Arthur M. Schlesinger, Jr. (New York: Chelsea House, 1973), 3493–3494.

10. Quoted in Stephen E. Ambrose, *Nixon: The Triumph of a Politician* (New York: Simon and Schuster, 1989), 144–145.

11. "Tony Blair Is Tough on Crime, Tough on the Causes of Crime," *New Statesman*, December 28, 2015, available at http://www.newstatesman.com/2015/12/archive-tony-blair -tough-crime-tough-causes-crime.

12. National Advisory Commission on Civil Disorders, *The Kerner Report*, 1; see also xxvii.

13. William Julius Wilson, *The Declining Significance of Race* (Chicago: University of Chicago Press, 1978).

14. William Julius Wilson, *The Truly Disadvantaged: The Inner City, the Underclass and Public Policy* (Chicago: University of Chicago Press, 1990); William Julius Wilson, *When Work Disappears: The World of the New Urban Poor* (New York: Vintage, 1997).

15. Andrew Greeley, *Why Can't They Be like Us?* (New York: Dutton, 1971), 14.

16. Richard J. Krickus, "The White Ethnics: Who Are They and Where Are They Going?" *City*, May–June 1971, p. 30.

17. Quoted in Philip Shabecoff, "Msgr. Geno Baroni, a Leader in Neighborhood Organizing," *New York Times*, August 29, 1984, available at http://www.nytimes.com/1984/08/29/ obituaries/msgr-geno-baroni-a-leader-in-neighborhood-organizing.html.

18. Irving Louis Horowitz, "Race, Class and the New Ethnicity," in *Ideology and Utopia in the United States, 1956–1976* (London: Oxford University Press, 1977), 67.

19. Nathan Glazer and Daniel P. Moynihan, introduction to *Ethnicity: Theory and Experience*, ed. Nathan Glazer and Daniel P. Moynihan (Cambridge, MA: Harvard University Press, 1975), 10, 15.

20. Michael Novak, *The Rise of the Unmeltable Ethnics: Politics and Culture in the Seventies* (New York: Macmillan, 1971).

21. Herbert Gans, *The Urban Villagers* (New York: Free Press, 1962).

22. Gerald D. Suttles, *The Social Construction of Communities* (Chicago: University of Chicago Press, 1972), 245.

23. National Advisory Commission on Civil Disorders, *The Kerner Report*, 245.

24. Jules Witcover, *Marathon: The Pursuit of the Presidency, 1972–1976* (New York: Viking, 1977), 302.

25. Ibid.

26. Ibid., 303.

27. Ibid., 305–306.

28. Nathan Glazer, "The Universalization of Ethnicity," in *Ethnic Dilemmas, 1964–1982* (Cambridge, MA: Harvard University Press, 1983), 253. The chapter was originally published in an altered form in *Encounter* in February 1975.

29. Stephen Steinberg, *The Ethnic Myth: Race, Ethnicity, and Class in America* (Boston: Beacon Press, 1981).

30. Martin Kilson, "Blacks and Neo-ethnicity in American Political Life," in Glazer and Moynihan, *Ethnicity*, 263–264.

31. Orlando Patterson, *Ethnic Chauvinism: The Reactionary Impulse* (New York: Stein and Day, 1977), 147–185.

32. National Advisory Commission on Civil Disorders, *The Kerner Report*, 154, 11, 144.

33. Fred Harris, interview by Bill Moyers, *Bill Moyers Journal*, March 28, 2008, available at http://www.pbs.org/moyers/journal/03282008/transcript1.html.

34. National Advisory Commission on Civil Disorders, *The Kerner Report*, 1.

Chapter 22

1. National Advisory Commission on Civil Disorders, *The Kerner Report* (Princeton, NJ: Princeton University Press, 2016), 365.

2. Ibid., 21.

3. Ibid., 115.

4. Ibid., 368.

5. Peter Waddington, *Liberty and Order: Public Order Policing in a Capital City* (London: UCL Press, 1994), 7.

6. Franklin D. Gilliam, Jr., and Shanto Iyengar, "Prime Suspects: The Influence of Local Television News on the Viewing Public," *American Journal of Political Science* 44, no. 3 (2000): 560–573.

7. Heinz Endowments African American Men and Boys Task Force, "Portrayal and Perception: Two Audits of News Media Reporting on African American Men and Boys," November 2011, available at https://www.opensocietyfoundations.org/sites/default/files/portrayal-and-perception-20111101.pdf.

8. Robert Entman and Kimberly Gross, "Race to Judgment: Stereotyping Media and Criminal Defendants," *Law and Contemporary Problems* 71, no. 93 (2008): 93–133.

9. Anthony C. Thompson, *Releasing Prisoners, Redeeming Communities: Reentry, Race and Politics* (New York: NYU Press, 2008), 13.

10. German Lopez, "When a Drug Epidemic's Victims Are White," *Vox*, April 4, 2017, available at https://www.vox.com/identities/2017/4/4/15098746/opioid-heroin-epidemic-race.

11. Erna Smith, "Transmitting Race: Los Angeles Riot in Television News," May 1994, available at https://shorensteincenter.org/wp-content/uploads/2012/03/r11_smith.pdf.

12. Daniel T. Rodgers, *The Age of Fracture* (Cambridge, MA: Harvard University Press, 2012).

13. Michelle Alexander, *The New Jim Crow: Mass Incarceration in the Age of Colorblindness* (New York: New Press, 2010); Elizabeth Hinton, *From the War on Poverty to the War on Crime: The Making of Mass Incarceration in America* (New York: Harvard University Press, 2016).

14. "The Los Angeles Riots, Race and Journalism," *NPR*, April 30, 2017, available at http://www.npr.org/2017/04/30/526250830/the-los-angeles-riots-race-and-journalism.

15. Matt Grossmann and David A. Hopkins, *Asymmetric Politics: Ideological Republicans and Group Interest Politics* (New York: Oxford University Press, 2016), 129–197.

16. Adam Johnson, "5 Times the Media Has Smeared Black Victims of Police Killings Since Michael Brown," *Alternet*, August 6, 2015, available at http://www.alternet.org/media/5-times-media-has-smeared-black-victims-police-killings-michael-brown.

17. Kevin McSpadden, "You Now Have a Shorter Attention Span than a Goldfish," *Time*, May 14, 2015, available at http://time.com/3858309/attention-spans-goldfish.

18. Sylvester Monroe, "'Burn, Baby, Burn': What I Saw as a Black Journalist Covering the L.A. Riots 25 Years Ago," *Washington Post*, April 28, 2017, available at https://www.washingtonpost.com/news/retropolis/wp/2017/04/28/burn-baby-burn-what-i-saw-as-a-black-journalist-covering-the-l-a-riots-25-years-ago.

19. Ronald N. Jacobs, *Race, Media, and the Crisis of Society: From Watts to Rodney King* (New York: Cambridge University Press, 2000).

20. Frank Newport, "Americans See Obama Election as Race Relations Milestone," *Gallup News*, November 7, 2008, available at http://news.gallup.com/poll/111817/americans-see-obama-election-race-relations-milestone.aspx.

Chapter 23

1. Alan Travis, "Thatcher Government Toyed with Evacuating Liverpool after 1981 Riots," *The Guardian*, December 29, 2011, available at https://www.theguardian.com/uk/2011/dec/30/thatcher-government-liverpool-riots-1981.

2. "Report of the National Advisory Commission in Civil Disorders: Summary of Report," February 29, 1968, available at http://www.eisenhowerfoundation.org/docs/kerner.pdf.

3. Black male life expectancy in the District of Columbia is 64.88 years. See Jennifer Welsh, "Race and Life Expectancy in All 50 States," *Live Science*, March 5, 2012, available at https://www.livescience.com/18835-race-lifespan-states.html.

4. Male life expectancy in the Gaza Strip is 72.3 years. See Central Intelligence Agency, "Middle East: Gaza Strip," in *The World Factbook*, available at https://www.cia.gov/library/publications/the-world-factbook/geos/gz.html (accessed October 2, 2017).

5. Gary Younge, "Farewell to America," *The Guardian*, July 1, 2015, available at https://www.theguardian.com/us-news/2015/jul/01/gary-younge-farewell-to-america.

6. Gary Younge, "A Day in the Death of America," *The Guardian*, June 9, 2007, available at https://www.theguardian.com/world/2007/jun/09/usa.usgunviolence.

7. Ibid.

8. Drew DeSilver, "Black Unemployment Rate Is Consistently Twice That of Whites," Pew Research Center, August 21, 2013, available at http://www.pewresearch.org/fact-tank/2013/08/21/through-good-times-and-bad-black-unemployment-is-consistently-double-that-of-whites.

9. Pew Research Center, "Incarceration Gap Widens between Whites and Blacks," September 6, 2013, available at http://www.pewresearch.org/fact-tank/2013/09/06/incarceration-gap-between-whites-and-blacks-widens.

10. Thomas Shapiro, Tatjana Meschede, and Sam Osoro, "The Roots of the Widening Racial Wealth Gap: Explaining the Black-White Economic Divide," February 2013, available at https://iasp.brandeis.edu/pdfs/Author/shapiro-thomas-m/racialwealthgapbrief.pdf.

11. Gary Younge, "We Used to Think There Was a Black Community," *The Guardian*, November 8, 2007, available at https://www.theguardian.com/world/2007/nov/08/usa.gender.

12. Erin McCann, "The Coin? Gold. Its 'Real Value'? Lady Liberty Is Black," *New York Times*, January 13, 2017, available at https://www.nytimes.com/2017/01/13/us/black-lady-liberty-us-coin.html.

13. Mariko Lin Chang, "Lifting as We Climb: Women of Color, Wealth, and America's Future," 2010, available at http://www.mariko-chang.com/LiftingAsWeClimb.pdf.

14. Eileen Patten, "Racial, Gender Wage Gaps Persist in U.S. despite Some Progress," Pew Research Center, July 1, 2016, available at http://www.pewresearch.org/fact-tank/2016/07/01/racial-gender-wage-gaps-persist-in-u-s-despite-some-progress.

15. Gary Younge, "The US Can't Keep Track of How Many People Its Police Kill; We're Counting Because Lives Matter," *The Guardian*, June 1, 2015, available at https://www.theguardian.com/us-news/commentisfree/2015/jun/01/the-counted-keeping-count-police.

16. Gary Younge, "No Surrender," *The Guardian*, May 24, 2002, available at https://www.theguardian.com/books/2002/may/25/biography.mayaangelou.

17. Jennifer Senior, "Review: *Another Day in the Death of America*, on Guns Killing Children," *New York Times*, October 27, 2016, available at https://www.nytimes.com/2016/10/28/books/review-another-day-in-the-death-of-america-on-guns-killing-children.html.

18. Gary Younge, *Another Day in the Death of America* (New York: Nation Books, 2016), 153–154.

19. "One Dead, Seven Shot during Violent Weekend in Chicago," Getty Images, November 25, 2013, available at http://www.gettyimages.co.uk/event/one-dead-seven-shot-during-violent-weekend-in-chicago-452418727#the-mother-of-18yearold-tyshon-anderson-signs-a-memorial-to-her-son-picture-id451955755.

20. Quoted in Gary Younge, "*Men We Reaped* by Jesmyn Ward: Review," *The Guardian*, March 6, 2014, available at https://www.theguardian.com/books/2014/mar/06/men-we-reaped-jesmyn-ward.

21. Younge, *Another Day in the Death of America*, 195.

22. Douglas S. Massey and Nancy A. Denton, *American Apartheid: Segregation and the Making of the Underclass* (Cambridge, MA: Harvard University Press, 1993), 75.

23. Ibid., 77.

24. Dale Russakoff, "Schooled," *New Yorker*, May 19, 2014, available at https://www.newyorker.com/magazine/2014/05/19/schooled.

25. John Berger, *Ways of Seeing* (London: Penguin Classics, 2008), 7.

26. U.S. Department of Justice Civil Rights Division, "Investigation of the Ferguson Police Department," March 4, 2015, available at https://www.justice.gov/sites/default/files/opa/press-releases/attachments/2015/03/04/ferguson_police_department_report.pdf.

27. Ibid.

Contributors

Oscar Perry Abello is a New York City–based journalist, covering community development and economic justice in the United States. Since 2011, his writing has appeared online in publications such as *Fast Company*, *Next City*, and *NextBillion*, on topics including economic development, community development finance, affordable housing, and worker cooperatives. A graduate of Villanova University, he holds a B.A. in economics and peace and justice studies. He was the inaugural corecipient of the Solidarity Award of Villanova's Center for Peace and Justice Education.

Elijah Anderson, Ph.D., sociology, is William K. Lanman Jr. Professor of Sociology at Yale University and one of America's leading urban ethnologists. Author of a number of acclaimed books, the most recent being *The Cosmopolitan Canopy: Race and Civility in Everyday Life*, he was the 2013 recipient of the prestigious Cox-Johnson-Frazier Award of the American Sociological Association and the 2017 recipient of the Merit Award of the Eastern Sociological Society.

Anil N. F. Aranha, Ph.D., is associate director (academic) in the Medical Education Office of Diversity and Inclusion with a joint faculty appointment in the Department of Internal Medicine at Wayne State University School of Medicine. His research interests include medical and public health education; geriatric health care; food, nutrition, and health behaviors; health care utilization; health services and outcomes; and patient satisfaction and medical intervention cost-effectiveness. He has published forty peer-reviewed articles in these fields.

Jared Bernstein, Ph.D., social welfare, is a senior fellow at the Center on Budget and Policy Priorities. He served as deputy chief economist in the Department of Labor, 1995–1996, and chief economist and economic advisor to Vice President Joe Biden during the Obama administration. He is the author of a number of books, including *All Together Now: Common Sense for a Fair Economy*, and is a regular contributor to the *Washington Post* and the *New York Times*.

Henry G. Cisneros, Ph.D., public administration, was the first Hispanic American mayor of a major U.S. city, San Antonio, Texas, and was selected as the Outstanding Mayor in the nation by *City and State Magazine*. He was secretary of Housing and Urban Development during the administration of President Bill Clinton and is a former president of the National League of Cities and a former president and CEO, and current board member, of Univisión Communications. He is the author or editor of several books, including *Interwoven Destinies: Cities and the Nation*.

Elliott Currie, Ph.D., is professor of criminology, law, and society at the University of California, Irvine, and adjunct professor in the Faculty of Law, School of Justice, Queensland University of Technology, Australia. He is the author of many books on crime, delinquency, drug abuse, and social policy, including *The Roots of Danger: Violent Crime in Global Perspective*. His book *Crime and Punishment in America*, revised and expanded in 2013, was a finalist for the Pulitzer Prize in general nonfiction in 1999. He is coauthor of *Whitewashing Race: The Myth of the Colorblind Society*, which was the winner of the 2004 Book Award from the Benjamin L. Hooks Institute for Social Change.

Alan Curtis, Ph.D., president of the Milton S. Eisenhower Foundation, has degrees from Harvard, the University of London, and the University of Pennsylvania. He was a task force codirector on President Lyndon Johnson's National Violence Commission, executive director of President Jimmy Carter's Urban Policy Group, and urban policy advisor to the secretary of Housing and Urban Development in the Carter administration. Currently replicating the Quantum Opportunities evidence-based model in inner-city neighborhoods, Dr. Curtis is author or editor of twenty books, Eisenhower Foundation book-length reports, and Kerner updates, including (as Lynn A. Curtis) *Criminal Violence, American Violence and Public Policy, Youth Investment and Police Mentoring, The Millennium Breach, Locked in the Poorhouse,* and (as Alan Curtis) *Patriotism, Democracy, and Common Sense.*

Linda Darling-Hammond, Ed.D. with highest distinction, is the Charles E. Ducommun Professor of Education Emeritus at Stanford University and president and CEO of the Learning Policy Institute. She is the founder of the Stanford Center for Opportunity Policy in Education, faculty sponsor of the Stanford Teacher Education Program, which she helped design, and currently serves as chair of California's Commission on Teacher Credentialing. She was executive director of the National Commission on Teaching and America's Future and was the leader of President Barack Obama's 2008 education policy transition team. Among her more than five hundred publications are several award-winning books, including *The Right to Learn* and *Preparing Teachers for a Changing World*.

Martha F. Davis, J.D., is professor of law and associate dean for Experiential Education at Northeastern University School of Law, where she is also faculty director for the law school human rights program. She held the Fulbright distinguished chair at the Raoul Wallenberg Institute of Human Rights and Humanitarian Law in Lund, Sweden, and served as vice president and legal director of the NOW Legal Defense and Education Fund. She is the author of many scholarly articles and several books on human rights, women's rights, and social justice issues, including her most recent book, *Global Urban Justice: The Rise of Human Rights Cities*.

E. J. Dionne, Jr., D.Phil., Oxford University, Rhodes scholar, is a senior fellow at the Brookings Institution and professor in the Foundations of Democracy and Culture at Georgetown University where he teaches in the McCourt School of Public Policy and the Government Department. In 1975, he went to work for the *New York Times* covering state, local, and national politics and also served as a foreign correspondent. He joined the *Washington Post* in 1990, first as a political reporter, then to write a regular column for the *Post*, which is now syndicated in 240 newspapers. He is the author of six books and the editor of seven more. His most recent book is *Why the Right Went Wrong: Conservatism—from Goldwater to Trump and Beyond*.

Marian Wright Edelman, J.D., is the founder and president of the Children's Defense Fund. A graduate of Spelman College and Yale Law School, she was the first African American woman admitted to the Mississippi bar and served as director of the NAACP Legal Defense and Education Fund office in Jackson, Mississippi. She has spent her entire professional life as a passionate and highly effective advocate for disadvantaged Americans. She is the recipient of the Albert Schweitzer Humanitarian Prize, the Presidential Medal of Freedom, the nation's highest civilian award, and the Robert F. Kennedy Lifetime Achievement Award for her writings, which include *The Sea Is So Wide and My Boat Is So Small: Charting a Course for the Next Generation*.

Delbert S. Elliott, Ph.D., is Distinguished Professor Emeritus of Sociology at the University of Colorado, Boulder, where he is also founding director of the Center for the Study and Prevention of Violence and research professor at the Institute of Behavioral Science. He is a fellow and past president of the American Society of Criminology, a fellow in the Academy of Experimental Criminology, the principal investigator of the National Youth Survey, a thirty-year longitudinal study of criminal behavior and drug use in the United States, and the science editor of the U.S. Surgeon General's Report on Youth Violence (2001). He is the author of several widely cited books, including most recently *Good Kids from Bad Neighborhoods* and *The Prevention of Crime.*

Carol Emig, M.P.P., John F. Kennedy School, Harvard University, is president of Child Trends, an independent, nonpartisan research center, headquartered in Washington, D.C., that works to improve the lives and prospects of children and youth by conducting high-quality research and applying the resulting knowledge to public policies, programs, and systems. She was the executive director of the Pew Commission on Children in Foster Care, a blue-ribbon panel of child welfare experts, and deputy director of the National Commission on Children, a bipartisan congressional-presidential panel.

Jeff Faux is founding president and distinguished fellow and board member at the Economic Policy Institute, the nation's leading think tank on political and economic issues. Educated at Queens College, George Washington University, and Harvard University, he has studied, taught, and published on a wide variety of issues—from the global economy to neighborhood community development, monetary policy, and political strategy. He is the author or coauthor of six books, the latest of which is *The Servant Economy: Where America's Elite Is Sending the Middle Class.*

Ron Grzywinski was the cofounder, CEO, and advisor to the board of directors of ShoreBank Corporation, which was the nation's first and largest certified community development finance institution. In 1996, he created ShoreBank Pacific, the nation's first environmental development bank. A visiting scholar at the Center for Urban Research and Learning at Loyola University, Chicago, he is the recipient of numerous honors, including the Theodore Hesburgh Award for Ethical Business Practices from the University of Notre Dame, the Independent Sector's John W. Gardner Leadership Award, and an honorary doctorate of business from Northern Michigan University.

Fred Harris, J.D., a former U.S. senator from Oklahoma, is University of New Mexico emeritus professor of political science and director of its

Fred Harris Congressional Internship Program. He served as a reform-minded national chair of the Democratic Party. He has produced nineteen nonfiction books on policy, government, and politics, including *The New Populism* and, as coeditor with Roger Wilkins, *Quiet Riots: Race and Poverty in the United States*. He is recognized (with New York City mayor John Lindsay) as one of the two activist leaders of the Kerner Commission and is now its only living member; he is chairman emeritus of the Eisenhower Foundation.

Michael P. Jeffries, Ph.D., is associate professor of American Studies at Wellesley College, where he teaches courses on American popular culture and the politics of race, class, and gender. He is the author of three books, including *Barack Obama and the Meaning of Race in America*, and is a regular contributor to the *Boston Globe*, the *Atlantic*, and the *Guardian*.

Lamar K. Johnson, M.D., is a fourth-year resident in the Combined Internal Medicine/Pediatrics program at Wayne State University School of Medicine/Detroit Medical Center. He holds an undergraduate degree in biology from Howard University in Washington, D.C., and completed his medical degree at Meharry College, Nashville, Tennessee. His interests include global and urban health, as well as medical education and public policy. He plans to pursue a career in primary care.

Celinda Lake is a prominent pollster and political strategist for progressives, currently serving as president of Lake Research Partners. Her polling and strategic advice have helped elect an impressive number of candidates to the U.S. Senate and House, especially women candidates, and she was the pollster for the 2008 presidential campaign of Senator Joe Biden. She has been a key participant in campaigns launched by such groups as the AFL-CIO, the Sierra Club, and Planned Parenthood and in message projects that helped redefine language on the economy, inequality, big money in politics, climate change, public schools and teachers, and criminal justice reform. Coauthor of the book *What Women Really Want*, she is a recipient of the American Political Consultant Award and the Opportunity Agenda Creative Change Award.

Marilyn Melkonian, J.D., is the president and founder of the Telesis Corporation, which, in collaboration with residents and local partners, builds urban communities that are livable, beautiful, and diverse. She was a member of the staff of Senator Edward Brooke, Republican of Massachusetts, a member of the Kerner Commission. She was a partner in the law firm of Tufo, Johnston and Zucotti, specializing in land use and housing development. During the administration of President Jimmy Carter, she served as deputy assistant secretary for Housing at the Department of

Housing and Urban Development. She is founder and chair of the National Housing Trust, dedicated to preserving the nation's supply of affordable housing, and a member of the board of the Brooking Institution's Center on Urban and Metropolitan Policy.

Gary Orfield, Ph.D., is distinguished professor of education, law, political science, and urban planning at UCLA; professor emeritus of education and social policy at Harvard University; and cofounder and codirector of the Civil Rights Project, begun at Harvard and now at UCLA. His many books, articles, and studies focus on the relationship between housing and education, as well as on desegregation and the operation of school choice. His books include *Must We Bus? Segregated Schools and National Policy* and, most recently, *Educational Delusions?* In a recent rating from *Education Week*, he was named the most influential education policy scholar in the United States for 2015.

Diane Ravitch, Ph.D., is a historian of education, an educational policy analyst, and a research professor at New York University's Steinhardt School of Culture, Education, and Human Development. She served in public positions in the administrations of Presidents George W. Bush and Bill Clinton. On the basis of her experience, she renounced her earlier support for testing and choice as both unworkable and harmful. In 2010, she authored the best-selling book *The Death and Life of the Great American School System: How Testing and Choice Undermine Education* and has become a tireless and influential activist against privatization and high-stakes testing, believing that the best predictor of low academic performance is poverty—not bad teachers.

Laurie O. Robinson is the Clarence J. Robinson Professor of Criminology, Law, and Society at George Mason University after more than three decades of engagement in national criminal justice policy. She served as director of the Criminal Justice Section of the American Bar Association and director of the master of science program at the University of Pennsylvania's Department of Criminology. In both the Bill Clinton and the Barack Obama administrations, she was assistant attorney general, heading the Department of Justice Office of Justice Programs. She was also cochair of President Obama's Task Force on 21st Century Policing. She is a member of the Committee on Law and Justice of the National Academy of Sciences.

Herbert C. Smitherman, Jr., M.D., is vice dean of Diversity and Community Affairs and associate professor of General Medicine at Wayne State University School of Medicine. He is president and CEO of the Health Centers Detroit Foundation, the first Federally Qualified Health Center designated in Detroit. His research and expertise focus primarily on creating sustainable systems of care for urban communities. He is the coauthor of a new health policy book, *Taking Care of the Uninsured: A Path to Reform*.

Joseph E.Stiglitz, Ph.D., is an economist and professor at Columbia University. He is cochair of the High-Level Expert Group on the Measurement of Economic Performance and Social Progress at the Organization for Economic Cooperation and Development and chief economist at the Roosevelt Institute. A recipient of the 2001 Nobel Memorial Prize in Economic Sciences, he is former senior vice president and chief economist at the World Bank and, during the administration of President Bill Clinton, was a member and chair of the President's Council of Economic Advisers. On the basis of academic citations, he is the fourth-most influential economist in the world, and in 2011, he was named by *Time* magazine as one of the one hundred most influential people in the world. He is the author of numerous acclaimed and best-selling books, including *The Great Divide: Unequal Societies and What We Can Do about Them*.

Dorothy Stoneman, Ed.D., is founder and former CEO of YouthBuild USA, the support center for 260 U.S. locations and 80 foreign countries. In YouthBuild, low-income unemployed young people ages sixteen to twenty-four without a high school diploma enroll full time for six to twenty-four months to work toward their high school equivalent or diploma—while getting paid to build affordable housing for homeless and low-income people in their neighborhoods. She helped found and now works with Opportunity Youth United, a national network of deeply engaged urban and rural young people from all racial and ethnic groups. She is a recipient of the 2000 John Gardner Leadership Award and a 1996 MacArthur Fellowship.

Kevin K. Washburn, J.D., is professor of law and the former dean of the University of New Mexico School of Law. He served as assistant secretary for Indian Affairs in the Department of the Interior during the second term of President Barack Obama and, in that role, was the highest-ranking official for federal Indian policy, overseeing the nearly eight thousand employees and budget of $2.8 billion of the Bureau of Indian Affairs and Indian Education. He has produced several books, including the *Cohen Handbook of Federal Indian* Law. He and his wife and children are citizens of the Chickasaw Nation of Oklahoma.

Valerie Wilson, Ph.D., is an economist and the director of the Program on Race, Ethnicity, and the Economy at the Economic Policy Institute in Washington, D.C., and was formerly vice president of the National Urban League Washington Bureau, where she was responsible for planning and directing the bureau's research agenda. She has written extensively on issues affecting economic inequality in the United States and, through the State Department's Bureau of International Information Programs, delivered the keynote address on Minority Economic Empowerment at the Nobel Peace Center in Oslo, Norway.

Gary Younge is an award-winning author, broadcaster, and editor at large for the *Guardian*, based in London, and writes a monthly column, "Beneath the Radar," for *Nation* magazine. He has reported from all over Europe, Africa, the United States, and the Caribbean and was the U.S. correspondent for the *Guardian* from 2003 to 2015. He is the author of five books, including *No Place Like Home: A Black Briton's Journey* and *Another Day in the Death of America*, which won the 2017 J. Anthony Lukas Book Prize from Columbia Journalism School and Nieman Foundation. Currently a visiting professor at London South Bank University, he holds honorary doctorates from his alma mater, Heriot Watt University, and London South Bank University.

Julian E. Zelizer, Ph.D., is the Malcolm Stevenson Forbes Class of 1941 Professor of History and Public Affairs at Princeton University and a CNN analyst. He edited a new version of the Kerner Report, published by Princeton University Press, and is the author of many scholarly articles and book chapters, as well as eighteen books on American political history, the latest being *The Fierce Urgency of Now: Lyndon Johnson, Congress, and the Battle for the Great Society*. In addition to his scholarly work, he has published some seven hundred newspaper editorials and regularly appears on television to comment on the news.

Index